COMPARATIVE POLITICS TODAY

PRINCIPAL CONTRIBUTORS

GABRIEL A. ALMOND	*Stanford University*
FREDERICK C. BARGHOORN	*Yale University*
LEWIS J. EDINGER	*Columbia University*
HENRY W. EHRMANN	*Dartmouth College*
CHARLES W. GOSSETT	*Stanford University*
G. BINGHAM POWELL, JR.	*University of Rochester*
RICHARD ROSE	*University of Strathclyde*
ROBERT E. SCOTT	*University of Illinois*
JAMES R. TOWNSEND	*University of Washington*

SECOND EDITION

COMPARATIVE POLITICS TODAY

A World View

GENERAL EDITORS

GABRIEL A. ALMOND *Stanford University*

G. BINGHAM POWELL, JR. *University of Rochester*

LITTLE, BROWN AND COMPANY *Boston Toronto*

Library of Congress Catalog Card No. 79-87605

First Printing

Published simultaneously in Canada by Little, Brown & Company (Canada) Limited

Printed in the United States of America

Photograph Credits

Page 3, Henri Bureau/Sygma; 9, Tass from Sovfoto; 19, Bernard Pierre Wolff/Magnum; 26, Hilmar Pabel-Stern/Black Star; 30, Mary Ellen Mark/Magnum; 37, Eastfoto; 40, © 1979 Sipa Press from Black Star; 43, David Seymour/Magnum; 57, Charles Harbutt/Magnum; 61, Eastfoto; 66, Wide World Photos; 73, Mark Godfrey/Magnum; 78, © 1978 Sipa Press from Black Star; 82, Camera Press/Photo Trends; 90, © Harvé Glodguen/Viva from Woodfin Camp and Associates; 97, Sygma; 103, Raghu Rai/Magnum; 112, Fred Maroon/Louis Mercier; 118, Wide World Photos; 122, J. Boerig/Sygma; 131, Eastfoto; 138, Marc Riboud/Magnum; 144, © 1979 Sipa Press from Black Star; 153, T. R. Jones/Magnum; 173, Peter Marlow/Sygma; 195, A. DeAndrade/Magnum; 222, A. Bracelle/Sygma; 235, C. Raimond-Dityvon/Viva from Woodfin Camp and Associates; 249, C. Raimond-Dityvon/Viva from Woodfin Camp and Associates; 280, Bossu/Sygma; 292, Wide World Photos; 305, Sven Simon/Katherine Young; 324, Sovfoto; 341, Tass from Sovfoto; 357, Tass from Sovfoto; 386, Eastfoto; 410, Eastfoto; 425, Eastfoto; 439, Richard Melloul/Sygma; 483, Tanzania Information Service; 497, Marc Riboud/Magnum; 517, Eastfoto.

Preface

The second edition of *Comparative Politics Today: A World View* has been improved over the first edition in country coverage, analytic integration, and thematic balance.

It now includes a chapter on West Germany by Lewis Edinger, thus rounding out its European, advanced industrial offerings to include England, France, West Germany, and Russia. From the developing nations it again presents China, Mexico, and Tanzania. As the world's most populous nation, China is interesting in and of itself, but in addition its ideology and developmental strategy have had exemplary consequences in the rest of the "Third World." Our neighbor Mexico, one of the most rapidly growing Latin American nations, gives us insight into the politics of a partly industrialized nation combining democratic and authoritarian tendencies. Tanzania exemplifies the search among some of the new nations for a distinctive and equitable strategy of modernization.

The second major improvement is the effort of the authors to adhere to a common theoretical framework. We took seriously the requests of many of the users of the first edition that the theoretical chapters and country studies be more effectively integrated. The "system, process, policy" framework has been followed throughout the book. Our seven countries are systematically used, along with others, as illustrations in our theoretical chapters. Teachers and students wanting to make systematic comparisons will find their efforts greatly facilitated by the Analytic Appendix, which provides page references relating the theoretical discussions with the appropriate topical materials in the seven country studies. The Analytic Appendix also provides comparative questions for class discussion.

Finally *Comparative Politics Today* in its second edition gives more appropriate stress to the themes of constitutional and governmental organization, and public policy and performance. Chapters Seven and Eight of the theoretical introduction and the introductory and concluding parts of each country study treat these themes in some detail.

Comparative Politics Today continues to draw from the analytic and country studies of the Little, Brown series in *Comparative Politics*. The theoretical framework presented in Parts One and Two is adapted from Gabriel A. Almond and G. Bingham Powell, Jr., *Comparative Politics: System, Process, and Policy*. The chapters on political culture and socialization draw on Gabriel A. Almond and Sidney Verba, *The Civic Culture: Political Attitudes and Democracy in Five Nations*, and from Richard E. Dawson, Kenneth Prewitt, and Karen Dawson, *Political Socialization*. Five of the country studies presented in Part Three are revised, briefer versions of recent editions of Richard Rose, *Politics in England*; Henry W. Ehrmann, *Politics in France*; Lewis J. Edinger, *Politics in West Germany*; Frederick C. Barghoorn, *Politics in Russia*; and James R. Townsend, *Politics in China*.

We also acknowledge the assistance of others who helped us in this enterprise. We want to acknowledge again the important contributions of Neil K. Friedman, Robert J. Mundt, Andrew J. Perry, and Lawrence E. Rose to the first edition. Lewis Edinger wishes to acknowledge the assistance of Robert C. A. Sorensen of Columbia University in the preparation of the chapter on Germany; James R. Townsend, the assistance of Diane Fathi, Barbara Mahr, and Phillip Wall in the preparation of the chapter on China; Frederick Barghoorn, the assistance of Mr. Paul K. Cook in providing charts and data for the chapter on the U.S.S.R.; Charles Gossett, the advice and guidance given him by Professors David Abernethy and Goran Hyden in the preparation of the chapter on Tanzania; and Richard Rose, the assistance of the staff at the Centre for the Study of Public Policy at the University of Strathclyde. The work owes much to Lois Renner of Stanford University who handled the circulation of outlines and the processing of some of the draft chapters.

At Little, Brown our gratitude is owing to Richard Boyer and Gregory Franklin who shepherded the second edition from planning to fruition, to Barbara Garrey and Susan Warne who supervised the production process, and to Dale Anderson who carried through the copy-editing.

Gabriel A. Almond
G. Bingham Powell, Jr.

Contents

PART ONE

INTRODUCTION

GABRIEL A. ALMOND
G. BINGHAM POWELL, JR.

CHAPTER ONE

The Study of Comparative Politics

The comparative approach is as old as political science itself. Through the centuries, theorists have sought to understand and explain variations between the procedures and achievements of political systems. They have compared monarchy with democracy, constitutional rule with tyranny, bourgeois capitalist democracy with proletarian dictatorship, traditional regimes with modern ones, and the like.

When the social or political scientist studies human and social behavior he or she tries to be scientifically precise, observing changes in social and political phenomena in different periods of time, or noting differences in institutions and practices in different societies. If country A has a stable two-party system and country B has an unstable multiparty system, what other characteristics explain the difference? Like a laboratory scientist conducting an experiment, the political scientist tries to hold constant as many conditions as possible in an effort to find the special factors that may explain each country's distinctive characteristics.

Because their controls are less exact, the findings of political scientists are less scientifically reliable than those of biologists and physicists, but the intentions and logic of the comparative method are similar to those used in the more exact sciences. Aristotle, in his *Politics*, contrasted the economies and social structures of the many Greek city-states in an effort to determine how social and economic arrangements affected political institutions and organizations and the policies followed by these regimes. A modern political theorist, Robert Dahl, in his study *Polyarchy*, compares the economic characteristics, the cultures, and the historical experiences of the more than one hundred nations in the contemporary world in an effort to discover what combination of conditions and characteristics are associated with democracy.[1]

In comparing institutions and processes we normally go through three steps. The first step is simple description. Like the biologist who travels about collecting plants and animals, the political scientist looks at whole political systems or at their parts — legislatures, bureaucracies, party systems, court systems, and other political institutions — in various countries and at various times.

With many cases in hand we can carry out the second step, which is to sort out the findings, classify-

[1] Robert A. Dahl, *Polyarchy: Participation and Opposition* (New Haven, Conn.: Yale University Press, 1971).

ing the phenomena or grouping them into types. We discover that some political systems have bureaucracies and others do not; some have organized interest groups and others do not; some have relatively impartial courts and others do not. Among countries with political parties, some have only one party, some have two, others have a great many. More significantly, we observe that in some political systems the parties seem to be very important in selecting leaders and building support for policies, while in others, they merely express points of view, or try to encourage attitudes that support an authoritarian regime.

In the third stage of comparison, the political scientist looks for regularities in the relations among variables, such as the social and economic conditions usually present in stable democracies, the conditions that lead to civil disorder, the political consequences of industrialization, and the like. With many cases and examples, classified into types, and with the use of imagination and logic, we can develop theories about social and political relationships. By examining more cases, we can test our theories and thus increase confidence in their validity. As we gain confidence in our theories, we can use them to explain, and even to some degree predict, the political causes and consequences of new events.

Comparative studies are more than the beginning of political science; they provide the beginnings of political understanding and judgment. They give us perspective on our own institutions — their virtues and shortcomings — and what makes them the way they are. Examining the institutions of other countries permits us to see the range of political alternatives, their costs and advantages.

Political systems perform many functions. Here the police in Mexico restrain crowds cheering the arrival of Pope John Paul II in January 1979.

SYSTEM AND ENVIRONMENT: AN ECOLOGICAL APPROACH

Three concepts — system, structure, and function — provide the unity and coherence of this book. *System*, as we use the word, is an ecological concept implying an organization interacting with an environment, influencing it and being influenced by it. It also suggests that there are many interacting internal parts. The political system is part of the arrangements that a society has for formulating and pursuing its collective goals. The political system in a society is especially distinguished by its relation to accepted (legitimate) coercion: the policies made by the political system can legitimately be backed up by coercion and obedience compelled.

The collective goals of a society are pursued in many areas. Political systems wage war or encourage peace; cultivate international trade or restrict it; open their borders to the exchange of ideas and artistic experiences or close them; tax their populations equitably or inequitably; regulate behavior strictly or less strictly; allocate resources for education, health, and welfare, or fail to do so; pay due regard to the interdependence of man and nature, or permit nature's capital to be depleted or misused.

In order to carry on these many activities, political systems have institutions, or *structures*, such as parliaments, bureaucracies, courts, and political parties, which carry on specific activities, or *functions*, which in turn enable the political system to formulate and enforce its policies. System, structure, and function are all part of the same continuing process. They are essential for an understanding of how politics is affected by its natural and human environments, and how it affects them. They are the conceptual components of an ecological approach to politics.

Figure 1.1 suggests that a political system exists in both a domestic and an international environment, molding these environments and being molded by them. The system receives *inputs* of demands and support from these environments and attempts to shape them through its *outputs*. Let us suppose that Ruritania is a primarily agricultural, rural society, with a largely illiterate population. Much of the agricultural land is held by a small number of large landholders, and most of the people work on these large estates, depending on the landowners for their subsistence and protection. Their religion teaches them to accept their fate, that the principal virtues in life are hard work and obedience.

This kind of society, economy, and culture is unlikely to sustain a vigorous democracy, with competitive political parties, active trade unions, and chambers of commerce. It is more likely to have a traditional authoritarian regime, perhaps like Nepal, or Ethiopia before the military coup of 1974. The royal family and large landowners would be dominant in politics. Without popular elections, there would be no organized political parties. With little industry and commerce, there probably would not be influential trade unions or business organizations. In the diagram the arrows labeled "inputs," leading from the larger society to the *polity* (the politically organized segment of the society), would carry the demands of the aristocracy. The arrow labeled "outputs," leading from the polity to the larger society, might carry little more than regulatory and tax policies designed to maintain order and to provide the limited services such a society would require.

Ruritania engages in diplomatic, economic, cultural, and military interactions with its neighbors in the international environment, and must therefore have institutions for making and implementing foreign policy. If one or more of its neighbors follow aggressive policies toward Ruritania, or if Ruritania follows aggressive policies toward its neighbors, then it will have to build up its armed forces, increase taxation, or get foreign loans and support. Thus the Ruritanian political system is influenced by the structure and culture of its society and by relations with its neighbors.

However, the Ruritanian political system in its turn influences its society and its foreign neighbors. Suppose that a young king comes to power and joins forces with liberal landowners in an effort to modernize Ruritania. He institutes a public school system, builds roads, and fosters the development of industry. The population becomes literate, reads newspapers, and is interested in what is going on outside of its villages. The cities begin to grow. Ruritania begins to have people in business and the professions and industrial workers. These new social classes demand improvements: more schools, more industries, more roads, more pay, and shorter hours. Landowners and religious leaders, on the other hand, might demand an end to these policies, since they are changing the structure of power and the culture of Ruritanian society. Thus Ruritanian politics produces changes in Ruritanian society, and these changes feed back into politics, introducing new issues and new forms of political struggle.

What happens inside Ruritania affects its neighbors as well. The changes taking place in Ruritania become known in neighboring countries. Mauretania and Aquitania start to imitate it and adopt modernizing policies. Moravia and Groovia oppose these modernizations and suppress groups in their own societies that advocate following the Ruritanian example. The leaders of Moravia and Groovia may view these developments as so serious a threat that they increase their armed forces and threaten to invade Ruritania if it continues to follow its modernizing policies. As a consequence, Ruritania has to expend more of its resources on arms in order to defend its security. This may slow down its modernization. The arrows between Ruritania and its neighbors move both ways, reflecting the two-way interaction, just as the arrows within Ruritania move both ways between its society and political system.

The advantage of the ecological perspective is that it directs our attention to the larger issues of

Figure 1.1

The Political System and Its Environments

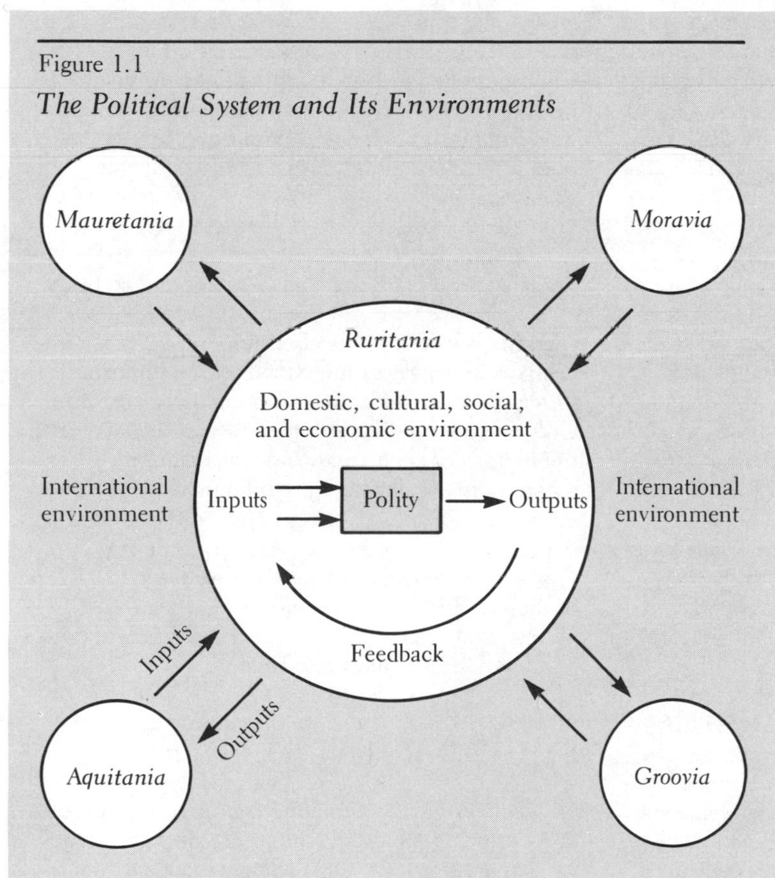

politics. If we are to make sound judgments in politics we need to place political systems in their environments, recognizing how these environments both set limits on and provide opportunities for political choices. The internal organization and procedures of a political system need to be understood within the framework of a basic question: what structures are most suitable for the policies pursued by that system?

The system-environment approach keeps us from reaching quick and biased political judgments. If a country is poor in natural resources and lacks skills necessary to exploit what it has, we cannot fault it for having a low industrial output or poor educational and social services. Similarly, a country dominated and exploited by another country with a conservative policy cannot be faulted for failing to introduce social reforms.

Up to this point we have been stressing the relation of the parts of a system to its overall foreign and domestic policy and performance. A nation pursuing an aggressive foreign policy will have to expand its military and create a larger civilian bureaucracy to support and control the larger armed forces. It will have to tax its people heavily, and it may have to control, regulate, and suppress opposition to its aggressive policy. In many important respects, therefore, the internal structure of a political system will vary with external policies. The same may be said of internal policies and the institutions and organizations needed to perform them. A nation that seeks to suppress opposition will have to expand its police forces, control the press, censor correspondence and newspapers, take over radio and television, and develop an intelligence apparatus in order to discover what people are thinking and whether they are likely to revolt.

The notion of interdependence goes even further than this relationship between policy and institutions. The institutions or parts of political systems are also interdependent. If a government is based on popularly elected representatives in legislative bodies, then a system of election must be instituted. If many people enjoy the right to vote, then the politicians seeking office will have to mobilize the electorate and organize political parties to carry on election campaigns. As the policy-making agencies of the political system enact laws they will need administrators and civil servants to implement these laws, and they will need judges to determine whether the laws have been violated, and what punishments are to be imposed on the violators.

POLITICAL STRUCTURES OR INSTITUTIONS

Figure 1.2 locates within the polity the familiar structures of the political system: interest groups, political parties, legislatures, executives, bureaucracies, and courts. The difficulty with this sixfold classification is that it will not carry us very far in comparing political systems with one another. Britain and France, for example, have all six types of political institutions, but they are not organized in the same way. Both countries have legislatures with two chambers (the House of Commons and House of Lords in Britain and the National Assembly and Senate in France); and both countries have councils of ministers (the Cabinet in Britain, the Council of Ministers in France). But Britain has a monarch and France does not. Britain has a prime minister and France has both a president and a prime minister. Britain tends to have a two-party system; France has more than half a dozen parties. Britain has one large trade-union organization; France has Communist, Socialist, and Catholic trade-union organizations.

But this institution-by-institution comparison, even for Western industrial democracies, would not bring us far toward understanding the important similarities and differences among these countries. Only when we see what role these institutions play in the pattern of performance do we begin to get at meaningful similarities and differences. The significance of the differences between the unified British and the fragmented French trade-union movements becomes clear when we trace the effect of these differences on the party system, the policy-making process, and the distribution of power and income in Britain and France.

STRUCTURE AND FUNCTION

Only when we begin to ask questions about process and performance can we attach meaning to structural characteristics. Only when we can say that spe-

Figure 1.2
The Political System and Its Structures

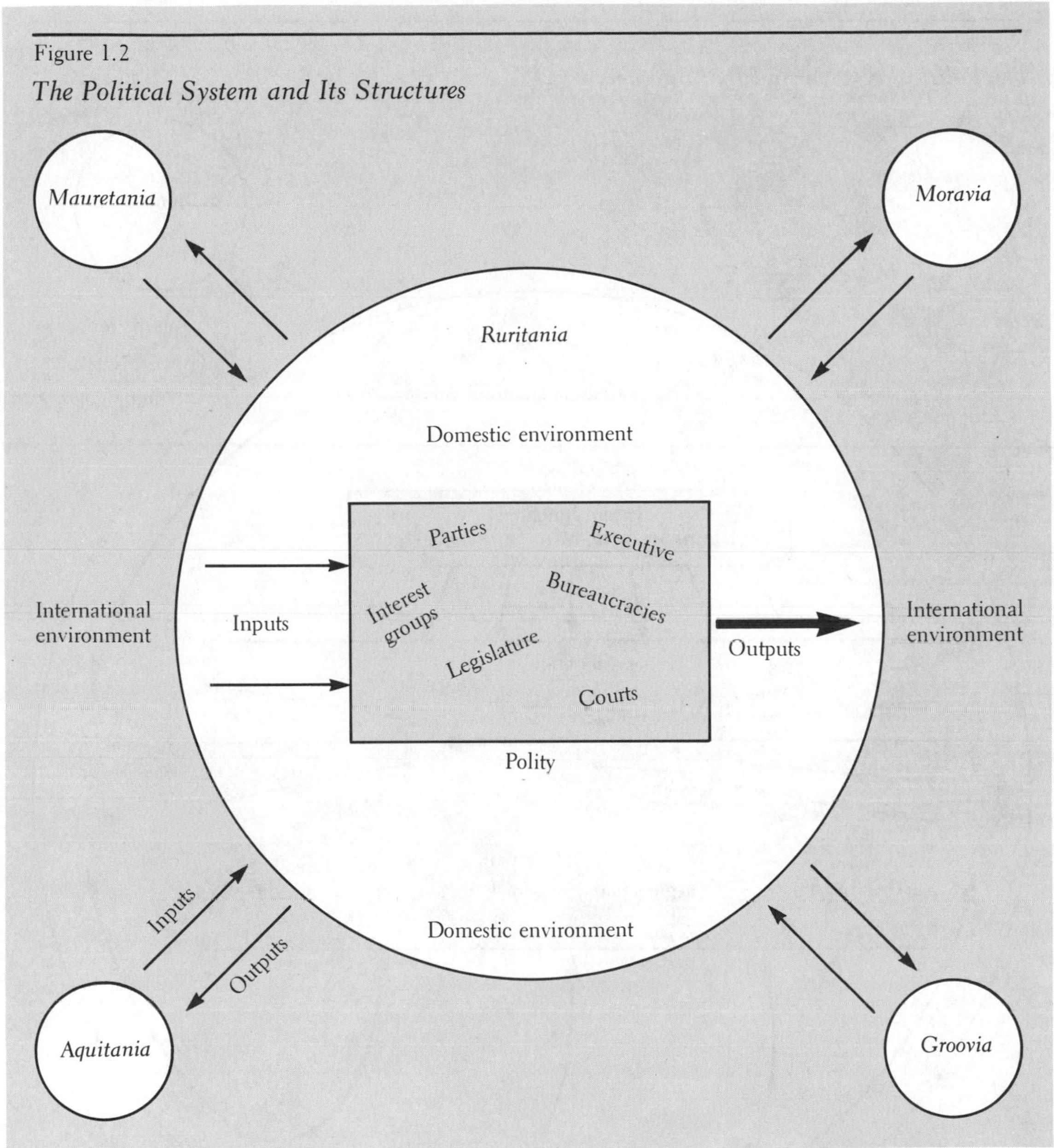

Figure 1.3
The Political System and Its Functions

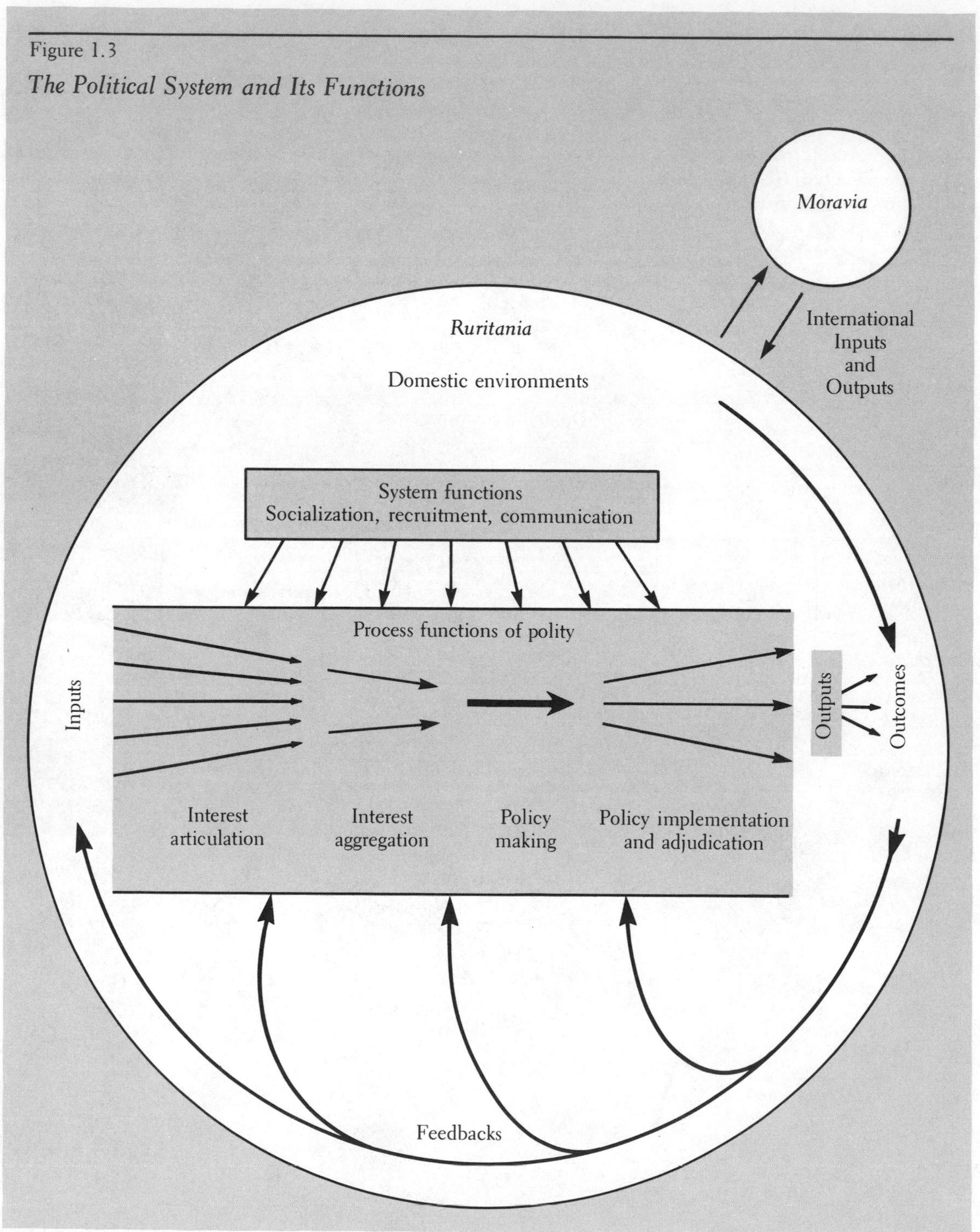

in the world today: Britain, France, and West Germany are industrialized democracies; the U.S.S.R. is an industrialized communist nation; China is a communist nation in the early stages of industrialization; Mexico is a partially industrialized, partially democratic nation; and Tanzania is a new country just embarking on economic and political development.

KEY TERMS

political system
structure
environment
interest aggregation
implementation
political socialization
political communication
demands
feedback
ecological approach
function
interest articulation
policy making
adjudication
political recruitment
inputs
supports
case studies

CHAPTER TWO

The Environment of the Political System

In our introductory discussion of political systems we suggested that the social and international environments have great impact on political processes. These environments shape the issues of politics. They confront the political system with sets of problems, such as economic growth, inflation, or national security, and possibilities and limitations in resources with which to meet these problems. A large, industrial, wealthy society such as the United States faces a different set of problems and has different levels of resources than a smaller, agricultural society such as Tanzania. We may think of the structural-functional arrangements in a nation as a basic strategy for dealing with these issues — a strategy, however, that is further shaped by many more specific policy efforts. In this chapter we want to outline some of the most important of the environmental features that shape political issues.

OLD NATIONS, NEW NATIONS

Almost the entire land surface of the globe today is divided into independent national territories. Two centuries ago, at the time the United States was gaining its independence, most independent nations were in Europe, with much of the rest of the world parceled out as colonies belonging to one or another of the European empires. The great shift in recent history has been from empire to nation. More than half of the one hundred and fifty or so contemporary states have acquired their independence since the end of World War II.

Figure 2.1 shows the explosion of nations that began in the nineteenth century, when the Spanish and Portuguese empires in Latin America broke up into twenty independent nations. Between World War I and World War II, six new nations in North Africa and the Middle East acquired their independence from the Ottoman, French, and British empires, and the collapse of the Russian and Austro-Hungarian empires resulted in nine additional independent states in Eastern Europe. Since World War II, forty new nations have replaced the European colonies in sub-Saharan Africa; fifteen newly independent countries emerged in the Islamic areas of North Africa and the Middle East; seven new nations were created in Latin America; and fifteen nations in South, Southeast, and East Asia broke free from British, French, Dutch, and Japanese control. The

Figure 2.1
Formation of Nations Since the Eighteenth Century

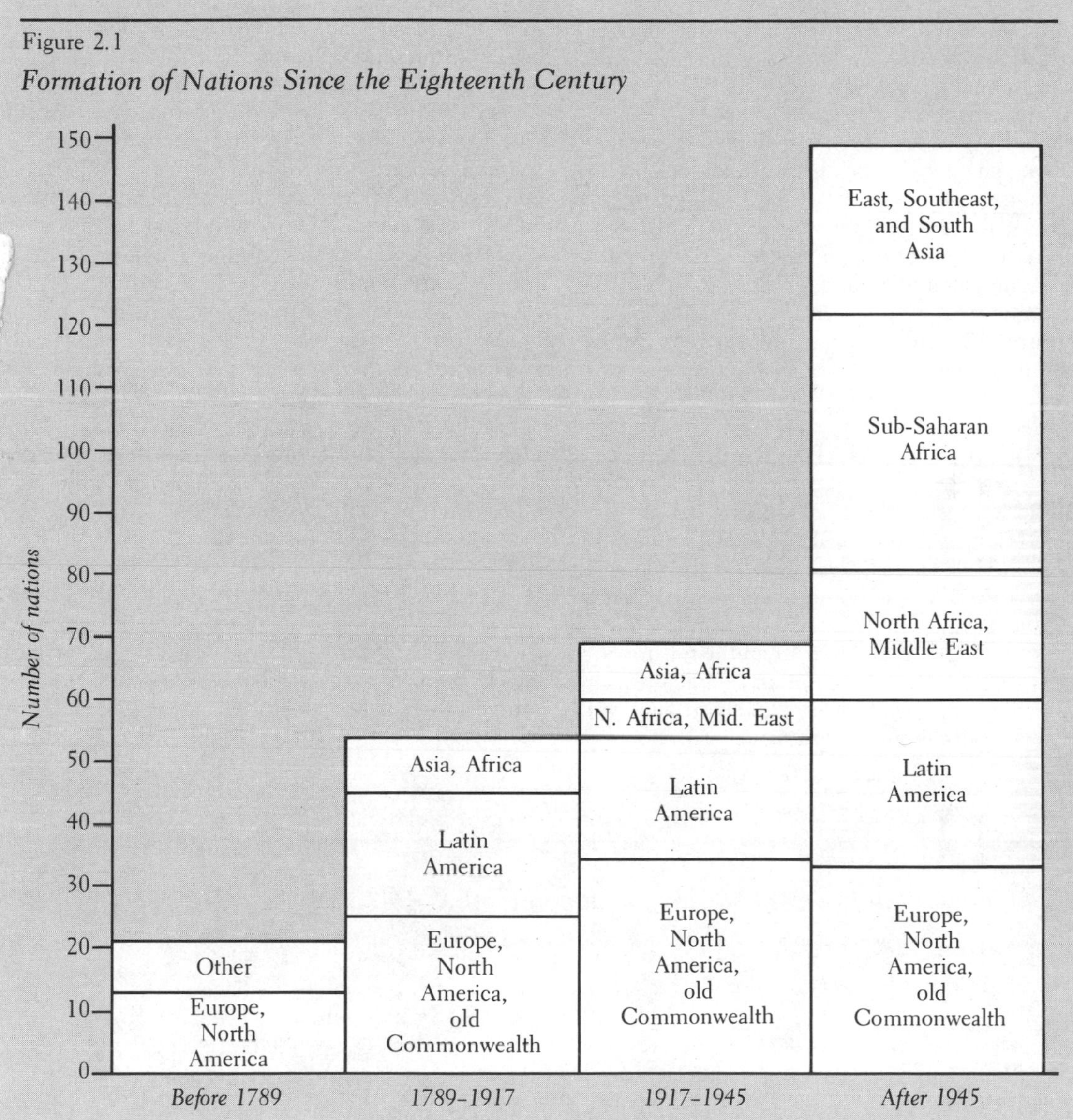

Source: Data to 1945 from Charles S. Taylor and Michael C. Hudson, *World Handbook of Political and Social Indicators,* 2nd ed. (New Haven, Conn.: Yale University Press, 1972), pp. 26 ff.; data after 1945 from *The World Almanac* (New York: Newspaper Enterprise Association, 1978), pp. 511 ff.

number of nations in Europe declined by one: although Germany split into two states and Cyprus acquired its independence, the Soviet Union annexed Latvia, Lithuania, and Estonia.

All these nations — new as well as old — share characteristics. They have legal authority over their territories and people; they have armies, air forces, and in some cases, navies; they send and receive ambassadors; almost all of them belong to the United Nations; they collect taxes; and they seek to regulate their economies and maintain order through parliaments, ministries and departments, courts, police, and prisons. But they also vary enormously, and in many different ways.

BIG NATIONS, SMALL NATIONS

Consider territorial size. The largest nation is the Soviet Union, with over 8,500,000 square miles. It is more than 35,000 times larger than Singapore, which occupies only 225 square miles. The United States and China cover over 3,600,000 square miles, an area nearly a thousand times larger than the territory of Lebanon.

Contrasts in population are equally striking (see Table 2.1). But the political significance of population size and geographic area is not obvious, or easily evaluated. It does not follow that only big countries are important and influential. Albania defies the Soviet Union; Cuba successfully challenges the United States; Israel stands off the entire Arab world. Nor does it follow that area and population size determine a country's political system. Luxembourg and the United States are both democracies; China and Albania are both Communist. Traditional authoritarian regimes can be found in countries that are small, medium, or large. These enormous contrasts in size show only that the nations now making up the world differ greatly in their range of physical and human resources. And although area and population (as well as geographic location) do not strictly determine politics, economics, or culture, they are important factors affecting economic development, foreign policy and defense problems, and many other issues of political significance.

RICH NATIONS, POOR NATIONS

At least as significant as physical size and population are such things as the availability of natural resources, the level of economic and social development, ethnic and cultural characteristics, and the

Table 2.1

Estimated Populations of Nations by Region, 1975–1977

Region	*Largest*	*Smallest*
Latin America	Brazil: 109,180,000	Grenada: 100,000
Middle East and North Africa	Turkey: 40,160,000	Qatar: 100,000
Sub-Saharan Africa	Nigeria: 64,750,000	São Tomé and Príncipe: 80,000
South Asia	India: 610,080,000	Maldives: 120,000
Southeast Asia	Indonesia: 139,620,000	Singapore: 2,280,000
East Asia	China: 852,130,000	North Korea: 16,250,000
Western Europe and North America	United States: 216,817,000	Luxembourg: 360,000
Eastern Europe	U.S.S.R.: 257,900,000	Albania: 2,550,000

Source: The World Almanac & Book of Facts, 1978 edition (New York: Newspaper Enterprise Association, 1978), pp. 511 ff. Copyright © 1977 by the Newspaper Enterprise Association.

An environment of low economic growth and underdeveloped human skills, exemplified here in Rajasthan (India), severely limits political capabilities.

rate of economic growth and social change. Furthermore, it may be misleading to distinguish among nations on the basis of total mineral resources, gross national production, and the like. Wealth, income, opportunity, and even historical memories and language are not evenly distributed within a nation. A high gross national product may conceal significant inequalities in the distribution of economic and social amenities and opportunities. A high rate of national growth may benefit only particular regions or social groups, leaving large areas or parts of the population unrewarded or even less well off than before.

Figure 2.2 gives the gross national product (GNP) per capita for eleven nations from all parts of the world. (Seven are the countries studied in this book. The remaining four extend the range and variety of comparison.) Gross national product is an estimate of the value of goods and services produced by the people in a country in a given year. As it is only an estimate, the figure must be used cautiously. The figure for the GNP of poorer nations, for instance, tends to underestimate goods and services produced and consumed by individuals themselves, particularly when they are engaged in subsistence agriculture. Although we must be cautious in using these figures, there can be no question that the range of difference between the GNP of rich nations and poor nations is enormous.

Let us compare Figure 2.3, which measures the proportion of the working population engaged in agriculture, with Figure 2.2, measuring GNP per capita. We find that the United States, with the highest per capita national product, has the second smallest proportion of work force in agriculture, and that China, the fourth lowest in per capita national product, has 67 percent of its workers in agriculture.

Figure 2.2

Per Capita Gross National Product for Selected Nations 1975 (in U.S. Dollars)

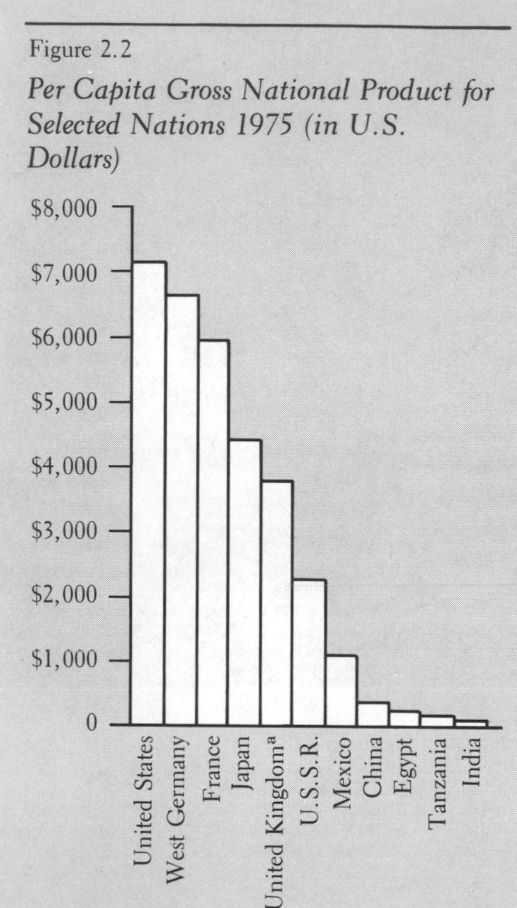

[a] Statistical data for cross-national comparisons in most cases refer to the United Kingdom, which includes both Great Britain (England, Scotland and Wales) and Northern Ireland, rather than to Britain alone. Tables in Chapters 1–8 reflect that fact, although we shall often discriminate between the very different political situations in Britain and Northern Ireland in our discussion.

Source: World Bank, *World Bank Atlas* (Washington, D.C.: World Bank, 1977), pp. 6–7.

Figure 2.3

Percentage of Labor Force in Agriculture for Selected Nations

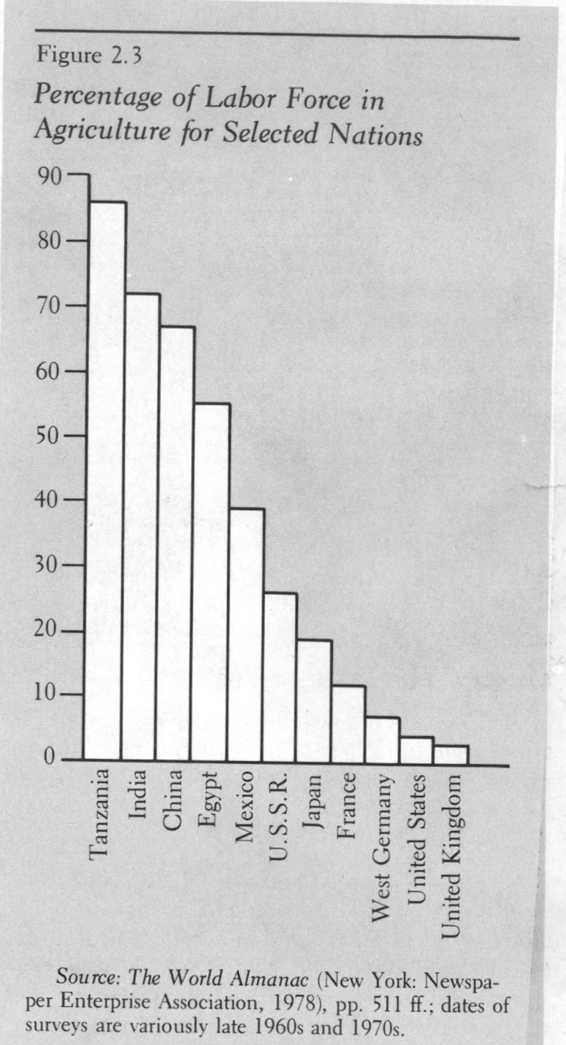

Source: The World Almanac (New York: Newspaper Enterprise Association, 1978), pp. 511 ff.; dates of surveys are variously late 1960s and 1970s.

The rich countries, on the whole, prove to be predominantly industrial, commercial, and urban while the poor countries, consistently, are predominantly agricultural and rural.

To be rich and industrialized also means to be literate, educated, and to have access to the larger world of complex events, activities, and values. In the six most industrialized countries in our list — Britain, France, West Germany, the United States, the U.S.S.R., and Japan — practically everyone over the age of fifteen years can read and write, while in India, Tanzania, and Egypt only one-third of the population or less has this minimal degree of educa-

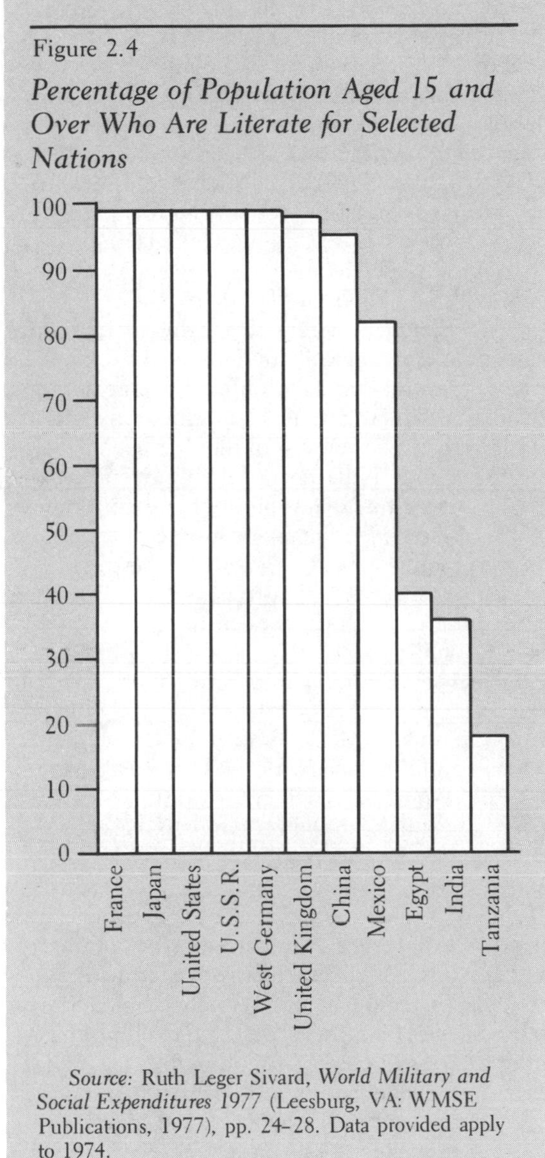

Figure 2.4

Percentage of Population Aged 15 and Over Who Are Literate for Selected Nations

Source: Ruth Leger Sivard, *World Military and Social Expenditures* 1977 (Leesburg, VA: WMSE Publications, 1977), pp. 24–28. Data provided apply to 1974.

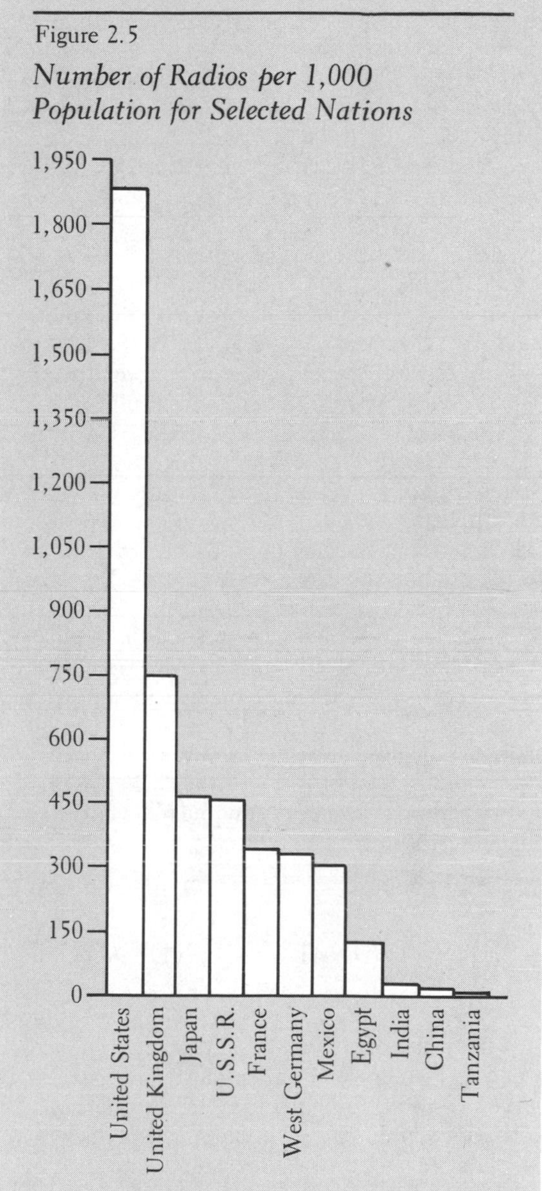

Figure 2.5

Number of Radios per 1,000 Population for Selected Nations

Source: UNESCO Statistical Yearbook, 1977 (Paris: UNESCO, 1978), pp. 1002–1007. The data are from 1975 except for the United Kingdom, U.S.S.R. and Mexico, which are from 1974, and China, which are from 1970.

tion. (See Figure 2.4.) Moreover, the countries with the fewest literate citizens are also most lacking in radios and other communication devices that do not require literacy. (See Figure 2.5.)

Industrialization, education, and exposure to the media of communication are associated with better nutrition and medical care. In the economically advanced countries fewer children die in infancy, and people on the average live longer. In recent years the average citizen of Britain, France, Germany, Japan, the United States, and the U.S.S.R. has had a life expectancy of seventy years or more at birth. The average newborn Mexican, however, has had a life expectancy of a little more than sixty-two years, the average Egyptian a little more than fifty-two years, and the average Indian or Tanzanian a little more than forty years (see Table 8.5).

These characteristics — material productivity, education, exposure to the media of communication, longer and healthier lives — are closely interconnected. Only when a country becomes economically productive can it afford better education, communications media, and nutrition and health care. In order to become more productive it needs the resources to develop a skilled and healthy labor force and build the factories, productive farms, and transportation systems that material welfare requires. Preindustrial nations face most urgently the issues of economic development: how to improve the immediate welfare of their citizens, yet also build and invest for the future. Typically, these are also newer nations, and face as well the challenge of creating national awareness and building effective political institutions.

INTERNATIONAL DEPENDENCE AND INDEPENDENCE

The international setting has important influences on political issues. Among the most important aspects of the international setting are the questions of international political and economic dependence on other political systems. The nations treated in this book have substantial political independence, although some of them, such as Britain, France, and Germany, have become members of international organizations (the European Economic Community) with important roles in domestic life. Other nations, such as Poland, Czechoslovakia, and Hungary, are more thoroughly dominated. The Soviet Union invaded Czechoslovakia in 1968 when it disapproved of the direction of that country's domestic political reforms, and maintains armed forces and at least a constraining overall policy direction in a number of other nations. One cannot reasonably discuss the political process in such penetrated nations without taking into account the role played by other political systems in their policy making.

Economic dependence in the international sphere is also an important feature of the environment of the political system. Typically, it has been the poor and economically underdeveloped nations of the world that have suffered from economic dependence. Their national economies have often had a large foreign trade sector that has been a major basis for income. With most of their citizens employed in agriculture of low productivity, this foreign sector has often been the major source of resources for governmental activities, whether investment for the future or spending on current welfare. But often the foreign trade sector is concentrated on a single product, such as sugar in Cuba or copper in Chile, and subject to fluctuating international prices. Often, too, trade is concentrated on a single other nation, as the trade of Mexico is with the United States, or Cuba's and Bulgaria's with the U.S.S.R. In such cases, the resources on which the domestic system depends are subject to the economic policies of, and perhaps political manipulation by, the leaders of other countries.

Table 2.2 provides some measures of economic dependence and interdependence for the nations we have been discussing. The relatively fortunate position of the great industrial powers, the United States and the Soviet Union, is very clear. Less than 10 percent of their GNP comes from foreign trade, and they are not dependent on a single commodity or a single foreign nation for exports. Japan and the Western European nations have large international sectors, but are relatively diversified. Even these data may be somewhat misleading; they may hide some problems. The dependence of the United States and many other industrialized countries on imported oil has given rise to great concern about the impact of Arab oil policies on their economies. Nor do such data reflect the important role of the huge multi-

Table 2.2

International Economic Dependence: Measures for Selected Nations, 1965

Country	*Foreign trade as percentage of GNP*	*Concentration of export commodities*[a]	*Concentration of export receiving countries*[a]
Tanzania	42.1%	23	9
Egypt	32.7%	37	8
West Germany	31.5%	10	7
United Kingdom	29.1%	9	5
France	21.7%	6	8
Japan	19.7%	9	9
Mexico	13.9%	9	31
U.S.S.R.	9.8%	na	7
India	9.1%	17	10
United States	7.3%	8	7
China	6.0%	na	na

[a] The concentration indices reflect the dominance of total export values by a few large products or exports to only a few countries. Technically, the index is calculated by the formula $c = \Sigma p_i^2$ where p_i is the proportion of total value of exports accounted for by the ith commodity or country.

Source: Charles S. Taylor and Michael C. Hudson, *World Handbook of Political and Social Indicators*, 2nd ed. (New Haven, Conn.: Yale University Press, 1972), pp. 366 ff. By permission.

national corporations, with budgets as large as those of many countries, whose decisions can sharply affect international economic outcomes.

Mexico has a smaller international trade sector, but nearly one-third of it is with the United States alone. Egypt and Tanzania, at the more dependent end of the scale, have substantial foreign trade sectors, and their trade incomes are strongly tied to a single commodity, cotton for Egypt and coffee for Tanzania. These cases are not as extreme as those of some other nations not included in Table 2.2. For example, in 1965 over half of Cuba's GNP was produced by foreign trade; 75 percent of foreign trade was accounted for by sugar alone, and 25 percent of it went to a single nation, the U.S.S.R. No wonder the issue of economic independence and diversification is so important in such nations.

ECONOMIC INEQUALITY WITHIN NATIONS

The political processes of a country may be affected sharply by internal divisions of income, wealth, and occupation, as well as by economic dependence or poverty. Table 2.3 compares wealth and income inequality for those on which we have data, substituting Czechoslovakia and Bulgaria for the U.S.S.R. (Unfortunately, no data were available for the U.S.S.R. or China.) The table makes two very clear points. First, as several studies have shown, the command economics of communist nations can be used to ensure relative equality of income for the bulk of the population. (However, such measures do not reflect the substantial privilege and greater access

Table 2.3

Selected Nations Ranked by per Capita GNP and Equality of Income Distribution, Recent Years

Country[a]	*Ranking in GNP per capita*	*Ranking in equality of income distribution before taxes*[b]
United States	1	4
West Germany	2	7
France	3	8
Japan	4	5
United Kingdom	5	3
Czechoslovakia	6	1
Bulgaria	7	2
Mexico	8	11
Egypt	9	9
Tanzania	10	10
India	11	6

[a] No data available for China or U.S.S.R.

[b] Rank is based on share of income going to wealthiest 20 percent of population, according to data from the 1960s or early 1970s.

Source: For 1975 GNP rank, World Bank, *World Bank Atlas* (Washington, D.C.: World Bank, 1977), pp. 6–7. For income distribution, Hollis Chenery et al., *Redistribution with Growth: An Approach to Policy* (London: Oxford University Press, 1974), pp. 8–9, except for Egypt, which is an estimate based on Charles S. Taylor and Michael C. Hudson, *World Handbook of Political and Social Indicators*, 2nd ed. (New Haven, Conn: Yale University Press, 1972), pp. 263 ff.

to luxury goods and services that accompany political position in such systems.) Second, there tends to be a positive association between economic development and equality of income, at least past a certain stage in economic growth. Wealthy nations like the United States and the European nations tend to have more equitable income distributions than poorer countries, like Tanzania and Mexico.

The association of industrialization and high productivity with more equal distribution of income has been true historically and tends to be true today. The trend toward greater equality in industrial societies is more marked with respect to income — that is, wages, salaries, and the like — than to wealth — ownership of land or other forms of property. The first stages of industrialization and modernization may actually *increase* inequality in the distribution of income by creating a dual economy and society — a rural sector, with wide variation of landholding and status, and an urban industrial commercial sector, with its own differentials in income and consumption patterns. These inequalities, already present in most preindustrial societies, tend to increase at the same time that education and communication are spreading, which helps explain the political instability of many developing countries. It also helps explain their susceptibility to radical ideologies and egalitarian political movements. Inequality, then, is an issue that must be faced by all developing nations. We shall examine some of the strategies applied to that problem later.

The fact that inequalities are often less extreme in the advanced industrial nations does not mean that the issue of inequality is unimportant there. Britain, among the countries with a more equal distribution of income, is frequently agitated by intense conflicts between industry and labor over the distribution of wealth, income, and opportunity. The failure of British industry to grow rapidly has compounded these problems. And some industrial nations, such as France and Italy, have very substantial income inequality, a major issue associated with the development of strong Communist parties in these two nations. When a study in 1975 showed that France had the most inequitable post-tax income distribution of twenty-four relatively industrialized nations, the French Communist and Socialist parties intensified demands for redistribution.

Table 2.4

Selected Nations Ranked by Degree of Ethnic-Linguistic Heterogeneity

Rank	*Country*
1	Tanzania
2	India
3	U.S.S.R.
4	United States
5	United Kingdom
6	Mexico
7	France
8	China
9	Egypt
10	West Germany
11	Japan

Source: Charles S. Taylor and Michael C. Hudson, *World Handbook of Political and Social Indicators*, 2nd ed. (New Haven, Conn.: Yale University Press, 1972), pp. 271 ff. By permission.

CULTURAL HETEROGENEITY WITHIN NATIONS

Nations are not only divided horizontally according to disparities in income, wealth, and opportunity; they are often divided vertically by language, culture, and religion. Table 2.4 ranks our selected nations according to the degree of ethnic-linguistic heterogeneity, that is, by the diversity — the sheer number — of different languages and ethnic strains found among their populations. Tanzania, ranking highest, contains more than a hundred tribal groups speaking different languages and dialects, although Swahili is commonly used throughout the country. The largest tribal group includes under 10 percent of the population. However, the extreme cultural fragmentation of Tanzania is in itself a form of insurance against ethnic conflict, since there is no dominant tribe capable of exploiting smaller tribes. India is also divided into many linguistic-cultural groups, but a dominant language — Hindi — is spoken by almost 40 percent of the population. Efforts to make Hindi the official language produced major violent clashes in the mid-1960s, and will no doubt continue to trouble Indian politics in the future.

Racial conflict has agitated American politics, particularly in recent decades. Ethnic problems are serious in the Soviet Union, but they rarely break above the surface because of governmental repression. Britain suffers ethnic cleavages in Northern Ireland, Wales, and Scotland, as well as in England, with the recent influx of blacks and Asians. In Northern Ireland the cleavages are accentuated by religious and nationalist differences that have produced a civil war. Although the countries at the bottom of the scale are less troubled by ethnic-linguistic conflicts, even Japan, the most culturally homogeneous nation on our list, has an "untouchable" minority, the Buraku-Min, who number about two million and who are confined to lowly occupations and segregated in ghettos.

The Russian invasion of Czechoslovakia in 1968 demonstrated overt international domination; an old woman cries at the ouster of her national leaders, whose photographs she holds.

PROBLEMS CONFRONTING INDUSTRIAL AND PREINDUSTRIAL NATIONS

Consideration of various features of the domestic and international environments shows that we must distinguish sharply between the problems confronting industrial and preindustrial nations. Table 2.5 contrasts these types of problems and the difficulties that industrial and preindustrial nations have in coping with them.

The table begins with the problems of governmental organization. The advanced industrial nations have for the most part well-established agencies for making and implementing policy, with experienced political leaders and civil servants performing the various jobs. Their advantages here stem in part from their longer historical independence, as we saw in Table 2.1, in part from the greater social and economic skills and resources they command, and in part from the greater compatibility of modern organizations with their more rationalized modern culture.

But we do not mean that industrial nations have no problems of governmental organization. The growth of government in advanced industrial societies, and the increased rates of taxation and public expenditure required for that growth, have been meeting increased public resistance, demands for cutbacks in government programs, pressure for greater efficiency in governmental performance, and efforts to limit and reduce taxation and government expenditure. In communist advanced industrial societies there are similar policy conflicts over the efficiency and productivity of government organiza-

Table 2.5

Policy Problems Confronting Industrial and Preindustrial Nations

Policy problem	*Industrial nations*	*Preindustrial nations*
Governmental organization	*Maintaining* and *adapting* existing policy-making and implementing agencies (e.g., reform of parliament, reorganization of provincial and local government)	*Creating* effective governmental agencies; recruitment and training of governmental personnel
National unity	*Coping with* persistent tendencies toward ethnic and subcultural fragmentation	*Creating* national identity and loyalty
Economic development	*Maintaining* satisfactory growth rate through some combination of public and private investment and use of fiscal controls and incentives	*Accumulating* capital from domestic and foreign sources for investment in industry and industrial infrastructure (e.g., transportation, education)
Economic stability	*Combining* satisfactory growth rate with control of inflation; *maintaining* balance of payments equilibrium and adequate employment	*Coping with* fluctuations in demand for raw materials, extreme inflation resulting from rapid and uneven growth, and acute unemployment problems due to urban migration
Social welfare	*Maintaining* educational opportunity, medical care, old-age assistance, etc. in time of limited growth and taxpayer resistance	*Creating* educational and welfare systems
Participation	*Responding to* demands for popular participation and from disadvantaged racial, ethnic, status, age, and sex groups; *coping with* demands for greater participation in industry and local communities	*Creating* organizations for participation: political parties, interest groups, communications media, local community organizations
Quality of life	*Coping with* problems of industrial growth, urban blight, and consumption of natural resources	*Coping with* environmental deterioration, the crowding caused by urban migration, and beginning conservation
Foreign and security policy	*Maintaining* national security through weapons development and alliance systems; *seeking* to reduce risks of war through disarmament negotiations and effective foreign trade diplomacy	*Dealing with* economic and security dependency through integration in Western or Eastern camp, or *maintaining* a neutral posture; *coping with* foreign trade and investment problems

tion and performance, but these conflicts are largely hidden, and the solutions are limited to those consistent with a centralized, penetrative, authoritarian organization. In the advanced industrial nations — communist or not — solutions to problems in organization usually take the form of adaptations of the already existing and widely accepted government institutions. Their organizational problems are different from those encountered in the Third World.

Some democratic industrial nations, of course, have quite powerful revolutionary movements. Both France and Italy have large Communist parties whose supporters favor fundamental changes in governmental organization and power. But this problem is still different from that confronting many preindustrial nations, which have to develop, for the first time, effective governmental and political agencies through which the central authorities can reach into the countryside, extract resources from people, provide benefits for them, regulate their behavior, and provide organizations through which their needs and demands may be expressed. These problems are not of the same order throughout the Third World. The problems of governmental organization in a country like India differ greatly from those facing a country like Tanzania. In India, where the British left an effective governmental machinery and personnel, the government still has difficulty reaching into the villages, where most of the Indian people live. But Tanzania must create governmental machinery where almost none existed before.

A second point of contrast is in the area of national unity or identity. The industrial nations are all relatively old countries. The sense of being French, Japanese, American, British, or Russian is well established, and much of the population has a sense of national loyalty, a readiness to make sacrifices for the interests of the nation and comply with national laws. Most of the advanced industrial nations may be said to have this problem of national unity under control, although we must not forget such recent manifestations of ethnic conflict as Britain's problems in Northern Ireland, Scotland, and Wales, and Canada's difficulties with the French-speaking in Quebec.

In the preindustrial nations, many of which have existed for only a decade or two, the problem of national identity and loyalty may be far more serious. For example, the notion of being a Nigerian rather than primarily a member of a tribe — an Ibo, a Yoruba, or a Hausa-Fulani — is new, and traditional tribal allegiances are difficult to reconcile with the need for compliance with national laws and policies.

The problems of economic policy facing industrial and preindustrial nations break into three parts: maintaining economic growth; maintaining economic stability in terms of prices, wages, and employment; and responding to demands for improvements in social services. Even the most advanced industrial nations must maintain a satisfactory rate of growth through some combination of public and private investment, and through the use of fiscal controls in order to meet rising expectations among various groups in the population for improvements in their welfare. In the advanced industrial democracies the reconciliation of economic growth, stable prices, and adequate employment has recently become an increasingly difficult problem. But maintaining a satisfactory rate of growth, price stability and adequate employment is different from introducing modern industry and commerce, the problem confronting preindustrial nations. Before preindustrial nations can move toward industrialization they must find capital for investment in industry and supporting services, make the right investment decisions, and train a skilled labor force.

After a period of overoptimism regarding the possibilities for rapid industrialization and modernization in the new nations, it has been generally recognized that the processes will be slow and difficult. But in the meantime, the spread of modern communications media causes the people of the new nations to demand modern products and services. Thus their weak economies and fragile political institutions are overwhelmed by demands for a share in the benefits of modern industrial civilization that are beyond their capacities to provide.

Although all countries are troubled by inflation and unemployment, these are particularly difficult for preindustrial and newly industrializing nations. Many of them are dependent upon a single raw material, such as coffee, cocoa, or sugar, exported to foreign markets. Prices for these products in the international markets often fluctuate widely, producing boom and depression, with serious economic and political consequences. It is true that the energy shortage has given advantages to those preindustrial nations with oil resources; but they are only a small minority in the Third World, and the oil reserves are limited, and in some areas nearing depletion. Thus in both areas of economic policy — growth and stability — the preindustrial nations face far more difficult problems without the skills and resources required to cope effectively with them.

Problems of social-welfare policy in the industrial nations occur in the form of demands for the extension of educational opportunity or the provision and maintenance of adequate medical care, old age or unemployment assistance, and the like. These continued pressures on scarce resources create serious problems, but a country that is increasing its productivity can make incremental improvements in the level of welfare expenditures out of the fiscal dividend, the increase in tax yields resulting from the imposition of the same level of taxation on an increasing tax base.

In preindustrial nations the problem is different. Welfare demands increase; the tax base does not grow as rapidly; and other claims on scarce governmental resources may be even more compelling. This combination of a slow rate of economic growth, extreme fluctuations in markets, and rising demand for social services creates a set of economic problems that would overload any political system, particularly a system in which people are free to organize political groups and seek to influence public policy. But political parties, trade unions, and commercial and professional organizations formed in preindustrial nations tend to be new organizations with inexperienced leaders and without modern systems of communications. Thus the impact of popular demands is quite volatile and uneven.

This is not to suggest that there are no problems of political participation in industrial nations. Indeed, democratic industrial countries often face demands from previously disadvantaged racial, ethnic, status, age, and sex groups for opportunities to participate; and in authoritarian industrial countries intellectuals and other disaffected groups occasionally demand freedom or even revolt. But, without minimizing the gravity of these demands, they occur in political systems where organizations and traditions of political participation already exist and where incremental responses are possible.

Quality of life as a political issue is unique to the industrial nations. Indeed, it is industrialization that is responsible for the problem. Environmentalism and quality-of-life issues came to a head in the late 1960s as the social costs of industrialization became increasingly evident. For the first time, on a significant political scale, the absolute value of industrial growth and material welfare began to be questioned, and steps were taken to control industrial pollution and urban blight, to reduce the exploitation of natural resources and the aesthetic deterioration of the environment. Though preindustrial nations may be exhausting their resources and contaminating their environments, the demands for industrialization and increasing material welfare so greatly outweigh these longer-run considerations that they can hardly be said to constitute political problems. In Third World areas having valuable raw materials such as oil there is some concern for conservation, but the politics of aesthetics and environmentalism cannot be said to have reached the Third World yet.

In the industrial nations, problems of foreign and security policy occur in the form of questions like the following. What shall we invest in weapons development, and what shall be the size, composition, and method of recruitment of the armed forces? How can national security be enhanced and the costs of military expenditures reduced through diplomacy and alliances? How can foreign trade be enhanced through foreign economic policy and diplomacy? In the industrial nations the problem of foreign and security policy naturally varies substantially from country to country, particularly in relation to their power and strategic significance. The United States and Russia, as the two leading, ideologically opposed, industrial powers are more preoccupied by and involved in international conflict than most other nations. For the United States and the Soviet Union, foreign policy imposes a far greater burden on national resources than it does on the other advanced industrial nations.

Unusually complex and intractable problems of foreign trade, balance of payments, and instability in the value of currencies have arisen as a result of the energy crisis. This may be only the first major challenge to the policy ingenuity and creativity of the advanced industrial nations as the supply of essential raw materials begins to run low. Still, their general

Children in Northern Ireland take occupation forces nearly for granted; the ethnic conflict between Catholics and Protestants has cost over two thousand lives and much hardship.

economic productivity gives the industrial nations a powerful basis from which to approach trade problems.

The problems of foreign policy for the preindustrial nations are different. Without industry or economic diversification, they tend to become dependent, both economically and politically, on one or the other, or both, of the two competing power blocs. Having economies of low productivity, they often need outside aid and investment in order to achieve economic growth. Their often undeveloped sense of national identity makes them particularly vulnerable to outside intervention designed to mobilize ethnic and regional groups. The weakness of political and military organization makes defense against external intervention by other powers difficult unless assistance can be found.

INDUSTRIALIZATION AND DEMOCRATIZATION AS DEVELOPMENTAL GOALS

For well over a century, the goals of industrialization and democratization have been taken for granted in the West. Even the Marxist-Leninists who made the Russian Revolution viewed these values as absolute ends, differing from the liberals of Western Europe and America only in their sense of timing and strategy. The Russian Revolution was the starting point for an enormously costly and largely successful effort at industrialization. Some other partially developed communist countries have achieved high rates of industrial growth by controlling capital and suppressing demands for consumption and welfare. Of the twin democratic values they have opted for equality at the cost of liberty. However, not all growth rates in communist Eastern Europe have been equally impressive,[1] and although they have eliminated inequality based on the private ownership of wealth and large income differentials, they have introduced inequalities of their own based on the special access of political elites and other privileged groups to scarce goods and services.

The success of communist industrialization, as well as the collapse of some democratic regimes among the new nations, has shaken Western faith in the inevitability of democracy in history. Similarly, the spotty efforts of both capitalists and communists to stimulate rapid economic growth among the preindustrial nations has shaken faith in the capacity of the new nations for economic modernization under any system. And even as these disillusionments from outside the Western world have shaken its confidence in the superiority and exportability of its values and institutions, values have begun to change internally. Particularly among the young, educated members of the middle class in Western European and American society, there is a growing ambivalence about material values, the absolute virtue of hard work and achievement. It is a mood that fosters social experimentation, a new attitude toward nature, a greater emphasis on spiritual values and the cultivation of human relationships.

It is quite unlikely that these tendencies among the educated young in the West will lead to a dismantling of industrial civilization. But that they are more than youthful excesses is suggested by growing anxiety in Western countries over industrial and other forms of environmental pollution, urban blight, the exhaustion of natural resources, and the deterioration of moral standards and respect for government and the law. No one can predict how values will change in the industrial West, but there can be little question that faith in the universal appeal of democracy and material welfare has given way to more sober second thoughts about the trends of history and about the goals and tactics of Western politics and public policy.

[1] For example, Abram Bergson's careful comparative study of economic growth in Communist nations and non-Communist nations at similar modernization levels, shows rather similar growth rates over a decade. And he found a great deal of variation within each type of system. Abram Bergson, "Development Under Two Systems," *World Politics*, 23:4 (July 1971), pp. 579–617.

CHALLENGES TO THE NATION-STATE

Ironically, the new nations come into nationhood just as the viability of the nation-state as an independent political entity is coming into question. The power of modern weaponry, the interdependence of the world economy, the international character of problems of environmental pollution and energy conservation, and the internationalization of the media of communication — all challenge the capacity of individual nation-states to survive as independent, self-sufficient political units.

These international challenges may in time lead to a further development of international law, and the development of international problem-solving mechanisms. The nation-state, after all, was a response to challenges beyond the problem-solving capacity of petty principalities and kingdoms. The present surfacing of international problems seems bound to produce some increase in international institution building. It will surely not mean the end of the nation-state, but it may lead to a new division of labor and authority between the state and supranational agencies. From this perspective the extreme nationalism of some of the new nations (as well as the old) may be a bit out of date.

The European Economic Community (EEC) illustrates the advantage of regional coordination for trade and economic growth. Its example may lead to similar supranational efforts elsewhere. The proliferation of multinational corporations like the Exxon Corporation, International Telephone and Telegraph (ITT), and International Business Machines (IBM) may be leading toward international institution building. These massive corporations, with their huge budgets and their installations, property, and activities all over the world, escape effective regulation simply because their foreign operations are beyond the reach of individual nation-states. Multinational corporations seem to require some form of multinational regulation, if they are to be regulated at all.

The predominance of the nation-state is threatened not only by supranational problems and institutions, but also by internal tendencies toward decentralization. The capacity of large centralized bureaucracies to respond to the special needs of particular regions, groups, and communities is increasingly being questioned, and efforts have been made to reemphasize and strengthen the functions and resources of regional governments.

In the Western countries, a restless democratic conscience is searching out disadvantaged social groups to emancipate, and surviving areas of privilege to conquer. The movements for civil rights and equal opportunities, the reduction of the voting age, and the granting of equal rights to women are all indications of a continuing democratic vitality.

We live in an age when established guidelines have become blurred and when old beliefs and expectations are coming into question. Crises of this kind are threatening, but they are also the moments in history for considering new options and new directions in political life.

KEY TERMS

independence
Gross National Product
literacy
income inequality
cultural heterogeneity
economic development
Multinational Corporations
interdependence
industrialization
foreign trade dependence
wealth inequality
"quality of life" issues
equality vs. liberty
developmental goals

PART TWO

SYSTEM, PROCESS, AND POLICY

GABRIEL A. ALMOND
G. BINGHAM POWELL, JR.

CHAPTER THREE

Political Socialization and Political Culture

Social scientists use the term *socialization* to refer to the way children are introduced to the values and attitudes of their society and how they learn what will be expected of them in their adult roles. *Political socialization* is the part of this process that shapes political attitudes, suggesting how each member of the society is expected to participate in the political system. Most children, at a relatively early age, acquire distinctive political attitudes and expectations. One recent study[1] of British and French children in their early teens revealed some striking differences in attitudes toward political authority.

The interviewer used a story-completion technique in which the child was given the beginning of a narrative and asked to complete it.

Interviewer: One day the Queen was driving her car to a meeting. Because she was late, she was driving very fast. The police stop the car. Finish the story.

Susan: Well, really, the police wouldn't really stop the Queen driving the car, because somebody would be escorting the Queen to the meeting and that would stop the rest of the cars so she wouldn't really need to be going fast. People have got time to wait for the Queen. She wouldn't really be late.

Interviewer: Let's suppose for the purpose of this question that the Queen was driving by herself in a car and she wanted to go out and away from all the other people and the police stopped her for going fast.

Susan: Well, the police might have stopped her, but as soon as they saw it was the Queen they wouldn't take her in for speeding or anything like that.

Interviewer: What do you suppose the policeman would say?

Susan: I think he would be astounded, because really the Queen, she doesn't drive the car on her own. And she knows Britain's speed limit, so she wouldn't have gone really fast.

These assumptions about monarchic power are not the result of deliberate teaching by the schools. They appear, rather, to have been casually absorbed from family, friends, books, radio and television, and from reasoning about how things "must work."

[1] Fred I. Greenstein and Sidney Tarrow, "Political Orientations of Children: The Use of a Semi-Projective Technique in Three Nations," in H. Eckstein and T. R. Gurr (eds.), *Sage Professional Paper in Comparative Politics* Series, vol. 1 (1970). The excerpts from this study are reprinted by permission of the Publisher, Sage Publications, Inc., Beverly Hills, Ca. Copyright © 1970 by Sage Publications, Inc. See also Fred I. Greenstein, "Children's Images of Political Leaders in Three Democracies," paper presented at the annual meeting of the American Political Science Association, New Orleans, September 4–8, 1973.

A French girl, Janine, when asked how she would explain the president of the Republic to a foreign child, replied, "Is it required to answer him [the foreign child]?" Surprised, the interviewer asked her to repeat herself.

Janine: Is it required to answer the child who asked the question?

Interviewer: That would be a nice thing to do.

Janine: If a child agrees to answer the other child, the two of them would go out into the school yard for him to explain it. The French boy explains. But perhaps after several explanations the foreign child doesn't understand and [still says], "Explain it to me." [Getting impatient at this] the French child says, "The President of the Republic is the one who rules, like a king. Everyone must obey him." And perhaps the foreign child now will understand what he has been told — even if he doesn't agree.

Apart from the political wariness apparent in Janine's comments, there is also an assumption about the nature of political leadership that English or American children would have difficulty understanding. Janine's conception of the president as a stern and distant leader occurred again in her explanation of why the president is more important than the prime minister: "The President is like a king and the Prime Minister must carry out all his orders — he isn't the one who gives the orders."

Françoise, a much less authoritarian storyteller than her compatriot Janine, did not balk at telling an imaginary questioner about the president of the Republic, but when she was asked, "How would you vote?" — a question British and American children answered without hesitation — this conversation followed:

Françoise: I would say to him [the questioner] that I know who I would vote for.

Interviewer: You wouldn't say any more?

Françoise: No.

Interviewer: You wouldn't give his name?

Françoise: No.

Interviewer: No? Is it a secret?

Françoise: Yes.

POLITICAL SOCIALIZATION

Political socialization, then, refers to the processes through which political attitudes and patterns of behavior are acquired.

Some persons acquire only elementary political concepts as they mature, while others continuously elaborate and revise their political beliefs, values, motivations, and activities as they pass through childhood and adult life. This development of political belief sometimes involves conscious adaptation to an otherwise confusing social environment. More often, it results from taking cues and examples from such convenient sources as family, school, peers, and the communications media.[2]

Political socialization is also the way one generation passes on political standards and beliefs to succeeding generations, a process called *cultural transmission*.

Two points about political socialization need to be emphasized. First, socialization continues throughout an individual's life. Attitudes established during infancy are always being adapted or reinforced as the individual passes through a variety of social experiences. Early family influences, for example, can create a favorable image of a political party, but subsequent education, job experience, and the influence of friends may dramatically alter that early image. Furthermore, certain events and experiences — a war or a depression — leave their mark on a whole society. For older members of the society, these experiences may bring about *resocialization*, drastic changes in their attitudes toward their political institutions. Events such as these seem to have their greatest impact, however, on the younger members of the electorate, who have more flexible attitudes toward the system.

A second point is that political socialization may take the form of either direct or indirect transmission and learning. Socialization is direct when it involves the explicit communication of information, values, or feelings toward politics. Civics courses in public high schools are *direct political socialization*, as are efforts by the Communist party to create "the Soviet man" or "the Cuban socialist man." *Indirect political socialization* may occur with particular force in a child's early years — with the development of an accommodating or aggressive stance toward parents, teachers, and friends, a posture likely to affect adult

[2] Jack Dennis, Leon Lindberg, and Donald McCrone, "Support for Nation and Government among English Children," *British Journal of Political Science*, 1:1 (January 1971), p. 25.

attitudes toward political leaders and fellow citizens. For example, overt antigovernment sentiment, especially toward federal authority, has long been a characteristic of the Appalachian version of American political culture. Another characteristic of the same area is a high degree of family disruption. The father may be a powerless figure, unemployed or absent. If the Appalachian child sees a parallel between the father figure in her family and the authority structure of the larger political system, she is not very likely to think kindly of either.[3]

Political socialization shapes and transmits a nation's political culture. Political socialization may also maintain a nation's political culture as it passes the culture on from old to young. It transforms the political culture insofar as it leads the population, or parts of it, to view and experience politics in a different way. In time of rapid change or extraordinary events, such as the formation of a new nation, political socialization may even create a political culture where none existed before. Maintaining, transforming, and creating — these are the tasks that political socialization performs for the political culture.

Political cultures are often most dramatically transformed as a result of wars and revolutions. Sometimes the transformation is deliberate — the goal of political leaders or groups. It may also stem from the more or less unplanned and uncontrolled response of groups or whole societies to the impact of major events. West Germany and Cuba illustrate these processes.

Political Resocialization

WEST GERMANY In post–World War II Germany those in authority have deliberately sought to transform the national political culture. Political socialization of a less structured kind has also occurred, however, chiefly as a consequence of Germany's catastrophic defeat in World War II and its rapid economic recovery in the 1950s. Allied occupation forces and, over a longer period, the postwar government sought to alter German political values and behavior to make them more supportive of the democratic political structures created for the postwar era.

The transformation of German political culture in the last three decades has been extraordinary. Students of contemporary German politics attribute these remarkable changes — the greatly increased trust in government, commitment to democratic processes, and readiness to participate in politics; the increasingly moderate partisanship; and the general climate of political consensus and stability — to four factors. First, the older generations, who had retained their identification with the pre–World War I monarchy, or with the Nazi system, were being outnumbered by those age groups who have been socialized in the peace and prosperity of the postwar period and exposed to deliberate efforts to inculcate democratic attitudes. The second factor is said to be the absence of a credible alternative to the democratic Bonn regime, the impossibility of uniting East and West Germany, and the military powerlessness of Germany in the post–World War II world.

The third factor has been the postwar modernization of Germany. With the loss of the Eastern part of the country, West Germany became more homogeneously urban and industrial, and the rapid rate of economic growth in this period accentuated these tendencies. The German family became more egalitarian, and parent-child relations more permissive. The educational level of the population increased, and civics instruction in the schools seems to have had some effect.

Finally the German political and economic systems have performed successfully. Early legislation equalized the burdens of the defeat, and helped reintegrate the refugees from the eastern territories. Economic reconstruction rapidly turned West Germany into the leading European industrial power. Fiscal and social policy were effectively employed to maintain economic growth and stability, high levels of employment, and relatively high standards of education, health care, housing, and recreation.

There can be no doubt that German political culture has been transformed into a stable democracy, and that deliberate efforts at democratic socialization through the schools, political parties, and civic organizations have contributed to this resocialization.

[3] D. Jaros et al., "The Malevolent Leader: Political Socialization in an American Subculture," *American Political Science Review*, 62:2 (1968), pp. 564–575.

Cuba's vast socialization campaign here takes the form of a roll call of Young Pioneers in front of a house in which Fidel Castro had prepared an assault during the Revolution.

But it is also clear that the political and international constraints and the performance of the regime played crucial roles in this significant transformation of political culture.[4]

CUBA Since coming to power, the revolutionary government in Cuba has sought to create a new political culture. From the beginning, the revolutionary leaders rejected the old — especially the urban — culture, condemning it for inequity, materialism, and corruption, and for its dependence on American culture. During the 1960s, Cuban political socialization has sought the creation of a "new Cuban man," revolutionary and Communist, whose qualities include attachment to the values of cooperation, political equality, hard work, self-improvement, obedience, and incorruptibility. Though Cuba's leadership has attempted to socialize all Cubans, regardless of age and status, their special targets have been the young, believing them most likely to respond to the revolutionary experience with an enthusiasm for Communist orthodoxy. In recent years the regime has engaged as many Cubans as possible in some form of productive farm work. Thousands of children are sent for several weeks of work and study in rural areas; other young people have taken up semipermanent residence on the Isle of Youth, the intention being to form "the first generation of true communists in a setting of equality

[4] For a thorough analysis of these changes in German political culture see David P. Conradt, "Changing German Political Culture," in Gabriel A. Almond and Sidney Verba, eds. *The Civic Culture Revisited* (Princeton, N.J.: Princeton University Press, 1979). For a more detailed discussion of German resocialization, see Chapter 11 of this book.

and sacrifice."[5] And adults in the capital city of Havana are expected to help make the urban community self-sufficient in foodstuffs by cultivating adjacent lands. It may also be that the use of Cuban troops on a large scale in combat, training, and indoctrination missions in Angola, Mozambique, Ethiopia, and elsewhere in Africa is viewed not only as a way of exporting revolution, but also as a means for indoctrination and ideological hardening of young Cubans.

After almost two decades the emerging, transformed Cuban political culture probably still depends more heavily on a revolutionary environment and on the organizations and communications media controlled by the Communist party, rather than on strongly held values and beliefs among the general population. As in the past, peasant families are reluctant to send children to the new schools; labor absenteeism is chronic; and many Cubans still resist pressure to participate in public life. Even so, most Cubans seem to appreciate the regime's part in improving, markedly, the circumstances of their daily lives; and there is widespread — if sometimes weakly held — feeling that everyone should contribute to the nation's development efforts. Perhaps most significant of all, the values associated with the Hispanic-American upper and middle classes — materialism, strong family ties, and hierarchy — seem to have broken up in Cuba, partly because many who cling most fervently to those values have emigrated, but also because the revolutionary experiences and the socialization programs have left their mark.

Agents of Political Socialization

Political socialization is accomplished through a variety of institutions and agents. Some, like civics courses in schools, are deliberately designed for this purpose, among others. Still others, like play and work groups, are likely to affect political socialization only indirectly.

THE FAMILY The direct and indirect influences of the family — the first socialization structure that an individual encounters — are powerful and lasting. The most distinctive of these influences is the shaping of attitudes toward authority. The family makes collective decisions, and for the child these decisions may be authoritative — failure to obey may lead to punishment. An early experience with participation in family decision making can increase the child's sense of political competence, provide him with skills for political interaction, and make him more likely to participate actively in the political system as an adult. By the same token, the child's pattern of obedience to decisions can help to predispose his future performance as a political subject. The family also shapes future political attitudes by locating the individual in a vast social world; establishing ethnic, linguistic, and religious ties and social class; affirming cultural and educational values and achievements; and directing occupational and economic aspirations.[6] An increasing interest in politics, and in political activism, among women has profoundly affected the family's function as a socializing agent. Education reduces the rate of political apathy among women in all countries, but in the United States — and to a lesser extent in Great Britain — women tend to be politically informed, observant, and emotionally involved in the political life of their communities. In the United States and Great Britain, ideas about political events and issues tend to be brought into the family by both marriage partners, and political discussions reflect this shared interest. Some scholars suggest that a family open to reciprocal discussion of political issues provides a type of political socialization that enables children to develop within the family itself a sense of political competence and obligation, and to learn to tolerate the ambiguities of politics and political controversy.[7]

THE SCHOOL Educated persons are more aware of the impact of government on their lives, pay

[5] Richard R. Fagen, *The Transformation of Political Culture in Cuba* (Stanford, Calif.: Stanford University Press, 1968), p. 149. For a detailed discussion of political resocialization in a Communist country in the early stage of industrialization, see Chapter 13 on China.

[6] Richard E. Dawson, Kenneth Prewitt, and Karen Dawson, *Political Socialization*, 2nd ed. (Boston: Little, Brown, 1977) ch. 7.

[7] Gabriel A. Almond and Sidney Verba, (eds.), *The Civic Culture* (Princeton, N.J.: Princeton University Press, 1963), pp. 387 ff.

more attention to politics, have more information about political processes, and undertake a wider range of activities in their political behavior.

Schools provide the adolescent with knowledge about the political world and his role in it. They provide children with more concrete perceptions of political institutions and relationships. Schools also transmit the values and attitudes of the society. They can play an important role in shaping attitudes about the unwritten rules of the political game, as the traditional British public schools instill the values of public duty, informal political relations, and political integrity. Schools can reinforce affection for the political system and provide common symbols for an expressive response to the system, such as the flag and pledge of allegiance. Teaching cultural history serves a similar function in a new nation, as in Africa.[8]

PEER GROUPS Although the school and family are the agents most obviously engaged in socialization, several other social units also shape political attitudes. One is peer groups, including childhood play groups, friendship cliques, and small work groups, in which members share relatively equal status and close ties. Individuals adopt the views of their peers because they like or respect them or because they want to be like them. A peer group socializes its members by motivating or pressuring them to conform to the attitudes or behavior accepted by the group. An individual may become interested in politics or begin to follow political events because her close friends do so. A high school senior may choose to go on to college because other students with whom he identifies have chosen to do the same. In such cases, the individual modifies his or her interests and behavior to reflect those of the group in an effort to be accepted by its members.[9]

OCCUPATION Jobs, and the formal and informal organizations built around them — unions, professional associations, and the like — are also channels for the explicit communication of information and beliefs. Individuals identify with a particular group, such as a union, and use that group as a political reference point. They become sensitive to the group's norms and evaluate its actions according to their sense of what is best for the group and what it stands for. Participating in collective bargaining or a strike can be a powerful socializing experience for worker and employer alike. The striking laborer learns that she can shape decisions being made about her future, and also gains knowledge of specific skills, such as demonstrating and picketing, which may come in handy as she participates in other political activity.

Occupational and professional associations such as the American Medical Association are among the most universal and influential secondary groups affecting political attitudes in modern and modernizing societies. They enlist large numbers of trained professionals, and assure their loyalty by defending their members' economic and professional interests. Because these associations relate to occupational strata, they promote and intensify occupational and class-related political values.[10]

MASS MEDIA Modern societies cannot exist without widespread and rapid communication. Information about events occurring anywhere in the world becomes general knowledge in a few hours. Much of the world, particularly its modern parts, has become a single audience, moved by the same events and motivated by similar tastes. We know that the mass media — newspapers, radio, television, magazines — play an important part in transmitting modern attitudes and values to the new nations. In addition to providing specific and immediate information about political events, the mass media also convey, directly or indirectly, the major values on which a society agrees. Certain symbols are conveyed in an emotional context, and the events described alongside them take on a specific emotional color. Controlled mass media can be a powerful force in shaping political beliefs.[11]

[8] Dawson, Prewitt, and Dawson, *Political Socialization*, 2nd ed., ch. 8.

[9] Dawson, Prewitt, and Dawson, *Political Socialization*, 2nd ed., ch. 6, 9.

[10] Dawson, Prewitt, and Dawson, *Political Socialization*, 2nd ed., ch. 9.

[11] Dawson, Prewitt, and Dawson, *Political Socialization*, 2nd ed., ch. 10.

After his return from exile in 1979, the Ayatollah Khomeini attempted to transform Iran's political culture by drawing upon religious symbols and his own charisma.

POLITICAL PARTIES   Specialized political structures, such as interest groups and parties, play a deliberate and important role in political socialization. Political parties attempt to mold issue preferences, arouse the apathetic, and find new issues as they mobilize support for candidates. Political parties — such as the Republicans and Democrats in the United States, and Labour and Conservatives in Britain — typically draw heavily on traditional symbols of the nation or a class and reinforce them. A competitive party system may focus criticism on the government's *incumbents* (officeholders), but it often reinforces support for the basic structures and processes. Parties also keep citizens in contact with the political structures. Most individuals are concerned with politics only in a limited way, but a steady flow of party activities, culminating in an election every few years, keeps citizens involved in their citizenship, their participant roles.

In competitive party systems, party socialization activities can also be divisive. In their efforts to gain support leaders may appeal to class, language, religion, and other ethnic divisions, and make citizens more aware of these differences. In the 1960s in Belgium, the small Flemish and French separatist parties emphasized language differences and split the traditional Belgian party system, which had been stable for fifty years; aroused massive political conflict; and brought about major policy changes, including constitutional revisions. Many leaders in preindustrial nations oppose competitive parties because they fear such divisiveness in their new nations. In communist nations, and in many preindustrial nations, governments use a single party to attempt to inculcate common attitudes of national unity, support for the government, and ideological agreement. The combination of a single party and a controlled mass media is potent: the media present a single point of view, and the party activities reinforce that perspective by involving the citizen more directly and personally.

DIRECT CONTACTS WITH GOVERNMENTAL STRUCTURES In modern societies, the wide scope of governmental activities brings citizens into frequent contact with various bureaucratic agencies. Although the scope of government intervention in daily life is not as great in the United States as in many Western European nations — or, of course, as in the Communist nations — even American citizens have sufficient direct governmental contacts to shape their evaluations. A recent study, for example, found that 72 percent of adult Americans had interacted with at least one government agency in the preceding year; about a third had interacted with more. The most frequent contacts were with tax authorities, school officials, and the police.[12] No matter how positive the view of the political system that has been taught in school, a citizen who is harassed by the police, ignored by welfare agencies, or unfairly taxed is unlikely to feel much warmth towards the authorities.

In their study of citizen attitudes in five nations, Almond and Verba found marked differences across countries in the expectations that citizens had of their treatment by police and bureaucrats.[13] Italians, and particularly Mexicans, had quite dismal expectations as to equality and responsiveness of treatment. American blacks also reported quite negative expectations in these 1960 interviews. Quite likely, these expectations are in large measure a response to actual patterns of treatment by government.

[12] Robert G. Lehnen, *American Institutions: Political Opinion and Public Policy* (Hinsdale: Holt, Rinehart and Winston, 1976), p. 183.

[13] Almond and Verba, *The Civic Culture*, pp. 108–109. And see Dwaine Marvick, "The Political Socialization of the American Negro," *Annals of the American Academy No. 361* (September, 1965), pp. 112–127.

THE SOCIAL AND CULTURAL ENVIRONMENT We have already emphasized that specific events, such as war, depression, or prosperity, can be powerful socialization influences. Fundamental cultural style, expressed in a consistent manner through many socialization agents, can also have great effect. An important example is the implicit message of modern technology and scientific culture. Alex Inkeles and David Smith's study of the development of modern attitudes in six nations emphasizes how factory experience can create an awareness of the possibilities of organization, change, and control over nature. They report how one Nigerian worker replied to a question about how his new work made him feel:

> "Sometimes like nine feet tall with arms a yard wide. Here in the factory I alone with my machine can twist any way I want a piece of steel all the men in my home village together could not begin to bend at all."[14]

They found that factory work, education, and mass media exposure all contributed in major ways to information on national issues and leaders, openness to new experiences, appreciation of technical skill, readiness for social change, and personal and political self-confidence. For almost two centuries now the secularizing influences of science and control over nature have shaped political cultures, first in the West, increasingly throughout the world.

THE POLITICAL SELF

These agents, experiences, and influences, as they shape individual attitudes, create what may be called the political self, a combination in varying proportions of several feelings and attitudes.

First, there are basic attitudes and beliefs, such as nationalism, tribal or class identification, ideological commitment, and a fundamental sense of one's rights, privileges, and duties in the political system. Second, there are less emotional commitments to and knowledge about governmental and political institutions, such as the electoral system, the structure of the legislature, the power of the executive, the

[14] Alex Inkeles and David H. Smith, *Becoming Modern* (Cambridge, Mass.: Harvard University Press, 1974), p. 158.

structure of the courts, and the penal system. Finally there are more fleeting views about current events, policies, issues, and personalities. All of these attitudes change, but those in the first group tend to be more durable than later ones.

There is evidence, however, to suggest that even so basic an attitude as nationalism may undergo change as conditions change and as socialization experiences are modified from generation to generation. A study[15] conducted in four western European countries in the 1960s, for example, found a variation between adults and youth in relative degree of "European-ness." In response to the question, "To what extent are you in favor of, or opposed to, the efforts being made to unify Europe?" the youth of three of the four countries were overwhelmingly favorable, by a majority (93 to 95 percent) that swamped all such differences as social class, sex, or religion. Among adults in these three countries the majority supporting European integration was much smaller. For young Europeans growing up in a period of European integration, it would appear that enthusiasm for a unified Europe is now competing with their national loyalties.

Political socialization never really ceases. As we become involved in new social groups and roles, move from one part of the country to another, shift up or down the social and economic ladder, become a parent, find or lose a job, age — all these common experiences modify our political perspective.

Some general trends in the development of the political self are apparent in the industrial democracies. First, political participation tends to increase during early adulthood, reaching a peak at the age of forty or fifty years, when family, community, and other responsibilities are greatest, and declining thereafter. Second, new political attachments develop, although usually within bounds established by the deep, persistent orientations of childhood. Most adult Americans rarely alter their basic identification with a political party. In some other countries, however — France, for example — partisan identifications apparently do not develop early in childhood for many citizens, and volatility of partisan attitudes persists. Third, even basic attachments and identifications sometimes change in adulthood. The impact of war, defeat, and vast social upheaval on many adult West Germans, as we discussed, provides a good example. Fourth, geographical mobility, especially from rural to urban areas, can have significant impact on the political self, by exposing the individual to new socializing experiences.

[15] Ronald Inglehart, "An End to European Integration?" in Mattei Dogan and Richard Rose (eds.), *European Politics* (Boston: Little, Brown, 1971), pp. 120–129.

POLITICAL CULTURE

A political culture is a particular distribution of political attitudes, values, feelings, information, and skills. As people's attitudes affect what they will do, a nation's political culture affects the conduct of its citizens and leaders throughout the political system. We can compare aspects of political culture in different nations, and so understand the propensities for present and future behavior. In approaching any specific political system it would be useful to develop a map of the important contours of its political culture, as well as a corresponding map of its structures and functions.

System Propensities

One way of mapping a nation's political culture is to describe citizens' attitudes to the three levels of the political system: system, process, and policy. At the system level we are interested in the citizens' and leaders' views of the values and organizations that hold the political system together. How is it and how should it be that leaders are selected and citizens come to obey the laws? At the process level we are interested in individuals' propensities to become involved in the process: to make demands, obey the law, support some groups and oppose others, and participate in various ways. At the policy level we want to know what policies citizens and leaders expect from the government. What goals are to be established and how are they to be achieved?

Perhaps the single most important aspect of system propensities is the level and basis of *legitimacy* of the government. If citizens believe that they ought to obey the laws, then legitimacy is high. If they see no reason to obey, or if they comply only from fear, then legitimacy is low. Because it is much easier to

The continuing weight of history in French political culture is symbolized by these placards (at a 1935 congress) depicting literary giants — who also represent political subcultures.

get compliance when citizens believe in the legitimacy of the government, virtually all governments, even the most brutal and coercive, try to make citizens believe that their laws ought to be obeyed, and that it is legitimate to use force against those who resist. A government with high legitimacy will be more effective in making and implementing policies, and more likely to overcome hardships and reversals.

Citizens may recognize a government as legitimate for many different reasons. In a traditional society, legitimacy may depend on the ruler inheriting the throne and on the ruler's obedience to certain religious customs, such as making sacrifices and performing rituals. In a modern democracy, the legitimacy of the authorities will depend on their selection by citizens in competitive elections and on their following constitutional procedures in lawmaking. In other political cultures, the leaders may base their claim to legitimacy on their special grace, wisdom, or ideology, which they claim will transform citizens' lives for the better, even though they do not respond to specific demands or follow prescribed procedures.

Whether legitimacy is based on tradition, ideology, citizen participation, or specific policies has important implications for the efficiency and stability of the political system. These bases of legitimacy set the rules for a kind of exchange between citizens and authorities. Citizens obey the laws and in return the government meets the obligations set by its basis of legitimacy. As long as the obligations are met, citizens should comply and provide support and appropriate participation. If customs are violated — the constitution subverted, the ruling ideology ignored — then authorities must expect resistance and rebellion.

In systems in which legitimacy is low, and the

bases of legitimacy not accepted, resort to violence and brute force is often a solution to political disagreements. Three serious problems for legitimacy are the following: (1) failure of all citizens to accept the national political community (as in Northern Ireland); (2) lack of general acceptance of the structural-functional arrangements for recruiting leaders and making policies (as in Germany's Weimar Republic, 1919–1933); (3) failure of the leaders to convince citizens that they are fulfilling their part of the bargain of making the right kinds of laws or following the right procedures (as during the Nixon administration).

Process Propensities

As shown in Figure 3.1, in a hypothetical modern industrial democracy a sizable proportion (60 percent) of adults may be involved as actual and potential participants in political processes. They are informed about politics and can and do make political demands, giving their political support to different political leaders. We call these people *participants*. Another 30 percent are simply *subjects;* they passively obey government officials and the law, but do not vote or involve themselves in politics. A third group (10 percent) are hardly aware of government

Figure 3.1

Models of Political Culture: Orientations Toward Involvement in the Political Process (in percentages)

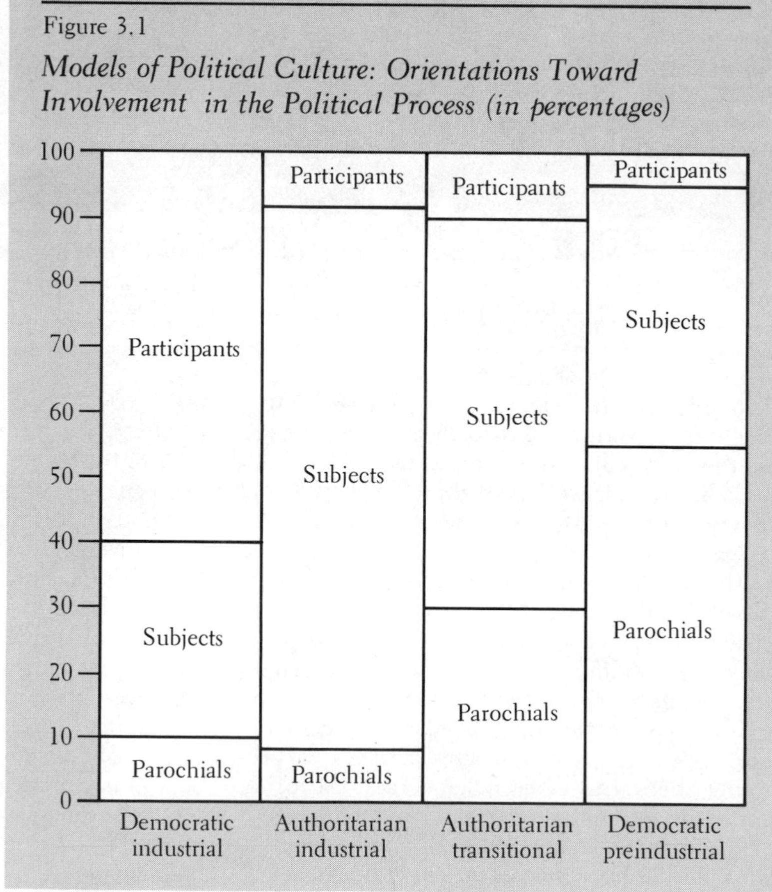

and politics at all. They may be illiterate, rural people living in remote areas, or older women unresponsive to female suffrage who are almost entirely involved in their families and communities. We call these people *parochials*.

Such a distribution would not be unusual in modern democracies. It provides enough political activists to ensure competition between political parties and sizable voter turnout, as well as critical audiences for debate on public issues and pressure groups certain to propose new policies and protect their particular interests.

The second column in Figure 3.1 depicts a largely industrialized authoritarian society, such as the U.S.S.R. or Czechoslovakia. A rather small minority of citizens becomes involved in the huge one-party system, which penetrates and oversees the society, as well as decides its policies. Most of the rest of the citizens are mobilized as subjects by the party, the bureaucracy and the government-controlled mass media. Citizens are encouraged and even coerced to cast a symbolic vote of support in elections, and to pay taxes, obey regulations, accept assigned jobs, and so forth. Thanks to the effectiveness of modern societal organization and communications, and to the efforts of the authoritarian party, few citizens are unaware of the government and its impact on their lives. Hence, we see that most of the society is made up of subjects, rather than parochials or participants.

The third model is of an authoritarian system that is only partly industrial and modern, perhaps a country like Brazil. In spite of an authoritarian political organization, some participants — students and intellectuals, for example — would oppose the system and try to change it through persuasion or more aggressive acts of protest. Favored groups, like businessmen and landowners, would discuss public issues and engage in lobbying. But most people in such a system would be passive subjects, aware of government and complying with the law, but not otherwise involved in public affairs. The parochials, peasants and farm laborers working and living in large landed estates, would have little conscious contact at all with the political system.

Our fourth example is the democratic preindustrial system, perhaps like India, which has a predominantly rural, illiterate population. In such a country there would be only a few political participants, chiefly educated professionals, businessmen, and landowners. A much larger number of employees, workers, and perhaps independent farmers would be directly affected by government taxation and other official policies. But the largest group of citizens would be illiterate farm workers and peasants, whose knowledge of and involvement with the public sector would be minimal.

Another relevant feature of process culture is peoples' beliefs about other groups and themselves as group members. Do individuals see the society as divided into social classes, regional groups, or ethnic communities? Do they identify themselves with particular factions or parties? How do they feel about groups of which they are not members? The question of political trust of other groups will affect the willingness of citizens to work with others for political goals, and the willingness of leaders to form coalitions with other groups. The governing of a large nation requires forming of large coalitions, and substantial amounts of trust in other leaders to keep bargains and be honest in negotiations. Beyond the question of trust, but related to it, is the question of hostility, an emotional component to intergroup and interpersonal relations. The tragic examples of ethnic and religious conflict in many nations show how easily hostility can be converted into violence and aggressive action. One need only think of the terrible toll of civil war in Nigeria, Lebanon, or Northern Ireland.

Policy Propensities

If we are to understand the politics of a nation, we must understand the issues people care about and the underlying images of the good society and how to achieve it that shape their opinions. Citizens in different nations differ as to the importance they attach to various policy outcomes. In some societies private property is highly valued, in others communal possessions are the rule. Some goods are valued by nearly everyone, such as material welfare, but societies differ nevertheless: some emphasize equality and minimum standards for all, while others emphasize the opportunity to move up the economic ladder. Some cultures put more weight on welfare and security, others value liberty and procedural justice. Moreover, the combination of learned values,

Table 3.1
Respondents' Self-Locations on a Left-Right Continuum in Eight Countries

Country	Self-Locations[a]						
	Left	*C-L*	*Center*	*C-R*	*Right*	*Total*	(N)
United States	5.0	13.2	48.9	24.0	8.9	100%	(1162)
West Germany	3.1	20.6	44.6	23.6	8.1	100	(2126)
Switzerland	4.1	19.7	42.8	24.0	9.4	100	(1097)
United Kingdom	8.6	18.2	40.0	22.9	10.4	100	(1211)
Austria	5.3	20.2	34.4	27.3	13.0	100	(1190)
Netherlands	9.2	22.8	32.1	26.2	9.7	100	(1085)
Italy	23.6	25.8	37.3	8.9	4.4	100	(1500)
Finland	13.0	26.7	34.7	16.3	9.3	100	(1132)

[a] The ten points of the original scale are collapsed as follows: Left = 1, 2; Center-Left = 3, 4; Center = 5, 6; Center-Right = 7, 8; Right = 9, 10.

Source: Adapted from Giacomo Sani and Giovanni Sartori, "Frammentazione, Polarizzazione E Cleavages: Democrazie Facili E Difficili," *Rivista Italiona Di Scienza Politica*, vol. 9, no. 3, pp. 339 ff. The larger study from which the data in this article were taken is under the direction of S. H. Barnes of the University of Michigan and is being published in two volumes, S. H. Barnes, Max Kaase, et al., *Political Action: As Participation in Five Western Democracies* (Beverly Hills, Ca.: Sage Publications, Inc., 1979) and P. Pesonen and H. Kerr, *People and Their Polities*, forthcoming.

strategies, and social conditions will lead to quite different perceptions about how to achieve desired social outcomes. A recent study showed that 73 percent of the Italian Parliament strongly agreed that a government wanting to help the poor would have to take from the rich in order to do it. Only 12 percent of the British Parliament took the same strong position, and half disagreed with the idea that redistribution was laden with conflict.[16] Similarly, citizens and leaders in preindustrial nations disagree about the mixture of government regulation and direct government investment in the economy necessary for economic growth.

Political cultures may be consensual or conflictual on issues of public policy and on their views of legitimate governmental and political arrangements. In a recent study of advanced industrial societies, respondents in eight countries were asked to locate their political positions on a ten-point scale ranging from extreme left to extreme right. Table 3.1 reports the distribution of self-locations in the various samples, showing substantial differences in the size of left, center, and right tendencies. These differences and patterns are brought out more clearly in Figure 3.2. The eight countries fall into three groups. Four — the United States, Germany, the United Kingdom, and Switzerland — have normal curves: most of the respondents are concentrated in the moderate center (from 40 percent for the United Kingdom to almost 50 percent for the United States). The extreme left and right wings are quite small. These four countries would seem to have consensual political cultures, as most people tend to take moderate positions on political issues. The second pattern is that of the Netherlands and Austria: the curve of distribution is flatter, meaning the political culture is more conflictual, more polarized, because the distance be-

[16] Robert Putnam, *The Beliefs of Politicians* (New Haven, Conn.: Yale University Press, 1973), p. 108.

Figure 3.2

Patterns of Left-Right Distributions in Eight Countries

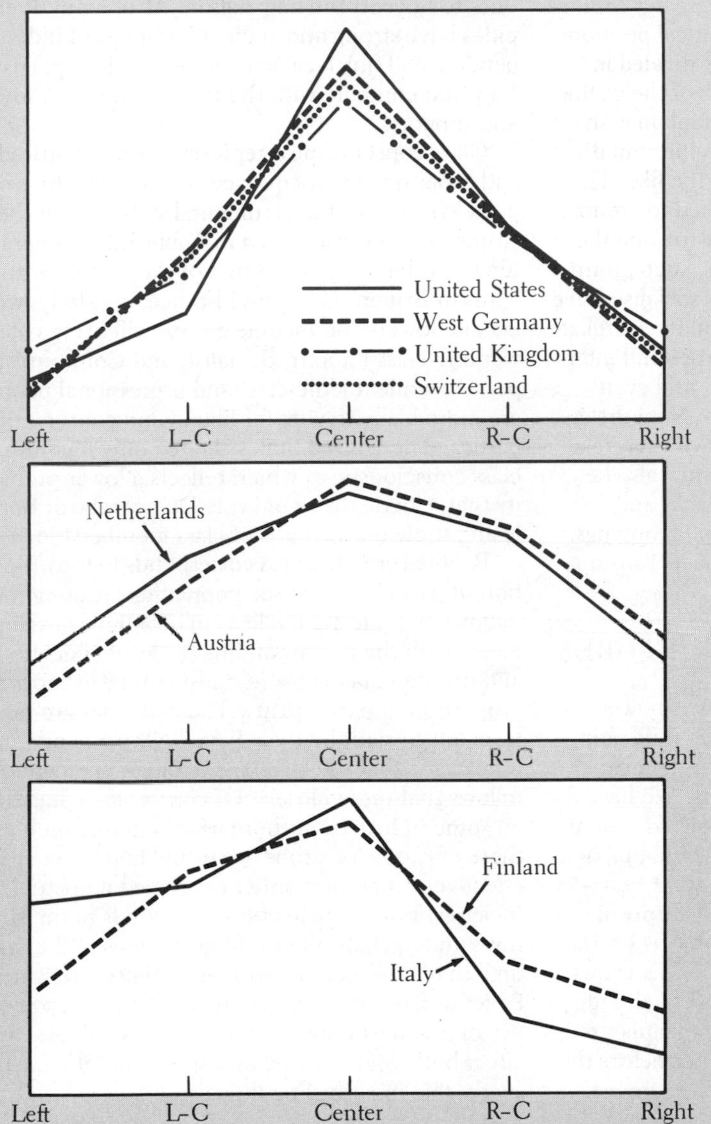

Source: Adapted from Giacomo Sani and Giovanni Sartori,"Frammentazione, Polarizzazione E Cleavages: Democrazie Facili E Difficili," *Rivista Italiona Di Scienza Politica*, vol. 9, no. 3, pp. 339ff. The larger study from which the data in this article were taken is under the direction of S. H. Barnes of the University of Michigan and is being published in two volumes, S. H. Barnes, Max Kaase, et al., *Political Action: As Participation in Five Western Democracies* (Beverly Hills, Ca.: Sage Publications, Inc., 1979) and P. Pesonen and H. Kerr, *People and Their Politics*, forthcoming.

tween political groups is greater. In the Italian and Finnish pattern, the curve is also fairly flat and shows a strong leftward leaning reflecting a greater conflictual tendency and polarization of political positions.

When a country like Italy is deeply divided in political attitudes and values we speak of the distinctive groups as *political subcultures*, which may share common national sentiments and loyalties but disagree on basic issues, ideologies, and the like. The term political subculture may be applied to groups less opposed to one another, as in Austria and the Netherlands. In these latter countries, such groups as Catholics, Protestants, liberals, and socialists have distinctive points of view on political matters, affiliate themselves with different political parties and interest groups, have separate newspapers, and even separate social clubs and sport groups. Nonetheless, relationships between these groups have been relatively amicable. Political subcultures may also be based on ethnic groupings, such as blacks and Chicanos in the United States, or tribal groupings, such as the Sukuma, Haya, or Makonde in Tanzania.

COMPARING POLITICAL CULTURES

Table 3.2 summarizes much of what we know about differences in national political cultures. The ratings are rough estimates based on public opinion surveys and descriptions by informed observers. We have divided up these aspects into attitudes toward system, process, and policy, following our general approach.

A sense of national identity is important to national cohesion and stability. It may be surprising to find Italy, which has a long history, rated as having the same intensity of national identity as Tanzania, a nation in existence for only a little over a decade. The explanation, apparently, is that Tanzania's regime has systematically campaigned since before the founding of the nation to develop public support. Tanzania's president, Julius Nyerere, has traveled about the country from village to village, appealing to the Tanzanian population for support of the Tanzanian nation and for participation in its activities. Italy, on the other hand, though a relatively modern country with a literate population, became a nation in the middle of the nineteenth century, with the union of preexisting kingdoms and principalities. The Roman Catholic Church opposed national unification for many decades, and urged all Catholics to boycott the new nation. Also, many Italian cities have strong and ancient traditions of independence. Thus localism and regionalism persist in Italy and compete with the Italian nation for loyalty and support.

Class consciousness represents a set of attitudes with important consequences for the structure of party systems and governmental stability. All the European countries listed in Table 3.2 are characterized as having a high sense of class consciousness. Thus in Britain, Germany, France, and Italy, workers and lower-paid income groups will likely vote for working-class Labour, Socialist, and Communist parties, while middle-class and professional people are more likely to vote for liberal and conservative parties. The United States is rated only medium in class consciousness, which reflects a lower probability that Americans would vote Democratic or Republican purely on the basis of class membership.

Political effectiveness corresponds to the proportion of participants in the population. Among the nations in Table 3.2 the level of economic development, with the corresponding levels of education and mass media exposure, most strongly shapes the proportion of participants. The countries are ranked from left to right by their 1965 GNP per capita, and we can see that effectiveness of citizen perceptions follows that quite closely. Of course, if we had data on some industrial authoritarian systems, such as those of Eastern Europe, we would find lower citizen effectiveness among rather developed industrial societies. For political culture responds to the structures and opportunities offered citizens at the same time that it affects the working of those structures. Belief in freedom and in equality, finally, represent two of the most important policy propensities, which affect both goals desired by citizens and the means acceptable in achieving them.

CHANGE IN POLITICAL CULTURE

Before we place too much emphasis on these data, we need to stress how timebound many of these attitudes may be. Most of the research for Table 3.2 was gathered in the 1950s and 1960s. The evidence is

Table 3.2

Aspects of Political Culture in Selected Nations[a]

Aspects	United States	Great Britain	West Germany	France	Italy	Japan	Mexico	Egypt	India	Tanzania
System propensities										
Sense of national identity	H	H	MH	H	ML	H	M	M	L	ML
Trust of government	H	H	MH	M	ML	MH	M	ML	M	M
Process propensities										
Class consciousness	M	H	H	H	H	MH	M	M	L	L
Political effectiveness	H	H	M	M	M	M	ML	ML	L	ML
Policy propensities										
Belief in freedom	H	H	MH	MH	M	ML	ML	ML	L	L
Belief in equality	MH	M	MH	M	ML	M	ML	ML	L	M

[a] *Scale:* H = high; MH = medium high; M = medium; ML = medium low; L = low.

Source: Adapted from Dirk Berg-Schlosser, *Politische Kultur* (Munich: Ernst Vogel, 1972), pp. 116 ff. By permission.

Figure 3.3

Growing Distrust of Government in the United States, 1952–1973

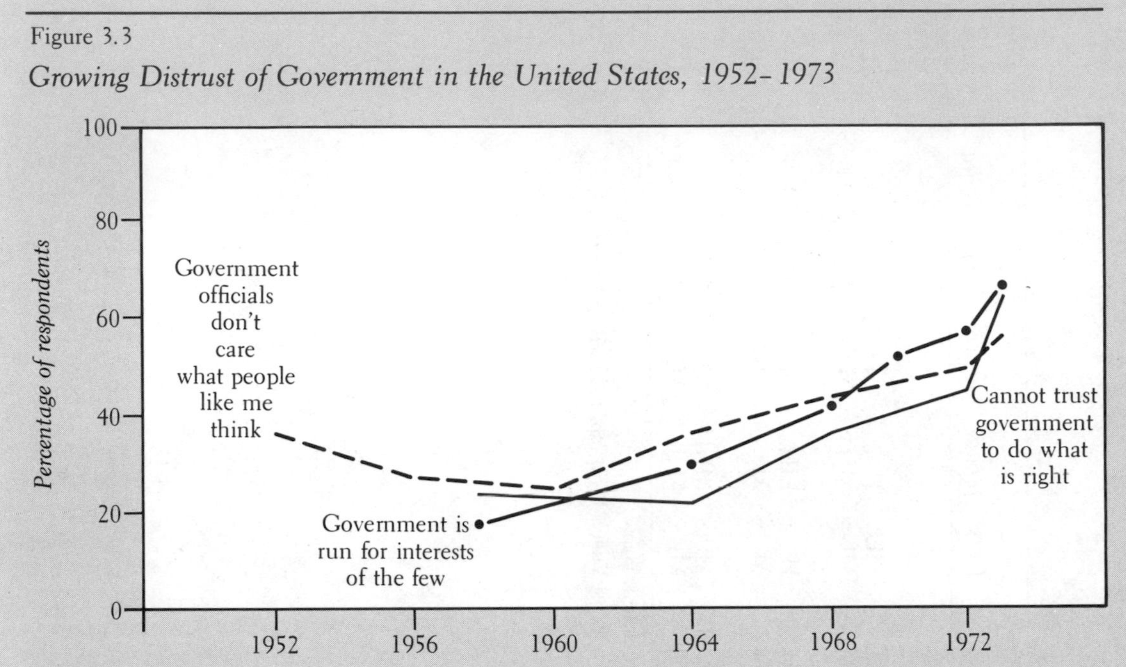

Source: From Norman H. Nie, Sidney Verba, and John Petrosik, *The Changing American Voter*, Figures 15.6 and 15.7. Copyright © 1976 by the Twentieth Century Fund. Reprinted by permission of the publisher, Harvard University Press.

impressive that attitudes reported for these countries may have undergone considerable change in recent years, at least in some respects and among some groups. Figure 3.3 shows how much the level of trust in government has declined among Americans in recent years. By any of these measures, citizens' trust in the American government declined throughout the 1960s, as the nation was wracked by internal conflict over racial inequality and a disastrous war. The revelation of national political scandal and the disregard of constitutional procedures by the Nixon administration led to another sudden decline in 1973. Clearly, the legitimacy of the national government was severely undermined by these events.

Of course, the legitimacy of any government rests upon a complicated mixture of procedure and policy. But in traditional societies the time frame is a long one. If crops fail, enemies invade, and floods destroy, then, eventually, as in Imperial China, the emperor may lose the mandate of heaven, or the chiefs their authority, or the feudal lords their claim to the loyalty of their serfs. But in a modern secular society there is a more direct and explicit connection between acceptable policy outcomes and the granting of legitimacy to the government. The belief that man can shape the environment puts pressure on political leaders to perform well. If they do not, they will lose legitimacy, and their ability to govern will be undermined, perhaps even the regime threatened if the incumbents are not replaced.

A study of American college students found striking changes in their attitudes toward the principal values of American culture. It reported a rejection of materialistic values, mechanization, and bureaucratic organization, and a widespread preference for communal rather than individual values — for the expression of feeling rather than intellectualism — as well as a search for sacredness in nature.[17]

These and other studies report significant changes in basic political and cultural attitudes in the United States and Western Europe and make it clear that political culture is not a static phenomenon. While the evidence we have is insufficient to justify predicting fundamental changes in the political cultures of advanced industrial societies, it does bring into question the stability of the attitude patterns shown in Table 3.2.

[17] Daniel Yankelovich, *The Changing Values on Campus* (New York: Washington Square Press, 1972), pp. 167 ff. See also Ronald Inglehart, *The Silent Revolution* (Princeton, N.J.: Princeton University Press, 1977), pp. 1–115.

KEY TERMS

socialization
political socialization
political resocialization
agents of political socialization
political self
political culture
legitimacy
participants
subjects
parochials
political subcultures
consensual political culture
conflictual political culture

CHAPTER FOUR

Political Recruitment and Political Structure

Voting is one of the commonest political actions in the contemporary world. The frequency of elections varies, but nations that hold no elections are unusual. Voting is also one of the simplest political actions. The citizen enters a voting booth and indicates his support for a political leader or policy. The number of voters can easily be counted and the result determined. Table 4.1 shows the proportion of eligible voters turning out in elections in the 1960s in different nations. In most contemporary nations the majority of citizens are eligible to vote, and among the examples in Table 4.1 between 50 and 100 percent of them actually did so.

Despite its simplicity, the implications of the vote are profound. Few structures illustrate so clearly the need for a structural-functional approach to describing political systems. For although electoral structures may be fairly similar in the nations in Table 4.1, with the use of ballots and a principle of one-citizen, one-vote, the functions of the electoral structures of the different nations differ. In the U.S.S.R. a citizen can only vote for the nominee of the Communist party. In that political system, as in China, voting only plays a role in political socialization, serving as a symbolic input of citizen support for the government. In Tanzania, only one party is allowed, but there may be competing candidates. In fact, important incumbents have often been defeated. In Mexico, more than one party is allowed, and elections have been important at the local level. But the dominant party, the Partido Revolucionario Institucional (PRI), has controlled the national electoral process through a variety of means, and elections are not important in the selection of new top leaders or policies. On the other hand, in the United States, the Western European nations, and Japan, citizens choose between competing political parties, and their choices affect which leaders assume the top offices of government. The desire for office, to attain or remain in power, often brings leaders to modify policies to meet citizen expectations; and shifts in citizen support can bring to power new coalitions committed to new policies. In India, too, elections have significant impact on the recruitment of leaders and on approaches to policy.

Even a brief consideration of electoral structures underlines three points. First, we must take a structural-functional perspective, and look at what elections actually do, not simply at whether or not they are held. Second, the political system is a sys-

Table 4.1

Electoral Turnout in a Representative Election of Selected Nations, 1960s

Country	*Percentage of eligible citizens voting*	*Voters as percentage of population over 20 years old*
U.S.S.R.	99.9	97.7
Czechoslovakia	99.4	100.0
Egypt	98.5	n.a.
West Germany	86.4	77.6
France	80.0	66.5
Tanzania	76.9	49.0
United Kingdom	77.1	72.4
Japan	71.1	72.3
United States	58.7	56.8
Mexico	54.1	49.8
India	53.1	55.8

Source: Charles S. Taylor and Michael C. Hudson, *World Handbook of Political and Social Indicators*, 2nd ed. (New Haven, Conn.: Yale University Press, 1972), pp. 54 ff. By permission. For Tanzania, column 1 is percent of registered voters going to the polls; column 2 is percent of potentially eligible voters who are both registered and voted (see Table 15.3, pp. 495).

tem, and the implications and workings of electoral structures depend on other structures and functions also. Is there freedom to organize new parties? What are the present party alternatives and how do parties choose leaders? Is information freely available? How are policies actually made? Is retaliation or coercion of deviant voters possible? Third, recruitment is an especially important function, a system function that in many ways affects the working of the political process and the resulting policies. Which citizens are participating in elections? How do elections affect elite recruitment? Are elites anticipating citizen voting, and working to build electoral backing as they engage in day-to-day politics?

DEMOCRATIC AND AUTHORITARIAN POLITICAL STRUCTURES

The most important structural-functional distinction in classifying political systems is between democratic and authoritarian systems. Other important distinctions can be made at other levels, as between nations in preindustrial and industrial environments, or between nations with conservative or change-oriented policy tendencies. But in describing structures and functions we stress initially the degree of democratization. At the level of nation-states, democracy consists of political structures that involve citizens in selecting among competing political leaders. The more citizens are involved and the more meaningful their choices, the more democratic the system.

No simple criterion of democracy exists. The sheer number of citizens voting is no guide. Both citizen participation and meaningful choices between competing elites are essential. As political systems become larger, more complex, and more capable of penetrating and shaping the society, the probability of some form of citizen involvement increases, but the question of the meaningfulness of participation also becomes more serious. In a modern society it is possible for the government to control and shape the flow of information and communication, the formation of attitudes and culture, and the recruitment of elites at all levels. On the other hand, it is also possible for independent social and political subsystems to exert autonomous influence on politics. High levels of education and information can build a participant political culture. Specialized social, economic, and political groups of all kinds can be springboards for the average citizen to make political demands, and mobilize other people into political activity, even to build new political parties and support new alternatives in leadership. Thus more developed political systems, especially in industrial societies, have greater potential for authoritarian control of citizens on a mass scale, and also for democratic control by citizens on a mass scale.

Figure 4.1 illustrates the democratic-authoritarian distinction in national political structures, and shows how that distinction becomes more dramatic and clear-cut as a national political system develops more specialized and inclusive organizations for controlling the society. At the top right and top left of the figure are Britain and the U.S.S.R., both systems having many specialized structures for shaping their societies, including schools, mass media, party systems, and vast bureaucracies, and both able to draw upon literate and skilled populations. But in Britain these many structures and the involved population give citizens great ability to control their leaders. In the U.S.S.R. the policies made by the top leaders are used to direct and control citizens, whose information sources, freedom to form groups, and patterns of involvement with the government are carefully directed from above. In such systems as India, Tanzania, and Egypt, the development of specialized and integrated structures is much less complete. They show democratic or authoritarian leanings, but both citizen capacity for input and leaders' capacity for manipulation and control are lesser.

CITIZENS' INVOLVEMENT IN POLITICS

Citizens become involved in the political process in two different ways. *Participant activities* are those in which the average citizen makes some attempt to influence policy making. She may write a congressman to urge passage of fair-housing legislation, or work to help a candidate favoring industrial development rather than environmentalism. *Subject activities* are those in which the average citizen is involved in policy implementation. Laws have been made, and the citizen responds to them, whether as tax payer, welfare recipient, or simple law abider. These supports, which citizens put into the process as subjects or resist putting in, are important in determining the effectiveness of policies. Table 4.2 shows the major types of citizens' involvement in politics, and some examples of each type.

Citizens as Participants

In the next three chapters we shall discuss the input functions of interest articulation, interest aggregation, and policy making. As we can see in Table 4.2, citizens can become involved in each of these functions. In interest articulation citizens make requests, demands, and pleas for policies. Some interest articulation involves only a citizen and his family, as when a veteran writes his congressman for help in getting his benefits approved, or when a home owner asks the local party precinct leader to see if she can have her driveway snowplowed regularly. These narrow, personal demands on the political system are called *parochial contacts*. Citizens become involved in politics this way in all political systems, even the most repressive. In the vast bureaucracies of contemporary communist systems citizens may be almost continually involved in trying to get improvement in their conditions and treatment

Figure 4.1
Democracy and Authoritarianism in Selected Contemporary Political Systems

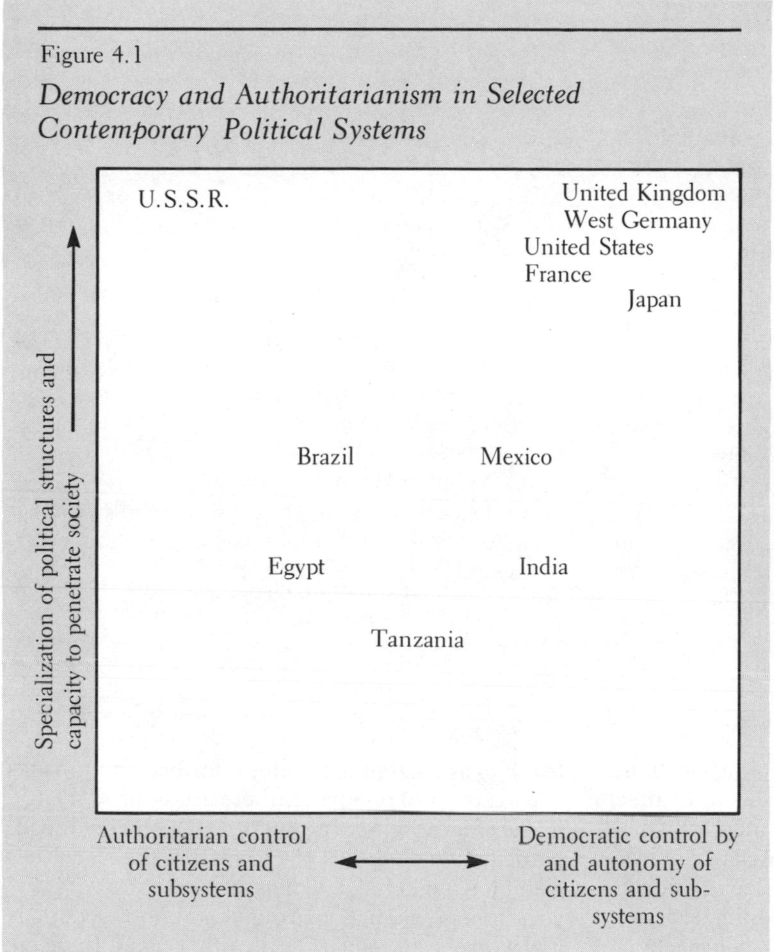

within the bounds of official policy. Citizens may also become involved in politics as members of interest groups, discussed in detail in the next chapter. They may include formal groups organized for interest articulation, such as professional groups like the American Medical Association, or they may be informal local groups, like the signers of a petition submitted to a city council, or they may even be the spontaneous gathering of outraged ghetto dwellers, whose smoldering resentment of poverty and injustice erupts in a sudden riot over an accusation of police brutality. In authoritarian systems, interest group activities are much more carefully limited and regulated than in democratic systems.

Interest aggregation activities are those in which the citizen provides active political support — commits political resources — to a political leader or faction. The two major categories of citizen interest aggregation activities are voting and campaign activity in competitive elections. The great and ingenious invention of representative democracy makes these activities possible for the average citizen. By allowing freedom to organize and communicate, and to form political parties, and by making the recruitment of

Table 4.2

Types of Citizen Involvement in Politics

Participant activities	*Subject activities*
Interest Articulation	Resource provider
Parochial contacting	Tax payer
Informal group activity	Military draftee
Formal group activity	Juror
Interest aggregation	Resource receiver
Voting in competitive elections	Social security recipient
Party work in competitive elections	Welfare recipient
Policy making	Veterans' benefit recipient
Voting in referendum	Behavior regulatee
Member of town meeting, workers' council	Obeyer of laws
	Parent sending child to school
	Manufacturer obeying safety regulations
	Symbol receiver, provider
	Giver of pledge, loyalty oath
	Listener to political speeches
	Voter in noncompetitive election

top policy makers dependent on winning elections, the structures of democracy allow citizens to affect policies. Citizens affect policies not merely by making requests or appealing to the conscience of leaders, but by being counted in the choice of leaders. Where citizens can take part in choosing leaders, other input activities, such as demands made by interest groups, will also receive more attention. A citizens' action group, labor union, or business lobby which can offer the votes of many members, or which can contribute money or stuff envelopes before election day, will receive serious attention when it raises policy issues.

Even in democratically oriented nations, of course, it is difficult for citizens to be very involved in direct policy making. The average citizen, by definition, does not make his living in politics, and his time is therefore somewhat limited. And apart from an occasional referendum, most national policies cannot be fruitfully decided with mass participation. Drafting legislation is a complicated process. But at the local level citizen involvement is somewhat more feasible, as citizens are better informed about issues and events. On one hand, there are some special forms of local self-government in which very broad participation does take place, such as the New England town meeting and Yugoslavian forms of self-government, such as apartment and house councils and workers' councils. On the other hand, there are local policy-making roles that are part-time elite roles. American city council members, and many other local officials in many societies, are not full-time officials. They just cross the borderline between citizen and elite activity.

Who Participates? Citizen Recruitment

The data on citizen participation in Table 4.3 show that even nations with similar political systems vary substantially in the amount of citizen activity in politics. Americans vote less frequently than the Dutch or Austrians or West Germans. They contact officials about personal and family problems less

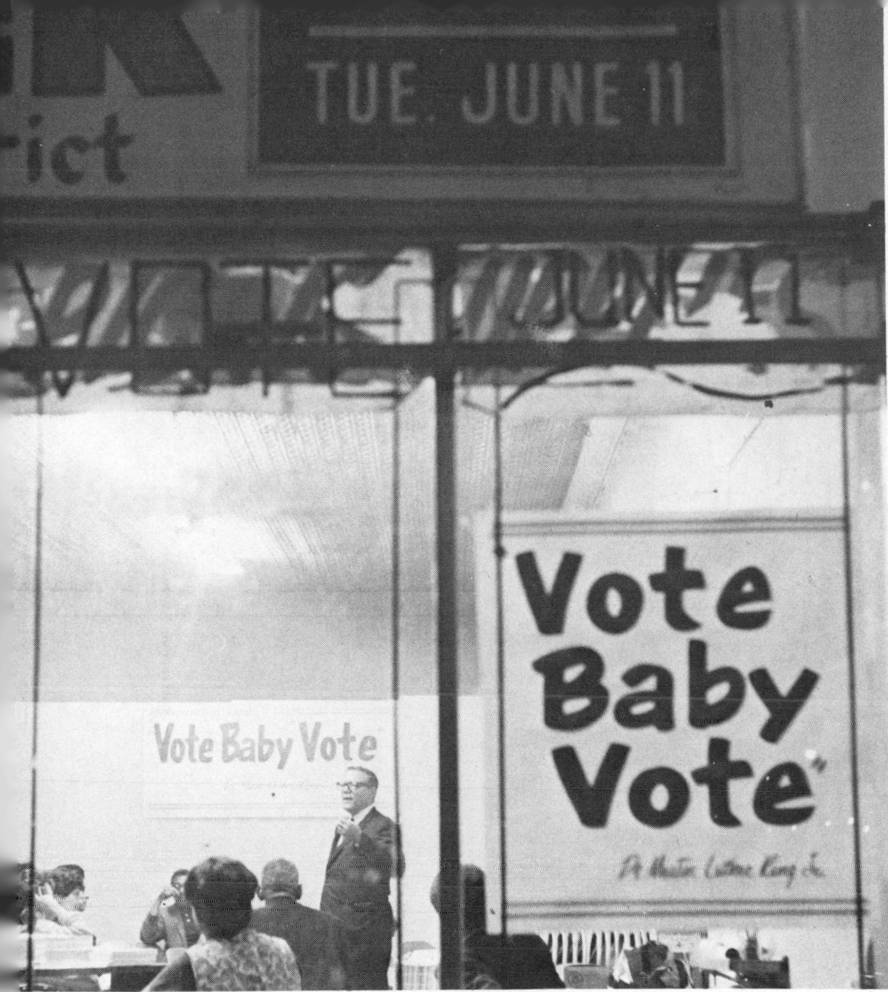

Participation in competitive elections is an important interest aggregation role; registration of blacks has had significant impact on American politics in the last twenty years.

than Austrians or the Dutch, although more frequently than Nigerians. But they are more likely to be active members of groups involved in community affairs than citizens in these nations and, like the Japanese and Indians, are more likely to work for a political party. As these differences suggest, there is no simple answer to the question of who participates and why. It depends on the type of participation.

But some patterns can be found, and studies of political behavior are increasing our understanding of citizen participation.[1] First, we note that many sorts of participation depend on the eligibility and encouragement established by the political system itself. Authoritarian systems typically do not allow party competition, and carefully control and limit the activities of groups, foreclosing large-scale citizen involvement in interest aggregation or recruitment. Nations with some degree of democratization, such as Tanzania, allow widespread citizen campaign and voting activity within a single party, with different candidates for nomination as the different choices. Even highly democratized systems, such as the United States, the Western European nations, and Japan, vary in eligibility requirements for voting. At least until recently, the United States made voting registration quite difficult for persons who change residence, while registration in Europe is much easier, if not automatic. In Italy, citizens receive free rail transportation home to vote. In some nations voting has been required, and nonvoting penalized by fines.

[1] See Robert Lane, *Political Life* (Glencoe, Ill.: Free Press, 1959); Gabriel A. Almond and Sidney Verba, *The Civic Culture* (Princeton, N.J.: Princeton University Press, 1963); Sidney Verba and Norman Nie, *Participation in America: Social Equality and Political Democracy* (New York: Harper and Row, 1972); and Verba, Nie, and Kim, *Modes of Democratic Participation*, ch. 5, 6.

Table 4.3

Citizen Participation in Seven Nations: Percentage Performing Each Act in the Three Years Preceding the Study

Type of participation	*Austria*	*India*	*Japan*	*Nether-lands*	*Nigeria*	*United States*	*Yugo-slavia*
Interest articulation							
Local parochial contacting	16%	12%	7%	38%	2%	7%	20%[a]
Active member of formal organization taking part in local affairs	9	7	11	15	28	32	57[b]
Interest aggregation							
Vote in competitive national election[c]	96	59	72	78[d]	66	72	—[e]
Work for party	10	25	25	10	—[f]	26	—[e]
Party member	28	6	4	13	—[f]	8	—[e]

[a] Contacting includes both local and extralocal officials.

[b] Organizational activity includes formal and informal groups.

[c] Due to citizens' feeling that they should have voted, surveys of voting turnout, such as this, tend to produce higher voting rates than actually occurred. Compare these voting data with those in Table 4.1.

[d] Voting is for municipal elections only.

[e] No competitive elections.

[f] Activity is illegal.

Sources: Sidney Verba, Norman H. Nie, and Jae-on Kim, *Modes of Democratic Participation* (Beverly Hills, Calif.: Sage Publications, 1971), p. 36. Copyright © 1971 by, and by permission of, Sage Publications, Inc.; and Sidney Verba, Norman H. Nie, Ana Barbic, Galen Irwin, Henk Molleman, and Goldie Shabad, "The Modes of Participation: Continuities in Research," *Comparative Political Studies*, 6:2 (July 1973), pp. 235–250.

Second, we know that political parties and various organizations are extremely important in encouraging citizens to become politically involved. In some countries, the system of parties offers rather drastic choices of policy, ideology, and group benefits, as in the conflict between the Communist and Christian Democratic parties in Italy. In other countries, such as the United States, the parties offer less contrasting alternatives to voters. Where choices are dramatic and different parties are clearly linked to particular groups of citizens, those citizens are more likely to get involved.[2] Obviously, some parties also make great organized efforts to get out the vote. In India and Mexico, the parties, especially the governing parties, have often sent out trucks to round up voters in the rural areas. In many nations, party organiza-

[2] For a study of the impact of such factors as registration laws, compulsory voting, and party alternatives on voting turnout, see G. Bingham Powell Jr., "Voting Turnout in Thirty Democracies," in Richard Rose, ed., *Party and Electoral Systems* (Beverly Hills: Sage Publications, 1979.)

tions make elaborate efforts to contact voters and see that they get to the polls. As these organizations are very elaborate and thorough in some nations, such as Austria and the Netherlands, moderately extensive in others, such as West Germany and France, and quite weak in others, including most parts of the United States, voting turnout is shaped accordingly.

Parties also offer a variety of incentives for membership and campaign work, such as public housing opportunities, better treatment by government bureaucrats of the ruling party, and automatic membership through party-linked occupational groups. Activity through formal groups will also depend on the extensiveness of these groups in the society, and the benefits they offer members. Citizens may join PTA groups due to pressure from children to meet teachers, or join labor unions due to job pressures, but be alerted by these organizations to various political needs and channels of action.

Candidates with particularly strong personal appeal can bring many apolitical people into political activity. Dwight Eisenhower was able to capitalize on the American people's fondness for him as a hero of World War II in his presidential victories in the 1950s. Julius Nyerere in Tanzania and Fidel Castro in Cuba are two charismatic leaders of developing countries who have mobilized masses of people into at least intermittent and sometimes sustained political activity.

Finally, all these surrounding conditions will be utilized in different ways by citizens with participant attitudes. Citizens who are well-informed, confident in their ability to influence others, attentive to political affairs, or who think it their duty to get involved, will make use of opportunities for participation. Skill and confidence are especially important in complicated activities like organizing new groups or rising to be a leader in an organization involved in community affairs. Much cross-national research has shown that better educated, wealthier, and occupationally skilled citizens are more likely, on the average, to develop the attitudes that encourage participation.[3] The personal resources that such people accumulate in their private lives can be easily converted into political involvement when duty calls or need arises. Consequently, these studies have shown that the better-off citizens in a society tend to be most active in politics. This tendency is least pronounced in voting participation, most pronounced in forming groups.

To understand who participates, then, either in a single nation or in different nations, we must understand how the rules of eligibility and control, the recruitment efforts of parties and organized groups, and the attitudes of individuals all fit together. In a general sense, then, we can understand how in the United States the difficulty of voting requirements, the weakness of party organizations and alternatives and working-class groups like unions, and the strength of organizations of the educated middle class all bring the better-off citizens to the polls much more frequently than the poor. In Japan and Austria strong socialist parties and labor unions, simpler voting requirements, and strong support by citizens for some parties tend to counterbalance the greater information and awareness of the better off, and turnout is relatively equal among classes.

Citizens as Subjects

One of the most pervasive of all citizen roles, and that which has generated more citizen resistance to the efforts of authorities to promote compliance than any other, is the role of tax payer. The recent tax revolt in the state of California illustrates this resistance dramatically. Through a referendum held in the summer of 1978, 63 percent of those voting supported a state constitutional amendment to reduce the permissible property tax rate to less than half of what it had been.

Resources must be extracted from the society for a wide range of types of governmental activities. Modern nonsocialist societies extract from a quarter to a half of all the national income in taxes and levies of various kinds; communist political systems extract from half to three-fourths of national income through taxation and profits on national industries (see Chapter 8). Many devices are used to compel citizens to become obedient providers of the necessary resources. The United States relies heavily on

[3] Almond and Verba, *Civic Culture*; Verba, Nie, and Kim, *Modes of Democratic Participation*; and Alex Inkeles and David H. Smith, *Becoming Modern* (Cambridge, Mass.: Harvard University Press, 1974).

direct income taxes. The government withholds the income of individual earners, as well as corporations, who must file annual statements to request refunds when they have overpaid, or make additional payments when they have underpaid. An agency of the government, the Internal Revenue Service, monitors citizen taxation. Many state and local governments also tax incomes or use a host of indirect taxes, such as sales taxes. Although the primary sanction for compliance is coercion, with severe penalties provided for tax evasion, a normative emphasis on obedience to the law and good citizenship supplements coercion. In fact, some European nations have much higher levels of tax evasion than the United States. In France, for example, tax evasion is virtually a time-honored custom, and governmental budget forecasters always anticipate a substantial shortfall.[4]

Citizen roles as receivers of governmental benefits are assumed much more readily, although here too government agencies must typically engage in substantial public education campaigns to inform citizens of the availability of benefits and how to receive them. Aid to the handicapped, to war veterans, to the aged, to the poor, and to various special groups takes a great variety of forms. Patterns of bureaucratic implementation typically require citizens to register, or make special applications, for the benefits in question, whether these are welfare benefits, medical care, or loans to small business or for disaster relief. The agency must then monitor the system to see that only eligible citizens receive the benefits.

Modern societies are also covered by networks of regulations. Parents, for example, are commonly required to send children of certain ages to school for specific periods of the year. Compliance is achieved through a combination of incentive and coercion. On one hand, education is emphasized as a positive benefit to children and families. On the other hand, penalties are provided for failure to comply, unless educational requirements are met otherwise. It is, indeed, difficult to think of occupational and other major social and economic roles in modern societies that are not somehow linked to a form of government regulation. From traffic regulation to antitrust laws, the citizen in a complex society faces regulatory action. Yet, here too there is variation. In authoritarian political systems the regulation is typically more pervasive, often more arbitrary, and extends to the control of internal travel, public gatherings, and public speech.

A final form of citizen subject role is of particular interest: the symbolic involvement role. Most political systems attempt to involve citizens with symbols of the community, regime, and authorities. In some countries, school children must learn and recite the pledge of allegiance, and complex legal battles have been fought in the United States over the efforts of citizens to resist this requirement for religious or ethical reasons. The mass media are filled with efforts by political leaders to invoke and reinforce symbols of national history and unity.

Contemporary authoritarian systems, particularly the one-party states, press the symbolic involvement of citizens much further. In major efforts to socialize citizen attitudes through symbolic role playing, these systems typically mobilize every citizen to cast a vote for the single party's candidate on election day, and to participate in parades, work groups, and the like. For the same purpose, many have instituted vast recreational programs, particularly to further the involvement of the young. The penetrative party and bureaucratic organizations in these regimes are usually highly effective in mobilizing citizens to perform these symbolic roles, although the effect on attitudes cannot be determined.

THE RECRUITMENT OF ELITES

Becoming Eligible: Bias Toward The Better Off

Every political system has procedures for the recruitment, or selection, of political and administrative officeholders. In democracies such as the United States, Britain, and France, political and administrative positions are formally open to any candidate with sufficient talent. But political recruits, like political participants, tend to be people of middle- or upper-class background, and those coming from the lower classes who have been able to gain access to

[4] See Hugh Heclo, Arnold Heidenheimer, and Carolyn Teich Adams, *Comparative Public Policy* (New York: St. Martin's Press, 1975), ch. 8.

Contemporary authoritarian systems emphasize recruitment of citizens into symbolic support for government and leaders, as in this massive rally in China.

education.[5] Of course, this somewhat overstates the case. The trade unions or leftist political parties in some countries may serve as channels of political advancement for people lacking in economic advantage or educational opportunity. Thus the Labour party delegation in the British House of Commons and the Communist party delegation in the French National Assembly include a substantial number of workers. However, the workers have usually acquired political skills and experience by holding offices in trade unions or other groups.

There is a reason for this bias in political recruitment. Political and governmental leadership, particularly in modern, technologically sophisticated societies, requires knowledge and skills hard to acquire in any way other than through education and training. Natural intelligence and experience in a trade union or cooperative society may, to a limited degree, take the place of substantial formal education. But even in leftist parties, the higher offices tend to be held by educated professional people rather than by members of the working class.

Communist countries, despite their ideologies of working-class revolution, have not been able to avoid this bias. As they advance into industrialism, or as they seek to do so, they depend increasingly on trained technicians. Even the running of an effective revolutionary party calls for technical competence and substantial knowledge. In the Soviet Union, the Central Committee of the Communist party has increasingly been composed of persons with higher education who are recruited from the regional

[5] See the general review of many studies by Robert Putnam, *The Comparative Study of Political Elites* (Englewood Cliffs, N.J.: Prentice-Hall, 1976).

party organizations, the army, and the bureaucracy. The emergence in communist countries of an educated, technically competent, and privileged ruling class is in violation of their revolutionary populist ideology, and some friction has resulted. Thus we observe a cycle of recruitment of the technically competent followed by ideological and populistic attacks on bureaucracy and privilege. Nowhere has this been more marked than in China, where the Great Proletarian Cultural Revolution of the late 1960s sought to destroy the powers and privileges of the party leadership and the governmental bureaucracy and bring power back to the people. Yet if the communist countries are to make and implement developmental programs, they cannot escape this dependence on education and competence.

Selection of Elite Policy Makers

From among those who have been recruited to lower levels of the political elite, a much smaller number must be selected for the top roles. Historically, the problem of selecting the individuals to fill the top policy-making roles has been critical for maintaining internal order and stability of government. Monarchs, presidents, commanders, and party chairmen exercise great power, personally and over policy directions. A major accomplishment of stable democracies has been to regulate the potential conflict involved in succession, and confine it to the mobilization of votes instead of weapons. When we refer generally to "recruitment structures," we are thinking of how systems choose the top policy makers and executives.

Table 4.4 shows these recruitment structures in a number of contemporary nations. The most familiar structures in the table are the presidential and parliamentary forms of competitive party systems. In the presidential form, as in the United States and France, parties select candidates for nomination, and the electorate more or less directly chooses between these. The Mexican system is similar, but the PRI has such control over the electoral process that for half a century the electorate has merely ratified the party's presidential nominee. That nomination itself has been achieved after complex bargaining between party factions and with other powerful groups.

In the parliamentary form, the chief executive is not selected directly by popular election. Rather, the parties select leaders, and the electorate votes to determine the strength of the party in the assembly. If a single party wins a majority, its leader becomes prime minister. If no party wins a majority, bargaining takes place to enable some prime minister to emerge who can command a coalition majority in the parliament — or at least not be defeated by one. In some cases, as has happened rather often in Italy, a prime minister may exist on the sufferance of a hostile assembly, which can force the leader from office at any time, but refrains to do so because no replacement can win either. In both the competitive presidential and parliamentary systems, the tenure of the chief executive is periodically renewed, as new elections are held, and either a successor is selected or the incumbent retained. As long as the party and the election or assembly structures provide clear majorities, and all actors abide by the results, these systems work with great stability, and tie recruitment directly to interest aggregation and policy creation.

Table 4.4 also illustrates the role of noncompetitive parties. In the Mexican case, as we have noted, selection takes place through a rather open process of oligarchic bargaining within and around the PRI and the incumbent president, who cannot succeed himself (see Chapter 14). Despite the somewhat closed nature of the recruitment process, the rule of no reelection forces periodic change in personnel, and often in policy, and the party and the semicompetitive elections do bring about popular involvement. In the communist systems of the U.S.S.R. and Czechoslovakia, Communist parties select the first secretary or its equivalent. Negotiations between top party leaders in the Presidium and the Central Committee are typically not available for full analysis, so generalizations must be made cautiously. But it is safe to conclude that succession is not a simple matter, because these systems provide for no limited term for incumbents — hence the incumbent must always be aware of the possibility of a party coup of the type that ousted Nikita Khrushchev from the Soviet leadership in 1964. As systems, however, the heirarchical party selection structures have been quite successful in maintaining themselves.
In the Eastern European countries, some sort of negotiation or approval by the Soviet Union is also typically involved. It is apparent, especially since the

Table 4.4

Recruitment of Chief Executive in Selected Contemporary Nations, 1977

Country	*Chief executive structure*[a]	*Recruitment structures*[b]	*Frequency type of government has survived succession*[c]
United States	President	Party and electorate	Very often
France	President	Party and electorate	Twice
West Germany	Prime minister	Party and assembly	Often
Great Britain	Prime minister	Party and assembly	Very often
Czechoslovakia	Party secretary	Party and U.S.S.R. party	Often
Israel	Prime minister	Party and assembly	Often
U.S.S.R.	Party secretary	Party	Often
Italy	Prime minister	Party and assembly	Very often
Japan	Prime minister	Party and assembly	Often
Mexico	President	Party and elites	Very often
Yugoslavia	President and first secretary	Party	No experience
Peru	President	Military	One
Brazil	President	Military and elites	Often
Egypt	President	Military and elites	One
China	Party chairman	Party and military	One
India	Prime minister	Party and assembly	Often
Nigeria	President	Military	Twice
Tanzania	President	Party	No experience

[a] "Party secretary" refers to that position or a similar one as head of party in communist regime.

[b] "Party and assembly" refers to the typical parliamentary system.

[c] "Often" means that at least three successions have taken place; that is, that a new individual has assumed the chief executive role three different times under that type of government.

Soviet suppression of the Hungarian uprising in 1956 and the Czechoslovakian intervention in 1968, that the selection systems in these nations cannot be considered independently from the Soviet Union, which is willing to intervene militarily to maintain its veto over personnel and policy.

The poorer nations, moving down the column of Table 4.4, show substantially less stability, and the regimes have usually had less experience at surviving succession crises. In the cases of Yugoslavia and Tanzania, the national founders of the regime remain in control, and it remains to be seen if the one-party selection structures can function in choosing a replacement. These regimes have been successful in controlling lower-level recruitment. The military regimes in Peru and Nigeria are typical of military governments in many nations not shown: no other structure shows signs of replacing the military command or junta in selecting leaders, but individuals have seldom remained in command for very long without a coup. In Egypt and Brazil, mixed civilian-military oligarchies have demonstrated some substantial staying power, responding to and controlling internal power factions through a mixture of involvement and coercion. In China the Communist party has remained in power, but has suffered several periods of internal strife, and the army has been involved in recruitment at all levels.

It is indicative of the great need to mobilize broadly-based political resources behind the selection of chief executives in contemporary political systems that political parties are important selection structures in so many cases. The frequent appearance of parties also reflects, no doubt, the nature of legitimacy in secular cultures: the promise that actions of the rulers will be in the interests of the ruled.

Control of Elites

Performance of the system functions is crucial for the stability of a political system. Elite recruitment is one of the most essential system functions. Traditional empires and dictatorships, in which self-perpetuation was a major goal of the rulers, seem to have focused on recruitment as the system function to be most carefully regulated. Lesser elites were controlled through the careful selection of loyalists to fill the supervisory roles in the military and civilian bureaucracies, and through the provision of powerful inducements for continuing loyal performance. The conquering general or authoritarian dictator mixes rewards to favorites with severe penalties for failure or disloyalty.

Modern authoritarian systems have discovered that more efficient and effective control is achieved through simultaneous manipulation of political socialization, political recruitment, and political communication. Socialization efforts are made to instill loyalty, to recruit loyal activists, and to limit and regulate the flow of information.

But if recruitment is made a part of a larger pattern of control, it is hardly neglected. Selection in the U.S.S.R., for example, is accomplished through a device called *nomenklatura*. Under this procedure important positions are kept under the direct supervision of a specific party agency whose officials have the final word on the advancement of anyone to such an office (see Chapter 12). Moreover, a complicated set of inducements is offered to make sure that chosen officials perform as they are supposed to. These inducements make it difficult for any but the topmost officials to have much freedom of action. Maximum control is ensured with normative incentives, such as appeal to party, ideology, and national idealism; financial incentives, such as better salaries, access to finer food and clothing, better housing, and freedom to travel; and coercive control, such as reporting by police, party, and bureaucrats. Demotion or imprisonment are penalties for disapproved actions. To avoid that bane of authoritarian systems, the coup by police or military forces, the varied command layers and inducement structures are interwoven.

Democratic systems, too, use selection and regulation to attempt to control the performance of government officials. As we have already emphasized, periodic renewal of the tenure of elected officials is a fundamental device for ensuring the responsiveness of democratic elites. But other recruitment and expulsion structures exist also. In many parliamentary systems the prime minister and cabinet can be forced to resign office if they lose the confidence of a majority of members of a parliament. In the American system the Supreme Court has the authority to declare congressional or presidential actions unconstitutional, and impeachment procedures can be used against the incumbents in top roles, even the president (as seen in the events forcing President Nixon from office) or a Supreme Court justice, if their activities stray too far beyond permissible bounds. Military officers and civil servants are also subject to removal from office or demotion for violating their oaths of office or for failing to perform their duties. These devices to ensure that the powerful perform their duties as expected are an essential part of political recruitment.

COERCIVE AND VIOLENT POLITICAL PARTICIPATION

Nations offer different opportunities for legitimate participation by citizens and leaders. In most countries citizens can vote, although that vote may perform different functions, and in all they can and must pay taxes. Elites may run for office and openly mobilize citizen support in some nations, work their way up the hierarchy of the authoritarian party in others. But in all nations there is also an alternative form of political action, which may or may not actually be used. Most obvious and important is the possibility of coercion and violence, which are illegal except when used by the government itself, but which can be used by citizens nonetheless. The appearance of widespread violence is usually a sign that the stability of the form of government itself, not to mention the particular incumbents, is threatened.

Some forms of participation are legitimate in some nations, but not in others. A good example is the protest demonstration. Peaceful protest demonstrations are legitimate in most democratic nations, at least within certain bounds. They are usually an unconventional form of interest articulation, designed to publicize the demonstrators' feelings of injustice or concern and gain the attention of leaders or the public. As Table 4.5 shows, over a thousand such demonstrations were counted in the United States between 1958 and 1967, reflecting both the relative (and increasing) legitimacy of the type of action and the great breadth of citizen discontent. The number of such demonstrations increased tremen-

Table 4.5

Coercive Forms of Political Activity in Selected Political Systems, 1958–1967

Country	*Protest demonstrations*[a]	*Armed political attacks*	*Attempted military coups*[b]
United States	1151	523	None
France	133	485	1958, 1961
West Germany	89	25	None
Great Britain	116	26	None
U.S.S.R.	9	20	None
Japan	107	6	None
Spain	65	56	None
Mexico	26	50	None
Egypt	5	0	None
China	3	657	None
India	135	1507	None
Nigeria	11	393	1966, 1966 1967, 1967
Tanzania	4	16	None

[a] Includes only peaceful demonstrations.

[b] Not all attempted coups were successful.

Source: Charles S. Taylor and Michael C. Hudson, *World Handbook of Political and Social Indicators*, 2nd ed. (New Haven, Conn.: Yale University Press, 1972), pp. 88–93; and William R. Thompson, *The Grievances of Military Coup-Makers* (Beverly Hills, Calif.: Sage Publications, 1973); pp. 67 ff.

dously from the previous decade, as black citizens sought full rights and improvement of living conditions, and as the young became increasingly alienated from the unpopular war in Vietnam. In other democracies, too, protest demonstrations were common in the 1960s, to the point that they virtually became accepted as conventional, rather than unusual, forms of political action. In authoritarian systems, however, protest demonstrations were illegal, and demonstrators severely punished. Consequently, unrest in these nations was either stifled or took more violent form.

Table 4.5 also shows armed attacks made by individual citizens and, more usually, small terrorist groups against the government or political opponents. Such attacks were all too frequent in the United States also, demonstrating the severity of internal racial conflict in particular, but they were much less common than protest demonstrations. Indeed, Table 4.5 shows that in most of the industrial democracies peaceful protest was more common than violent attacks, while in the authoritarian systems the reverse was the case. France, where the secret army terrorist group, the OAS (Organisation de l'armée secréte), sought to force the government to reverse its policy of independence for Algeria, was a conspicuous exception in the early 1960s. But in the late 1960s and 1970s peaceful protest became more common in France also. China, in the throes of the Cultural Revolution, Nigeria, rapidly approaching civil war and the breakdown of civil authority, and India, torn by ethnic conflict over language and religion, all show high levels of armed attacks.

Finally, the table shows the frequency with which military groups attempted to move against the government. Coup attempts by the armed forces are

In parliamentary systems a majority party leader becomes prime minister; Japan's Ohira receives banzai *("long live") cheers following his selection at the Liberal Democratic party convention.*

usually associated with the breakdown of government. Indeed, in Nigeria and Indonesia coups directly resulted in either civil war or massive retaliatory bloodshed. But in many nations military forces have been able to take over the government and force changes in personnel and policy with relative ease and lack of opposition. In the nations in Table 4.5 coup attempts are rather rare, because they are rare among the wealthier nations of the world, where political systems of greater resources have been more successful in managing conflict, keeping it within legitimate bounds. But in many poorer nations, operating in preindustrial environments and facing a host of problems and pressures, military coups are a frequent occurrence, often almost a last means of holding together a collapsing society, or a reflection of the loss of support of more popularly based governments. Among the 110 nations that were independent in 1960, military forces had attempted a coup at least once in forty-two by the end of 1969. In thirty-four countries, at least, the coup efforts were successful. In some countries there were repeated interventions by the armed forces: in Syria there were eight known military coup efforts in the 1960s, of which five were partially successful. Across the full range of countries, slightly over half the attempted coups were at least partially successful.[6]

HOW MUCH PARTICIPATION?

One aspect of the participation explosion is a widespread belief, particularly among younger people, in participant democracy. The main thrust of this belief is that even in democratic countries political decisions are made by the establishment — the economically privileged and the politically powerful. The solution to this problem, claim the proponents of participant democracy, is to bring decision making down to the level of the community and small groups, back to the people. As a result, citizens would be able to grasp the issues and act politically in their own interests.

Those who argue for participant democracy are critical of political theorists who argue that even in democracies there must be a division of political labor and influence, and that a country in which most people would be politically active much of the time would be impossible to govern.[7]

It is not surprising that ideas and political arrangements long taken for granted should be questioned in recent times. Our discussion of the remarkable rise of civil disorder in the United States and other democratic countries in recent years reflects serious dissatisfaction with the political institutions and policies of modern democracies. Previously apathetic minority groups and college students, who at an earlier time were referred to as the silent generation, have burst into political activity and changed the structure of politics in important ways.

The fundamental question is whether a direct, participant democracy is possible in modern nations confronted with contemporary conditions and problems. Robert Dahl has faced this question and presented an analysis deserving of attention.[8] His argument starts with the idea that the preferences, values, and interests of all members of political communities should be taken into account in the decisions of democratic political systems. If all or most members of the community have the same interests and preferences, then there is no problem. But since this unanimity never occurs, some kind of rule of decision is essential. The majority principle would seem to be an ethically acceptable solution, but in some cases majority rule may be impossible, since the interests of some minority may be so important that its members would not tolerate rule by majority. Language, religion, and property rights are examples of issues over which the application of majority rule may result in civil war, national fragmentation, and the destruction of democracy. In democracies majority rule is normally limited in some areas, either through the acceptance of mutual guarantees pro-

[6] These estimates of coup frequency and motivation were calculated from data in Thompson, *Grievances of Coup-Makers*, pp. 67 ff.

[7] See, for example, Seymour Martin Lipset, *Political Man* (London: Mercury Books, 1963); Harry Eckstein, *A Theory of Stable Democracy* (Princeton, N.J.: Center of International Studies, Princeton University Press, 1961); Almond and Verba, *Civic Culture*.

[8] Robert A. Dahl, *After the Revolution* (New Haven, Conn.: Yale University Press, 1971).

tecting the interests of minorities (permitting free practice of religion, the right to speak and be educated in minority languages, and so forth), or through a reserved area of autonomous decisions where government is prohibited from interfering (freedom of speech, press, assembly, petition, and so forth). But these limits on majority rule are only the beginning of sound democratic logic.

In order for people to accomplish their purposes, they have had to form ever larger and larger political associations. Even the nation-state, at least as presently constituted, may be too small in the modern world. Modern military, industrial, medical, and communications technology has made many important decisions about man's physical survival and safety the domain of the international level; the alternative is destruction through war, pollution, overpopulation, and the exhaustion of resources. Although some urgent problems can still be faced at the national or subnational level, others require multinational cooperation, through associations like the European Economic Community. This leaves only some decisions to be made at the local or community level. As we move from the community and local levels up through the national level to the international level, the preference of individuals matters less and less. When tens and hundreds of millions of people are involved, and when the issues are as complicated as nuclear disarmament, the control of population and pollution, and the development of new sources of energy, more and more decision making must be delegated to political representatives or to trained professionals.

Participant democracy must also be reconciled with the principle of economy. The investment of time and effort by people in participation, and the benefits they reap from their investment vary widely now and probably always will. As Dahl points out:

> At one extreme is the inactive member of an association who does not enjoy taking part, is pretty well satisfied with the way things turn out, thinks his participation cannot change things much, sees little difference in the alternatives, does not feel very competent, and perhaps believes that what the association does is not very important anyway. To him any time spent in the affairs of the association is bound to look like time wasted. At the other extreme is the frantic activist who would rather politic than eat, believes that the future of mankind depends on his association, sees vast issues at stake in every decision, feels confident of his competence, and is equally certain not only that he can shape the outcome, but that disaster will strike if he does not participate.[9]

Dahl argues that the ideal of participant democracy must confront not only the sheer numbers of people involved, the differences in interests and preferences, and the need for competence; it must also confront the economic aspects of participation, that is, what people must forego in the way of time, energy, and money if they are active in politics. He concludes that its cost to the individual limits the role that direct participation can play in democratic government. Delegation of power to representatives (held accountable, to be sure, through elections) and to nonelected professionals and specialists is a necessary and desirable alternative.

Dahl concludes his discussion of the limits of participant democracy with the metaphor of Chinese boxes, the ancient toy consisting of a large box that contains smaller and smaller boxes. Just as there is a range of box sizes, political problems occur in all dimensions and at all levels. Problem-solving organizations must exist at each level if the problems are going to be solved at all. The big box is analogous to the international level, where, it becomes increasingly evident, problem-solving apparatus and capacity will have to develop if man is to survive. The tiny box is analogous to the local community, where direct participation of individuals in local political decisions like sewage disposal, education, and road maintenance is both possible and feasible, since many individuals not only want to solve these problems but are competent to judge the effectiveness of alternative solutions and are motivated to pay the costs of participating. As one moves from the tiniest box to the largest one, specialized competence becomes more important and the costs of participation become greater, necessitating reliance on elected representatives and appointed professionals.

None of this, however, argues that the ideal of participation has been fully realized in the con-

[9] Dahl, *After the Revolution*, p. 47.

temporary nations characterized (properly) as democracies. Recent experiments in local community participation and in participation by workers and their representatives in the decision making of economic enterprises suggest that there are still opportunities for democratic creativity. And the recent mobilization and politicization of members of underprivileged minority groups, women, and young people in industrial democracies show that there are still bastions of privilege and inequality to conquer.

KEY TERMS

democracy
participant activities
subject activities
interest articulation
interest aggregation
policy-making
political recruitment
recruitment structures
presidential recruitment
parliamentary recruitment
nomenklatura system
participant democracy

CHAPTER FIVE

Interest Articulation and Interest Groups

Every political system has some way of formulating and responding to demands. As we saw in Chapter 4, the most simple form of interest articulation in all political systems is the individual making a plea or request to a city council member, legislator, tax or zoning officer, or, in a more traditional system, village head or tribal chieftain. Interest groups formed to increase the strength and effectiveness of individual demands have been active in politics throughout history.

During the last hundred years or so, as societies have industrialized and the scope of governmental activity has widened, the quantity and variety of interest groups have grown proportionately. Interest group headquarters, sometimes numbering in the thousands, are to be found in capitals like London, Washington, Paris, Bonn, and Rome. Some of these headquarters are in buildings which are almost as imposing as those housing major governmental agencies. In those countries where power is decentralized, these organizations will have headquarters in each seat of power throughout the system.

TYPES OF INTEREST GROUPS

Interest groups vary in structure, style, financing, and support base, among other things, and the variation for any given nation may greatly influence its politics, its economics, and its social life. Table 5.1 attempts to distinguish among interest groups according to their social bases or goals.

While interest groups are also organized on the basis of tribal membership, race, national origin, religion, or policy issues, the most powerful, largest, and financially strongest groups are those based on occupation or profession, largely because the livelihoods and careers of men and women are affected most immediately by governmental policy and action. Most countries therefore have labor unions, manufacturers' associations, farm groups, and associations of doctors, lawyers, engineers, and teachers.

Interest groups may also be separated according to organizational characteristics. The United States Chamber of Commerce, for example, with its impressive limestone building a short distance from the White House, its hundreds of staff members and

Table 5.1
Examples of Interest Groups Defined by Social Bases or Goals

Social base or goal	*Examples*
Tribal	Alaskan Federation of Natives (Eskimos, Indians, Aleuts) (United States)
	Ibo Federal Union (Nigeria)
Racial	British West Indies Association (Great Britain)
	Chinese American Citizens Alliance (United States)
	Congress of Racial Equality (United States)
Ethnic	Mexican-American Political Association (United States)
	Polish National Alliance (United States)
	Quebec Liberation Front (Canada)
Religious	American Friends Service Committee (United States)
	Burma Muslim Organization (Burma)
	Independent Catholic Action (France)
	Society for the Propagation of the Gospel in Foreign Parts (Great Britain)
Occupational-professional	American Medical Association (United States)
	Federation of Housewives (Japan)
	General Confederation of Beetgrowers (France)
	General Confederation of Italian Industry (Italy)
	Transport and General Workers Union (Great Britain)
	Wheatgrowers Federation (Australia)
Issue- or policy-oriented	Association for Returning Okinawa Islands to Japan (Japan)
	Committee for the Green Foothills (United States)
	Council on Foreign Relations (United States)
	Italian Union of Women (Italy)
	Society for the Preservation of Rural England (Great Britain)
	Temperance Alliance (Australia)

employees, and its annual budget in the millions, can hardly be lumped with a group of neighbors getting together to protest a zoning regulation at a meeting of the local planning commission.

Individual Contactors

Individuals may act alone in contacting political officials, and under some conditions these activities may be quite important. We have already seen in Table 4.2 that contacting about narrow personal or family matters remains common in the modern world. Indeed it has probably increased in complex industrial societies with large government bureaucracies. So also there may be an increase in individuals' efforts to articulate their opinions on broader issues, as when they write their senator on foreign policy, or approach their local zoning board about neighborhood improvement. Purely personal efforts may become important when many people act on the same type of problem or when a single contactor is too influential to be ignored, as when a wealthy campaign contributor brings a personal problem to the attention of a politician, or the king's minister asks a favor for his child. However, individual efforts to articulate interests on broader issues become closely intertwined, typically, with group awareness and intermittent group activities (see below).[1]

More interesting is the creation of networks of individual supporters by political leaders, who try to build followings with the exchange of favors and support with each citizen in the network. The politician provides benefits, such as cutting red tape or securing government loans or services, in return for the citizen's votes, campaign activities or contributions, or personal favors. Such networks, often called *patronage networks*, or *patron-client networks*, may be especially prevalent in societies where many individuals survive on a narrow economic margin, and where formal organizations to sustain them are not effective.[2] Many sets of personal arrangements between politicians and individual followers may make it hard to build broad and stable organizations, as leaders may move from one organization or party to another, taking their followers along.

In authoritarian societies, where a small elite makes most decisions, and in all societies where bureaucracies have much power, personal networks built by individual leaders take on added importance. Students of Soviet politics have written of the patronage followings established by Josef Stalin, Khrushchev, and other leaders in their rise to power, and the effects of these networks on the careers of both leaders and followers.[3] Networks of personal supporters are a special kind of political structure, because their members are not drawn together by a shared interest in making policy demands, but are held together by the skill and resources of the leader in satisfying the needs of the followers.

Anomic Groups

Anomic groups are the more or less spontaneous groups that form suddenly when many individuals respond similarly to frustration, disappointment, or other strong emotions. They are flash affairs, rising and subsiding suddenly. Without previous organization or planning, individuals long frustrated may suddenly take to the streets to vent their anger as a rumor of new injustice sweeps the community or news of a government action touches deep emotions. Their actions may lead to violence, but do not necessarily. James Coleman provides a good example of an anomic interest group in eastern Nigeria, where women carried on much of the trading:

> The rumor that women were to be taxed . . . precipitated a women's movement that spread like wildfire through two of the most densely populated provinces. Chiefs and Europeans were attacked indiscriminately and there was widespread destruction of property and goods, belonging mainly to trading firms. The riot was not quelled until the police, in an overwhelming show of force, killed fifty women and injured an equal number. An unusual feature was that the women, all illiterate, not only initiated but also were the only participants in the uprising. The whole affair was entirely spontaneous and received no support from either the men or the literate elements of the provinces.[4]

Much of what passes for anomic behavior may, of course, be no more than the use of unconventional, violent means by organized groups, as with urban guerrillas in recent years. But, particularly where organized groups are absent, or where they have failed to obtain adequate representation of their interests in the political system, smoldering discontent may be sparked by an incident or by the emergence of a leader, and may suddenly explode in unpredictable and uncontrollable ways. For example, after a long period of domestic quiet, Egypt was swept by riots in 1977 as people protested an increase in government-regulated food prices. Some political systems, including the United States, Italy, India and the Arab nations, have been marked by a rather high frequency of such violent and spontaneous group formation; others are notable for the infrequency of such disturbances (for comparative data see Table 8.7).

Events in the past decades in developed societies reflect anomic group activity. In the communist countries of Eastern Europe, violent, generally spon-

[1] See Sidney Verba, Norman H. Nie, and Jae-on Kim, *The Modes of Democratic Participation* (Beverly Hills, Calif.: Sage Publications, 1971).

[2] These clientelist or patronage structures are discussed further in the next chapter, in terms of their role in interest aggregation.

[3] See the essays in G. F. Skilling and F. Griffiths (eds.), *Interest Groups in Soviet Politics* (Princeton, N.J.: Princeton University Press, 1971).

[4] James S. Coleman, *Nigeria: Background to Nationalism* (Berkeley: University of California Press, 1958), p. 174.

taneous protest appeared in East Berlin and Hungary in the 1950s; in Czechoslovakia in 1968 during the period of Soviet occupation; and in many Polish cities in 1970, when working-class communities demonstrated against governmental policies they found threatening. In the United States, spontaneous political action occurred in many black areas in the aftermath of Martin Luther King's assassination and on many college campuses after the American invasion of Cambodia. Wildcat strikes, long a feature of the British trade-union scene, also occurred frequently in the early 1970s in such continental European countries as Germany and Sweden. And in southern Italy in 1970 there was a massive uprising in Reggio di Calabria after the city was not granted the politically and economically important status of regional capital.

We must be cautious, however, about characterizing as anomic political behavior what is really the result of detailed planning by interest groups. Farmers' demonstrations in France and Britain and at Common Market headquarters in Brussels in the early 1970s, for example, owed much to indignation but little to spontaneity.

Nonassociational Groups

Like anomic groups, *nonassociational groups* are rarely well organized and their activity is episodic. They differ from anomic groups because they are based on common interests of ethnicity, region, religion, occupation, or perhaps kinship. Because of these continuing economic or cultural ties, nonassociational groups have more continuity than anomic groups. Subgroups within a large nonassociational group (such as blacks or workers) may, how-

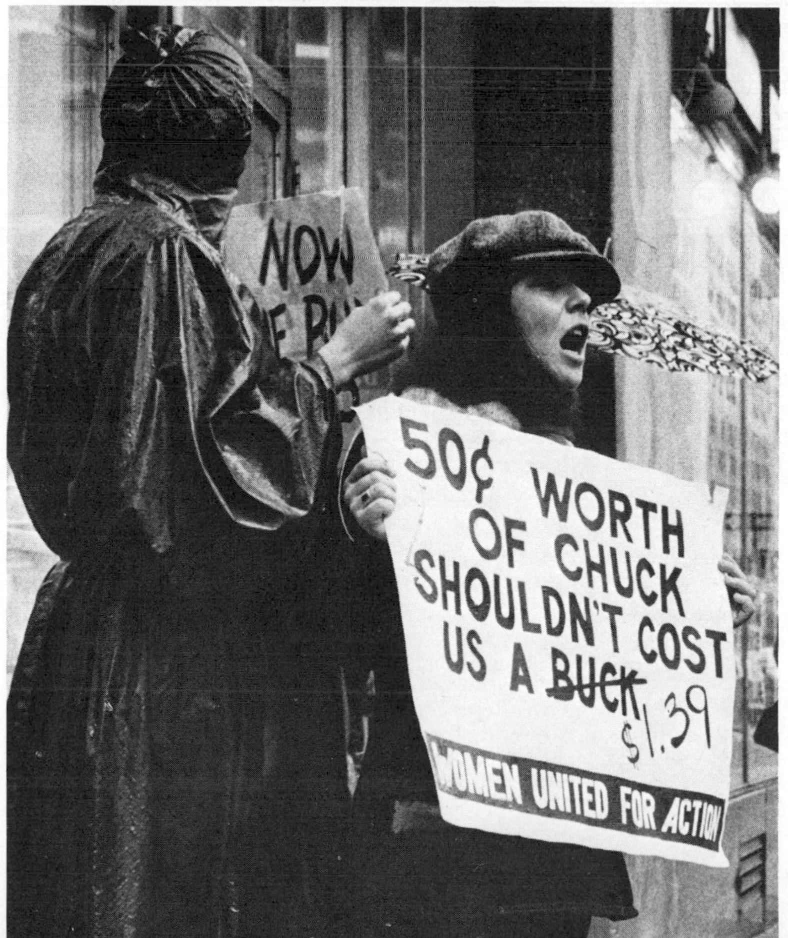

Rapid inflation encourages the spontaneous formation of many new groups in the United States, as in these efforts by angry consumers to boycott beef retailers.

ever, act as an anomic group, as in a spontaneous riot by a small number of blacks or an unplanned demonstration by one union local. There are two especially interesting kinds of nonassociational groups. One is the very large group that has not become formally organized, although its members perceive, perhaps dimly, their common interests. The best example may be the consumer interest group, such as all coffee drinkers, but many ethnic, regional, and occupational groups also fit into this category. The problem in organizing such groups is that with so many members sharing a rather small problem, it is difficult to find leaders who are willing to commit the effort and time needed to organize.

A second type of nonassociational group is the small kinship, lineage, economic, or ethnic subgroup, whose members know each other personally. Here, too, there is long-term continuity and only intermittent and unspecialized articulation of interests. But the small, face-to-face group has some important advantages, and may be highly effective in some political situations. If its members are well-connected, or its goals unpopular or illegal, the group may prefer to remain informal, even inconspicuous. Examples of the action of such groups include the work stoppages and petitions demanding better wages and hospital conditions by doctors in Mexico City in the 1960s;[5] requests made by large landowners asking a bureaucrat to continue a grain tariff; and the appeal of relatives of a government tax collector for favored treatment for the family business. As the last two examples suggest, personal interest articulation may often have more legitimacy and be put on a more permanent basis by invoking group ties and interests. Leaders similarly invoke such connections in building personal support networks.

Institutional Groups

Political parties, business corporations, legislatures, armies, bureaucracies, and churches often support *institutional groups* or have members with special responsibility for lobbying. These groups are formal and have other political or social functions in addition to interest articulation. But either as corporate bodies or as smaller groups within these bodies (legislative blocs, officer cliques, higher or lower clergy, religious orders, departments, skill groups, and ideological cliques in bureaucracies), such groups express their own interests or represent the interest of other groups in the society.

In France, civil and military bureaucracies do not simply react to pressures from the outside; in the absence of political directives they often act as independent forces of interest representation. In Italy, groups formed especially for interest articulation are forced to compete with many institutional groups. The Roman Catholic Church, especially, has used its influence in Italian politics, even if much of its intervention has taken the form of religious education. In 1948, for example, the pope and bishops repeatedly admonished Catholics, under penalty of sin, to use their votes to defeat socialists and communists. In 1978, the Permanent Council of the Italian Bishops' Conference denounced "Marxists and Communists" in a warning against allowing the Communist party to become a member of the governing coalition. Less overtly, the church seeks influence by having members of the clergy call on officeholders.

Where institutional interest groups are powerful, it is usually because of the strength provided by their organizational base. In authoritarian regimes, which prohibit or at least control other types of groups, institutional groups play a very large role. Educational officials, party officials and factions, jurists, factory managers, officers in the various military services, and groups composed of many other institutionally based members have had significant roles in interest articulation in communist regimes.[6] In preindustrial societies, which usually have few associational (groups and where such groups usually fail to mobi-

[5] Evelyn P. Stevens, "Protest Movements in an Authoritarian Regime," *Comparative Politics*, 7:3 (April 1975), pp. 361–382.

[6] See Skilling and Griffiths, *Interest Groups in Soviet Politics*; the essays by Barghoorn and Skilling in Robert A. Dahl, *Regimes and Oppositions* (New Haven, Conn.: Yale University Press, 1973); Roman Kolkowicz, "Interest Groups in Soviet Politics," *Comparative Politics*, 2:3 (April 1970), pp. 445–472; and Chapter 12 below.

lize much support, the prominent part played by military groups, corporations, party factions, and bureaucrats is well known. We already pointed out the frequency of military intervention in coups in such societies (see Chapter 4), but even where the military does not seize power directly, the possibility of such action forces close government attention to military requests. In industrial democracies, too, bureaucratic and corporate interests use their great resources and special information to affect policy. In the United States, for example, the military-industrial complex consists of the combination of personnel in the Defense Department and defense industries who mobilize in support of military expenditures.

Associational Groups

Associational groups include trade unions, chambers of commerce and manufacturers' associations, ethnic associations, religious associations, and civic groups. Associational groups characteristically represent the expressed interests of a particular group, employ a full-time professional staff, and have orderly procedures for the formulation of interests and demands.

In Great Britain, for example, the British Iron and Steel Federation, composed of directors of leading companies, negotiates with the government on matters affecting the steel industry.[7] The chief political work of the federation involves bargaining outside the channels of party politics with civil servants about regulations and legislative proposals. The federation also attempts to influence public opinion through advertising campaigns, like one mounted against nationalization of the steel industry.

Studies have shown that associational interest groups — where they are allowed to flourish — affect the development of other types of groups. Their organizational base gives them an advantage over nonassociational groups; their tactics and goals are often recognized as legitimate in the society; and by representing a broad range of groups and interests, they may effectively limit the influence of anomic, nonassociational, and institutional groups.

ACCESS TO THE INFLUENTIAL

To be effective, interest groups must be able to reach key decision makers. Groups may formally or informally express the interests of their members and yet fail to penetrate and influence decision makers. Interest groups vary in the tactics used to gain access to the influential, and political systems vary in the ways they organize and distribute influence.

If, for example, only one major legitimate access channel is available — as in a political system dominated by a single party — it becomes difficult for all groups to achieve access. Demands transmitted through that channel may be distorted as they work their way to key decision makers. The leadership thus may be prevented from getting information about the needs and demands of important groups in the society. Over the long run, this can easily lead to miscalculations by the leadership and to unrest among the dissatisfied groups. Another problem in a one-party system is that groups that have already established access may block the access of new groups. Guinean students rioted in 1961 to protest the arrest and trial of five prominent intellectuals. The inability of students and intellectuals to make themselves heard through the narrow channels of a one-party state, clogged by entrenched interests of the older and more established groups, seems to have been a major factor in the dissatisfaction. That student restiveness came as a surprise to most Guineans seems to confirm the point.[8]

In communicating political demands, individuals representing interest groups or themselves usually want to do more than merely convey information. They wish to make their views apparent to those leaders making decisions relevant to their interests, and they wish to express their needs in the manner most likely to gain a favorable response. So interest

[7] See Richard Rose, *Influencing Voters* (London: Faber and Faber, 1967), pp. 110–114.

[8] Victor D. Du Bois, "Guinea," in James S. Coleman and Carl C. Rosberg (eds.), *Political Parties and National Integration in Tropical Africa* (Berkeley: University of California Press, 1964), p. 210

groups look for special channels for transmitting their demands and develop special techniques for convincing decision makers that these demands deserve attention and response. Interest group leaders and lobbyists realize that the impact of a given message will vary according to many factors. One factor is the relation between the information conveyed and the perceptions and knowledge of the recipient. Control over special knowledge needed by decision makers is always a powerful tool for an interest group. But impact also depends on the attitudes of the decision makers — feelings of hostility or sympathy toward the interest group or individual, belief in the legitimacy of the claim, and so forth. Of particular importance is the decision maker's perception of the consequence of rejecting or agreeing to the demand.

The avenues for expressing opinions in a society have great importance in determining the range, effectiveness, and tactics used by interest groups. Where legitimate, conventional channels seem effective, groups will use them. Where such channels are not available or seem useless, an interest group may either give up trying, or turn to unconventional and even illegitimate channels, such as demonstrations, strikes, riots, and terror tactics. The most important types of access channels, the reasons for their prominence, and the consequences of their availability will now be discussed.

Personal Connection

One important means of access to political elites is through personal connections — the use of family, school, local, or other social ties. An excellent example is the informal network among the British elite based on old school ties originating at Eton or Harrow or in the colleges at Oxford and Cambridge universities.

Although personal connections are commonly used by nonassociational groups representing family or regional interests, they serve other groups as well. This is true in all political systems, perhaps largely because face-to-face contact is one of the most effective means of shaping attitudes. Where the contact occurs in an atmosphere of cordiality and friendship, the likelihood of a favorable response increases. Demands communicated by a friend, a relative, or a neighbor carry much more weight than a formal approach from a total stranger. Even in very modern political systems, personal connections are usually cultivated with care. In Washington, D.C., for example, the business of advising interest groups and individuals on access problems has become a profession, involving the full-time efforts of individuals with personal contacts influential in government.

Direct Representation

Direct representation in legislatures and bureaucracies provides a group with direct and continued communication of its interests by an involved member of the decision-making structure. In Italy, for example, labor unions enjoy constant representation on legislative committees. The legislatures of the United States, Great Britain, France, Germany, and other nations include many representatives of interest groups. Members of governmental institutional interest groups also have daily contact with active decision makers.

Indirect representation may also serve as a channel for interest groups that have no other means of communication. In the 1830s and 1840s in Great Britain, some aristocratic and middle-class members of Parliament took it upon themselves to express the demands of the working class. They were not responding to pressures and demands from below, but acting as self-appointed guardians of these neglected and suppressed interests. Their work did much to promote the passage of legislation to improve working conditions in factories and mines. Indirect representation occurs today in the developing areas where a modern political system — with effective associational groups and an effective party system — has yet to appear or fails to reach a majority of citizens. But it is an unreliable form of communication, since it often results in miscalculations on the part of the decision-making elite.

Mass Media

The mass media — television, radio, newspapers, magazines — constitute one method of communication, although the confusion created by the number of messages and by their lack of specific direction limits their effectiveness for many less important groups. Where the mass media are controlled by political elites and messages are subject to censorship, the media are to some degree eliminated as a useful channel of access, or reserved only for favored groups. In an open society, however, the use of the mass media to convey political demands serves as a major approach to decision makers.

Political Parties

Political parties are an important institutional means of communication, but a number of factors limits their usefulness. A highly ideological party with a hierarchical structure, such as the Communist party, is more likely to control affiliated interest groups than to communicate the demands of those interest groups. Decentralized party organizations, like those in the United States, whether inside or outside the legislative organization, may be less receptive to demands than individual legislators or blocs would be. In a nation like Great Britain, on the other hand, the various components of the party organization, particularly parliamentary committees, are important channels for transmitting demands to the Cabinet and the party in power. In nations like Mexico, where a single party dominates the political system, the party provides a vital channel for the articulation of many interests.

Legislatures, Cabinets, Bureaucracies

Standard lobbying tactics include appearances (and testimony) before legislative committees, providing information to individual legislators, and similar activities. Contacts with the bureaucracy at various levels and in different departments may be particularly important where the bureaucracy has decision-making authority; where the group is more interested in shaping procedures than in affecting policies; or where interests are narrow and directly involve few citizens outside the group. A study of access channels used by groups in Birmingham, England, showed that on broad issues involving class, ethnic, or consumer groups, the associations tended to work through the political parties. But on narrower issues, involving few other groups and less political conflict, the associations tended to turn to the appropriate administrative department.[9]

The relationships between interest groups and bureaucracies have been studied extensively. The appearance of regular channels for consultation and negotiation with interest groups, such as the committees, conferences, and informal communications found in the British system, provides an unusually explicit form of interest-group access to the bureaucracy. But a multitude of less formalized relationships have been analyzed in the United States, France, Italy, and Germany, and in developing nations like Egypt, Thailand, and the Philippines.

Protest Demonstrations

Protest demonstrations, strikes, and other forms of nonviolent, but dramatic and direct, pressure on government are ways of interest articulation that may be legitimate or illegitimate, depending on the political system and the actions of the demonstrators. Such demonstrations may be either spontaneous actions of anomic groups or, more frequently, an organized resort to an unconventional channel by organized groups. In democratic societies, protest demonstrations may be efforts to mobilize popular support — eventually electoral support — for the group's cause. The demonstrations for civil rights and against the Vietnam War of the 1960s were examples of such activity. In nondemocratic societies such demonstrations are more hazardous, and represent perhaps more extreme dissatisfaction with the alternative channels. As we saw in Chapter 4, the use of peaceful protest is more frequent in democratic systems, due no doubt to the greater controls on such activity in authoritarian systems.

Protest demonstrations have been aptly described as a tactic of society's powerlessness, those who do not have access or resources to influence decision makers, and hence must turn to unconventional means

[9] K. Newton and D. S. Morris, "British Interest Group Theory Reexamined," *Comparative Politics*, 7 (July 1975), pp. 577–595.

Frustrated in their efforts to block the new Tokyo International Airport through peaceful appeals, radical students and local farmers turned to violent obstruction — also unsuccessfully.

to appeal for response and support.[10] As it is a tactic of the powerless, protest activity is typically used by minority groups and young people, who are not among the elite. Yet, within the group whose goals set the protest in motion, we tend to find patterns of motivation and involvement similar to those that initiate many other forms of participation. The better off, the educated, and members of other social and political organizations are the most likely to participate in protests. Their better information, skills, and general resources facilitate involvement; other organizations provide coordination and communication networks. The less fortunate are more likely to repress their frustration, or find an outlet in violence.

Coercive Tactics

It is useful to distinguish between legitimate, or constitutional or conventional access channels, such as those we have been describing, and illegitimate, coercive ones. There are two kinds of political resources that can be used in trying to get elites to respond. One is established by the legitimate structures of the government, which designate which resources can be used in policy making. In an electoral, legislative, democratic form of government, the appropriate resources may be votes in the national assembly. Various factions may attempt to gain control

[10] James Q. Wilson, "The Strategy of Protest," *Journal of Conflict Resolution*, 5:3 (September 1961), pp. 291–303; see also Michael Lipsky, "Protest as a Political Resource," *American Political Science Review* 62:4 (December 1968), pp. 1144–1158.

of these legislative votes through winning elections, or through bargaining, persuasion, or promises of support.

But regardless of the acceptable tactics, violence and coercion remain a possibility for those individuals and groups who feel that they are otherwise powerless. A leading authority writes that political violence is "episodic in the history of most organized political communities and chronic in many."[11] Surely, political violence has been etched in the minds of most Americans by events during the past decades in the United States.

Bruce L. R. Smith provides an insight into the function of demonstrations, protests, and acts of violence as forms of political participation:

> Violence has always been part of the political process. Politics does not merely encompass the actions of legislative assemblies, political parties, electoral contests, and the other formal trappings of modern government. Protest activities of one form or another, efforts to dramatize grievances in a fashion that will attract attention, and ultimately the destruction or threatened destruction of life and property appear as expressions of political grievances even in stable consensual societies.[12]

Most scholars who have written on the subject see acts of protest and collective violence as closely associated with the character of a society and the circumstances that prevail there. In his studies of civil strife, Ted Robert Gurr has developed the concept of "relative deprivation" to explain the frustration or discontent that motivates people to act aggressively. Gurr defines relative deprivation as "a discrepancy between people's expectations about the goods and conditions of life to which they are entitled, on the one hand, and, on the other, their value capabilities — the degree to which they think they can attain these goods and conditions."[13]

But feelings of relative deprivation do not by themselves lead to outbreaks of violence or disruptive acts of protest. Relative deprivation is only a source of frustration and discontent. Of course, the more such discontent persists, the greater the chance of collective violence. But whether or not this discontent leads to protest and violence is usually dependent upon several other conditions. The incidence and form of violence are ultimately linked to social conditions and attitudes shaped by them. Graham and Gurr have summarized this view:

> People are most strongly disposed to act violently on their discontent if they believe that violence is justifiable and likely of success; they are likely to take violent political action to the extent that they regard their government as illegitimate and responsible for their frustrations. The extent, intensity, and organization of civil strife is finally determined by characteristics of the social system; the degree and consistency of social control, and the extent to which institutions afford peaceful alternatives to violent protest.[14]

This general analysis of violence should not blind us to the differences between types of violent political activity. A *riot*, for example, involves the spontaneous expression of collective anger and dissatisfaction by a group of citizens. Though riots have long been dismissed as aberrant and irrational action by social riff-raff, modern studies have shown that rioters vary greatly in their motivation, behavior, and social background.[15] Most riots in fact seem to follow some fairly clear-cut patterns, such as confining destruction or violence to particular areas or targets. Riots are often directed against property rather than persons, as was seen in most American ghetto riots, where the overwhelming majority of deaths were caused by untrained troops attempting to restore order, not by rioters. Relative deprivation seems to be a major cause of riots, but the release of the frustrations is not as aimless as often supposed. Reinhard Bendix has even spoken of collective bargaining by riot in discussing the period of English

[11] Ted Robert Gurr, *Why Men Rebel* (Princeton, N.J.: Princeton University Press, 1970), p. 317.

[12] Quoted by Jerome H. Skolnick in the preface to his report to the National Commission on the Causes and Prevention of Violence, *The Politics of Protest* (New York: Simon and Schuster, 1969), p. xvi.

[13] Ted Robert Gurr, "A Comparative Study of Civil Strife," in Graham and Gurr (eds.), *Violence in America*, pp. 462–463.

[14] Hugh Davis Graham and Ted Robert Gurr, "Conclusion: The Sources of Violence," in Graham and Gurr (eds.), *Violence in America*, p. 631.

[15] See James F. Short and Marvin E. Wolfgang (eds.), *Collective Violence* (Chicago: Aldine-Atherton, 1972); and see Anthony Oberschall, *Social Conflict and Social Movements* (Englewood Cliffs, N.J.: Prentice-Hall, 1973).

political history when labor unions and other forms of combination were prohibited by law.[16]

And while deprivation may help fuel the discontent, *strikes* and *obstructions* — as well as many violent demonstrations that are called riots but should not be — are typically carried out by well-organized associational or institutional groups. According to Ann Wilner, for example, public protests in Indonesia during the rule of Achmad Sukarno were largely state-managed, "instigated, provoked, and planned by one or several members of a political elite," in order to test their strength, gain support from the undecided, frighten others from joining the opposition, and challenge higher authorities.[17] James Payne suggests that in Peru, violent demonstrations and riots under the civilian regimes of the early 1960s were "fully a part of the Peruvian pattern, not merely distasteful, peripheral incidents." The labor unions, in particular, found such tactics crucial to their survival: "to ask the Peruvian unionists to use collective bargaining and refrain from violence is tantamount to urging dissolution of the labor movement."[18]

The success of such tactics has varied, depending on the legitimacy and sympathies of the government and coercive pressure, pro and con, from other groups. General strikes in Belgium were instrumental in bringing about the expansion of suffrage early in the twentieth century, but were disastrous failures for the sponsoring organizations in Italy in 1922 and Britain in 1927. And, like the massive truckers' strike that helped bring down the government in Chile in 1972–1973, these unsuccessful actions left deep bitterness in the societies. The peasant farmers' tactics of seizing public buildings, blocking roads, and the like won major concessions from the French government in the early 1960s, in part because the government was threatened by terrorism from right-wing army groups and discontent elsewhere, and badly needed peasant support. But by the late 1960s, a stronger regime was able to ignore or suppress peasant obstructions.[19]

Finally, *terrorism* has been used, including deliberate assassination, armed attacks on other groups or government officials, and provocation of bloodshed. Table 4.2 showed the frequency of such attacks in a number of societies. The use of terrorism typically reflects the desire of some groups to change the rules of the political game. The tragedies in Northern Ireland, and the frequent kidnappings and attacks by groups in the Middle East seeking to dramatize the situation of the Palestinians, speak of the continuing use of such tactics.

Violent tactics have been chosen by groups who feel that they have least to lose from chaotic upheaval and whose expectations from the political system cannot be achieved through legitimate means. Payne notes that among the factors shaping the development of structured violence in Peru were the nonrepresentative conditions of the electoral system, the exclusion of the opposition from formal decision making, the centralization of decision making in the executive, the uncertainty in the bargaining process, and the absence of adequate channels of communication among workers, management, and government.[20] Groups that have access to effective nonviolent means of communication are less likely to resort to violent behavior.

EFFECTIVENESS OF INTEREST GROUPS

What factors make interest groups effective? A group's ability to mobilize the support, energy, and resources of its members is surely an important factor. So is the extent of its resources — financial strength, membership size, political skills, organizational cohesiveness, and prestige among the general public or governmental decision makers. In addition to its own attributes, however, an interest group's ef-

[16] Reinhard Bendix, *Nation-Building and Citizenship* (New York: Wiley, 1964), p. 72.

[17] Ann Ruth Willner, "Public Protest in Indonesia," in Ivo K. Feierabend, Rosalind Feierabend, and Ted Robert Gurr (eds.), *Anger, Violence, and Politics* (Englewood Cliffs, N.J.: Prentice-Hall, 1972), pp. 355–357.

[18] James Payne, "Peru: The Politics of Structured Violence," in Feierabend, Feierabend, and Gurr (eds.), *Anger, Violence, and Politics*, p. 360.

[19] See Suzanne Berger, *Peasants Against Politics* (Cambridge, Mass.: Harvard University Press, 1972).

[20] James L. Payne, *Labor and Politics in Peru* (New Haven, Conn.: Yale University Press, 1965), ch. 13 and 14.

fectiveness is affected by the public issues and policies relevant at any given time.[21] For example, policy may at one time emphasize aerospace developments, granting greater influence to interest groups whose members have special knowledge and interest in aerospace technology; but if policy shifts to emphasize social service, interest groups specializing in urban planning, housing, transportation, medicine, and social welfare will gain influence.

An interest group's effectiveness is also determined partially by governmental structure. In the American system, for example, with effective federalism and separation of powers, groups frequently need to influence not one but many groups of decision makers, dispersed geographically and institutionally throughout the political system. In the British system, however, groups need only influence the important policy-making group, Cabinet members and senior civil servants. Yet the British system may provide difficulties for many interest groups because decision makers have important independent sources of power — such as strong party discipline or career tenure — whereas the more numerous American decision makers are less easily able, in their separate spheres, to resist pressure.

The autonomy or independence of interest groups also contributes to their effectiveness. In France and Italy, many associational interest groups, such as trade unions and peasant organizations, have been controlled by the Communist party or the Roman Catholic Church. Usually, these groups tend to mobilize support for the political parties or social institutions that dominate them. This lack of autonomy can have serious consequences for the political process. The denial of independent expression to interest groups may lead to outbreaks of violence. Furthermore, the subordination of interest groups by political parties may limit the adaptability of the political process, create monopolies in the political market, and even stalemate the political system. In Italy, trade unionism has long been divided among unions dominated by the Christian Democrat, Socialist, and Communist parties. More recently, however, these trade unions seem to have been reducing their dependence on the parties and engaging in closer cooperation on primarily economic matters.

The best example of interest groups' lack of independence occurs in communist systems, where the dominating party organizations penetrate all levels of the society and exercise close control over such interest groups as are permitted to exist. In the Soviet Union, the party elite tries to penetrate the entire society. Interest articulation is indirect or in the form of very low-level suggestions within specific bounds. Important, overt interest articulation is limited to members of the leadership, who can use their positions in political institutions as a base from which to express their demands.

Chosen tactics are also relevant to success. Even when used deliberately violence threatens to pass beyond the control of its promoters. It has serious liabilities as a form of access, not the least of which is the danger to life and property for those who use it. Furthermore, the complex forces that lead to violent outbursts are not easily interpreted by decision makers, and adequate response to such demands becomes difficult. For example, although the demands articulated by black civil rights groups are often practical and specific, it may be difficult — even for sympathetic leaders — to interpret or respond constructively to events like the 1965 Watts riots.

POLICY PERSPECTIVES ON INTEREST ARTICULATION

As we pointed out in Chapter 1, we need to look at the structures performing political functions from both a process and a policy perspective. If we are to understand the formation of policies, we need to know not merely which groups articulate interests, but what policy preferences they express. Many associational interest groups, for example, specialize in certain policy areas. The list of associational groups in Table 5.1 has already suggested the tendency of such groups to organize themselves around specific issues. The concerns of other interest groups, such as anomic or institutional ones, may be less easily

[21] Harry Eckstein, "The Determinants of Pressure-Group Politics," in Mattei Dogan and Richard Rose (eds.), *European Politics* (Boston: Little, Brown, 1971), p. 328.

The British Society of Civil Servants, a well-organized and usually effective associational interest group, assembles for an orderly meeting in a London hall to plan a 24-hour work stoppage.

discerned, but are equally important for the policy process.

Table 5.2 provides an overview of interest articulation. The far left column indicates the types of groups that commonly articulate interests in modern societies. The next columns provide examples of interest articulation by each type in respective policy areas: extractive, distributive, and regulative policies in the domestic arena, and a few examples of international policies. A third dimension is provided by the symbols, which indicate when coercive, illegitimate channels were used, rather than constitutional ones. Careful examination of each case will provide a more precise classification of the access channels, for instance, elite representation by American black congressmen, the use of party channels by the Italian Catholic Church, and the use of terror by the French OAS. In this table we have used examples from many nations in order to suggest the varieties of possibilities, and to fill in all the categories with reasonably obvious cases. If we were studying interest articulation patterns in a single nation, of course, we should attempt to build up the table showing the structures, policies, and channels involved during a particular period.

Although we have focused on relatively specific policy articulations, expressions of discontent can be much more vague and diffuse. Another distinction to make is the level at which the demand is made. Rather than distinguishing between requests for different policies, for example, we might distinguish between demands for minor policy changes, for changes in the processes of decision making and implementation, and for changes in the basic system itself, particularly in elite recruitment. Students of the Soviet system, for example, have used terms such as

Table 5.2

Process and Policy Perspectives on Interest Articulation

	Examples of interest articulation in various policy areas			
Types of interest groups	*Domestic extractive policy*	*Domestic distributive policy*	*Domestic regulative policy*	*International policy*
Individual	Peasant family seeks patron's aid with tax law.	Austrian worker asks party official for housing aid.	U.S. family business seeks relief from pollution standards.	British farmer writes MP against Common Market.
Anomic groups	Nigerian women riot over 1950s rumor on taxes.*	Polish workers' strikes over wage policies.*	Venezuelan students and citizens strike against dictatorship, 1958.*	U.S. students demonstrate over Cambodia policy.†
Nonassociational groups	Mexican business leaders discuss taxes with president.	U.S. Black Caucus in Congress call for minority jobs.	Soviet writers demand more freedom of speech, 1960s.	Saudi Arabian royal family factions favor oil embargo.
Institutional groups	Catholic Church urges Italian Christian Democrat party oppose Vatican tax.	U.S. Corps of Army Engineers proposes new river locks.	Soviet jurists ask more due process in parasite laws, 1960s.	U.S.S.R. Politburo faction opposes placing Soviet missiles in Cuba, 1962.
Associational groups	AFL-CIO president calls for U.S. tax cut, 1974.	British Medical Association negotiates salaries under Health Service.	U.S. retail druggists lobby to pass fair trade laws.	French OAS launches terror bombing over Algeria policy, 1960s.*

* Use of coercive, unconstitutional access channels and tactics.

† Use of coercion by some elements or subgroups.

subversive or integral opposition to refer to actions calling for basic change in the communist system,[22] as opposed to factional or sectoral interests articulated by institutional groups on policy questions.

INTEREST GROUPS IN POLITICAL SYSTEMS

Modern Industrialized Systems

Political leaders in all modern societies need specialized organizations to respond to demands or to manipulate and control them. However, the variety of arrangements which appear is impressive. In particular there are sharp contrasts between the autonomous groups, which press demands in the democratic systems, on one hand, and the carefully regulated, primarily institutional groups, which predominate in authoritarian societies. Following are brief descriptions of how political structure and political culture affect interest group organization and function in Great Britain, France, and the U.S.S.R.; this subject is discussed in more detail in Chapters 9, 10, and 12.

In Britain, political parties and interest groups are relatively separate. Most British trade unions are affiliated with the Labour party, but the parliamentary party — especially those members of Parliament who are also government ministers — often acts independently of trade-union pressure. However, in 1969 the Labour government abandoned — in the face of trade-union pressure — legislation that would have regulated unions, suggesting that a Labour government is more vulnerable to union pressure than a Conservative one. Similarly, British trade associations and chambers of commerce align with the Conservative party, even if Conservative cabinets and the parliamentary party nevertheless remain relatively independent of those influential groups. At the same time, of course, associational interest groups engage in extensive formal and informal bargaining, negotiation, and sometimes collaboration or collusion with governmental administrative agencies.

[22] See Barghoorn and Skilling in Dahl, *Regimes and Oppositions*.

Because the British government spends vast sums for public services, institutional groups like the armed forces, the nationalized industries, and the major government departments play an active part in shaping legislation. Nonassociational patterns of interest articulation have been prominent in this century, particularly during Conservative administrations in the 1950s; and elite political activity still quite frequently assumes such forms, though decreasingly so. Violent forms of activity have been extremely infrequent in British politics generally, although conspicuous in Northern Ireland.

In France during the Fourth Republic (1947–1959), interest groups and political parties were not clearly separated and tended to divide into three main ideological families. The communist family included the Communist party, the Communist-dominated general trade union (CGT), and, particularly in the Paris region, a variety of Communist-operated, ostensibly nonpolitical agencies providing occupational and welfare services and recreational facilities. The socialist system consisted of the Socialist party (SFIO) and the trade union organization Force Ouvrière. The Catholic system included the church hierarchy and clergy; Catholic Action, a church organization with a network of specialized groupings based on age, sex, and occupation; and a Catholic trade union (CFTC) and political party (MRP). With such ideological families, interest groups found it difficult to transmit specific proposals not shaped along ideological lines. And a relatively ineffective Cabinet and legislature meant that powerful interest groups (such as big business and agriculture) and small merchant groups often had greater influence in both the National Assembly and the bureaucracy than did political parties. Nonassociational interest articulation continued to come from important families (particularly in rural areas), from groups in the bureaucracy, and from business interests. Less powerful interests or groups less well represented in the population were neglected in the process. Anomic and violent activity occurred much more frequently than in Britain — in part a reflection of cultural tradition, but also an indication that the system had failed to allow important regional and agrarian interests adequate representation.

The political structure of the Fifth Republic (created in 1959) has substantially changed the role of interest groups in France and limited their access to decision making. The new constitution provided for presidential authority, which made it possible for the government to survive despite interest group pressure. The rapid economic growth of the 1960s produced new interest groups and encouraged the older ones to engage in economic bargaining rather than ideological confrontation. The events of May 1968, when students opposed the government in the classic French style — confrontations, marches, and barricades in the streets — suggest that problems of participation have not been solved. Large segments of the working class quickly followed the students, in some cases through strikes organized by official union leadership, but more often through spontaneous wildcat strikes that union leaders could only subsequently endorse. When open and regular channels of interest representation are inadequate, such anomic episodes are predictable.

The Soviet Union has often been described as a political system in which interest-group conflict is completely absent; the only interest group is the political party, apparently itself not differentiated into interest groups. Articulation and aggregation of interests, however, do take place in authoritarian systems, largely under the surface, through the interplay of interest groups and factions. Among the groups struggling over power in the Soviet Union are cliques competing for control of the higher levels of the party apparatus; conflicting bureaucratic groups; regional groups conflicting with each other and with the central government and the party bureaucracy; professional groups of artists, scientists, and educators; peasants; non-Russian ethnic groups; and religious groups. Demands are made in some form by each of these groups, but combining these demands into alternative policy proposals is carried on largely through a covert political process.

In the Soviet Union, communication of needs by such groups as consumers, wage earners, and collective farmers has been primarily indirect and diffuse, although artists and scientists have in recent years openly demanded freedom of expression. But it is primarily at the top levels of party and government bureaucracy that policy alternatives are explored; and it is at this level that interest-group activity is most intense. Such activity, of necessity, largely takes the form of negotiation and coalition formation between institutional interest groups in the bureaucracy, the party, and the military.

Developing Systems

If there is one element of political development about which everyone seems to agree, it is that socioeconomic change seems to reshape political structure and culture. One of the consequences of modernization — particularly important for interest articulation — is a widespread belief that the conditions of life can be altered through human action. The changes also foster urbanization, education, a radical growth in public communication, and in most cases an improvement in the physical conditions of life.

Socioeconomic modernization increases the capability of the political system to tap the resources of the society, both by increasing such resources and by creating a greater potential for effective political administration. More important, these changes greatly increase both the need for coordinated social action to solve new problems and the likelihood of increased political participation and political demands from members of the society.

Socioeconomic change can directly affect several aspects of political culture: the level of political information, degree of political participation, feelings of political competence, and perception of the impact or potential impact of government on the individual. These components of political culture are affected not through some mysterious transference, but by the fact that socioeconomic development greatly increases the flow of information and contact among parts of the society and the level of education, wealth, and status of members of the society. And the evidence suggests that increases in educational level and socioeconomic status are closely related to increases of political awareness, participation, and feeling of political competence.

While participant attitudes emerge in the political culture of societies undergoing modernization, the specialization of labor leads to the formation of a large number of special interests, which can be the basis for associational interest groups. The processes by which associational groups emerge and sustain themselves are complex; but the growth of the mass media, of a more extended bureaucracy, and of other political structures provides additional channels through which emergent groups can make their interests known.

Some theorists argue that as a society experiences socioeconomic change, more numerous and varied means of political interest articulation will emerge. Others, however, believe that while rates of social mobilization are high and desires for political participation are expanding, the accompanying rates of political organization and institutionalization are frequently low, with resulting political instability and disorder. That is, many interests are being expressed, but relatively few are satisfactorily accommodated. Kinship, racial, and religious groups are supplemented by occupational and class groups. As such social forces become more varied and, usually, express their demands more intensely, the political system increases in complexity to undertake more tasks efficiently and authoritatively. But this political development has often failed to occur in modernizing societies during the twentieth century.

The problem may be larger than simply a failure to develop within the political sphere. If socioeconomic change undermines the more traditional bases of association, people need to develop new forms of association in order to present their demands effectively. Yet this is by no means automatic. Societies vary widely in the extent to which people engage in associational activity.[23] Edward Banfield pointed to the extreme case of an Italian village within which almost no associational activity occurred, with people unwilling to trust anyone outside their immediate family.[24] In the ideal case, modernization would supplement family and other primary groups with effectively organized interest groups. But in some societies, modernization may weaken existing structures while failing to foster the development of effective associational groups or political parties. The outcome might well be heightened political demands by individuals and groups with no structures able to respond to those demands. In such circumstances, anomic, nonassociational, and institutional groups may predominate, and instability, political coups, and authoritarian regimes may be a common consequence.

[23] Gabriel A. Almond and Sidney Verba, *Civic Culture*, ch. 11.

[24] Edward C. Banfield, *The Moral Basis of a Backward Society* (New York: Free Press, 1958).

KEY TERMS

patronage or "patron-client" networks
anomic interest groups
nonassociational groups
institutional groups
associational groups
relative deprivation
riots
strike
political terror tactics
channel of political access

CHAPTER SIX

Interest Aggregation and Political Parties

Because we often think of parties and interest aggregation together, we discuss both this important structure and this important function in this chapter. Modern political parties first took shape as excluded groups strove to compete for power and dominant groups sought public support to sustain themselves. Interest aggregation is the activity in which demands of individuals and groups are combined into alternative policies. Political parties are particularly adept at interest aggregation, as they nominate candidates who stand for a set of policies, then try to build support for these candidates. In democratic systems a number of parties compete to mobilize the backing of interest groups and voters. In authoritarian systems, a single party tries to mobilize citizens' support for its policies and candidates. In both systems, interest aggregation may well take place within the parties, as party conventions or party leaders hear the demands of different groups — unions, consumers, party factions, business organizations — and create policy alternatives. In authoritarian systems, however, the process is more covert and controlled.

Taking the structural-functional approach draws our attention to the fact that different structures may perform the same function, and the same structures may perform different functions. Here, we shall first look at political parties, their variety of types and some of the functions they perform in different systems. Then we shall consider the variety of structures performing interest aggregation, and the special role of parties.

THE SOCIAL BASES AND GOALS OF POLITICAL PARTIES

Organized political parties came into existence in the late eighteenth and early nineteenth century in Western Europe, as the result of efforts by groups outside positions of political power to compete for public office and control over governmental policy. When these middle-class and working-class movements began to press the upper classes for a share of decision-making power, the governing groups were forced to appeal for public support in order to maintain their dominance. Thus, political parties linked people and government. Today, over three-fourths of independent nations have one or more political parties, and in most of these nations the parties play a very important part in linking citizens and the political system. Parties perform key functions in both the most democratic and the most authoritarian regimes.

Contemporary nations without political parties are found chiefly in the Middle East, South and Southeast Asia, and sub-Saharan Africa. These are mainly of two sorts. First, there are traditional dynastic regimes like the tiny sheikdoms of the Persian Gulf or traditional kingdoms like Saudi Arabia and Nepal. Second, there are military regimes, like those in Nigeria and Chile, in which political parties have been suppressed. But the political party is such a useful way to link people and their leaders, and is capable of performing such a variety of functions, that most nations today encourage the development of some sort of parties. With the penetration of modern ideas and values, and the increased citizen involvement in politics that typically accompanies these, the appearance of parties is increasingly likely in those nations that still do not have them.

Political parties can be described by their size, organization, goals, and bases of support. Table 6.1 lists most of the parties to be found in the countries we have been discussing. The following brief descriptions of some of them will help illustrate the great variety of party characteristics.

The British Conservative party has approximately 3 million members, organized in over six hundred constituency associations (local units), each responsible for trying to elect one Conservative member to the House of Commons. As of this writing, the Conservative was the largest party in the House of Commons, and the party leader, Mrs. Margaret Thatcher, had just been chosen prime minister with a solid Conservative majority, following the 1979 elections. The Conservative party is strongest among the middle and upper classes. However, it receives support from all kinds of people — upper, middle, and working classes; English, Scots, and Welsh; high churchmen, dissenters, and Catholics.

The Social Democratic party of West Germany is, as of this writing, the largest party in the Bundestag, the legislature, and the most important partner in the governing coalition. It is a moderate socialist party supported by the German trade unions. Its voters and members are substantially from the working class, but also include professionals, intellectuals, and even businessmen.

The French Communist party is the third largest party in the National Assembly. In coalition with the other parties of the left, it supported the Socialist leader, Mitterand, in the presidential election of 1974, when he came within a percentage point of victory. In the legislative elections of 1978 it appeared likely that the Socialist-Communist coalition would win a majority, but in the last months before the election the Communists broke the alliance and the Guallist-Republican coalition and its allies won 59 percent of the seats. The party seeks fundamental social and economic change in French society, and basic political changes as well. The Communist party in France draws most of its support from nonchurch-going workers and intellectuals, and is highly organized, offering many supplemental organizations to involve and shape its members' lives.

The Janata coalition of India is a group of parties and movements that allied to defeat Indira Ghandi and her Congress party supporters and reinstitute constitutional government in India. It includes remnants of the Congress party and a number of older conservative movements. It is conservative in social and economic policy.

The Institutional Revolutionary party is the dominant in Mexico, receiving well over 80 percent of the vote. However, other parties are permitted to operate and run candidates for the Mexican legislature. The party is a federation of working-class, agrarian, professional, and middle-class organizations.

The Arab Socialist Union was the only legal party in Egypt. Its goal is the mobilization of the Egyptian population around the diffuse socialism and pan-Arabism of the Egyptian leadership. Its strength is concentrated in urban areas.

The Tanzanian African National Union is the only political party allowed in Tanzania. However, the party does encourage some controlled competition within its own ranks. The party links the top leadership and local organizers, and is committed to mobilizing the people of Tanzania into support for the modernizing policies of the national leader and president, Julius Nyerere.

The Communist party is the only party in the U.S.S.R. Its top leadership controls both the party and the government. The party is represented and functions as the leading group in all the organizations of Soviet society — government agencies, factories, collective farms, professional societies, the military services, schools, and universities. Its youth

Table 6.1

Political Parties in Selected Nations

Country and parties	*Election*	*Percentage of seats in national assembly of four largest parties*			
United States	1976				
Democratic		67			
Republican			33	—	—
France	1978				
Gaullist		32			
Socialist			21		
Communist				18	
Republican					15
West Germany	1976				
Social Democratic		43			
Christian Democratic			38		
Christian Social				11	
Free Democratic					8
Great Britain	1979				
Conservative		53			
Labour			42		
Liberal				2	
Other					3
U.S.S.R.	1979				
Communist		100	—	—	—
Japan	1976				
Liberal Democratic		49			
Socialist			24		
Komeito				11	
Democratic Socialist					6
Mexico	1976				
Institutional Revolutionary		83			
National Action			9		
Popular Socialist				5	
Authentic Revolutionary					3
Egypt	1971				
Arab Socialist Union		100	—	—	—
China	1978				
Communist		100	—	—	—
India	1977				
Janata and allies		55			
Congress and allies			30		
Communist party of India				4	
Other					1
Tanzania	1975				
Tanzanian African National Union		100	—	—	—

Recently, the Italian Communist party, the major opposition party, has made special efforts to mobilize women to its cause, as at this 1976 election rally.

and children's organizations — the Young Pioneers and the Komsomol — include almost all young people in the Soviet Union.

These brief sketches of different political parties in existence today, which may be explored further in the chapters on individual countries, suggest what all parties have in common and some of the ways they differ. All the parties in Table 6.1 take part in elections and have seats in the legislature. But they differ in social composition and in other respects. Social class and religious practices, for example, are bases of party formation in the Social Democratic party of Germany and the Communist party of France. Ethnic differences are the basis of the Scottish Nationalist party and Plaid Cymru (Welsh nationalist party) of Britain. Religion is a basis of party formation in the Democratic Christian party of Italy.

The existence of religious, tribal, ethnic, and class differences in a society does not automatically mean that political parties form around them. What creates political parties is some set of historical experiences that heightens the political consciousness of one or more groups. The dominance of one tribe over another, historical conflicts between religious groups, a dominant culture seeking to impose its language and history on another culture, the dominance of an aristocracy or an industrialist class over farmers or workers — all these situations may lead to the formation of political parties.

Political parties also differ according to their goals, and in this regard the political parties listed in Table 6.1 break into three divisions. First is the *representative party*, accepting a competitive party system and seeking to win a maximum number of seats in the legislature. The Conservative party of Britain, the Liberal party of Japan, the Janata party of India, the Communist party of France, the Social Democratic party of West Germany, and the two American parties, fall into this class (as do other parties in those nations). They often form governments or constitute the principal opposition party.

Another group — *nation-building parties* — includes the Tanzanian African National Union, whose major goals include the creation of a common sense of national identity and the suppression of narrow tribal interests. The Arab Socialist Union of Egypt is a similar nation-building party.

A third group, the *mobilization* or *integration parties*, include the Institutional Revolutionary party in Mexico, the Communist party of China, and the Communist party of the Soviet Union. These parties tend to be monopolistic, suppressing competition and mobilizing the population around the goals of the regime's leaders, rather than fostering participation and representation for the various groups in the society. But these mobilization parties differ. The Mexican party tolerates a limited amount of political competition from outside political movements and also permits bargaining among major interest groups within the structure and processes of the party itself. The Communist parties of the Soviet Union and China preempt the political arena. Other political movements are prohibited, and competing factions or interests within the party are suppressed or are granted only limited expression. The party is controlled by an elite that also controls the entire government.

THE FUNCTIONS OF POLITICAL PARTIES

The activities carried on by political parties depend on the groups that form them and the goals they seek. A revolutionary party may strive to transform the governmental organization, culture, society, and economy of a country; if successful, it may control every significant organized activity in the society. A conservative party, on the other hand, may be little more than an aristocratic clique trying to keep things as they are. The Communist party of the Soviet Union (CPSU), the Conservative party of Britain, and the Tanzanian African National Union (TANU) are illustrations of the degree to which parties may differ in the extent, scope, and variety of their activities. (The three parties are discussed in greater detail in Chapters 12, 9, 15, respectively.)

Political Socialization

Every society has ways of socializing its population into politics, but the socialization role played by political parties differs greatly. In the Soviet Union, the CPSU and its related youth movements, the Young Pioneers and the Komsomol, are the most important socializing agencies. Families and occupational, ethnic, and religious groups somehow escape the elaborate socializing network of the party, which helps to explain why dissent persists among artists, writers, scientists, peasants, Jews, and other minorities in the Soviet Union.

The Conservative party of Britain also has a political socialization function, but on a limited scale and in competition with the Labour and Liberal parties. In Britain, moreover, political parties are just one among many competing institutions and agencies that openly and legitimately carry on these processes. The British family is far more important and autonomous in its socializing activities than the Soviet family is. Schools, neighborhood and peer groups, churches, professional and work groups, trade unions and businessmen's associations, and the mass media also share in political socialization. The socializing activities of the Conservative party take place in the constituency associations and local clubs and societies affiliated with them. The Conservative constituency associations seek to recruit and indoctrinate new members. They canvass voters and distribute literature, and their candidates make speeches. At the leadership or elite level, clubs, party meetings, and parliamentary committees are constantly training and indoctrinating party members.

TANU is the only political party in Tanzania. The country has been independent only since 1961, and TANU has been in existence in its present form since 1966. As in other newly independent nations, party activities are to a considerable extent still on the drawing boards, so we must speak of intentions and goals rather than of well-established patterns of performance. TANU hopes to transform a society of more than a hundred tribal groups into a single nation with a sense of national identity, whose people accept and participate in the activities of government and politics.

The organization chart for TANU looks a bit like the organization chart for the CPSU, but these structural similarities are misleading. The political system of Tanzania has not yet transformed and modernized Tanzanian society. The Tanzanian population is largely rural, carrying on subsistence rather than commercial agriculture. It is largely preliterate, or only partially literate, and is still quite local in its political structure and culture. Tanzania's leaders are still shaping their own ideology. They favor a mild form of cooperative socialism, and major efforts have been made to transform Tanzania into a society of communal, cooperative villages. The party wants to have, in each village, a TANU cell for every ten families, to carry on propaganda and development activities. While the effectiveness of this cooperative socialist program is still to be demonstrated, there can be little doubt that much progress has been made by TANU in disseminating a sense of Tanzanian identity, loyalty, and commitment.

Recruitment: Citizen Participation

In modern times political parties have been founded as larger numbers of people have been granted voting rights and as groups have demanded that they be given the right to vote and to compete for public office. The Communist party of the Soviet Union controls all political participation within the framework of the party-dominated elections. Any other form of mass political participation is both prohibited by the constitution and repressed by the police and the organization of the party. The Conservative party of Britain competes with other parties in mobilizing voters. In Tanzania, TANU plays an important role in organizing mass political participation. It competes, however, not with other political parties, but with traditional tribal and village communities that resist TANU's efforts to mobilize their members.

Recruitment of Elites

Parties vary in their patterns of recruitment of citizens into specialized roles. The CPSU either directly selects and appoints political and government officials or closely supervises their appointment and tenure. Even scientists and writers who resist the party's guidelines may find themselves sidetracked, or worse. A major issue of Soviet politics is the requirement of party loyalty as a qualification for holding any position in Soviet society. The demands of a modern economy and social organization make it impossible to press these requirements at the expense of competence. But in the central political decision-making roles, and even in such fields as the arts, loyalty to the party is often pressed to the point that competence and performance are seriously affected.

The recruitment function of the British Conservative party is far more restricted. For one thing, it must compete with other parties in recruiting. Also, outside government, it has a very limited patronage: loyal party workers may, for example, hope for jobs or directorships in business and industry run by loyal Conservatives.

TANU dominates political recruitment in Tanzania. A principal difference in this regard between TANU and the CPSU is that politics and government are less important in the economic and social life of Tanzania than they are in the U.S.S.R. A second difference is that the bureaucracy is much more autonomous and powerful in Tanzania. A third is that open electoral competition is permitted between two TANU nominees in each district.

Communication

Another function of political parties is the communication of political information, issues, and ideas. In the Soviet Union, press, radio, television, and even direct face-to-face communication are generally dominated by the CPSU. Although this aspect of Soviet politics has been substantially liberalized since the death of Stalin, it is still risky for Russians to communicate with one another about political questions, and most questions of any importance tend to be defined as political. Political discussion is supposed to be carried on within the party — in the primary cells, in party committees and congresses, and in party-controlled agencies like the trade unions and professional associations. Press, radio, and television are controlled by the party.

Political communication in Britain differs from the Soviet pattern in two important respects. First, the press, radio, and television tend to be politically neutral. Where political preferences exist, alternative points of view are expressed in competing newspapers and radio and television programs. Thus, although some newspapers in Britain support the Conservative party, others support the Labour party. Second, political discussion in the government-controlled radio and television system and in private television must be divided so that each party receives a share of the time.

TANU provides the major organized, modern system of communication in Tanzania. In the largely preliterate and rural society spread over many sparsely populated areas, modern communications through organizational networks or mass media must compete with the hundreds of local primary communications systems. The little evidence we have about TANU's performance in communication suggests that although great progress has been made in disseminating information about the political party and its goals, local tribal and village communications systems are still quite important.

Interest Articulation

The three parties we are comparing differ significantly in the extent to which they make and transmit demands to government. In the Soviet Union, all associations and interest groups are assumed to operate within the CPSU. Nevertheless, in recent years the formulation of demands in the U.S.S.R. has been a much more complicated process than the one described as legitimate in authoritative Soviet sources. Local interests are permitted a certain amount of autonomy at the regional level. Even in organizations of scientists and artists, the party is flexible, sometimes permitting scientific and artistic autonomy and at other times insisting on party orthodoxy. Within the central agencies of the Soviet establishment — at the upper levels of the bureaucracy and among the military services — there is some tolerance of interest group bargaining, in which the spokesmen for heavy, light, and distributive industries and for the navy, air force, and army are permitted to press their points of view. A kind of covert bargaining system exists within the framework of the CPSU and the government, and even to some extent outside the communist system.

The Conservative party in Britain is in competition with the Labour and Liberal parties for the loyalty and support of society's various interest groups. To win this support, the Conservative party invites economic, regional, and local interest groups to make their claims and to influence party policy through the activities of the constituency associations and the annual party conferences and in the party committees in Parliament. The major difference between the British and Soviet patterns lies in the British system of autonomous associational groups, and in the necessity that parties compete for their support. The Conservative party can bargain with interest groups, but it cannot control them.

Most of the Tanzanian population has not yet learned that it can make demands on the government. Interest group activity and interest articulation are therefore on a relatively small scale, much of it carried on at the local traditional level and satisfied within those limits. TANU has difficulties with political demands. It wants to stimulate and mobilize local populations into new expectations, but at the same time it wants to prevent this mobilization from overwhelming the political process or diverting the party from the plans of the leadership. Interest articulation is thus coordinated within the framework of the party; organized interest groups like trade unions and chambers of commerce are affiliated with it.

Interest Aggregation

Interest aggregation describes how demands initiated by different groups are combined into alternative policies. In democratic societies, parties formulate political programs and make proposals to legislative bodies, and candidates for public office bargain with interest groups, offering support for their positions in exchange for their support and votes. The aggregative function of the British Conservative party is performed on a market basis. The party leadership offers legislation when in control of the government and proposes alternatives when in opposition. In both cases, it engages in a bargaining process with interest groups, offering inducements to business and labor, specific industries, various regions, and so forth. But it does this in competition with the Labour party and, to a lesser extent, with the Liberal and Scottish Nationalist parties. Thus the policy alternatives are publicly formulated and become issues debated in Parliament and the mass media, and informally in pubs or living rooms.

Interest aggregation is also performed in political systems where competition between political parties is not open. In the Soviet Union, aggregation takes place within the higher branches of the CPSU as well as within the bureaucracy and the various military services. The demands and needs of the consumer, the party elite's concern with investment for economic growth, and the demands of the military services for weapons development are combined and reconciled by the government bureaucracy, the party bureaucracy, and ultimately the top policy-making organ of the CPSU, the Politburo. Competition over policy alternatives, however, occurs under the surface.

In Tanzania, TANU tolerates a certain amount of competitive policy aggregation within the framework of its own organization, but it will not permit other groups to run candidates. It does, however, require that two candidates be nominated for each seat in the Parliament, and to some extent it permits these candidates to take different positions on public issues. Hence something like competitive aggregation is carried on in Tanzania, but within the constraints of the party organization.

Policy Making

The enactment of government policy in the Soviet Union is dominated by the highest echelons of the CPSU, particularly the Politburo. The ministries and bureaucracies in Russia are implementing agencies, or at best initiators of policy. The formal equivalents to parliaments in democratic systems — the soviets — simply function as legitimators after the decisions have already been reached.

In Britain, the Conservative party is involved in policy making as the government or as the opposition. Thus it competes, as an opposition party or with an opposition party. In addition the higher reaches of the British civil service are important in policy making. Higher civil servants' background of experience and access to information gives them a large share in the formation of policy. The Conservative party leadership competes over policy not only with the Labour party leadership but also with the bureaucracy.

Julius Nyerere is both the president of TANU and the dominant figure in the government of Tanzania. Policies are decided by Nyerere and a small group of his associates, their principal power base being the civil service. They use the party organization more as a mobilizing and policy-implementing organ than as a policy-making one.

Policy Implementation

The CPSU oversees the implementation of public policy in the U.S.S.R. through the departments of the Secretariat and through regional and local party bureaus and their secretariats. The party carries out this function through the work of several hundred thousand paid party officials in Moscow and throughout Russia in the republic, regional, and district secretariats. In addition, a party-state control committee functions as a kind of inspector, to make sure that the lower echelons of both party and government carry out the policies adopted at the center.

The Soviet system contrasts sharply with that in Britain. The British parties are less involved in policy implementation; oversight of the civil service is carried out by the Cabinet and higher Ministry officials. The efforts of the opposition parties to expose administrative blunders and government policy failures does serve to check bureaucratic waywardness. And the party in power is quick to respond to complaints, from its own members, as well as from opposition and the press, about implementation failures.

In Tanzania, as we suggested earlier, TANU's regional and local organizations try to realize goals of modernization and development. But this effort to employ the party organization as an implementing structure is just beginning.

Adjudication

In recent decades the Soviet Union has moved toward a more impartial administration of justice. But the CPSU still decides what is to be considered a political offense, and reserves the right to act arbitrarily whenever it considers the regime to be in danger. Judicial procedure in the Soviet Union still falls far short of providing an adversary process in the defense of persons accused of crime.

In Britain, a long and well-established tradition of judicial impartiality, providing procedural protection for accused persons, shields adjudication from intervention by political parties.

Politics in traditional Tanzanian society has long been organized principally around the settlement of disputes, not the development of programs and policies and the enactment of statutes. The local organizations of TANU, particularly the primary cells of the party organization, have become heavily involved in settling disputes.

STRUCTURES PERFORMING INTEREST AGGREGATION

Just as parties perform many functions other than interest aggregation, interest aggregation may be performed by structures other than parties. Even a single individual can evaluate a variety of claims and considerations in adopting his policy position. If he controls substantial political resources, as an influential party leader or a military dictator, his personal role in interest aggregation may be considerable. But large national political systems usually develop more specialized organizations for the specific purpose of aggregating interests and mobilizing resources behind policies. Political parties are just such organizations. Here we shall compare the role of parties with that of other structures.

Individual Elites and Clients

We saw in the last chapter that individual leaders may establish networks of individual supporters on the basis of exchanges of favors and support. Such networks may allow the leader to accumulate substantial political resources, and hence play a significant role in shaping policy alternatives. He can deliver votes or other manifestations of support from his following because he provides them with personal rewards or favors. The collective interests of the following are not being expressed, nor do they constitute an interest group, as they may not perceive common interests. Rather, their political resources are being aggregated by the leader.

Although such personal networks are to be found in all societies, they have been especially important in Japan, in Southeast Asia, and Latin America. In recent years, political scientists, often drawing upon the work of anthropologists, have analyzed many aspects of these patron-client relationships.[1] Typically, these networks involve a diffuse pattern of exchange between patron and client. The patron provides land, equipment, marketing services, loans for poor harvest years, protection from bandits (and tax collectors), and negotiations with state officials to secure public works, loans, favors, and the like. The client provides labor on the land, personal services, and whatever political resources he possesses, including voting as the patron directs. But patron-clientism may also pervade modern society, as Japan illustrates.

Personal networks have often been important for the careers of individual politicians, and can help to integrate citizens into the society by providing them with needed benefits — especially if they exist on the margin of subsistence, as in many peasant societies. However, domination of interest aggregation by patron-client ties typically means a static pattern of overall policy formation. In such a political system, the ability to mobilize political resources behind unified policies of social change, or to respond to crises, will be difficult, as doing so depends on ever-shifting agreements between many factional leaders. In modern societies, as citizens become aware of larger collective interests, and have the resources and skills to work for them, personal networks are regulated, replaced, and incorporated within broader organizations. As we see in Table 6.2, extensive performance

[1] See, for example, Nobutaka Ike, *Japanese Politics: Patron Client Democracy in Japan* (New York: Knopf, 1972) ch. 1; John Duncan Powell, "Peasant Society and Clientelist Politics," *American Political Science Review*, 64:2 (June 1970), pp. 411–425; Rene Lemarchand and Keith Legg, "Political Clientelism and Development," *Comparative Politics*, 4:2 (January 1972), pp. 148–178; James C. Scott, "Patron-Client Politics and Political Change in Southeast Asia," *American Political Science Review*, 66:1 (March 1972); James C. Scott, "The Erosion of Patron-Client Bonds and Social Change in Rural Southeast Asia," *Journal of Asian Studies*, 32:1 (November 1972); and Carl H. Lande, "Networks and Groups in Southeast Asia," *American Political Science Review*, 67:1 (March 1973), pp. 103–127.

Table 6.2
Structures Performing Interest Aggregation in Selected Contemporary Nations[a]

	Extensiveness of interest aggregation by actor				
Country	*Patron-client networks*	*Associational groups*	*Competitive political parties*	*Non-competitive parties*	*Military forces*
United States	Low	Moderate	High	Low	Low
West Germany	Low	High	High	Low	Low
France	Low	Moderate	High	Low	Low
Japan	Moderate	High	High	Low	Low
Great Britain	Low	High	High	Low	Low
U.S.S.R.	Low	Low	Low	High	Low
Mexico	Moderate	Moderate	Low	High	Low
China	Low	Low	Low	High	Moderate
Egypt	High	Low	Low	Moderate	Moderate
Nigeria	High	Low	Low	Low	High
Tanzania	High	Low	Low	High	Low
India	High	Moderate	Moderate	Moderate	Low

[a] Nations are ranked by 1975 GNP per capita. Extensiveness of interest aggregation rated as low, moderate, or high only. Rating refers to broad level performance, and may vary in different issue areas, and at different times.

of interest aggregation by such personal networks is confined largely to the least economically developed countries.

Interest Groups

Many of the interest groups discussed in the last chapter can perform interest aggregation. Non-associational groups based on religion, language, kinship, and tribe can be used to develop policy backing among many individuals and subgroups. Such nonassociational ties may give a larger group meaning to patron-client networks. And associational groups possess by their very nature an internal organization designed to learn the opinions of their members, and to mobilize their activities in favor of particular policies. Whether formed on the basis of specific issues or on class or ethnic group identity, associational groups can mobilize considerable electoral or financial resources merely by alerting their members to matters of common interest and coordinating their activities. The great peak associations of many Western European interest groups, such as the Federation of German Industry or the British Trade Unions Congress, represent a variety of associated organizations, and aggregate diverse and conflicting demands into policy alternatives to press on party or bureaucracy. Table 6.2 indicates that such groups are important as interest aggregators, as well as interest articulators, in most of the economically developed democracies.

Looking at large associational groups indicates the subtle dividing line between interest articulation and aggregation that can easily be crossed by organizations with powerful resources. Although often operating merely to express demands and support major political contenders, such as parties, associational groups can occasionally wield sufficient resources to become contenders in their own right. The power of the labor unions within the British

Labour party, for example, has rested on the unions' ability to develop coherent policy positions, and mobilize the votes of their members to support those positions. In many European nations, national decision-making bodies have been set up outside the normal legislative channels, bodies with substantial authority to make national policies in special areas, such as the Dutch Social and Economic Council or the Austrian chamber system. These bodies incorporate labor unions' and employer associations' representatives.

Outside the constitutional arena, we must also keep in mind the ability of large unions or business associations to call nationwide strikes or shut down key industries, which may get them direct political power to shape national policies. In Britain in 1974 the coal miners' strike crippled the national economy, and the unions played a rather direct role in national policy formation, aggregating the powerful resources of workers in an essential economic area. In Chile in 1972 and 1973, the long and devastating strikes by the Confederation of Truck Owners against the Allende government created shortages in food and raw materials throughout the nation, which initially encouraged the government to bring the military officers into the cabinet and later played an important role in the breakdown of government legitimacy preceding a military coup.

Institutional groups like bureaucratic and military factions can also be important interest aggregators. Indeed, the bureaucracy acts as a kind of interest aggregator in most societies. Although established primarily for the implementation of policies whose broad outline is set by higher authorities, the bureaucracy may negotiate with a variety of groups to find their preferences or mobilize their support.

Interest groups in strategic positions can aggregate resources; the truckers' strike in Chile in 1972–73 created national food shortages, gravely weakening the government.

Agencies may even be "captured" by interest groups and used to support their demands. The desire of bureaucrats to expand their organizations through the discovery of new problems and policies, and to increase their ability to solve problems in their special areas, often leads them to create client support.

Military interest groups, with their special control over the instruments of violence, have great potential power as interest aggregators. If the legitimacy of the government breaks down and all groups feel free to use coercion and violence to shape policies, then the united military can usually be decisive. We pointed out in Chapter 4 that in the 1960s, almost 40 percent of nations were confronted with military coup attempts, and these were at least partially successful in changing leaders or policy in about a third of all nations. However, less than half of these coup attempts were concerned with general political issues and public policy. Most military coups seem motivated by grievances and the military's fears that their professional or career interests will be slighted or overlooked by civil authorities.[2]

Competitive Party Systems

Parties vary greatly in their goals and structures, as well as in the political settings in which they operate. Naturally, they also vary greatly in their performance of interest aggregation. We suggested some of these differences in our comparison of the functions performed by the British Conservative party, the Communist party of the Soviet Union, and the Tanzanian African National Union. In analyzing parties it is especially important to keep in mind the sharp distinction between competitive parties, seeking primarily to build upon electoral support, and noncompetitive parties. This structural distinction does not depend on the closeness of electoral victory, or even upon the number of parties. It depends on the primacy of winning votes as a prerequisite for control of policy making, on one hand, and on the possibility for several parties to form and organize to seek those votes, on the other. Thus, a party can win most of the votes in a given area or region, or even a given national election, but nonetheless be a competitive party. Its goals involve winning elections, either as a primary objective or as means for policy making; its predominance at the polls is always subject to challenge by other parties; its organization thus involves arrangements for finding out what voters want and getting supporters involved.

In analyzing the role of competitive parties in interest aggregation, we need to consider not only the individual party, but the structure of parties, electorates, electoral laws, and policy-making bodies that interact in a competitive party system. Typically, interest aggregation in a competitive party system takes place at one or more of three different levels: within the individual parties, as the party chooses candidates and adopts policy proposals; through electoral competition, as voters give varying amounts of support to different parties; and through bargaining and coalition building in the legislature or executive.

At the first level, individual parties develop a set of policy positions. Typically, these positions are believed to have the backing of large or cohesive groups of voters or they reflect the continuing linkages between the party and organized interest groups, such as labor unions or business associations. In the United States, the national party conventions are the focus of development of policy positions, both through the formation of the party platform, and, perhaps more importantly, through the selection of candidates committed to certain policies.

The parties then offer their chosen candidates for office. They not only present candidates, but attempt to publicize them and mobilize electoral support, through rallies, mass media promotion, door-to-door campaigning, and systematic efforts to locate sympathetic voters and get them to the polls on election day. In the elections, citizens directly participate in interest aggregation by voting for different parties. Such votes are converted into legislative seats and, in presidential systems, control of the chief executive. In the last decade political scientists have done a great deal of research on the dynamics of citizens' voting decisions, and the causes and effects of appeals to voters.[3] The effects of electoral laws, which

[2] William Thompson, *The Grievances of Military Coup-Makers* (Beverly Hills, Calif.: Sage Publications, 1973).

[3] One review can be found in Norman H. Nie, Sidney Verba, and John Petrosik, *The Changing American Voter*

may often greatly benefit some parties at the expense of others, have also been carefully studied.[4]

If a party committed to some clear-cut positions wins control of the executive, either directly or indirectly, and control of the legislature, it will be able to pass and implement its policies. This has happened when, for example, Social Democratic parties committed to expansion of the governmental sector have won control of the legislature in various European nations. Gerald Pomper's study of American parties and their campaign platforms indicates that the Republicans and Democrats have also been fairly responsible in keeping their promises.[5] Another study suggests that because Democratic candidates for Congress were almost always more liberal on welfare policy than Republicans, domestic welfare policy would have been quite different in the 1960s if the election outcomes had been dramatically shifted.[6] However, if no party wins a clear majority, as in many multiparty systems, the final stage of interest aggregation by parties takes place as different parties bargain to form coalitions within the assemblies and executives.[7] If, as in the United States, the parties are not internally cohesive on many issues, aggregation also takes place between party factions within the legislature.

In Table 6.3 competitive party systems are classified as to type, with examples given for each

(Cambridge, Mass.: Harvard University Press, 1976). Also see Philip E. Converse, "Public Opinion and Voting Behavior," in Fred Greenstein and Nelson Polsby (eds.), *Handbook of Political Science* (Reading, Mass.: Addison-Wesley, 1975); and Gerald Pomper, *Voters' Choice* (New York: Dodd, Mead, 1975), as well as the *American Political Science Review*. On party strategies, the classic analysis is Anthony Downs, *An Economic Theory of Democracy* (New York: Harper and Row, 1957).

[4] Especially see Douglas Rae, *The Political Consequences of Electoral Laws* (New Haven, Conn.: Yale University Press, 1967, 1971).

[5] Gerald Pomper, *Elections in America* (New York: Dodd, Mead, 1968), ch. 7–10.

[6] John L. Sullivan and Robert E. O'Connor, "Electoral Choice and Popular Control of Public Policy," *American Political Science Review*, 66 (December 1972), pp. 1256–1268.

[7] For a study of the effect of number and division of parties, instability in representation, and polarization as they affect cabinet stability, see Lawrence C. Dodd, *Coalitions in Parliamentary Government* (Princeton, N.J.: Princeton University Press, 1976).

type. We distinguish between two-party and multiparty systems, and rate them according to their relative antagonism or polarization.[8] The number of major parties has an impact on legislative activity and the business of forming governments, as does the stability of the party representation and leadership. But a large number of parties in and of itself does not necessarily cause governmental instability. More important is the degree of antagonism or polarization among the parties. We refer to a system as *consensual* if the parties commanding most of the legislative seats are not too far apart on policies, and have a reasonable amount of trust for each other. If the legislature is dominated by parties that are very far apart on issues, or highly distrustful and antagonistic, we would classify that party system as *conflictual*. If a party system has mixed characteristics, that is, both consensual and conflictual elements, we classify it as *consociational* or *accommodative*.

The United States, Britain, and West Germany are contemporary examples of consensual two-party systems, although they differ in the degree of consensus. These three are not perfect two party systems. Britain, in addition to the Labour and Conservative parties, has the Liberal party, the Scottish Nationalist party, and a smaller Welsh party. West Germany has the Free Democratic party which is an essential part of the present governing coalition. The United States has had third-party movements intermittently in its history. Nevertheless, two parties dominate each of these systems. Good examples of consensual multiparty systems are found in Scandinavia. In Norway and Sweden there are four or five parties — socialists, agrarian, liberals, conservatives, and small Communist movements. The three or four larger parties have usually been able to construct long-lived governments, singly or in coalition since World War II.

Austria between 1918 and 1934 is the best example of a two-party conflictual system. Antagonism between the Socialist party and the other parties was so intense that in the mid-1930s it produced civil war, a conflict resulting in the suppression of the Socialist party, the collapse of democratic government, and the erection of an authoritarian, Catholic, one-party

[8] This classification is adapted from Arend Lijphart, "Typologies of Democratic Systems," *Comparative Political Studies* (April 1968).

Table 6.3
Types of Competitive Party Systems

	Two-Party	*Multiparty*
Consensual	United States Britain West Germany	Norway Sweden
Conflictual	Pre–World War II Austria	France Italy Weimar Germany 1919–1933
Consociational (accommodative)	Austria 1948–1966	Netherlands Belgium Lebanon 1946–1975

system. France, Italy, and Weimar Germany are good examples of conflictual multiparty systems, with powerful Communist parties on the left and conservative or fascist movements on the right. Cabinets had to be formed out of centrist movements, which were themselves divided on many issues, thus making for instability and poor government performance.

The mixed system we call consociational arises in countries in which there is considerable conflict and antagonism on the basis of religion, ethnicity, or social class. Through historical experience the leadership of competing movements have found bases of accommodation that provide mutual guarantees to the various groups. In the consociational systems of Austria and Lebanon, the two major groups — socialists and Catholics in Austria, and Christians and Moslems in Lebanon — worked out a set of understandings making it possible for stable governments to be formed. Austria's accommodation was based on a two-party system, Lebanon's on many small, personalistic religious parties. These two examples have gone in opposite directions in recent years. Austria since 1966 has begun to move toward a consensual two-party system, while Lebanon has been penetrated and fragmented by the Middle Eastern conflict and has fallen victim of civil war.

The Netherlands and Belgium continue to be examples of consociational multiparty systems. Belgium is divided ethnically and linguistically between the French and Flemish speakers, and by social class. The Netherlands is divided by religion between Protestants and Catholics and by social class. In both countries tacit understanding among these groups has made stable government possible, although the language question in Belgium continues to be explosive.

All this suggests that while the number of parties is of some importance in relation to stability, the degree of antagonism among parties is of greater importance. Where multiparty systems consist of relatively moderate antagonists, stability and effective performance seem possible. Where systems consist of highly antagonistic elements, collapse and civil war are ever-present possibilities, regardless of the number of parties. Lebanon, prewar Austria, and the Weimar Republic are tragic examples.

Noncompetitive Political Parties

Noncompetitive parties are also specialized interest aggregation structures: they deliberately attempt to develop policy alternatives and to mobilize support for them. But they do so in a different way from the competitive parties we have been discussing. With noncompetitive parties aggregation takes place within the ranks of the party, or in interactions with institutional groups in the bureaucracy or military. We distinguish two major variants of the noncompetitive party, according to the degree of internal hierarchical control and the party's relationship with subgroups.

THE CORPORATIST POLITICAL PARTY

The corporatist party permits some autonomous formation of demands within its own ranks or by associational groups associated with it. The degree of aggregation and open bargaining may be substantial and takes many forms. In Mexico the PRI dominates the political process and there has been little chance of another party winning a national election. The PRI has maintained general popular support since the creation of a broad coalition by Lázaro Cárdenas in the 1930s, and also controls the counting of the ballots. Its actions are not shaped by electoral competition. But the party incorporates many associational groups within it, with separate sectors for labor, agrarian, and popular interests. In addition to these formal components, the party has recognized informally rather distinct and well-organized political factions grouped behind figures such as former President Cárdenas on the Left and former President Miguel Alemán on the right.

Various Mexican leaders mobilize their factions within the PRI and in other important groups not directly affiliated with it, such as big business interests. Bargaining is particularly important every six years, when a new presidential nominee must be chosen by the party. The legal provision that the incumbent president cannot succeed himself guarantees some turnover of elites and may facilitate more open internal bargaining. Recent discontent has suggested, however, some of the difficulties in incorporating all interests, particularly those of urban and rural poor who have not shared in Mexico's general economic growth (see Chapter 14).

We have already discussed the interesting variation of the corporatist party of Tanzania, where the party controls nominations, but requires that two candidates be nominated in each district for the elections. The presence of two candidates permits local interests to form behind one or the other, and encourages the party toward more open aggregation of interests. The defeat of many Cabinet members by unknown local candidates suggests that the competition is more than an illusion. At the same time, control over the nomination and the prohibition against other parties obviously limits the policy stances allowed to mobilize support.

Neighboring Kenya has had a more personalistic, factionalized, and tribal-oriented set of conflicts within the Kenyan African National Union (KANU), and less central party control over candidates. But in both Kenya and Tanzania the electoral process has contributed to substantial turnover, and hence to pressure for attention to constituent needs, as well as citizen perception of elite responsiveness. In Kenya in 1969, half of the former members of Parliament who ran for reelection were defeated, including five ministers. Moreover, the electoral process has played an important role in shaping competition within elite groups. According to Henry Bienen:

> It must be emphasized that elections counted in Kenya despite the fact that they were often highly constrained. . . . National leaders had to be able to hold their constituencies. They had to make a good showing in elections and where possible to use their influence to help their supporters win election.[9]

THE HIERARCHICAL GOVERNING PARTY

The hierarchical governing party, unlike the corporatist party, does not openly recognize the legitimacy of internal interest aggregation, nor of interest aggregation by autonomous social groups. Limited interest articulation may be permitted to controlled institutional or associational groups, but the open mobilization of support for alternative policy positions is not permitted. In such regimes as the Soviet Union and China, the party mobilizes mass support behind the policies developed at the top. The Chinese regime has not typically recognized the legitimacy of any large internal groups. In these systems, interest articulation by individuals, within certain bounds, may be permitted, the mobilization of

[9] Henry Bienen, *Kenya: The Politics of Participation and Control* (Princeton, N.J.: Princeton University Press, 1974), p. 112.

wide support before the top elite has decided is not.[10] The parties do play important roles in the mobilization of support for policies. An unchallenged ideological focus provides legitimacy and coherence, and the party is used to penetrate and organize most social structures in its name, and in accordance with centralized policies.

Of course, as we indicated in talking about interest articulation, the hierarchical ruling party may be the focus of more internal aggregation at various levels than is commonly recognized, or legitimately permitted (see Chapter 5). Internally, various groups may coalesce around such interests as region or industry, or behind leaders of policy factions. Generational differences or differences of temperament may distinguish hard-liners and soft-liners on ranges of policy. Either openly or covertly, beneath the supposedly united front, power struggles may erupt in times of crisis, with different leaders mobilizing backing for themselves and their positions. Succession crises are particularly likely to generate such power struggles, as demonstrated at the death of Stalin in the U.S.S.R. and recently at the death of Mao Zedong in China.

The party itself may also be challenged by other political structures, and may appear only as one among several policy and resource aggregators. An example is the period of the Cultural Revolution in China, when Mao apparently used students and the army against the entrenched party bureaucracy to force a more populist policy. Other examples are in governing parties in Eastern Europe, which have been constrained in their actions by pressure from the U.S.S.R., which sets limits on policy alternatives for them.

As an instrument designed for unified mobilization, the hierarchical governing party has seemed attractive to many leaders committed to massive social change. The party that successfully mobilized a colonial people behind independence, for example, might be used to penetrate and change an underdeveloped society. However, as the experiences of many new nations have underlined, the creation of a hierarchical and penetrative governing party that could be used for social transformation is extremely difficult. The protracted guerrilla warfare that contributed to the development of the Chinese party is not easily replicated, nor is the external Soviet involvement that was essential in Eastern Europe and North Korea. Indigenous communism in Yugoslavia has taken a more decentralized and corporatist form, as a matter of policy and in recognition of the party's linkage to peasant supporters.[11] The stable one-party regimes in most underdeveloped nations have for the most part been involved in military coalitions, as in Egypt, or are corporatist, as in Tanzania, Kenya, the Ivory Coast, and Mexico. The hierarchical governing parties attempted in some African states have had limited penetrative capacity, and Kwame Nkrumah's spectacular effort in Ghana was easily toppled by a military coup.

Indeed, as the outburst of coups in the single party African systems in the late 1960s and early 1970s conclusively demonstrates, the development of a stable corporatist party system is no easy matter either. The relative success of the corporatist systems in Mexico, Kenya, and Tanzania should not blind us to the frequent failure of efforts to establish such structures in many other systems. Moreover, many of the corporatist systems exist in uneasy and unstable coalition with the armed forces.[12] We might tentatively say that the single party systems in Egypt, Burma, and the Congo play the crucial interest aggregation role on a day-to-day basis, but there is no doubt of the crucial importance of the military in sustaining the chief executive or of its predominance in affairs touching its interests.

Military Governments

We cannot leave our consideration of structures performing interest aggregation without discussing military governments. The last decade has seen the overthrow of many of the single-party and multiparty regimes established in the new nations after inde-

[10] See Chapter 13 below; see also Franz Schurmann, *Ideology and Organization in Communist China* (Berkeley: University of California Press, 1966).

[11] See Bogdan Denis Denitch, *The Legitimation of a Revolution: The Yugoslav Case* (New Haven, Conn.: Yale University Press, 1976).

[12] See the excellent discussion of fluid parties and quasi-parties by Giovanni Sartori, *Parties and Party Systems*, (Cambridge, Eng.: Cambridge University Press, 1976), ch. 8.

pendence. In some cases one party regime was replaced with another. But more frequently the new regime was based on the military as the decisionmaker, or at least as one of the most important interest aggregators. Even where civilian rule was later reestablished, the experience of successful military intervention seems to interject the military permanently as a major contender. In Brazil the military played a crucial interest aggregation role in the democratic processes before 1964, and played the dominant aggregating and decisionmaking roles after 1964. In Nigeria the collapse of democracy into civil war has resulted in continuing military rule. In Ghana the overthrow of Nkrumah has been followed by military rule interspersed with experimentation with competitive parties. In Peru military governments have been the rule for a decade. And in many other nations, including Syria, Pakistan, Indonesia, Mali, Uganda, Bolivia, and Chile, the military has become the dominant, or at least a major, interest aggregator.

Table 6.4 estimates the most important interest aggregation structure in the 118 sizable independent nations, as of the beginning of 1976. These figures must be taken only as approximations, because of our limited knowledge of the politics of some nations and because the relative importance of a structure in interest aggregation will vary with different issues and circumstances within a single nation. But the table provides a rough idea as to the importance of the three major forms — competitive party-assembly systems, one-party structures, and military organizations. Strikingly, systems in which the military predominates are about as common as each of the

Parties try to draw on familiar symbols as they aggregate support; Mrs. Indira Gandhi appealed to the memories of her father (Nehru) and Mahatma Gandhi as she organized a new party in 1978.

Table 6.4

Regimes Classified by Predominant Interest Aggregation Structure in 1976, by Region

	Predominant Interest Aggregation Structure					
Region	*Competitive party-assembly system*	*Non-competitive party system*	*Military*	*Other*[a]	*Total*	*Nations*[b]
Atlantic[c]	88%	6%	6%	0%	100%	(17)
East Europe and North Asia	0	100	0	0	100	(11)
Middle East[d]	20	20	33	27	100	(15)
South and Southeast Asia	36	36	19	9	100	(22)
Sub-Saharan Africa	3	48	48	0	99	(33)
Latin America	30	15	45	10	100	(20)
Total	28	36	29	8	101	(118)
(Nations)	(33)	(42)	(34)	(9)		

[a] Includes the traditional monarchies of Saudi Arabia, Iran, Jordan, and Nepal, as well as the apparently primarily executive and bureaucracy based aggregation systems of the Philippines, Paraguay, and Haiti. (Note: In 1978, the Iranian monarchy was overthrown, and replaced by an "Islamic Republic" whose political resource bases were as yet undefined.)

[b] Only nations with over 1 million population are included.

[c] Atlantic region includes Western Europe, the United States, and Canada.

[d] Middle East region includes Greece and Turkey.

Source: Estimates based on a variety of sources including Arthur Banks, *Political Handbook of the World, 1976* (New York: McGraw-Hill, 1976); *The Statesman's Year Book, 1975–76*; and Giovanni Sartori, *Parties and Party Systems* (Cambridge, Eng.: Cambridge University Press, 1976), ch. 8.

party-dominated systems. Military dominated governments are particularly found in Africa and Latin America, and play a large role in the Middle East.

The virtual monopoly of coercive resources held by the military give it great potential power as a political contender. The major limitation on military organizations as contenders is that their internal structures are not well designed for interest aggregation across a range of issues or outside the coercive arena. The military is primarily organized to facilitate downward processing of commands involving the implementation of coercion. It is not set up to aggregate internal differences and affect a compromise, nor to mobilize wide support of all components behind policy. Also, military organizations are not easily adapted to rally or communicate with social groups outside the command hierarchy. Thus, the military lacks those advantages in mobilizing support held by party systems. These internal limitations may be less serious when the military is dealing with common grievances, and putting pressure on — or seizing power from — incumbent authorities. But these limitations become a major problem when a military government needs to mobilize backing for, say, economic development policy. Legitimate authority and communication of the regime's political and ideological goals to many social sectors are then needed.

After some experience with intervention or as a governing bureaucracy, the military organization may attempt to develop, at least informally, more specialized internal aggregation structures. The Brazilian military, for example, seems to have developed fairly clear-cut interest factions in the late 1960s, and to have had policy making structured by these coalitions. Or the military leaders may encourage formation of a subordinate single party to assist the civilian bureaucracy in gaining popular support for policies.

Military intervention is often undertaken to suppress polarization in society, or to remedy failures of the existing party structures. But unless it can develop a successful alternative, it may fall back on the use of raw force to determine the strength of internal factions and suppress dissent. As it is difficult to determine the support of such resources before they are used, the military may reflect continuing instability — with coup following coup or with a series of bloody purges — or may become immobilized in a desire to avoid internal conflict. Or its leaders may decide to return the nation to civilian rule, while continuing to play an important aggregation role in some policy areas.

THE SIGNIFICANCE OF INTEREST AGGREGATION

How interests are aggregated is an important determinant of what a country's government does for and to its citizens. The factors that most interest us about government and politics — stability, revolution, participation, welfare, equality, liberty, security — are very much a consequence of interest aggregation. Through interest aggregation the desires and demands of citizens are converted into a few policy alternatives. In terms of policy, this means that many possible policies have been eliminated, and only a few remain. In terms of process, it means that political resources have been accumulated in the hands of relatively few individuals, who will decide policy. The remaining policy alternatives are serious or major alternatives, because they have the backing of plenty of political resources. Policy alternatives such as the government taking over all heavy industrial production in the United States, or government allowing free and competitive elections in the U.S.S.R., are not serious, because no set of leaders commanding major political resources favors these, even though these policies are implemented in other countries.

Narrowing and combining policy wishes can be seen easily in the working of competitive party systems. Of the many possible policy preferences, only a few are backed by parties, after the parties choose leaders and establish platforms to run on. In the elections, voters give backing to some of these parties, and thus shape the strength of party representation in the legislature. Even at the legislative stage, some further consolidation and coalition building takes place between party factions or party groups. But at some point the majority of policy possibilities have been eliminated. Either they were never backed by parties, or parties supporting them did badly in the elections. In noncompetitive party systems, or in military governments, or in monarchies, aggregation works differently, but with the similar effect of narrowing and combining policies and resources. It may be that on some issues, aggregation will virtually determine policy, as when power is held by a military government, a faction of an authoritarian party, or a disciplined party majority in a competitive system. In other cases the legislative assembly, military council, or party politburo may contain several different factions of similar strength.

One characteristic of interest aggregation in all systems is whether it polarizes or depolarizes. In Chapter 3 we discussed consensual and polarized political cultures. We showed there that the United States, West Germany, Britain, and Switzerland were consensual, with most citizens preferring moderate positions. Italy and Finland were examples of polarized cultures, with larger concentrations of citizens on the left and fewer in the center.

Polarization in the policy-making body should look pretty much like polarization in the political culture. In a consensual society, like West Germany, the Bundestag is made up of largely moderate and tolerant parties. In conflictual Italy, the stalemated Parliament is dominated by deeply divided parties — the Communists and the Christian Democrats.

But politics shapes its environment, as well as reflects it. Interest aggregation often alters the amount of polarization that the political culture might be expected to project into policy making. That is one reason that politics is so fascinating. Well-organized and well-led political parties might, at least for a while, be able to dominate politics and limit the strength of extremist groups in the legislature, as in the consociational model we mentioned earlier. Conversely, well-organized extremists might be able to appeal to the fears and prejudices of some groups, and get them more effectively to the polls, thus gaining more legislative strength in an otherwise consensual country.

Of course, noncompetitive interest aggregation structures may very likely create a political power balance that is far from reflecting popular opinion. In a highly divided and conflict-ridden society, such unrepresentativeness may be seen as a great virtue. Leaders of military coups in many nations have justified their overthrow of party governments by claiming to depolarize politics and rid the nation of conflict it cannot afford. Similarly, heads of authoritarian parties typically claim that their nation must concentrate all its energies and resources around common purposes, and that to allow party competition would be too polarizing. One justification for democracy is that it leads political leaders to act as the people wish. In a polarized political culture, the cost of interest aggregation that reflects division and uncertainty may be seen as too high a price to pay for citizen control. As the frequent instability in authoritarian and military governments indicates, though, it may be easier to do away with the appearance of polarization than the reality. Cultural divisions may end up being reflected through military factions or intraparty groups, instead of through party competition, and the citizens may end up without freedom and participation, or stability.

KEY TERMS

representative party
nation-building party
mobilization or integration party
Communist Party of the Soviet Union (CPSU)
British Conservative Party
Tanzanian African National Union (TANU)
interest articulation
interest aggregation
soviets
patron-client relationship
multi-party system
two-party system
consensual system
conflictual system
consociational system
corporatist political party
hierarchical governing party

CHAPTER SEVEN

Policy Making and Implementation

Policy making is a pivotal stage in the political process. Interests are being articulated. Policy preferences and political resources are being combined and aggregated. Contenders who are committed to various alternatives and who command various political resources have emerged. The lineup of political forces has taken shape. Now authoritative policies must be enacted: bills proposed and passed by the legislature, edicts issued by the ruling military council, the new five-year plan approved by the politburo. Later, policy goals must be implemented, their implications dealt with.

The study of policy making is complicated. First, we must recognize that policy making often involves the final act of using the political resources that contenders have aggregated. To understand policy making, we must understand the rules for the use of political resources in decision making. What amount and type of resources must be presented for the elite to accept that a policy is authoritative? Is it a majority vote in the legislature, a decree issued by the monarch, signed unanimous agreement by military field commanders, or official backing by two-thirds of the politburo? Or is it merely the whim of the military dictator?

Second, we must understand the political and policy background to the final use of political resources. Where are policies initiated, considered, and accepted before decisions are made? In Britain enacting legislation requires a majority of Parliament to vote for a bill, rather than oppose it. But formulating the bill and building support for it may not take place in Parliament at all. In Britain, and in most democracies, the majority of the work — specifying and evaluating the options and alternatives, writing the legislation, and determining the funds to be allocated for achieving the goals — will take place in the bureaucracy and the Cabinet. If the party, parties, or factions that control the executive also control a disciplined parliamentary majority (as is usually, though not always, true in Britain), then the final legislation is merely formal ratification of the work that has taken place in the Cabinet and the bureaucracy. The aggregation of resources by the party system, on one hand, and the expertise of the bureaucracy, on the other, have greatly reduced the role of Parliament as the policy-making structure. Parliament remains important to policy making because the accepted rules make its votes essential, and because party leaders must have the assent of their party members in Parliament, and cannot completely control them. But its part in policy making is limited.

We begin with a brief description of some of the different features of decision rules that govern the use of political resources in policy making. Then, we shall discuss the working of some of the most important structures involved in policy making and policy implementation: assemblies, executives, and bureaucracies. We must build, of course, on the discussion of interest aggregation and the structures that perform it in the last chapter. Given that we understand how competitive parties, authoritarian parties, the armed forces, and other organizations aggregate policies and resources, we can consider how policies are made and implemented in the final stages.

GOVERNMENTAL RULES FOR POLICY MAKING

Americans are familiar with a written constitution, a document setting forth the procedures, or at least some of them, by which laws can be made and funding authorized. The Constitution of the United States describes in general how authoritative policies can be made by a majority vote of both houses of Congress with presidential agreement, or by two-thirds vote of both houses to override a presidential veto. The Constitution also forbids some kinds of policy making, and places limits on others, as well as providing for the general nature of congressional representation. The Constitution can be and has been changed, following a described set of procedures, and as properly altered it establishes the rules for policy making. Elites follow those rules, for the most part.

Other nations may have no single document, but a long accepted and highly developed set of customs, buttressed by major statutes. In Britain, for instance, the rules provide that authoritative policy must be made through a majority vote of the elected House of Commons and assent by the House of Lords. In yet other nations, there may be an elaborate document that is completely or partially ignored by a party or military government. Nonetheless, that government usually attempts very quickly to establish its own working set of rules for making decisions, its working constitution. Even a military government or dictatorship based on coercion attempts to have a working set of arrangements for having decrees proposed, considered, and adopted. *Decision rules* are the basic rules governing how decisions are made, spelling out the policy-making roles, dividing them territorially and functionally, and the like. They set the terms of the political contest. Individuals and groups seeking to influence policy have to operate within the framework of these rules. If a nation decentralizes policy-making authority, so that to preserve the environment it is necessary to get majority votes in many state legislatures, a great effort will be needed for groups to initiate new conservation measures. If the working constitution merely requires a formal decree from the commander of the armed forces, or a declaration by the politburo, a different approach will be needed to influence those crucial policy makers. The decision rules shape political activity, because they determine what political resources to seek — whether legislative seats or the support of regional military commanders — and how to acquire and use them.

The basic decision rules or constitutions of political systems may be compared in three ways: (1) the geographic distribution of authority; (2) the structural separation of authority; and (3) the limitations on government authority.

Geographic Distribution of Government Power

Classifying systems according to the geographic division of power gives us *confederal systems* at one extreme, *unitary systems* at the other extreme, and *federal systems* in the middle. The United States under the Articles of Confederation was a confederal system. The central government had power over foreign affairs and defense, but it had to depend on financial and other support from the states to implement this power. Under the Constitution, adopted in 1787, the American government changed from confederal to federal, that is, both central and state governments had spheres of authority and the means to implement their power. Today, United States, West Germany, India and Tanzania are federal systems in which federal and local units each have autonomy in particular spheres of public policy. These policy areas and powers are, however, divided among central and local units in varying ways in these countries.

France, China, and Japan are unitary governments, with power and authority concentrated at the center. Regional and local units have only those powers specifically delegated to them from the central government, which may change or withdraw the powers at its discretion. Britain has recently moved to devolve some policy-making authority to Scottish and Welsh elective assemblies. It may be moving toward a federal structure, although mixed referenda results in the spring of 1979 left the situation in doubt.

In comparing confederal, federal, and unitary systems, however, we must keep in mind the distinction between formal and actual distribution of power. In unitary systems, in spite of the formal concentration of power at the center, regional and local units may acquire authority that the central government rarely challenges. In federal systems over the last century or so, power has steadily moved from regional units toward the center. Thus the real differences between federal and unitary systems may be considerably less significant than those their formal arrangements suggest. An extreme example of the discrepancy between formal and actual federalism is the Soviet Union, which consists of "federated" republics, three of which are represented in the United Nations. But the Soviet governing apparatus is the Communist party, a highly centralized body exercising authority both at the center and at the periphery, suggesting that Soviet federalism is more theoretical than real. Similarly, Mexican federalism has been largely eroded, and power is concentrated in the center.

Separation of Governmental Powers

Comparing governments according to the concentration or separation of policy-making authority, at any geographic level, reveals several types. These are illustrated in Table 7.1. In *authoritarian* regimes, such as the U.S.S.R., China, Egypt, Mexico and Tanzania, there is no fully settled delegation of authority to legislatures, courts, or similar structures outside the office of chief executive. In such systems, power may either be concentrated in a political bureau or military junta, or, typically, consist of an uneasy balance of military factions, bureaucrats, and party leaders. But none of these groups, as they bring their political resources to bear on policy making, are faced with an accepted need to compete for citizen support. Such systems vary greatly in the extent to which they attempt to regulate all aspects of social and economic life. They also vary in the amount of debate and even contestation allowed within the party or military. Mexico and Tanzania, as shown in Table 7.1, are relatively more open in this respect. But in all of the authoritarian systems the rules of governmental policy making involve a concentrated focus on executive action.

Parliamentary regimes, such as those of West Germany, Great Britain, Japan, and India, are characterized by a combination of the political executive and the assembly. This does not mean that prime ministers and cabinets in parliamentary governments lack settled spheres of authority and power. Rather, it signifies that the executive (usually called a cabinet or council of ministers) is selected from the assembly and holds office only as long as it can command the support of a majority in the assembly.

Policy-making authority is most sharply separated in the *democratic presidential regime*, of which the United States is the outstanding example. The principal characteristics of this regime are that the political executive is independently elected, holds office for the entire term whether or not he has the legislature's support, and has substantial authority in policy making, as in the American president's veto power. At the same time, the executive must deal with an independently elected legislature that also has policy-making authority; this distinguishes the democratic presidential regime from many authoritarian regimes called presidential. Of course, if the same party controls both presidency and legislature, and the party has internal agreement, this effective aggregation of political resources will create a situation much like that in parliamentary regimes with stable party governments or coalitions.

France under the Fifth Republic (since 1959) is an interesting example of a *mixed parliamentary-presidential regime*. The president of France is elected by popular vote and holds office for a seven-

Table 7.1

Attributes of Decision Rules

Geographic distribution of authority

Centralized ←→ *Decentralized*

Unitary	*Formally federal*	*Federal*	*Confederal*
France Japan Great Britain China	U.S.S.R. Mexico	United States under Constitution West Germany India Tanzania	United States under Articles of Confederation United Nations European Economic Community

Structural separation of authority

Concentrated ←→ *Separated*

Authoritarian		*Parliamentary*	*Mixed*[a]	*Democratic presidential*
U.S.S.R. China Egypt	Mexico Tanzania	West Germany Great Britain Japan India	France	United States Chile (to 1973) Venezuela

Judicial limitations on governmental authority

Unlimited ←→ *Limited*

Nonindependent courts	*Independent courts*	*Power of judicial review*
U.S.S.R. China Egypt	France Great Britain India Tanzania	United States West Germany Japan

[a] Parliamentary and presidential.

year term, whether or not he is supported by the National Assembly. The French prime minister and Cabinet, on the other hand, depend on a majority in the National Assembly. Thus far in the Fifth Republic, the system has been sustained by a National Assembly majority supporting both president and prime minister. The test of the system may occur when this majority dissolves and a contest occurs between the president and the National Assembly. Some tensions have already been generated by the fact that President Valéry Giscard d'Estaing heads the smaller party in the government's coalition, while the prime minister heads the larger.

Limitations on Government Powers

Parliamentary, presidential, and parliamentary-presidential regimes are characterized by some form of legal or customary limitation on authority; authoritarian regimes are not. Systems in which the powers of various government units are defined and limited by a written constitution, statutes, and custom are called *constitutional regimes*. Constitutional regimes typically restrict government power. Citizens' rights — like that to a fair trial and freedom to speak, petition, publish, and assemble — are protected against government interference except under unusual and specified circumstances. The courts are crucial institutions in the limitation of governmental power.

Governments may be divided into those, at one extreme, in which the power to coerce citizens is relatively unlimited by the courts, and those, at the other extreme, in which the courts not only protect the rights of citizens but also police other parts of the government to see that their powers are properly exercised. The United States is the best example of a system in which political power is limited by the courts. Its institution of *judicial review* allows federal and state courts to rule that other parts of the government have exceeded their powers. Most other constitutional regimes have independent courts that can protect citizens against the improper implementation of laws and regulations, but cannot overrule the assembly or the political executive. The substantive rights of citizens in these systems are protected by custom, self-restraint, and political pressure, rather than by judicial process.

POLICY-MAKING STRUCTURES

In addition to political parties, which we discussed in the last chapter, three important types of institutions are involved in policy making: the executive, whether elective or appointive; the higher levels of bureaucracy; and the assembly. Political executives — presidents and their appointees in presidential systems; prime ministers and cabinets in parliamentary systems; and politburos or presidia in communist systems — tend to be the main formulators of public policy. But the distribution of policy-making predominance among the three institutions varies from country to country and from issue area to issue area.

The central decisions in a foreign policy crisis are generally made by the top executive, the president (John F. Kennedy in the Cuban Missile Crisis) or prime minister (Sir Anthony Eden in the Suez Crisis). Ordinarily, though, individual ministers or department heads have substantial autonomy. Under the leadership of a strong and capable Cabinet officer, for example, an agency in the American executive branch may attain a highly autonomous position by using congressional connections, administrative discretion and competence, and the technique of ignoring undesirable presidential requests. Richard Fenno has provided us with a fascinating account of the "political fiefdom" established by Jesse Jones, as the head of Franklin D. Roosevelt's Reconstruction Finance Corporation. Within limits, Jones was able to ignore certain of Roosevelt's proposals, overcome financial cuts that the Bureau of the Budget attempted to impose, and generally operate the RFC as an independent force in its area.[1]

Similarly, bureaucratic agencies and higher civil servants may acquire substantial power in their spheres. For a number of decades J. Edgar Hoover could resist control by the president and attorney general and manipulate Congress. The Central Intelligence Agency has similarly operated independently, often committing the United States to a foreign policy course independently of the political executive and legislative agencies. In Britain, Richard Crossman records with frustration his efforts to control his ministry (Housing and Urban Affairs) in opposition to the views of his permanent secretary, the top civil servant. He became aware of a network of higher civil servants throughout the bureaucracy, which in some circumstances could fight the prime minister and Cabinet to a standstill.[2]

Finally, assemblies and their committees may enjoy some autonomy, but more often this is true in a negative sense of vetoing initiatives from the political executive and higher civil service. Many dramatic examples of this come from American experience, where powerful committee chairmen have dominated legislation within their jurisdiction. Committees of the German Bundestag and of the French National Assembly, while not as powerful as their

[1] Richard F. Fenno, Jr., *The President's Cabinet* (Cambridge, Mass.: Harvard University Press, 1959), pp. 234–247.

[2] Richard Crossman, *Diary of a Cabinet Minister* (London, England: Macmillan, 1975).

The independent power of the American legislature was demonstrated in the Watergate hearings in 1973. Here former Counsel to the President John Dean testifies to the cover-up of illegal activities by the executive.

American counterparts, take an active and substantial part in policy making. If the government in a parliamentary system does not command a majority, or if its coalition is fragile, the parliament may repeatedly frustrate government's attempt to make policy. A minority government, or one composed of a coalition of parties that disagree on important issues, may be able to stay in power only by refusing to make policy in areas of disagreement.

ASSEMBLIES

Almost all contemporary political systems have assemblies, variously called chambers, senates, diets, soviets, and the like. As of 1971, one hundred and eight of the one hundred and thirty-eight independent countries had such governmental bodies, and since that time another half dozen countries have instituted them.[3] Bodies of many members that proceed by formal deliberation and voting, assemblies are generally elected by popular vote and hence are accountable at least formally to the citizenry. Thus, they are at least legitimating agencies. The almost universal adoption of them suggests that in the modern world a legitimate government must at least formally include a representative popular component.

The Functions of Assemblies

All assemblies have many members — from under a hundred to over a thousand — who deliberate, debate, and vote on policies that come before them.

[3] Jean Blondel, *Comparative Legislatures* (Englewood Cliffs, N.J.: Prentice-Hall, 1973), pp. 144 ff.

Most important policies and rules must be considered and approved by these bodies before they have the force of law. Although legislative approval is needed to give authority to policy, the actual formulation of legislation in most countries is carried on elsewhere, usually by the political executive and the upper levels of the bureaucracy.

When we compare assemblies on the basis of their importance as political and policy-making agencies, the United States Senate and House of Representatives, which play a very important role in the formulation and enactment of legislation, are at one extreme. The other extreme is represented by the Supreme Soviet of the U.S.S.R., which meets infrequently and does little more than listen to statements from Soviet leaders and legitimize decisions made elsewhere. Roughly midway between the two is the House of Commons in Britain, where legislative proposals are sometimes initiated or modified by ordinary members of Parliament, but where public policy is usually made by the Cabinet or ministers (who are, to be sure, chosen from the members of the parliamentary body). The assembly primarily debates, amends, and formally enacts legislation.

Assemblies perform a wide variety of functions other than policy making. The British House of Commons contributes importantly to the creation of popular attitudes and values affecting government and politics. Most noteworthy political events in Britain occur in Commons — statements by the prime minister or other ministers, attacks on the government by the opposition, questioning of ministers, debates on the current issues and policies, and critical votes. The centrality of the House of Commons in the British political system and the importance attached to its activities by the mass media mean that the political values, practices, and substantive decisions of Commons are constantly passed on to the population. Thus, beyond learning about specific issues and votes, British citizens are informed of basic attitudes characterizing the relationship between government and opposition, appropriate kinds of behavior for political leaders in their relations with one another, and approved limits on government power.

The United States Senate, House of Representatives, and state and local assemblies also contribute to the political socialization of Americans, affecting basic political attitudes and values. But since power is shared among assemblies, executives, and courts, the impact of any one of these bodies is more limited and the total effect more dispersed and conflicting than is true in Britain. The Soviet Union's soviets are much less significant as agents of political socialization. Their meetings are less frequent, and there is little if any debate, except locally. The principal image transmitted by the soviets is that the people's deputies accept unanimously, without debate, decisions made by the party leadership.

Assemblies are of even greater importance in the socialization of political leaders. Most national political leaders in the United States spend some part of their careers in Congress, although service in the assembly is not as important as it is to British ministers, who are chosen from among the members of Parliament. In the Soviet Union, executives are also members of soviets, but experience there has far less importance than membership and experience in the Communist party and the bureaucracy.

Assemblies may perform valuable roles in the recruitment of political leaders. Members of the British Cabinet are usually selected from the House of Commons after long years of service as back benchers or as junior ministers. If in a parliamentary system the cabinet loses its majority, it usually resigns, or the assembly is dissolved and new elections are called. Indeed, any weakening of the majority in parliamentary systems is often associated with some shift in the composition of the cabinet and ministry, in efforts to meet the dissatisfaction of the majority party or coalition.

In presidential systems like the United States, recruitment, though still important, is performed differently. Membership in legislatures at the state and national levels leads to higher political office, but less regularly. Five out of the last eight American presidents came from Congress. But President Eisenhower was elected after a distinguished military career; Roosevelt's prior political experience had been as governor of New York; and Jimmy Carter's was as governor of Georgia.

Although communist political leaders are typically elected to soviets, membership in these bodies is not particularly relevant to political advancement. More important is performance in party committees and bureaus or valuable service in the bureaucracy.

American and British assemblies influence the policy-making process by expressing the interests of different economic and social groups in the population and combining these interests into policy alternatives. But the concentration of legislative power in the British Cabinet means that interest-group demands on Parliament have less effect on legislative outcomes in Britain than they do in the United States, where Congress and state legislatures act independently of the executive. Almost no interest articulation and aggregation occur in the Soviet Union's Supreme Soviet or its republic soviets. In local soviets, however, issues pertaining to local affairs sometimes become the subject of debate.

In the actual formulation and enactment of legislation, Congress is of greater importance than the House of Commons, while soviets have little if any importance. Both Congress and Parliament implement rules. Both inquire into and investigate the performance of administrative agencies, although in different ways. The investigative powers of American congressional committees give them more influence than their counterparts in Commons. Congressional committees using their powers of investigation often conduct proceedings seemingly judicial in character, in which they may compel people to testify, hold individuals in contempt, and impose punishments. In Britain, select committees have special responsibilities in these areas, and members of the House of Commons can ask questions about administrative efficiency and performance that the appropriate ministers are required to answer. The British also have a parliamentary commissioner (ombudsman), an official responsible to the House of Commons who must hear citizens' complaints regarding failures or improprieties of administrative performance in individual cases. In the Soviet Union, criticism of administrative performance occurs in a limited way in the local soviets. At the central level, control is exercised by the party.

Some assemblies engage in adjudication, although in rather special ways. In Britain, the House of Lords constitutes the highest formal court of appeals. In fact, however, the judicial function of the House of Lords is performed by the lord chancellor — head of the judiciary and presiding officer of the House of Lords — and nine appointed law lords. In the United States, in the event of crimes committed by public officials, impeachment proceedings may be invoked, in which the House of Representatives indicts and the Senate tries.

This brief comparison of the functions performed by assemblies in the United States, Britain, and the Soviet Union should set to rest the simplified notion that assemblies legislate. All assemblies in democratic systems have an important relationship to rule making, but not a dominant one; their political importance lies not just in this relationship, but also in the great variety of other political functions they perform.

Differences in Structures of Assemblies

Assemblies differ in their organizational patterns as well as in their powers and functions. About half of the parliaments or congresses consist of two chambers, which have different powers and different ways of selecting members.

In Europe, parliaments developed out of estates, bodies representing different sociopolitical groups intermittently called together by kings or other hereditary rulers for consultation and gathering revenue. In France, for example, there were three estates: the higher clergy, the higher aristocracy, and the so-called third estate, representing other classes. In England, estates were early organized in two chambers — the lords spiritual (the bishops) and temporal in the House of Lords, and knights and burgesses elected from the counties and boroughs in the House of Commons. But this basis of parliamentary organization persists today only in England, where the House of Lords is still dominated numerically by the hereditary aristocracy.

Most of the democratic countries, and some of the authoritarian ones, have a bicameral (two-chamber) assembly. Federal systems provide simultaneously for two forms of representation: one chamber for constituencies based on population, the second for constituencies based on federal units. Even in unitary systems, bicameralism is a common practice, but the purpose of the second chamber is to break up the process of policy making and provide for longer and more cautious consideration of legislation. The emphasis in these systems is on general separation of power, rather than the distinct representation of special geographic entities.

The formation of the American Congress reflected a concern for both federalism and separation of powers. The House directly represents the populace, with districts made of roughly equal numbers of citizens, giving a voice to various local interests and, in the aggregate, the popular majority. The fifty American states are equally represented in the Senate; thus federal units have special access to one of the two legislative chambers and are in a position to protect their interests. But the American congressional system is also connected with the other branches in the federal separation of powers and checks and balances; thus the Senate must approve or disapprove treaties and executive appointments as a way of checking the executive, and all measures involving taxation or appropriations must be initiated in the House.

The American system, in which the two chambers seem practically equal in power, is unusual. In most bicameral systems one chamber is dominant, and the second (for example, the British House of Lords and the French Senate) tends to play a primarily limiting and delaying role. As we have pointed out, cabinets in parliamentary systems are usually chosen from the majority party or parties' leadership in the more popularly representative chamber. Governments in parliamentary systems depend on majority support to continue in office. If the cabinet is chosen from among the majority party in one of the chambers, then the cabinet is responsible to that chamber, which will, consequently, acquire a more important position in policy making than the second chamber.

Assemblies also differ in their internal organizations, in ways that have important consequences for policy making and implementation. There are two kinds of internal organization in assemblies and parliaments — party organization and formal organization (presiding officers, committees, and the like). A party system may function differently in a presidential government than it does in a parliamentary government. Parliamentary parties in Britain, as in most parliamentary systems, are disciplined, in that members of Parliament rarely vote in opposition to the instructions of party leaders. Because cabinets generally hold office as long as they can command a majority of the assembly, deviating from party discipline means risking the fall of the government and new elections.

In presidential systems, the executive and members of the assembly are elected for definite terms of office, and the fate of the party and of its members is less directly and immediately involved in voting on legislative measures. In American legislatures, party discipline operates principally with respect to procedural questions, like the selection of a presiding officer or the appointment of committees. On substantive legislative and policy issues, Democratic and Republican legislators, federal and state, are freer to decide whether or not to vote with party leaders. A comparison of roll-call votes in the American Congress and the British House of Commons would show much more consistency in party voting among British representatives.

All assemblies have a committee structure, some division of labor permitting specialized groups of legislators to deliberate on particular kinds of issues and recommend action to the whole assembly. Without such a sublegislative organization it would be impossible to handle the large flow of legislative business. But the importance of committees varies, as we have noted.

The power of committees generally varies with the relative power of the assembly and the executive. A parliamentary government with a strong and stable cabinet system usually has weak committees. The cabinet decides whether or not a bill will be enacted into law, and the parliament usually adopts it without basic changes. Where power is divided, as between a separately elected executive and assembly, the committees are more likely to acquire relative stability in membership, expertise in one field, and considerable influence on policy.

POLITICAL EXECUTIVES

All political systems have some form of central leadership, concentrated in an individual or a small group. When large numbers of people pursue collective goals, initiatives are inevitably taken, deliberative processes are organized and presided over, conflicts are resolved, and decisions are made and then implemented. In political systems, the agent or source of these processes is the *political executive*.

Types of Executives

Political executives have many names and titles, and their duties and powers also vary enormously. Even the functions and authority of the world's few remaining monarchs are strikingly different. Some political executives are called presidents, but their powers and functions may differ substantially. Some political executives are called prime ministers or premiers, others chairmen. Political executives can also be collective, with such titles as cabinet, council of ministers, politburo, or presidium.

Titles don't specify the functions these officials perform, but executives may be distinguished as shown in Table 7.2. Political executives are *effective* only if they have genuine powers in the enactment and implementation of laws and regulations. If they do not have these powers, they are symbolic or *ceremonial*.

Individual effective executives include the American presidency, an office with very substantial powers affecting all processes of government. Although the American executive includes collective bodies such as the Cabinet and the National Security Council, they advise the president instead of acting as collective decision makers. The French presidency is also a powerful individual executive, but we do not know yet how this office may develop in relation to the Council of Ministers, which is responsible

Table 7.2

Types of Political Executives: Examples from Selected Countries

Effective	*Ceremonial*
Individual	
President of the United States	Swedish king
Prime minister of Sweden	President of West Germany
President of France	British queen
Chancellor of West Germany	Japanese emperor
British prime minister	Chairman of the Supreme Soviet, U.S.S.R.
General secretary of the Central Committee, U.S.S.R.	President of India
President of Mexico	
Prime minister of India	
President of Tanzania	
Collective	
British Cabinet	British royal family
Japanese Cabinet	Presidium of the Supreme Soviet, U.S.S.R.
Politburo, U.S.S.R.	
Politburo, China	
Swiss Federal Council	

to the National Assembly. Thus far, French presidents have had the support of a majority in the National Assembly, hence the premier and the Council of Ministers have tended to be subordinate to the president. At the extreme of concentrated power was an executive like President Idi Amin of Uganda, who retained judicial power in his own hands and did not share his power in a consistent way with any other agency.

Saudi Arabia is an example of a surviving traditional kingship, in which a large concentration of power is regulated and limited by custom and tradition. Ministerial councils or cabinets may occur in these systems, but they tend to be dominated by the monarch. The first secretary of the Central Committee of the Soviet Union's Communist party is also an individual political executive. Under the regimes of Stalin, Khrushchev, and Leonid Brezhnev, the first secretary was the dominant figure in the Soviet system.

Sorting out political systems on the individual-collective scale is a bit more complicated. In Britain — in wartime — the political executive tends to be a prime minister. Strong prime ministers even in less troubled times may dominate their cabinets, but for the most part the British executive is a collective unit. The Cabinet meets regularly, makes important decisions, and acts on the basis of group deliberation. The Federal Council of Switzerland (Bundesrat) is an extreme example of a collective executive. The chairman of the Federal Council is elected annually and seems to be little more than a presiding officer. The power of the Soviet Politburo, another collective executive, varies. Under Stalin, particularly in his later years, the Politburo virtually ceased functioning; under Khrushchev, the Politburo met and made decisions; under Brezhnev, the executive became more of a collective, but in recent years Brezhnev has assumed a dominant role. There seems to be a pattern in Soviet leadership succession. In the beginning leadership is collective; as time goes on one individual becomes dominant.

Though we may speak of the political executive as being individual or collective, we are talking about the distribution of power and authority in it, not simple numbers. All executives have many members. They consist of elective and appointive officials who have policy-making power. A British prime minister makes some one hundred ministerial and junior ministerial appointments, a German chancellor may make a similar number. In the United States President Carter, on taking office, had some two thousand political appointments to make, of which two hundred were key policy-making positions in the executive branch.

A word or two about ceremonial executives may be appropriate. Monarchs like the British queen and Scandinavian kings are principally ceremonial and symbolic officers with very occasional political powers. They are living symbols of the state and nation and of its historical continuity. Britain's queen opens Parliament and makes statements on important holidays and anniversaries. When there is an election, or when a government falls, the queen appoints a new prime minister. She is the transmitter of legitimacy. Normally she has no choice in selecting a prime minister, since she picks the candidate likely to have a majority in Commons; but if there is doubt about which leader has a majority or who leads the party, the queen's discretion may be an important power.

In republican countries with parliamentary systems, presidents perform the functions that fall to kings and queens in parliamentary monarchies. German and Italian presidents issue statements, make speeches on important anniversaries, and designate prime ministers after elections or when a government has resigned.

A system in which the ceremonial executive is separated from the effective executive has a number of advantages. The ceremonial executive tends to be above politics and symbolizes unity and continuity. The American presidency, which combines both effective and ceremonial functions, risks the likelihood that the president will use her ceremonial and symbolic authority to enhance her political power, or that her involvement in politics may hamper her in performing her symbolic or unifying role. The Soviet Union and other communist countries tend to separate the ceremonial and the effective executives. In a formal sense, the chairman of the Supreme Soviet is the top executive. He greets distinguished visitors, opens and presides over meetings of the Supreme Soviet, and appoints ministers. When Brezhnev, the party first secretary, assumed the office of chairman of the Supreme Soviet, it was a departure from common practice.

Britain's royal family is an example of a collective ceremonial executive. So many occasions call for the physical presence of the monarch that members of the royal family share appearances. The activities of the royal family are reported daily in the press, giving legitimacy to a great variety of events. There is much riding in carriages, parading, and ritual in British public life. In contrast, the Scandinavian monarchies are more humdrum, and the Scandinavian royal institutions are sometimes called bicycle monarchies.

Functions of the Executive

Political executives typically perform important system functions. The executive is the locus of leadership in the political system. Lenins, Ataturks, Roosevelts, de Gaulles, and Adenauers hold the chief executive positions, and their energy, ideas, imagination, and resolution provide stabilizing and adaptive capacity to the political system.

Studies of childhood socialization show that the first role perceived by children tends to be the top political executive — the president, prime minister, and king or queen. In early childhood there is a tendency to identify the top political executive as a parent figure; as the child matures he begins to differentiate political from other roles, and among different political roles (see Chapter 3). The conduct of the political executive affects the trust and confidence which young people feel in the whole political system, and which they carry with them into adulthood. People who have experienced Roosevelt, Churchill, de Gaulle, or Adenauer in their childhoods bring different expectations into their adult political lives than would people who were children

In modernized nations monarchs are usually ceremonial executives, living symbols of political legitimacy; here Sweden's King Carl Gustaf conducts Spain's King Juan Carlos on a tour of Stockholm.

under Johnson or Nixon, MacMillan or Wilson, or Hitler.

The role of the political executive in recruitment is obviously important. Presidents, prime ministers, and first secretaries have large and important appointive powers, not only of cabinet and politburo members and government ministers, but of judges as well. Typically the political executive is the source of honors and distinctions to members of the government and private citizens — they give distinguished service medals, the Order of Lenin, knighthoods and peerages, and prizes of various kinds.

The political executive plays a central role in political communication, the top executive playing the crucial one. Presidents' press conferences, prime ministers' speeches in parliaments, cabinet members' testimony in committees, and the party leaders' speeches at the party congress may communicate important information regarding past, present, and future trends of domestic and foreign policy. These high level communications may be appeals for support or for improved performance in various sectors of the society and economy, or may outline new policies.

The executive is of central significance in the performance of the process functions. The executive may serve as an advocate of particular interests, as when a president supports the demands of minority groups or the business community or a prime minister supports the interests of pensioners or depressed regions. Cabinet members typically speak for particular interests, such as labor, business, agriculture, children, minority groups, and the like. They may play a crucial role as interest aggregators as they seek to build coalitions favoring legislation. Typically the executive is the most important structure in policy making. The executive normally initiates new policies, and depending on the division of powers between the executive and the legislature, has a substantial part in their adoption. The political executive also oversees the implementation of policies, and can hold subordinate officials accountable for their performance.

Whatever dynamism a political system has tends to be focused in the executive. A bureaucracy without an executive tends to implement past policies, not initiate new ones; and without direction of politically motivated ministers bureaucracies tend toward inertia and conservatism. The decision of a president, prime minister, cabinet, or politburo to pursue a new course in foreign or domestic policy will usually be accompanied by structural adaptations — the appointment of a vigorous minister, increasing the staff, establishing a special cabinet committee, and the like. Where the political executive is weak and divided, as in Fourth Republic France or contemporary Italy, this dynamic force is missing. Initiative then passes to the bureaucracy, legislative committees, and powerful interest groups, and general needs, interests, and problems may be neglected.

While the executive consists of the cabinet heads for all the policy areas its policy thrust will be reflected by its composition. New departures in foreign policy or welfare policy may be reflected in new appointments or rearrangements, and sometimes by the direct assumption of responsibility for a policy area by the chief political executive.

THE BUREAUCRACY

Modern societies are dominated by large organizations, and the largest organizations in these societies are the government bureaucracies. As governments increase efforts to improve the health, productivity, welfare, and security of their populations, the size of government organizations keeps increasing. In the centrally planned and coordinated communist societies, the vast majority of the population works for the government, and is thus part of the government bureaucracy. Table 7.3 estimates government employment as a percentage of all workers in a number of countries in the early 1960s. The figures include central and local employees at all levels of government, workers for public service enterprises like the post office, and employees of nationalized manufacturing industries. More recent figures would probably show even larger government sectors, at least outside agriculture, where even some communist nations have found private ownership necessary for good production. The figures are enormous, ranging into the millions for larger countries. Even in developing nations like India and Tanzania, government employees constitute a major part of the work force performing modern tasks.

Table 7.3
Size of Government Bureaucracies: Public Employees and Workers in Government-Owned Industries

Country[a]	Population[b] 1961	Active labor force, 1961[b]	Number of government and public enterprise workers, 1960[b]	Percentage of labor force employed by government
United States	183.7	69.9	8.9	13%
Britain	52.9	24.6	3.7	15
France	46.0	19.7	2.2	11
West Germany	54.0	26.8	2.6	10
Israel	2.2	.7	.2	29
U.S.S.R.	218.0	109.8	64.8	59
Japan	94.1	44.0	2.7	6
Kenya	8.5	3.3	.2	6
Nigeria	35.8	18.3	.2	1
India	442.2	189.0	6.5	3

[a] Countries ranked in order of 1960-GNP/Capita
[b] In millions.
Sources: Bruce Russett, et al., *World Handbook of Political and Social Indicators* (New Haven, Conn.: Yale University Press, 1964), pp. 70 ff; World Bank, *World Bank Tables, 1976* (Baltimore: Johns Hopkins University Press, 1976), pp. 614 ff; Frederic L. Pryor, *Property and Industrial Organization in Communist and Capitalist Nations* (Bloomington: Indiana University Press, 1973), pp. 46–47; Ellen Mickiewicz, *Handbook of Soviet Social Science Data* (New York: Free Press, 1973), p. 55.

Structure of the Bureaucracy

Of course, not all government employees are equally significant in the political process. Most important are the highly trained expert personnel of the top civil service. In his analysis of policy-making in Britain, F. M. G. Willson argues that "The policy-making centre of British government . . . consists of a group at most 3,500 strong, of whom only 100 are politicians or in any sense 'party political' appointees. These figures can be reduced to a nucleus of some 350, of whom not more than 50 — and probably nearer 30 — are 'party political.'"[4] Willson observes that the government consists of some one hundred front-bench members of Parliament, some twenty of whom serve in the Cabinet, and the remainder of whom serve as ministers, junior ministers, and parliamentary secretaries in charge of the government departments. This relatively small group of political policy makers confront some three thousand permanent higher civil servants largely recruited as young men from the universities directly into the higher civil service. They spend their lives as an elite corps, moving about from ministry to ministry, watching governments come and go, and becoming increasingly important as policy makers as they rise into the top posts.

The importance of the permanent higher civil service is not unique to Britain, though perhaps it has been most fully institutionalized there. In Swe-

[4] F. M. G. Willson, "Policy-Making and the Policy-Makers," in Richard Rose (ed.), *Policy Making in Britain* (New York: Free Press, 1969), pp. 360–361.

den and France, too, the higher civil service is filled with powerful generalists who can bring long tenure, experience, and technical knowledge to their particular areas. In the United States, many top positions go to presidential appointees, rather than permanent civil servants, but despite this difference, and a greater emphasis on technical specialization, there are permanent civil servants in the key positions just below the top appointees in such agencies as the Internal Revenue Service, the Central Intelligence Agency, the National Institute of Health, and all the cabinet departments. These men tend to be specialists, such as military officers, diplomats, doctors, scientists, economists, and engineers, and they exert great impact on the formulation and execution of policies in their specialties.

In the U.S.S.R. we may distinguish between the top party bureaucrats (the *apparatchiki*) who staff the secretariats of the Communist party, and the top officials of the various ministries and government agencies. The party secretariat is directly under the control of the Politburo of the Central Committee, and is the guardian of the party line laid down by the Politburo. It is the instrument of the political executive in enforcing party policy on the government ministries. Many students of communist politics in the past have pointed to the conflict between the ideological propensities of the central party elites and the rational-technological propensities of the officials in the government ministries. But a recent study concludes that there has been a trend toward the "emergence of a technical-managerial stratum of political leaders and a declining importance of ideological considerations in decision-making" and recruitment.[5] This suggests that the political executive, the politburo, has been using the party secretariat as a broadly supervisory corps, and as a means of reconciling the claims of various ministries with the general goals of the party elite.

Functions of the Bureaucracy

A functional analysis of the bureaucracy may suggest why this governmental organization has acquired such enormous significance in most contemporary societies. We have often stressed that most political agencies and institutions perform a number of different functions. The bureaucracy is almost alone in carrying out its function — the enforcement or implementation of laws, rules, and regulations. In a sense bureaucracies monopolize the output side of the political system. (Occasionally, of course, policy makers take the law into their own hands. The establishment of the "Plumbers" unit in the Nixon White House, and their performance of what are normally police and security functions, is an example of policy makers attempting directly to control implementation.)

In addition to this near monopoly of enforcement, bureaucracies greatly influence the processes of policy making. Most modern legislation is general and can be effectively enforced only if administrative officials work out regulations elaborating the policy. The extent to which a general policy is carried out usually depends on bureaucrats' interpretations of it and on the spirit and effectiveness with which they enforce it. Moreover, much of the adjudication in modern political systems is performed by administrative agencies, whether organized as independent regulatory bodies or as units in regular operating departments.

We discussed in Chapters 5 and 6 how bureaucratic agencies may serve as articulators and aggregators of interests. Departments like those for agriculture, labor, defense, welfare, and education may be among the most important spokesmen for interest groups. And when an agriculture department obtains agreement on policy among different agricultural interest groups, or when a labor department draws together competing trade unions around some common policy, bureaucrats are performing a significant interest-aggregating function.

Finally, bureaucracies are instrumental in performing the communication function. Even in democratic systems, the bureaucracy is one of the most important sources of information about public issues and political events. News reporters are constantly knocking at the doors of administrative officials in search of the latest information on all spheres of foreign and domestic policy. Although an aggressive press in a modern democracy may force considerable information out of the bureaucracy, bureaucrats

[5] William A. Welsh, "Communist Political Leadership," in Carl Beck, et al., *Comparative Communist Political Leadership* (New York: David McKay, 1973), p. 305.

Political communication is one of the important functions performed by the executive; here President Carter appeals on television for support for his program of energy development.

clearly have some control over the amount of information they divulge and the way it is interpreted. The decisions made by a political elite, whether executives or legislators, are also based to a considerable extent on the information they obtain from administrative agencies. Similarly, interest groups, political parties, and the public are dependent on the information transmitted by administrative officials.

The truth of the matter is that modern, complex societies cannot get along without bureaucracies, and it also seems to be practically impossible to get along with them. The title of a recent book, *Implementation: How Great Expectations in Washington Are Dashed in Oakland*, expresses this dilemma.[6] Public policies are statements of intent enacted by the executive and the assembly. They allocate resources and designate responsibility for the realization of these goals. But realization depends on the bureaucracy and the responsiveness of the groups affected by the policies. Policies may be lost in the thicket of bureaucratic infighting or twisted out of recognition by bureaucratic misunderstanding or opposition.

Creating and maintaining a responsive and responsible bureaucracy is one of the intractable problems of modern and modernizing society — capitalist or socialist, advanced or backward. It is a problem that can never be solved thoroughly, but only mitigated or kept under control by a variety of countervailing structures and influences.

Mark Nadel and Frances Rourke suggest the variety of ways that bureaucracies may be influenced and controlled externally or internally, through gov-

[6] Jeffrey Pressman and Aaron Wildavsky (Berkeley and Los Angeles: University of California Press, 1973).

Table 7.4
Typology of Controls for Bureaucratic Responsibility

	Formal	*Informal*
External	Directly or indirectly elected chief executive: president, prime minister, governor, etc. Elected assembly: congress, parliament, city council, etc. Courts Ombudsman	Public opinion Press Public interest groups Constituencies Competing bureaucratic organizations
Internal	Representative bureaucracy where legally required Citizen participation where legally required Decentralization	Perception of public opinion (anticipated reaction) Professional standards Socialization in the norms of responsibility

Source: Taken from Mark V. Nadel and Frances E. Rourke, "Bureaucracies," in Fred I. Greenstein and Nelson W. Polsby (eds.), *Handbook of Political Science*, Vol. 5. © 1975, Addison-Wesley, Reading, Mass., p. 416. Reprinted with permission.

ernment and nongovernment agencies and forces (see Table 7.4).[7] The major external government control is, as we have suggested, the political executive. Although presidents, prime ministers, and ministers formally command subordinate officials and have the power to remove them for nonperformance of duty, there is actually mutual dependence and reciprocal control between executives and bureaucracies. The power of the executive is typically expressed in efforts at persuasion; only rarely does it take the extreme form of dismissal or transfer. Centralized budgeting and administrative reorganization are other means by which the executive controls bureaucracy. The reallocation of resources among administrative agencies and the changing lines of authority may bring bureaucratic implementation into greater conformity with the aims of the political executive.

Assemblies and courts also exercise significant external controls over bureaucracy. Committee investigations, questions put to administrative agencies by assembly members, judicial processes controlling administrative excesses — all may have some effect on bureaucratic performance. The recent invention and rapid diffusion of the institution of the ombudsman is another indication of the problem of the control of bureaucracy from the perspective of injury or injustice to individuals.[8] In the Scandinavian countries, Britain, West Germany, and elsewhere

[7] Mark V. Nadel and Frances E. Rourke, "Bureaucracies," in Fred I. Greenstein and Nelson W. Polsby (eds.), *Handbook of Political Science*, Vol. 5 (Reading, Mass.: Addison-Wesley, 1975), pp. 373–440.

[8] See D. C. Rowat (ed.), *The Ombudsman: Citizen's Defender* (London: Allen and Unwin, 1965).

the ombudsman investigates claims of injury or of damage made by individuals as the result of government action, offering a procedure more expeditious and less costly than court action. Ombudsmen report to the legislative body for remedial action.

Among the extragovernmental forces and agencies that attempt to control bureaucracies are public opinion and the mass media; interest groups of various kinds, particularly the newer variety of public interest groups (like "Nader's Raiders"); and the constituencies of bureaucratic agencies, such as business, labor, farmers, minority groups, and the like.

Bureaucratic responsiveness and responsibility are also affected by internal controls, such as advisory committees formed of people representing many parties and many interest groups, and decentralization, which brings the bureaucracy closer to the groups it affects. Finally the attitudes and values of the bureaucrats themselves affect their responsiveness and responsibility. Different bureaucracies have different attitudes toward public opinion, the media, and political parties. The norms and values that bureaucrats bring with them as they are recruited into public service, and the standards and obligations they are taught to respect within public service, has an important bearing on bureaucratic performance.

The variety and kinds of controls we have been discussing operate in the advanced industrial democracies. Authoritarian systems lack many of these controls, particularly the external ones of elected political executives and legislators, independent courts, mass media, and interest groups. Communist systems seem particularly to be prone to bureaucratic inefficiency and conservatism, and their social costs must even be greater in view of the greater size of the public sector and greater scope of governmental activities. The principal controls are the agencies of the Communist party such as the politburo, the central committee and its secretariat, and the control committee. But in the absence of free and competitive elections, autonomous interest groups, and a free press, the effectiveness of these controls is limited.

Bureaucracy, in the sense of inefficiency and inertia, is pandemic. It is truly a dilemma since people are unlikely to invent any schemes for carrying out large-scale social tasks without the organization, division of labor, and professionalism that bureaucracy provides. Its pathologies can only be mitigated. The art of modern political leadership consists not only in the prudent search for appropriate goals and policies, but also in the attempt to learn how to interact with the massive and complex bureaucracy — how and when to press and coerce it, reshuffle it, terminate its redundant and obsolete parts, flatter and reward it, teach it, and be taught by it.

KEY TERMS

policy making
confederal systems
unitary systems
separation of powers
presidential regime
effective vs. ceremonial executive
permanent/career civil service
decision rules
federal systems
parliamentary regime
constitutional regime
bicameral vs. unicameral assembly
individual vs. collective executive
ombudsman

CHAPTER EIGHT

Public Policy

Public policies express the goals that emerge from policy making. Policies are intended outcomes. They also contain the means by which policy makers think to achieve these outcomes. A housing policy, for example, may set minimum housing standards for a society, and specify what efforts will be made to achieve those standards. These efforts may range from construction of all housing units by the government, as in the U.S.S.R., through financial encouragement of private construction by tax benefits and loan guarantees, as in the United States, to an absence of intervention in housing. The different goals and efforts in different systems indicate that leaders value different things, face competing goals, and have different ideas and means for achieving them.

There always will be a substantial gap between policy intentions and policy consequences. Policies are changed as they are implemented by the bureaucracy. Beyond these changes, the effect of policy on society is never certain. The yield of a tax depends upon the performance of the economy, the effectiveness of collection, and the attitudes of taxpayers. There may be long term, unintended consequences, as when tax benefits encourage new types of investment or saving. An appropriate metaphor for the efforts of policy makers is a crew guiding a vessel into a harbor. Constant soundings and sightings are necessary if the helmsman is to move the vessel towards its objective. Constant adjustment is necessary, in response to feedback about the consequences of the last effort. The politician, like the helmsman, cannot be sure of the responsiveness of his crew and vessel to his instructions, and cannot accurately predict current and wind in his environment. Policy implementation, output, outcome, feedback, and new policy efforts — these constitute the elements of public policy and policy performance. In this chapter we analyze the public policy level of political systems, considering in turn outputs, outcomes, evaluation, and development strategies.

POLITICAL PERFORMANCE

The outputs of the political system, both domestic and international, can be classified under four headings. First is the extraction of resources from the domestic and international environments: money, goods, persons, services. Second is distributive activity: what goods and services are distributed, and to whom? Third is the regulation of human behavior — the use of compulsion and inducement to enforce extractive and distributive compliance or otherwise bring about desired behavior. Finally is symbolic performance, referring to the political speeches, holidays, rites, public monuments and statues and the like used by leaders to exhort citizens to desired forms of conduct, to provide inspiring examples, to edify the population, and to socialize the young.

Extractive Performance

All political systems, even the most simple, extract resources from their environments. When primitive peoples go to war, for example, specific age groups may be called on to fight. Such direct extraction of services is still found in the most complex of modern states, in the form of military duty, other obligatory public service like jury duty, or compulsory labor imposed on those convicted of wrongdoing. In Table 8.1 we show the size of the military recruitment in selected countries, both in absolute terms and relative to the working age population. Israel is added to our usual list of countries to illustrate the great burden which that country's military efforts place upon her population. We can see that although Israel's army was slightly smaller than Egypt's, a much greater proportionate burden was placed upon the population to sustain those forces.

The most common form of resource extraction in contemporary systems is taxation. Taxation is the extraction of money or goods from members of a political system, considerations for which they receive no immediate and direct benefit. In Britain, for example, citizens earning $50,000 in wages pay half of that in personal income taxes; in West Germany, they would pay about 40 percent; in the United States or France, about 25 percent, if they did not take advantage of special exemptions.[1] Table 8.1 also shows the total revenues extracted both in absolute amounts and as a percentage of the gross domestic product of the society. Several important points are clear. First, we see that the Soviet Union, with its centralized command economy directly extracts about half of its national product, the largest proportion of any country in the table, although it is not as large as the proportion in some other communist nations. Second, we see that the size of the economy greatly affects the amount of resources a nation has to work with, both in absolute terms and relative to its population. The United States extracts less relative to production than other industrialized nations, but its great size and wealth give it more available resources than any other country. Finally, we see the plight of poorer nations, such as India. With limited resources, limited government capacity, and much of its domestic product supporting the farmers who produce it, India can only extract a small percentage of its resources. As it is a preindustrial nation, those resources are not great on a per capita basis, so relative to its population the political system has little with which to work. But in absolute terms, because of the country's vast size, the government has substantial revenue, which can be concentrated on particular projects. This explains why such a poor country as India can develop a substantial defense force and develop nuclear weapons, yet have a hard time in dealing with education and welfare needs or investing for economic growth.

The revenues in Table 8.1 do not come entirely from income taxes, as Table 8.2 shows. The United States and Japan obtain revenue largely from income taxes and other direct taxes; Germany and France, as well as the very poor nations, rely less on direct taxes; the Soviet Union uses them very little. Social security contributions, some paid by employers, are important revenue sources in most industrialized nations. Indirect taxes, such as property and sales taxes, and what are called turn-over and value-added taxes, in which taxes are collected from manufacturers, wholesalers, and retailers, and passed along indirectly to consumers, are major income sources in most nations. The poorest nations rely especially heavily on such indirect means as excise taxes on imported goods.

The special system of the Soviet Union and other centralized communist economies is also suggested in the table. The major tax is the turn-over tax, in which an average of 40 percent or 50 percent is added to the price of goods and taken in taxes. Additional revenue comes from the profits from the vast system

[1] Richard Musgrave, *Fiscal Systems* (New Haven, Conn.: Yale University Press, 1969).

Table 8.1

Extractive Performance in Selected Nations: Military Recruitment and Governmental Revenues

	Military recruitment		*Government revenue: 1973*		
Country[a]	*Total*	*Percent of population*	*Percent gross domestic product*	*Absolute in billions*[b]	*Per capita*[b]
United States	2,100,000	1.03	32	$484	$2268
West Germany	490,000	.77	41	174	2817
France	505,000	.94	38	128	2417
Japan	277,000	.25	22	108	976
United Kingdom	333,600	.60	38	87	1554
Israel	342,500	11.42[c]	39	5	1407
U.S.S.R.	3,375,000	1.35	51[d]	325[d]	1300[d]
Mexico	70,000	.12	9[e]	7	118
China	3,250,000	.41	n.a.	n.a.	n.a.
Egypt	349,000	1.05	28	3	78
Nigeria	250,000	.31	15[f]	1	22
Tanzania	15,000	.10	17[e]	1	29
India	941,000	.15	16	13	23

[a] Ranked by 1975 GNP per capita

[b] Calculated by multiplying previous column by absolute and per capita gross domestic product. (The available data are for GDP, rather than GNP, which we have used in earlier chapters. The two figures, however, are of similar magnitude for these nations.)

[c] Includes 300,000 on immediate mobilization status; standing military force is 42,500 which is 1.42 percent of population.

[d] All revenue data for U.S.S.R. are calculated from the estimated size of government sector [in Richard A. Musgrave, *Fiscal Systems* (New Haven, Conn.: Yale University Press, 1969), p. 43]. His estimate is for 1964. That percentage is multiplied by 1975 GNP [World Bank, from *World Bank Atlas* (Washington, D. C.: World Bank, 1977), pp. 6–7] to get the following columns. Because of the great differences in organization, comparisons between communist and less centralized economies should be regarded as only rough estimates. Also, all data are supplied by governments and should be used with caution.

[e] Central government only.

[f] 1970 data.

Sources: Robert C. Sellers (ed.), *Armed Forces of the World: A Reference Handbook*, 4th ed. (New York: Praeger, 1977); World Bank, *World Bank Tables*, 1976 (Baltimore: John Hopkins University Press, 1976), pp. 440–446; United Nations, *Yearbook of National Account Statistics*, 1976 (New York: United Nations, 1976).

Table 8.2

Sources of Government Revenue in Selected Nations, 1975

Country	Direct taxes	Indirect taxes	Social Security contri-butions and fixed fees	Profits and interest from state enterprise	Total
United States	42%	30%	24%	4%	100%
West Germany	29	31	36	4	100
France	17	35	40	8	100
Japan	44	30	24	2	100
United Kingdom	41	33	19	7	100
Israel	26	54	14	6	100
U.S.S.R.	7	38	22	32	99
Nigeria	23	57	7	13	100
India	19	73	2	6	100

Sources: United Nations, *Yearbook of National Account Statistics*, 1976 (New York: United Nations, 1976) for all nations except the U.S.S.R. The data for the U.S.S.R. are from Richard A. Musgrave, *Fiscal Systems* (New Haven, Conn.: Yale University Press, 1969), p. 43, and are for 1965. Data for Nigeria are for 1969. Expenditures may be greater than revenues, as revenues do not show the various forms of deficit financing.

of state-run industries. Because the government sets prices, these profits can be shaped by direct government policies.[2]

Sources of revenue are interesting because they determine who pays how much of the taxes. Income taxes in most nations are *progressive*; those who make more pay larger percentages of what they make. Thus, in the United States and Britain, the tax rate approximately doubles as income rises from $20,000 to $40,000. Indirect taxes tend to be more *regressive*; those making less money pay higher proportions of what they earn. A tax on food or clothing, for example, tends to be regressive because these items bulk larger in the budgets of the poor. Social security contributions are also regressive, especially if the employee pays all of them. Due to special provisions in the laws, however, it is often very difficult to say how progressive or regressive a particular tax system may be. Careful studies have cast doubt on whether the American tax system, one of the most carefully examined, is really progressive, despite its high reliance on the income tax.[3] In 1967 399 Americans with in-

[2] See Musgrave, *Fiscal Systems*, and Franklyn D. Holzman, "Economic Organization of Communism," in D. E. Sills (ed.), *International Encyclopedia of the Social Sciences*, Vol. 3 (New York: Macmillan, 1968), pp. 146 ff, for a more complete account.

[3] See Joseph A. Pechman and Benjamin A. Okner, *Who Bears the Tax Burden?* (Washington: The Brookings Institution, 1974.)

comes over $100,000 paid no tax at all on a combined income over $185 million, and 23 persons with incomes in excess of $1 million paid no tax on a combined income of $95 million.[4] Despite some changes since then, the overall picture is much the same. The substantial progressivity in the income tax is to a great extent counterbalanced by regressive taxes at other levels. Table 8.2 suggests that many other countries have even less progressive tax systems, although studies are not available to answer the question clearly.[5]

Distributive Performance

Our information on the varying amounts and incidence of extractive performance is limited, as comparative studies have only begun to make progress. Similar limitations face analysis of distributive performance: who benefits and to what degree. We know more about the rough efforts made by various political systems in different issue areas than we know about which individuals benefit from them. Table 8.3 indicates the efforts made by governments in different policy areas as a percentage of total domestic product. Although these figures are drawn from a variety of sources, especially from data released from the governments in question, and cannot be guaranteed as to accuracy, they are rough indicators of the countries' efforts.

Beginning with education, we see that expenditures range from a high of 7 percent in the Soviet Union to around 3 percent in India and Mexico. Education is one of the most important aspects of distributive performance, as the population's education level is closely related to its skill and productivity. Education is also an important personal and political resource, encouraging those who possess it to improve their own welfare, and to make demands on the political system. Despite its importance, poor nations have difficulty making great strides in education. United Nations studies show that percentage expenditures for education were rising throughout the world in the 1960s, but they rose faster in the industrialized nations than in the poor ones. And we recall from Table 8.1 that the different income bases of these nations mean that differences in absolute expenditures, and expenditures relative to need, were rising much faster than the percentages. The gap between rich and poor has been increasing.

In expenditures on defense we see an even wider range, from nearly a third of national product in Israel (and a fifth in Egypt) to 2 percent or less for Japan and Mexico. Defense is one area where per capita wealth has little relationship to spending in percentage terms. Nations locked in tense international confrontations, or undertaking efforts at widespread influence, make major defense efforts, even at the cost of a great drain on other areas and on total resources. Thus, Israel and Egypt show extremely high expenditures due to the Middle East confrontations; and the United States and the Soviet Union make large efforts reflecting their mutual tension and their arms race.

Social security and health expenditures, on the other hand, are affected by levels of wealth. It is difficult for poor nations to spare the resources for welfare programs, given their limited budgets and many demands, as Harold Wilensky's study of sixty-four nations shows.[6] In both absolute and relative terms expenditure on social security in poor nations tends to be limited. This is due only in part to the rather young age of their populations and the role of the extended family in caring for the elderly and infirm. All the wealthier nations make efforts to assist the aged and unemployed; however, differences in expenditures reflect policy and historical experience. The United States made a much greater effort, and much earlier, in mass education than did most European nations; on the other hand, Americans began spending on social insurance and public services much later, and still do much less. Americans have historically put much more emphasis on equality of opportunity, less on welfare obligations, than Europeans.

Wilensky also found that centralized governments, well-organized working-class parties and movements, and low military expenditures were all associated with stronger efforts in welfare. Interest-

[4] Bernard P. Herber, *Modern Public Finance* (Illinois: Richard Irwin, 1971), p. 147.

[5] See Arnold Heidenheimer, Hugh Heclo, and Carolyn Teich Adams, *Comparative Public Policy* (New York: St. Martin's Press, 1975), ch. 8.

[6] Harold Wilensky, *The Welfare State and Equality* (Berkeley: University of California Press, 1975).

Table 8.3

Distributive Performance in Selected Nations as Percentage of Gross Domestic Product, 1974

	Government Expenditures					
Country[a]	*Public education*	*Defense*	*Welfare*[b]	*Other*[c] *government*	*Non-governmental*[d] *sector of national product*	*Total national product*
United States	6%	6%	13%	7%	68%	100%
West Germany	4	4	18	12	62	100
France	5	4	22	5	64	100
Japan	4	2	10	1	83	100
United Kingdom	6	5	16	12	61	100
Israel	4	31	12	11	42	100
U.S.S.R.	6	12	10	23	49	100
Mexico	3	1	n.a.	n.a.	n.a.	100
China	4	6	n.a.	n.a.	n.a.	100
Egypt	6	20	n.a.	n.a.	n.a.	100
Nigeria	4	4	2	5	85	100
Tanzania	4	4	n.a.	n.a.	n.a.	100
India	3	3	2	5	87	100

[a] Ranked by 1974 GNP per capita.

[b] Includes social security and public health expenditures.

[c] Calculated by subtracting the sum of columns 2, 3, and 4 from total government disbursements.

[d] Calculated by subtracting total governmental disbursements from Gross Domestic Product and dividing by Gross Domestic Product.

Sources: Ruth Leger Sivard, *World Military and Social Expenditure 1977* (Leesburg, Va.: WMSE Publications, 1977), pp. 20–31; United Nations, *Yearbook of National Account Statistics, 1976* (New York: United Nations, 1976); Richard A. Musgrave, *Fiscal Systems* (New Haven, Conn.: Yale University Press, 1969), p. 41; Charles S. Taylor and Michael C. Hudson, *World Handbook of Political and Social Indicators*, 2nd ed. (New Haven, Conn.: Yale University Press, 1972), pp. 30–37; and Harold Wilensky, *The Welfare State and Equality* (Berkeley: University of California Press, 1975), pp. 122–124.

ingly, among wealthier nations, the communist systems of Eastern Europe and the democracies of Western Europe show similar levels of welfare efforts.[7] In Table 8.3 we see that the Soviet Union makes a slightly less substantial effort than the United States and that both are well behind Britain, France, and West Germany. We would find, however, Czechoslovakia's effort is quite comparable to France's.[8] We can see here that policy efforts reflect a combination of available resources, competing so-

[7] Wilensky, *Welfare State*, ch. 3–4. A similar conclusion is reached by Frederick L. Pryor, *Property Public Expenditures in Communist and Capitalist Nations* (Homewood, Ill.: Irwin, 1968).

[8] Wilensky, *Welfare State*, pp. 122–124.

Political systems extract many kinds of resources. Here the deputy commander in China's People's Liberation Army coaches a woman in China's Militia in firing practice.

cial needs and demands, and leaders' preferences and strategies. All political systems must choose how much to extract and how and for what purposes they will distribute what they extract. The wealthy systems can extract more easily, and face less painful decisions on distribution. But the recent tax rebellion in the United States, and the unrest over the level of taxation in other industrial democracies suggests that limits have been exceeded.

The last category of government expenditures in Table 8.3 includes a variety of government activities, including administrative costs, debt payments, minor subsidy programs, economic spending, housing, and the like; and capital investment in the economy. In most governments these expenditures account for some 5 to 10 percent of national product. However, in communist governments — at least in the relatively industrialized states of Eastern Europe on which we have data — this area accounts for a quarter to a half of national product. For the U.S.S.R. this area accounts for nearly a quarter of national product, and nearly half of government spending. These figures emphasize the differences between the market-oriented regimes, in which much, if not most, economic investment is left to private enterprise, and the command economies of Soviet-style communism. In the latter, government capital investment, reflecting government ownership of major industries, is responsible for huge government spending.[9] In these systems, investment is a matter of government direction and decision.

Regulative Performance

Regulative performance refers to the exercise of control by a political system over the behavior of in-

[9] Musgrave, *Fiscal Systems*, ch. 2.

dividuals and groups in the society. Although we usually associate regulation with legal coercion or its threat, political systems commonly control behavior through exhortation and material or financial inducements as well.

The regulative activities of modern political systems have proliferated enormously over the last century or so. Industrialization and urban concentration have produced interdependence, and problems in traffic, health, and public order. Growth in industry has created problems with monopolies, industrial safety, and labor exploitation. At the same time, the growth of science and the predominance of the attitude that man can control the environment have led to a recognition of the possibility of meeting these problems with government actions. Modernization has produced a blanket of regulatory activities.

The pattern of regulation varies not only with the broad socioeconomic and cultural changes associated with modernization, but with changes in other cultural values. Thus, in recent years the scope of regulation in the United States has extended to include the protection of voting rights, racial segregation, prohibition of discrimination against minority groups and women in employment, control of pollution, and the like. At the same time, regulation of birth control, abortion, divorce, and sexual conduct in most modern nations has lessened.

In characterizing the regulative performance of a political system we answer the following questions:

1. What aspects of human behavior and interaction are regulated and to what degree? Does the government regulate such domains as family relations, economic activity, religious activity, political activity, geographical mobility, professional and occupational qualifications, and protection of person and property?
2. What sanctions are used to compel or induce citizens to comply? Does the government use exhortation and moral persuasion, financial rewards and penalties, validation of some types of action, physical confinement or punishment, and direction of various activities?
3. What groups in the society are regulated, and with what procedural limitations on enforcement? Are these sanctions applied uniformly or do they affect different areas or groups differently?

Of course, all modern nations use all these sanctions in varying degrees. But the variety of patterns is great, and reflects values, goals, and strategies. Governments have taken over various industries in most nations, for example, but the range is very different. In 1960, one study shows, government in the United States employed only 1 percent of the persons engaged in mining and manufacturing and 28 percent of those working for utilities; in France, the corresponding figures were 8 percent and 71 percent; in the Soviet Union they were 93 percent and 100 percent.[10] Even in the Soviet Union, however, and to a greater degree in Eastern Europe, performance difficulties and peasant opposition have led to the retention of substantial private production in agriculture.

Although space compels us to treat the critical area of regulative performance briefly,[11] one final aspect must be emphasized: government control over political participation and communication. We noted in Chapter 4 that the presence or absence of political competition was an essential structural feature of political systems. Political systems vary from authoritarian regimes that prohibit party organization, the formation of voluntary associations, and freedom of communication, to democratic systems, where such rights are protected. Government regulatory performance in this area has a crucial effect on the political processes.

Table 8.4 shows the ratings of civil liberties in a variety of countries, as reported by the Freedom House "Comparative Survey of Freedom" for 1977. The countries are ranked by their level of GNP/Capita for that same year. In the countries rated "1" the press is free to criticize the government and regularly does so, and individuals are free to discuss politics without fear. The second level countries aspire to this degree of liberty, but various government infringements, such as controls introduced to check terrorism in West Germany and Israel in 1977, prevent its full realization. Those nations we usually

[10] Frederick L. Pryor, *Property and Industrial Organization in Communist and Capitalist Nations* (Bloomington: Indiana University Press, 1973), pp. 46–47.

[11] A much more extensive discussion of all forms of performance, outcome, development strategy, and political goods can be found in Gabriel Almond and G. Bingham Powell, *Comparative Politics: System, Process, Policy* (Little, Brown, 1978), ch. 11–14.

Table 8.4
Regulative Performance: Civil Liberties Ratings for Selected Nations, 1977

Country[a]	*Rating of civil liberties*[b]
United States	1
West Germany	2
France	2
Japan	1
United Kingdom	1
U.S.S.R.	6
Israel	2
Mexico	3
Nigeria	4
China	6
Egypt	4
Tanzania	6
India	2

[a] Ranked by 1977 GNP per capita, estimated by World Bank, *1978 World Bank Atlas* (Washington: World Bank, 1978), pp. 27–30.

[b] Freedom House's "Comparative Survey of Freedom" ratings are based on a variety of criteria; the civil liberties ranking emphasizes above all the freedom of the press and other mass media from government control. The highest ranking, for greatest civil liberties, is a "1"; the lowest is "7."

Sources: Raymond D. Gastil (ed.), *Freedom in the World: Political Rights and Civil Liberties 1978* (Boston: Freedom House and G. K. Hall and Co., 1978), pp. 10–17.

characterize as democracies fall into one of the first two categories. In Mexico the government limits the criticism of an often vigorous press through control of newsprint supplies and sometimes through direct intervention. In such nations as Egypt and Nigeria there are some elements of press criticism and/or civil rights, but there are also broad areas of systematic repression. In the nations ranked "6" the government exerts complete control over all the mass media, and no individual rights rank ahead of those of the government, as in the Communist regimes of the U.S.S.R. and China. Tanzania also checks freedom of dissent closely in all areas. These estimates provide a general overview of government regulatory performance in limiting internal criticism and freedom.

Symbolic Performance

A fourth category of political system outputs is symbolic performance. Much of communication by political leaders takes the form of appeals to history, courage, boldness, wisdom, and magnanimity embodied in the nation's past; or to values and ideologies, such as equality, liberty, community, democracy, communism, liberalism, or religious tradition; or promises of future accomplishment and rewards. Political systems differ in citizens' confidence in their leaders and faith in their political symbols. Symbolic outputs are also intended, however, to enhance other aspects of performance: to make people pay their taxes more readily and honestly, comply with the law more faithfully, or accept sacrifice, danger, and hardship. Such appeals may be especially important in time of crisis. Some of the most magnificent and most successful examples may be found in Winston Churchill's stirring speeches to the British people during the dangerous moments when Britain stood alone after the fall of France in World War II. But symbolic performance is also important in less extreme circumstances. Political leaders seek to influence citizen behavior in energy crises, or in times of drought, famine, and disaster. Jawboning — exhorting business executives and labor leaders to go slow in raising prices and wages — is a frequently employed anti-inflation measure. Public buildings, plazas, monuments, holidays with their parades, and civic and patriotic indoctrination in schools all contribute to the sense of governmental legitimacy among the population, and their willingness to comply with public policy.

OUTCOMES OF POLITICAL PERFORMANCE

In discussing political performance we have emphasized that outputs should be regarded as efforts, not accomplishments. How extractive, distributive, regulative, and symbolic efforts affect society is not dependent on effort alone. It also depends on the existing state of the society and on other changes taking place in the environment. The American government may modify its tax policy in times of high unemployment, giving a tax rebate to increase consumption and stimulate the economy, but if extremely cold weather hits and the rebate may be spent on increased heating costs, or if a sudden rise in international oil prices increases fuel expenses, the rebate may fail to stimulate the economy. A full discussion of the outcomes of political performance is beyond the scope of this chapter, but we can provide a few examples of some of the most important aspects of political outcomes.

Domestic Welfare Outcomes

One of the most important areas of public policy is domestic welfare. Table 8.5 offers data on some aspects of material welfare in our selected political systems. First we examine distribution of income, which is affected by tax and social security policies. The first column shows the nations' per capita gross national product, the total goods and services produced divided by the population. The second column shows a rough measure of the distribution of income in a country, the proportion of income received by the wealthiest fifth of society.

The most equitable systems in these terms are the United States and Britain, where the top fifth receives about 39 percent of income before taxes. We

Table 8.5

Welfare Outcomes in Selected Nations

Country	*GNP per capita 1975*	*Income share of top 20 percent*[a]	*Yearly growth rate of GNP per capita, 1960–75*	*Life expectancy at birth*[b] *Men*	*Women*	*Rooms per person*[c]
United States	$7120	39%	2.5%	69 years	77 years	1.7
West Germany	6670	53	3.5	68	75	1.2
France	5950	54	4.2	69	76	1.1
Japan	4450	40	7.7	71	76	.9
Great Britain	3780	39	2.2	68	74	1.4
U.S.S.R.	2550	n.a.	3.8	64	74	.7
Mexico	1050	64	3.2	63	67	.3
China	380	n.a.	5.2	60	63	n.a.
Egypt	260	n.a.	1.5	52	54	.6
Tanzania	170	61	3.0	40–41	40–41	n.a.
India	140	52	1.3	42	41	.4

[a] Figures are for various years in the 1960s and reflect income before taxes but after transfer payments.

[b] Years are mostly in the 1970s, except for India and Egypt, where the most recent data are from 1960.

[c] Figures are for the 1960s.

Sources: World Bank, *World Bank Atlas* (Washington, D.C.; World Bank, 1977), pp. 8–9; Hollis Chenery et al., *Redistribution with Growth* (London: Oxford University Press, 1974), pp. 8–9; United Nations, *United Nations Demographic Yearbook, 1976* (New York: United Nations, 1977), pp. 130–136; United Nations, *United Nations Statistical Yearbook, 1976* (New York: United Nations, 1977), pp. 880–887.

have no data on the Soviet Union; however income distribution statistics for Bulgaria and Czechoslovakia show substantially more equal distributions in these centrally controlled systems, with the top fifth receiving only about one-third. Least equitable of these systems is Mexico, where economic growth has been associated with great concentration of income since World War II, with the top fifth receiving 64 percent of the income in the late 1960s.

Another crucial economic indicator is growth. Richer nations, with few exceptions, enjoy more rapid growth than poor nations, in part because of lower rates of population growth. Mexico's per capita growth rate in 1960–1975, for example, was half of its absolute growth because of its high rate of population increase. Egypt's per capita growth rate was very low because of population increases, a pattern also clear in India. Japan's impressive expansion, on the other hand, is supported by a relatively stable population. And although their growth rates are lower, population stability in France and the U.S.S.R. produced very healthy increases in per capita growth.

Table 8.5 shows two other indicators of welfare: life expectancy and housing facilities. Life expectancy at birth is strongly shaped by the general control of disease, and especially by the likelihood that babies will survive their first year. As we can see, life expectancy is generally high in most wealthier nations, much lower in poorer ones. Finally, the table shows housing facilities, in terms of the average number of rooms available for each person. Here we see the effects of general prosperity, government policies, and income equality. In the United States and Britain, wealthy nations with rather equal income distribution, there are about one and one-half rooms for each citizen. Britain's extensive government housing construction has probably increased the equity of these figures. France is a wealthy nation, but income equality is less, and average housing is a little over one room per person. The Soviet Union is a substantially wealthy nation, and has high equality, but government policies over the last two decades have stressed growth of defense and heavy industry, not increases in consumer goods. Housing is therefore limited. Mexico has the most limited housing facilities of all, reflecting both its relatively limited national income and its unequal distribution. India is also inadequately housed, but that reflects limitations of its resources, rather than inequality of distribution.

The figures in Table 8.5 are crude indicators of some aspects of citizen welfare. A more complete glimpse of policy effects is shown in Table 8.6, which focuses on education, an important aspect of welfare. In the first column we see each country's education goals, the number of years that children are required to attend school. The next three columns describe education policy performance. First, we see the expenditure on public education as a percentage of GNP. The next column shows how that effort translates into actual dollars. Then we see those dollars relative to population size, a crude measure of the amount available for the children who must be educated. We can see that rather small efforts in Germany translate into much greater expenditures per child than the proportionally greater effort in Egypt, or the equivalent one in China. The Soviet Union makes a greater effort to get the same per capita output as Japan, and less than the United States.

The final two columns show the policy outcomes in the short run and the long run. The short run-effort is the percentage of the five to nineteen year-olds in school. This percentage is greatly affected by the dollars actually spent, although differences in efficiency and emphasis on mass or elite education also shape this outcome. Finally, we see the long-term outcome in terms of literacy. Literacy is affected by education programs, but only slowly, unless very substantial adult education programs are undertaken. In countries like India and Tanzania, the older generation is largely illiterate, and it will take a long time for the education of the younger generation to have its effects. China has made more of an effort at adult education, although these data must be treated with caution, as they are merely estimates.

Table 8.6 reveals the sobering difficulties of trying to change societies, even in an area such as literacy, where modern methods and technology are available. It is hard for a poor country to spend a high percentage of its GNP on education because that means sacrifices elsewhere. And in any case, the country's revenue is probably limited, because much of the national income simply feeds the producers. No matter how large the country's percentage effort may be, it does not translate into much per child, be-

Table 8.6
Education Policy in Selected Nations

		Educational performance outputs in 1974			Educational Outcomes	
Country	Policy goals: years of required education	Effort: percentage GNP spent on public education	Absolute output (in millions of U.S. dollars)	By need: education dollars per capita	Percentage of 5–19 year olds in school	Percentage of adults literate
United States	10–12	5.6	$80,300	$379	84%	99%
West Germany	9	4.1	15,772	254	67	99
France	10	5.3	14,363	273	69	99
Japan	9	4.0	17,908	163	68	99
United Kingdom	11	5.9	11,377	203	84	98
U.S.S.R.	8	6.0	42,000	166	64	99
Mexico	6	2.5	1,595	28	56	82
Egypt	6	5.4	555	15	41	40
China	n.a.	4.0	8,200	10	62	95
Tanzania	7	3.6	75	5	21	18
India	5	2.0	1,881	3	38	36

Sources: UNESCO, *Statistical Yearbook* (Paris: UNESCO, 1976), pp. 123–143; Ruth Leger Sivard, *World Military and Social Expenditures*, 1977 (Leesburg, Va.: WMSE Publications, 1977), pp. 20–31.

cause the resource base is so small and the population is growing rapidly, pouring children into the new schools. The older population is largely illiterate, so that the net effect on literacy is small.

Domestic Security Outcomes

Personal safety and security are also highly valued policy outcomes. Indeed, maintaining order and national security and protecting person and property are the most fundamental responsibilities of government. Table 8.7 illustrates the relative size of internal security forces, a measure of regulative output, and shows several different measures of internal security outcomes. The size of internal security forces, as we see, is a poor predictor of crime rates or political unrest. The absence of a relationship reflects the fact that other factors influence the expression of violence, such as the disciplined party system and control of communication in the U.S.S.R., and the relative size of the military.

Despite the general rise of crime in many modern societies, we have relatively little comparative data. Murder rates are usually considered the most reliable statistics, although they are often not closely related to other crime levels. We see in Table 8.7 that there is a great variation in the countries for which we have data, with the United States and Mexico having much higher rates than the European nations and Japan. We do not know much about the causes of these rates, although much research is now being done on the effect of cultural values, the prevalence of handguns in the society, the number of people between fifteen and twenty-five, and the like. But there

Table 8.7

Domestic Security Outcomes in Selected Nations

		Security outcomes			
				Deaths from political violence, 1958–1967	
Country	*Regulative output: security forces per 1000 working population, 1965*	*Murders per million, 1967*	*Riots (yearly average), 1958–1967*	*Total*	*Yearly average per million*[a]
United States	3.5	138	61.3	289	.14
West Germany	3.6	25	2.9	4	.01
France	4.7	18	.4	101	.21
Japan	2.3	28	6.5	2	.00
Great Britain	2.7	15	3.8	3	.01
U.S.S.R.	2.6	n.a.	2.9	299	.12
Mexico	n.a.	319[b]	5.2	280	.66
China	1.6	n.a.	12.0	6224	.89
Egypt	6.6	n.a.	.2	0	0
Tanzania	.2	n.a.	1.2	86	.82
India	2.1	n.a.	30.8	3203	.66

[a] Uses 1965 population.

[b] Data are for 1960.

Sources: Charles S. Taylor and Michael C. Hudson, *World Handbook of Political and Social Indicators*, 2nd ed. (New Haven, Conn.: Yale University Press, 1972), pp. 42 ff, 94 ff, 110 ff; Central Statistical Office, *Social Trends* (London: Her Majesty's Stationery Office, 1972), p. 179; and President's Commission on Law Enforcement, Task Force Report, *Crime and Its Impact: An Assessment* (Washington, D.C.: Government Printing Office, 1967), p. 39.

is little disagreement that in this regard, domestic security outcomes in the United States are not very satisfactory.

The other columns show the number of riots and deaths by political violence. The absence of riots indicates the ability of groups in a society to resolve issues short of violence, and the degree of people's satisfaction with government. But it also reflects the extent to which nations successfully impose discipline on their populations, the amount of freedom they accord them, and the amount and incidence of policing. The figures on deaths by political violence have been translated into relative terms, to indicate the immediate impact on citizens, although both riots and deaths are often confined to particular areas and groups. We might note also that riots are much more likely to result in deaths when they reflect direct antagonism between ethnic groups, rather than economic or political discontent with the government. All these data must be viewed with great caution, as they have been taken from the public press, which is more reliable in some nations than others.

The data also hide great fluctuations from year to year. In France the incidence of riots was high under the Fourth Republic in the 1950s, but death by violence was highest in 1962, when the secret terrorist organization (OAS) was attempting to force the government to change its Algerian policy. In the United States there was an explosion of rioting in the 1960s associated with the black rebellion and the Vietnam War. The Chinese figures reflect the beginning of the Cultural Revolution, those for India, ethnic conflict. British figures would be much greater in the following decade, as both the number of security forces and the incidence of violence escalated in Northern Ireland. Egypt faced a major burst of violence over food prices in 1977.

Outcomes in the International Arena

Thus far, we have discussed outputs and outcomes in the domestic sphere. Of course, international events and actions affect all domestic outcomes, as we suggested in Chapter 2. Nations extract resources from the international sphere through many devices, ranging from confiscating spoils of war to forcing favorable trade agreements to obtaining international aid and loans. Similarly, nations distribute resources internationally, as they face unfavorable trade arrangements, pay war reparations, or make loans or grants to other nations. International performance has a substantial impact on domestic welfare, reflected in growth of the economy or internal wealth. The impact of the increase in oil prices following the pricing agreements of the oil producing nations is one recent example of the domestic effects of international outcomes.

Perhaps the most important international area, however, is the regulation of conflict. Table 8.8 shows international security outcomes since 1816 in terms of the number of wars and battle deaths incurred by each country. Over time these costs of international security have escalated. Most of the deaths

In times of crisis the distributive performance of government can be a matter of life and death. Here flour from the United States is distributed during a famine in Kasai (Congo).

Table 8.8

International Security Outcomes for Selected Nations, 1816–1965

Country	*Years in international system*	*Number of wars*[a]	*Battle deaths*[a]	*Battle deaths per year*
Russia	150	15	9,662,560	64,417
Germany[b]	141	6	5,353,500	41,181
China	106	8	3,110,500	29,344
Japan	99	7	1,365,300	13,791
France	148	19	1,943,840	13,134
United Kingdom	150	19	1,295,280	8,635
United States	150	6	608,000	4,059
India	19	3	5,000	263
Egypt	29	2	5,000	172
Mexico	135	3	19,000	141
Tanzania	5	0	0	0

[a] Does not include civil wars.

[b] Figures are for Prussia before unification in 1871.

Source: J. David Singer and Melvin Small, *The Wages of War 1816–1965* (New York: John Wiley, 1972), pp. 275 ff.

are concentrated in the twentieth century and civilian deaths, which the table does not show, have escalated even more rapidly. With the development of nuclear weapons large-scale war promises to become far more destructive to lives and property and far more random in its victims.

The tension between security output and outcome is also suggested by the introduction of a new measure of human battle costs, "mega-deaths," which would be appropriate in a post–nuclear war version of Table 8.8. Up until 1914 the incidence and magnitude of war seemed to bear some relationship to public policy. The alliance that defeated Napoleon in 1815 viewed the Europe constituted by the Treaty of Vienna as an outcome worth the costs in blood and treasure of the long Napoleonic wars. Victorious Prussia under Otto von Bismarck could view the Austrian and French wars of the mid-nineteenth century as reasonable costs for German unification under Prussia. It is well to note, however, that the Franco-Prussian War was in some sense a prelude to World War I; as World War I was prelude to World War II, when the relationship between war as means and the reasonableness of its outcome began to grow apart. With the development and use of nuclear weapons at the end of World War II, this relationship may be said to have been broken.

However, even though actual resort to large-scale war is viewed as unthinkable, budget allocations for military purposes, the development of more versatile weaponry, and the deployment of such military means continues to be a crucial component of international policy, intended to maintain or alter an inherently unstable balance of terror. International disarmament efforts to reduce the danger that these capabilities will be used are still in an early stage.

Feedback

The outcomes of policy making are not the end of the process. As we indicated in Chapter 1 (see Figure 1.3), outcomes feed back into the system as new inputs. These feedback effects are moderated by the political culture of the society. Citizens react to a growth of 5 percent in the GNP, or increases in the murder rate, or deaths in battle. Their interpretation of these events leads to changes in their policy demands, in their supports for leaders, and in their obedience to the law. As demands are articulated through interest groups and parties, policy making begins again. Or, more accurately, it continues, in a perpetual interaction between the political system and its environment, as individuals and groups seek to achieve their purposes.

POLITICAL GOODS AND POLITICAL PRODUCTIVITY

Our approach to political analysis leads us from process to performance to evaluation. If we are to compare and evaluate the workings of different political systems, we need a checklist to direct our attention to the variety of goods that can be produced by political action. One society or one group of citizens may value order and stability; another may value participation and liberty. They may value these with different intensity, and their preferences and the intensity of them may change with time and circumstances.

A System, Process, and Policy Approach to Political Goods

Evaluation of political performance is inescapable, even when we think we are being completely unbiased. A long tradition in political analysis has emphasized the system goods of order, predictability, and stability. Descriptions and analyses stressed, at least implicitly, the undesirable features of system breakdown, of too frequent changes of regime or rulers. Another school of thought has emphasized goods associated with process, citizen participation and freedom of political competition. Democracy is good and authoritarianism is bad, according to this school of thought, which directs research to the maintenance of democracy. Systems rejecting it or failing to sustain it are considered unsuccessful. Recent interest in human needs, in the quality of life, and in the tremendous problems of economic development has led to a concern with policy goods, such as economic welfare and personal security. A political system that improves welfare, decreases inequalities, or cleans up its environment becomes the model.

These schools of thought are all concerned with important practical goods valued by most people in varying degrees and under varying circumstances. Without accepting any particular theory about basic human needs and values, we can say that each of these goods, and others not listed here, have been valued by many people in many societies. Table 8.9 draws on our three-level analysis of political systems, and on the work and thought of a number of scholars and thinkers, to present a brief checklist of goods that can be produced by political systems. In describing any particular political system, we at least need to consider the domestic and international goods depicted here. Future research will doubtless suggest additional goods for inclusion, and further illuminate the relationships between these goods and their production in different environments.

We cannot deal with these items at great length, but we can emphasize a few of the ideas involved. System goods have to do with the regularity and predictability of the working of political systems, and with the ability of systems to adapt to environmental challenges and changes. Regularity and adaptability are typically somewhat in conflict. On one hand, most people feel anxiety if there are serious interruptions and changes in the routine and behavior of political life. Successions of military coups or the continuing collapses of cabinet governments or resignations of presidents create a sense of unease and unpredictability. On the other hand, as conditions change — as wars, rebellions, and economic disasters occur — or as aspirations change, people feel a need for the political system to respond.

At the process level, we identify such goods as effective, satisfying participation, which is typically desired by most citizens if given a choice and which produces generally positive views of the political sys-

Table 8.9

The Productivity of Political Systems

Levels of political goods	*Classes of goods*	*Content and examples*
Systems level	System maintenance	Regularity and predictability of processes in domestic and international politics
	System adaptation	Structural and cultural adaptability in response to environmental change and challenges
Process level	Participation in political inputs	Instrumental to domestic and foreign policy; directly productive of a sense of dignity and efficacy, where met with responsiveness
	Compliance and support	Fulfillment of citizen duty and patriotic service
	Procedural justice	Equitable procedure and equality before the law
Policy level	Welfare	Growth per capita; quantity and quality of health and welfare; distributive equity
	Security	Safety of person and property; public order; national security
	Liberty	Freedom from regulation, protection of privacy, and respect for autonomy of other individuals, groups, and nations

tem. Participation is not merely valued instrumentally, as a means to force political elites to respond, but for its own sake, because it increases the individual's sense of competence and dignity. Compliance can also be a good, as individuals seek to avoid penalties or to respond to the powerful impulse to serve others, which can be one of man's most gratifying experiences. President Kennedy in his inaugural address called on such impulses to serve and sacrifice when he said, "Ask not what your country can do for you, but what you can do for your country." Young people, especially, in national crises in many countries have almost always volunteered their services with an enthusiasm that cannot be explained by any simple calculation of the individual benefits from increasing policy effectiveness. Procedural justice (trial by jury, habeas corpus, no cruel and unusual punishment) is another crucial process value, whose deprivation is a severe blow to citizens, and without which other goods may be impaired.

At the policy level we come to the values of welfare, its quantity, quality, and equity; personal and national security; and freedom from interference in a life of reasonable privacy. We have already discussed, indirectly, some of the welfare and security goods, but more must be said about liberty, which is sometimes only viewed as a purely negative good, a freedom from governmental regulation and harassment. Freedom is more than inhibition of government action, since infractions of liberty and privacy may be initiated by private individuals and organizations. In fact, liberty may be fostered by government intervention, when private parties interfere with the liberty of others. Much recent legislation regarding racial segregation may be understood in these terms. At such points, of course, different groups and perspectives may come to conflict over liberty. We should also emphasize that liberty feeds back into many other goods. Liberty to act, organize, obtain information, and protest is an indispensable part of effective political participation. Nor is it irrelevant to such policy goods as social, political, and economic equality. We have seen that in the command economies of Eastern Europe, incomes are more equitably distributed than in most of Western Europe. Yet, the large proportion of national income taken by the government and spent on investment or defense limits the consumer's freedom to choose how to spend personal income. Little choice is offered in goods produced, even for that amount of income left to the individual to allocate. Equality of income may be greater than in many other systems, but liberty is constrained.

Trade-Offs and Opportunity Costs

One of the hard facts about political goods is that all are desirable but cannot be pursued simultaneously. A political system has to trade off one good to obtain another. Spending funds on education is giving up the opportunity to spend them on welfare, or to leave them in the hands of the consumer for her own use. These trade-offs and opportunity costs are found not only in simple decisions about giving up education for better health care, but also in complicated decisions about investment for the future as opposed to consumption today. Even more difficult are the trade-offs between security and liberty or stability and adaptation, where the very concepts imply giving up some of one for some of the other. The extreme of liberty, where each person is totally free to act, would be a highly insecure world where the strong would bully the weak and where it would be difficult to arrange collective action. Yet, without some liberty to act, security is of little value, as the prisoner is too well aware.

Goods do not only have negative trade-offs, and the trade-offs are not the same under all circumstances. Under some conditions increasing liberty somewhat will also increase security, because riots against censorship will end. Under some conditions investment in education will be paid back many times in health and welfare, because trained citizens can care better for themselves and work more productively. One of the important tasks of social science is to discover the conditions under which positive and negative trade-offs occur. If a system beset with coups and violence, disease and physical suffering, suppression and arbitrary rule, can be replaced with a more stable, more participatory one that makes some progress in economic development, few will doubt that the trade-off is positive.

We must stress, however, that analogies from economics are no more than analogies. Political science has no way of converting units of liberty into units of safety and welfare. And since politics involves life on a large scale, it is important to acknowledge that we can never calculate the value of a political outcome gained at the cost of human life. People act as though they know how to make such conversions; but political scientists can only point to values that people have used and indicate the range of goods considered. The weight given to various goods will vary in different times and cultures. The advantage of a clear-cut ideology is that it provides people with apparently sound schemes for telling how much one value should be traded off against another, and thus offers orderly sequences of action leading to what is viewed as the best outcome. Such schemes may be invaluable for those pressed to action in the terrible circumstances of war, revolution, and famine. But there is no ideology, just as there is no political science, that can solve all these problems objectively.

STRATEGIES FOR PRODUCING POLITICAL GOODS

A Typology of Political Systems

All political systems embody strategies for producing political goods. The strategies may be oriented to goods on one level or another, or to goods intended for the few or the many. The strategies may be shaped primarily by challenges imposed from the environment, by inheritance from the past, or by the self-conscious efforts of present-day politicians. We can in any case classify political systems by strategies. The typology guiding most contemporary political research, and the division of courses, reflects such a perspective. We saw in Chapter 2 that the major environmental feature of the political system was its economy, either preindustrial or industrial. All preindustrial nations face a host of similar problems, the most challenging being increasing welfare goods. Because of similarities in challenges, resources, and goals, we usually treat the preindustrial nations as a major category for study, further subdividing them by the political structures and strategies they adopt in their effort to increase welfare goods.

The industrial nations face a somewhat different set of problems. One of the major questions they must consider is how to handle process goods, particularly participation. We saw in Chapters 3, 4, and 5 that socioeconomic development brings increased citizen awareness of and participation in politics. In the industrial nations political input structures must be developed to deal with this potential for citizen participation on a large scale. One major strategy is to introduce a controlled, nonautonomous party to contain, direct, and mobilize citizens under government control. The other major strategy is to recognize competing parties that mobilize citizens behind leaders representing different goods and strategies. We refer to the first of these strategies as authoritarian and to the second as democratic. Within these major classifications, we further classify systems by the conservatism of their policy, the degree to which they limit the role of the political system in directing production of policy goods. This approach distinguishes, then, the following varieties of political systems:

I. Industrial nations
   A. Democratic
      1. Conservative
      2. Liberal
   B. Authoritarian
      1. Conservative
      2. Radical
II. Preindustrial nations
   A. Neotraditional
   B. Populist
   C. Authoritarian
      1. Technocratic
      2. Technocratic-distributive
      3. Technocratic-mobilizational

Political Structure and Strategy

INDUSTRIALIZED DEMOCRATIC NATIONS The industrialized democratic nations must reconcile rising income levels and pressures to extend and expand government services with the need to accumulate resources for investment in economic growth. Where rising income and expanded social services are both pursued, the rate of growth may be retarded and inflation is likely. This dilemma, which faces all of the industrial democracies, may be dealt with conservatively, as in France and Japan. In these two countries, and in West Germany until the late 1960s, dominant conservative parties favored capital accumulation, investment, and growth. While this economic policy may produce rapid growth, it also tends to accentuate inequalities in the distribution of income. These inequalities are likely to bring support to parties favoring income redistribution, as has occurred in the Social Democratic victories in Germany and the increased strength of leftist parties in France.

Britain has pursued the liberal strategy, a high degree of economic equality is maintained, but at the cost of stability and growth. International trade problems and low domestic productivity exacerbate this problem. Sweden has used a more productive economy, very high social services, and equally high taxes, to combine growth, private ownership of industry, and income equality. But here, as in the unusual American combination of high education performance and conservative social and economic policy, contemporary pressures for growth and equity are difficult to reconcile.

Adding to the welfare policy difficulties of the industrial democracies is their preoccupation with environmental problems, and the severe conflicts these impose in relation to the energy crisis. The simultaneous burdens of pollution control and diminishing resources add to public and private industrial costs, and tend to introduce new political cleavage. The long-range maintenance of the system good of stability, the process goods of participation and compliance, and the policy goods of safety of person and property are dependent on satisfactory outcomes in these welfare areas. In the last decade, however, success in these areas has not been very impressive in most of the industrial democracies.

INDUSTRIALIZED AUTHORITARIAN NATIONS Two principal strategies are followed by the industrialized authoritarian nations. The Soviet Union is an example of the radical strategy, which is also followed to varying degrees by the nations of Eastern Europe that it dominates. Because it means thorough centralization of power and penetration of society, such a system may, to a point, disregard popular reaction to policies. Thus its leaders have greater leeway in deciding what proportion of resources should be allocated to investment in industrial growth and national defense, and what proportion should be allocated to the production of consumer goods. The division of resources among growth, security, and consumption is a significant policy issue in the authoritarian nations, but the form the problem takes is different from that in the democracies. The authoritarian elites not only have greater discretion in policy making, but they can cope with price, wage, and other problems through administrative decisions. However, they face substantial problems of productivity and inefficiency, due to the problems of coordinating vast government enterprises, and the absence of a price-setting market economy. The Eastern European nations have also all faced substantial domestic discontent, reflected in riots and some elite protests, which Soviet forces have kept in control either by invading or by the threat that they might.

Economic growth in the authoritarian systems with penetrative, centralized economies has varied substantially. Some countries have had impressive growth rates, while others have lagged badly. Abram Bergson's research shows similar average growth

The regulation of international conflict is a deadly matter; these pastry figures of Carter and Brezhnev playing chess with nuclear missiles appeared in a Vienna shop window at a time when the two leaders were bargaining in Vienna over the terms of Salt II.

rates in Eastern and Western Europe, with great internal variations within both groups.[12] The command economy approach does not seem a sure answer to economic policy problems, at least at this stage. And while distributive records are impressive, a substantial price is paid in these countries in suppression of free participation, autonomy, and privacy.

Until the death of Francisco Franco in 1975 and the adoption of a constitution in 1976, Spain was a good example of the conservative version of the industrialized authoritarian system. Popular political organization and demand were suppressed, and the regime and private industries had considerable freedom in allocating resources. Franco's Spain followed a policy of rapid economic growth while holding down wage levels and restricting social services. Thus, rapid growth has been associated with inequalities in the distribution of wealth and income. The political system was less centralized and penetrating than the Soviet Union. Some influence and bargaining was shared by industrial, banking and commercial interests, large landholders, and the Roman Catholic church. Groups representing the interests of the lower classes had to operate underground and at relatively great risk.[13]

PREINDUSTRIAL NATIONS The preindustrial nations face common problems posed by the challenge of modernization. We classify these nations by the strategy they adopt to meet these challenges. *Neotraditional* political systems emphasize the system good of stability. Many of the regimes of sub-Saharan Africa would fall into this category. These largely static systems are characterized by low growth rates, low literacy, and low rates of urbanization and industrialization. They have survived into the modern era with their traditional social structures and cultures largely unchanged. Their primary modern development has been the introduction of modern military institutions and technology, which in many cases has enabled groups of officers to seize and keep power. Where these systems stabilize, the elite maintains cohesion through a system of police suppression, patronage, spoils, and privileges distributed through urban interest groups and tribal elites. A good many systems that began as democracies have reverted to this strategy of merely coping with their existing circumstances, with generally low productivity.

The *populist* strategy emphasizes system, process, and policy goods, and has relatively open and competitive participation. These protodemocracies were established in many new nations upon independence. However, the tremendous strains of competitive participation in a preindustrial setting soon became apparent. With the emergence, sooner or later, of leaders appealing to the poorest members of the society, policy demands for more equitable distribution, as well as for growth, became difficult to resist. Conflicts between growth and equity became difficult to resolve, and the mobilization of participation also brought ethnic and tribal differences to the fore. Such ethnic conflicts are difficult to manage stably even in industrial systems, but with the limited resources of preindustrial societies, the problems are more severe. The result has been the disappearance of many of the populist, democratic systems, although they can still be found in countries such as India, Turkey, and Venezuela. The African populist regimes fell in the 1960s, either to military coups or to one-party machines, themselves often swept away later by coups. And in Latin America the much older democratic systems in Uruguay and Chile were also overwhelmed by internal pressures for equality under conditions of low growth and high inflation.

The other three categories of preindustrial nations reflect various authoritarian strategies. They sacrifice competitive participation, to greater or lesser degrees, in an effort to achieve stability and economic growth. The *authoritarian technocratic* approach has been successful in Brazil, where a coalition of military and civilian technocrats and middle-class business interests has suppressed participation and kept distribution unequal. Income inequality has increased markedly, but economic growth has been rapid. The governments of Peru and South Korea have adopted an *authoritarian technocratic-distributive* strategy, which suppresses participation,

[12] Abram Bergson, "Development Under Two Systems," *World Politics*, 23: 4 (July 1971), pp. 579–617.

[13] Juan J. Linz, "An Authoritarian Regime: Spain," in E. Allardt and Y. Littunen (eds.), *Cleavages, Ideologies and Party Systems* (Helsinki, Finland: Westermarck Society, 1964).

but encourages some income distribution as well as growth. Peru has adopted an explicitly leftist orientation, and tried to develop a corporatist economy under military rule, while Korea has used a market economy with government stimulation. Early land reforms, rapid education development, labor intensive, export-oriented industrialization, and heavy American advice, support, and pressure have marked the Korean experiment.

Last of all, the *authoritarian technocratic-mobilizational* strategy has been exemplified primarily by preindustrial communist countries, but to a lesser extent as well by such countries as Taiwan, Tanzania, and Mexico. What distinguishes this approach is the use of a single political party to mobilize and involve citizens in the political process. Competitive participation is suppressed or limited, but citizens are involved through the party organization. These systems vary substantially in success and in their emphasis on distribution or growth. Taiwan has been successful in combining growth and some distributive equity under the domination of the Kuomintang party. Mexico has been dominated by the PRI, and despite an earlier distributive phase, experienced substantial growth in the 1960s at the cost of increasing inequality. Tanzania is at the very beginning of economic development. The single party controls competitive participation and attempts to transform the economy. Government intervention in the economy has recently been tempered by encouragement of private agriculture.

Opting for political order, mobilized participation, high compliance, and economic growth, at the expense of competitive participation, liberty, and procedural justice, these systems show a variety of specific patterns. Three of them, China, Mexico, and Tanzania, are discussed in later chapters of this book.

We should emphasize that the problems of the preindustrial nations are so formidable that no single strategy is sure to achieve even the goals of growth. One of the tragic aspects of efforts to increase productivity is that a nation can sacrifice liberty and competition, but still not achieve growth or equity. The cases mentioned above are the relatively successful ones. But many military regimes have failed to achieve the growth of Brazil; the Peruvian experiment is already in great doubt; and efforts at building mobilizational systems in Guinea and Ghana failed. There is, as suggested by the title of a recent study of participation and developmental strategies, *No Easy Choice*.[14]

[14] Samuel P. Huntington and Joan N. Nelson, *No Easy Choice; Political Participation in Developing Countries* (Cambridge, Mass.: Harvard University Press, 1976).

KEY TERMS

public policies
distributive policies
symbolic policies
direct taxes
progressive taxes
political performance
trade-off
technocratic
extractive policies
regulative policies
command economy
indirect taxes
regressive taxes
feedback
opportunity cost
neo-traditional political system

PART THREE

COUNTRY STUDIES

The United Kingdom
(Standard Statistical Regions)
ATLANTIC
OCEAN
North Sea
Irish Sea
English Channel
SCOTLAND
Aberdeen
Glasgow
Edinburgh
NORTHERN IRELAND
Belfast
REPUBLIC OF IRELAND
Dublin
ENGLAND
Newcastle
Tyne R.
NORTH
YORKSHIRE AND HUMBERSIDE
Leeds
Sheffield
Liverpool
Manchester
Mersey R.
NORTH WEST
EAST MIDLANDS
WEST MIDLANDS
Birmingham
EAST ANGLIA
WALES
Cardiff
Severn R.
Bristol
SOUTH EAST
Greater London Council
Thames R.
SOUTH WEST
FRANCE
0
100
Scale of Miles

CHAPTER NINE

RICHARD ROSE

Politics in England

INTRODUCTION: PAST SUCCESS BREEDS FUTURE CONCERN

England today suffers the aftereffects of early success. Two centuries after creating the first Industrial Revolution, England labors with an aging economy. Industrial equipment is not as modern as in Germany or Japan, or Brazil, which started industrializing later. English firms that once bought cotton in America for milling in Lancashire and sale in Asia now cannot compete with native manufacturers. Trade unions that have preserved craft traditions through generations of depression and prosperity hesitate to abandon obsolete practices that they regard as a customary right. Whereas Americans write about living in a technologically innovative post-industrial society, the English worry more about deindustrialization.

A century and a half since Victorian innovators began adapting traditional political institutions to the world's first urban, industrial society, England is alleged to suffer from the overinstitutionalization of government. Change is said to be stifled by the resistance of old line political institutions that give priority to interests reflecting the past, rather than future needs. Political stability can be another way of describing political stagnation.

Understanding England is important, because for generations it has been the prototype of a country enjoying both representative government and economic wealth. All the largest nations of Europe have lacked England's political stability, and some still lack its wealth. The colonies now forming the independent nations of the British Commonwealth have looked to England as an exemplar of good government. What has been said of England's American colonies is true of other countries as well: "The pattern of political activity in the colonies was part of a more comprehensive British pattern, and cannot be understood in isolation from that larger system."[1] Parliaments can be found in India, Kenya, and Canada, as well as in Westminster. The responsible party system of England has long been admired, and even at times recommended for emulation in the United States. The British civil service has served as the model for many developing nations, and imita-

[1] Bernard Bailyn, *The Origins of American Politics* (New York: Vintage, 1970), p. ix.

tion has continued after the force of empire has been withdrawn. Even the Republic of Ireland, which owes its independence to armed revolt against the Crown, has modeled many of its institutions on Westminster.

In America, England is now cited as a negative example, a country that must be understood in order to avoid following its course. In a farewell interview as president, Gerald Ford cautioned, "It would be tragic for this country if we went down the same path and ended up with the same problems that Great Britain has."[2] Memories are short. Ten years earlier Americans saw themselves as having worse problems than any other modern nation. An American journalist in London, Anthony Lewis, then wrote:

> Of course there are things wrong with Britain today. What seems unjustified is any national sense that in these sins Britain is worse than other countries, and must therefore suffer. A moment's consideration of the United States, with its terrifying problems of war, and poverty and social division, should make clear the absurdity of any such guilty notion. . . . In Britain, after all, the problem is only money.[3]

A half century ago, the distinguished French writer, Andre Siegfried, diagnosed England's position thus: "To turn the corner from the nineteenth into the twentieth century, there, in a word, is the whole British problem."[4] Since then, England has achieved great change. In the turbulent world of today, it faces a new challenge: to prepare for entry into the twenty-first century.

THE CONSTRAINTS OF HISTORY AND PLACE

Every country is constrained by its history, for past actions limit present alternatives. Past events can also be important when they leave no heritage. For example, in the eighteenth century, English slave traders exported slaves to the New World, but not to England, thus avoiding the legacy of racial problems that torments the United States. The past has not left England free of all problems, however. The 1921 Anglo-Irish Treaty gave independence to two-thirds of the population of Ireland, but left a challenge to political authority in Ulster.

Compared to other countries, England has been fortunate in that it solved many of the fundamental problems of governing before the onset of industrialization. The Crown was established as the central political authority in late medieval times, and the supremacy of secular power over spiritual power was settled in the sixteenth century, when Henry VIII broke with the Roman Catholic church to establish the Church of England. The power struggle between Crown and Parliament in the civil war of the 1640s was resolved by the Restoration of 1660 and the Glorious Revolution of 1688. The monarchy continued, but with less power than before. At the onset of industrialization in the late eighteenth century the Constitution was mixed, with authority divided between Crown and Parliament. The result was limited government, but not ineffectual government.

The continuity of England's political institutions is outstanding. The heir to an ancient Crown pilots jet airplanes and a medievally styled chancellor of the exchequer pilots the pound through the deep waters of the international economy. Clement Attlee characterized the government when he summarized the interpenetration of different periods of the past in a tribute to Winston Churchill:

> There was a layer of seventeenth century, a layer of eighteenth century, a layer of nineteenth century and possibly even a layer of twentieth century. You were never sure which layer would be uppermost.[5]

Symbols of continuity often mask great changes in English life. For example, Parliament was once a supporter of royal authority; then it was a restraint upon it, deposing monarchs. It then became a lawmaking body, and today is primarily an electoral college, making or unmaking cabinets.

[2] "Ford Fear of Carter Promises," *Daily Telegraph* (London), 4 January, 1977.

[3] Anthony Lewis, "QE2 and Other Sore Points," *Sunday Times* (London), January 12, 1969.

[4] Andre Siegfried, *England's Crisis* (New York: Harcourt, Brace, 1931), p. 13. For contemporary views see Dennis Kavanagh and Richard Rose (eds.), *New Trends in British Politics* (Beverly Hills, Calif.: Sage Publications, 1977), and William B. Gwyn and Richard Rose (eds.), *Britain: Progress and Decline* (New Orleans: Tulane University Press, 1980).

[5] Clement Attlee, *The Guardian* (Manchester), April 21, 1963.

The Making of Modern England

Industrialization, not political revolution, was the great discontinuity in English history. By the early eighteenth century England had already developed the commercial skills and resources needed to industrialize an agricultural and handicraft economy; by the middle of the nineteenth century, England had become the world's first industrial society. The repeal of the Corn Laws in 1846, signifying the shift from an agrarian society producing its own food to an industrial economy exchanging its industrial goods for food from other countries, is a landmark of this change.

There is no agreement among social scientists over when England developed a modern system of government. A political historian might date the change at 1485, an economic historian from about 1760, and a frustrated egalitarian reformer might proclaim that it hasn't happened yet.[6] The simplest way to date the advent of modern government is to say that it came about in Victorian times. During this era, from 1837 to 1901, the principal features of the old Constitution were altered and supplemented by new devices so that government could cope with the problems of a society that was increasingly industrial, urban, literate, and critical of unchanged traditions.

The 1832 Reform Act started a process of enfranchising the masses that led to the grant of the vote to a majority of English males by 1885. Concurrently party organization began to develop along recognizable modern lines. Innovations promoted by followers of the rationalism of Jeremy Bentham led to the development of a large, effective civil service. By the last quarter of the nineteenth century, England had a constitutional bureaucracy capable of organizing everything from saving candle ends to laws that were prototypes of the modern welfare state.

The transformation of society, economy, and government in the nineteenth century was great. From 1800 to 1900 the population of the United Kingdom increased from 16 to 41 million people. The gross national product increased more than eleven times in total size; this was an increase of 434 percent per capita. Government spending as a share of gross national product grew by only 2 per cent in the century, because of the fiscal dividend of economic growth. In 1900, public expenditure was equal to 14 per cent of the national product.[7]

World War II brought about great changes within England. The wartime all-party coalition government of Winston Churchill sought to provide "fair shares for all" while mobilizing the population for all-out war. From this coalition emerged the Beveridge Report on Social Welfare, John Maynard Keynes's Full Employment White Paper of 1944, and the Butler Education Act of 1944. These three measures — the first two named after Liberals and the third after a Conservative — remain landmarks of the mixed-economy welfare state today.

The fair-shares policy was continued by the Labour government of Clement Attlee, elected in 1945. It maintained rationing and controls to ensure that everyone observed the austerity required when rebuilding a peacetime economy. The National Health Service was established, providing free medical care for all. Mines, utilities, railways, and transportation and steel industries were nationalized into government ownership. By 1951 the Labour government had exhausted the catalog of policy innovations about which there was agreement, but its economic policies had yet to produce prosperity. A much reformed Conservative party under Winston Churchill returned to power.

For more than three decades since, successive Conservative and Labour governments have sought economic prosperity, generous welfare services, and increased take-home pay for ordinary citizens. The 1950s saw a marked rise in living standards. Consumer goods once thought to be the privilege of a few, such as automobiles and refrigerators, became widely available. Some observers interpreted the boom in mass consumption as the start of a classless society. The Conservatives won general elections by unprecedented increases in their parliamentary majority in 1955 and 1959. Prime Minister Harold

[6] For a much fuller discussion of modernization in England, see Richard Rose, "England: a Traditionally Modern Political Culture," in Lucian W. Pye and Sidney Verba (eds.), *Political Culture and Political Development* (Princeton, N.J.: Princeton University Press, 1965), pp. 83–129.

[7] See Jindrich Veverka, "The Growth of Government Expenditure in the United Kingdom since 1870," *Scottish Journal of Political Economy*, 10:2 (1963), pp. 114 ff.

Macmillan summarized the economic record of the 1950s by saying "Most of our people have never had it so good."

The creation of a modern system of government did not make the problems of governing disappear. What it did do was give politicians institutions useful for responding to the challenges that have confronted twentieth-century England.

The first of these challenges has been national defense in a war-torn world. In World War I, Britain and France held Germany at bay in a trench war of bloody attrition, finally winning with latter-day American support in 1918. In 1940 and 1941, Britain stood alone against Nazi Germany until the war broadened to include Russia, the United States, and Japan. Britain once again emerged on the winning side.

The second great challenge, the incorporation of the working class into the full rights of citizenship, was met gradually. The bulk of the populist demands made by the Chartists in 1837 were met by 1918. The supremacy of the elected House of Commons over the artistocratic and hereditary House of Lords was established by legislation in 1911. In 1918, the right to vote was granted all adult men aged 21 or above and all women aged twenty-eight; women were given the right to vote at the same age as men in 1928. The Labour Party, founded in 1900 to secure the representation of manual workers in Parliament, first formed a minority government briefly in 1923.

The third challenge was to distribute the fruits of economic growth, which the government did through welfare policies benefiting the mass of citizens. Compulsory primary education was introduced in 1870. The Liberal government of 1906–1914 laid a foundation for the welfare state by guaranteeing old-age pensions. Interwar governments expanded the provision of welfare services. The British government was relatively well placed to increase public spending. The country's GNP more than doubled between 1913 and 1938, a rate of growth faster than that of France, Germany, or Sweden. But Macmillan was also cautious about the future. In 1957, he warned: "What is beginning to worry some of us is, 'Is it too good to be true?' or perhaps I should say, 'Is it too good to last?.' Amidst all this prosperity, there is one problem that has troubled us — in one way or another — ever since the war. It's the problem of rising prices."[8]

The 1960s cast a shadow of doubt upon the government's ability to guarantee continued affluence, for the British economy was growing more slowly than European competitors. In an effort to encourage economic growth, the Macmillan government turned to economic planning and in 1961 applied unsuccessfully to join the European Common Market. In opposition, Labour leaders argued that socialism provided a better means to develop the economy in an era of technological change. But this promise was not matched by the performance of the 1964 – 1970 Labour government under Harold Wilson, for the economy suffered.

The sixties was also the beginning of publicly expressed disillusionment with British government. Continuities with the past were attacked as evidence of the dead hand of tradition. Satire — on television and the stage and in print — mocked what was formerly held in esteem. A stream of books, pamphlets and articles were published on the theme "what's wrong with Britain?" and a series of royal commissions and inquiries were launched to propose reforms of the civil service, local government, Parliament, education, the mass media, industrial relations and the Constitution. New titles were given to government department offices, signifying the desire for change for its own sake. Behind the entranceway to these restyled offices, the same people went through the same administrative routines as before.

The experience of Conservative government under Edward Heath from 1970 to 1974 and Labour government under Harold Wilson and James Callaghan from 1974 to 1979 demonstrated that the difficulties of governing England are not the fault of particular individuals or parties.

In trying to limit wages, Heath risked the authority of his office in 1974 in a confrontation with the National Union of Mineworkers, which was defying government policy. The impasse was broken by the election of February 28, 1974. The electorate returned a vote of no confidence in both major parties.

[8] Quoted in Dennis Kavanagh and Richard Rose, eds., *New Trends in British Politics*. (Beverly Hills: Sage Publications, 1977), p. 13.

The Queen with her Consort, Prince Philip, riding in a state coach during the Jubilee celebrations of her twenty-five years as reigning monarch in 1977.

The Conservative share of the vote dropped to 37.9 percent, Labour's to 37.2 percent, the lowest level of support for each party in generations.

A minority Labour government was formed under Harold Wilson. In an October 1974 election it won a bare parliamentary majority with 39.2 percent of the vote, the lowest share for any majority government in British history. By 1977, due to by-election defeats and defections by sitting MPs (members of Parliament), the Labour government required a pact with the Liberal party to guarantee it a Commons majority.

The major achievement of the 1974–1979 Labour government was to maintain a political consensus in the face of the country's most severe economic difficulties since the interwar depression. Instead of confrontation with the unions, the Labour government sought a "social contract." This was intended to allow unrestrained wage increases and provide higher welfare benefits. In 1975, this policy became economically unviable, and a wage freeze was introduced. By the beginning of 1979, the economy had gone from bad to worse. Unemployment stood at 1.5 million, the highest since the 1930s; prices had doubled since 1974; real wages had fallen, and the economy had actually contracted, instead of growing, in two of the past four years.

The British general election of May 3, 1979 saw the two major parties reversing roles. The Labour Government under James Callaghan argued against the risk of change. The nominally Conservative party led by Margaret Thatcher called for a radical change in the country's economic policy. The Conservatives won an absolute majority in Parliament, but the party gained only 43.9 percent of the popular vote. Labour's share of the popular vote fell to 36.9

percent, its lowest since 1931. The Liberals and Nationalists continued to poll relatively well, together taking nearly 18 percent of the popular vote. The electorate's greater confidence in Mr. Callaghan's personality as against Mrs. Thatcher could not, however, overcome the unpopularity of the Labour government's record. Mrs. Thatcher thus became the first woman prime minister of a major European country.

A Mixed Inheritance

Most Englishmen have enough perspective on their past and present to believe that while conditions could be better, they could also be worse. England's present is not compared with other nations, but with England's past. Given great past advantages, the implicit premise of political action is the assimilation of the present in the past, rather than the radical rejection of the past for an unknown and untested future. The spirit is summed up in the motto of Lord Hugh Cecil's study of conservatism: "Even when I changed, it should be to preserve."[9]

The greatest asset England has to preserve is its centuries-old heritage of representative government. The prior resolution of fundamental political issues means that there is not the violence against the state that occurs in Italy. The creation of a national identity among the English confines nationalist breakaway movements to the periphery of the kingdom, rather than the center, as in Canada or Belgium. The acceptance of the limits of law by the government makes the English secure against authoritarian rule, as in Eastern Europe. Because parties peacefully exchange roles as government and opposition, citizens have an effective choice in elections, a condition not yet met in the French Fifth Republic.

But past success, while a great source of confidence, cannot guarantee the future. The fact that Victorian leaders successfully modernized their institutions may encourage their heirs, but it cannot resolve today's problem, the challenge of remodernizing England.

[9] Lord Hugh Cecil, *Conservatism* (London: Williams and Norgate, n.d.), p. 243.

Insularity and Involvement

The island position of Great Britain is its most significant geographical feature; insularity is one of its most striking cultural characteristics. London is physically closer to France than to the geographical center of England, but the English Channel has for centuries fixed a deep gulf between England and continental Europe, although there is no other continent to which the island could conceivably be assigned. In the words of a French writer, "We might liken England to a ship which, though anchored in European waters, is always ready to sail away."[10]

England's military dependence upon the United States is as meaningful politically as its geographical propinquity to France, Belgium, and the Netherlands. Historical links with Commonwealth countries on other continents further reduces the significance of physical geography. Politically, England may claim to be equally close to or distant from Europe, North America, and the nations of the global Commonwealth.

Insularity is not to be confused with isolation. The British empire drew together territories as scattered and various as India, Nigeria, and Palestine, as well as the old dominions of Canada, Australia, the West Indies, New Zealand, and South Africa. The end of the empire began with the grant of independence to India and Pakistan in 1947. The empire has been replaced by a free association of more than two dozen sovereign states, the Commonwealth. The independent status of its chief members is shown by the removal of the word "British" from the title of the Commonwealth. Meetings of Commonwealth countries today emphasize political and social conflicts among its heterogeneous worldwide membership.

British foreign policy since 1945 is a story of contracting military and diplomatic commitments. Britain retains one of the five permanent places in the Security Council of the United Nations, and it is still a member of 126 different international bodies. But British official reports now question whether the country needs or can afford diplomatic commitments that it took for granted a half-century ago.

The British economy is unusually involved in the

[10] Andre Siegfried, *England's Crisis*, p. 303.

world economy. England must export to live. England must import much of the food that it eats, and major industries must import many raw materials as well. To pay for these imports, England exports a wide range of manufactured goods, as well as such "invisible" services as banking and insurance. The City of London is one of the world's great financial centers. England disperses its trade more widely among the countries of the world than any other nation.

Because Britain's inflation rate has been higher than that of other major Western nations, the value of the pound has declined relative to other major international currencies. Until 1949, the pound was worth $4.20, and from then until 1967, $2.80. It was then devalued to $2.40 and since 1972 has been allowed to float in international exchange markets. Its price is basically determined by supply and demand. At one point in 1976, it floated down to a value of less than $1.60, before rising above $2.00 in 1979 with an improvement in the British economy and continued troubles with the American economy.

While the British government's influence upon the national economy has been growing, the influence of international market forces upon the British economy has grown even more. To meet balance of payments problems, Britain has had to go to the International Monetary Fund time and again to secure loans. In negotiating these loans, British governments have had to promise to undertake economic measures that they knew would be unpopular with the national electorate, such as squeezing consumption and increasing unemployment, in order to forestall other difficulties, such as inflation or devaluation of the pound.

As Britain's relative position has declined in the world, its governments have looked to Europe, hoping to secure continued economic growth and a share of diplomatic influence by joining with the six increasingly prosperous founder countries of the European Community, or Common Market as it is often called to stress its economic rather than political significance. Concurrently, many economic and social changes in European societies were drawing the nation into closer links with its continental neighbors. Britain joined the European Community on January 1, 1973, but there has been a question mark behind its membership ever since. In 1975, the Labour government called a national referendum to determine whether or not Britain should remain a member of the European Community. The referendum showed a majority of 67 to 33 percent in favor. But the one-third that voted against have not abandoned their opposition, and opinion polls have shown that support for membership has waned since then.

Economic arguments were the chief ones given for entering the Common Market. The British economy was pictured as likely to benefit from the stimulus of wider markets and competition, and the risk of exclusion from continental markets if Britain remained outside was depicted as a risk the country could not afford. But benefits did not follow as expected, since the October 1973 oil crisis triggered a world recession. Common Market membership has been blamed by its critics for many of the economic difficulties that have befallen Britain since.

Politically, membership in the Common Market has drawn British politicians and civil servants closer to Europe. They are involved in endless bargains about large numbers of community regulations that become binding laws in Britain. In addition, the prime minister meets regularly with the heads of other community governments to discuss common economic problems.

But even as Britain becomes more closely tied to other countries, many prefer more distance. In 1978, 51 percent of respondents told the Gallup Poll that they would like to see the country become more like Sweden or Switzerland; only 31 percent said they wished England to try to be a leading world power.[11]

England's future place in the world is not determined by popular wish alone. The constraints of history and place limit the extent to which the government can insulate the country. Today, the effective choice is not between England being big and rich or small and rich, but between remaining a big, rich country or becoming a big, relatively poor country. In refusing to face this choice, England's leaders demonstrate the aptness of the judgment of the

[11] *Gallup Political Index*, London, No. 216 (July, 1978), p. 14.

American diplomat, Dean Acheson: "Great Britain has lost an empire and has not yet found a role."[12]

One Crown and Many Nations

The English Crown is the oldest and best known in the world, yet there is no such thing as an English state. In international law, as in the title of the Queen, the state is the United Kingdom of Great Britain and Northern Ireland. The island of Great Britain, the principal part of the United Kingdom, is divided into three parts: England, Scotland, and Wales. England, smaller than Alabama or Wisconsin, constitutes 55 percent of the land area of Great Britain. The other part of the United Kingdom, Northern Ireland, consists of six counties of Ulster that have preferred to remain under the Crown rather than join the independent Irish Republic ruled from Dublin.

In social and political terms, the United Kingdom is a multinational state.[13] The great majority of Welsh people think of themselves as Welsh, and Scottish people think of themselves as Scots. In Northern Ireland there is no agreement about national identity; Catholics tend to see themselves as Irish, and Protestants see themselves as British or Ulstermen. Except in Northern Ireland, these distinctive identities can be harmonized with British identification.

Scotland was once an independent kingdom, united with England by an accident of dynastic succession in 1603, and directly since 1707. Scots retain distinctive legal, religious, and educational institutions. In 1885, a separate minister for Scottish affairs was established in the British government. The Scottish Office gradually accumulated administrative responsibilities for health, education, agriculture, housing, and economic development. Its policies have remained consistent with those applied in England as long as the head of the Scottish Office has also been a Cabinet minister.[14]

The most distinctive feature of Wales is its language, but the proportion of Welsh-speaking people in its population has declined from 53 percent in 1891 to 27 percent in 1971. Within Wales there are very sharp contrasts between the English-speaking, industrial, and more populous south, and the Welsh-speaking, rural, and less populous northwest. Since the sixteenth century, when Wales was amalgamated with England, it has almost invariably been governed by the same laws as England. In 1964, a separate Welsh Office was established for administrative purposes; its head was made a Cabinet minister. The laws that the Welsh Office administers have normally been acts of Parliament that apply equally to England and Wales.[15]

Northern Ireland is the most un-English part of the United Kingdom. Formally Northern Ireland is a secular state, but in practice differences between Protestants and Catholics dominate its politics. Protestants, two-thirds of the population, maintain that they are British, and wish to be under the Crown. Until 1972, they exercised extensive local powers, including police powers, with a home-rule style Parliament at Stormont, a suburb of Belfast. Many Catholics did not support this regime, wishing instead to leave the United Kingdom and join the Republic of Ireland.[16]

Since the start of civil rights demonstrations by Catholics in Northern Ireland in 1968, the land has been in turmoil. Demonstrations turned to street violence in August 1969, and the British Army intervened. The illegal Irish Republican Army (IRA) was revived, and in 1971 began a military campaign to remove Northern Ireland from the United Kingdom. In retaliation, Protestants have organized illegal forces too. Since the killing started in August 1969, through December 31, 1979, about 2,000 have died in political violence, a proportion equivalent to more than 70,000 dead in Britain or 275,000 in America.

British policy in Northern Ireland has been erratic

[12] Dean Acheson, "Britain's Independent Role About Played Out," *The Times* (London), December 6, 1962.

[13] See Richard Rose, "The United Kingdom as a Multi-National State," in R. Rose (ed.), *Studies in British Politics*, 3rd ed. (New York: St. Martin's Press, 1976), pp. 115–150.

[14] See James Kellas, *The Scottish Political System*, 2nd ed. (New York: Cambridge University Press, 1975); and Jack Brand, *The National Movement in Scotland* (London: Routledge and Kegan Paul, 1978).

[15] See Alan Butt Philip, *The Welsh Question* (Cardiff: University of Wales Press, 1975).

[16] See Richard Rose, *Governing without Consensus* (Boston: Beacon Press, 1971); and Richard Rose, *Northern Ireland: Time of Choice* (Washington, D.C.: American Enterprise Institute, 1976).

and unsuccessful. In 1971, the British Army helped to intern hundreds of Catholics without trial in an unsuccessful attempt to break the IRA. In 1972, the British government abolished the Stormont Parliament, placing government in the hands of a Northern Ireland Office under a British Cabinet minister. In 1974 the government created a short-lived Northern Ireland executive, sharing power between one faction of Protestant Unionists and the Catholic Social Democratic and Labour party. The executive collapsed in the face of a general strike organized by Protestant workers. Today, the Northern Ireland Office administers Ulster in what is described as temporary direct rule.

In the 1970s, nationalist parties have challenged the monopoly of votes of British parties (see Table 9.1). The challenge has been most successful in Northern Ireland, where neither the Conservative nor Labour parties have contested seats. In Scotland, in October 1974, the Scottish National party came second in popular votes with 30 percent of the total, only 6 percent less than that won by the front-running Labour party. In Wales, Plaid Cymru, a nationalist party, has consistently polled about one-tenth of the vote since 1970. In October 1974 it reached a high in parliamentary terms, winning three of the principality's thirty-six seats. The most distinctive feature of Welsh politics, however, continues to be the disproportionately high Labour vote.

In response to the rise in nationalist votes in Scotland and Wales, the Labour government in August 1974 pledged to "devolve" some government responsibilities to popularly elected assemblies in Scotland and Wales. In 1978 Parliament approved devolution acts. The measures were put to popular vote in Scotland and Wales. In the March 1, 1979 referendum in

Table 9.1

The Division of the Vote in the United Kingdom, 1974–1979

	Conservative	*Labour*	*Total, two main parties*	*Liberal*	*Nationalist*
England					
10 October 1974	38.9%	40.1%	79.0%	20.2%	n.a.
3 May 1979	47.2	36.7	83.9	14.9	
Scotland					
10 October 1974	24.7	36.3	61.0	8.3	30.4%
3 May 1979	31.4	41.6	73.0	9.0	17.3
Wales					
10 October 1974	23.9	49.5	73.4	15.5	10.8
3 May 1979	32.2	48.6	80.8	10.6	8.1
Northern Ireland					
10 October 1974	—	—	—	—	100[a]
3 May 1979	—	—	—	—	100
United Kingdom total					
10 October 1974	35.8	39.2	75.0	18.3	5.8
3 May 1979	43.9	37.0	80.9	13.8	4.3

[a] All Northern Ireland parties are classified as Nationalist because, while they disagree with each other about many things, none runs as part of a British party.

Source: Figures supplied by F. W. S. Craig, Parliamentary Research Services.

Wales, the voters rejected the devolution of authority to a Welsh Assembly: 79.7 percent voted against, and 20.3 percent favoured devolution. The principal arguments used against devolution were that it would create one too many tiers of government, and that it might threaten to separate Wales from England.

In Scotland, a narrow majority of Scots voting gave approval to devolution: 51.6 percent voted yes, and 48.4 percent voted no. But Parliament stipulated that if less than 40 percent of those eligible to vote failed to approve, the devolution acts should be returned to Parliament for further consideration. The proportion of voters endorsing devolution was 32.8 percent of the Scottish electorate. The House of Commons decided that this was insufficient to justify the major constitutional innovation of creating a separate Scottish legislative Assembly, and voted not to put into effect the Act they had previously passed.

The May 3, 1979 general election confirmed the strength of Unionist (that is, pro-United Kingdom) as against Nationalist sentiments in both Scotland and Wales. The vote of the Scottish National Party dropped to 17.3 percent, and it lost nine of its eleven Members of Parliament. The vote of the Welsh Nationalists dropped by 2.7 percent, and it lost one of its three MPs.

Politics in England is the subject of this chapter because England dominates the United Kingdom. Its people constitute five-sixths of the population, and the remainder is divided unequally among three noncontiguous nations. In politics, the people outside England are expected to adapt to English ways. What is central to England will never be overlooked by any United Kingdom government, and politicians who wish to advance in British government must accept the norms of English society.

A Multiracial England?

Through the centuries England has received a small but noteworthy number of immigrants from other lands, principally Europe. The present Queen is immediately descended from German royalty. George I came from Hanover to assume the English throne in 1714, succeeding the Scottish Stuarts. Until the outbreak of anti-German sentiment in World War I, the surname of the royal family was Saxe-Coburg-Gotha. By royal proclamation, King George V changed the family name to Windsor in 1917.

In the late 1950s, immigrants began to arrive in England from the West Indies, Pakistan, India, and other parts of the Commonwealth. Most immigrants have been attracted to England by jobs, whether as a doctor, a factory worker, or a hospital orderly. The census estimates of nonwhite population of the United Kingdom rose from 74,000 (0.2 percent) in 1951 to 1,500,000 (2.7 percent) in 1971.

The immigrants have little in common upon arrival. West Indians speak English as their native language, although some speak with a calypso accent; most are skilled manual workers. Many immigrants from India and Pakistan are unskilled workers and are not fluent in English. Muslims and Sikhs follow religious practices that make them even more distinctive. The small number of African immigrants are distinctive from others and divided among themselves by tribe and citizenship. These cultural differences, reflected also in differences in skin color, have made it difficult for immigrants to establish a political movement as blacks have in the United States. Instead, there is a hetereogeneous assortment of nonwhite groups.

From the first, public opinion has opposed immigration of nonwhites. Conservative and Labour governments responded by passing laws in 1962, 1968, and 1971 intended to limit the number of nonwhite immigrants. The measures were meant to prevent the sudden influx of hundreds of thousands of Indians or Pakistanis, and to allow time for the integration of nonwhite immigrants already in Britain.

To encourage racial integration, laws have established community relations agencies in the central and local governments, and antidiscrimination measures have also been enacted. The policies are often modeled on American legislation, except that provisions for the judicial enforcement of immigrants' rights are much weaker in England than in the United States. This follows from the absence of a bill of rights and of courts with the powers of American courts. The government-sponsored Commission on Racial Equality relies primarily on investigation and conciliation, rather than prosecution, in combating discrimination.

An imperial heritage has made England a multiracial society in fact, but not yet in political values and legislation. Politicians have concluded that the transition from an all-white to a multiracial society is so difficult that the slower the pace and the fewer people involved, the less friction. One question for the 1980s is whether this characteristically gradual approach will lead to the acceptance of the children of Commonwealth immigrants as black Britons, or even their assimilation as black English, or whether a reaction will create a small but politically alienated group who are first and foremost identified as blacks rather than Britons.

THE CONSTITUTION OF THE CROWN

England has no written constitution; its absence is considered a great advantage by many who write about British politics. Not being obligated to a written document is said to permit the government to adapt its actions and institutions to changing circumstances and demands without procedural difficulties. Flexibility arises from vagueness about the powers and procedures of government. When there is a major dispute about government actions, both sides appeal rhetorically to so-called constitutional principles; disputes are usually resolved by superior political power. As the immediate cause of controversy recedes into the past, all sides usually come to accept yesterday's resolution of disputed actions as part of today's constitutional practice.

In everyday political conversation, English people do not talk about the Constitution but about government. The term government is used in many different senses. One may speak of the Queen's government, to emphasize enduring and nonpartisan features, or use the name of the current prime minister to stress personal and transitory features, or refer to a Labour or Conservative government to emphasize partisanship. The term government officials usually refers to civil servants.

Collectively, the executive agencies of government are often referred to as Whitehall, after the London street in which many major government offices are located. Downing Street, the home of the prime minister, is a small lane off Whitehall, and Parliament — the home of both the House of Commons and the House of Lords — is at the bottom end of Whitehall. The clustering of government offices in Westminster symbolizes the centralization of government, just as the increasing dispersion of government offices throughout London symbolizes the growing complexity of central government.

The Crown symbolizes the sum of government powers. This does not mean that the monarch personally determines the major activities of what is referred to as Her Majesty's Government. Queen Elizabeth II is almost exclusively concerned with the ceremonial aspects of government. The Queen gives formal assent to laws passed by Parliament; she may not publicly state an opinion about legislation. The Queen is also responsible for naming the prime minister and dissolving Parliament before a general election. In these actions, the Queen is expected to respect the will of Parliament, as communicated to her by the leaders of the governing party. She usually also receives the prime minister once a week to discuss current affairs. No modern prime minister has suggested that he followed a policy because of the monarch's wishes.

The question thus arises: what constitutes the Crown? No simple answer can be given. The Crown is an idea to which people are asked to give loyalty. It is a concept of indefinite territory; it does not refer to a particular primordial community of people. The idea of the Crown confuses the dignified parts of the Constitution, which sanctify authority by tradition and myth, with the efficient parts, which carry out the work of government.

Cabinet and Prime Minister

If British government is to be characterized in a single phrase, it is best described as Cabinet government.[17] As Walter Bagehot noted, the Cabinet is the efficient secret of the English constitution, securing "the close union, the nearly complete fusion of the executive and legislative powers."[18] Fusion results from the fact that Cabinet ministers, the heads of the major departments of central government, come

[17] For a variety of studies of this institution, see Valentine Herman and James E. Alt (eds.), *Cabinet Studies: A Reader* (London: Macmillan, 1975).

[18] Walter Bagehot, *The English Constitution* (London: World's Classics, 1955), p. 9.

from the majority party in the House of Commons, thus assuring government control of legislation. Because the parliamentary parties normally vote as blocs, no Cabinet expects to be turned out of office by losing a vote of confidence as long as its party has a Commons majority.

Endorsement by the Cabinet is the strongest sanction a policy can have. Many major decisions, especially in economic and foreign affairs, do not require an act of Parliament. Rather, the Cabinet approves what should be done within broad grants of authority. Once the Cabinet has approved a policy, the endorsement of its action by the Commons can normally be taken for granted, and civil servants are expected to work faithfully to carry out the decision, however much they may disagree with it.

The convention of Cabinet responsibility requires that all ministers, including many too junior actually to sit in the Cabinet, give public support to a Cabinet decision, or at least refrain from making public criticism. Cabinet ministers usually go along silently with their colleagues, even when they disagree with a decision, in return for colleagues endorsing their departmental actions. If a minister does not wish to go along with colleagues, it is conventional for the minister to resign. But such is the political pain and risk of giving up office that only eight members of the Cabinet have resigned on political grounds since 1945.

If the party in office lacks an absolute majority in the House of Commons, the Cabinet cannot be certain of securing a parliamentary majority for every decision. From March 1974 to 1979 the Labour government intermittently lacked a majority in the Commons. In March 1977 it took the unusual step of concluding a pact with the Liberals to ensure support for government legislation. As long as a party has a majority, a Cabinet is secure for up to five years, the maximum life of a Parliament.

Notwithstanding the Cabinet's formal importance, it normally ratifies rather than makes decisions. One reason is the pressure of time. A second reason is bureaucratic: the great majority of matters going up to Cabinet have normally been discussed in great detail beforehand in Whitehall committees. Ministers meet in Cabinet committees to review the preliminary reports of civil servants, and to dispute and resolve outstanding political issues. Whenever possible, Cabinet ministers prefer to resolve their differences by bargaining in a committee or by informal negotiations. By doing so they can enter full Cabinet meetings with a recommendation that is difficult to challenge.

Within the Cabinet, the prime minister occupies a unique position. Sometimes he is referred to as *primus inter pares* (first among equals), but as Winston Churchill once wrote, "There can be no comparison between the positions of number one and numbers two, three or four."[19] As leader of the majority party in the House of Commons as well as chairman of the Cabinet and the party's chief election campaigner, the prime minister personally represents the fusion of legislative and executive authority. Status in one role reinforces status in another.

The prime minister's authority arises first of all from the fact that, as the leader of the largest party in Commons, she can claim to be the legitimate spokesman for all that party's MPs. In 1975, Mrs. Margaret Thatcher successfully challenged the incumbent Conservative party leader in opposition, Edward Heath, securing a plurality of votes on the first ballot and winning election by an absolute majority on the second. In 1976, six Cabinet ministers sought election as Labour leader, following the retirement of Harold Wilson. On the third ballot, James Callaghan was elected Labour party leader, thus becoming prime minister, only to lose office subsequently in the 1979 general election.

Patronage is the second source of a prime minister's influence. The prime minister determines which of several hundred MPs serve as the twenty or so Cabinet ministers (the number of Cabinet departments is determined by the prime minister, and varies). In addition, the prime minister also appoints sixty or more MPs to variously titled subordinate posts within departments as ministers, undersecretaries, or parliamentary secretaries. Collectively, these ministers constitute the front bench of the governing party (all other MPs in the party are back benchers). In addition, another thirty or so backbench MPs act as unpaid parliamentary private secretaries (political aides) to individual ministers.

[19] Winston Churchill, *Their Finest Hour* (London: Cassell, 1949), p. 14.

These patronage appointees equal about one-third of the governing party, and two-thirds of the votes required to give the prime minister a vote of no confidence in a party caucus.

In Whitehall, the prime minister's authority derives from chairing Cabinet meetings, and being its authorized spokesman in the Commons, on television, or in discussions with foreign governments. As chairman of the Cabinet, the prime minister can, in former Prime Minister Clement Attlee's words, "extract the opinion of those he wants when he needs them." Votes are virtually never taken in the Cabinet. A discussion is concluded by the prime minister's summing up. In Attlee's words: "The job of the Prime Minister is to get the general feeling — collect the voices. And then, when everything reasonable has been said, to get on with the job and say, 'Well, I think the decision of the Cabinet is, this, that or the other. Any objections?' Usually there aren't."[20]

The prime minister is also the party's leading campaigner. General election campaigns concentrate great attention on the personality and statements of party leaders. By entering Downing Street as the victor of a general election, a prime minister can claim the personal backing of the electorate. Once in office, a prime minister riding high in the opinion polls can intimidate colleagues by asserting that they must accept his views to ensure victory in the next election. However, a prime minister who relies on electoral authority is vulnerable. For example, Edward Heath was made prime minister in 1970 by the national electorate, but lost his post as party leader in 1975 after leading the Conservatives to defeat in both general elections of 1974.

The formal powers of the prime minister change slowly, if at all, but the significance of the office varies according to the political circumstances of the day and how the incumbent defines the role (see Figure 9.1). Individual prime ministers set very different sights. Clement Attlee, Labour prime minister from 1945 to 1951, was a nonassertive spokesman for the lowest common denominator of views within the Cabinet. This self-denying role kept him apart from the clash of personalities among his senior ministers. When Winston Churchill succeeded in 1951, he concentrated on foreign affairs, exerting little influence in domestic policy. Anthony Eden failed to define a role for himself in domestic politics after succeeding Churchill in 1955. In foreign affairs Eden took initiatives without consulting colleagues, leading to Britain's unsuccessful Suez War of 1956. Eden's health broke in the resulting controversy, and his resignation followed in 1957.

Harold Macmillan was ready to intervene in both domestic and foreign policy, but his directives were not so frequent as to cause friction with his Cabinet. Macmillan was exceptional in that he had previously held major posts concerned with both the economy and foreign affairs. After five years in office, however, political setbacks and ill health weakened Macmillan's ability to set policy guidelines; the party welcomed his resignation on health grounds in October 1963. Sir Alec Douglas-Home had the good health to take an active part in government, but lacked any knowledge of economic affairs, the chief problem at the time. Sir Alec was also distrusted by many Cabinet colleagues because of the way a party caucus had secured him the post.

Both Harold Wilson and Edward Heath assumed office committed to an activist definition of the Prime Minister's job. In 1964, Wilson encouraged British journalists to compare him with John F. Kennedy, perceived in London as a powerful doer of things. But Wilson's fondness for publicity led critics to describe him as more interested in public relations than in policies. In reaction, Edward Heath entered office in 1970 with the declared intention of stressing action, not words. Heath pursued major domestic and foreign policy objectives, and sought to reorganize the Whitehall machine to enhance the power of the prime minister. But the crisis of 1974 marked a retreat from the ideal of an activist prime minister. Heath's aggressive direction of the economy was rejected by the electorate, and Harold Wilson appeared as a political conciliator, promoting consensus in place of confrontation. James Callaghan avoided aggressive leadership, emphasizing instead the reconciliation of diverse interests. Emollient words replaced the promise of action as the dominant image of a prime minister. The election of Margaret Thatcher in 1979 once again returned to Downing Street a prime minister committed to an activist role.

[20] Quoted in Francis Williams, *A Prime Minister Remembers* (London: Heinemann, 1961), p. 81.

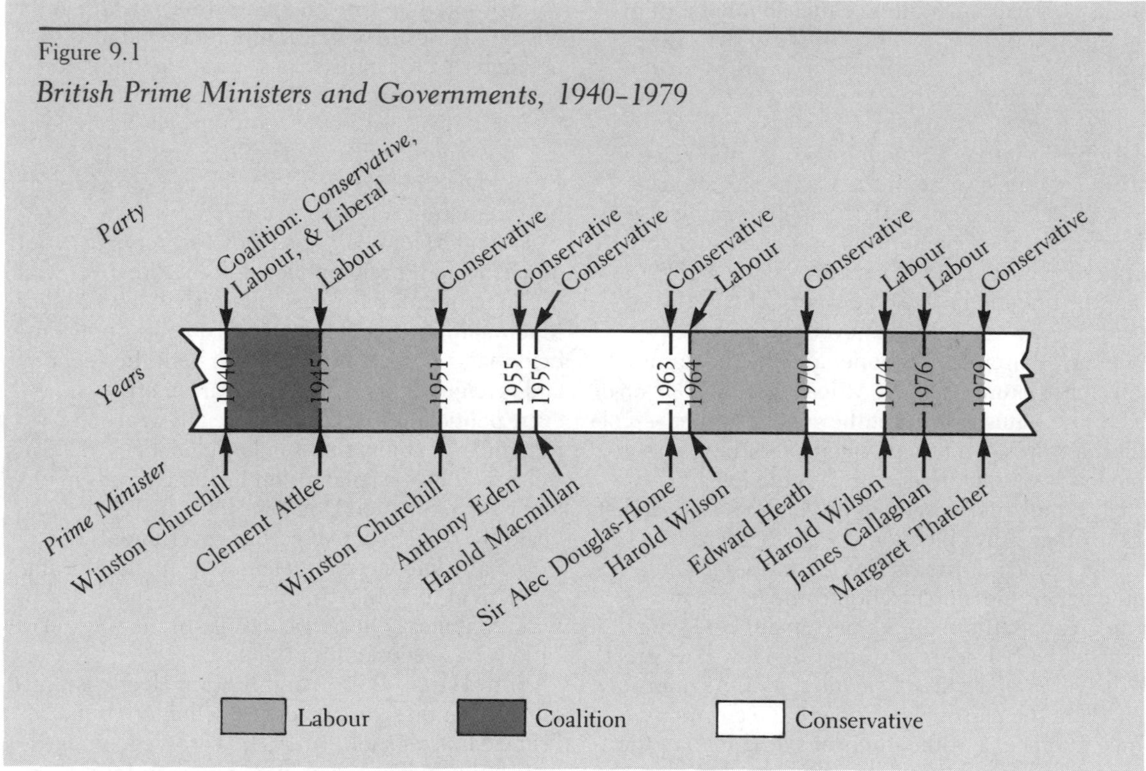

Figure 9.1

British Prime Ministers and Governments, 1940–1979

As an individual politician, a British prime minister has less formal authority than an American president. The president is directly elected by the nation's voters for a fixed term of office. A prime minister, by contrast, is chosen by his colleagues in the Commons for an indefinite term. The president is thus more secure in office than a prime minister. A president can dismiss Cabinet appointees with little fear of the consequences, whereas a prime minister sees potential rivals for the leadership among senior colleagues. The president is the undoubted leader of the federal executive. The most commanding phrase in Washington is: the president wants this. The equivalent phrase in Whitehall is: the Cabinet has decided that.

However, because British government is more subject to Cabinet direction, the office of prime minister is more powerful than the American presidency. Armed with the authority of Cabinet and support from the majority party in the Commons, the prime minister can be certain that virtually all legislation introduced will be enacted into law. By contrast, a president must suffer the slings and arrows of congressional delays, amendments, and opposition nullifying much of his legislation. The prime minister is at the apex of a unitary government, embracing local as well as central government, and without judicial limitations. The president is only the leading man in the executive branch of the federal government, without formal authority over Congress, and with even less authority over state and local governments and the judiciary.

Every prime minister, however, must live with the fact that, while she is on top of the Whitehall machine, the number of things she can do is limited by the number of hours in the week. What can be done by the government as a whole is determined by the departments headed by individual members of the Cabinet. If the Cabinet is the keystone of the arch of central government, the departments are the building blocks. Every Cabinet decision must be administered by a department or by interdepartmental collaboration. The great bulk of decisions are taken within departments, especially if they are not expected to cause political controversy.

From time to time, politicians or professors suggest that the involvement of Cabinet ministers in departmental affairs prevents the Cabinet from being a proper planning body. These critics usually advocate a small Cabinet of half a dozen persons to act as overseers of Whitehall. Except in wartime, no prime minister has accepted this view. The majority have agreed with a former leading minister, Herbert Morrison, that "a Cabinet without departmental ministers would be deficient in that day-to-day administrative experience which makes a real contribution to collective decisions."[21]

Unlike the American Cabinet, the British Cabinet is not fixed. Which departments are included in the Cabinet is determined by the prime minister, and the number varies. Every Cabinet has some departments organized primarily in terms of clients, and others by services. When Mrs. Thatcher formed her Cabinet in May, 1979, the departments were:

1. *Economic affairs* — treasury; trade; industry; employment; energy; agriculture, fisheries, and food
2. *External affairs* — Foreign and Commonwealth Office; defense
3. *Social services* — health and social security; education and science
4. *Environmental and territorial* — environment (including English local government and housing); the Scottish Office; the Welsh Office; the Northern Ireland Office
5. *Law* — Lord Chancellor's Office; Home Office; the attorney-general and the solicitor-general for England and Wales; the lord advocate and the solicitor-general for Scotland
6. *Managerial or nondepartmental* — leader of the House of Commons (job doubled with the nondepartmental portfolio of chancellor of the Duchy of Lancaster); lord president of the Council (job doubled with leader of the House of Lords); paymaster general; lord privy seal; parliamentary secretary of the Treasury (chief whip in the House of Commons); civil service department

Departments are not single-purpose institutions with a clear hierarchy of tasks, but each is an agglomeration of more or less related administrative units brought together by government expansion, fusion, and fission. For example, the creation of a Ministry of Technology by the Labour government in 1964 simply placed a new Cabinet minister on top of a collection of bureaus previously responsible to a variety of ministers. The abolition of this ministry by the Conservatives in 1970 did not mean the wholesale dismissal of civil servants, but rather the reassignment of the parts of the ministry to other ministries, especially the new Department of Trade and Industry. In 1974 the new Labour government divided this department into separate departments of trade and industry.

The Treasury and the Home Office illustrate the differences among Whitehall departments. The Home Office has a staff of approximately 25,000 and the Treasury, 1,000. Because of the importance of its tasks, the Treasury has more senior civil servants than the Home Office. The Home Office has more staff at lower levels because of its much greater volume of routine work. The Home Office has many tasks that are administratively separate: it supervises police, fire, prison, drugs, cruelty to animals, control of obscene publications, and race relations. The Treasury, by contrast, has a few major interrelated tasks: management of the economy, protecting the balance of payments, and control of public expenditures. The job of home secretary is thus much more burdensome. More paper work is required, and the home secretary is always vulnerable to adverse publicity, for example, if a convicted murderer escapes from a prison for which the home secretary is responsible.

Every minister has many roles, but ministers differ in the emphasis given to each.[22] In policy terms, a minister may initiate policies, select among alternatives brought forward from within the department, or avoid making any decision at all. A Cabinet

[21] Lord Morrison of Lambeth, *Government and Parliament*, 3rd ed. (London: Oxford University Press, 1964), p. 48.

[22] See Bruce W. Headey, *British Cabinet Ministers* (London: George Allen and Unwin, 1974).

minister is also the executive head of a large bureaucracy, formally responsible for all that is done by thousands of civil servants. In addition, a minister is a department's ambassador to the world outside, representing the department in the Cabinet and the Commons, in discussions with pressure groups, and in the mass media.

The Civil Service

While government could continue for months without new legislation, it would collapse overnight if hundreds of thousands of civil servants stopped administering laws concerning taxes, pensions, housing, health, and other responsibilities of the welfare state. Because British government is big government, even a middle-rank civil servant may be responsible for a staff of several thousand people or for spending tens of millions of pounds. Only if these duties are executed routinely — that is, quietly and effectively — will leading ministers have the time and opportunity to debate and make new policies.

Nearly three in every ten British workers is paid by public money, but the overwhelming proportion do not work for the civil service. The largest single group (3,000,000) work in local government. About 750,000 workers are officially classified as part of the civil service.

Civil servants are divided into a variety of classes unequal in size and political significance. The most important group is also the smallest: the administrative class that advises ministers and oversees the work of bureaus. It consists of about 7,500 persons. The largest group (about 200,000) consists of clerical staff, typing and filing the paperwork that is the stuff of bureaucracy or undertaking other tasks with little discretion.

Top civil servants deny they are politicians because of the partisan connotations of the term, but their work is political because they are not so much concerned with the details of management as with what government should do. It is also political in that they are often expected to make public choices, albeit on relatively minor matters, without reference to their minister. Senior civil servants do not administer particular programs. Instead, they advise on the policies that the program are meant to achieve.

One major concern of senior civil servants is to look after "their" minister. They must decide which problems and appeals go to the minister and which they may dispose of. Civil servants are expected to advise on the administrative practicability of policy proposals. An active minister may have enthusiasm dampened by a chilling note from a civil servant stating that a proposal is impracticable. Such a statement is not a veto of ministerial action, but it is advice that cannot lightly be ignored. Civil servants are also expected to be on the alert for potentially awkward political consequences in activities of the department, to alert the minister if a public controversy threatens, and to provide arguments in defense of the department in the event of a political storm.

The second major concern of senior civil servants is to maintain good government whatever the party in power. While civil servants report to a minister, they are also servants of the Crown, that is, committed to seeing that the Queen's government is carried on without disruption or disturbance because of the wishes of a passing politician. As permanent members of permanent institutions, civil servants are concerned with protecting long-term interests of government. Because promotion is determined by superior civil servants, each individual wishes to cultivate a reputation for adhering to civil service standards of good behavior. Civil servants are also conscious that, in the course of a forty-year career in Whitehall, individuals whom they oppose in one interdepartmental committee may be colleagues another year.

Ministers and civil servants need each other. A minister looks first to civil servants for information about what is happening within the department, especially about real or potential controversies. When controversies arise, a minister wants civil servants to identify the available alternatives and point out the difficulties and attractions of each. A minister also needs civil servants to translate the party's broad policy objectives into concrete policy alternatives and eventually to write the bills that can be introduced and enacted in Parliament. The chief criticism that ministers make of civil servants is that they lack expertise.

Civil servants want their minister to make clear and prompt decisions, and to stick to a decision if it attracts criticism as well as praise. Civil servants also like a minister to be successful as the department's ambassador, winning battles in Cabinet, defending the department from criticism in Parliament, in the governing party, and in the press, and securing public recognition and praise for its achievements. A minister who is indecisive when action is imperative, or who is inconsistent and unpredictable, makes life difficult for civil servants. A minister who is unsuccessful as an ambassador makes the department a loser in the competition for scarce public funds and legislative time, and will depress departmental morale by failing to answer public criticism.

The difficulties of British government have made reform of the civil service a perennial topic. It is assumed that changing the institutions or personnel of government would be sufficient to change the impact of policies on society. The 1970s have seen the introduction of special advisers to Cabinet ministers to perform political functions that civil servants are barred from or unsuited for. These special advisers provide political companionship for ministers who may feel lonely surrounded by civil servants. They read Cabinet papers from other departments, commenting on them in the light of party concerns; they act as liaison between the minister and party groups specially concerned with the work of the department; and they read files, attend meetings, and hold political discussions for which the minister lacks time.

Notwithstanding much talk and some action on reform, criticisms of the civil service continue.[23] It is significant (though little noted) that most of the criticisms of the civil servants are equally applicable to ministers. For example, both are generalists; neither is expected to have professional skills or expertise relevant to the substantive problems of the department, whether it is the treasury, education, agriculture, or social services. Neither MPs nor civil servants have training or experience in managing large organizations, except what they learn on the job. Ministers are shuffled from department to department in response to the political exigencies of the moment, and civil servants too may be posted to another place soon after mastering the technical details of one job.

[23] See the Fulton Committee, *Report: The Civil Service*, Vol. I (London: Her Majesty's Stationery Office, Cmnd. 3638, 1968), and L. J. Sharpe, "Whitehall — Structures and People," in Kavanagh and Rose (eds.), *New Trends in British Politics*, pp. 53–81.

Because Whitehall is run by a combination of ministers and civil servants, anything that affects one part affects the whole system. If the caliber or skills of the civil service deteriorate, this affects the performance of the Cabinet. If a prime minister or the Cabinet is uncertain or unrealistic in setting policy objectives, civil servants cannot perform up to their full potential. Either way, the aggregate capability of government is diminished.

The Role of Parliament

In its ceremonial role, Parliament is very impressive.[24] In terms of efficient power, Parliament is not so impressive, because its policy-making role is strictly limited. The Cabinet controls its proceedings. The prime minister can be sure that any proposal the government puts forward will be promptly voted on in Parliament, and voted on in the form desired, for the executive drafts legislation and controls amendments. Furthermore, the Cabinet enjoys the power of the purse: the budget prepared by the executive is debated at length in Parliament, but rarely altered.

In the United States, each house of Congress controls its own proceedings independent of the other and of the White House. When one party controls the presidency and the other Congress, party loyalty reinforces the independence of each. An American president may ask Congress to enact a bill, but he cannot compel a favorable vote, and a bill may come to him for signature with amendments that reduce or destroy its value to the White House. Moreover, Congress may reduce or increase presidential requests for appropriations. The president's budget is not a final document but an attempt to persuade Congress to provide funds for executive programs. Members of Congress invoke their budget-cutting powers to maintain their influence over executive activities throughout the year. Parliament lacks each of these powerful checks on the executive.

In a year's parliamentary business, the government can secure the passage of every bill it introduces; this has happened eight times since 1945, and

[24] The term Parliament can refer either to the House of Commons or both the House of Commons and the largely hereditary House of Lords.

since then governments have secured an average of 97 percent of the legislation introduced during a full Parliament (see Table 9.2). The ability of the government to get its way is not influenced by which party is in power.

The bills the government promotes are often amended in the House of Commons, but the government almost invariably determines whether or not proposed amendments will be enacted. In three full sessions from 1967 to 1971, the government moved a total of 1772 amendments in the committee and report stages; 1770 were approved by Parliament. By contrast, 4,198 amendments were moved by MPs and government party back benchers; of these, only 210 were approved by the government.

THE HOUSE OF COMMONS The principal division in the central government does not run between Parliament and Cabinet, but within the House of Commons between the majority party — which controls the Commons and Cabinet — and the opposition. The government consistently wins votes in the House of Commons because it has a majority and because of party loyalties. The party line on voting in the Commons is stated officially in a weekly memorandum issued by the party's chief whip. MPs of the governing party accept the whip's memorandum because they recognize that only by voting as a bloc can their party continue to control government. To defy the whip by abstaining, or even by voting for the other side, is acceptable only if it does not lead to the downfall of the government. The government falls if it loses a vote of confidence on a major issue.

From 1945 to 1974, in seven-eighths of all divisions, voting was strictly along party lines, that is, not one of the 600 plus Conservative or Labour MPs voted with the other party. When an MP did vote

Table 9.2

The Proportion of Government Bills Approved by Parliament

	Bills introduced	*Approved*	*Percentage approved*
Parliament (government)			
1945–1950 (Labour)	310	307	99.1
1950–1951 (Labour)	99	97	98.0
1951–1954[a] (Conservative)	167	158	94.6
1955–1959 (Conservative)	229	223	97.3
1959–1964 (Conservative)	251	244	97.7
1964–1965[a] (Labour)	66	65	98.5
1966–1969[a] (Labour)	215	210	97.7
1970–1973 (Conservative)	192	189	98.4
1974–1978[a] (Labour)	260	236	90.8
Totals	1789	1729	96.6

[a] Omits final session of each Parliament, interrupted by government calling a general election, voiding all pending bills.

Sources: Valentine Herman, "What Governments Say and What Governments Do: An Analysis of Post-War Queen's Speeches" *Parliamentary Affairs*, 28:1 (1974) Table 1, Gavin Drewry, "Legislation," in S. A. Walkland and Michael Ryle (eds.), *The Commons in the Seventies* (London: Fontana, 1977), Table 1, and Ivor Burton and Gavin Drewry, "Public Legislation: A Survey of the Sessions 1977/8 and 1978/9," *Parliamentary Affairs*, forthcoming.

with opponents, it almost invariably meant that a rebel vote would not affect the outcome. In other words, an individual MP can express distinctive personal or constituent views as long as stepping out of line would not hurt the party's cause.

Within the governing party, there are opportunities for back-bench MPs to influence government, individually and collectively. The whip is expected to listen to the views of back-bench MPs dissatisfied with a particular government proposal, and convey their concerns to ministers. In the corridors and club rooms as well as the committee rooms of the Commons, back benchers can tell ministers what they think is wrong with their party's measures. Disagreement can be carried to Commons debate as well.

The opposition party cannot expect to alter major government decisions because it does not have enough votes. The opposition accepts the defeat of nearly every one of its motions for a period of up to five years, the maximum life of a contemporary Parliament, because it hopes for victory in the next election. As long as the two major parties alternate in winning control of a parliamentary majority at elections each can expect to enjoy all the powers of British government at least part of the time.

In the course of a typical year, the Commons spends less than half its time discussing legislation. Most of its time is devoted to debating the outlines or details of policies. Many ministerial decisions are statements of intention, since the government cannot unilaterally determine the outcome of international negotiations, domestic bargaining about wages or prices, or trends in the national and international economy. In advance of government action, parliamentary debates register the mood of the house, indicating what decisions or statements of intent would be popular. After the event MPs debate the wisdom and effectiveness of these policy decisions.

Among parliamentary activities, the first and foremost is weighing men, not measures. MPs continually assess their colleagues as ministers and potential ministers. A minister may win a formal vote of confidence but actually lose standing among colleagues if her arguments are demolished in debate or if she shows little understanding of the case that civil servants have briefed her to argue. The clublike atmosphere of the Commons permits MPs to judge their colleagues over the years, separating those who merit trust from those who do not.

Scrutinizing the administration of laws is a second major function of Parliament. An MP may write directly to a minister, questioning a seemingly anomalous or unfair departmental decision or policy called to his attention by a constituent or pressure group. If the MP is not satisfied with the results of this review, he can raise the issue at question time in the Commons. MPs can also raise administrative issues in the adjournment debate during the last half hour of every parliamentary day. The knowledge that dissatisfaction with a private reply can lead to public debate ensures that correspondence from back-bench MPs is given special attention within the minister's office.

MPs can request the parliamentary commissioner for administration (also known as the ombudsman, after the Swedish prototype) to investigate complaints about maladministration by government departments. But many areas are excluded from the commissioner's inquiry, in the first two years of work (the office was created in 1967) nearly three-fifths of all complaints received were rejected as outside the commissioner's jurisdiction. The commissioner's findings are reported to Parliament for debate, but have no power to order the reversal of a government decision.

The House of Commons also uses committees to scrutinize administration. A small group of MPs can give more time to an issue than can the whole house. Moreover, committees can interview civil servants and other experts and receive written reports. While committees can play the roles of important bodies — questioning ministers, civil servants, and outside experts; making field trips, and publishing reports — they lack significant political influence. As committees move from discussions of detail to more general questions of political principle that are issues of confidence in the government, party discipline makes the government secure against them.

Talking about legislation is a third function of the House of Commons. It is not concerned with actually writing the legislation. Ministers decide on the general principles of bills, which are then written by specialist lawyers acting on instructions from civil servants that detail ministerial wishes. Particular details are discussed at length with affected and interested parties before being introduced in the Commons. Laws are described as acts of Parliament, but it would be more accurate if they were stamped "made in Whitehall."

Such influence as the Commons exerts upon legislation is felt during drafting, when Whitehall seeks to anticipate what MPs will and will not attack in debate. Inevitably, Whitehall officials are less able than MPs to assess the collective opinion of Parliament. That is why both government and opposition amendments to legislation are brought forward during parliamentary deliberation.

The fourth function of MPs is to articulate political ideas and values outside as well as inside the House of Commons. An MP has much more access to the mass media than an ordinary citizen, and is also better able to raise party issues outside Parliament. Within Parliament, an MP can communicate ideas to a minister informally, through the minister's parliamentary private secretary, or in party committees that meet privately. If rebuffed in private conversations and meetings, a back-bench MP can carry disagreement to the floor of the Commons.

It is sometimes suggested that Parliament has a fifth function: mobilizing consent for particular government measures. But Parliament cannot sway mass opinion, because the mass of the electorate is not nearly as interested in the work of Parliament as are MPs or professors of politics. The average daily sale of *Hansard*, the journal containing a verbatim report of parliamentary debates, is about 2,000 copies. Only the quality newspapers read by one-tenth of the electorate report in any detail speeches made in the Commons. The public's lack of interest or exposure to debate is matched by that of MPs. Only one-sixth of back benchers regularly listen to their colleagues make speeches in the House of Commons, and less than one-third of MPs read or skim *Hansard* regularly. The majority of MPs rely on press reports or conversations with other MPs to find out what is going on in the Commons.[25]

A newly elected MP, contemplating her role as one among 635 individuals, is faced with many alternatives. She may decide to do no more than meet the whip's expectations for a party loyalist, voting as the leadership decides, without taking part in deliberations about policy. An MP who wishes to be more than a name in a division list must decide whether to make her mark by brilliance in debate, willingness to attend routine committee meetings as an acknowledged representative of a pressure group, or in a nonpartisan way, for example as a house wit or the head of its kitchen committee. An MP is expected to speak for constituency interests, but constituents accept that party discipline will prevent their MP from voting with their interest against the party policy when these conflict. The one role that an MP will rarely undertake is that of legislator.

[25] For data on this point, and much else about individual MPs, see Anthony Barker and Michael Rush, *The Member of Parliament and His Information* (London: George Allen and Unwin, 1970), pp. 135 ff.

THE HOUSE OF LORDS The House of Lords is unique among the upper chambers of modern Western parliaments because it is primarily hereditary. Hereditary peers constitute the majority of members of the Lords, but they do not dominate its proceedings. Since 1958, distinguished men and women can be appointed to life peerages. And many members are retired members of the House of Commons; appointed to peerages, they find the more relaxed pace of the Lords suited to their advancing years.

Like the Commons, the Lords weighs men as fit or unfit for ministerial office. Because of the high average age of peers however, few expect office; only in the Conservative ranks are there younger peers seeking to establish themselves politically. Since 1963 when it was first allowed, however, some of the most politically ambitious young peers have disclaimed their hereditary status and stood for election to the Commons.

The Lord's power to reject bills passed by the Commons was formidable until the Parliament Act of 1911 abolished its right of veto, substituting the power to delay the enactment of legislation. The power of delay is especially significant in the year before a general election. Occasionally the predominantly Conservative Lords uses its powers to delay the passage of a major Labour government bill or to oppose a nonparty measure, like the abolition of capital punishment. If this happens late in the life of a Parliament, the bill cannot be enacted until after another general election.

The Lords wishes to avoid rejecting measures

from the Commons, because doing so would raise questions about its own status. The Lords cannot claim to represent the nation, because its members are neither elected popularly nor represent a cross-section of the population. Moreover, the Lords has always had a Conservative majority. Before the passage of the Life Peerages Act, Conservatives outnumbered Labour peers by about eight to one; since then, the Conservative advantage over Labour has been about three to one.

The Lords can initiate or amend legislation. The government often introduces legislation in the Lords if it deals with technical matters, such as the consolidation of previous acts of Parliament or law reform. The government can use the Lords as a revising chamber to incorporate amendments suggested in either chamber. In addition, like the Commons, the Lords can discuss public issues without reference to legislation. The government or opposition may initiate a debate on foreign affairs, or individual peers may raise such topics as pornography or the future of hill farming. Peers may use their right to question ministers as a means of watching over the administration.

REFORM OF PARLIAMENT Parliament influences government in two major ways. First, back-bench MPs, especially in the governing party, can demand that the government do something about an issue or can voice opposition to a proposed government course of action. Second, the procedures of the Commons make the introduction of a major bill a lengthy and tiring effort for the minister involved, who must be prepared to explain and defend it clause by clause as the Commons discusses it in principle and in detail. Many MPs wait unsuccessfully because there is not time for all of them to speak in a major debate. And often ministers wait unsuccessfully for the Cabinet to grant scarce parliamentary time to them to put a major bill to Parliament.

The limited influence of both houses of Parliament has led to many reform proposals, particularly from younger MPs who wish to make their jobs as interesting and important as possible. Since 1964, MPs have gradually obtained better office space, improved secretarial assistance, and more generous expense allowances. The growth of committees has given MPs more opportunities to scrutinize procedural reforms and has allowed more time for MPs voices to be heard, but does not necessarily give them more to say.

Since 1963, reform of the House of Lords has been at a standstill. No government has feared the Lords sufficiently to give a high priority to the complex task of altering it, and peers wish to avoid a head-on clash with the government for fear that this might lead to elimination of a hereditary House of Lords.

Proposals to reform the Commons have languished because proponents of reform disagree about the part Parliament should take in government. Some reformers believe that Parliament should be able to prevent executive actions; others simply wish greater access to and influence on executive actions. One group wants to transfer power from Whitehall to the Commons; the other wants to improve the work of Whitehall by correcting its errors.

The most important obstacle to reform reflects the greatest grievance of back-bench reformers; the power of decision rests with the Cabinet and not with the Commons as a whole. Whatever MPs say as members of the opposition or on the back benches, once in the Cabinet they think that the present powers of Parliament are all that the executive can allow or afford.

A Community of Interests

In many crucial respects, British government is directed by a small community of people in Whitehall. While very few ministers or civil servants live in or near Whitehall, they spend many hours working there in great intimacy. At the top, Whitehall is not a sprawling impersonal institution like the University of London or the University of California. It is a small-scale institution like an Oxford college or an Amercan liberal arts college. The public is the intended beneficiary of government policies, but the public is distant from the world of Westminster. MPs, civil servants, and ministers respond to the demands of their offices and of each other so that the Queen's government can be carried on.

The tone of Whitehall is set by senior civil servants rather than ministers, because they are more numerous as well as more durable. At any one time, there are likely to be about a hundred ministers and about three thousand senior civil servants working in Whitehall. Of these, less than thirty ministers are likely to have much political influence; they must work in tandem with about three hundred very important civil servants.

Civil servants are not anonymous. Each has a reputation to maintain with his peers and superiors. He must be trustworthy. He must not withhold information crucial to colleagues in other departments. A senior civil servant should also be considered reliable and sound. Intelligence is demonstrated by showing an awareness of the complexities of a problem, by finding one more snag than anyone else has found, or by finding one more objection to an awkward proposal for change.

The personification of the English senior civil servant is the knowing impassive figure of the mandarin; the symbol of the Washington counterpart is the aggressive athlete, the man with clout. "Why are your officials so passionate?" a British Treasury official once asked American presidential advisor Richard Neustadt.[26] Neustadt turned the question around, to ask why British civil servants are so detached from the outcome of their activities. He concluded that American civil servants care about policies because their careers are wrapped up with the success of their departments and, even more, with their reputations for getting things done. To win a political battle is to advance personally, as well as to advance the common good. By contrast, English civil servants know that, come what may, their minister will get the credit or the blame.

The Constitution of the Crown is not a mechanism for solving problems, but for coping with or adapting to inevitable or perennially recurring problems. Whitehall officials talk about the machinery of government, but they do not believe that government is a machine, capable of manufacturing engineering-type solutions to political problems. Gardening metaphors are much more suitable for describing Whitehall attitudes toward institutions of government. Within a given year, there is a familiar cycle of planting, cultivating, and reaping a year's work, acts of Parliament, white papers, or the prevention of measures that could have spread like weeds. A gardener does not expect to control the weather but to respond to it, watering plants when rain is short, pulling weeds when they sprout, and pruning plants that grow too fast.

Gardening is continuous work, and the yield is uncertain. The great bulk of Whitehall work is dealing with the daily routine: preparing briefs for committee meetings or answers to parliamentary questions, repairing the damage done by past mistakes, or planting ideas or proposals that may blossom a year or two hence. Just as there are thousands of gardeners for every plant geneticist trying to improve the breed, so there are hundreds of civil servants trying to preserve the garden of Whitehall, for every person trying to improve on it.

The closeness of the community of Whitehall has its dangers. Generalizing from a study of financial control by the Treasury, Hugh Heclo and Aaron Wildavsky argue:

> Political administration in Great Britain is profoundly narcissistic, because each participant must and does care greatly about what his fellows are doing and thinking. To be more precise, it is not so much the individuals who are self-absorbed as the governmental apparatus of which they are a part and to which they must necessarily respond. To say that British political administrators care more about themselves than about the country would be wrong; to say that more of their time and attention is devoted to themselves than to outsiders would be closer to the truth.[27]

Whitehall's strength is the ease with which business can be dispatched. The method of governing emphasizes the morale of government more than the substance of policies. A good policy is defined as one that both ministers and civil servants of different departments find acceptable to administer and defend publicly. It is not necessarily a policy that produces a desired result. For example, leading ministers and civil servants enthusiastically devise new methods for managing the British economy, combining new elements and traditional strategies. Yet no matter how popular and convincing these policies have appeared in Whitehall, none has yet to make the desired impact in the world beyond Whitehall.

[26] Richard E. Neustadt, "White House and Whitehall," *The Public Interest* 2 (1966), p. 55.

[27] Hugh Heclo and Aaron Wildavsky, *The Private Government of Public Money* (Berkeley: University of California Press, 1974), p. 9.

POLITICAL CULTURE AND POLITICAL AUTHORITY

The political culture of England consists of values, beliefs, and emotional attitudes toward authority. Because of the continuity of political institutions, many contemporary cultural outlooks reflect events of the remote past transmitted to today's citizens by intergenerational political socialization. The political outlook of an elderly English person may combine norms from Victorian times with beliefs derived from events of the 1970s.

Allegiance to Authority: The Legitimacy of the System

Of all attitudes affecting government, the most important concern allegiance to political authority. The government of England can claim full legitimacy only if the values of citizens support authority, and favor compliance with basic rules. Support for a regime is not a judgment about the effectiveness or efficiency of government. English people simultaneously value their form of government, while making many specific criticisms of how it works. Nor do people comply with every law all the time.

The continuity of authoritative government in England makes the idea of overthrowing the existing regime inconceivable to many people. When people are asked what they think of government by elected representatives, 94 percent support it as a good way of governing, and only 3 percent consider it a bad way to run the country. MPs, too, give almost unanimous support to the established system; only 2 percent think there should be big changes in the way England is governed.[28]

The political difficulties arising from the worldwide oil crisis of 1973, the outcome of two elections in 1974, and the country's continuing economic difficulties have reduced the confidence of people in the effectiveness of England's government. But this reduced confidence has not made people doubt the legitimacy of parliamentary institutions. Nationalist parties in Scotland and Wales and many parties in Northern Ireland reject government from England, but not parliamentary government within their own territory. Notwithstanding the country's difficulties, in the October 1974 election candidates of the Communist Party of Great Britain secured the derisory total of 0.1 percent of the vote, and those of the white supremacy, antiimmigrant National Front only 0.6 percent.

The legitimacy of government is also evidenced by the readiness of English people to comply with laws. Law enforcement does not require massing of large numbers of armed police or the employing of masses of undercover agents. In proportion to its population, England's security forces are one-third smaller than those of America, West Germany, France, or Italy, and even in the troubled 1970s, street violence, kidnappings, and assassinations have not erupted in English political life. Crimes that are committed — fast driving, burglary, or homicide — are considered antisocial, rather than crimes against the state.

The very concept of a political crime is unknown in England. Northern Ireland is the only place in the United Kingdom in which politically motivated violations of the law have been consistently undertaken and have successfully destroyed established authority — although failing to constitute a new authority in its place. The political history of Northern Ireland is a reminder that the authority of Westminster is not inviolate. But it also demonstrates that the only determined and successful assaults on it in this century have been both literally and figuratively un-English.

The rise of unorthodox methods of political activity since the late 1960s — protest marches, rent strikes, sit-ins at public buildings, and violence to property and persons — has reaffirmed the commitment of the English to basic rules. Public opinion surveys show there is little support for political action outside the law (see Table 9.3). A majority say that they approve of signing petitions and lawful demonstrations *and* disapprove of eight other forms of political protest, ranging from boycotts and rent strikes to violence. Approval is low (16 percent) for unconventional but legal measures, such as unofficial strikes, as well as for measures that are illegal but well pub-

[28] See Committee on the Management of Local Government, *The Local Government Elector*, Vol. 3 (London: Her Majesty's Stationery Office, 1967), pp. 66 ff, and Robert D. Putnam, *The Beliefs of Politicians* (New Haven, Conn.: Yale University Press, 1973).

Table 9.3
Support for Unorthodox Political Behavior

	Approve	*Believe effective*	*Have done*
Sign petitions	86%	73%	23%
Lawful demonstrations	69	60	6
Boycotts	37	48	6
Rent strikes	24	27	2
Unofficial strikes	16	42	5
Occupying buildings	15	29	1
Blocking traffic	15	31	1
Painting slogans on walls	1	6	—
Damaging property	2	10	1
Personal violence	2	11	—

Source: This table, drawn from "Protest in British Political Culture" by Alan Marsh, is reprinted from *Protest and Political Consciousness*, Sage Library of Social Research, Vol. 49, © 1977, pp. 29–54, by permission of the Publisher, Sage Publications, Inc. (Beverly Hills/London).

licized, such as occupying buildings or blocking traffic.

The English commitment to lawful political actions reflects values about how people ought to act, not simply calculations about what will work. The proportion approving lawful protest is higher than that believing such measures are effective, and the minority believing unorthodox measures are effective is larger than that approving such measures. Since most people disapprove of unorthodox political behavior and do not believe it effective, it follows that very few have engaged in such protests; the highest number is 6 percent reporting involvement in boycotts, and 5 percent in unofficial strikes.

The commitment of the English people to established authority is also shown by their readiness to support the government in taking strong measures to defend itself when its authority is challenged. Surveys show that 80 percent approve courts giving severe sentences to protesters who disregard the police, and 73 percent approve of police using force against demonstrators. Only a minority, however, go so far as to endorse government actions that would conflict with individual rights, such as using troops to break strikes or declaring all public protest demonstrations illegal. Most English people reject unorthodox political action, but they also reject the government amending or bending the law to repress lawful disagreement with policy.[29]

The legitimacy accorded to government in England is not the result of carefully calculated policies pursued through the ages. In fact, politicians try to avoid raising constitutional issues, because they are so difficult to resolve in the absence of a written Constitution. In the words of journalist Hugo Young, "Constitutional issues exist in order to be denied, circumvented or reduced to an administrative inconvenience."[30]

The legitimacy of authority is the tacit premise of English politics. Because the subject is not often discussed or analyzed, it is not easy to explain why English people do accept authority. For centuries, English political philosophers have speculated about

[29] See Alan Marsh, *Protest and Political Consciousness* (Beverly Hills, Calif.: Sage Publications, 1977), Table 3.2.

[30] "Into the Golden Future," London *Sunday Times*, 7 August, 1977.

Margaret Thatcher, surrounded by political colleagues, displays the Conservative party manifesto for the 1979 British general election, which led to her becoming Britain's first woman Prime Minister.

the causes of this allegiance; they offer many and conflicting explanations. Moreover, their views are over the heads of the great mass of the population, who have never read them. The political outlook of the mass of English people are derived from experience, and not from books.

The symbols of a common past are sometimes invoked as a major determinant of legitimacy. The monarchy is the most prominent and personal symbol of the continuity of English history. But surveys of public opinion show that the Queen is of little political significance; she is viewed as a nonpolitical figure and emotional responses to the monarchy tend to be shallow. The popularity of a monarch is a consequence of political legitimacy, not a cause of it.[31] Moreover, in Northern Ireland, the Queen is not a symbol of legitimacy, but a symbol of divisions between Protestants proclaiming loyalty to the British Crown, and Republicans who reject the Crown.

In a survey asking people why they support the government, the most popular reason (77 percent) was "It's the best form of government we know." Constituted authority is not said to be perfect, or even trouble free: it is valued on the basis of experience. Popular endorsement of government — "It's the kind of government the people want" — is also viewed as a justification by 66 percent. A third reason endorsed by a majority (65 percent) is the inevitability of authority: "We've got to accept it whatever we think."[32] The effectiveness of government in providing the right things for people is relatively

[31] Richard Rose and Dennis Kavanagh, "The Monarchy in Contemporary Political Culture," *Comparative Politics*, 8:3 (1976), pp. 548–576.

[32] See Richard Rose and Harvé Mossawir, "Voting and Elections: A Functional Analysis," *Political Studies*, 15:2 (1967), pp. 182 ff.

unimportant; only 49 percent think it is a good reason for accepting authority. Contrary to what is sometimes argued by economic determinists of differing political views, popular allegiance is not bought by the provision of public benefits.

The Role of Law

Courts and law enforcement agencies are relatively unimportant in maintaining or changing political culture; the role of law is narrowly defined in England. In the past, judges proclaimed the doctrine of the rule of law to restrain royal absolutism. In the twentieth century, English judges have adopted a self-denying policy. They do not consider themselves arbiters of what government can do. Instead, they assert that it is up to Parliament, under the direction of the Cabinet, to decide. Unlike their American counterparts, English courts claim no power to declare an act of Parliament unconstitutional, nor will they accept a claim that an act should be set aside because it conflicts with a previous act of Parliament or with what claimants describe as natural rights. English judges believe that an unwritten Constitution must be constantly made and unmade, but they want no part of the job. That is for Parliament and the electorate. The final court of appeal is political rather than judicial.

Instead of reviewing constitutionality, as in the United States, the courts determine whether the executive acts within statutory powers. If an action of the central government or a local authority is *ultra vires* (outside its powers), the courts may order the government or authority to desist. The courts may also quash an action undertaken in a procedurally improper manner. But if a statute delegates discretion to a public authority, the courts do not question the reasonableness or the motives of the executive exercising discretion. And even if the courts rule against the executive, the effect of such a judgment can be canceled by a subsequent act of Parliament giving retroactive authority.

An English person who believes that the government has denied her basic rights will find it difficult to get the courts to redress her grievance. There are no primary rules in the unwritten Constitution or in legal documents that the citizen may invoke against an act of Parliament. The American Bill of Rights holds that some individual rights are superior to statute. In England, as long as the government has statutory authority for its actions, the courts will uphold it. And the government's statutory powers can be so broad as to sanction almost anything, as wartime illustrates.

The powers of the British government, however, are constrained by cultural norms dictating what government should and should not do. For example, public officials worry about the implications of population trends for public policy, but they do not propose laws to regulate family size. In the words of one High Court judge:

> In the constitution of this country, there are no guaranteed or absolute rights. The safeguard of British liberty is in the good sense of the people and in the system of representative and responsible government which has been evolved.[33]

The role of the police illustrates the presence of mutual trust between governing and governed. In England, police work on the assumption that their authority will be generally accepted and that those they seek to apprehend will be shunned by society at large. Police patrol unarmed; criminals are expected to be unarmed too. To a remarkable extent police in England are respected. This does not mean that they are never criticized, but the mass of the population considers police officers who are guilty of wrongdoing to be atypical.

England has no paramilitary security force to compel obedience to the law, or anything like the American National Guard for use in the event of domestic political disorder. The navy is England's major armed service, and by its nature, the navy cannot be deployed within Britain. The army, almost never used to enforce public order within England, is a source of ready manpower in a flood or a railway wreck.

The importance of English attitudes in maintaining law and order is best demonstrated by a comparison with Northern Ireland, the most disorderly part of the United Kingdom. Parliament has never been successful in efforts to export English institutions of police, courts, or military organization to Ireland,

[33] Lord Wright in *Liversidge* v. *Sir John Anderson and Another*, 1941, quoted in G. Le May, *British Government, 1914–1953* (London: Methuen, 1955) p. 332.

because these institutions can operate only with the full consent of the population. Irish Republicans have always rejected them, and Ulster Protestants, determined to maintain their own political hegemony, have accepted them only with reservations. Westminster's first reaction to civil rights disorders in Ulster was to encourage the Northern Ireland government to imitate English procedures. But by August 1971 the British government was ready to intern without trial hundreds of Catholics suspected of violence. By February 1973 it was interning Protestants too. England's rule of law, it was painfully clear, could not be exported successfully to all parts of the United Kingdom.[34]

Whose Authority?

The influence of individual English people is inevitably unequal, for governments are run by small groups of officeholders. The power of those governing is justified because they are believed to represent the country as a whole.

The justifications for representation are multiple. Three are specially important today.

In the *trusteeship* theory, leaders are meant to take the initiative in determining what government does. MPs and cabinets are not expected to ask what the people want, but to use their independent judgment to determine what is in the best interests of society. In the words of L. S. Amery, a Conservative Cabinet minister writing after World War II, England is governed "for the people, with, but not by, the people."[35]

The trustee view of government is summed up in the epigram, "the government's job is to govern." The outlook is popular with the party in office, because it justifies the government doing whatever it wishes. Reciprocally, the opposition party rejects this theory, because it does not enjoy the prerogatives of the government. Civil servants find the doctrine congenial because they permanently serve the governing party, and therefore see themselves as permanent (and nonelected) trustees of the public interest.

In predemocratic times, government by trustees was justified on the grounds that ordinary people should and did defer to their betters, defined by aristocratic birth or gentlemanly manners. Today, only a very small and aging proportion of English people are prepared to defer to others on the grounds of social status.[36] The electors' choice of MPs, both Labour and Conservative, shows that university education, rather than high birth, is now the most likely basis for securing entry to the ranks of the few who govern.

The *collectivist* theory of representation regards social groups as the constituent units of politics; government is the arena in which different groups compete for influence, with public policies the result of conflicting group pressures.

In England both parties and interest groups embody collectivist politics. The chief groups contending for political influence are the trade unions and industrial, commercial, and financial organizations. The unions are integrally a part of the Labour party. Most businessmen vote Conservative, and the Conservative party draws a significant portion of its funds from business organizations. In the collectivist view, individuals are politically significant only insofar as they are members of groups. But more than half the labor force and more than two-thirds of the electorate does not belong to a trade union. An even smaller proportion of English people are businessmen or own shares in business. Political parties are the groups that represent the largest segments of the electorate.

Individualist theories of representation emphasize the importance of each citizen's role in the political process. MPs are meant to represent constituencies in which each individual has a vote of equal value. Because ministers are expected to be accountable to a House of Commons in which each MP is accountable to constituents, individual voters, or at least a majority of voters, can, at one remove, theoretically control — if not positively direct — government.

Individualist values are more appropriate for a small society, or one in which few people have the

[34] See Richard Rose, "On the Priority of Citizenship in the Deep South and Northern Ireland," *Journal of Politics* 38:2 (1976), pp. 247–291.

[35] L. S. Amery, *Thoughts on the Constitution* (London: Oxford University Press, 1953), p. 21.

[36] See Dennis Kavanagh, "The Deferential English: A Comparative Critique," *Government and Opposition*, 6:3 (1971), pp. 333–360.

right to vote, such as early Victorian England. With an electorate of more than 40 million people, no one English person today can expect his voice or vote to exert a large amount of influence. Individuals must accept having their views aggregated by political parties in order to organize governing.

Individuals do enjoy influence, insofar as their status as citizens allows them to claim equality before the law. But this right affects how they are treated by government, not what government does. The use of referenda on Common Market membership in 1975 and Scottish and Welsh devolution in 1979 has given individual voters the chance to approve or reject decisions taken by Parliament. But the choice of whether to have a referendum and what the question is remains with the government.

These three cultural outlooks coexist within England because the political culture is a composite. Leading Cabinet ministers and civil servants often like to see themselves as trustees for the nation, acting as they think best. Lesser ministers and civil servants tend to be caught up in collectivist politics, negotiating to reconcile conflicts between and within parties and pressure groups. At election time, the votes of millions of individual English people decide who governs.

While MPs and civil servants both recognize the significance of individual voters, MPs see their primary role as that of representing collective groups or as trustees for the nation. In the words of a Labour MP:

> The essential thing in a democracy is a general election in which a Government is elected with power to do any damned thing it likes and if the people don't like it, they have the right to chuck it out.[37]

A Conservative member with an aristocratic background endorses the same view in characteristic mock diffidence:

> I personally consider myself capable of coming to decisions without having to fight an election once every four or five years, but on the other hand, the people must be allowed to feel that they can exercise some control, even if it's only the control of chucking somebody out that they don't like.[38]

[37] Quoted from Putnam, *Beliefs of Politicians*, p. 172.
[38] *Ibid.*, p. 173.

Cultural Limits on Policy

The diffuse legitimacy that English people confer upon government does not endorse doing anything or everything that leaders might wish. The norms of the political culture include a set of dos and don'ts about the scope of political authority. From the time of Magna Carta in 1215, English people have expected the Crown to recognize limits in what it may do. In theory, Parliament can enact any policy that the government recommends; in practice, the government is limited by what people will stand for.

Chief among the things that government is expected *not* to interfere with is liberty. Cultural norms about freedom of speech are an effective inhibition against political censorship, and allegations of police interference with individual's liberties are rarely heard, in comparison with the United States, where statute laws are less effective constraints on police actions than the cultural inhibitions of England.

Increasingly permissive cultural values have widened the individual's freedom from government regulation of social behavior. Even before the passage of permissive legislation in the 1960s, the enforcement of morality by statute was severely limited. For example, while the United States and Scandinavian countries were experimenting with the legal prohibition of alcohol to curb drunkenness, England adopted the simpler tactic of requiring public houses to close at specified hours each day. In the 1960s laws against sexual relations between consenting male adults were repealed, and censorship of books, films, and plays was virtually abandoned. Abortion was legalized in 1968, further reducing the scope of legislation affecting private morality.

Today, the most significant limits on the scope of government policy are practical, not cultural. This is most evident in the government's efforts to manage the economy. By undertaking this commitment, the British government has exchanged the authority of command for the uncertainties of influence. Government can influence the economy by the taxes it levies, and by the character of public expenditure. Successive Labour and Conservative governments have sought to expand the scope of government policy by exhorting labor and business leaders, by offering incentives for cooperation and, in difficult times, by appealing over their heads to their members, or even passing temporary legislation to regulate wages or prices. But the government cannot achieve what successive Labour and Conservative governments have sought since 1945, a rate of economic growth that is competitive with that of other major Western nations, and that is also sufficient to meet all the growing spending commitments of the government.[39]

No government accepting responsibility for managing the economy can ignore the influence of unions. A major political dispute today concerns whether the government has the right to regulate the activities of trade unions. Nineteenth-century laws inhibiting the right to strike make British unions, by contrast with European or American counterparts, anxious to avoid government legislation governing their activities. In 1969 a Labour government proposal for a new industrial relations act was vetoed by trade union pressure on the Cabinet. In 1971, a Conservative government passed an industrial relations act, but the unions refused to cooperate with it, and it was subsequently repealed by a Labour government.

POLITICAL SOCIALIZATION, PARTICIPATION, AND RECRUITMENT

Socialization influences the political division of labor. Children learn early that people differ from each other, and these differences gradually become salient in political contexts. A young person not only learns about differences between political parties and political roles, but also the part that he or she may be expected to take in politics. Socialization differentiates persons into Conservative, Labour, or Liberal supporters or a voter not identifying with any particular party.[40] It also divides the electorate into a small minority actively participating in politics, and a large mass active only intermittently.

The Influence of Family

The influence of the family comes first in time; political attitudes learned within the family become intertwined with primary family loyalties. A child may learn little of what the Labour or Conservative party stands for except that it is the party of mom and dad. If both parents support the same party and let their offspring know which party it is, then there is at least a two-in-three likelihood that this identification will persist throughout most of the young person's life.

Religious identification is likely to be acquired from parents as well. While church attendance is low and politics is secular, religion retains a residual influence on party loyalties. Voters who have been raised in a Church of England family are more likely to support the Conservatives, and Labour supporters are more likely to belong to nonconformist Protestant denominations, or to be Catholics or Jewish.

Parental influence is most evident when a child born into a politically active family enters politics. It is like going into a family business. The eldest son of a hereditary peer knows he is guaranteed a seat in the House of Lords if his father predeceases him. Prime ministers are disproportionately drawn from political families: Winston Churchill's ancestors had been in the Commons or Lords since the early eighteenth century. Churchill's son and grandson, as well as three sons-in-law, have also sat in the Commons. Harold Wilson's parents and grandparents, though never in Parliament, were keenly interested in politics; he claims, "I was born with politics in me."[41]

Political attitudes and activities are not identical from generation to generation for two reasons. First, the historical circumstances in which people learn about politics change from generation to generation. Today's parents are likely to have begun learning about politics in a period of wartime and postwar austerity. Their children are learning about politics in a time of relative propersity. Grandparents formed

[39] See Richard Rose and Guy Peters, *Can Government Go Bankrupt?* (New York: Basic Books, 1978), ch. 2–4.

[40] For a detailed examination of social influences upon party loyalties, see David Butler and Donald Stokes, *Political Change in Britain*, 2nd ed. (New York: St. Martin's Press, 1974); and Richard Rose, "Britain: Simple Abstractions and Complex Realities," in Richard Rose (ed.), *Electoral Behavior* (New York: Free Press, 1974), pp. 481–541.

[41] Quoted in "The Family Background of Harold Wilson," in Rose (ed.), *Studies in British Politics*, 3rd ed., p. 75.

party allegiances when there was a choice of three large parties: Conservative, Liberal, and Labour. Differences in historical experience influence profiles of party support among age groups. The oldest voters tend to be Conservatives because Labour was weak when they first formed party attachments and because middle-class and women voters, who are disproportionately Conservative, are longer lived.

A second source of generational differences is the greater volatility of youth. Young voters tend more toward Labour than their elders, but young voters also tend to shift voting patterns more than their elders. As young people become older, their party loyalties become more fixed; the experience of one election tends to reinforce previous experiences. Overall, class rather than age is the more important determinant of young voters' party choice. In every age group, a majority of the working class vote Labour, and a majority of the upper-middle class vote Conservative.

Sex Similarities and Differences

From childhood, boys and girls learn different sex roles, but studies of political attitudes show that there is virtually no difference in political interest or outlooks among boys and girls.[42]

The chief influence upon the voting behavior of women, as on that of men, is class. While women are slightly more likely to vote Conservative than men, the difference averages only 6 percent. This is much less than the difference in party support along class lines.

All political parties are interested in the votes of women, but they do not seek them primarily by offering feminist policies. Womens' votes are sought on similar grounds to those of men. Economic issues have far more prominence than feminist issues. Because women constitute slightly more than half the electorate, all parties wish to avoid offending women, and are thus open to lobbying by women's pressure groups. The 1975 Sex Discrimination Act, prohibiting discrimination in employment, followed from a document published by a Conservative government, and was enacted by a Labour government.

Sex differences do lead to differences in political participation. Moreover, these differences cannot be explained as a function of lower interest in politics. Among women, 15 percent describe themselves as having a great deal or some interest in politics, compared to 24 percent of men. Whereas women constitute more than half the electorate, less than one-third of elected councillors in local government are women. In national politics, from 5 to 7 percent of candidates are women, with a lower proportion being elected. In the Parliament elected in 1979, 19 of the 635 MPs are women. At Cabinet level, women are usually recruited on the basis of political skills, and not as token representatives of their sex. Margaret Thatcher was elected leader of the Conservative party in 1975 because of her political standing and in spite of her sex.

Schooling

English schools teach "life adjustment" as well as academic subjects. Implicitly as well as explicitly, schools prepare young persons for adulthood by emphasizing behavior and attitudes appropriate to adult roles, as well as by teaching basic skills.

In England education has always assumed inequality.[43] The great majority of the population has been considered fit for only a minimum of education; until the end of World War II, the majority left school at fourteen. Today, the majority are expected to leave school at sixteen. The highly educated, a small fraction of the population, are expected to play a leading part in politics. When secondary education was made compulsory by the 1944 Education Act, pupils were sent to separate schools according to academic ability, determined by an examination taken at age eleven and older. About one-quarter were sent to academic grammar schools, the remainder were said to have failed. They attended secondary modern schools offering an education for manual work or a very routine white-collar job.

In 1965 the Labour government requested all local authorities to reorganize secondary education

[42] Robert E. Dowse and J. A. Hughes, "Girls, Boys and Politics," *British Journal of Sociology*, 22:1 (1971), pp. 53–67.

[43] The discussion that follows excludes Wales, where education has historically been valued differently and where language presents distinctive issues, and Scotland and Northern Ireland where education is differently organized with state-supported segregation of schools by religion.

to abolish the selective examination. While the circular met opposition from Conservative-controlled local authorities, its policy has gradually become effective throughout the country. By 1977, 80 percent of young people were attending comprehensive schools, mixing pupils of all abilities. The effects of this change, whatever they are, can only work slowly through the society, for the majority of voters will be products of the old selective system until about the year 2000.

Secondary schools discriminate according to social status as well as intelligence. Public schools — that is, private, tuition-charging, and often boarding institutions — accept pupils with a wide range of intellectual abilities but with one thing in common, their parents pay high annual tuition. Boarding schools allow young people to be raised among their social peers rather than among more heterogeneous neighbors. Entrance to the most prestigious public schools, like Eton, may also be aided by family connections. The brightest public school students at the best schools are likely to receive an academic education superior to that received at the average state secondary school; at the poorest public schools, however, they are likely to receive an inferior education. Approximately 4 percent of young persons attend public schools. The great majority of ex-public school students seek careers in industry or commerce, which have the most numerous job opportunities. Only a small proportion aspire to a career in the civil service or in older professions traditionally associated with politics.

Approximately one secondary-school student in eight moves on to higher education. About half of those attend universities, another quarter are at colleges of education, and the remainder are in a variety of full-time and part-time institutions, such as polytechnics. By comparison with the United States, England has historically had few universities; sixteen of the thirty-three English universities were founded between 1961 and 1967.

University students have shown considerable volatility in their political outlook while there. After graduation, the extent of change is even greater, as members of the Cabinet of the 1964–1970 Labour government illustrate. Nearly half, including Prime Minister Harold Wilson, were graduates of Oxford. But in their student days, these Labour ministers had belonged to four different parties: Labour, Liberal, Conservative, and Communist. Wilson himself had been a Liberal.

Differences in schooling imply differences in adult life. The more education a person has, the more likely he is to favor the party most closely identified with educational elitism, the Conservatives, to show interest in politics, and to be active in politics. But, again, class differences are much more important. Among upper-middle-class persons with a minimum of education, 66 percent are Conservatives; among working-class people with the same minimum, only 35 percent are Conservatives. Length or type of education seems to have little influence on interest in politics: it accounts for less than 1 percent of the variation between those most and least interested.

Education is most strongly related to active participation in politics. The more education a person has, the greater the possibility of climbing the political ladder. English people with a minimum of education constitute nearly three-quarters of the electorate but less than half the local government councillors and less than one-tenth the MPs, ministers, and senior civil servants. Moreover, those with a maximum of education, the 2 percent with a university degree, constitute more than half the MPs, ministers, and senior civil servants. The Labour party, claiming to represent working-class interests, draws more than half of its MPs and Cabinet ministers from the small fraction of its supporters who are university graduates.

Education often reflects family background and, in the case of expensive public schools, social status. Leading civil servants tend to have a prestigious secondary education. The typical Conservative MP or minister has a public school education and has earned a university degree. While two-fifths of Labour MPs have no education to brag about, whether viewed in terms of prestige or merit, the average Labour minister has an education that is both prestigious and meritorious. Whatever the party or office, a politician whose only asset is passing examinations and winning scholarships is at a disadvantage compared to one who has been to public school.

Class

Class is a concept as diffuse as it is meant to be pervasive; sometimes it is used as a label for the cumulative effect of all socialization. Occupation is the most commonly used index of class in England, although to group people together by that does not mean that they are identical in every other respect. A coal miner usually lives in a mining village where his occupation is integrally related to a whole network of social relations, with family, friends, and neighbors. But a taxi driver working in central London usually lives in a suburb; work relationships are divorced from other ties.

Nearly every definition of occupational class places about two-thirds of English people in the working class, and one-third in the middle class. In politics, it is particularly important to to distinguish differences among nonmanual workers. The handful of upper-class people living solely on inherited capital are politically less significant than the 5 percent of upper-middle-class people who dominate the professions and large organizations, including government.

Whatever measure is used, class differences produce significant differences in party preference and in political interest and participation. The influence of class on party preference has been documented by every voting study ever undertaken in England (see Table 9.4), although three qualifications must be made. First, a proportion of the electorate has no party preference or votes Liberal or Nationalist. Second, the relationship between class and party is asymmetrical. The middle class is more strongly Conservative than the working class is Labour; the most homogeneous category is the upper-middle class. The third qualification follows from the second: the relationship between party and class is partial, not complete.

The relationship between class and party increases when one takes into account the parents' class. People in the same class as their parents are likely to be Conservative if middle class and Labour if working class. Upwardly mobile people favor the Conservatives, but by a lesser margin than those born into the middle class. A plurality of downwardly mobile people are Labour, but less strongly so than those born in the working class.

More sophisticated theories of the influence of class emphasize the role played by class institutions such as trade unions in socializing people. For example, a division is created within the working-class based on union membership. This division produces differences in political outlook. In those working-class families without a union member (approximately 50 percent of working-class families), voters divide evenly between the Conservative and Labour parties; in families of manual workers in trade unions, 60 percent favor Labour.

The distinctive housing pattern of English society makes it possible to study the political effect of living in a homogeneous neighborhood. One-third of English families live in a publicly owned and subsidized council house. Council houses are usually grouped together in substantial numbers. This not only creates identification with the council estate, but also makes persons identifiable as council tenants. About four-fifths of council-house tenants are working class. In 1979, 56 percent of working-class council tenants supported Labour, as against 26 percent of

Table 9.4

The Influence of Class on Party Preference

Class	*Conservative*	*Labour*	*Liberal*	*Nationalist and none*	*Total in population*
Middle	59%	17%	16%	8%	13%
Lower middle	50	26	15	10	23
Working	35	42	12	11	64

Source: Calculated by the author from unpublished Gallup Poll, May 1979.

working-class voters who owned their own homes. Among the lower middle class, a majority of council tenants favored Labour, and a majority of homeowners favored the Conservatives.

Analyzing the relationship of class and political participation is difficult, because full-time politicians, by definition, have middle-class jobs. The great majority of Conservative MPs come from middle-class homes; politics neither raises nor lowers their occupational status. The Labour party, by contrast, has always drawn a significant proportion of its MPs from working-class families; the power of trade unions to nominate their members in many safe Labour seats maintains this pattern. Educational changes since World War II have created a third type of Labour MP, a person born into a working-class home who assumes a middle-class career by being a university graduate. The civil service disproportionately recruits the offspring of middle-class families because it draws primarily from the universities, and students there are disproportionately middle class. The higher the political job, the greater the likelihood that it will be filled by someone who began in the middle class.

While class differences affect party loyalty and, even more, recruitment into active political roles, they do not lead to political attitudes based on assumptions of class conflict. When people are interviewed about class-related issues, differences are found within the middle class and within the working class. The two groups are not cohesive and opposing in views. Approximately one-fifth of the electorate sees party politics in class terms, but fewer see politics in terms of mutually exclusive, as distinct from differing, class interests.

The Cumulative Effect

In the course of a lifetime, every English citizen is subject to a variety of social experiences; some emphasize differences among individual citizens, others emphasize a common identity. Because English society is very homogeneous in terms of race, religion, national identity, and urban life-style, socialization emphasizes many common values. France, Germany, Belgium, and the Netherlands — not to mention the United States and Canada — are far more pluralistic in social structure.

The English are said to differ politically along class lines because only class differences are substantial in size and political impact. The greatest degree of partisanship is shown by the smallest social groups within English society: middle-class rural Protestants (Conservative advantage, 45 percent). The largest group — urban Protestant manual workers — shows the most even division of partisanship (the Labour advantage is but 9 percent).

When all the socialization influences described here are combined in a complex statistical equation they explain less than one-third (31.7 percent) of the variation between Conservative and Labour voters. Parent's class and party identification account for nearly two-thirds of the variance that can be explained. One reason that English people do not vote strictly along class lines is that most do not have socialization experiences consistent with idealized definitions of middle-class Conservatives and working-class Labour supporters. Changes such as the collapse and resurgence of the Liberal party also encourage discontinuities in behavior. Political socialization influences the probabilities of political action; it does not determine such action.

Popular Participation

If a government is to govern everyone must participate, and virtually everyone does in England, if participation is defined as paying taxes and drawing benefits. The mixed-economy welfare state provides benefits at every stage of life, from maternity and children's allowances through schooling, housing, and health to a pension in old age and a death benefit for the next of kin. Up to three-quarters of the population lives in a household drawing a weekly cash benefit from government and even more are part of a family that annually enjoys such major benefits as health care, education, or a pension.

Elections provide the one opportunity that English people have to influence government directly. Virtually every British citizen age eighteen or over is eligible to vote. The burden of registration is undertaken by local government officials, and registration lists are revised annually to maintain accuracy. The wide dispersal of polling stations, the compactness of the territory, and the individual sense of citizen duty result in a high turnout compared to that in the

United States, though not compared with other European countries. In the ten general elections since 1950, turnout has averaged 77.4 percent of the electorate.

Of the total electorate, 19 percent say they have a great deal of interest in politics outside an election campaign. The working class provides a majority both of those interested and of those not at all interested. When voters are asked to identify major politicians, the average respondent names three persons; only 5 percent can name one Liberal, three Conservative, and three Labour front benchers.

The Conservative and Labour parties maintain constituency associations throughout England, and the Liberals wish to do so. There are no restrictive entrance rules; the parties seek as many members as are willing to join. With only a little initiative or effort, a person may become a ward secretary of a local party or a member of its general management committee. In the Labour party, nearly 90 percent of the party's supporters are affiliated through trade unions; party dues are paid as part of union dues. Some of these "members" do not know that they belong to the Labour party. The Labour party has an estimated 300,000 individual members; the Conservatives have an estimated 1 million members. For most party members, paying dues is the extent of their participation.

Another measure of political involvement is participation in local political activities, from voting to standing as a candidate for public office. One survey found that 7 percent of the English electorate engages in at least five of ten common political activities.[44] A majority of these vote, help in fund-raising efforts, urge people to vote, hold office in an organization, recommend that people contact an MP, make a public talk, and present their views to an MP. The activists are almost evenly divided between Conservative and Labour supporters. The activists are not a representative cross-section of the society, but they do include substantial numbers from all ages, classes, and educational backgrounds, and both sexes.

Many English people indirectly participate in politics by belonging to organized interest groups. These range from an anglers' club concerned with the pollution of a local stream to the Automobile Association representing motorists. An estimated 61 percent of the population belongs to at least one organization (see Table 9.5). A total of 14 percent are officers or committee members of a voluntary organization.

In the 1970s ad hoc protest groups appeared in local and national politics. Many of these groups reflect local concern over a single issue. The concentration of politics in London makes it possible for London-based protest organizations to appear as nationwide organizations, by hiring a hall and advertising a meeting. Overall, only 6 percent of the electorate say they have taken part in a lawful street demonstration, and even fewer have participated in illegal protests.[45]

The majority of English people participate in national politics by voting and belonging to a voluntary organization.[46] A number of indicators show 5 to 14 percent of the electorate regularly involved in politics. If holding elected office is the measure of involvement, the proportion drops below 1 percent. By this standard one could argue that the proportion of the adult population actively participating in politics in England today is scarcely higher than it was before the passage of democratic franchise reforms in the nineteenth century.

Recruiting for Central Political Roles

There are two contrasting approaches to studying central political roles. One is to define the tasks of a political job, then recruit individuals with appropriate skills. This is the approach of management theory. The other is to proceed inductively, analyzing the attributes that influence recruitment and ask: given their skills, what kind of job can these politicians do? Because of the constraints that history and contemporary conventions place on recruitment in England, the inductive approach is more suitable.

The holders of central political roles can be

[44] Robert M. Worcester, "The Hidden Activists," in Rose (ed.), *Studies in British Politics*, 3rd ed., pp. 198–203.

[45] Marsh, *Protest and Political Consciousness*, p. 45.

[46] The most thorough British surveys of participation, from which much of the data in Table 9.5 is drawn, are M. Horton, *The Local Government Elector*, and Louis Moss and Stanley Parker, *The Local Government Councillor*, vol. 2 (London: Her Majesty's Stationery Office, 1967).

Table 9.5

Involvement in National Politics

	Estimated number of people (in millions)	*Estimated percentage of adults*
Eligible electorate, 1978	41.2	98
Voters, 1979	29.2	76
Organization members	24.0	61
Receiving weekly cash benefit	12.8	47
Great deal of interest	8.0	19
Official post in organization	5.5	14
Political activists	2.8	7
Protest demonstrations	2.5	6
Individual party members	2.0	5
MP, senior civil servant	0.0	0.1

Sources: Electorate and voters: Home Office. Organization members and officers, *The Local Government Elector* (London: Her Majesty's Stationery Office, 1967), pp. 113 ff. Cash benefits, estimated from: *Social Trends*, (London: Her Majesty's Stationery Office, Vol. 9, 1979), pp. 106ff; Political interest. *SSRC British Electoral Survey*, October 1974, Q. 44; Political activists: Robert M. Worcester, "The Hidden Activists," *New Society*, June 8, 1972; Protest demonstrations: Alan C. Marsh, *Protest and Political Consciousness*, pp. 45 ff; Individual party members: estimate by author; MP, senior civil servant: derived by the author from official statistics.

grouped under three broad headings: Cabinet ministers, senior civil servants, and intermittent public persons. Members of Parliament are not central to government unless they attain ministerial position. Ministers must be elected to Parliament and then selected for promotion. Civil servants first compete by examination and then gain promotion by seniority and selection. Intermittent public persons depend on patronage for appointment to public bodies or owe their prominence to positions of leadership in major pressure groups independent of government.

A few generalizations can be made about those in central political roles. First, experience is positively valued. Starting early on a path that can lead to political eminence is almost a precondition of success. Those who seek leading roles are not expected to start at the bottom in local politics and work their way gradually to the top in Westminster. Instead, an individual must early become a "cadet" in a London position qualifying for a central political role, then gradually accumulate seniority and skill. The process might be described as working one's way sideways, for seniority will carry a person a substantial distance forward.

A second influence upon recruitment is geographical. MPs, senior civil servants, and most intermittent public persons spend all their working lives in London. MPs are not required to have lived in the constituency that nominates them, or even to take up residence there upon election. Jobs outside London are remote from the centers of power. Election to the Commons is virtually a precondition for selection as a Cabinet minister. Nomination for winnable or safe seats involves competition among aspirants for the favor of the local party's selection committee. There are no American-style popular primaries.

Once elected, at least two-thirds of MPs can count on a career of fifteen years or longer in the Commons, because most parliamentary seats are safe for reelection. In promoting an individual to a ministerial post, a prime minister may use any of three criteria: representativeness, loyalty, and competence. An MP may be offered an appointment as a representative of women, of Scots, or of a political tendency within the parliamentary party. Even opponents may be offered posts, to gain their silence through collective responsibility. Loyalty to the prime minister is important to counterbalance potential opposition in the Cabinet and to encourage back-bench MPs in the belief that loyalty brings rewards. A prime minister's discretion in recruiting ministers is limited by the fact that there are over one hundred jobs to distribute among approximately two hundred eligible MPs. Many back benchers are ruled out on the grounds of parliamentary inexperience, old age, extremism, personal unreliability, or lack of interest in office. A majority of all MPs elected three times or more are given a ministerial post.

Experience in the Commons does not prepare an individual for a minister's work. The chief concerns of an MP are dealing with people and talking about ideas. These attributes are useful in Whitehall too, but a minister must also be able to handle paperwork, know how to appraise policy alternatives, and know how to relate political generalities to a specific technical problem.

The recruitment procedure ensures that ministers have had ample experience in one of their important tasks: handling parliamentary business. But it does not provide persons with substantial knowledge of their departments' subjects. The restriction of appointments to established MPs prevents a nationwide canvass for specialists. Little more than 10 percent of ministers are appointed to departments where they can claim some expertise.

The one way in which a minister can be sure of learning about a department's work is to learn on the job. The amount of time required to learn the ropes of a department varies with the department's complexity. Anthony Crosland, a Labour minister with an unusually analytical mind, reckoned: "It takes you six months to get your head properly above water, a year to get the general drift of most of the field, and two years really to master the whole of a department."[47] It can take more than two years for a minister to see a measure through.

[47] Quoted in Maurice Kogan, *The Politics of Education* (Harmondsworth: Penguin, 1971), p. 155.

The conventions of patronage cause a frequent reshuffling of ministers from department to department. From 1955 to 1970 the average minister in a major department stayed in one office only 2.2 years. The speed of ministerial turnover is one of the highest in Western nations, and is increasing. When a minister is moved, he invariably goes to a department where he has had no previous experience.

The recruitment of ministers has come under criticism as part of a general cry for reform. Industrialists argue the need for more businesslike ministers, and economists the need for more economic expertise. Some praise the American system of recruiting for the federal executive from large organizations outside Washington — whether state governments, universities, or profit-making companies. Only in wartime emergencies, when persons with management experience were required to run the administrative apparatus of modern war, has a prime minister made a special effort to recruit ministers from outside Parliament.[48]

In the 1970 Conservative government, and in subsequent governments of both parties special advisers were recruited from outside Parliament and the civil service. The advisers are intended to assist ministers, particularly in remembering the broader concerns of the party they claim to represent. In the 1960s, it was assumed that technical expertise was lacking in Whitehall. Today, some reckon that political expertise is lacking there.

The recruitment of senior civil servants has been a controversial subject for generations. Most of the controversy has concerned the class origins of recruits to the Civil Service, especially the Foreign Office. Less attention has been given to the skills required of recruits. In 1968, the Fulton Committee on the reform of the civil service claimed that civil servants should be recruited on the basis of relevant knowledge, "minds disciplined by the social studies, the mathematical and physical sciences, the biological sciences or in the applied and engineering sciences."[49] It did not, however, indicate why scientific or engineering subjects should necessarily be more relevant to the work of Whitehall administrators than

[48] See Rose, *Problem of Party Government*, ch. 14–16 for a discussion of the impact upon government of existing methods of recruiting ministers and civil servants.

[49] Fulton Committee, *Report*, pp. 27 ff.

history or classics. The committee also failed to agree about a straightforward test for relevant knowledge. The Civil Service Commission has since remedied this deficiency. Candidates for the highest posts are now examined for verbal aptitude and their ability to summarize lengthy papers, to resolve a problem by fitting specific facts to general regulations, to draw inferences from simple statistics, and to follow diagrams. But most senior civil servants today were recruited under rules, which allowed a wide choice of academic studies; the majority specialized in medieval and modern history or in Latin and Greek.

Because bright young people enter the civil service with few specialist skills and spend decades before reaching senior posts, role socialization is particularly important. Civil service recruits, whether descended from coal miners or aristocrats, are expected to learn what to do by following the procedures of their seniors. Senior civil servants determine the promotion of their juniors. Co-option ensures the transmission of established assumptions about how government works, although it need not imply agreement about what should be done in particular policy areas. A civil servant is promoted because he knows how things should be done, and not because of his views about policies. He is inoculated against deep involvement in subject matter by frequent transferrals from post to post; the average administrator lasts 2.8 years in a particular job.

Many individuals are only intermittently involved in politics and may not see themselves in a political role. If all persons holding government appointments are political, then the archbishop of Canterbury, the director general of the British Broadcasting Corporation, the regius professor of Greek at Oxford, and the astronomer royal are politicians. If challenged, each would probably deny that he or she was a politician, yet each would also claim to be carrying out official duties with regard for the public interest.

Tens of thousands of English citizens are recruited into part-time government service — most without salary — through appointments to bodies concerned with public policy. Civic-minded people are expected to serve without reluctance on a council, committee, or commission, or to assist law enforcement as a justice of the peace. Many members of government committees are there because they have jobs in organizations affected by the committee's deliberations. Interest-group appointees are often balanced as committee chairmen by a "lay gent," a person whose amateurism implies neutrality about government work. The Treasury is said to keep a list of "the great and the good" to act as lay representatives of the public on committees.

A very small proportion of those in central political roles are temporary recruits to a full-time government post. The contribution of any temporary recruit is limited by the vice of his virtue: the more novel the perspective an individual brings to Whitehall, the greater the number of procedures must be learned to operate effectively. The more the recruit learns, the less novel his perspective.

No precise estimate can be made of the number of people intermittently involved in central political roles. The number is certainly far greater than the number of MPs or senior civil servants, because these latter groups are small. Public persons usually have two things in common. They have never been a candidate for elective office and they have never been an established civil servant. Protestations to the contrary, these intermittent public persons are as much (and sometimes more) involved in the policy process than the average MP.

Politicians and Society

Traditionally, the leaders of English society were simultaneously social, economic, and political personages. But the twentieth century has brought about the rise of the full-time professional politician, just as it has brought professionalization to many other social roles, from sports to scholarship. Aristocrats, businessmen, or trade union leaders cannot expect to translate their high standing elsewhere into an important post within politics. Since the end of World War II no leader from the business world has been a senior Cabinet minister, and only two leading trade union officials have.

Intensive apprenticeship is a prerequisite for success in most aspects of English life today. Just as a Cabinet minister must usually spend years as an MP, so a trade union secretary must start as a shop steward, a professor as a university lecturer, and a general as a lieutenant. In consequence, political leaders in England today are far more distant from other leaders in society than in the predemocratic era. After years of interviewing men in leading positions in many different areas of English life, Anthony Sampson concluded:

> My own fear is not that the Establishment in Britain is too close, but that it is not close enough, that the circles are overlapping less and less and that one half of the ring has very little contact with the other half.[50]

The extent to which political recruitment is regarded as closed depends on the size of the political class within society. Nothing could be more selective than a parliamentary election that results in one person becoming prime minister out of a country of 55 million people. Yet nothing is considered more representative, because an election is the one occasion in which every English adult participates in politics with equal effect.

The greater the scope of activities defined as political, the greater the number of people participating in politics. Growing government intervention in the economy has made company directors and shop stewards at least intermittent politicans. Yet their economic position gives them freedom to act independently of government. Workers can vote with their feet by an unofficial strike. Businessmen can vote with their pocketbooks by investing money outside the United Kingdom.

Like success in polo, success in politics is due to skill and experience. But the readiness and opportunity to play the game and develop the skills are not determined by natural aptitudes. They depend also on personal and family circumstances, as well as on general social characteristics.

Among active political participants, intense socialization into the role of politician is likely to override other influences. This is illustrated by what happens when an opposition party is elected to office. The new leaders can alter policy, but accession to office may also alter the men. Lord Balneil, the heir to one of the oldest titles in Britain, has noted that existing patterns of politics are preserved "not so much by the conscious efforts of the well established, but by the zeal of those who have just won entry, and by the hopes of those who still aspire."[51]

[50] Anthony Sampson, *Anatomy of Britain* (London: Hodder and Stoughton, 1962), pp. 222–223.

[51] Lord Balneil, "The Upper Classes," *The Twentieth Century*, No. 999 (1960), p. 432.

ARTICULATING INTERESTS

Political demands are put before the government in two ways: through such communication media as television and the press, and through specialized political institutions, such as organized interest groups and political parties.

The liberal model of English politics demands a great flow of information between governing and governed. The greater the supply of information, the better informed the public and, since the public is expected to be the ultimate arbiter of policy, the better the policies of government. In the liberal model, the government is expected to supply information freely to the governed because the public has the right to know. By contrast, the Whitehall model of communication is very different. Information is assumed to be a scarce commodity and, like all scarce commodities, it is not freely exchanged. Publicity is thought to be costly not only because of the time required, but also because public discussion of policy might interfere with private negotiations among spokesmen for affected groups. Many laws and Whitehall conventions assume that publicity is not in the public interest. Both points of view are expressed in politics; the Whitehall model is predominate.

Political Communication

The mass media are large and complex industries. Television and radio are highly centralized but competitive channels of political communication. The British Broadcasting Corporation (BBC) provides two television networks, four radio networks, and local stations throughout the United Kingdom. The Independent Broadcasting Authority (IBA) licenses fifteen companies to produce programs for regional audiences; they exchange programs to provide network services. Commercial local radio stations are also operated under IBA auspices.

Because of technical limitations on channel availability and economic limitations on program competition, the broadcasting industry is subject to government licensing. The BBC's board of governors is appointed by the government, as are the members of the IBA. Each body operates under a government charter subject to periodic review and renewal. The BBC depends for much of its revenue upon a license bought by each household with a television set; the annual revenue of independent television companies revenue comes primarily from advertising.

The general public trusts the impartiality of the broadcasting media. In one national survey, only 9 percent attributed any political bias to BBC news, and only 7 percent found bias in commercial television. Weekly current-affairs programs are similarly viewed as impartial. This confidence is not shared by politicians. One criticism, from members of both major parties, is that broadcasting does not give enough time to programs viewers ought to watch, that is, programs concerning Parliament. Politicians' complaints may be motivated by the belief that their unpopularity rests not with themselves and what they do, but with those who communicate news about them.

Studies of audience reaction to politics on television emphasize the little effect programs have on basic political outlooks. People judge programs in the light of their party loyalty; they do not choose a party in response to their program preference. Long-time Conservatives like Conservative programs best, and veteran Labour supporters like Labour programs best — regardless of program content.[52]

The English press, unlike that in the United States and in many continental European countries, is centralized. Seven morning newspapers printed in London circulate throughout England, thanks to special shipping facilities. London-based papers account for two-thirds of daily circulation, and nearly all Sunday circulation. The concentration of production is made necessary by the high costs of newspaper operation and the great influence of advertising. A popular newspaper has difficulty breaking even with a circulation of 1 million because it may not attract sufficient advertising. National papers with circulations smaller than 1 million require a specialist readership to justify premium advertising rates.

The influence of a paper on the political outlook of its readers is not independent of other influences. A reader's views will be affected by class and party loyalty as well as by the paper; class influences the choice of paper as it does that of party. Not surprisingly, Conservative families are more likely to read pro-Conservative papers, and Labour families prefer pro-Labour papers.

Both the press and broadcasting influence political discussion through their decisions about what is worth reporting and what is not. Ministers complain that their difficulties and failures are always news, but claims of success by ministers will also be printed, if the minister has high political status. In the words of a political journalist, "You may not believe what a man is saying, but if he is Prime Minister, he has a right to have his views known."[53] Competition among papers makes it all but impossible for the government to repress or disguise events defined as newsworthy.

Although their professional interests are different, communicators and politicians need each other. Journalists need politicians as news sources; politicians need journalists to publicize their views and themselves. Members of the general public, however, may neither notice nor care about the publicity that results.

Many conventions and laws in English political life emphasize noncommunication rather than communication. Politicians fearing public embarrassment avoid public discussion whenever possible. Civil servants often dislike public discussion because it involves controversy and delays. Official Whitehall policy is that information about policy questions should be published "whenever reasonably possible." Whitehall is the sole judge of what is reasonable.

The obstacles to communication result in imperfect communication; even ministers do not know everything they wish to know. Time is one problem. There are not enough hours in the day for any minister to read everything about her department or to draft or sign every statement issued in her name. A minister must communicate views in general terms, so that staff can apply them in particular instances without direct communication. The complexity of government is another inhibiting factor. A minister cannot keep informed about all that goes on in his

[52] See Marplan, *Political Index* (January 1970), p. 5; and BBC Audience Research Department Report, "The February 1974 General Election on Television," in Rose (ed.), *Studies in British Politics*, 3rd ed., pp. 292–304.

[53] Private conversation of the author with well known Fleet Street journalist.

department. When scandals occur, the minister is formally responsible, but can truthfully plead that he did not know what was being done in his name. The flow of information between central and local government is also inhibited by geographical and institutional distance.

The doctrine of ministerial responsibility, and the corollary of civil service anonymity, remains powerful because it appeals to the most important people in government, ministers and civil servants. Ministers do not wish to have news of differences within their department discussed in public prior to their decision. Civil servants regard confidentiality as the basis of trust for the exchange of opinions and advice between them and ministers.

Noncommunication between government and governed can create problems of credibility, a point increasingly realized in Whitehall. Outside groups — the press, academics, and MPs — are pressuring Whitehall to reveal more about what is going on inside government. Moreover, some Whitehall officials now believe that public discussion of policy alternatives in advance of a final decision helps to anticipate criticism and remove defects from legislation, as well as mobilize consent.

Busy policy makers want help, not information for its own sake. Whitehall departments will encourage interest groups to articulate their interests if they are unsure about popular acceptance of various alternatives. They will discourage discussion if they feel confident about what they wish to do. A policy maker's readiness to listen to interest articulation is not a function of the quality of information, but of political realities.

Interest Groups

Interest groups and parties are the most familiar organizations articulating political demands. Interest groups are distinct from parties because they do not seek to control the government by contesting elections. Instead, they seek to influence the decisions of government, whichever party is in office.

British interest groups, especially trade unions, are highly integrated into party politics. In the Labour Party, trade unions provide nearly 90 percent of the party's affiliated members, more than 85 percent of votes at party conferences, and 85 percent of its income. They control eighteen of the twenty-eight seats on its National Executive Committee and sponsor more than one-third of Labour MPs. The relationship between British unions and the Labour party is much closer than similar relationships in the United States, where the AFL-CIO has no institutional voice or vote in the Democratic party convention. It is also different from the pattern in France or Italy, where union members divide along political lines into socialist-, communist-, and Christian-oriented unions.

The Conservative party existed long before industry rose to political influence, and its structure was established independently of business groups. Businessmen disliking a Labour government have no choice but to support the Conservative cause: the Liberals' weak position gives them little appeal to business interests. There is no formal institutional connection between business groups and the Conservative party; support is chiefly in the form of financial contribution.[54]

Many interest groups advocate demands remote from partisan controversies, for example, one organization represents ex-servicemen who have lost arms or legs. A study of organized urban interest groups found that more than four-fifths of their demands had little salience to party controversy.[55] But the growth of government influence on the mixed economy has tended to politicize many issues that interest groups would prefer to regard as nonpolitical, that is, demands that the government, regardless of party, should grant.

The more durable, frequent, numerous, and intense the contacts among individuals, the easier they are to organize for political action. Miners have all the characteristics that lead to cohesive organization. They usually work at mining all their lives; their work is always in contact with fellow miners, and they frequently meet miners outside the pits, because they live clustered in mining villages. And because homes are near the pits, the future of a mine becomes the future of a community. By contrast, members of a group traveling on a charter flight are virtually incapable of organization, for they meet

[54] For the complexities of business involvement in politics, see Wyn Grant and David Marsh, *The Confederation of British Industry* (London: Hodder and Stoughton, 1977).

[55] See Kenneth Newton and David Morris, "British Interest Group Theory Re-examined," *Comparative Politics*, 7:4 (1975), p. 587.

only once. A feature distinguishing British interest groups is their degree of formal organization. Whatever the interest affected by a government policy, one or more organizations probably claim to represent it and seek to influence the government.

Of all the political resources that interest groups command, strategic location is the most significant. An organization is in a strategic position if it can, like the National Union of Mineworkers, quickly create a political crisis by withdrawing cooperation. Electricity-supply workers and bankers, for example, have stronger strategic positions than garment manufacturers. In extreme instances, a group may exit from the authority of government. Bankers may do business outside Britain when they fear devaluation, or trade union leaders may refuse to recognize government-established negotiating and arbitration procedures. A union crucial to the everyday activities of society may also exert pressure by calling a strike. The loyalty of members to leaders is another group resource. Group votes in elections are of little importance, because few group leaders can sway individual votes from the powerful pull of established class and party loyalties. Publicity is useful, but it is employed as the sole resource only by those with no other advantages.

Whitehall prefers to deal with cohesive interest groups, because that is administratively convenient. An agreement made between a government department and an organized group is more likely to be carried out, or so it is believed in Whitehall. But decades of attempting to secure agreement about how to improve the British economy have shown that group leaders cannot guarantee that any bargain they make with a Whitehall department will be carried out if group members do not deem it in their interest. Group leaders can articulate members' demands but they cannot force their members to accept them. As one experienced British economist has noted:

> Neither the trade unions nor management have systems of private government that can send plenipotentiaries to negotiate on their behalf and commit them to settlement, save on limited issues and particular occasions, when the negotiators can keep in touch with their constituents as the negotiations proceed.[56]

[56] E. H. Phelps-Brown, "The National Economic Development Organization," *Public Administration*, 51 (Autumn 1963), p. 245.

Interest groups exert influence within a framework of political values and institutions. The likelihood of any group gaining wide support for its demands depends on the congruence between group demands and the values, beliefs, and emotions of the culture. One belief is accepted throughout the culture: the right of affected interests to be consulted before the government announces its decision. Interest group officials realize that their demands will not always be met by the government, but they expect that the government will listen to them before making policy. The more a group's goals are consistent with cultural norms, the easier it is for the group to equate its interest with the national interest.

The structure of the political system is an important influence on the activities of interest groups. Techniques and strategies customary in England would often be inappropriate in the United States, for the decentralization of American government, both in Washington and at lower levels, requires influence to be directed toward many institutions and makes institutions more accessible to influence. The centralization of the British government focuses virtually all interest group attention on Whitehall departments.

Interest groups give most attention to senior civil servants and departmental ministers because many key decisions affecting the groups are made within a department. Competing group demands tend to reduce the influence of any single group. In economic affairs, which attract the largest number of interest groups, the claims of finance, industry, and commerce, for example, are often opposed to those of trade unions. Members of groups are themselves subject to conflicting loyalties. A businessman who wishes taxes lowered may, as a parent and motorist, wish more public money spent on education and on roads.

The extent of group influence depends chiefly on the scope and scale of the decision sought. The wider the decision's implications, the greater the likelihood it will be controversial among conflicting groups. Where the spending of public funds is involved, the Treasury acts as a further restraint. And some decisions sought by groups will be rejected as unacceptable to the government. In 1945, for example, the Labour government entered office committed to nationalizing a number of industries. It was not concerned with negotiating the principle — whether the mines or the railways should be nationalized — but with deciding how nationalization should take place. Business interests thus had the choice of cooperating in their own demise, or fighting government on principle — and losing.

The most important influence on a group's success is the pattern of policy of the government. In part, this reflects long-term commitments made by previous governments. But parties, rather than interest groups, decide whether or not a group's demands are regarded as nonpartisan. By making a political issue of its activities, say the cost of pharmaceuticals to the National Health Service, a group of drug manufacturers can be dragged into political controversy against their will, and forced to bargain with government from weakness. A group is subject to perpetual tension: should it seek nonpartisan status by a strategy of responsibility, cooperating with the government in hopes of securing amendments in its interest? Or should it be outspoken in articulating its interests, even when this leads to controversy with the government, and threatens the gain of concessions?

Interest groups seek four things from government: information about government attitudes and policy shifts likely to affect their interests; the good will of the administrators who carry out policy; influence over government policy; and symbolic status (allowing an organization to add the prefix "royal" to its title, or awarding a knighthood to its general secretary). Government, in turn, seeks four things from groups: information about society that is not available from other sources; advice on what groups think should be done and their reaction to various policy alternatives; cooperation with the law; and rarely, the administration of government policies on its behalf.

Because most of these needs are complementary, interest groups and the government find it easy to negotiate. Negotiations proceed without threats of coercion or bribery, because each needs the other. The object of negotiation is agreement. Public officials and group spokesmen know that, if there are many interests and points of view, it is most convenient to reach a compromise or consensus. Agreement is convenient for participants because it avoids decisions being made by outsiders in Cabinet or Parliament (i.e., politicians) who know and care less about details than those involved.

THE PARTY SYSTEM: AGGREGATION AND CHOICE

British government is party government.[57] Parties organize the selection of candidates, the preparation of policies, and the conduct of elections. In a general election, a voter does not vote for preferred policies, but for the party that is deemed best at aggregating the interests and values of millions of citizens. Voters do not determine who governs, but which party shall govern.

Electoral Choice

The prime minister determines when an election is held. An election must occur at least once every five years, but within that time the prime minister is free to request the Queen to dissolve Parliament and call a general election at any time of the governing party's choice. Thus, the person with the most to win or lose by an election can try to select the most favorable date.

The ballot offers each voter a simple choice. A voter is confronted with a small sheet of paper giving the name, address, occupation and party label of the several persons who seek to become the sole MP from one of the 635 constituencies into which the United Kingdom is divided for electoral purposes. The ideas and arguments of tens of thousands of political activists and the decisions of many party committees are aggregated by the ballot paper into a choice between a few standard bearers.

The choice of an individual voter reflects personal characteristics and social influences as well as issue preferences. Images of a party are derived from its past achievements and the voter's past experiences. When voters are asked what they like or dislike about the Conservative and Labour parties, they say such things as "it knows how to run the country" or "it doesn't know how to run the country"; "it's good for the working class" or "it's bad for the working class." The images imply a judgment that past performance will persist in the future. Voter attitudes are sensitive to historical achievements. By comparison with

[57] For a detailed exposition of the subject, see Rose, *The Problem of Party Government*.

party images, the images of individual leaders or local parliamentary candidates are ephemeral and insignificant.

Because shifts in voting tend to cancel out, the net fluctuation in the vote for the two major parties is small (see Figure 9.2). Since 1945 the Conservative share of the national vote has varied by 13.9 percent and the Labour share by 11.9 percent. In the United States, by comparison, the Republicans share of the total vote has varied by 22.2 percent, and the Democratic share by 23.6 percent.

The logic of the electoral system favors the single strongest party, however small or large its share of the vote. To win election to Parliament, a candidate need not gain an absolute majority, but only a plurality, as in an American congressional election. From 1945 through 1970, about three-quarters of all MPs were elected with more than half the vote in their constituency. But the proportion fell to 40 percent in 1974.

The electoral system usually manufactures a majority party in Parliament from a minority of votes. No party has won more than half the popular vote since the 1935 general election. Yet at every election since then, except for February 1974, one party has won an absolute majority of seats in the House of Commons. In the extreme case of October 1974, the Labour party won a bare majority of 318 seats with only 39.2 percent of the popular vote. By contrast, the Liberals won only 13 seats with 18.3 percent of the vote. The system is not meant to provide parliamentary representation proportional to votes, but to give one party absolute control and complete responsibility for what government does.

The May 3, 1979 general election reinforced the two-party system. The electoral system gave the Conservatives an absolute majority in the House of Commons, with 339 of the 635 seats. The Conservatives, however, gained this majority with 43.9 percent of the popular vote, a lower share than the losing party received in elections in the 1950s. Labour saw its popular vote drop to 37.0 percent of the total, its lowest share since 1931. The Liberals won 13.8 percent of the popular vote, but with 11 MPs could only claim 1.7 percent of the membership in the Commons. The Liberal, Nationalist, and Ulster parties between them secured nearly one in every five votes.

Britain can be said to have a two-party system by one measure only: the number of parties that have formed a government since 1945. Since then, government has been in the hands of either the Labour party or the Conservative party, others have been excluded from office. The Liberals were even excluded from office in 1977–1978, when the Labour government depended on the votes of thirteen Liberals for a working majority. Liberals gained the right to discuss pending legislation with the government, but not to sit in government or, as it turned out, to exert significant positive influence on legislation.

In electoral terms, however, Britain has a multiparty system. This is clearly and consistently shown in four ways. First, in most constituencies three or more candidates normally contest a seat: Labour, Conservative, and Liberal or Nationalist. In May 1979, a total of 2,576 candidates contested 635 seats, an average of 4 candidates per seat. Second, the two major parties do not monopolize the popular vote. They came closest to doing so in 1951, when they collectively secured 96.8 percent of the popular vote. But they have not secured more than 90 percent of the vote since 1959. In October 1974, they took only 75 percent; in May 1979 the figure rose to 80.9 percent. Third, the two major parties do not monopolize seats in the House of Commons. The electoral system has on average awarded Conservative and Labour parties 97 percent of the seats in the House of Commons. But in 1950 and in 1964 a small third group prevented the government from holding a secure Commons majority for five years. And fourth, outside England, many parties win significant numbers of seats and votes. In the extreme case of Northern Ireland, parties are organized around two religions — Protestant and Catholic — and since 1974 the British Labour and Conservative parties have not nominated any candidates there. In Scotland, the Scottish National party won the second largest share of the popular vote in 1974, and in 1979 it won 17 percent of the Scottish vote. In Wales, the combined strength of Liberals and the Welsh Nationalists left the two major parties with 80.8 percent of the Welsh vote in 1979.

The party system is better described as multiparty than three-party, because the name and number of relevant parties differs from election to election, as well as from area to area of the United Kingdom.

Figure 9.2

Votes Cast in British General Elections, 1918–1979 (in percentages)

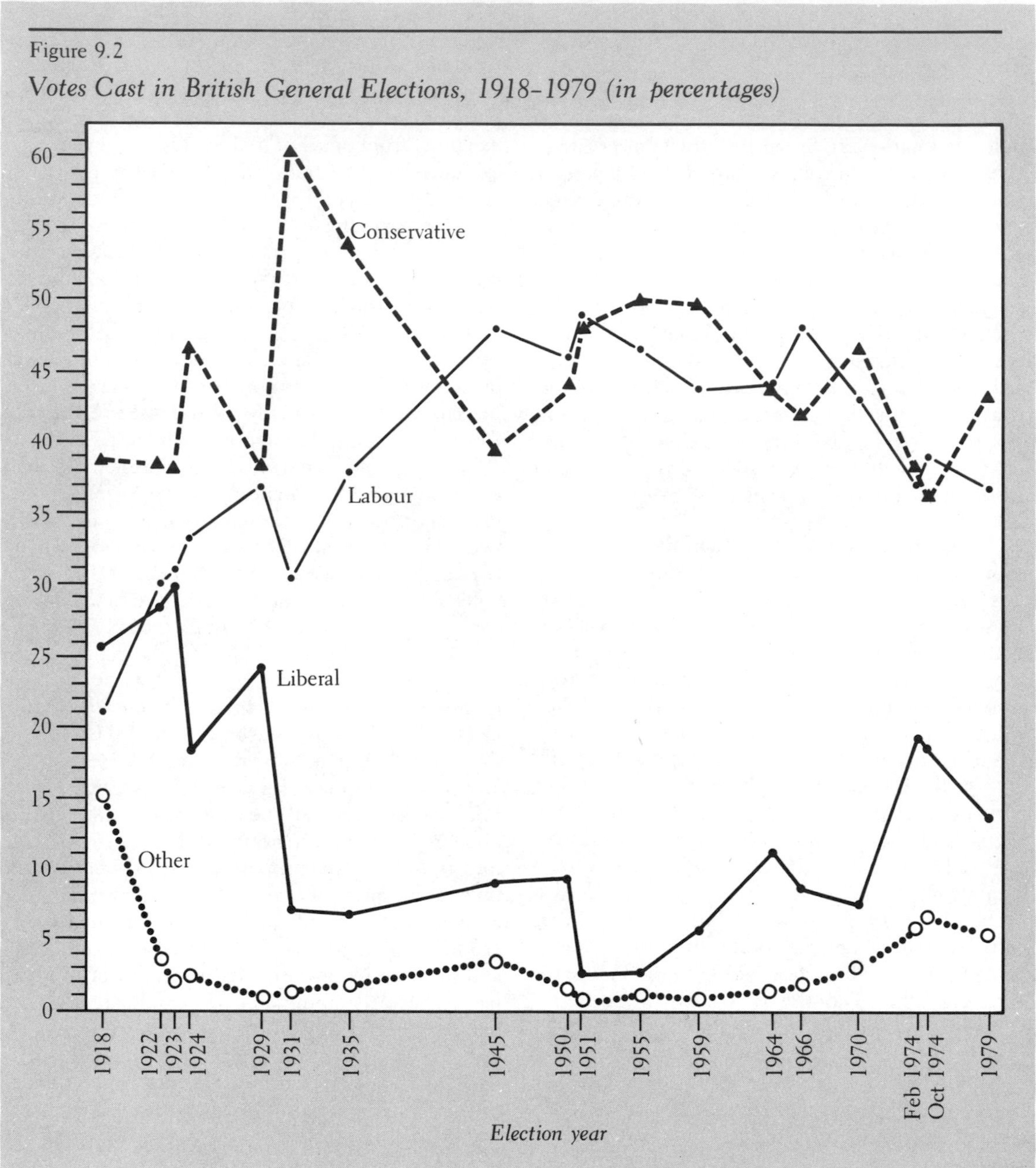

The Liberals have consistently run third in total votes in the United Kingdom, but they have not won more than fourteen MPs in any election since 1945. In Scotland, the Scottish National party was third in total votes, but fourth in seats won following the 1979 election. In Wales, Plaid Cymru was fourth in total votes, but third in Welsh MPs. In Northern Ireland, party labels are multiple and fast changing. The two poles of electoral competition are constant, but labeled by religion.

There is always a third choice, even when only two parties are on the ballot: not voting. The level of voluntary or involuntary abstention is low in England by comparison with the United States, but high by European standards. While nonpolitical reasons appear to explain most abstentions, it is noteworthy that the proportion of eligible voters not voting at a general election has risen from 16.1 percent in 1951 to 27.2 percent in 1970.

Control of Organization

Party organizations are often referred to as machines, but the term is a misnomer. The parties do not manufacture votes at election time and a party headquarters cannot necessarily manufacture support for a leader being criticized; nor is party organization designed to convert voter preferences into government policy by any mechanical process recognizable, even metaphorically.

British parties are organizations with formal institutions and offices, established by written constitutions, and staffed by bureaucrats whose careers depend on loyalty to the organizations, not to individual politicians or financial supporters. Yet fragmentation is a dominant feature of party structure. Different people rule at different levels of organization — constituency, headquarters, and Parliament. Moreover, power is distributed differently in the Conservative and Labour parties.

Constituency parties are local party units that select the party's parliamentary candidate; collectively, the elected choices of constituency parties constitute the party in the House of Commons, the pool of talent from which a prime minister selects a Cabinet. At no stage in the selection of parliamentary candidate are the voters of the constituency consulted, as they are in an American primary. The decentralization of candidate selection allows the selection of MPs with a wide variety of political outlooks and interests. Once elected to the Commons, three-quarters of MPs have safe seats and need not fear rejection by the voters. As long as they avoid antagonizing their local constituency party, they are sure to be readopted as a candidate; nomination is nearly tantamount to election.

The party in Parliament expresses the policy of the national party. Once the party takes a position in Parliament, its position becomes a political fact. In a crisis commitments must be made without time to consult with the party outside Parliament. This is especially true of the governing party. The need of speed and the constitutional conventions greatly limit consultation by the party leadership, sometimes even excluding consultation with back benchers in their own party.

The party leader is strongest when also prime minister. Constitutional conventions and Cabinet patronage strengthen a prime minister's hand. Moreover, an open attack on a prime minister threatens loss of office through intraparty conflict. The opposition leader has no powers of patronage, and influence will vary with the expectation of followers about whether the leader will be prime minister or a loser after the next election.

A prime minister is likely to reach the height of influence midway in tenure. At this stage, the prime minister will have had the opportunity to establish her personality and preferences among the party followers. In theory, the prime minister could retire at the height of influence. Stanley Baldwin, who left office voluntarily in 1937, was the last to do so until Harold Wilson stepped down as Labour prime minister in March 1976. Every other leader in between retired after age, ill health, or political failures visibly reduced influence.

The influence of the Labour party leader is complicated by the status accorded the party's annual conference, which debates and votes on policy resolutions. R. T. McKenzie has argued that the party's constitution is at variance with the British constitution. A nonelected party conference has no right to dictate to an elected parliamentary Labour party, whether it is in or out of office. The party's constitution recognizes that the annual conference cannot bind MPs dealing with complex and changing events;

they are expected "to give effect as far as may be practicable to the principles from time to time approved by the Party Conference" (clause IV.3). At the height of the dispute in 1960 about the role of party institutions in stating policy about Britain's nuclear weapons, the party's general secretary wrote:

> Within the party there are three centers of decision making: the Annual Conference, the National Executive Committee and the Parliamentary Labour Party. . . . None of these elements can dominate the others. Policy cannot be laid down; it must be agreed.[58]

The same problem does not arise in the Conservative party because the party leader is not formally accountable to the conference of the constituency associations, the National Union. Moreover, the Conservative party's central office does not issue policy statements as does Labour's National Executive Committee.

"Stratarchy" is the best term to describe the distribution of power within British parties. Parties are not hierarchical organizational weapons, led from the top like an army. They are stratarchies, characterized by different groups ruling at different levels, or strata. Local councillors can run their local constituency party as an adjunct of local concerns; the party's chief full-time officers are primarily concerned with bureaucratic problems of coordination; and the parliamentary leader runs the party in the Commons in the way best suited to that environment.

Policy Preferences

The extent to which parties stand for differing policies is a matter of dispute; moreover, parties are likely to change a position if it is electorally unpopular. While parties may differ about their vision of an ideal society, election manifestos are not presented as the logical conclusion of an ideology. The Conservative party does not even describe the party's goals in its constitution. Moreover, many of the parties' described aims (peace, prosperity, and liberty) are not peculiar to it.

A review of popular attitudes on a variety of issues — economic, social, and moral — shows that a plurality of Conservative and Labour voters hold the same view on a majority of eighteen issues.[59] Many issues on which supporters of the two parties agree have moral overtones: treatment of immigrants, capital punishment, control of political demonstrations, and abortion. Even agreement that farmers are paid too little might be considered altruistic, coming from a heavily urban electorate. Agreement usually involves endorsing the more conservative of the two policy alternatives.

Disagreement between Labour and Conservative supporters is greatest about economic issues, a pattern that has persisted for decades. Differences in economic views can be interpreted as differences of interest rather than principle. This interpretation is reinforced by the fact that partisan differences do not extend to moral questions, where general principles are likely to determine attitudes. The two issues showing the highest interparty difference — nationalization of the steel industry and the power of trade unions — do not reflect sharply conflicting preferences between partisans. In both instances, the interparty difference appears high as a consequence of the virtual unanimity of Conservatives, as against a major division of opinion among Labour voters. Conservatives are more likely to agree among themselves than are Labour voters.[60]

The policy preferences of MPs cannot confidently be predicted from their voting records, because party discipline encourages MPs to vote with the party in public, even though they may disagree in private. But MPs are sometimes allowed free votes on moral or conscience issues. Opinion surveys show that a majority of Conservative MPs disagree with a majority of Labour MPs on ten of fifteen major policy issues. Labour MPs show a higher degree of intraparty cohesion in their votes on conscience issues than on issues for which party whips set the voting patterns.[61]

Taken together, surveys emphasize how the policies preferred by MPs differ from those of the

[58] Morgan Phillips, *Constitution of the Labour Party* (London: Labour Party, 1960), p. 4. The relative importance of these three organs was again opened up by votes at the October, 1979 Labour Annual Party Conference.

[59] For details of survey data discussed here, see Rose, *The Problem of Party Government*, ch. 11.

[60] Richard Rose, *The Problem of Party Government*, p. 308.

[61] Richard Rose, *The Problem of Party Government*, p. 313.

electorate. This can be demonstrated by comparing attitudes of voters and MPs on seven issues common to the two investigations. Conservative and Labour voters tend to show the highest profile of agreement; the difference between them averages 16 percent. Conservative MPs and Conservative voters are next in their tendency to agree; the average difference between these two groups is 27 percent. By contrast, the average difference between Labour MPs and their voters, 38 percent, is higher than the average difference between Labour voters and Conservative MPs.

The English electoral system does not allow voters to voice a preference on only one issue: they must vote for the party that offers the most appealing package of policies. An analysis of party platforms for the 1970 election shows that on the issues we just analyzed, the Conservative platform was in agreement with the views of the majority of Conservative voters in twelve of fifteen instances. By contrast, the Labour platform agreed with the majority view of its partisans on only four issues: foreign affairs, comprehensive schools, farm incomes, and pensions. The Conservative party draws support across class lines because its supporters tend to agree on issues. Labour maintains its support because of social solidarity within the working class, rather than agreement on issues.

In effect, British political parties are coalitions of groups with a variety of policy preferences. Before a party takes a firm position, groups within the party compete to determine the policy, around which the whole party is meant to coalesce. The party's collection of policies may not coincide with the competing preferences of individual voters. For example, one person might favor reformist social policies ad-

Coal miners advance their interests by acting politically through the Labour party and by their union's threatening strikes against the state-owned National Coal Board.

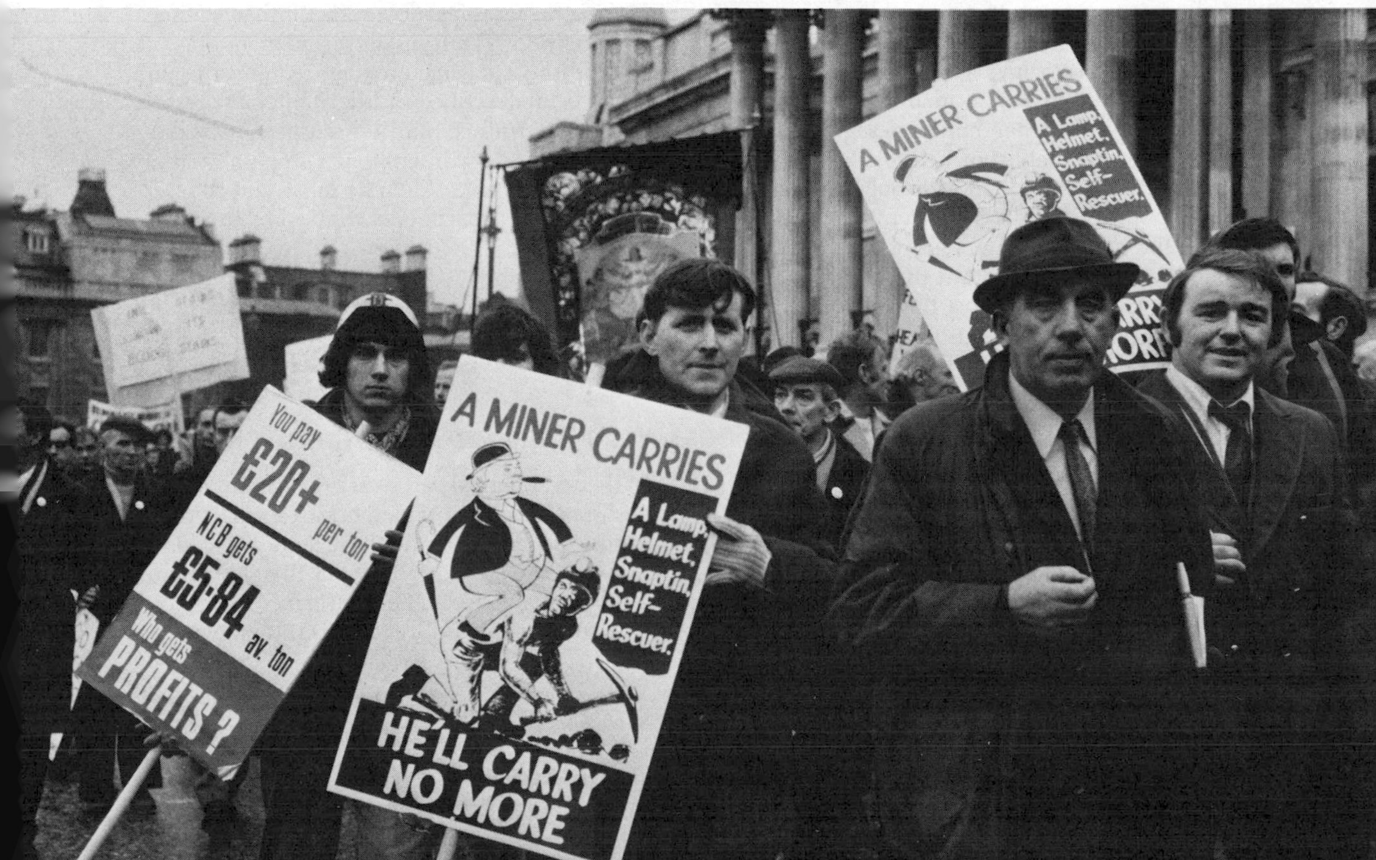

vocated by the Labour party, but prefer economic doctrines advocated by the Conservatives. The largest group of voters is in the center of a scale measuring attitudes toward the two parties, finding things to like and dislike about each of them. The party that a voter favors tends to be determined by such factors as family background and class.

The extent of coalition and competition between the parties can be measured by voting in the House of Commons. While party discipline requires that MPs of a party vote together, it does not require that opposition MPs always vote against all measures of the governing party. A division of MPs takes place in the Commons only if the Opposition requests it. When a bill is likely to be popular, such as the provision of greater welfare benefits, the opposition party will hesitate before going on record against it. It will confine criticism to amendments challenging the operation of the bill, but not its principles.

Notwithstanding the rhetoric of confrontation between the parties that has arisen in the 1970s, the practice of legislation shows very limited competition between the parties. In the 1970–1974 Parliament, the Labour opposition voted against the principle of only 21 percent of the 177 government bills introduced by the Conservative administration. Of these measures, 45 percent were primarily concerned with administrative rather than policy measures. When the Labour government returned to office in March 1974, the Conservative opposition only voted against 23 percent of the 247 bills the government introduced in the next five years. Part of the time Labour lacked an overall majority, but the Conservatives divided the Commons against the government on only a minority of legislation. One reason for this is that 45 percent of the Labour bills dealt with administrative rather than major policy concerns.[62]

By comparison with America, British parties cover a different ideological spectrum. American parties include a larger right-wing element, in political, economic, and cultural terms. There is, for example, no British electoral equivalent for the relative success of George Wallace in presidential and primary contests in 1968 and 1972. Also, the British Labour party represents a larger left-wing element on economic issues than would be found in the Democratic party in America. The greatest distinction between the parties of the two nations is the greater cohesion — both in organization and in policy — of the two largest British parties. In England, the voter chooses between the parties. In America, in primary, state, and federal elections, a voter chooses within parties as much as between them.

[62] For details, see Ivor Burton and Gavin Drewry's analyses in *Parliamentary Affairs*, 28:2 (1975), 29:2 (1976), and 31:2 (1978), and Richard Rose, *Do Parties Make a Difference?* (London: Macmillan, 1980).

POLICY MAKING AND IMPLEMENTATION

Government policies are statements of intent, not accomplishment. Stating a policy intention is meaningless if it is not followed by actions directing government institutions toward the realization of policy objectives. But passing an act of Parliament is not proof that intentions will be realized; the record of any Parliament includes monuments to good (and sometimes bad) intentions that never come to pass.

Making policy is far more difficult than stating policy intentions. To translate a statement of good intentions into a specific program requires running what has been described as "the Whitehall obstacle race."[63] A determined minister must secure agreement within his department that a proposal is administratively practicable. Then he must gain consent from other departments affected by the proposal. Then the Treasury must grant its approval if money is to be spent. Once over these hurdles, the minister must ask the Cabinet to approve and to find room in a crowded parliamentary timetable to introduce and pass a bill, if legislation is required.

The Limits of Centralization

In theory, political parties are the institutions that unite disparate groups of people into a single governing force. But British parties have demonstrated that it is far easier to state desired goals than to prepare detailed programs for achieving them.

The conventions of British government work

[63] Hugh Dalton, *Call Back Yesterday* (London: Muller, 1953), p. 237.

against the opposition party preparing detailed plans for governing. The opposition has no chance of any of its parliamentary motions becoming law, hence it must be negative rather than constructive. The more unpopular the government, the greater the opposition's incentive to make its chief policy "throw the rascals out." Opposition MPs have no staff to aid them in drawing up draft bills, and the flow of information from Whitehall to the Commons does not tell MPs enough about the mechanics of administration. Parliament emphasizes fluency in oral discussion and not the skills needed for drafting legislation or administrative orders. The party headquarters have research departments, but they are overworked and understaffed. The practical problems of implementing policies may not be noticed by MPs until they become ministers. Emanuel Shinwell, a Labour MP placed in charge of nationalizing the mines in 1945, recalled:

> We are about to take over the mining industry. That is not as easy as it looks. I have been talking of nationalization for forty years, but the complications of the transfer of property had never occurred to me.[64]

Many issues of importance within the departments are unlikely to have been mentioned or anticipated in a party platform. Sir William Armstrong, when permanent head of the civil service, said that ministers entered office with a vain optimism about the ease with which their intentions can be translated into policy. The civil servants then call the minister's attention to "ongoing reality," that is, circumstances they regard as inhibiting or dooming the realization of these intentions.[65]

If a minister does have clear ideas and an understanding of how to shape, resolve, or accommodate the ongoing problems of a department with the policy intentions of the party, change can occur. If not, there is likely to be much continuity in policies from a Labour to a Conservative government and vice versa. As a former Conservative chancellor of the exchequer said of his Labour government successors, they inherited "our problems and our remedies."[66]

Elective office offers one great advantage to the winning party. If a front-bench MP can get on top of his department, he has the whole weight of the Whitehall machine behind him to lend its authority to what is done in the name of the party. What is true for individual ministers is particularly true for the prime minister.

The prime minister is party leader, dispenser of Cabinet patronage,chairman of Cabinet discussions, and chief spokesman for the government in the Commons, in the mass media, and in world politics. Because of this, a number of writers have argued that Britain has prime ministerial government. While often invoked, the phrase is rarely defined. R. H. S. Crossman, a former Labour minister, has argued that "primary decisions" are made by the prime minister and "secondary decisions" are made by departmental ministers in consultation with the Cabinet; any decision taken solely by a minister becomes by definition "not at all important."[67]

The weaknesses of the theory that British government is prime ministerial government are several. The first is vagueness. The distinction between important and unimportant decisions is never defined. The decisions in which the prime minister is not involved are collectively more important than matters that receive her attention. Another argument, that the prime minister's significance arises simply from an ability to remain in office, treats the prime minister like a constitutional monarch.

The literature on prime ministerial power rarely considers the problem of overload, resulting from responsibilities growing without a comparable expansion of capabilities. The greatest limitation on a prime minister is the clock. She has only so many hours in which to discharge all responsibilities, including many only remotely connected with execu-

[64] Alan Watkins, "Labour in Power," in Gerald Kaufman (ed.), *The Left* (London: Blond, 1966), p. 173.

[65] Sir William Armstrong, "The Role and Character of the Civil Service" (text of a talk to the British Academy, London, June 24, 1970), p. 21.

[66] David Butler and Michael Pinto-Duschinsky, *The British General Election of 1970* (London: Macmillan, 1971), p. 62. For a view from the inside, see the three volumes of *Diaries* by a Labour minister of the period, R. H. S. Crossman (London: Hamish Hamilton, 1975–1977).

[67] See R. H. S. Crossman, "Introduction" to Walter Bagehot, *The English Constitution* (London: Fontana, 1963), pp. 51 ff; and J. P. Mackintosh, *The British Cabinet*, 2nd ed. (London: Stevens, 1968).

tive decision making. Time is scarce, and it is exhaustible. To negotiate in an industrial dispute is to forego the opportunity of discussing other matters. One person cannot keep abreast of the complexities of foreign affairs, economic policy, industrial relations, the environment, housing, education, health, social security, and public order — especially when there are other tasks besides. Many observers — including retired prime ministers, writing in their memoirs — emphasize the time spent on foreign affairs.

The prime minister's ability to extend influence is further limited by the smallness of her staff and because most staff members are civil servants rather than political lieutenants capable of acting as surrogates on policy questions. The prime minister's private office consists of no more than ten persons, in contrast with the staff of the White House.

The prime minister, while the most important single person in government, cannot be the central figure in government. Describing the prime minister as at the apex of government aptly symbolizes the small space occupied, and how far the person on top is from events on the ground.

The Cabinet is constitutionally the chief mechanism for coordinating government policy. It is large enough to include persons with day-to-day executive responsibilities for major policy areas, yet small enough so that every member can sit around a table and participate in its deliberations. In theory, the most important persons in government deliberate in the Cabinet on the general wisdom of particular measures. In practice, according to one former minister, "The one thing that is hardly ever discussed is general policy."[68] The fullness of the files accompanying the Cabinet agenda is a sign that an uninvolved minister can contribute little that has not already been thoroughly discussed. Moreover, if every minister spoke on each item, there would be time to discuss only two or three items per meeting. In such circumstances, Cabinet ministers tend to remain silent on matters outside their responsibility, expecting that other ministers will do likewise.

Cabinet ministers cannot discuss or resolve all their differences in full Cabinet. As the activities of government expand, the problems of interdepartmental conflict multiply. This has resulted in a greatly expanded role for Cabinet committees. These committees have the time and political power to settle issues among departments. Cabinet committee decisions usually meet with little opposition in the full Cabinet.

Civil servants, rather than ministers, are the most important coordinating personnel. Every Cabinet committee is shadowed by a committee of civil servants from the same departments. Because civil servants are more numerous than ministers and have fewer demands on their time outside Whitehall, they have more time to invest in interdepartmental contacts. As permanent officials, civil servants accumulate more knowledge of Whitehall than ministers, who come and go. They also have less incentive to press short-term departmental views, because job changes may place them in the seat of those with whom they negotiate. As administrators, they are concerned with making sure that any government policy is workable in interdepartmental terms, as well as in their own department. Not the least of their characteristics in negotiation is that they seek agreement.

Insofar as money is needed, the Treasury is the potential coordinator of government policy. Before a new measure is put to the Cabinet, the Treasury must be consulted about its cost, and it must have Treasury approval before consideration in Parliament. The annual budget cycle provides another opportunity for review of policies, especially if they involve a noteworthy increase in expenditure. Implications of long-term expenditures are reviewed in the five-year projections of the Public Expenditure Survey Committee. Moreover, the Treasury's responsibilities for general economic policy lead it to issue, at irregular intervals, directives requesting increases or cuts in public spending, depending on whether the economy needs spurring or restraining. Until the establishment of the Civil Service Department in 1968, the Treasury was also responsible for personnel, including promotion of senior civil servants.

While the organization of the Treasury is subject to recurring changes, its problems remain constant. All areas of economic policy are or ought to be interrelated, but the number of tasks involved are more

[68] L. S. Amery, *Thoughts on the Constitution* (London: Oxford University University Press, 1953), p. 87.

than one minister can handle. Three crucial Treasury activities are interrelated, yet each is so substantial that they are separately managed — and at times can conflict. First, the Treasury is manager of the domestic economy. Second, it is responsible for maintaining a favorable balance of payments in trade. A third Treasury function, budgeting annual expenditures, is no longer an end in itself. Given the impact of government expenditure on the private as well as the public sector, it has now become a means to the end of managing the economy.

Because of conflicts between these activities and because of the effects, often negative, that measures taken in one field have on another, British governments since World War I have intermittently sought to undertake economic planning. The history of Whitehall's efforts shows a slow but gradual increase in the Treasury's economic sophistication, with new forms of planning being introduced, then abolished, leaving behind some gain in knowledge. But administrative machinery cannot, of itself, resolve political conflicts or guarantee economic success.

The limits upon central direction to government led Edward Heath, when newly installed as Conservative prime minister in 1970, to establish a Central Policy Review Staff (CPRS) within the Cabinet Office. The unit was intended to provide a comprehensive review of government strategy, evaluating policy alternatives and considering how policies of different departments related to the party's objectives. With a staff of fifteen, less than one per government department, the CPRS cannot be compared with the United States Office of Management and Budget. Its creation was evidence of weaknesses perceived in Downing Street. When asked to name the CPRS's major achievement, its first head, Lord Rothschild, said:

> I don't know that the government is better run as a result of our work. I think the highest compliment I ever got paid was from a Cabinet minister who said: "You make us think from time to time." I thought that was a great achievement, considering how much ministers have to do. They don't have much time to think.[69]

[69] Lord Rothschild, "Thinking about the Think Tank," *The Listener*, December 28, 1972.

The Limits of Decentralization

The responsibilities of government today are so varied and numerous that the powers of the center can only be exercised by decentralization. Only by delegating unimportant matters can Cabinet ministers gain time to attend to important ones.

Many motives lead ministers to decide not to direct policies the government supports, indirectly or directly. Ministers may wish to avoid charges of political interference (the National Theatre), to allow flexibility in commercial operations (the Electricity Board), to lend an aura of impartiality to quasi-judicial activities (the Monopolies Commission), to respect the extragovernmental origins of an agency (the British Standards Institution), to allow qualified professionals to regulate technical matters (the Royal College of Physicians and Surgeons), to remove controversial matters from close proximity to Whitehall (Family Planning Association), or to permit the concentration of special skills (a fund for disaster relief).

Decentralization may give a special purpose agency limited responsibilities covering the whole country (for example, the National Coal Board or the Arts Council). Or it may give multiple powers to agencies operating within designated areas (the Welsh Office). Some agencies combine both attributes. The BBC, for example, is national for many purposes but divides into regional units for some programs; New Town Corporations are multipurpose bodies operating within a limited geographical area.

Many agencies operate with government authorization, yet outside the framework of government departments. *Whitaker's Almanack*, a standard reference book, requires seventy-four double-column pages to list government and public offices. In addition, it separately catalogues commissions, banks, the armed services, churches, universities and schools, nationalized industries, and museums and art galleries, each of which also affects the public interest.

The functional agencies of the Crown described in the following paragraphs exist in a political no-man's-land, because they are not controlled by elected representatives, whether Cabinet ministers or local councillors. They are fringe bodies, on the margin of central government, yet not immediately under a minister's direction. They are a part of government because their duties are sanctioned by law, they are often public monopolies, their funds are derived from taxation, and their directors are normally appointed by the department that is ultimately responsible for them. Any catalog of these paragovernmental functional agencies can only be illustrative, for the boundary between public and private is not easily drawn in a land where the largest church is a state church. But the following examples show the variety and types of such groups.

EXECUTIVE AGENCIES NOT DIRECTLY UNDER MINISTERIAL DEPARTMENTS The Board of Inland Revenue and the Royal Mint are formally independent of departments, out of a desire to retain flexibility and freedom from political intervention. Yet both agencies only apply policies decided elsewhere. The Mint cannot coin money without Cabinet authority, nor can the Inland Revenue alter tax laws on its own.

NATIONALIZED INDUSTRIES The government not only owns the corporations that operate nationalized industries, but also appoints the boards that direct them, provides investment capital, and underwrites losses. Yet each industry is formally independent of Whitehall, and its employees are not civil servants. This is intended to increase the freedom of action of the industries, coal, electricity, gas, the railways, airlines, steel, and others. The relationship between department ministers and leaders of nationalized industries is confused by the coexistence of multiple and sometimes conflicting objectives: profitability, an undefined fair rate of return on investment, services to consumers, and the protection of jobs.

PUBLICLY MAINTAINED REGULATORY OR ADMINISTRATIVE AGENCIES A regulatory agency such as the Independent Broadcasting Authority grants licenses to commercial television companies, and monitors the program content of the companies it licenses. An administrative agency, such as the Social Science Research Council, draws funds from the Treasury and its council is appointed by government. But its activities are administered by staff whose work is monitored by SSRC committees composed of academic experts and lay persons.

PUBLICLY ASSISTED AGENCIES While originating outside government, these bodies receive substantial government aid. The Royal Opera House did not commence under government or royal sponsorship, but today, it can present operas up to international standards thanks only to a substantial Treasury subsidy.

Fringe bodies are a paragovernmental jungle surrounding the central Whitehall departments. They are paragovernmental because they discharge their functions around but not in the Whitehall policy process. They are a jungle because of their complexity and density. Any Whitehall official, minister or civil servant, is well advised to secure a survival kit before rushing into that jungle hunting for more influence on the agencies.

Local government is the chief territorial means of decentralization. Within a given city or county, local authorities are not the only government agency delivering services locally. A few Whitehall departments also have major local field offices, for example, for pensions and social security, employment, and the post office. In addition, many functional agencies are important in local areas. Nationalized industries such as electricity, gas, and transportation are prominent local employers, and in steel or mining towns, a nationalized industry may be the single largest employer.

In constitutional theory, English local government reflects a "top-down" conception of authority. All local authorities operate on the basis of powers and institutions prescribed by Parliament. The *ultra vires* rule prohibits local authorities from doing anything not authorized by Parliament. It has been an important constraint on local government initiative, both legally and psychologically. In the United States, by contrast, the Constitution leaves states with the residual power to do anything not exclusively granted to the federal government. The boundaries and powers of all local authorities are determined by the central government, which can change both, as it did most recently in the Local Government Act of 1972.

Efficiency has been the overriding aim in reforming local government. Whitehall views local government as a major mechanism for delivering services to citizens. As such, it wishes the services to be of a reasonable standard and at a reasonable cost, for the central government pays for a substantial portion of local government services. Popular election of local government leaders is recognized as politically inevitable but, in the words of one leading expert on central-local relations, "mayors and aldermen and councillors are not necessary political animals. We could manage without them."[70]

Reorganization of local governments in the 1970s was based on the assumption that there were too many small local authorities, and that bigger ones would be better, that is, would provide higher standard services at the same or less cost. Trebling the size of the average authority was assumed to produce economies of scale, as in assembly-line manufacturing.

The reformed structure divides England into three different jurisdictions: the shire counties, with 59 percent of the population; metropolitan county councils in major cities, with 25 percent of the population; and the Greater London Council, with 16 percent. Each of these authorities has a tier of elected government beneath it: district councils in the counties and metropolitan areas, and borough councils in Greater London. County councils were given responsibility for education, land-use planning, and roads, transportation, and personal social services. In metropolitan areas, the district councils were given responsibilities over education and personal social services, assigned to the county councils in the shire counties. Housing, a major concern in a country where more than one quarter of the population lives in municipally owned houses, is primarily a district council responsibility. In the Greater London Council area, the bulk of responsibilities were given to the lower-tier boroughs.

Within each local authority, control is vested in the hands of an elected council comprised of unpaid part-time representatives. This limits the time councillors can give to local politics and reduces the number of people who can afford to participate. Low turnout for local elections — often half the turnout of a parliamentary election — is an indicator of limited public interest in local government. Disciplined parties contest council elections and provide guidelines for policy making.

The financial powers of local authorities are very much affected by the central government, both positively and negatively. Central government departments exercise a variety of supervisory powers as well. Inspectors examine schools and police and fire service. Auditors examine small and large expenditures to make sure they are sanctioned by statute. The salaries and terms of appointment of many local employees are also affected by central government decisions. Land-use decisions of local authorities may be appealed to the central government, even when the dispute lies within a single local authority's area. In extreme cases, a minister can override decisions made by elected local councils, suspend councillors, or assume administrative powers directly.

Notwithstanding its right to authorize activities and set standards, the central government has consistently rejected responsibility for the administration of most major welfare services. Education is administered locally, as are many services by social workers. Local authorities build and manage housing. A variety of planning, road, and environmental services, and police and fire protection are also locally administered. The resistance of doctors to local control led to the establishment of regional hospital boards outside the control of local authorities, but outside the immediate control of Whitehall departments as well.

The paradox of central authority and administrative devolution is summed up by John P. Mackintosh:

> Central government can plan, control, guide, review, audit and so on, but never actually execute. Foreign students find it scarcely credible that in Britain Ministries of Housing have never built a single house and Ministries of Education have never run a single school.[71]

The lack of direct control — of functional bodies as well as of local authorities — results in the central government spending much effort issuing instruc-

[70] J. A. G. Griffith, *Central Departments and Local Authorities* (London: George Allen and Unwin, 1966), p. 542.

[71] John P. Mackintosh, "The Report of the Review Body on Local Government in Northern Ireland, 1970," *Public Administration*, 49 (Spring 1971), p. 20.

tions, requests, or advice to other institutions of government.

Decentralization exists because the central government cannot administer all its services in all parts of the United Kingdom without overloading the center. The desire to push administration out of Whitehall has become a prominent feature of reorganization. Yet central government does not wish to reduce its power to constrain the authorities it has created. Only Whitehall supervision, it is assumed, can ensure territorial justice for its subjects, that is, equal services and opportunities throughout the United Kingdom.

The critics of central direction argue that local decision making is morally superior and that local authorities are likely to know and care more about local concerns. In the non-English parts of the United Kingdom, nationalists go so far as to argue that self-government, rather than efficient government from Whitehall, is the best government. But even some advocates of national independence make clear that they do not wish to do away entirely with financial aid from Whitehall.

The complexity of the policy process restricts both centralization and decentralization. Centralization in the hands of a single decision maker is limited by the number and variety of organizations involved in most major decisions. A proposal to establish a new town with a population of 100,000 people will involve four or five major departments, plus two or more major local authorities, and a host of functional agencies, both governmental and nongovernmental. In such circumstances decisions are not made, they emerge. Many organizations influence policy at some point in the process; the more-or-less intended result is the outcome of interorganizational bargaining and adjustment among groups, rather than the product of a single decision maker.

The dilemma of centralization and decentralization is illustrated by a dispute in land-use planning between a nationalized industry and a local authority. An industry claims that the industrial use of land is in the public interest; a local authority wishes to keep land free from industry because it views green spaces as even more important. Central government cannot eliminate disagreement, but it can hear appeals and determine which substructure has the most persuasive notion of the public interest.

A Ruling Clique?

In a complex political system like England's, we cannot expect all types of policies to be determined in the same way. Decisions about war and peace tend to be centralized, decisions about land-use planning depend on local knowledge. An elaborate analysis of a variety of major British government decisions undertaken by C. J. Hewitt has identified six different patterns of power characterizing policy making.[72]

A *ruling clique* model is most appropriate to describe foreign-policy making. Major decisions about diplomacy and defense are consistently made by a single group of people, centered on the prime minister, the Foreign Office, the Ministry of Defence, and, when financial considerations are significant, the Treasury. To describe these persons as a single group is not to suggest agreement among everyone involved, but to note their relative isolation from influences outside their narrow circle. One constraint on the ruling clique in foreign affairs arises from dependence of British foreign policy on limited manpower and public money. Another constraint is the foreign policy of other nations.

Balance-of-power pluralism, in which a few groups consistently compete about the same policy, with each winning some of the time, characterizes the making of domestic economic policy. Typically, business and financial interests are arrayed on one side and unions on the other, with the government's senior economic officials acting as something more than disinterested brokers. The weight of each side varies with changing economic and political circumstances.

Social welfare policies illustrate *segmented pluralism*. The cluster of groups concerned with education are few and stable, as in the balance-of-power model, but they differ from the cluster of groups involved with health. These in turn differ from the groups involved in social services for the poor and the handicapped. The narrow scope of

[72] See C. J. Hewitt, "Elites and the Distribution of Power in British Society," in P. Stanworth and A. Giddens (eds.), *Elites and Power in British Society* (London: Cambridge University Press, 1974), pp. 45–64; and "Policy-making in Postwar Britain," *British Journal of Political Science*, 4:2 (1974), pp. 187–216.

each group's concern (teachers and doctors, for example, have different professional associations) produces a high degree of institutional organization within each policy area. Policy making requires lengthy negotiations because broad policies involve many groups protecting their interests. Thus welfare policies are changed less quickly than economic policies.

Amorphous pluralism describes policy arenas in which those with interests to defend or articulate are constantly changing from issue to issue. Controversies arising out of land-use planning always have to do with specific plots of land. Whereas planners are concerned with the consistency of principles from case to case, nearly all other participants are concerned with saving or developing what may literally be their own back yard.

Policy making is *populist* when the mass of the electorate is directly involved in determining the outcome. When government policy depends on consumer response, the decisions of masses of consumers become crucial. Some mass consumer decisions affect policy unwittingly. For example, the decision of many English to buy cars and rely less on railways and buses has greatly influenced transportation policy. In race relations, popular opinion (as reflected in MPs' perceptions as well as in opinion polls) has increasingly been used to justify laws intended to restrict (not always successfully) the immigration of nonwhite Commonwealth citizens.

A *veto* model describes the frustration of government policy. Occasionally, policy proposals are vetoed by the public opposition of strategic interest groups. More often, the veto power of a group prevents an issue being put on the political agenda that would threaten one of its central interests. For example, the Trades Union Congress has successfully prevented governments from proposing legislation affecting them, as well as vetoing legislation once proposed. Parliament is even more hesitant to debate legislation affecting the state church, the Church of England, fearing that ecclesiastical officials would challenge Parliament's right to legislate about matters of faith.

The foregoing review emphasizes that any model of the policy process is likely to fit some issue areas but not others. Moreover, it shows that the role of a group in policy making is not only a function of its resources, but also a function of the policy area. The resources of bankers, trade unions, prelates, or motorists cannot be generalized across all policy areas, though they are important in some.

Cabinet ministers and civil servants are consistently involved in the policy process, in contrast to most groups, which are involved intermittently. Ministers do not dominate all policy areas; business and unions, for example, have a great influence upon economic policy. But those in the government are consistently able to extract advantage from whatever maneuvering room there is in a given political situation, and government has the advantage of declaring the terms of every policy bargain struck with groups.

THE PROOF OF POLICY

The raw materials of government are few but potentially powerful: laws, taxing and spending money, organizing public officials, and mobilizing symbols for collective commitment. But the resources of government do not necessarily produce the effects policy makers intend. Hence, to evaluate the performance of British government, we must not only examine the performance of government, but also outcomes in society, to assess whether public policies produce their intended results.

Policy Performance

In war and peace, the British government is successful in extracting money and military manpower from its citizens. In the total war of World War II, civilians were conscripted for war industries, as well as the armed services. Military conscription remained in effect for more than a decade after the war, then was abandoned as part of the scaling down of the country's international commitments. Stringent wartime rationing of food was kept for nine years after the war. The English people accepted such regulation of their behavior as necessary to carrying out postwar reconstruction for their collective welfare.

Today, taxes represent the chief tribute that government extracts from its citizens. In total, taxes take more than two-fifths of the nation's gross national product. About 35 percent of the total tax comes from income tax, with another sixth from social security contributions financed partly by employers and partly by employees. An additional quarter of tax revenue comes from sales and excise taxes, including a standard 15 percent value added tax (VAT), levied on the sale of almost all goods and services. Property taxes paid to local government come next in importance, accounting for 9 percent of revenue. Taxes on corporate profits brought in 4 percent of government revenue in 1976, a bad year for profits.[73]

In addition, Britain has been financing high levels of public expenditure and private consumption in the 1970s by borrowing heavily from foreign banks. Total borrowing has financed up to one-sixth of public expenditure in years when public deficits have been unusually large. These loans must be paid for by future tax levies.

The income tax rates in Britain are high by European standards. The standard rate of income tax is 30 percent; rates rise quickly on above average earnings to a maximum of 60 percent. Since social security contributions must also be paid, the average worker pays about 36 pence on every additional pound earned, as well as paying indirect sales taxes when earnings are spent. A retired couple living on a pension finds that sales and income taxes claim more than one-quarter of the pension.[74]

Thanks to the fiscal dividend of economic growth, take-home pay as well as tax bills increased in the 1950s and 1960s. Government was able to count on receiving increasing revenues from taxation, as extra earnings and inflation pushed wage earners into higher and higher tax brackets and increased the revenue from sales taxes too. Equally important, the population was generally willing to pay taxes voluntarily. By contrast with France or Italy, British tax collectors reckon that the income declared for tax purposes approaches a person's true income. In the 1970s, however, high inflation made taxes bite harder. From 1971 to 1976, the government's tax revenue more than doubled. Taxes themselves contribute to inflation by pushing up the cost of living. Yet the government cannot cut its demands for taxes easily, for the simple reason that, even with heavy borrowing, it needs more money to meet the costs of public policy.

The money that government collects in taxes is spent for a variety of public purposes. Government statisticians calculate that about 40 percent of families, especially the elderly, the unemployed, and those with large families, are likely to receive more in benefits than they pay out in taxes.

The great bulk of public money in Britain is spent on what people normally think of as good goods. Pensions and other social security payments account for nearly one-quarter of total public expenditure (see Table 9.6). Spending on defense and law and order (both regarded as vital by most English people) comes second, accounting for one-sixth of the total. The next two major spending programs — education, and health and personal social services — each account for about one-seventh of the total. (Housing subsidies are conceived as welfare programs, rather than as capital investment.) Together, these four major pillars of the contemporary British welfare state account for 58.5 percent of all public spending. The sums spent on welfare programs are increasing steadily. From 1972 to 1978, spending on social security increased by 23 percent, primarily to protect the elderly against inflation. Housing subsidies increased even more, 42 percent, because of changes in the law and rising costs of construction and borrowing.

A significant amount of public spending — £3.9 billion — is devoted to aid to industry, trade, and agriculture. The bulk of this money is not spent in subsidizing nationalized industries. Instead, two-thirds of it is devoted to subsidizing privately owned industries or private enterprise farmers.

Because of its unique command of laws, government can try to direct society by enacting regulations as well as by spending money. The bulk of government regulation is directed at economic activities. English people do not believe in the sanctity of private property to the same extent as Americans. The Crown, rather than the individual, has the final right to determine how property is used.

After long periods under Labour government, many industries that in the United States might be subject to government regulation (the airlines, railways, or energy producing companies) are now state owned. This eliminates some sources of complaints

[73] Calculations from data in *Social Trends*, Vol. 8 (London: Her Majesty's Stationery Office, 1977), Table 7.6.

[74] *Social Trends*, Chart 6.21.

Table 9.6
Public Expenditure in Great Britain, 1977–1978

	Total	*Percentage*
Social security	£13,226	23.6
Defense and domestic order	9,048	16.1
Education	8,010	14.2
Health and personal social services	7,390	13.1
Roads, transportation, and environment	4,372	7.8
Housing	4,290	7.6
Industry, trade, and agriculture	3,982	7.1
Miscellaneous	4,002	7.1
Debt interest	1,900	3.4
Total	£56,220	100.0

Source: From *The Government's Expenditure Plans, 1978–79 to 1981–82* (London: Her Majesty's Stationery Office, Cmnd. 7049–I), pp. 18–19. All spending totals are in 1977 survey prices. Reprinted by permission.

about regulation heard from American businessmen. In England, the characteristic complaint comes from socialists, who argue that government-owned industries are not sufficiently subject to regulation by Parliament. From the nationalized industries the complaint is that government directives are unclear or contradictory. For example, the government may ask a nationalized firm to perform a social role, avoiding laying off workers in regions with high unemployment or even selling products at a loss to support government antiinflation policies. Simultaneously, however, the Treasury expects nationalized industries to show a profit, as a private firm unhindered by these directives would seek to do.

The British government is also quick to intervene in the problems of particular industries, or even individual firms, whose difficulties threaten to make large numbers of workers unemployed or reduce exports. Free-enterprise critics of such intervention have denounced this as a government policy of caring for the lame ducks of industry, firms that should go out of business because they are losing money. But successive Conservative as well as Labour governments have responded to political pressures to do something about ailing or failing firms by subsidizing them.

Unlike many continental European countries, England has a centuries-old tradition of free speech. The office of government censor has been unknown. Only plays were subject to review, and the permissive era of the 1960s abolished theatrical censorship. Unlike the United States government, the British government has always been jealous of having its activities closely scrutinized in the press. The 1911 Official Secrets Act empowers Whitehall to keep secret many activities of government not affecting national security. The doctrine of collective responsibility and civil service anonymity are used to justify keeping private much public business. Newspapers are increasingly breaching regulations to report scoops to their readers, but this happens in spite of, rather than because of, government policy.

The potential strength of political symbols was made manifest during World War II when the government, under Winston Churchill's leadership, used patriotic symbols to encourage English people to fight on alone in 1940 and 1941, when a rational analysis might have suggested that the country sue for peace with Nazi Germany. Today, British politicians harken back to this era, calling upon citizens to show the Dunkirk spirit in the face of economic adversity. (Dunkirk, it should be noted, was a British military disaster.)

The most familiar political symbols — the Queen, the Union Jack, the national anthem, and images of green fields and medieval castles — are all peculiarly unsuited for the political problems of the moment. The problems of England today are those of an aging industrial economy that must make major changes in its industrial structure and trade if it is to prosper in future as in the past. Computer scientists, export managers, and coal miners are unlikely to be moved by an appeal to traditional symbols of rural England. They require different symbols or material inducements or threats, or all of these, to intensify their effects.

Insofar as the problems of the British economy are diagnosed as caused by attitudes of English people, government seeks symbols that appeal to the hearts and minds of persons in British industry. Moreover, doing so respects the wish of many English people not to have government fix wages, prices, and profits permanently, as is done in the command economies of Eastern Europe.

The apparatus of economic planning that British governments periodically unveil is to a significant extent symbolic. Both Conservative and Labour prime ministers have used speeches with grim metaphors in efforts to alert the country to the danger of living beyond its means, that is, enjoying more public and private consumption than can be paid for by the nation's economic product. Politicians have followed this up by calling leading businessmen and trade unionists together, and by setting up a variety of planning councils, industrial boards, productivity teams, and economic development councils. Legislation, often called temporary, as in the case of wages policies, is invoked only in the last resort. Analysis of the powers, organization, and achievements of these initiatives, which are often abolished or abandoned after a few years, emphasizes their lack of substantive weight.

Policy Outcomes

The performance of a polity is not determined solely by the actions of the government. No British government can, by itself, produce national security in the face of a world war. Nor can it secure the health of an economy when the economy is increasingly interdependent with that of other nations. Yet if a government cannot unilaterally produce policy outcomes, it can nevertheless influence these outcomes, if only by deciding how to adapt to the events that it cannot control. As a mixed-economy welfare state, the British government is also expected to accept responsibility for much that happens in society, even if the causes are beyond its control.

The greatest political success that British government can claim — the avoidance of involvement in a major war for more than three decades — results from the global balance of power, not primarily from the actions of British government. It is important nonetheless in bringing the English relief from the great losses of the two world wars in the first half of the twentieth century. Since 1945, England has enjoyed a longer period of peace than at any time since the 43-year period between the end of the Crimean War in 1856 to the commencement of the Boer War in South Africa in 1899.

Skillful diplomacy and the conjunction of British and American interests in Europe have been primarily responsible for the era of peace. From 1945 to 1951, the Labour government was very active in promoting the development of European economic recovery through the American-financed Marshall Plan, and military security through NATO (the North Atlantic Treaty Organization). It also participated in the Korean War of 1950–1953 as an act of mutual security, but since then has carefully disengaged from military confrontation in Asia, and since the failure of the 1956 Anglo-French attack on the Suez Canal in Egypt, it has eschewed the use of force on any significant scale. Its only war has been the internal war in Northern Ireland.

The British government was astute in making military alliances from relative strength after World War II, for its military manpower and the technology and resources available for armament have since declined substantially. The progressive scaling down of military commitments has been an adaptation to the fact of Britain's international weakness.

In managing the economy, British government can say it has presided over (or more arguably, been responsible for) success, when judged absolutely: the GNP has been rising steadily, so that the country is richer today in real terms than ever before. The economy has grown in twenty-four of twenty-seven years from 1951 through 1978, more than doubling the total wealth available for public and private consumption. The growth rate in the 1950s (2.3 percent annually) rose in the 1960s to 2.9 percent, then fell, as it did elsewhere in the Western world, to 1.6 percent in the 1970s. In the postwar era, Britain has maintained a higher annual rate of growth than at any earlier period in the twentieth century. The fact that this higher rate applies to a larger economy increases substantially the absolute value of the fiscal dividend of each year's growth.

However, the British economy has not grown as quickly as Britain's major European competitors. Its average growth of 2.8 percent from 1951 through 1977 is less than half the annual growth rate of Germany, and 2.0 percent less than that of France and Italy. It is only 0.5 percent less than that of the United States, but the United States had the advantage of entering competition for postwar growth with a much richer economy, endowed with a better supply of agricultural and natural resources than Britain. In 1961, Britain ranked ninth in per capita wealth among twenty-five nations in the international Organization for Economic Cooperation and Development. In 1976, it ranked eighteenth, a bigger fall than that experienced by the United States, which moved from first to fourth in the same period.[75]

Income distribution has been changing gradually through the decades. In 1939, the top 5 percent of the population received 25.3 percent of total income after taxes; in 1973, it received 12.9 percent. The share of income received by the middle half of the population has increased, but the earnings of the bottom 30 percent have hardly altered, going from 15.4 percent in 1939 to 15.9 percent in 1973. In absolute terms, though, the poorest have had their standard of living rise, sharing in proportion in the general rise of living standards and gaining many welfare benefits from the state.[76]

[75] For comparative details, see Rose and Peters, *Can Government Go Bankrupt?*, ch. 2.

[76] For details, see *Social Trends*, ch. 6; and Royal Commission on the Distribution of Income and Wealth, *Report No. 1* (London: Her Majesty's Stationery Office, Cmnd. 6171, 1975).

On all major indicators of well being, the British people enjoy a higher standard of living today than a generation ago. Health has improved significantly during the era of the National Health Service. The rate of infant mortality has declined by more than half, from thirty-one deaths per thousand in 1951 to fourteen in 1977. From 1951 to 1977 life expectancy at birth rose by three years for a male, and four and a half years for a female. The average woman can expect to live to the age of 76, the average man to nearly 70.[77]

In education, government effort has expanded, and so has the number of educated people in the population. In elementary schools, classroom size has fallen from thirty pupils per teacher in 1951 to twenty-four in 1977. At the same time, the proportion of sixteen- and seventeen-year-olds in school has increased from 11 percent to 46 percent. More young people are in higher education too; the proportion has risen from 3 percent in 1951 to fourteen percent in 1977.

Housing has also improved in quality. From 1951 through 1976, local authorities built nearly 4 million modern council houses to let at subsidized rents to working-class and middle-income tenants. Private builders, encouraged by government policies, have built another 4 million houses. In consequence, millions of slum houses lacking baths or indoor toilets have been torn down and residents rehoused. In 1976, 46 percent of the population lived in modern postwar houses; only 32 percent was living in houses built before 1918.

The security of the ordinary English person from crime has declined in postwar years. The number of indictable offenses known to the police has increased 480 percent from 1951 to 1977. The increase primarily reflects much higher levels of theft and robbery. Crimes of violence are relatively few. The proportion of security forces required to protect the population is 20 percent lower in Britain than in the United States, and the murder rate is only one-ninth the American rate (see Table 8.7). These statistics omit Northern Ireland.

In one important respect, road travel, England is

[77] For detailed statistics of health, education, housing, and public and road safety, see the relevant chapters in the annual British government publication, *Social Trends*.

becoming safer, because of the provision of safer roads and more stringent regulation of cars and motorists. The number of casualties from road accidents fell from 350,000 to 340,000 between 1961 and 1976, even though the total number of automobiles nearly doubled, and the number of miles traveled by car also doubled. In England, as in other countries, young motorists account for a disproportionate number of road accidents.

The administration of justice is normally considered fair minded by English people. It could be argued that the avoidance of courts is a better indicator of public order than heavy reliance on judicial confrontation. The work of the courts is much less an issue in Britain than in the United States, for two reasons. The first is the lower level of crime. The second is the absence of a written Constitution specifying citizen rights, which encourages Americans to use the courts in their self-interest far more than is the case in Britain.

The proportion of people making use of government-funded legal aid does show an increase. In 1975, 837,000 people did so, an increase of more than 140 percent since 1970, because government legislation made legal advice more easily available. About 45 percent of the consultations involve criminal proceedings, one-quarter involve divorce or family problems, and the rest cover miscellaneous civil problems.

Public participation in politics has declined slightly, judging by the conventional measure of turnout. It reached its postwar height of 83.9 percent in the general election of 1950, and a low of 72.0 percent in the 1970 election. Even the lowest turnout for a national election in Britain is almost 10 percent greater than the highest turnout for a postwar American presidential election.

An important feature of English life, often taken for granted by citizens but not by visitors from other parts of the world, is individual liberty. Freedom of speech is a tradition far older in English history than the right to vote. The era of protest demonstrations was met in England by a police force accustomed to deal peacefully with demonstrators, allowing them to march and display protest banners without violence and death following. To avoid violence at demonstrations requires well-disciplined police, as well as demonstrators prepared to act within the law. The British police have maintained public order without recourse to firearms, which would be unthinkable in many parts of the world. Firmness in drawing lines and holding them, along with support by public opinion and the government, whatever its party, has meant that protests are heard, but rarely erupt into violence.

Adaptability and Stability

England is distinctive in the modern world, because its government demonstrated the ability to adapt successfully to changing conditions over the centuries. The institutions of parliamentary government have adapted to challenges as diverse as those presented by the American Revolution, the Industrial Revolution, and the Russian Revolution.

As England enters the 1980s, continuities with the past remain evident. But the ability to adapt to future challenges is less certain. During the 1960s, both Labour and Conservative politicians voiced optimism about the prospects of reforming almost everything in society, except their own particular customs. The 1964–1970 Labour government and its 1970–1974 Conservative successor tried to introduce numerous procedural and substantive changes. But the net effect of these efforts has been a loss of confidence in reform. Today there is a greater concern with holding what England has, rather than changing in the hope of betterment. This mood is reinforced by developments in the world economy, which are a constant reminder that changes can be for the worse. Yet no government can stand still — even if it wished to do so — and reformers argue it should consciously try to change.

A characteristic of English political culture is empiricism, reacting to events as they occur. The reaction is likely to involve doing what is familiar and agreeable, rather than what is most effective. But often the first reaction of the government, however suitable it may seem, does not work as intended. The government then muddles through. Critics of British government emphasize the extent of the muddle; proponents, the fact that the government usually wins through. Britain's record in winning two world wars, if only narrowly, can be cited as evidence supporting either point of view.

Familiar ways are valued because of the achievements of British government through the years. There is good reason for satisfaction, as long as comparison is confined to the past economic performance of England or the past political performance of its neighboring countries in Europe. There is pride, rather than shame, in the past.

A readiness to conserve past and present achievements is found even among those seeking to change society. A study of innovative young English persons found that they used "the language of the future when talking of modernization, but they seek to join this with the values of the past: balance, stability and unity."[78] A majority of these would-be innovators explicitly stated that what they like most about England — moderation, tolerance, and a capacity for compromise and continuity — is also the cause of what they dislike most — resistance to change.

[78] Erwin C. Hargrove, *Professional Roles in Society and Government: The English Case* (Beverly Hills, Calif.: Sage Professional Papers in Comparative Politics, 01–035, 1972) pp. 14 ff.

KEY TERMS

deindustrialization
National Health Service
"invisible" service exports
Cabinet responsibiliy
theories of representation: trusteeship, collectivist, individualist
"public" schools
Trades Union Congress
Welsh National party (Plaid Cymru)
Beveridge Report on Social Welfare
The Commonwealth
Whitehall
vote of confidence
British Broadcasting Corporation (BBC)
Scottish National party
Central Policy Review Staff (CPRS)
Alternative policy models
Conservative party
Devolution
Labour party
Liberal party
deference

France
(New Regional Organization)
North Sea
ENGLAND
BELGIUM
English Channel
Lille
NORD
LUX.
GERMANY
HAUTE
PICARDIE
NORMANDIE
BASSE
Seine R.
Paris
REGION
PARISIENNE
CHAMPAGNE
LORRAINE
Rhine R.
Strasbourg
ALSACE
BRÊTAGNE
PAYS
DE LA LOIRE
Loire R.
CENTRE
Nantes
BOURGOGNE
FRANCHE-
COMTÉ
SWITZERLAND
POITOU-
CHARENTE
Bay of Biscay
LIMOUSIN
Clermont-
Ferrand
AUVERGNE
Lyon
RHONE-ALPES
St. Étienne
Grenoble
ITALY
Bordeaux
Garonne R.
Rhone R.
AQUITAINE
MIDI-PYRENÉES
PROVENCE-
CÔTE D'AZUR
Nice
Toulouse
LANGUEDOC
Marseilles
Toulon
CORSE
0
100
Scale of Miles
SPAIN
Mediterranean Sea

CHAPTER TEN

HENRY W. EHRMANN

Politics in France

INTRODUCTION

France is one of the most perplexing countries to judge and interpret. The French Enlightenment made an enormous contribution to what was later termed the "world revolution of the West" encompassing both sides of the Atlantic. When it severed the connection between state and monarchy, the French Revolution solidified the historical process initiated by the United States. Yet the same events left a legacy that has recently made France the prototype of a country with a fragmented political culture. Political scientists whose task it is to explain the rise and the demise of political institutions have found in the record of past French regimes ample material for study and reflection.

The fascination that the present French republic holds for many French, as well as the outside world, consists not only in its somewhat surprising stability. The student of comparative politics also notes that by combining two models of democratic government, the presidential and the parliamentary, the Fifth Republic is engaged in a constitutional experiment that, while not entirely new, has not been successful in the past but has served France well since its adoption.

The Frenchman Montesquieu once remarked that those nations are happy whose history is boring to read. To the extent that this is true, France is an unhappy country, for its history has been fascinating and turbulent, not boring. No wonder that its political systems have invited unending and frequently passionate comments from French and foreign observers alike.

A Historical Perspective

One of the oldest nation-states of Europe, France has had a remarkably stable population mix, and the French have a strong sense of national identity. The sometimes violent protest movements by certain ethnic minorities is a recent phenomenon to be discussed below, p. 240. The revolution of 1789 brought an end to the French monarchy that had brought the country under a centralized administration. The period of unstable revolutionary regimes that followed ended in the seizure of power by Napoleon Bonaparte, who proclaimed himself first consul and, later, emperor. The other European powers formed an alliance and forced Napoleon's surrender as well as the restoration of the Bourbon monarchy. But another revolution, in 1830, drove the last Bourbon from the French throne and replaced him with Louis Philippe of the House of Orléans, who promised a more moderate rule bounded by a new constitution.

Growing dissatisfaction among the rising bourgeoisie and the urban population produced still another Paris revolution in 1848. With it came the proclamation of the Second Republic (1848–1852) and a promise of universal suffrage. However, conflict between its middle-class and lower-class components kept the republican government ineffective, and out of the disorder rose another Napoleon, Louis, nephew of the first emperor. Louis Napoleon, crowned Napoleon III in 1852, brought stability to France for more than a decade, but his last years were marked by growing indecision and ill-conceived foreign ventures. His defeat and capture in the Franco-Prussian War (1870) began another turbulent period: France was occupied and forced into a humiliating armistice; radicals in Paris proclaimed the Paris Commune, which held out for two months until crushed by conservative forces. In the commune's aftermath, the struggle between republicans and monarchists led to the establishment of a conservative Third Republic in 1871. In the words of one of the leading politicians of the time, it was "the Republic which divides us least." In spite of such inauspicious beginnings, the Third Republic proved to be the longest regime in modern France, surviving World War I and lasting until France's defeat and occupation by Nazi Germany in 1940.

General Charles de Gaulle entered liberated Paris in 1944 with the hope that sweeping reforms would give France the viable democracy it had long sought. After less than two years, he resigned as head of the Provisional government, impatient as he was with the country's return to traditional party politics. In fact the Fourth Republic (1944–1958) disappointed earlier hopes and proved unable to cope with the tensions created by the cold war and the Algerian crisis. When civil war threatened in 1958, General de Gaulle was invited to return to power and help the country establish more stable institutions. Since then France has lived under the Constitution of the Fifth Republic, enacted by a referendum in 1958.

In spite of its tumultuous political history, France has developed a national mythology with roots reaching far into the past. Yet the French have never been able to agree on the political system most appropriate to their common goal of greatness. If every French citizen loves France, this does not preclude his poorly concealed contempt for the French outside his own immediate or political family. When the country falls on mediocre times, the French citizen is inclined to blame his fellow citizens, while the genius of the nation remains unimpaired in his eyes.

Economy and Society

Geographically France is at once Atlantic, Continental, and Mediterranean, and hence it occupies a unique place in Europe. Fifty-three million people, about one-fourth the population of the United States, are concentrated in an area one-fifteenth the size of the United States. If France were as densely populated as other major European countries, there would be more than 125 million French.

Urbanization has come slowly to France, in contrast to its neighbors, but it has had an important impact nonetheless. Before World War II, 48 percent of the population lived in rural communities of fewer than 2,000 inhabitants; only 30 percent do so at present. In 1936 only sixteen French cities had a population of more than 100,000, now twenty-one cities and urban agglomerations have a population of more than 300,000. This puts the country almost in line with such highly urbanized nations as West Germany and Great Britain.

Over one-fourth the total urban population — almost one-fifth of the entire nation — lives in the metropolitan region of Paris. This creates staggering problems, as it does in other metropolitan areas of the world. But in a country with centuries-old traditions of administrative, economic, and cultural centralization, it has also produced a dramatic gap in human and material resources between Paris and the rest of the country. With over one-fourth of the total French industrial production, the Paris region supports a per capita income about 60 percent higher than the national average; the regions that rank next in wealth barely reach that average.

Uneven development is striking in the nation: France west of a line running roughly from Le

Havre to Marseilles is as underdeveloped relative to the rest of France as southern Italy is compared to northern Italy. (See Figure 10.1.) Development is particularly rapid in the northeast quadrant of France, while other regions are losing population and lagging in investment, productivity, and, with some exceptions, new industry. Conflict persists between the dynamic and the static parts of the country, and governmental intervention cannot easily reconcile them without slowing growth.

Overall, French economic development has been more than respectable. In per capita gross national product, France ranks among the wealthiest nations of the world ($8,850 in 1978), well ahead of Great Britain and more than twice as prosperous as Italy. (For further comparisons, see Figure 2.2.)

By comparison with other highly developed industrial countries, the agricultural sector of France remains important in both economic and political terms. (For comparisons between the agricultural labor force in France and other countries, see Figure 2.3.) Cultivated acreage amounts to about half that of the original six Common Market countries combined. In spite of the population shift to the cities, agricultural production has not declined, and the increase of productivity is far higher in farming than in the rest of the economy. But this impressive performance hides the fact that one of three farms is estimated to be too small to be commercially viable. Because the political stability of the Third Republic depended on a large and stable peasantry, French agriculture was supported with protective tariffs that helped French farmers (and small businessmen) cling to their established routines. Only since 1945 have serious efforts been made to modernize agriculture, and stubborn individualism now seems to be on the wane. More attention is being paid to the possible advantages of farm cooperatives; marginal farms are being consolidated; technical education has been vastly improved; and further mechanization and experimentation are being used as avenues for long-range structural reforms. Even so, subsidies to the agricultural sector still cost the government almost as much as its total revenue from income taxes.

The business counterpart of the family farm is the family firm. Close to 80 percent of commercial firms do not employ a single salaried employee, and only 17 percent employ more than fifty. Although the number of corporations has more than doubled during the last ten years, family firms and partnerships still claim a considerable share of total business transactions. The largest French firms are small by American standards: the annual sales of the largest French corporation would rank fifty-fifth among American firms, eighteenth among all European firms. Development of many family firms has been handicapped by the extreme individualism, secretiveness, and conservatism of the paternalistic heads. Pressures for change, however, are emerging from the modernized sectors of the economy, from the new European institutions, such as the Common Market, and from younger members of business and the bureaucracy. The values of stability, privilege, and merely individual achievement are almost everywhere in conflict with arguments in favor of competition, innovation, and cooperation. Frequently government policies reflect contradictory pressures. (A discussion of the impact of policy on the everyday life of French citizens and of the likely future shape of policies and institutions is found in the concluding part of this chapter.

Constitution and Governmental Structure

The Constitution of 1958 is the sixteenth since the fall of the Bastille in 1789. Past republican regimes, known less for their achievements than for their instability, were invariably based on the principle that Parliament could overturn a government no longer backed by a majority of the elected representatives. Such an arrangement can work satisfactorily, as it does in most of Western Europe, when the country (and Parliament) embrace two or a few well-organized parties. The party or the coalition that has obtained a majority at the polls forms the government and can count on the almost unconditional support of its members in Parliament until the next elections. At that time, it is either kept in power or replaced by an equally disciplined party.

Why France never had the disciplined parties necessary for such a system will be explained below. The point for now is that the Constitution that General de Gaulle submitted for popular approval in 1958 offered to remedy previous failings. In preceding republics the president had been little more than a

Figure 10.1

Distribution of Employment in France

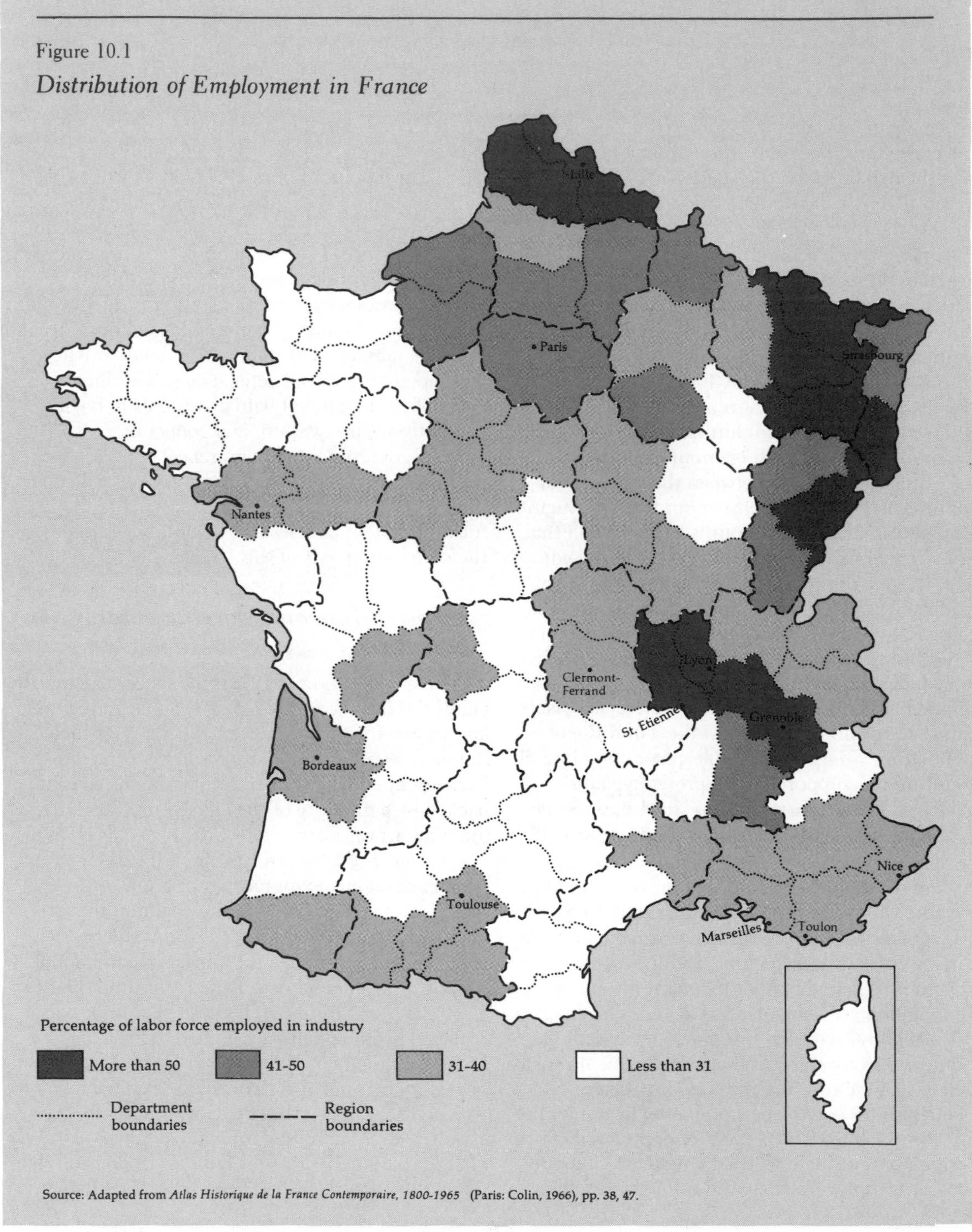

Source: Adapted from *Atlas Historique de la France Contemporaire, 1800-1965* (Paris: Colin, 1966), pp. 38, 47.

figurehead. According to the new Constitution, the president was to become a visible chief of state. He was to be placed "above the parties" to represent the unity of the national community. As guardian of the Constitution he was to be an arbiter who would rely on other powers — Parliament, the Constitutional Council, or the people — for the full weight of government action. He can appeal directly to the people in two ways: he can submit any legislative proposal to the electorate as a referendum and he can dissolve Parliament and call for new elections.

In case of grave threat "to the institutions of the republic" (and in a number of other situations vaguely described), the Constitution grants the president emergency powers. It is true that the president can be checked. He can be indicted for high treason by a majority vote in the two houses of Parliament and then tried by a high court of justice. But experience indicates that in a tense situation he who holds power and controls the means of communication will be likely to forestall an indictment by open ballot in Parliament.

According to the new Constitution, the president was to be elected by an electoral college composed of local notables. But in 1962 a referendum replaced the original design by the popular election of the president for a renewable term of seven years. This change endowed the powerful presidency with the legitimacy of a popular vote. De Gaulle, in a press conference, outlined his view of the office and its significance for the policy process. Power, he said, "emanates directly from the people, which implies that the Head of State, elected by the nation, is the source and holder of this power." He insisted "that the individual authority of the State is entrusted completely to the President by the people who elected him, that there is no other authority — either ministerial, civilian, military, or judicial — which is not entrusted or maintained by him."[1]

At the same time, de Gaulle also rejected an American-type presidential system as unsuitable for France. The Constitution stipulates that the prime minister "shall direct the operation of the government" and that the government "shall determine and direct the policy of the Nation." As in previous republics, the government of the Fifth Republic needs the support of a majority in Parliament to function and to stay in office. The Constitution therefore combines features of the presidential and parliamentary systems in a way frequently criticized as ambiguous. Yet the system has survived without a major crisis, since three succeeding presidents have been able to count on a majority in Parliament for supporting the governments of their choice. (For an organizational chart of the decision-making structure at the national level, see Figure 10.2.)

Parliament is composed of two houses: the National Assembly and the Senate. The National Assembly is elected directly for five years by all citizens over eighteen; it may be dissolved at any time, though not twice within a year.

The instability of previous regimes had been attributed mostly to the constant meddling of Parliament with the activities of the executive. Distrust of executive authority had given Parliament a predominant role in the policy process, quite apart from its ability to overthrow governments without having to fear its own dissolution. The Constitution of 1958 strove to put an end to the subordination of government to Parliament. The framers of the new text started with the assumption that French voters could never be expected to send coherent majorities to the National Assembly. The Constitution and the so-called organic laws, enacted in conjunction with it, imposed strict rules of behavior on each deputy and on Parliament as a body. This, it was hoped, would ensure the needed equilibrium.

Now the Cabinet, rather than Parliament, is in control of proceedings in both houses and can require priority for bills it wishes to promote. The president rather than the prime minister chooses the cabinet members. Most of them are, but need not be, deputies elected to the National Assembly. Parliament still enacts laws, but the domain of such laws is strictly defined. Many areas of modern life that in other democracies are regulated by laws and debated and approved by Parliament are turned over to rule making by the executive.

The French government has the power to force the final parliamentary vote on a bill with only those amendments it has been willing to accept. When the budget is being discussed, amendments that would reduce receipts or increase expenditures are disallowed. Should Parliament fail to accept the budget submitted by the government within seventy days,

[1] William G. Andrews, ed., *European Political Institutions* (Princeton: Van Nostrand, 1966), pp. 56–60.

Figure 10.2

Relationship Between French Public Authorities on the National Level

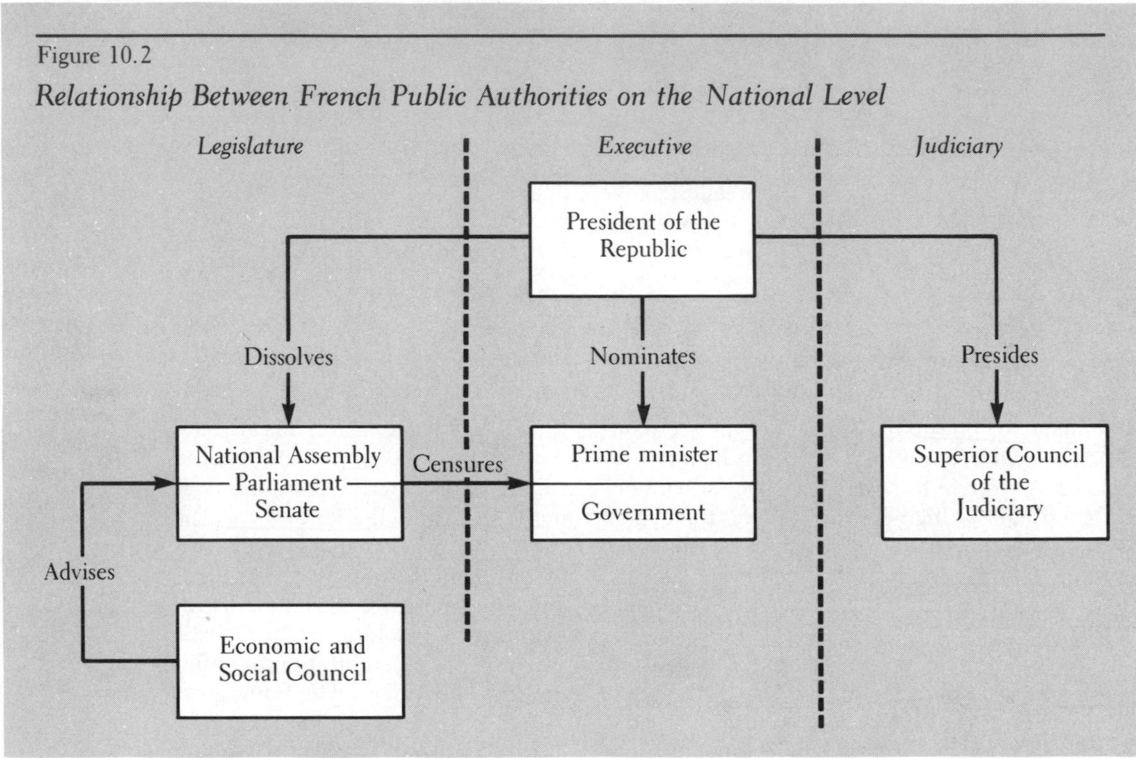

the Cabinet can enact the budget by ordinance. The nineteen standing committees of the National Assembly under the Fourth Republic have been reduced to six, and the committees were made large — from 60 to 120 members — to prevent interaction among highly specialized deputies or senators who could become effective counterparts to the ministers.

It is not surprising that the new Constitution spelled out in detail the conditions under which the National Assembly could overthrow a government. An explicit motion of censure must be formulated and passed by one half of the house. Even after such a motion of censure, the government might resist the pressure to resign: the president can dissolve the Assembly and call for new elections. During the first year after these elections a new dissolution of parliament is prohibited by the constitution. Hence the President would have to appoint a government which has majority support in parliament, even though the President might disapprove of its policies. Should such a situation ever occur, it is considered likely that the President would resign. The vote of censure is the only way Parliament can effectively criticize the conduct of government. As in the past, Parliament can obtain information from the government by means of debate, confrontation with the prime minister or Cabinet, written and oral questions, or formal investigations. Under the new regime, however, the government has denied the Assembly the right to appraise information thus obtained by a vote or a resolution.

The upper chamber of Parliament, the Senate, is elected by a large electoral college that designates senators for a nine-year term. This electoral college is made up mostly of municipal and departmental councillors in a way that gives predominance to the rural sector. (For a chart illustrating the hierarchy of government at various levels, see Figure 10.3.) The Senate shares with the National Assembly the right to initiate legislation; all bills must be approved by both houses.

Another organ of representation is the Economic and Social Council, which the constitution of 1958 took over almost unchanged from previous regimes. Appointed either by major interest groups or the government, the members of this council deliberate on all bills that have an economic or social impact. But since it is only an advisory board, the council's opinions can be ignored, as they have been.

France has no tradition of judicial review. As in other countries with civil law systems, and in Great

Figure 10.3
The Hierarchical Structure of French Government

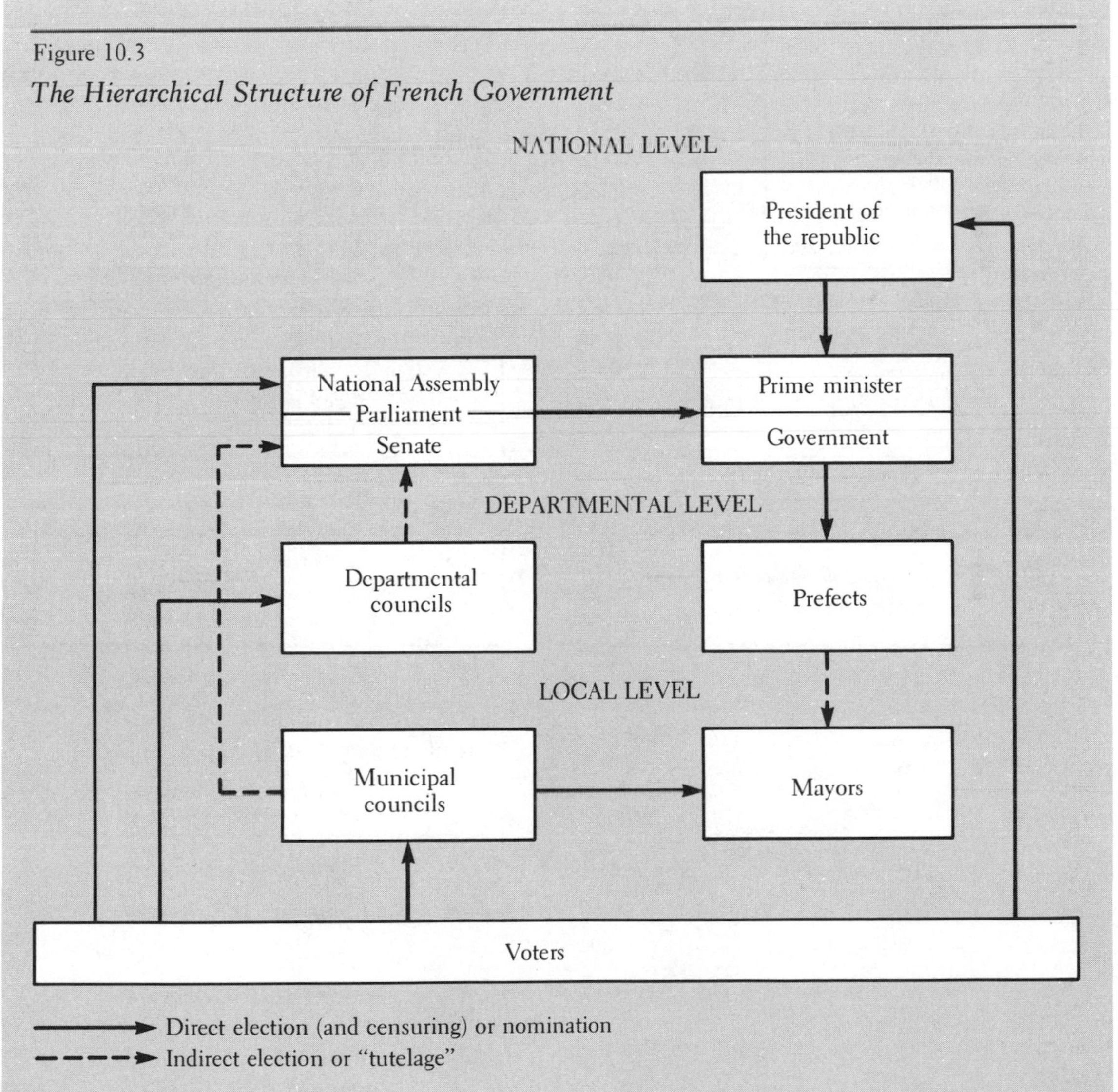

Figure 10.4

The Regular (Ordinary) Courts of the Fifth French Republic

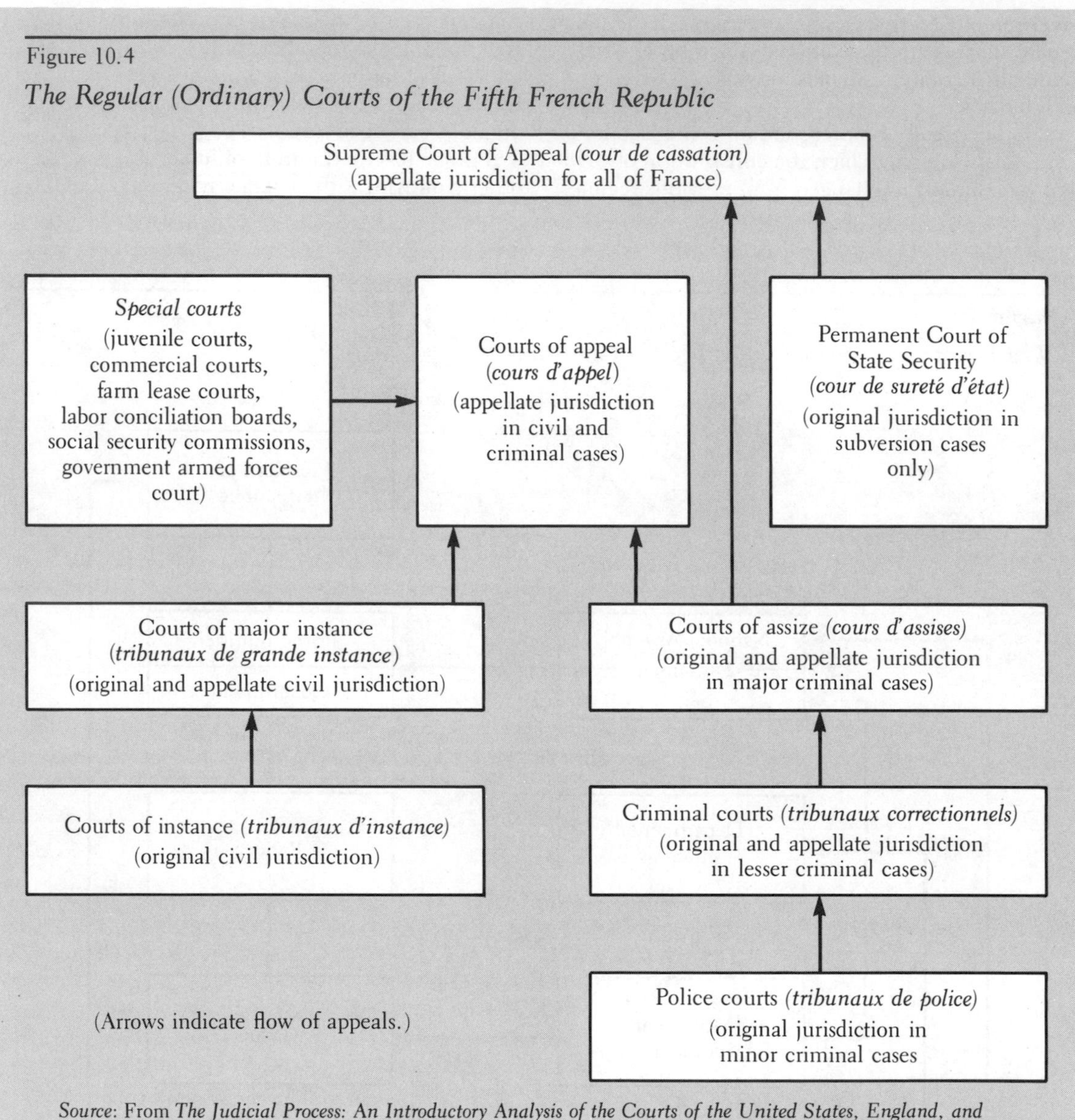

Source: From *The Judicial Process: An Introductory Analysis of the Courts of the United States, England, and France*, 3rd ed., by Henry J. Abraham. Copyright © 1962, 1968, 1975 by Oxford University Press, Inc. Reprinted by permission.

Britain as well, the sovereignty of Parliament means that the legislature has the last word and that a law enacted in constitutionally prescribed forms is not subject to the courts' scrutiny. The Constitution of 1958 created a Constitutional Council that in certain cases must examine legislation and international treaties and decide whether they conform to the Constitution. The council can also investigate laws on the request of the president, prime minister, speakers of the two houses, or sixty members of either house. A provision declared unconstitutional may not be promulgated. The selection of the nine council members (each serving for a nonrenewable nine-year term) is political: the nomination is in the hands of the president and the speakers of both houses of Parliament. So far this has resulted in the nomination, among others, of ex-ministers and former ambassadors; if they were legally trained at all, hardly any of them was a specialist in constitutional law.

The Fifth Republic undertook a series of reforms designed to streamline and modernize a partly outdated court system. The present court structure, as it pertains to civil and criminal cases, is illustrated in Figure 10.4. An elaborate structure of administrative courts was left virtually untouched. The role that the apex, the Council of State, has played at times in the policy process will be discussed below.

POLITICAL CULTURE AND SOCIALIZATION

Themes of Political Culture

THE BURDEN OF HISTORY Historical thinking can prove both a bond and — as the American Civil War demonstrates — a hindrance to consensus. The French are so fascinated by their own history that feuds of the past are constantly superimposed on the conflicts of the present. This passionate use of historical memories, resulting in seemingly inflexible ambitions, warnings, and taboos, complicates political decision making. In de Gaulle's words, France is "weighed down by history."[2]

[2] Charles de Gaulle, *War Memoirs III: The Salvation* (New York: Simon and Schuster, 1960), p. 330.

ABSTRACTION AND SYMBOLISM In the Age of Enlightenment the monarchy, in an effort to compensate for the servility it imposed on the educated classes, left them free to voice their views on many topics, provided the discussion remained general and abstract. The urge to discuss a wide range of problems, even trivial ones, in broad philosophical terms has hardly diminished. This exaltation of the abstract is reflected in the significance attributed to symbols and rituals. Rural communities that fought on opposite sides in the French Revolution still pay homage to different heroes, nearly two centuries later. They seem to have no real quarrel with each other, but inherited symbols have kept them apart so that their political and religious habits have remained disparate.[3] This helps explain why a nation united by almost universal admiration for a common historical experience holds to conflicting interpretations of its meaning.

REPRESENTATIVE VERSUS PLEBISCITARIAN TRADITIONS In France's political development, the opposition between two patterns of government has been of even greater significance than the controversy between monarchists and republicans. One pattern is the tradition of representative democracy, the other is populist, with emphasis on direct elections and frequent national referenda.

In the early days of the revolution, the newly established political system reflected a belief that the intentions of the people could be expressed validly only through elected representatives. The Constitution of 1793 rejected this view by denouncing "representative despotism," and tried to organize the general will through annual elections and referenda. Revolutionary rule, climaxing in Napoleon's rise to power, prevented this constitution from ever being applied, but Bonapartist rule proved as hostile to representative rule as it was to the absolute monarchy of the old regime.

These two forms of authority experienced within a decade developed into the opposite poles between which French political life has moved ever since.

[3] Laurence Wylie, "Social Change at the Grass Roots," in Stanley Hoffmann, Charles P. Kindleberger, Jesse R. Pitts, et al., *In Search of France* (Cambridge, Mass.: Harvard University Press, 1963), p. 230.

Almost invariably, politics under a given regime has been determined by one or the other. Direct democracy has been historically identified with the two Napoleons and advocated by many critics of representative democracy. They are scornful of intermediaries in state and society that stand between the unorganized masses and the popularly elected executive. Accordingly, in this system the importance of the legislative branch is reduced and political life carefully circumscribed. Infringement of laws by the executive is given legitimacy by popular approval, expressed in a referendum.

The representative tradition established itself firmly with the Third Republic and remained in force, with only short interruptions, till turmoil in Algeria returned de Gaulle to power. For this tradition, the essence of democratic government consists in close control of an ever-suspect executive and in the defense of constituency interests, however fragmented. The deputy, an elected representative, must decide personally, without directives from an extraparliamentary body, even a political party, how best to resist authority.

DISTRUST OF POLITICS AND GOVERNMENT The French share in the widespread ambivalence of modern times that combines distrust of government with high expectations from it. The French citizen's simultaneous distrust of authority and craving for it feed on both his individualism and his passion for equality. The ethos produces a self-reliant individual convinced that he is responsible to himself, and perhaps to his family, for what he is and may become. Obstacles are created by the outside world, the "they" that operate beyond the circle of the family, the family firm, the village. Most of the time, however, "they" are identified with the government.

Memories reaching back to the eighteenth century justify a state of mind that is potentially, if seldom overtly, insubordinate. A strong government is considered to be reactionary by nature, even if it pretends to be progressive. Since the citizen feels that no one but himself can be entrusted with the defense of his interests, he is inclined to shun cooperation. He fears that the discipline required by cooperation might constrain him. When he participates in public life, he hopes to weaken authority rather than encourage change, even when change is overdue. At times this individualism is tainted with anarchism. Yet the French also accommodate themselves rather easily to bureaucratic rule. Since administrative rulings supposedly treat all situations with the same yardstick, they satisfy the sharp sense of equality possessed by a people who feel forever shortchanged by the government and by the privileges those in power bestow on others.

CRISIS AND APATHY Even though the revolution of 1789 did not break with the past as completely as is commonly believed, it has conditioned the general outlook on crisis and compromise, continuity and change. Sudden change rather than gradual mutation, dramatic conflicts couched in the language of mutually exclusive, radical ideologies — these are the experiences that excite the French at historical moments when their minds are particularly malleable. At the end of the nineteenth century, history itself appeared to an illustrious French historian, Ernest Renan, as a "kind of civil war." In fact, what appears to the outsider as permanent instability is a fairly regular alternation between brief violent crises and prolonged periods of routine. The French have become accustomed to thinking that no thorough change can ever be brought about except through a major upheaval. Since the great revolution, every French adult has experienced — usually more than once — occasions of political excitement followed by disappointment. This leads to moral exhaustion, and widespread skepticism about any possibility of change.

Whether they originated within the country or were brought about by international conflict, each of France's emergencies has resulted in a constitutional crisis. Each time, the triumphant forces have codified their norms and philosophy, usually in a comprehensive document. The constitutions of 1791, 1830, 1875, and 1946 enshrined the representative principle; those of 1793 and of 1848 belong partly, and those of 1852 and 1958 (especially as amended in 1962) more frankly, to the plebiscitarian tradition. This explains why constitutions have never played the role of fundamental charters. Their norms have been satisfactory only to one segment of society and hotly contested by others.

The high sensitivity of the public at moments of crisis and its withdrawal into apathy during periods of unexciting routine are different aspects of the same phenomenon. An approaching major crisis is usually foreshadowed by a lack of support for the regime, a lack that may be expressed in the success of extremist parties, in tax evasion or outright resistance to tax collection, and in fiery debates on the next, and better, constitution.

Political Socialization

An individual's attitudes toward the political system, its institutions, and its values are paramount in understanding the peculiarities of a nation's politics. Understanding the limitations that an inherited political culture imposes on political development is of particular importance in studying an old country like France. In France more than elsewhere political institutions, even if they seem new, are shaped by the political culture. The French who designed the Constitution of the Fourth Republic after World War II had a mandate to establish a regime quite different from the one that had led the country into disaster in 1940. Yet the intended change was frustrated by the attitudes and beliefs of the political actors inside and outside Parliament, and those of French citizens as voters and as members of interest groups and parties. When de Gaulle was called in to prevent threatening disaster, he did not create anew but drew on other traditions, equally anchored in political culture. Much can be made of the difference in the style of politics before and after de Gaulle's reentry into politics, but during both periods the style was conditioned by the political socialization the actors and their followers had undergone.

THE CHURCH AND RELIGION Until well into the present century, the conflict between believers and nonbelievers has shaped the political culture. France is a Roman Catholic country — at least 92 percent of the citizenry has been baptized in the Catholic faith — yet one the church considers partly dechristianized. According to a 1977 public opinion poll, 55 percent of Catholic males (62 percent of Catholic workers) never attend church.

Since the revolution, conflict over religion has divided society and politics at all levels. While French Catholics viewed the revolution as the work of satanic men, enemies of the church became militant in their opposition to Catholic forms and symbols. With the establishment of the Third Republic in 1871, differences between the political subcultures of Catholicism and anticlericalism deepened further. After a few years militant anticlericalism took firm control of the republic. Parliament rescinded the centuries-old compact with the Vatican, expelled most Catholic orders, and severed all ties between church and state, so that "the moral unity of the country could be reestablished." Hostility between Catholics and anticlericals almost broke out into generalized violence. In rural regions, where Catholic observance had become a matter of habit rather than of genuine faith, dechristianization spread, spurred on by new legislation that deprived the church of all official prestige.[4] At the same time, representatives of the small-town bourgeoisie that had replaced the upper-middle class as political leaders swelled the membership of the organized antichurch — the Freemasonry. The number of Freemasons, it is estimated, never exceeded 50,000. But since they were distributed over many organizations, both public and private, Freemasons exercised, at least until 1914, a greater influence on the minds of French republicans than their number would suggest.

The militance of the republican regime was matched by the pope, who excommunicated every deputy voting for the separation laws. Faithful Catholics were driven to the view that only the overthrow of the regime could overcome their isolation.

Opposition between the political right and left was frequently determined by attitudes toward the Roman Catholic church. In those rural regions where religious practice continued to be lively and where the advice of local clergy counted on election day, conservative candidates carried the vote. But

[4] Gordon Wright, *France in Modern Times* (Chicago: Rand McNally, 1962), p. 332.

even governments of the center usually did not invite the support of conservative deputies whose anticlerical lineage was dubious. From 1879 to 1939, very few practicing Catholics obtained Cabinet rank. The political isolation of the Catholics has been compared to that of the Communists since 1947, since which time every government left of center has found it necessary to disclaim Communist support even when it was offered.[5]

The separation of church and state has now lost the rigidities that characterized the earlier republican regimes. How fundamentally feelings have changed is well illustrated by the results of a poll conducted during the presidential election campaign of 1969: 38 percent of those answering the poll preferred a churchgoing president, only 10 percent frowned on one, and 43 percent were indifferent.

After World War II, diverse Catholic movements and the church hierarchies changed methods and worked toward the rehabilitation of Roman Catholicism. Catholic organizations, publications, and teachings were far more flexible than they had been in the past, both socially and politically. On the other hand, the Socialist party and certain leftist movements have lately attracted a relatively large number of faithful young Catholics.

Simultaneously, Freemasonry is no longer important in political life. The vanishing significance of the fight against clericalism has weakened the Masonic lodges. From time to time specific issues still activate anticlerical feelings, which then erupt, volcanolike. In 1960, 11 million signatures were quickly gathered, especially in rural regions, to oppose legislation pro-

[5] See Francois Goguel and Alfred Grosser, *La Politique en France*, 4th ed. (Paris: Colin, 1970), p. 30.

Valéry Giscard d'Estaing and his wife among young Alsatians. Although constitutionally placed "above politics," the President of the Republic participates actively in all election campaigns.

posing public subsidies to and official recognition of parochial schools. But the protests grew out of traditions that have lost political and even ideological vitality. The legislation, once passed, worked smoothly and without incident.

For many reasons, French Jews (numbering about 600,000 since the recent exodus from North Africa) had been so integrated into French society that they did not need to be discussed as a separate element of political culture. This changed, at least temporarily, with de Gaulle's criticism of Israel, which created for the first time a Jewish vote opposed to the government majority. Under de Gaulle's successors the phenomenon seemed to have subsided, but it could be revived, if and when the French Foreign Office voices openly its traditional pro-Arab sympathies.

By contrast to the traditional attitude of the Jewish population, the Protestants (800,000 strong, or 1.6 percent of the total population) have, at least until recently, lived somewhat apart, with heavy concentrations in Alsace, in the Paris region, and in some regions of central and southeastern France. About two-thirds of Protestants belong to the upper bourgeoisie, so that Protestantism was marked socially and economically by a clannishness and a rather deliberate style of life. Until recently, French Protestants usually voted more to the left than others in their socioeconomic position or in the same region. They identified themselves with advanced republicanism because of the Catholic identification with the right and antirepublicanism. Even though they were culturally different from other republicans, the proportion of Protestants in high public positions was and is very large.

The new alignments among Catholics have had a corresponding impact on the beliefs and attitudes of Protestants. Since the liberation of 1944 Protestants have not voted left with any consistency. Their electoral behavior, like their activities in cultural and economic associations, is now determined by factors other than religion. They too have been fully integrated into the mainstream of French political culture.

FAMILY For those French who view their neighbors and fellow citizens with distrust, and the institutions around them with cynicism, the family is a safe haven. At least in the past, the French were always sociable to outsiders met on neutral ground. But distance was otherwise maintained and intimacy rarely granted. Concern for stability, safe income, property, and continuity were common to bourgeois and peasant families, though not to the urban or agricultural workers. The training of children in bourgeois and peasant families was marked by close supervision, incessant correction, and strict sanctions. In recent times this pattern of patriarchal authority has been seriously shaken, as young people assert their independence by leaving the family residence altogether. Moreover, in the rapidly urbanizing society of higher mobility, which France has become, prolonged absences of the father from home are more frequent. And because of better training and new experiences, the sons of farmers or of small businessmen no longer accept unquestioningly the outmoded working methods of their fathers.

What is most striking is a general change in atmosphere. In a dynamic society, family members, including children, bring into the family circle the results of their varied experiences, instead of merely receiving and passing on traditions. Leisure activities, especially watching television but also traveling, have influenced the style of family living and often the family's relationship with the world outside. The family's search for equilibrium and balance is, of course, not abandoned. But to enable the family to continue its role as one of the molders of individual motivations, a fresh equilibrium is sought, to take into account new forces pressing from the outside.

CLASS AND STATUS Feelings about class differences shape a society's authority pattern and the style in which authority is exercised. The French, like the English, are very conscious of living in a society divided into classes. But since equality is valued more highly in France than in England, deference toward the upper classes is far less developed, and resentful antagonism is widespread. The number of those who are conscious of belonging to a class is high, solidarity within classes intense. In a 1977 public opinion poll, 68 percent of all respondents and 73 percent of males declared that they belonged to a class; only 26 percent denied it. Among the workers, 76 percent classified themselves as working class; among workers habitually voting for the Communist party, 82 percent did. One study of the question concluded that although class conflict may have declined, class has undoubtedly remained the fundamental political unit.[6] The nation's elites continue to be recruited from an extremely small sector of the society. Upward social mobility exists, but it is frequently awkward and slow, especially into the ranks of the upper bourgeoisie. There are very few self-made men, and mobility by marriage remains infrequent, testimony to the solidity of the bourgeois family.

The fissure between bourgeoisie and working class has molded French history for more than a century, producing a divided political culture with different symbols, flags, and holidays. As a reaction to the lag in reform benefiting workers, the working class developed a creed called *ouvriérisme* (workerism). Workers, it was believed, should never entrust their defense to members of the bourgeoisie, not even to those in Parliament who mouth socialism; to send workers to Parliament was acting the part of a mother who sold her daughters into a house of prostitution. In the absence of expectations that their lot as individuals would be improved by the action of the government, the proletariat was finally reduced to harboring dreams of sudden emancipation.

When prosperity spread after World War II, large groups of wage earners were able to live in a style previously unobtainable, which had earlier been tainted as a bourgeois style. The availability of durable consumer goods and the development of consumer credit, the "motorization" of almost everybody, the multiplication of television sets, the high value placed on leisure activities — and the correspondingly high budget for the month-long paid vacation — all have produced attitudes upsetting the ingrained habits of the traditional proletarian culture. The common patterns of a mass culture are emerging at last, even in the style of celebrations and of sports events.

Among the respondents who in the 1977 public opinion poll had classified themselves as belonging to a class, 61 percent agreed with a statement that "little by little" manual and white-collar workers would be "integrated into a broad middle class." Only 22 percent disagreed, and there were no significant differences of opinion according to the respondent's social class.[7]

ASSOCIATIONS Interest groups and other associations, numerous though they are, do not play as significant a socialization role in France as they do in other countries. A bias against all authority has led to suspicion of tightly organized groups. But the ambivalence toward organized group activity is more than an expression of apathy; such ambivalence also reflects a lack of confidence in the value of cooperation.

Group affiliation plays a role in socialization only when it determines activities and attitudes. Some observers suggest that membership in French organizations involves less actual participation than it does in American or British organizations, and hence has less impact on social and political attitudes.[8] In France, as to a lesser extent in the United States, class makes a difference in group membership. Outside the limited circle of the urban upper bourgeoisie, associations other than interest groups have little importance and affect the lives of their members very little.

Lately there are indications that membership in associations is becoming more rewarding. Its value is no longer assessed exclusively in terms of the associations' influence as the representative of a group interest. Cultural clubs have swept aside the traditional barriers of class, denomination, and political conviction. Young blue-collar and white-collar workers, young farmers, young businessmen, and students express their intentions of affiliating with professional associations, trade unions, and so forth in significantly greater numbers than did their elders. Associations are regarded as necessary and normal elements of modern society. In a public opinion poll of 1977, 50 percent of all respondents (and 69 percent of those between twenty-five and thirty-four) stated that groups and associations should play a greater role in public life than they do.

[6] Suzanne Berger et al., "The Problem of Reform in France: The Political Ideas of Local Elites," *Political Science Quarterly*, 84:3 (1969), pp. 443 ff.

[7] For the results of the 1977 poll see SOFRES, *L'Opinion Française en 1977* (Paris: Presses de la Fondation Nationale des Sciences Politiques, 1978), tables 9, 10, 12.

[8] Eric Nordlinger, "Democratic Stability and Instability: The French Case," *World Politics*, 18:1 (1965), pp. 127–157.

EDUCATION The most important way a community preserves and transmits its cultural and political values is through education. Napoleon Bonaparte recognized the significance of education, and well into the second half of the twentieth century the French educational system has remained an imposing historical monument, in the unmistakable style of the First Empire. The edifice Napoleon erected combined education at all levels, from primary school to postgraduate professional training, into one centralized corporation: the imperial university. Its job was to teach the national doctrine through uniform programs at various levels.

The strict military discipline of the Napoleonic model has been loosened by succeeding regimes, but ruling groups have discovered that the machinery created by Napoleon was a convenient and coherent instrument for transmitting the values — both changing and permanent — of French civilization. The centralized imperial university has therefore never been dismantled, and the minister of education continues to control curriculum and teaching methods, the criteria for selection and advancement of pupils and teachers, and the content of examinations.

Making advancement at every step dependent on passing an examination is not peculiar to France. What is distinctly French is a widespread cult of competitive examinations that draws its strength from an obsessive and quite unrealistic belief that everybody is equal before an examination. Success or failure in the examination shapes not only the candidate and his family, but the milieu to which he will belong. French society is strewn with individuals who failed an examination, or received a lower than expected grade, and who have suffered irreparable psychological damage.

On the other hand, centralization of authority in a far-removed national government has often resulted in a beneficial weakening of controls and lessening of community pressure that might have become oppressive. The idea that education is an effective weapon for emancipation and social betterment has had popular as well as official recognition. Farmers and workers regard the instruction of their children, a better instruction than they had, as an important weapon in the fight against "them," which in this case may even include the instructors.

The *baccalauréat* — the certificate of completion of the secondary school, the *lycée* — has remained almost the sole means, and until recently also a guarantee, of access to higher education. But with forty to fifty students in each secondary school graduating class, and hundreds of students in university lecture halls, such a system suits and profits only those self-motivated individuals for whom it was designed. Moreover, it works to the disadvantage of the gifted child who comes from other than the bourgeoisie. The distance between teacher and pupil, the absence of good teaching methods, and the emphasis on the cultivated use of language widen the cultural gap further.

The bourgeois child who succeeds easily in an educational system uniquely suited to the bourgeois milieu is convinced that his position in society is due to inborn talent. Postwar reforms have tried to counter such class snobbery by easing the transition among the various levels of the educational system and by moving teachers more freely from one level to another. Education in France remains a vehicle of social mobility, even if at a level far below what might be desirable. During the academic year 1974–1975 only 13.3 percent of working-class children attended universities (compared to 40.7 percent of the working class in the total labor force); by contrast 32.9 percent of the students were the children of parents in the professions, top management, and high civil service, a group which comprises only 4.9 percent of the labor force. These figures have changed little over the last ten years. (For comparison with other countries, see Table 8.7.)

Discussion of thorough reform of education has persisted since World War II. The pressure of numbers, many experts concluded, was bound to explode the old structures, to modify methods, and to transform the style of education. A secondary school system that in 1975 was expected to instruct 4.9 million adolescents and certify many of them for higher education could not remain identical to one that at the beginning of the century trained 200,000 students, and as late as 1945 taught only 700,000 students. Between 1958 and 1976 the number of students in higher education rose from 170,000 to over one million.

The teaching methods practiced at the lycées were entirely inappropriate for the socialization of the lower-middle classes winning entry into secondary education. Increased social mobility and nationwide modernization resulted in the university and the economy falling out of step. Reformers were constantly frustrated by both the extreme centralization of the system and the power of vested interests defended by professors, teachers, and administrators. Because the universities failed to respond to the demands of mass education, students' dissatisfaction with the content and methods of their education was intensified by anxieties about their professional careers. For a minority, the system's haphazard efforts to provide training for skills were distasteful because, in their eyes, such a design subjected higher education to the demands of technocratic capitalism.[9]

The conjunction of these two discontented groups produced, in May 1968, the spark of rebellion that spread to all universities, and to many secondary schools. When students and police were battling in the streets, 61 percent of Paris respondents to an opinion poll believed that the students' demands for educational reforms were justified; only 16 percent thought otherwise.[10] President de Gaulle himself attributed the crisis to the inability of those in charge "to adapt themselves to the modern necessities of the nation." He pledged that the system of higher education would be "reconstructed not according to centuries-old habits, but in line with the actual needs of the country's development."[11]

A new law was passed by Parliament to create an autonomous university system, and thereby to undo the Napoleonic structure. In many respects the new arrangements have remained a paper scheme. Budgetary limitations constrain the formal powers of universities and academic departments to select staff. The elaborate structures created by the law to ensure the democratic participation of teachers and students in university administration were unsuccessful. Nonetheless it should not be concluded that nothing has changed. New methods were tried before 1968 and in quite a few places traditional attitudes have given way to a new mentality. Yet the reform legislation has seldom proven helpful to the reformers.

A thorough restructuring of secondary education has long appeared as a key to cultural change and social promotion. Students in secondary schools (and occasionally the parent-teacher associations) have used strikes, street demonstrations, and mass meetings to manifest their discontent with schools inadequate to educate millions, a task for which neither their methods nor their curriculum were designed. Inadequacy results in the boredom of students and teachers alike; the gap between the traditional teaching style and a greater permissiveness in home and family life proves particularly irritating.

Numerous and often contradictory reform plans have been put forward, but so far most proposed reforms have floundered on the resistance of teachers, parents, bureaucrats, and politicians. The desire to reform is widespread. But with no agreement on desirable changes, the status quo prevails.

Conclusion

Why, it is frequently asked, has a nation whose history has inspired free people everywhere, and that is made up of self-reliant, rational, and mature individuals, had such great difficulties in establishing a stable democracy? The answer may be found in the fact that the values that individual French citizens accept as normal, and which many cherish, often conflict with the needs of a political system combining freedom and authority.

Tensions between the desire to assert the uniqueness of the individual and the centralized bureaucratic control of society have produced ambiguous attitudes toward authority. The distrust of others as threats to individual self-fulfillment invites rejection of conventions and beliefs established by others. The insistence on authoritatively enforced rules and the distrust of established authority and of the peer group produce a political culture that expects little from cooperation or broad participation in decision making.

The result of such attitudes has frequently been a

[9] See Stephen S. Cohen, *Modern Capitalist Planning: The French Model* (Cambridge, Mass.: Harvard University Press, 1969), pp. 239 ff; and Alain Touraine, *The May Movement: Revolt and Reform* (New York: Random House, 1971).

[10] *Sondages*, 30:2 (1968), p. 74.

[11] *L'Année Politique, 1968* (Paris: Presses Universitaires, 1969), p. 379.

lack of solidarity and of civic sense, which many French deplore even while they practice it. When it results in a stalemate that stalls overdue changes, the nation is likely to turn to an authoritarian pacifier to solve the crisis. To win legitimacy for the solution imposed, this pacifier will frequently resort to a heroic style, which appears far more acceptable than the tedium of laborious bargaining.

Despite superficial similarities, this is not identical with a people trying to be saved from themselves by totalitarian rule. Since French confidence in themselves as individuals is not impaired, they do not see the need for totalitarian manipulation of their minds. They still distrust their government and their neighbors, and they want to voice their distrust. The freedom left for such criticism and the unwillingness to enforce conformity distinguish the authoritarian from the totalitarian regime. The Fifth Republic, both under de Gaulle and since his retirement, has never been totalitarian. But neither has it been able to get to the roots of the citizens' ambivalence toward authority.

POLITICAL PARTICIPATION

Participation in Local Politics

In France, as elsewhere, local politics affects the socialization of the citizen at several levels. It continues the civic education that home and school have begun. It offers possibilities for political participation beyond, though also including, the right to vote for local officials. It is a vantage point from which politics can be watched closely. In many countries, France among them, the local scene also provides the training ground for political activists, for those who seek fulfillment in local government as well as for those who move on to national involvement. All these functions are interconnected. Whether, and how effectively, local politics discharges them depends on the place of local government in the institutional framework of the political system and on the political culture underlying both.

A marked characteristic of the French system is the extreme diffusion of local government units. There are 36,400 communes (the basic area of local administration), compared to fewer than 35,000 local school boards in the United States. But almost 35,000 French communes have fewer than 2,000 inhabitants, and of these 22,500 have fewer than 500. In quantitative terms, these communes offer unrivaled opportunities for political participation. Since every commune is administered by an elected municipal council, composed of between nine and thirty-seven members, there are more than 470,000 municipal councillors in France — 1.8 percent of the electorate.

The communes are combined into ninety-five departments, each presided over by an elective *conseil général*. Although it wields less power than do many municipal councils in its area, the higher body opens additional avenues of elective office. (For the structure of local government see Figure 10.3.)

Another characteristic of French local government differs sharply from American and British practice and has significant consequences for all local participation. Because of centralization, all powers exercised by local government units are granted by the national government. This means that every individual acting on behalf of either a department or a commune acts in a dual capacity. Whether directly or indirectly elected by the citizens, as are the mayors of the communes, or appointed by the minister of the interior in Paris, as are the administrative heads (the prefects) of the departments, every act is that both of a local government official and of an agent of the national government.

Local authorities are chosen by the electorate without the intervention of the state; yet under certain conditions they can be dismissed and, more important, their decisions can be annulled by the prefects, to whom they must be submitted for approval. But this does not condemn mayors to passivity. It means rather that they are expected to bargain incessantly with the authorities of the state for such approval.

The tone of prefectural directives may often be harshly authoritarian, and mayors never cease complaining about the lack of understanding shown by the representatives of the state, but more often than not relations between local authorities and their partners representing the central government are close and cordial. Within the commune an effective mayor performs as the powerful executive that law and custom permit. But at the same time national authorities value the mayor as the link between the human problems of the commune and the abstract power of the state.[12] The prestige of local office is enhanced by the fact that most national political careers start in the commune or in the conseil général. If local government does not always provide a suitable training ground, it serves nevertheless as a jumping-off point for the ambitious. To be taken seriously in Paris, a politician must have the credentials of local success.

Holding concurrently the offices of deputy or senator and mayor has traditionally been one of the goals of a political career. Such interlacing of national and local elective office has undoubtedly had a stabilizing influence on both levels: flash political movements without local ties usually lose momentum quickly; municipal affairs are not seriously disrupted by sudden upheavals.

But so close a relationship is also unsettling. The deputy or senator who knows he will be judged on the basis of his success in commune or department frequently devotes much of his time and energy to obtaining satisfaction for local demands. Bonds of sympathy between local authorities and their constituents are strong, mostly because of administrative efficiency but also because municipal administration is the natural symbol for a community of local interests that feel forever threatened by the central government and frequently by a neighboring town. And because the achievements of local government often fall short of expectations, the central government is regularly blamed and in the next national election citizens might react by casting a protest vote against the regime.

Since the local government is regarded as the dispenser of administrative efficiency and as the focus of community solidarity, a nonpartisan stance is fairly widespread both in elections and in office. In smaller communities political labels are quite meaningless. Election lists resemble the balanced ticket of an American municipality: representatives of various economic interests and social groups, local notables, and sometimes representatives of minority groups are all given a place. When an incumbent mayor stands for reelection, he enjoys an almost complete freedom from the restraints that well-organized political parties might place on their candidates or programs.

A high price is paid for this nonpartisan harmony, at least in small rural communities. Constant efforts to preserve consensus discourage dynamic action, indicating more interest in equilibrium than in progress. Political activity and problem solving are not carried to the marketplace, where bargaining would have to take place in public. Instead, success and failure depend on personal relations.

Such arrangements in turn affect citizen attitudes. Especially in rural communities, participation in local elections might be high, but once elections are over, citizens pay scant attention to the activities of local representatives. Meetings of the city council are rarely attended by the public. Nothing important seems to happen there, since most mayors make decisions and take action behind closed doors. If citizens feel aggrieved they will protest in front of the buildings housing the prefect or subprefect, rather than lay their case before the city council.

Such a system is unlikely to teach citizens the art of solving problems together. Generalizations are hazardous, however, especially since traditional attitudes seem to be giving way in more than a few localities. Some municipal councils grant a hearing before appropriate subcommittees to a variety of interests. Citizen groups are invited to cooperate with the local authorities on either a functional or geographical basis. The style and behavior of a younger generation of local leaders is often incompatible with traditional attitudes. Where old mayors sought distinction by living within a limited budget, the new notables, among them the mayors of larger cities, do not shy away from imposing new tax burdens on their constituents.

Voting in Parliamentary Elections

In the Third and Fourth Republics, the French voter looked upon his representative in Parliament as his personal ambassador in Paris. By his vote he entrusted that representative with the defense of his interests, without regard for the requirements of a coherent national policy.

In other Western parliamentary systems, the emergence of disciplined parties modified the earlier

[12] See Mark Kesselman, *The Ambiguous Consensus: A Study of Local Government in France* (New York: Knopf, 1967), pp. 38–52 and 66 ff., for an excellent composite portrait of mayors.

system of representation. Binding instructions from party or parliamentary groups leave representatives little room for independent decisions based on constituency considerations, but determine the party's course of action. In the United States, where parties do not wield such power, presidential rather than congressional elections give the electorate a voice in deciding who should govern. In the French republics of the past, there were neither disciplined parties nor popular elections of the executive.

This explains the traditional ambivalence of the French voter toward the parliamentary system. As guardians of constituency interests, deputies and senators still commanded respect. But when the deputies engaged in what de Gaulle called the "games, poisons and delights" of the system — when they made and unmade governments, seemingly without regard for the popular verdict in the preceding election — popular contempt engulfed both the representatives and the system.

Since the early days of the Third Republic, France has experimented with a great number of electoral systems and devices without obtaining more satisfactory results. The increased stability of the Fifth Republic cannot be attributed to the method of electing National Assembly deputies, for the system is essentially the same one used during the most troubled years of the Third Republic: as in the United States, rather small electoral districts (close to 500 of them in continental France) are represented by a single deputy. On the first election day only those candidates are elected who obtain a majority of all votes cast, a relatively rare occurrence because of the abundance of candidates. In run-off elections the choice is narrowed, usually to no more than two or three candidates, and a plurality is sufficient for election.

Remarkably enough, in both the Third and Fourth Republics disenchantment with parliamentary institutions never prevented a high turnout: with one exception, electoral participation after 1885 never fell to less than 71 percent of registered voters, and in most elections participation was much higher. Constituency interests and an individualized appeal to the voters kept interest high.

At first glance, it appears that voting participation, at least in the parliamentary elections of the Fifth Republic, has undergone a significant change (see Figure 10.5). In the elections of 1958 and 1962, only 77 and 69 percent of eligible voters went to the polls. But these two elections took place within weeks of important national referenda, in which voters accepted the constitutional proposals of de Gaulle. After this, many voters felt that their votes could only corroborate their earlier votes, and so they abstained. Participation in subsequent parliamentary elections rose back to normal, above 80 percent.

As in other countries, social class, age, and education are important factors in determining electoral participation: the least educated, the lowest income groups, and the youngest and oldest age groups vote less; employed women vote more frequently than those at home.

More pronounced in France than elsewhere has been the difference in rural and urban turnout. In general, voting has been so much heavier in the countryside than in the cities that it has offset other determinants, like education and income. This is usually attributed to the rural voter's more direct experience with campaigning and the deputy. In smaller districts, candidates' personal confrontations and printed judgments of each other and discussions among their followers are more intense and vehement. These local antagonisms usually mobilize voter interest.

Campaigning and political propaganda have acquired a national dimension in the Fifth Republic that they often lacked in the past. The national and regional press, radio, and television, and printed tracts and posters put candidates and issues before the voter. Campaigning has become more and more professionalized. The use of public opinion polls and public relations experts and the systematic observation of electioneering common in other countries have become widespread.

This does not mean that local electioneering has lost its individuality. The electoral system, with small constituencies and two ballots, invites a multiplicity and variety of candidacies, and ensures considerable decentralization and parochialism. Even though attendance at electoral meetings is no longer large, candidates cannot afford to neglect them.

Voting in Plebiscitarian Contests

As we have seen earlier, French traditions of representative government frowned on any direct appeals to the electorate, mainly because the two Napoleons had used the referendum to establish or

Figure 10.5

French Voter Abstention Since 1945

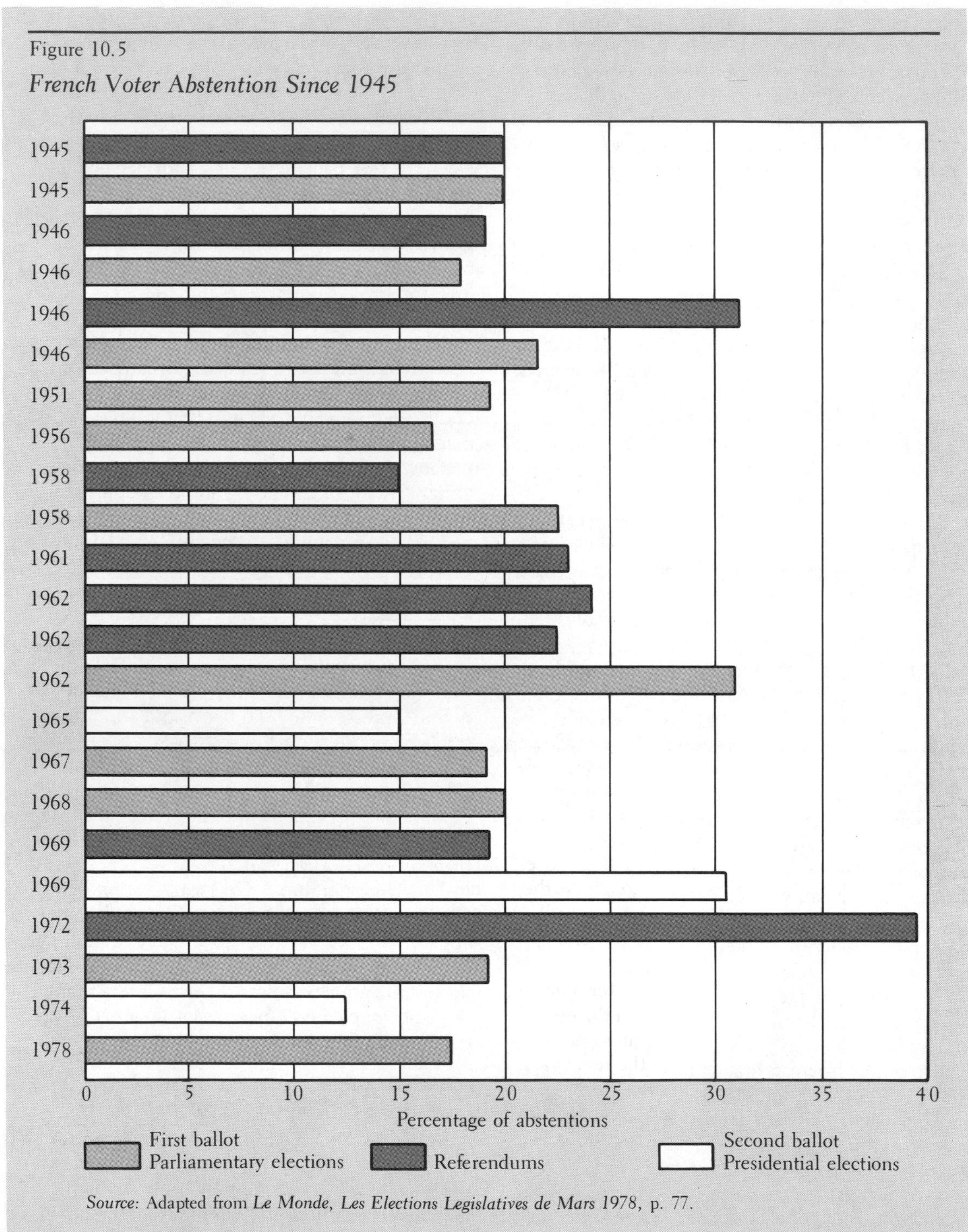

Source: Adapted from *Le Monde, Les Elections Legislatives de Mars* 1978, p. 77.

extend their powers. After the liberation from the Nazis, General de Gaulle held the reins of government and showed an inclination to obtain legitimacy for a new constitution by consulting the people directly.

Nonetheless, the 1958 Constitution of the Fifth Republic made only modest departures from the classical representative model. Although the Constitution was submitted to the electorate for approval, the direct appeal to the voters that it permitted under carefully prescribed conditions was hedged by parliamentary controls. As previously, Parliament was the only directly elected trustee of the nation. Popular election of the president was explicitly rejected as being too political; instead the president was to be appointed by an electoral college of about 80,000 local officials.

Between 1958 and 1972 the French electorate voted six times on a referendum. The attraction that the referendum held for de Gaulle, and the introduction of direct popular suffrage for presidential elections in 1962, transformed political institutions. Actually, all the referenda organized by de Gaulle should be qualified as plebiscites rather than referenda. (For the results of the voting see Table 10.1.) A referendum, in the American states and the Swiss cantons, is an invitation to the voters to approve or disapprove a legislative or constitutional issue. A plebiscite usually requires voters to approve or reject an already established policy, in circumstances such that a return to the prior system is either impossible or can be obtained only at an exorbitant price.

In 1958, a vote against the new Constitution might have involved the country in a civil war, which it had narrowly escaped a few months earlier. The two following referenda ambiguously endorsed the peace settlement of the Algerian war, successfully isolating the rebellious diehards who threatened order and prosperity.

Only six months after the second referendum on peace in Algeria General de Gaulle asked the electorate to endorse a constitutional amendment of great significance: to elect the president of the republic by direct popular suffrage. Such a method had been suspect to French republicans since Napoleon III had risen to imperial power through a popular majority in presidential elections. In 1962 all hesitations against this mode of electing the executive had not been overcome: only 46 percent of the registered voters approved. But since the referendum carried by a majority, the Constitution was changed.

Since then public opinion polls reveal that both the popular election of the president and the consultation of the electorate by referendum on important issues are widely approved. Undoubtedly the frustrations of voters who had felt before that parliamentary elections provided no leverage for them on major policy directives accounted in large part for the popularity of the referendum and of direct presidential elections. The political participation that plebiscites invite, however, is at best fleeting and frequently a sham, since the decisions have been reached beforehand. But where the confiscation of power by Parliament had been resented, a similar confiscation by the providential leader was accepted as commensurate with the prevalent style of authority. In a society where face-to-face relationships have been traditionally disliked, the plebiscites freed the citizens from active participation in the bargaining required of group decisions. The concentration of power in the hands of a popularly elected leader was tolerable because the distance between him and his followers was far greater than that between the voter and his deputy.

Favorable attitudes toward the referendum and the popular election of the president did not prevent the electorate from voting down, in 1969, another proposal submitted by de Gaulle, thereby causing his resignation. The legislation would have reformed the Senate and given new power to the regions into which the country is divided. (On these problems see pages 252 and 254.) Because he wished his leadership affirmed by another plebiscite, de Gaulle declared in the midst of the campaign that he would resign if there was not a majority of yes votes. But the electorate judged the proposals on their merits. Nothing in the Constitution compelled de Gaulle to resign, but his highly personal concept of his role, no longer accepted by a majority of the electorate, made his resignation inevitable.

When, after de Gaulle's retirement, his former Prime Minister Georges Pompidou acceded to the presidency, he expressed, at least by implication, little taste for wielding the weapon of a referendum soon. It had driven his predecessor from office and had plebiscitarian connotations that did not suit Pompidou's style of governing. Hence his announcement in the spring of 1972 that he was seek-

Table 10.1

French Voting in Referendums (R), 1958–1972, and Second Ballot of Presidential Elections (E), 1965, 1969, and 1974 (in metropolitan France)

	Registered voters	*Abstentions*		*"Yes" votes and votes for de Gaulle, Pompidou, or Giscard*			*"No" votes and votes for Mitterand or Poher*		
Date	*(in millions)*	*(in millions)*	*Percentage of registered voters*	*(in millions)*	*Percentage of registered voters*	*Percentage of votes cast*	*(in millions)*	*Percentage of registered voters*	*Percentage of votes cast*
9/28/58 (R)	26.62	4.01	15.1	17.67	66.4	79.2	4.62	17.4	20.7
1/8/61 (R)	27.18	6.39	23.5	15.20	55.9	75.3	5.00	18.4	24.7
4/8/62 (R)	26.99	6.59	24.4	17.51	64.9	90.7	1.79	6.6	9.3
10/28/62 (R)	27.58	6.28	22.7	12.81	46.4	61.7	7.93	28.8	38.2
12/19/65 (E)	28.22	4.36	15.4	12.64	44.8	54.5	10.55	37.4	45.5
4/18/69 (R)	28.66	5.56	19.4	10.52	36.7	46.7	11.94	41.6	53.2
6/15/69 (E)	28.75	8.90	30.9	10.69	37.2	57.5	7.87	27.4	42.4
4/23/72 (R)	29.07	11.48	39.5	10.50	36.1	67.7	5.01	17.2	32.3
5/19/74 (E)	29.80	3.60	12.1	13.10	43.9	50.7	12.70	42.8	49.3

ing approval by referendum for the treaty opening the Common Market to Great Britain and other countries caused surprise, but little enthusiasm. Pompidou's decision was motivated primarily by considerations of domestic politics. At the approach of parliamentary elections he wanted to consolidate his majority. That yes votes would outnumber the nos was enough of a foregone conclusion to deprive the campaign of drama. What had not been expected was the record number of abstentions. Hence the affirmative vote, while enough to give force of law to the treaty, amounted to a bare 36 percent of registered voters.

These experiences might induce future presidents to use the privilege of calling for a referendum sparingly, except in moments of political or constitutional crisis. This would mean that, as in the United States, the periodical presidential elections will be deemed a sufficient vehicle for the direct appeal to the electorate.

Ever since the presidential elections of 1965 it had become evident that the French voters derived great satisfaction from knowing that, unlike in past parliamentary elections, national and not parochial alignments were at stake, and that they were invited to pronounce themselves effectively on such issues. The traditional and once deeply rooted attitude that the only useful vote was against the government no longer made sense when almost everybody knew that the task was to elect an executive endowed with strong powers for seven years. Accordingly, turnout in presidential elections has been unusually high (see Figure 10.5). The one exception, the Pompidou election in 1969, when abstentions reached 31 percent, was not due to indifference, but to the abstention of Communist voters obeying a directive from the leadership, which for political reasons wanted to prevent the election of Pompidou's opponent. In the 1974 elections more registered voters than ever went to the polls.

The nomination procedures for presidential candidates reflect de Gaulle's dislike for giving any role to political parties, and make it very easy to put a candidate on the first ballot, comparable to the presidential primaries in the United States. So far, however, no presidential candidate, not even de Gaulle in 1965, has obtained the absolute majority needed to ensure election on the first ballot. In runoffs, held two weeks after the first ballot, only the two most successful candidates face each other. So far all serious candidates have been backed by a party or a coalition of parties, the provisions of the law notwithstanding. The French understood soon what the citizens of the United States learned during the seedtime of their republic: it is impossible to mount a national political campaign without the support, skill, and experience of a political party.

If all the presidential campaigns have fascinated French voters and foreign observers, this is not only due to the novelty of a nationwide competition in a country accustomed to small constituencies and parochial contests. Style and content of campaign oratory have generally been of high quality. Since the campaigns are short and concentrated, radio, television, and newspapers are able to grant candidates, commentators, and forecasters considerable time and space. The televised duel between Valéry Giscard d'Estaing and François Mitterand in May 1974, patterned after the Nixon-Kennedy debate but of far higher quality, was viewed by at least 50 percent of the population, and supposedly changed some 10 percent of the vote.[13]

In addition to the use of the mass media, impressive mass meetings were held throughout the country, attended mostly, but not exclusively, by young voters. Campaign literature, issued by hastily improvised headquarters, was abundant. Any direct election of a chief executive must personalize issues, and for this very reason it was enjoyed by the French voters.

As we shall see, political alignments have changed remarkably little during three stormy decades. But the involvement of citizens in a new electoral process has opened a new dimension for political participation.

RECRUITMENT AND STYLE OF ELITES

The Political Class

Until the advent of the Fifth Republic, Parliament provided the nucleus of French decision mak-

[13] For a lively and detailed account of the 1974 election campaign see Howard Penniman (ed.), *France at the Polls: The Presidential Election of 1974* (Washington, D.C.: American Enterprise Institute, 1975).

ers. Besides members of Parliament, elected officers of municipalities or departments, some local party leaders, and a few journalists of national renown were counted among the political class, which altogether totaled no more than 15,000 or 20,000 persons. All of them gravitated toward the halls of the National Assembly or the Senate, the lower and upper houses of Parliament.

In contrast to Great Britain, an inherited political career has become rare, although the family of the present president belongs to this exceptional species of a political family. Individual careers, however, have often been extremely long. Between 1877 and 1932, two-fifths of all deputies were reelected for four-year terms between three and ten times. Three percent of the deputies served at least seven times and typically kept their seats for about a third of a century.[14] Continuity and a fixed locale were intimately linked. An incumbent who sought reelection in his constituency was hardly ever dislodged. But such longevity, especially in times of crisis, also reinforced the voters' distrust of the political class as a self-perpetuating clique.

The professional, and especially the social, origin of members of Parliament has changed significantly since the establishment of the Third Republic in 1871, when the nobility and the upper bourgeoisie furnished, respectively, 34 and 36 percent of the deputies. In the first elections after World War I, the comparable figures were 10 and 30 percent, while the middle class was represented by 35 percent, and the lower-middle class by 15 percent. The trend has continued. But the number of deputies with working-class backgrounds has never exceeded 15 percent; most of them are Communists.

Among the politically active, intellectuals have always been conspicuous and numerically strong in France. In Parliament, the numbers of intellectuals — including teachers and professors, journalists, and doctors — has usually been higher than in other countries: about 38 percent in the Fifth Republic. The highly revered École Normale Supérieure in Paris, training ground for many university professors, especially in the humanities and social sciences, also functioned for many generations as a political seminar. Many parliamentary leaders, chiefly those of the left, discovered and sharpened their political ambitions while students at this school.

As in most representative regimes, lawyers have long made up the largest single professional group in Parliament. Before World War II, the legal profession supplied one-fourth of all deputies; because many were prominent, lawyers accounted for more than one-third of Cabinet posts. Most of these lawyers were local notables, trained in law and experienced in local administration. Rural constituencies, seldom represented by farmers, usually preferred lawyers over other candidates.

Since World War II, the number of lawyer-deputies has decreased drastically. In the Parliament elected in 1978, teachers, including university professors, are the largest professional group (90 out of 491). A new development in the social composition of Parliament is the large number of high civil servants who have decided to run for elective office, usually on the Gaullist ticket. They now number seventy, or almost 15 percent. This phenomenon, rare in the United States and Great Britain but also quite common in Western Germany, can be explained in part by the political sensitization of younger bureaucrats. More important even than their number is the considerable political weight of the bureaucrat-deputies. The six prime ministers who held office between 1958 and 1976 had all been civil servants before they ran for elective office. The numbers of businessmen, engineers, and industrial managers in Parliament have also greatly increased, though many so classified play a minor role.

The Bureaucracy

More than a century ago, Alexis de Tocqueville remarked that "since 1789 the administrative system has always stood firm among the debacles of political systems."[15] In the judgment of a recent observer, "the bureaucratic system of organization of French public administration is certainly one of the most entrenched of such closed systems of social action that has existed in the modern world."[16]

There are between 3,000 and 10,000 civil servants

[14] See Mattei Dogan, "Political Ascent in a Class Society: French Deputies, 1870–1958," in Dwaine Marvick (ed.), *Political Decision-Makers* (New York: Free Press, 1961), pp. 57–90.

[15] Alexis de Tocqueville, *The Old Regime and the French Revolution* (New York: Anchor, 1955), p. 202.

[16] Michel Crozier, *The Bureaucratic Phenomenon* (Chicago: University of Chicago Press, 1964), p. 308.

May 1968: fighting in the Quartier Latin. Historical memories of revolt and violence are relived by students soon to be joined in protest by millions of workers on strike and in their places of work.

in France whose functions correspond by and large to those of the former administrative class of the British civil service. Among the high civil servants, about three hundred can be singled out as active and often daily participants in political decision making. The selection of the highest civil servants as well as the lowest is the result of rigorous examinations, in which elaborate rites guard against favoritism and give the appearance of upholding the popular passion for equality. After World War II, Michel Debré (later the first prime minister of the Fifth Republic) established the École Nationale d'Administration (ENA) as a training ground for most of the prestige positions in the bureaucracy. He wanted, in the Napoleonic tradition, to open the civil service to talent, whatever its economic standing or family background. In order to break the quasi monopoly that the upper Parisian bourgeoisie had held on ranking positions and in order to enlarge the reservoir for recruitment without abandoning high standards of performance, the ENA opened its training facilities not only to qualified students, but also to those already serving in the less exalted echelons of the civil service. In the school they could prepare for advancement to the top bureaucratic levels.

The new school has undoubtedly had considerable impact on administrative development. But it has largely failed as an instrument of social promotion. By 1968 some 68 percent of those who had graduated at the top of their class, and were therefore free to choose the most prestigious positions, were the children of high civil servants or came from families with a professional or managerial background. Since then a slow increase in the number of candidates from the middle and lower middle classes is the only transformation that has taken place. Farmers and working-class families are hardly represented at all.

The members of the *grands corps* — the few

hundred ranking civil servants who graduated at the top of their classes — are extraordinarily mobile. They not only serve the agencies to which they are formally attached, but also act as troubleshooters for difficult assignments. They occupy top jobs in the important ministries and frequently head the personal staff of a minister or the president. They are in charge of numerous interministerial committees entrusted with preparing material needed for important decisions, though they do not always have direct control over decision making. They consider themselves, with much justification, the intellectuals in the administrative machinery.

The ethos of top ranking bureaucrats has always included the strong conviction that they are the principal, if not the sole, defenders of the public interest. One aspect of this conviction is the absence of corruption: rarely do scandals involve the financial integrity of high civil servants. But they might easily, and unfortunately, believe that they alone are virtuous. Until they run for elective office, they resent parliamentary institutions and their personnel because, influenced by special interests, the latter are likely to dismantle the reform proposals hatched in the administrative bureaus. Administrative centralization, even if excessive, is regarded as a necessity since only at the top can a sufficient regard for the public interest be mustered to resist arbitrariness and the pressure for privilege. An intended remoteness from such pressures has given bureaucrats an abstract perception of a mission entrusted to them by the state, rather than the feeling that they are servants of a specific community.

In the 1970s attitudes have changed and many high civil servants have admittedly lost faith in the classical bureaucratic model. Many of the benefits they expected to derive from modern management techniques have not really improved planning and output. Technocratic arrogance has made room for more moderate views as to what the state can and should do. Undoubtedly some of the rather brilliant achievements of private industry have impressed the civil servants to the point of persuading them to abandon their assumed role as the preceptors of the nation. A prewar practice has again become quite common: many civil servants leave even exalted positions in government for jobs in industry and banking. Obviously this deprives the civil service of some of its best and most experienced personnel. It also tends to erase, as it has in the United States, differences in attitudes of public servants and of managers of private wealth — possibly to the detriment of the governed.

INTEREST GROUPS

Interest Articulation

Means exist in every political community to bring the demands and desires of the society to the attention of decision makers. In France, as elsewhere, this function is served by a variety of structures. As in all modern states, associational interest groups that specialize in the articulation of interests through a more or less permanent organization are crucial in this process. But nonassociational groups, distinguished families, local or regional notables, prominent religious leaders, and especially modern business firms enjoy an influence in France that, although intermittent, often outweighs that of trade unions, trade associations, or other groups. In addition, interests are generated and articulated within the government itself. In France, the bureaucracy does not simply react to pressures from outside; its internal cleavages and relative independence from political directives have made it a frequent and autonomous agent of interest representation.

Frequently, and not without reason, organized interests in France are held responsible for the fact that a society with egalitarian traditions has so often reproduced and aggravated existing inequalities. Defense of the status quo is the dominant concern of interest groups in other countries, too. But in the stalemated society that France has been for so long, pressure groups did much to retard economic, social, and political development.

Yet protecting interests has never been done in a particularly scandalous way in France, nor has group pressure on the government been truly irresistible. Indeed the structure of most associational groups is less formidable in France than in many other countries, largely as a result of the general aversion to associations. In a society that was never as hierarchically organized as the state, industrialization grew slowly and the agricultural sector was isolated, so interest groups were often more coherent locally than nationally or regionally. Even then, their effectiveness at the local level was limited by the centralization of the government.

Actual membership in associations amounts to only a fraction of potential membership, a much smaller proportion than is true of Britain or Germany. Trade unions organize at most 22 percent of eligible wage earners, with a somewhat higher percentage of farmers in one or another of the numerous agricultural interest groups. The treasuries of many groups are often so depleted that they are unable to employ a competent staff. The well-qualified interest group official is a fairly recent phenomenon, found only in some sectors of the group system, such as business associations. The few organizations that count their membership in the millions are likely to serve narrow interests or broad ideas: home distillers of liquor, or friends or foes of the parochial schools.

Political and ideological divisions add to the fragmentation of group activities and increase the obstacles that stand in the way of effective articulation and defense of interests. The trade union movement and the agricultural organization embody the difficulties that exist for most groups.

The French labor movement has never looked upon itself as an interest group like the others, nor has it been regarded as such by outsiders.[17] All major labor confederations express anticaptitalism and, whereas most European trade unions combine demands for the material betterment of their constituents with a fight for emancipation, the heavy ideological baggage of French labor has interfered with normal trade union activities. Yet union members are well aware that whatever lasting reforms have been won are due either to legislation or to the intervention of state labor inspectors. Hence the relationship between improvements and union activities, especially as carried on by union members, appears tenuous.

From its beginning, the labor movement has suffered from extreme membership fluctuations. The membership of the largest and oldest confederation, the Communist-controlled Confédération Générale du Travail (CGT) has dwindled from more than 6 million in 1945–1946 to about 2 million (2.5 million according to its own claims) in the early 1970s; during the same period the number of its union locals has been about halved. Three other labor confederations, divided by outlook and strategy, total not more than 1 million members. The second strongest labor organization, the Confédération Française et Démocratique du Travail (CFDT) is the most original of all labor movements in Western Europe. An offshoot of a Catholic trade union movement, it now accepts many Marxist tenets of anticapitalism but rejects the Soviet model in favor of workers' self-management along the lines practiced in Yugoslavia. A third labor confederation, *Force Ouvrière* (FO) was founded in protest against communist control of the CGT. Its outlook is vaguely socialist but it shuns commitment to any political party. It has never been able to enlist much working class support.

The competition among different and often antagonistic trade union movements has led to a special pattern of bargaining procedures. The same group of wage earners may be represented by different organizations; this reduces the representativeness of the multiple trade union movements.

A similar long-standing division among agricultural organizations is more clearly political, the competition being among conservative Catholic and republican Freemason bodies and lesser groups of different persuasions. Attempts to forge a single agricultural confederation have been unsuccessful, and there remain nearly five hundred rural organizations on the national level alone. This is an expensive structure, possible only because many of the groups live in one way or another on public subsidies.

Within several interest groups, young members form an organization apart. This is not a functional division catering to the special needs of an age group, but an ideological alignment. The best known among these groups are the Young Farmers and the Young Employers, who offer ideas about rural organization or about new forms of capitalist enterprise and competition.

In addition to management, labor, and agriculture, interest organizations like students', ex-servicemen's, pensioners', parent-teacher associations, and taxpayers' groups are riddled by ideological and political dissensions. The result is a form of interest articulation that is neither pragmatic nor in-

[17] On the trade union movement, see Val Lorwin, *The French Labor Movement* (Cambridge, Mass.: Harvard University Press, 1954).

strumental and that is rarely as effective as its counterparts in the United States or Great Britain.

Given the ideological style of France's political culture, it is not surprising that groups devoted to the promotion of causes grow. At times their impact on public opinion has been considerable, but since many demand only a temporary commitment, they rarely need permanent and qualified staff, which only a few French interest groups can assemble.

Means of Access and Styles of Action

Interest groups are active wherever decisions can be influenced: in the electoral process and in Parliament; through contacts with the executive and with members of the bureaucracy; and through the mass media. By comparison with interest groups in other countries, however, most French groups appear less comfortable with propaganda or public relations techniques. This stems in part from uncertainty about the legitimacy of group activities. Organized business, for example, has long resisted efforts to develop a public image for itself.

Parliamentary and local elections usually stimulate strenuous group activity. The smallness of the constituency, the intensely personal relationship between representative and electorate, and, most important, the flabbiness of party organization and discipline, have driven interest groups to appeal directly to candidates. Before the election, candidates are asked to pledge to defend the group's concerns. Candidates are often prevented from discussing larger issues because of the din created by interest groups, which reinforces the tradition of narrow interest representation.

Groups play an important though obscure role in financing election campaigns, and thus in the selection of candidates. Given the high costs of modern campaigning, and in the absence of well-filled party treasuries, many candidates are obliged to rely on group support more likely to limit their freedom of action than the mere signing of pledges.

In preceding regimes, organized interests found Parliament the most convenient means of access to political power. During the Third and Fourth Republics, the highly specialized and powerful committees of both houses of Parliament were little more than institutional facades for interest groups.[18] "Study groups" brought deputies and group representatives together behind closed doors, and deputies joined "friendly societies" formed to discuss the concerns of various lobbies. Quite frequently groups substituted bills of their own design for those submitted by the government.

More often than not, however, the actual impact of group penetration into the parliamentary arena was more apparent than real. Many of the bills that deputies moved on behalf of lobbies were defeated because of parliamentary inefficiency. Whereas during election campaigns the absence of an effective party system increased the leverage of local interest groups, the situation was somewhat reversed in Parliament. Once individual representatives were identified as spokesmen for special interests, their effectiveness was greatly reduced. Some carefully planned lobbying by powerful groups in Parliament occasionally resulted in resounding defeats for the causes defended by organized interests.

The chief reason given by Gaullists for reforming and rationalizing Parliament was the desire to reduce the role of Parliament in the making and unmaking of governments. But many of the new rules established by the Constitution and legislation also diminished the role of organized interests in the legislative process. By and large this has been accomplished, but interest groups have not lost all influence on rule making and policy formation. To be effective, groups now use the channels that the best equipped have long found most rewarding, channels that give them direct access to the administration.

The indispensable collaboration between organized private interests and the state is institutionalized in advisory committees that are attached to most administrative agencies and composed mainly of civil servants and group representatives. These advisory bodies are frequently no more than additional channels of influence, and often not the most important ones. Some observers believe that the consultation that takes place in these bodies democratizes and humanizes administrative procedures; others say the process leads to undesirable

[18] Philip M. Williams, *Crisis and Compromise in the Fourth Republic* (New York: Anchor, 1964), pp. 374–377.

fragmentation of authority. Much seems to depend on the way bureaucracy uses the instruments of what is called administrative pluralism. When civil servants merely take into account the opinions and documentation presented to them before deciding, the effect is beneficial. But often decision makers defer to group suggestions, so that administrative functions are parceled out to socioeconomic groups.

Since administrative decision making in France is widely dispersed in spite of its formal centralization, interest groups must intervene in a great number of bureaus and agencies, even when concerned with just one decision. To be effective, a group needs more than one relationship — it must touch all the points where its interests are affected. In some of these encounters the public interest emerges unscathed; in others interest groups colonize parts of the administrative machinery and manipulate them at will. And often, of course, a mixture or less intense version of either extreme occurs.

Organized interests also bring pressure to bear on the political executive. For a long time the ministerial cabinets, the circle of personal collaborators who support every French minister, have been an important target. Inasmuch as the present regime has strengthened the position of the political executive, it has also enabled both the prime minister and the president to function more effectively as arbiters between competing claims and to exercise stricter control over many agencies and ministries.

In any system the style of group action is largely determined by the group's means of access to power and position in society. Most French interest groups rely extensively on the state for some kind of support. Labor unions carry on most of their business in publicly subsidized buildings. Chambers of commerce and chambers of agriculture have always received ample governmental subsidies, in recognition of their performance of functions like training apprentices, controlling weights and measures, and gathering statistical information. Employers' associations, trade unions, and rural groups are enmeshed in the administration of the comprehensive social security system, public insurance boards, and the like. With one foot in society and the other in government, these organizations form an institutional link between the state and the groups.

At the same time, French interest groups occasionally exhibit radicalism unusual in countries of similar development and more generally found in an earlier industrial era. But that is not really astonishing. Groups want to demonstrate that participation in administrative tasks and reliance on public support does not reduce their militancy. In a radical context, even the defense of purely economic, social, or cultural interests takes on a political coloration. In order to increase their political effectiveness, interest groups and parties organize temporary, combative alliances. While mergers of lobbies and political movements have shaken the system many times in the past few decades, their emphasis has usually been on protest rather than on demands for constructive action.

The dramatic events of the revolution of 1789, the significance of street fighting and barricades in the upheavals of the nineteenth century, and other romantically embellished reminiscences, have all made "violence into a sort of second nature of the French political temperament."[19] For the labor movement, the revolutionary strike seemed at one time the only means of mobilizing workers for some kind of participation. For groups and individuals, lawless action has remained an outlet for frustrations imposed by the dominance of government authority.

Even though the Fifth Republic has strengthened government authority in every domain, rebellions and political protests have not ceased. Time and again agitation in various parts of rural France has become violent, with loss of property and, occasionally, lives. Fearful of losing the rural vote, all the governments of the Fifth Republic have retreated on fundamental issues of agricultural policy. This also means that the French representatives on the European Common Market are compelled to fight rearguard actions and stem the tide of too rapid a modernization of European agriculture.

Union-led strikes, even where only bread-and-butter issues seem at stake, frequently acquire a political tinge. Strikes in public enterprises — by mail sorters, garbage collectors, and the workers in the

[19] René Rémond, *The Right Wing in France from 1815 to De Gaulle* (Philadelphia: University of Pennsylvania Press, 1969).

nationalized Renault works — are particularly bitter, for the striking personnel feel that the government is using its power to deny their demands instead of mediating between conflicting claims. When the government's views prevail, its victory is frequently Pyrrhic, for the strikes leave behind them bitterness and political resentment.

In the mid-1970s a new kind of interest group fought for its goal by using a mixture of normal pressure tactics and of violence: ethnic-linguistic minorities like the Corsicans, the Bretons, the Basques, and others are pleading for greater autonomy, if not for independence, occasionally with the help of dynamite.

So far no other political explosions of recent times have shaken France as much as those that surprised a prosperous country and a self-confident government in the spring of 1968.[20] Student revolts extended to most universities and many secondary schools before they opened a breach into which there rushed 7 to 8 million striking workers. Barricades in Paris streets and the occupation of factories throughout the country undermined the faith in the government's ability to act, and hence in its legitimacy. Eventually the tactical ability of President de Gaulle and the aimlessness of the rebels permitted the government to reestablish order without bloodshed. The Gaullists won the subsequent elections, said to be fought to "save the country from red totalitarian revolution,"[21] although the Communists' attitude during the decisive days had been more than cautious.

Typically, this latest in a series of violent social upheavals still haunts many Frenchmen, whereas in the United States the violent urban riots, as well as the student revolts of the sixties, seem largely forgotten. For years public opinion polls revealed that about half of French respondents believed that the country might face another crisis like that of May 1968. Such premonitions might have had little basis in fact, but they were something like a barometer of a continuing malaise produced by a lengthy list of unfulfilled promises made by the government to interests of all kinds.

[20] The number of books and articles dealing with the 1968 events is now staggering. The following accounts in English are the most interesting: Stanley Hoffman, *Decline or Renewal? France since the 1930s* (New York: Viking, 1974), pp. 145–184; Bernard E. Brown, *Protest in Paris: Anatomy of a Revolt* (Morristown, N.J.: General Learning Press, 1974). For a collection of (translated) statements by French participant-observers, see C. Posner (ed.), *Reflections on the Revolution in France: 1968* (Baltimore: Penguin, 1970).

[21] *L'Année Politique 1968* (Paris: Presses Universitaires, 1969), p. 382.

POLITICAL PARTIES

The Traditional Party System

French parties, like parties everywhere, exist to fulfill a variety of functions. Most important among them are: the aggregation, the sifting, of interests and demands and their transformation into policy alternatives; the mobilization of the citizenry for political participation and the integration of the citizenry into the system; the recruitment and selection of political leaders for executive and other posts; and the control of such leadership, especially the control of the government. Finally, parties are "alliances in conflicts over policies and value commitments within the larger body politic."[22] Not all of these functions will be served equally well by all parties or at all times. What must be explained is why French parties have done so badly, over long periods, on almost all counts. There are divergent explanations of this apparent weakness.

Some analysts of election data see a chronic and seemingly unalterable division of the French into two large political families, each motivated by a different mood or temperament and usually classified as The Right and The Left. If one views elections from this perspective, political alignments have remained surprisingly stable over long periods of history. As late as 1962, the opposition to de Gaulle was strongest where for more than a century republican traditions had had a solid foundation. The alignments in the presidential contest of 1974 and the parliamentary elections of 1978 mirrored the same divisions. Neither domestic upheavals nor interna-

[22] S. M. Lipset and Stein Rokkan, "Cleavage Structures, Party Systems, and Voter Alignments: An Introduction," in S. M. Lipset and Stein Rokkan (eds.), *Party Systems and Voter Alignments: Cross National Perspectives* (New York: Free Press, 1967), p. 51.

tional cataclysms have upset the geographical distribution or the proportional strength of the two sides. The electoral systems of the Third and Fifth Republics apparently favored this simplification of political alignments: in most constituencies run-off elections result in the confrontation of two candidates, each more or less representing one of the camps. A simple and stable division could have resulted in a pattern of two parties or coalitions alternating in having power and being in opposition, and hence giving valid expression to the voters' options. What has this not occurred?

Except for Socialists and Communists, French party organizations have largely remained as skeletal as were parties in other countries at the time of their nineteenth-century beginnings. French parties developed in a largely preindustrial and preurban environment, catering at first to upper-middle-class and later to middle-class elements. Their foremost and sometimes only function was to provide an organizational framework for the selection and election of candidates for local, departmental, and national offices.

Slow and irregular industrialization hampered the formation of a disciplined working-class party that would have challenged the bourgeois parties to overhaul their structures. The electoral system and a powerful upper house of Parliament, with heavy overrepresentation of the rural population, kept the workers in a position of electoral inferiority.

French parties that have represented the majority of the electorate throughout long periods were internally created, that is, they gradually emerged from groups inside the legislature. Political organization at the local and constituency level aimed mainly at assuring the election or reelection of members belonging to various legislative blocs or factions in Parliament.

An internally created party is almost always less disciplined and ideologically less coherent than one that has emerged outside the legislature. During election campaigns the candidates of legislative parties can expect little financial support from the organization. Between elections, those representing the traditional party formations are not responsive to any party directives coming from outside Parliament. Even within a parliamentary group or faction the formal institution of a whip, who maintains party discipline, is unknown. In most cases representatives vote solely in accordance with the commands of "career, conscience, and constituency."[23]

This form of representation and party organization survives largely because voters prefer it. An electorate that distrusts authority and wants representation to protect it against arbitrary government is likely to be suspicious of parties organized for political reform. For all their antagonism, the representative and plebiscitarian factions (see pages 219–220) have one thing in common: their aversion to well-established and strongly organized parties. Party membership has always been low, except during short and dramatic situations. According to recent estimates no more than 2 percent of registered voters are party members.

Organizational weakness and its underlying causes will easily result in a multipolar party system. But the primary cause of such division has been past conflicts over interests and values, many of them but dimly remembered except for the resentments they caused and which have persisted. Historical traditions have determined whether constituencies are regularly on the right or the left of the political spectrum. Different property laws under the monarchy, clerical or secular administration during the Old Regime, differences in agricultural crops or in the speed of industrialization, religious affiliation — all these have shaped political alignments which frequently have perpetuated themselves long after the original causes have disappeared.

Because of the large number of weak parties, most represent only a small section of the electorate. A party that cannot claim, without risking ridicule, to represent the interests of the entire electorate, or even of a large sector, takes on the characteristics of an interest group. It transmits to Parliament or to the government the undiluted narrow demands of its constituents. To avoid the suggestion that they represent no more than limited interests or personalties, these weak parties phrase even the most narrow political issues in lofty ideological terms.

The inconveniences of the French multiparty system were especially pronounced during the Third and Fourth Republics. Parliamentary majorities consisted to a large extent of temporary coalitions whose cohesion or disruption depended on whatever prob-

[23] Williams, *Crisis and Compromise*, p. 348.

lem was under consideration. As different problems arose, governments toppled or were condemned to immobility.

Neither right nor left could govern by itself for any length of time, because both lacked a permanent majority and included extreme groups that contested the legitimacy of the political order. To avoid losing the badly needed support of these extremes, both left-wing and right-wing coalitions had to make concessions to radicals, thereby narrowing the scope of possible action to such an extent that immobility was inevitable.

As a normal consequence of this party system, a center coalition has been in control of the government most of the time, no matter what the outcome of the preceding elections. Between 1789 and the advent of the Fifth Republic, republican France was ruled by governments of the center for all but thirty years. In a two- or three-party system, major parties normally move toward the political center in order to gain stability and cohesion. But where extreme party plurality prevails, the center is a swamp instead of a cohesive political force.[24] A centrist government cannot even pursue moderate policies for long without losing vital support, for there are no clear lines dividing government and opposition.

An opposition will behave responsibly if it knows it may have to act as the government in the foreseeable future and that it then will have to honor its promises. French centrists temporarily without a Cabinet post, however, were free to weaken the government by steady criticism, eventually causing its downfall. They knew that if they became part of the next shapeless center coalition they would probably never have to assume meaningful leadership posts, but would likely do no more than share some peripheral responsibility behind the smoke screen of shifting coalitions.[25]

Political parties have done little to integrate or simplify the multiplicity of attitudes that shape the political culture of France; instead they have rigidified and crystalized existing antagonisms. In 1958, the problems introduced by the Algerian War and decolonization and by France's entrance into the Common Market culminated in a major political crisis that the party system lacked the resilience to resolve.

The new republic created a new political framework that had a major, if gradual and mostly unforeseen, impact on all parties and on their relationship to each other. This shaped the functioning of the political system to a great extent. To explain this transformation the characteristics of the present parties, singly and as coalition partners, must be discussed. For the electoral strength of the parties through six elections see Table 10.2; for the distribution of seats in the National Assembly elected in March 1978 see also Figure 10.6.

Rassemblement pour la République (RPR)

The Gaullist party, thrown hastily together after de Gaulle's return to power in 1958, is the one novelty in modern French party politics. Only weeks after its birth, it won over 20 percent of the vote and almost 40 percent of the seats in the first Parliament of the new republic.

For the next ten years the Gaullists increased their share of the total vote in each parliamentary election, until in the first ballot of the landslide elections of 1968 they and their allies won over 10 million votes, 46 percent of the votes cast and 36 percent of the registered voters, enabling Gaullist deputies alone to hold a majority in the National Assembly — a record never obtained under a republican regime in France. If the more normal elections of 1973, the first after de Gaulle's death, brought a reflux, they did not deprive the Gaullist party of its status as the dominant party of the Fifth Republic. Yet only one year later, in the first ballot of the presidential elections, the party's candidate, Jacques Chaban-Delmas, a former prime minister, mustered not more than 14.6 percent of the vote and was eliminated from the race.

The Gaullist party has been first a team of Cabinet ministers, then a committee in charge of de-

[24] The center as a swamp has been analyzed by Maurice Duverger, "The Eternal Morass: French Centrism," in Mattei Dogan and Richard Rose (eds.), *European Politics: A Reader* (Boston: Little, Brown, 1971), pp. 237–246.

[25] See Giovanni Sartori, "European Political Parties: The Case of Polarized Pluralism," in Joseph La Palombara and Myron Weiner (eds.), *Political Parties and Political Development* (Princeton, N.J.: Princeton University Press, 1966), pp. 157 ff.

Table 10.2

First Ballot of French Parliamentary Elections, 1958–1973, and National Assembly Seats Won in Both Ballots (Voting in Metropolitan France)[a]

	1958			1962			1967			1968			1973			1978		
Registered voters (in millions)		27.24			27.53			28.3			28.2			30.6			35.2	
Percentage abstentions		22.9			31.3			19.1			19.9			19.1			17.2	
Parties	*Votes (in millions)*	*Percentage of votes cast*	*Seats in Parliament*	*Votes (in millions)*	*Percentage of votes cast*	*Seats in Parliament*	*Votes (in millions)*	*Percentage of votes cast*	*Seats in Parliament*	*Votes (in millions)*	*Percentage of votes cast*	*Seats in Parliament*	*Votes (in millions)*	*Percentage of votes cast*	*Seats in Parliament*	*Votes (in millions)*	*Percentage of votes cast*	*Seats in Parliament*
Communists (PC)	3.88	18.9	10	3.99	21.8	41	5.0	22.5	73	4.4	20.0	34	5.2	21.2	73	5.8	20.5	86
Leftist Socialists (PSU)	—	—	—	0.4	2.4	0	0.5	2.2	4	0.9	3.0	0	0.8	3.3	3	0.9	3.3	—
Socialists (SFIO now PS)	3.17	15.5	44	2.31	12.6	66	4.2[b]	18.7[b]	116[b]	3.6[b]	16.5[b]	57[b]	4.9[b]	20.4[b]	100[b]	6.4	22.6	104
Radicals and allied	1.71	8.3	33	1.38	7.6	39										0.6	2.1	10
MRP and Center	2.41	11.2	56	1.63	8.9	55	3.0	13.4	27	2.3	10.3	33	3.0[c]	12.4[c]	31	6.8[d]	23.8[d]	141[d]
Gaullists and majority	3.60	20.4	212	5.85[e]	31.9[e]	233[e]	8.4[e]	37.8[e]	244[e]	10.2[e]	46.0[e]	354[e]	9.4[e]	38.5[e]	261[e]	6.5[f]	22.6[f]	148[f]
Conservatives	4.74	22.9	118	2.54	13.9	35	0.8	3.7	15	0.5	2.4	0				—	—	—
Extreme right	0.67	3.0	0	0.16	0.9	0	0.2	0.8	0				0.7	2.8	0	—	—	—

[a] Unaffiliated deputies and splinter groups not listed.

[b] Allied in the Federation of the Left.

[c] In 1973, campaigning as "Reformers."

[d] Republicans and allied Center Parties (UDF).

[e] Votes cast for lists presenting both Gaullists and their various coalition partners.

[f] Gaullists (RPR).

signating candidates for elections to Parliament, and lastly, but only lastly, a party.[26] Such priorities were entirely in line with the views of de Gaulle, who had little use for any party, including his own. During the first years of the regime the upper echelons of the party hierarchy constituted almost without exception a peer group. Its members had belonged directly, or indirectly through a single intermediary, to General de Gaulle's entourage during the days of the Free French movement in London and Algiers or during the postliberation period. Since those troubled times had attracted men of widely different background to General de Gaulle, what bound them together was mostly their personal loyalty to the leader.

De Gaulle's second prime minister, Georges Pompidou, saw the need for a better organized party if future elections were to be won and an orderly succession of the charismatic leader was to ensure a Gaullism *sans* de Gaulle. New bylaws gave muscle to the party organization at all levels and promised to involve the membership in some decision making. From a membership of not more than 24,000 in 1959 the party supposedly rose presumably to between 150,000 and 200,000 in 1972.[27]

In reality, however, the role of the party's membership and of its activists, whether paid or voluntary, remained generally limited to assisting in propaganda efforts at election time. There also was no need for a party program as long as de Gaulle was the leader. The leadership would decide whatever action the circumstances demanded. When the leader's mantle fell on other shoulders than de Gaulle's, government policy and party objectives were determined the same way.

It was its constituency organization and the voting discipline of its elected representatives that distinguished the Gaullists from the parties of notables long characteristic of the French right.[28] But its lack of a program and of an input for the membership in policy making also made it different from the democratic mass parties in other European countries. Instead it took on the characteristics of a modern catchall party. For such a party the widest possible audience and immediate electoral successes remain the principal goals.

Table 10.2 illustrates how successful the Gaullists have been with such an appeal in all parliamentary elections. The strongest support has always come from women, farmers, and the old, while the young, the large cities, and the workers resisted the appeal of the Gaullists in a somewhat greater proportion. In one important respect the Gaullists failed to cash in on an advantage of a catchall party: instead of appearing politically colorless, its public image remained that of a party of the right, or even of the extreme right. That the Gaullists failed to gain a solid foothold in local government, held by the traditional conservative parties, was another weak point.

But as long as both the presidency and the premiership were in Gaullist hands (as was the case from 1958 to 1974) the predominance of the party in the political and administrative life of the country was assured. With the election of Valéry Giscard d'Estaing, never a Gaullist, to the presidency in 1974 and with the forced resignation in 1976 of Gaullist Jacques Chirac from the post of prime minister, the power of the Gaullist movement seemed seriously threatened. Its members no longer held any important ministerial posts. Although Gaullists were still the strongest single group in a Parliament elected before Pompidou's death, polls revealed that voters' sympathies had fallen to between 13 and 17 percent, which augured defeat in the next elections.

The decline of the party was turned around by the energy of Chirac, whose ascendancy had been typical of the young generation of French political leaders. A graduate of the ENA, he entered on a political rather than a bureaucratic career. He was elected to Parliament at thirty-four years of age and had oc-

[26] See the expert on the Gaullist movement, Jean Charlot, *The Gaullist Phenomenon: The Gaullist Movement in the Fifth Republic* (New York: Praeger, 1971).

[27] Like all other membership figures in France, these are subject to serious doubt. According to some well-informed estimates actual party membership might have amounted to not more than one-fifth of the official figures.

[28] For interesting portraits of two Gaullist deputies, probably typical for at least a number of the party's representatives, see Oliver H. Woshinsky, *The French Deputy* (Lexington, Mass.: Lexington Books, 1973), pp. 35–51 and passim. For the most insightful comments on de Gaulle's thinking on politics and the relationship between his thought and action see three excellent essays by Stanley Hoffmann, now reprinted in *Decline or Renewal? France since the 1930s* (New York: Viking, 1974), pp. 185–280.

cupied important Cabinet posts under Pompidou. He imposed his leadership on disgruntled Gaullist deputies, reminding them that only discipline would save them from the fate that had befallen all parties of the right. He then proceeeded to revamp the leadership and structure of the Gaullist movement, rechristened the Rally of the Republic. The ensuing revitalization of the movement as a constituency party in all regions of the country was phenomenal, even if outside observers believe that the official 1978 membership figures of 620,000 vastly overestimate actual membership (a realistic, and still respectable figure might be 150,000).[29] Some of the party's mass meetings in Paris and the provinces drew larger crowds than the rallies of any other political movement.

Chirac, who in the meantime had been elected mayor of Paris over the opposition of President Giscard, never broke with the government in power; yet he has kept his distance from government policies. As long as it seemed possible that the left might win the 1978 elections, he accused the government of being too soft on Socialists and Communists. Such redbaiting was thoroughly approved by the party's followers, who seem to be more rightist than the leadership of the old Gaullist movement. After the threat of electoral defeat had passed, Chirac criticized the government's social and economic policies as insufficiently daring. Whether bolder, and so far vaguely defined, reform policies will be supported by the RPR's voters, and whether strenuous efforts to win working-class support for the movement are going to be successful, remains to be seen.

At one time the new leadership of the RPR sought to give their party an image significantly different from that of the traditional and presumably discredited Gaullism. Yet when it turned out that at least as a myth Gaullism was still attractive, especially to a lower-middle-class audience, the party reversed its course and reaped the benefits of the myth's popularity. The RPR was returned to Parliament in 1978 as the largest single party (148 deputies), although its margin over the other parties of the government coalition is not as great as before. There is no doubt that the presidential ambitions of its leader will have to be reckoned with.

The Republicans and the Other Parties of the Center

By origin and nature the Republican party has been the typical party, or rather non-party, of French conservatism. It came into existence in 1962 when de Gaulle's strictures against European unity and his referendum on the popular election of the president estranged many conservatives who had been part of the Gaullist coalition. However, Giscard and a few fellow deputies found it inopportune to heed the injunction of their party to leave the government and join in a vote of censure against it. From that time on, these Republicans provided a small complement of the majority in Parliament and furnished some ministers to all the governments that served under de Gaulle and Pompidou. For most of this time Giscard himself was finance minister.

Although the mass media continuously provided much coverage of its leader, Giscard, the Republicans remained fragile as a political organization.[30] For more than four years no attempt was made to establish a party outside Parliament. At the approach of the 1967 elections a loose structure tied together the party's sympathizers in the provinces, many of them local notables of conservative leaning. The party's publications, like its strategy, steered carefully away from any doctrinal pronouncements, nor did they develop a well-defined program.

After Giscard was elected president in 1974, efforts were undertaken to transform the Republicans into a party that would be solidly established in every constituency, but little came of it. Only on the eve of the parliamentary elections of 1978 were the Republicans able to persuade the other parties and groups still crowding the center to join with them in the Union de la Démocratie Française (UDF), a loose al-

[29] See William R. Schonfeld, "The RPR: From a Rassemblement to the Gaullist Movement," in William Andrews and Stanley Hoffmann (eds.), *The Fifth Republic at Twenty* (Albany, N.Y.: SUNY Press, forthcoming).

[30] For an extensive discussion of Giscard's political career see Jerome King, "Valéry Giscard d'Estaing and the French Government," in Edward Feit (ed.), *Governments and Leaders: An Approach to Comparative Politics* (Boston: Houghton Mifflin, 1978), pp. 97–180.

Figure 10.6

Political Representation in the National Assembly as of March 1978

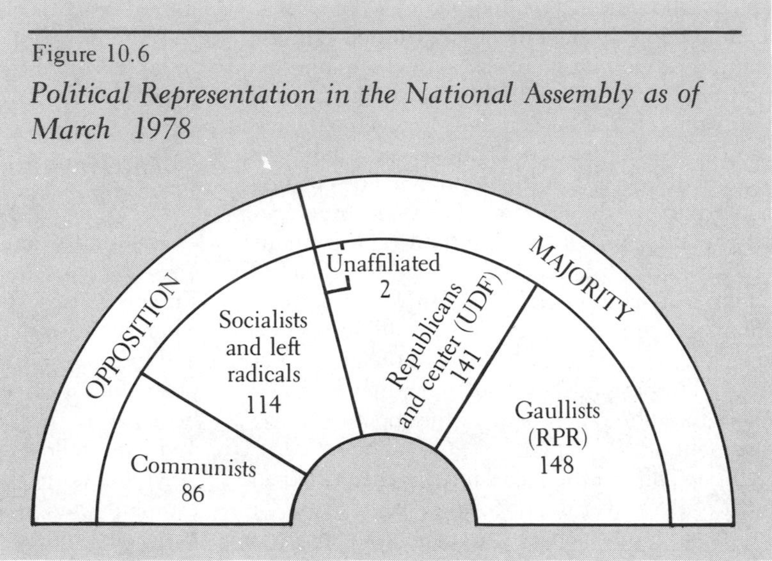

liance designed to counterbalance within the governmental majority the better organized Gaullists. In number of parliamentary seats the UDF almost equals the RPR. But it remains an amalgam of varied and often antagonistic personalities. Very few of the deputies belonging to it are supported by a constituency organization of any significance. Many derive their strength from positions as mayors or as other elected local offcals.

In Parliament the groups backing Giscard's government command a clear majority (see Figure 10.6); together with the so-called unaffiliated, who regularly vote with the government, the majority disposes of 291 votes as against 200 for the opposition. But the distribution of seats in Parliament does not reflect the almost equal division of the electorate into two political camps: in the run-off elections of 1978 only 50.71 percent had cast a ballot for the majority, 49.26 percent had voted for the opposition, composed of Socialists and Communists.

The Socialist Party

In comparison with the solid social-democratic parties in other European countries, the French Socialist party has lacked muscle almost since its beginnings in 1905. Slow and uneven industrialization and reluctance to organize have not only clogged the development of labor unions but have also deprived the Socialist party of the base of working-class strength that has come to other social-democratic parties from their affiliation with a trade union movement.

Unlike the British Labour party, the Socialist party also failed to absorb middle-class radicals, the equivalent of the Liberals in England. French doctrinaire Marxism prevented fusion with the neighbor to the right. The party was never strong enough to assume control of the government by itself. Its weakness reduced it to being at best one of several partners in the unstable coalition governments of the Third and Fourth Republics. Most of the working-class following of the Socialist party was concentrated in a few regions of traditional strength, such as the industrial North and urban agglomeration in the Center, but the party had some strongholds elsewhere. It had a large following among the winegrowers of the south, devotees of republican ideals, of anticlericalism, and of producers' cooperatives. The proportion of civil servants, especially teachers, and of people living on fixed income has at all times been far higher among Socialist voters than in the population at large. This made for a stable but not particularly dynamic following, especially since the young were no longer attracted by the party. In one respect only, albeit an important one, the Socialists outshine not only the ruling Gaullists but also their Communist competitors: their positions in local government remain strong, due to experienced personnel and honored traditions.

The party encountered considerable difficulties when it sought a new role under the changed conditions in the Fifth Republic. To be condemned to a permanent and increasingly impotent opposition was as unattractive as searching for new allies. Nationally, these could only be found on the left, but locally many Socialists relied on the support of the center. After several false starts, the old party dissolved and a new Socialist party (PS) saw the light in the summer of 1969.

The success of the party in acquiring a new image, attracting new members, and reversing its electoral decline has been far greater than expected. Its present leader, François Mitterand, came from outside the Socialist movement. He had held various Cabinet posts under the Fourth Republic and became one of the few non-Communists who voted against the Gaullist Constitution in 1958. In the first presidential election in 1965, Mitterand had proved his ability as a vote getter when, as the spokesman for the entire left, including the Communists, he won 45 percent of the popular vote. Thereafter, realizing that party organization remained an indispensable vehicle for political competition he entered the new PS and soon imposed his leadership.

Public opinion polls in 1976 and 1977 revealed that voter support of the PS had reached a high: between 30 and 32 percent of the voters preferred the party. Party membership was estimated at between 130,000 and 150,000. Mitterand's narrow defeat in the presidential contest of 1974 did not interrupt recruitment for the PS.

In terms of potential support the PS has also become something of a catchall party. It has mobilized support in regions where its predecessor had been notoriously weak and it has proven attractive to Catholic voters, especially young ones. Although its working-class support remains weak, the PS attracts employees, professionals, and technicians, among them a considerable number of high civil servants. However, unlike European social-democratic parties, its leadership does not mute the party's socialism to attract a wider following. It does not shun Marxist terminology, but emphasizes novel forms of a socialist order as an alternative to the existing society — and to the reforms proposed by the government.

In the first ballot of the 1978 elections, however, only 22.6 percent of the electorate voted Socialist, disappointing the PS and dashing the hopes for a victory of the left. To a large part, though not exclusively, this unexpected decline was due to the split between the PS and the Communists, just as the ascendancy of the PS owed much to the earlier agreement between the two on a common program. The reasons for both the temporary alliance and its breakup will be discussed below.

The PS, once more prevented from grasping governmental power that seemed within its reach, will probably encounter old difficulties. Internal tensions will come to the surface; a leadership crisis might ensue. Whether the loss of electoral support will prove to be only temporary or whether it indicates another period of decline is uncertain.

The Communists

In all democratic countries the Communists have been unlike other parties, because of their ties to a foreign nation, the Soviet Union. Because of the importance of France to the international position of the Soviet Union, the French Communist party (PC) for many decades and at dramatic moments altered its course abruptly, according to the demands of Russian foreign policy. Yet the party is a domestic force: a party which for thirty years has had an electoral following of between 19 and 26 percent of the voters in parliamentary elections, and which is represented by more than 20,000 city and town councillors and almost 800 mayors, administering municipalities with about 5 million people (more than 10 percent of the total population) — such a party impinges on the political game.

The Communist electorate has been more faithful than that of other parties. The party has always had its strongest following in the industrial regions of the North, except in those districts where Catholicism has remained strong, and in the red belt encircling Paris and Marseilles. In rural regions its support has waxed and waned with economic developments. If economic factors alone determined voting for the Communists, its voting strength should have been sapped with the spreading of prosperity and rising real wages. This, however, has not been the case. A vote for the PC is an expression of mixing indignation over injustice and mismanagement with more or less vague belief in a better society. At least emotionally, a fairly large share of the Communist vote corresponds to the indifference to the political system that millions of underprivileged citizens of the United States manifest by not voting.[31]

In 1966, 60 percent of the membership were, according to party sources, manual workers; 18 percent were white-collar employees; and 9 percent were intellectuals. Such a composition gave the PC more of a working-class character than any other party. Since then, according to unverifiable party sources, the membership has risen from 350,000 to between 500,000 and 600,000, but the proportion of manual workers has declined. During the last years, the party has more freely accepted intellectuals, professionals, and technicians; it has also increased the share of women members from about 25 to 30 percent. It is estimated that at least one-half, and perhaps as much as two-thirds, of the party are new members who have joined during the last decade. New members have been moved surprisingly quickly to positions of responsibility. If these changes were designed to give the party a new image, at the very least, they have been quite successful.[32] Yet the party's tight control of the country's strongest trade unions has in no way diminished.

Compared with other Communist parties in democratic countries, the French PC began very late to free itself from Stalinist dogmatism and the tutelage of the Soviet Union. International events and the emergence of new leadership have brought some of the changes that, among others, Italian Communists accepted much earlier. The Soviet Union is now freely criticized by party members and in the party's public pronouncements. A new party program dropped all reference to the dictatorship of the proletariat, and developed a platform of opposition to the government within the existing institutional framework.

What has not changed is the structure of the party, the French translation of the Leninist principle of democratic centralism. The limits of the party's liberalization remain those of a centralist organization: once policies are set from above they are binding, and factions are not tolerated. In this respect the PC and the RPR resemble each other: they are the only truly disciplined parties.

In the late 1960s the interests of the PC and the PS converged. The PC wished to overcome its isolation, the political ghetto in which it had been kept for over twenty years. At the same time, to dislodge the Gaullist-center majority, the new PS needed allies, which it could only find on the left. Experiences had shown that a mere electoral alliance between the two parties was not dynamic enough to convince the voters that the left offered a plausible alternative. Hence in June 1972 the PS, the PC, and the left radicals (in spite of its name a splinter group to the right of the Socialists) agreed on a comprehensive common program. The partners decided to set aside the considerable differences that divided them and spelled out detailed proposed policies for the five years of a normal parliamentary session. The core of the program was an ambitious proposal for comprehensive nationalization of industries and banking, but it also promised a wide range of other economic, social, and administrative reforms.

Whether the 13 million voters who in 1974 voted for Mitterand, the candidate of the united left, had truly decided for that program might be doubted. But even if their votes were mainly a rejection of a conservative government, they seemed to accept the logic that only a united left could dislodge the majority.

Subsequent by-elections and public opinion polls revealed that only the PS was profiting from increased popular sympathies, while the PC's following

[31] This comparison is suggested by the impressive analysis of non-voting in the United States in E. E. Schattschneider, *The Semi-Sovereign People* (New York: Holt, Rinehart & Winston, 1960), pp. 97–113.

[32] There is no longer a dearth of scholarly (as distinguished from merely polemic) studies of the PC. The most complete American study, with a rich bibliography, is Ronald Tiersky, *French Communism, 1920–1972* (New York: Columbia University Press, 1974). See also his "The French Communist Party and Detente," *Journal of International Affairs*, 28:2 (1974), pp. 188–205; and "French Communism in 1976," *Problems of Communism*, 25:1 (1976), pp. 20–47. The English edition of a book by one of the outstanding French experts on communism is Annie Kriegel, *The French Communists: Profile of a People* (Chicago: University of Chicago Press, 1972).

May 1968: Gaullists and war veterans demonstrating for order and an end to violence. The legacy of the days of turmoil were few lasting reforms but deep resentment between opposing groups.

stagnated, or even receded. Six months before the 1978 elections, when a victory of the left was generally predicted, the difference in support for the two allies amounted to ten percentage points of the total vote. Tensions between the two parties and an almost visceral distrust had been mounting for a long time. Faced with the possibility that they were to play the role of a junior partner in a government that would have to meet grave economic problems and possibly a major social crisis, the PC sought and found a pretext to break off the alliance with the PS and the radicals. It thereby destroyed the credibility of an alternative to the majority in power. The electorate reacted as could be expected and sent the left, once again divided, back to the opposition benches.

Within the PC, the events have provoked a crisis. Prominent party members have stridently critized the bureaucratization of the party's leadership and the harshness of democratic centralism. If the near-revolt had been able to achieve fundamental changes in the party's policies and structure, it could have made the PC over in the image of its Italian counterpart. But as a matter of fact the party leadership has once more silenced the opposition by isolating its spokesmen, most of them intellectuals from the working class membership.

POLICY PROCESSES

The Executive

The French constitution has a two-headed executive: as in other parliamentary regimes, the prime minister presides over the Cabinet; unlike in other parliamentary regimes, the president is far from being a figurehead. It was widely predicted that such an arrangement would almost necessarily lead to conflict. None has come to pass, however. Three presidents, for all their differences in outlook and style, and each of the prime ministers that have served under them, left no doubt that the executive had only one head, the president.

Georges Pompidou, the second president, had been de Gaulle's prime minister for more than six years. His successor, Valéry Giscard d'Estaing, had held the important post of minister of finance under de Gaulle and Pompidou for nine years. Both, therefore, had ample opportunity to observe closely the working of the constitutional system as it emerged. Upon assuming office both made it clear, by explicit statements and by practice, that they fully accepted the constitutional arrangements they inherited. As "supreme head of the Executive" the president was, in Pompidou's interpretation, "providing the fundamental drives, defining the essential directions and ensuring and controlling the proper functioning of the government." Giscard, in his first press conference, confirmed the "presidentialist interpretation of our institutions within the framework of existing legislation."

To control the proper functioning of government the president must nominate and dismiss the prime minister and other ministers. This has been the accepted practice in the Fifth Republic. In some cases the president has even dismissed a prime minister who was clearly enjoying the confidence of a majority in Parliament.

Hence the rather frequent reshuffling of Cabinet posts and personnel in the Fifth Republic is different from similar happenings in the Third and Fourth Republics. In those systems the changes occurred in response to shifts in partliamentary support and frequently in order to forestall, at least for a short time, the fall from power of the government. Now the president decides to appoint, move, or dismiss Cabinet officers on the basis of his own appreciation of the worth (or lack of it) of the individual member. This does not mean that presidential considerations are merely technical. They might be highly political, but they are exclusively his own.

Since all powers proceed from the president, the government headed by the prime minister has become essentially an administrative body, despite constitutional stipulations to the contrary. Its chief function is to provide whatever direction or resources are needed to implement the policies conceived by the chief of state. This means primarily enacting legislation whether they emanate from Parliament or directly from the executive, and budgeting funds, either by parliamentary vote or by substitutes. In many respects the government's position resembles that of the Cabinet in a presidential regime such as the United States, rather than that of a government in a parliamentary system such as Great Britain and the earlier French republics.

Although no domain of governmental activity escapes presidential initiative and control, members of the government are not deprived of all autonomy and spontaneity. Weekly meetings of the Council of Ministers, chaired by the president, have preserved the decorum of earlier days and are still a forum for deliberation and confrontation of viewpoints. Under Pompidou and Giscard the atmosphere at Cabinet meetings might have changed from that under the more authoritarian de Gaulle; but their exclusively advisory function has not.

The prime minister, in relation to Cabinet colleagues, is more than the first among equals. Among his many functions is harnessing the parliamentary majority for presidential policies, since according to the Constitution the regime cannot function correctly without a majority backing the government. This is what distinguishes France from a truly presidential regime such as the United States or Mexico.

The size of cabinets has varied in the different republics, but it has always been large, usually about forty members. Less than half, however, are full-fledged ministers; the others are classified as secretaries of state. They are part of the Cabinet and participate in its meetings, but they either head a smaller administration or are attached, like an American undersecretary, to a ministerial colleague.

In a parliamentary system it is normal that most, if not all, Cabinet members must be elected to Parliament. So far the governments of the Giscard administration have departed from this rule and reverted to a choice of personnel customary in the early Gaullist cabinets but subsequently abandoned. Important ministers of the Chirac Cabinet (those in charge of foreign affairs, finance, education, public health, and foreign trade) and several secretaries of state had never run for elective office, and were selected for their expertise. The same was true of Giscard's second Cabinet, formed by Raymond Barre, a professor of economics. In the first Cabinet of the Fifth Republic about 40 percent of the ministers had no electoral experience, most of them being ranking civil servants. By contrast, all members of Pompidou's first Cabinet had at one time been elected to one of the houses of Parliament. The earlier practice, which reflected de Gaulle's predilection for depoliticizing the affairs of state, was abandoned because of somewhat disappointing experience with the technicians and civil servants in the Cabinet. It first became apparent to the ranking bureaucrats that a minister with no support outside the civil service did not have enough political weight in the councils of government. This led many civil servants to ignore directives coming from a former colleague, although they were accustomed to accommodating a politician who had his own power base. Such rebuffs made some of the ministers understand the advantages to their own effectiveness and authority they could derive from a political mandate.

Government stability is one of the most striking differences between the present and preceding regimes. In its eleven years and five months, the Fourth Republic had twenty Cabinets and several lengthy periods of crisis during which an interim government held office until a replacement prime minister was found. De Gaulle had only three prime ministers, and Pompidou only two; each of their Cabinets identified closely with their policies. On the other hand, the constantly changing cabinets of the Fourth Republic included many of the same people, and the continuity of policies was impressive, but in the Fifth Republic, ministers have come and gone even while the same prime minister remained in office. The important ministries of agriculture and education have had frequent shifts in top leadership, leading to major policy shifts and considerable confusion about government policy.

The Civil Service

Because of its frank emphasis on the prestige and the procedures of the administrative state, and because of its dislike for party politics, the Gaullist regime was expected to increase the influence of the bureaucracy on policy. What has come about is a seemingly contradictory but actually consistent development. On one hand, the executive has subjected the bureaucracy to more political control; on the other, the domain open to decision making by the technicians in the civil service has been enlarged considerably.

The expansion of the government's lawmaking power at the expense of Parliament has resulted in numerous rulings being formulated and codified by the civil service. Contrary to widespread belief, the bureaucracy was not able to govern the Fourth Republic while ministries toppled; at the approach of a crisis all projects of more than routine nature were shelved. In the Fifth Republic, however, top-ranking bureaucrats have prepared important and detailed policy decisions without consulting Parliament or other elective bodies.

In most administrative quarters, this increased freedom from parliamentary control and interference was welcomed as a boon to efficiency. And even though ministers have changed fairly frequently, the civil service has generally welcomed the increased governmental stability. Even civil servants opposed to Gaullism on political grounds have been pleased by the increase in bureaucratic authority.[33] Decisions prepared by the civil service without consulting Parliament or other elective bodies have included the currency reform of 1958 and a host of economic measures and the thorough reforms of the court and the social security systems. The complete revamping of the administrative structure of the Paris region, affecting more than 9 million people, was briefly debated in Parliament, but in all essentials was shaped by governmental bureaus. Many important committees advising the government on long-range policy planning have been comprised exclusively of civil servants.

The reform that has been attempted often, and always been stalled, is of the administrative machinery and its methods. An almost automatic centraliza-

[33] An excellent, critical account of the workings and the mentality of the high bureaucracy in recent times is Ezra N. Suleiman, *Politics, Power, and Bureaucracy in France: The Administrative Elite* (Princeton, N.J.: Princeton University Press, 1974), p. 231. An interesting analysis of the all important Ministry of Finance is provided by Jack Hayward, *The One and Indivisible French Republic* (London: Weidenfeld and Nicholson, 1973), pp. 158–167.

tion is omnipresent. Every administration is rule-bound, but in France the rules are so dense and appear so rigid that they are swamped by exceptions. Yet since exceptions can only be granted by senior officials, responsibilities are continuously transferred to the highest administrative echelons. The traditional administrative way of problem solving — actually solution deferment — leads to a situation in which development is impeded by a blocking of decision making. The blocks can be blasted away only by a frankly political decision originating outside the bureaucracy. This was done by General de Gaulle when he opted for Algerian independence and set the country on the course of decolonization.

Regional Reform

The one major attack to overcome centralization and alter traditional structures is the regionalization of the country. In the early 1960s when modernization forged ahead it became apparent that the country's ninety-five departments, most of them carved out in the eighteenth century, were an obstacle to reform. At the present time a true regionalization of the overcentralized country would call for at least two major interconnected reforms: the areas need to be large and viable enough to develop and live, at least partly, on their own human and financial resources; and even without introducing a full-fledged federalism, which nobody has envisaged, those heading the new regions need to be less bound by directives from the capital.

The changes that have been introduced are far less sweeping. The country is now divided not into ten or twelve fairly large regions, which many economists have recommended, but into twenty-two regions that, with one exception, comprise several departments (see map on page 210). If one disregards the most and the least populous, Paris and Corsica, the twenty remaining regions vary in population between 4.7 million (Rhone-Alpes) and 0.7 million (Limousin); they also vary considerably in economic development.

A regional reform that set out to combat the sluggishness and developmental imbalance resulting in part from overcentralization, had to choose between decentralization or deconcentration. Decentralization would have meant that regional bodies, legitimized by elections and with adequate financial means and administrative structure, would have been put in charge of regional development. The French chose deconcentration, a new hierarchical arrangement by which the bureaucratic organs of the central government located in the regions are meant to initiate launching development projects without referring the final decision on every detail to Paris.

The chief executive of the regional organization is the prefect of the department in which the regional capital is situated. For the organizational relationship of the national and departmental levels, see Figure 10.3.

There is no room in the new legislation for either a popularly elected executive such as a United States governor or for an elected regional parliament, since direct elections would give the regions a democratic legitimacy and strength that is suspect to the traditional local notables and to the bureaucracy. Instead, each region is endowed with a regional council and an economic and social advisory committee, which meet annually for very short sessions.

However, for the viability of the new institutions, specific structures might be less important than the possibilities they offer for meaningful decisions on the regional level and for the democratic responsiveness of those making such decisions. Here the judgment must be guarded. So far the financial resources at the exclusive disposition of the regions are pitifully small — in 1975 six dollars per inhabitant — and are quickly distributed for highway maintenance and similar purposes. An important change would be to empower the regional governments to allocate the amount set aside in the national budget for development. New legislation on local finances is in preparation and could set the pace for a greater financial autonomy of the regions.

So far nothing permits us to conclude that regionalization as now set up has attacked the obstacles that the overcentralization of decision making puts in the way of vigorous economic expansion in the less favored regions. Nor has the cause of citizen participation been furthered to any significant degree.

Parliament

The Constitution had seriously curtailed the powers of Parliament both as a source of legislation and as an organ of control of the executive. The mere fact that both houses of Parliament are now confined to sessions of regulated length (a maximum of six months in every calendar year) has resulted in so much time pressure that effectiveness is impeded. In 1974, an average year, Parliament met for only seventy-nine days, far less than other parliaments in Western Europe, not to mention the United States Congress. Of a total of 543 hours of session, 264 hours were devoted to legislative business, 198 hours to budgetary debates. In this respect the situation has worsened under the Giscard administration. Since governments under Giscard submit many important bills to Parliament, both houses are frustrated at being inhibited by the Constitution.

During the early years of the Fifth Republic both the government and the members of Parliament adopted attitudes that narrowed the scope of parliamentary activities even more than was originally intended by the constitution makers. The executive was afraid that Parliament would overstep its bounds; the deputies and senators had difficulty adapting themselves to unaccustomed rules and roles. Little by little confrontation has given way to a modicum of collaboration. Of course, the emergence of a stable government majority in the lower house has facilitated a more relaxed handling of the rules. Over the years the players have come to understand their new roles, although some attitudes and expectations are still contradictory.

The legislative output of Parliament has been respectable. Merely counting laws is not meaningful, since their importance must be weighed. As the Constitution limits the domain of the law to vital fields, it is obvious that there are important statutes among the 1,300 laws enacted between 1958 and 1974 by both houses. All but 170 of these laws were proposed by the government, and many propositions put forward by members of Parliament failed, but neither fact is unusual in Western European parliaments; in postwar Great Britain private-member bills have dwindled to almost zero.

A dearth of information still seriously handicaps the effectiveness of majority and opposition members. In spite of recent improvements, working conditions remain inadequate; the average deputy or senator has little or no staff assistance. Parliamentary committees usually rely on the executive for the information needed to prepare reports or amendments. Public hearings on bills under consideration, an important source of information in the United States Congress, are practically unknown.

In one respect the situation in Parliament has undoubtedly taken a turn for the better recently. The Constitution, emulating British practices, stipulated that members' questions and ministers' replies be made a weekly priority. Yet during the early years oral questions were an unmitigated failure: there was none of the lively give-and-take of the British model; sessions devoted to questions were poorly attended; the deputies were inclined to clothe their questions in lengthy speeches, just as the members of the government read lengthy answers prepared by their staffs; and often ministers would send an assistant to represent them.

In 1970, when early tensions started to give way to a new view of the role of Parlianent, the National Assembly made room for a weekly session devoted to a new kind of question period, far more like the British and West German practice. A dozen or more brief questions are selected beforehand, and then the appropriate minister or secretary of state answers them succinctly and indicates remedies for any complaints. The opposition has not fared badly in these exchanges. The new practice reflects a greater eagerness on the part of the deputies to control rather than to attack, and less disposition on the part of the government to hide behind the cloak of official secrecy.

The possibility of controlling the executive machinery by ad hoc committees of investigation has always existed in the French republics, but every attempt to use them has produced meagre results. The committees have never been able to overcome administrative reluctance to disclose the truth. In the Fifth Republic a few matters have been made the subject of investigations; when the opposition suggested that seemingly scandalous situations be investigated, the government was frequently able to prevent the organization of a committee of inquiry. But even investigations that are permitted usually receive little publicity and their reports remain largely unknown. Also discouraging such committees is that their proceedings are strictly regulated.

During the years of the greatest imbalance between the powers of Parliament and the executive, deputies of all political persuasions intensified their defense of constituency interests. Such local concerns are easily preponderant in countries with weak parties. An electoral system with fairly small constituencies with only one representative, severely limited as a lawmaker and a watchdog of the executive, has encouraged the most active representatives, young and old, to be the agents of their constituents in the capital.

According to public opinion polls, voters approve of Parliament as an institution and of the role played by their deputies. Year by year the number of those who would like Parliament to be given a larger place in public life has risen. Deputies are judged to do a commendable job, and the hostile criticism directed against Parliament before 1958 has largely subsided.

The founders of the Fifth Republic had the notion that an indirectly elected upper house of Parliament in which the rural constituencies were overrepresented and institutions inherited from the Third and Fourth Republics, would function as a welcome counterweight against a possibly capricious National Assembly. Such hopes were frustrated. The membership of the Senate was never touched by the Gaullist groundswell characteristic of so many elections to the National Assembly. The Gaullists, who at times held a majority of seats in the National Assembly, have never been able to get more than thirty senators out of 283. The local notables making up a strong contingent of the Senate's electoral college regularly expressed their distrust of the regime, if not their outright hostility toward it, since they felt their status and influence were undermined by the personalization of political power and by the government's use of the mass media.

The Senate has disagreed with the government on many major policy decisions, rejecting or substantially amending bills approved by the National Assembly. This has not, however, proved a serious obstacle to the government, since the Constitution provides that if the two houses disagree on pending legislation, the government can appoint a joint committee. If the views of the two houses are no reconciled, it is up to the government to decide which will prevail. A weapon originally designed to discipline an unruly lower house could now be turned against the Senate.

Not only in France, but in all countries without a federal structure, the problem of how to organize a bicameral legislature is complex. How should its membership be defined without territorial units to be represented? Making it an appointed rather than an elected body removes democratic legitimacy. If, for that reason, it is denied equal powers with the popularly elected Parliament, how to avoid it being slighted, as is the British House of Lords and the French Economic and Social Council, if not totally ignored?

In the last referendum he submitted, de Gaulle proposed a novel formula for an allegedly modernized upper house. But in the referendum campaign the defense of the old Senate assumed a symbolic value and contributed to the defeat of the proposal. The oldest and also one of the most controversial of republican institutions had weathered another storm just at the time it was celebrating its centennial.

Checks and Balances

In a mixed regime such as the Fifth Republic, in which the president is constitutionally and politically able to overpower all other organs of government, the lack of an effective check on that power has often been decried. The Constitutional Council cannot assume the functions the Supreme Court exercises in the United States. In fact the council was designed by the drafters of the Constitution mainly as a safeguard against erosion of the constraints they had placed on Parliament. For years the council adhered faithfully to this task alone.

When, after de Gaulle's resignation, political tensions had abated, the council slowly changed its public image as the government's creature by a series of decisions. The first, rendered in 1971, declared unconstitutional a bill that had been approved by a large majority in the National Assembly but violated, according to the decision, the freedom of association, one of "the fundamental principles recognized by the laws of the Republic and solemnly reaffirmed in the preamble of the [1958] Constitution."

After *Marbury* v. *Madison* the United States Supreme Court waited half a century before it again exercised its power to annul national legislation; the Constitutional Council rendered, after a mere two years, two more decisions of lesser importance, but also striking down provisions it judged to abridge citizens' rights. Yet as long as access to the Constitutional Council was restricted to four officials close to the government and the parliamentary majority, the council could not be relied on to ensure the legality of executive and parliamentary enactments. This, however, is the essence of judicial review.

Before his accession to the presidency, Giscard and his party had spoken out in favor of a supreme court endowed with enough power and prestige to check the other branches of government. But the changes he envisaged would have necessitated a constitutional amendment, which the Gaullist deputies were clearly unwilling to approve. Instead, a modest modification of the existing provisions regulating appeals to the Constitutional Council has been introduced: now sixty deputies or sixty senators, supposedly speaking in the name of an overruled minority, can also submit cases to the Constitutional Council. This has already been done in several cases.

The much older Council of State is respected for all of its varied activities. Of its four sections, the judicial one has the most direct impact on the rights of citizens. By an extensive body of case law, the council has become "the great protector of the rights of property and of the rights of the individual against the State, the great redressor of wrongs committed by the State."[34] Whenever official acts are found to be devoid of a legal basis, whether they be those of a Cabinet minister or of a village mayor, the council annuls them and grants damages to the plaintiff. The council has steadily broadened its criteria for legality, and included equality before the law, freedom of speech and association, the right to natural justice, the right to be heard, the right not to be subjected to retroactive legislation, and other similar rights.

PERFORMANCE AND PROSPECTS

While French political culture has not prevented adaptation and change, it has accommodated alternate periods of immobility — when modernization was blocked or greatly slowed — and crisis. The change from one stage to another has often been abrupt rather than continuous or gradual. As a consequence, no French regime since the collapse of the old regime in 1789 has had the capacity for thorough self-reform. This has transformed almost every political crisis, many centering around problems of modernization, into a constitutional crisis. It has also meant that each of the sixteen constitutions produced since 1791 has had to seek legitimacy anew for the institutions it created and the values it sought to represent. Such discontinuity has proved traumatic and a continuous threat to democratic government.

Will the Fifth Republic be able to accomplish the changes required by continuous modernization, and will its rules and procedures be accepted as legitimate?

Obviously the Fifth Republic inherited many of the conditions under which it operates. Many barriers to modernization and to a more equitable distribution of resources must be attributed to traditional strains, rather than to failings of the new regime. Conversely, much of the vitality and many of the changes for which the new regime claims credit have resulted from attitudes that took root and reforms that were accomplished or well on the way before General de Gaulle returned to power in 1958.

The comparative data provided in Part II of this book indicate that in terms of extractive performance the French record is not notably different from other Western countries of similar development (see especially Tables 8.1 and 8.2). While the French economy, with its large public sector, is structurally different from those of the United States and West Germany, the amount of government revenues, both in per capita terms and as a percentage of gross national product, approximates those of other nations. However, the proportion of government revenues coming from direct taxes is far smaller, and the effective tax rates for the upper brackets substantially lower than elsewhere, including the United States.[35] The foremost reason for the prevalence of indirect taxation in France is the widespread and time-honored practice of tax evasion. French sources estimate that fraud is practiced by more than one-third of those with taxable incomes, a far higher figure than in the United States and Great Britain.

Further, it is officially recognized that loopholes,

[34] Joseph Barthélémy, *The Government of France*, B. J. Morris (trans.) (New York: Brentano's, 1924), p. 181.

[35] For more information on the French tax situation, see Adolf J. Heidenheimer, et al., *Comparative Public Policy: The Politics of Social Choice in Europe and America* (New York: St. Martin's Press, 1975), pp. 227 ff, and the sources there quoted. The definition of direct and indirect taxes varies greatly and confuses all comparative discussions.

exceptions, and exemptions leave at least 56 percent of business and 77 percent of agricultural income untaxed. Because of the high rate of evasion direct taxes fall heavily, and sometimes too heavily, on individual wage earners and on modern firms who have only limited possibilities for evasion. Personal income and inheritance taxes are far less progressive than they appear. In 1967, Giscard, then chairman of the Finance Committee in Parliament, lamented that "in France individual income taxes are a factor of fiscal inequity rather than of social justice."

Taxes, of course, indicate not only the extractive but also the distributive performance of a government. A system of taxation as iniquitous as the French one produces and reproduces inequality. In terms of government expenditures for public education and for welfare the French record is respectable (see Table 8.3 and 8.6). Social security benefits are substantial and, as opinion polls reveal, highly valued. It is true that satisfaction cannot be measured merely in terms of the level of expenditures. The continuing and widely resented malfunction of a fairly well-endowed educational system and its resilience to effective reform furnish an example.

In terms of the distribution of wealth and of post-tax income, France is the most unequal of nations of similar development. If one compares the incomes of the top and the bottom 20 percent of the population one arrives at a coefficient of inequality of 11.2 for France; for the United States the figure is 8.6, for West Germany 7.1, for Great Britain 6.4, and for the Netherlands 4.0. After taxes the poorest 10 percent of French households get 1.4 percent of total national income. The richest 10 percent receive 30.5 percent. In the United States the corresponding figures are 1.7 and 26.1 percent, in Great Britain 2.4 and 23.9 percent, in the Netherlands 3.2 and 21.8 percent.

As to national wealth, 5 percent of the population own 40 percent and the next 10 percent have an additional 30 percent, which means that 85 percent divide the remaining 30 percent among them. Of the original Common Market partners France still assigns the smallest share of its national income to wage earners but ranks highest in undistributed income of corporations. One of the principal economic advisors of President Giscard has calculated the total number of the underprivileged at 11.2 million (in a population of 53 million) and believes that without a drastic change in policies the number will still stand at 9.2 million in 1985.

The housing shortage occupies a special place among the social problems of long standing. In the first two decades after the war, construction of new housing units lagged dramatically behind the rates in West Germany and Great Britain. Since 1968 the situation has improved, but at the present rate of construction it would take a quarter of a century to fill the reasonable needs of a growing population no longer content to live in overage dwellings. Many, in and out of governnent, consider the dearth of suitable housing the tear in the French social fabric. But at the same time close to half a million luxury dwellings stand permanently vacant and the country holds the world record for secondary residences.

In a nation in which the urge for equality has been pronounced, and at times outweighed that for freedom, protests against inequities have sometimes taken violent forms. In a public opinion poll of people from eighteen to twenty-five "irritation about social inequalities" occupied the front rank of current preoccupations.[36]

Yet another failure of the system is mirrored in the widespread dissatisfaction with the court system. Young and old agree that the courts do not secure equality before the law: 68 percent (73 percent of the young) are convinced that the rich are better treated than the poor. Fifty-three percent believe that judges respond to pressures by the government, and 49 percent to those by their superiors. In the opinion of the respondents, judicial independence is badly secured.

Regulatory performance is distinctly better. Even during the more authoritarian phase of the Fifth Republic the government never resorted to those forms of compulsion practiced by totalitarian regimes. The Giscard administration has enacted, especially during its early days, a number of reforms pertaining to the life-style and living conditions of individual French of various categories. Through legislation,

[36] All the polling data in this section are quoted from SOFRES, *L'Opinion Française en 1977*.

abortion is now permitted during the first months of pregnancy and contraceptives are more readily available. A new divorce law has been passed and criminal procedures have been modified to allow discretion in setting punishment. The voting age and the age of legal responsibility has been lowered to eighteen. Political censorship of films and, presumably, the bugging of telephones have been stopped. A number of measures to protect the environment have also been passed. One of the first laws accepted by Parliament after Giscard's election thoroughly revamped the system of telecommunications, in an effort to reduce government control of radio and television. The heavy hand of the authorities in supervising the public stations had long been resented, especially since there is no private television at all.

This is a fairly impressive record touching the lives of millions of French, even if some changes can be criticized as surface reforms and if all will not be enforced as intended. But the president wanted more fundamental reforms, which he saw as indispensable for greater social justice and for a better balance between centralized decision making and democratic participation. When he tried to realize these reforms he encountered stubborn resistance from within his own majority, as deputies responded to constituency and group pressures. Some tax reform bills were so emasculated as to become almost meaningless; others had to be abandoned altogether. The relative failure of the regional reform, and thereby of effective decentralization, has been discussed above.

At the approach of the parliamentary elections of 1978, Giscard published a book explaining his concept of a modern pluralist democracy, opposed to classical liberalism and to what the author calls collectivism.[37] The book candidly raises a number of major problems that must be solved if France is to emerge as a fully modern democracy combining vigorous development with greater equality. What remains unanswered is how and with whose support Giscard hopes to arrive at these goals.

As long as the gap between promise and performance remains wide, and the pattern of decision making ill adapted to present demands, French society might remain stalled, with obstacles to change regularly overcome only in a crisis.[38] Remarkably enough, at least for the time being, the French no longer appear to harbor the mentality that looks to convulsion and drama for progress. In a 1977 poll, 57 percent expressed the belief that society would evolve by peaceful reform, only 22 percent foresaw crisis and violence as likely. At the time the poll was taken it was generally assumed that the opposition committed to a radical reform program would win the elections because of the unsatisfactory record of the government. Yet in most of their answers voters expressed an unsuspected consensus on the more fundamental questions of system performance.

The consensus embraces the institutional framework as it has developed since 1958. To have made the popular election of a strong executive legitimate remains one of the historical achievements of the regime. Whether the voters are truly in favor of a system combining parliamentary and presidential government is less certain. When polled, a large majority — not only on the left but also from the center — wishes to see Parliament endowed with broader powers, government and prime minister fully in control of policy making, and the president still elected directly, but with a less political stance. Undoubtedly such a redistribution of roles, resembling more the parliamentary model, would make politics easier if the president and parliamentary majority ever belonged to opposite political camps.

During the first twenty years of the Fifth Republic the concern that such a constellation might threaten institutional stability gave at each presidential and parliamentary election a renewed mandate to those already in power. Hence the regime has not yet met that test of democratic legitimacy, which consists in the peaceful transfer of power to the opposition and in the alternating of competing forces, whether single parties or coalitions. Because the elections of 1978 demonstrated once more how difficult it is under the prevailing system to dislodge an established majority, the ability of the government to combine stability and change will be crucial.

[37] Valéry Giscard d'Estaing, *French Democracy* (Garden City, N.J.: Doubleday, 1977).

[38] For a fascinating discussion see Michel Crozier, *The Stalled Society* (New York: Viking, 1973).

The outcome is uncertain. As long as French politics remain democratic, they will move more vigorously than the politics of other countries between the extremes of cohesion and diversity. This is fascinating, but it makes any predictions about the course of political change hazardous.

KEY TERMS

Charles de Gaulle
Fourth Republic
Fifth Republic
Parliament
plebiscite
Valéry Giscard d'Estaing
the political class
École Nationale d'Administration (ENA)
National Assembly
Senate
Constitution of 1958
motion of censure
Economic and Social Council
Constitutional Council
direct democracy
representative democracy
ouvriérisme
communes
prefects
referendum
grands corps
Confédération Générale du Travail
Rassemblement pour la République (RPR)
Rally of the Republic
Republican party
Union de la Démocratie Française
Socialist party
François Mitterand
Communist party
decentralization
deconcentration

WEST
BERLIN
EAST
BERLIN
DENMARK
Kiel
SCHLESWIG-
HOLSTEIN
Lübeck
Hamburg
Bremen
LOWER SAXONY
Berlin
Potsdam
Hanover
NETHERLANDS
GERMAN DEMOCRATIC
REPUBLIC
NORTH RHINE-
WESTPHALIA
Essen
Düsseldorf
Kassel
Leipzig
Cologne
Bonn
HESSE
BELGIUM
Frankfort
RHINELAND-
PALATINATE
LUX.
CZECHOSLOVAKIA
Nuremberg
SAAR
BAVARIA
Stuttgart
BADEN-
WÜRTTEMBURG
FRANCE
Munich
AUSTRIA
German Federal Republic
0
100
Scale of Miles
SWITZERLAND

CHAPTER ELEVEN

LEWIS J. EDINGER
with the collaboration of Robert C. A. Sorensen

Politics in West Germany

The recognition that the German Federal Republic is not what it used to be has in recent times startled both West Germans and foreign observers. West Germany is no longer merely an object of power politics, but a leading actor in European and world affairs. Its new status is directly related to the reduction of tensions in Central Europe and to its increasingly important position among economically interdependent states. The once troublesome German problem no longer bedevils East-West relations, and West German leaders have become less concerned with the popularity of their country abroad and are more assertive in promoting its international interests. In this context, it matters not so much that the Federal Republic is not a military superpower. More important, it stands in the front rank of the world's richest industrial countries.

The West German regime no longer appears tenuous and fragile, but well established and stable. Some thirty years after the founding of the Federal Republic, a good deal of evidence exists which can be used to compare the present with past German regimes.

THE MEANING OF THE PAST

What clues have West Germans derived from the past for what they should do and expect in contemporary politics? The basic lesson conveyed by most of their history books is that political controversies can lead to bitter conflicts, but autocracy is no cure.

The industrialization of nineteenth-century Germany led to intense conflicts between rural and urban interests, employers and employees, and ideological factions committed to divisive, exclusive dogmas. Under all earlier regimes, managing conflict was identified with a powerful state, strong executive leadership, weak legislatures, and minimal popular participation. Harmony in state and society rested more on the suppression than on the free expression of differences, and more on enforced compliance with formal rules handed down from above than on a popular, voluntary consensus achieved through bargaining and compromise.

Imperial Germany (1871–1918)

When unification first was achieved, by the German Empire in 1871, it was imposed from above through a policy of blood and iron — war and force — identified with Chancellor Otto von Bismarck. For almost half a century, Germans were taught that only a powerful state could safeguard their unity and survival. Authority was exercised by officials who served the interests of the state rather than the people. The role assigned to the ordinary citizen was that of the law-abiding subject.

Contemporary West Germans have been taught that the imperial regime failed to integrate preindustrial habits of thought and action with those produced by industrialization. Cleavages among interest groups were obscured rather than alleviated. Policy makers effectively resisted domestic demands for democratic reforms and committed the country to a foreign policy that exceeded its capabilities. By the time of Germany's defeat in World War I, political disintegration had proceeded too far to allow reform of the system, and the German Empire collapsed in 1918.

The Weimar Republic (1919–1933)

A democratic and republican regime was initiated in 1919 by a popularly elected constitutional assembly meeting in the town of Weimar. Responsibility for making peace and establishing a new political order was suddenly thrust on the imperial regime's critics, who had no governmental experience. For lack of alternatives, key positions in the economy, the armed forces, the judiciary, and the public administration remained in the hands of supporters of the old regime and its political culture.

The years of the Weimar Republic were marked by bitter conflicts between those seeking change and those resisting it, and among divided religious, cultural, and socioeconomic subcultures. Twenty-one different governments were formed, most not lasting more than six months, and eight parliamentary elections were held, with no party ever winning an absolute majority. The liberal democratic regime became increasingly discredited in the eyes of Germans who had learned to look to the state for authoritative guidance and who expected leaders to ensure order and harmony. While a substantial number of Germans belonged to political parties — especially the Social Democratic party, which supported the regime — many of those active in politics were intent on replacing the regime with an entirely different one.

Nazis and Communists separately promoted political instability, expecting that chaos would bring them into power. The holdover elites from the German Empire still mourned its passing, and their lack of support for the republic was supplemented by attacks on the regime by influential opinion makers — journalists, teachers, and religious leaders. Growing fatalism and lack of confidence undermined the determination of the defenders of the new German constitution and played into the hands of their successful opponents, the Nazis.

The Nazi Regime (1933–1945)

Mass and elite dissatisfaction with the Weimar system finally came to a head in a severe economic crisis that paved the way for Adolf Hitler's accession to power in 1933. To consolidate his rule, Hitler exploited the discontent of the old Prussian aristocracy, the military elite, the industrialists and big businessmen, the civil servants, and German nationalists and romantics. He destroyed the parties and interest groups of the Weimar Republic and transformed surviving structures into instruments of personal power.

In the new autocratic "leader state" all boundaries between state and society and between political and nonpolitical roles were to be eradicated. The new political culture, based on belligerent nationalism, anti-Semitism, radical romanticism, and brutal police control, was to reflect the spirit of the national collectivity as articulated by its embodiment, the omnipotent leader. But the Führer's erratic and intuitive style of government, along with the authoritarian organization of his state, caused tensions in Nazi Germany that became more pronounced as its fortunes declined. The one-sidedness of political communication in a system resting on command and obedience, and the dualism of government and Nazi party structures, led to widespread uncertainty over what kind of compliant behavior was expected, and to bitter jurisdictional disputes among the elites who were supposed to execute Hitler's orders faithfully. In the end, military defeat brought about the disintegration of the Third Reich.

Occupation and the Creation of the Federal Republic (1945–1949)

With the collapse of Hitler's regime in 1945, the Western occupying powers, the United States, Great Britain, and France, sought to eradicate what they took to be the principal elements of Nazi political and military power. They encouraged anti-Nazis and non-Nazis to assume responsibility for the gradual development of a free-enterprise system. During this enforced denazification West Germans were meant to obey commands from above, and most readily adapted themselves to foreign control. On the one hand, the authoritative decisions of the military governments were based on a punitive policy toward a people held collectively responsible for the actions of the Nazi regime, on the other hand they reflected an "enlightened despotism" aimed at preventing future German aggression. To implement the policies, the occupying powers held war crimes trials, conducted denazification purges, initiated educational reforms, dismantled industrial plants to pay for reparations, and carefully reshaped political structures.

Economic recovery and social reorganization began around 1948 and developed rapidly with the establishment of the Federal Republic one year later. As friction between Western and Soviet leaders increased over the next decade, foreign supervision of West German political affairs decreased. The new policy of the Western allies was to draw the Federal Republic into a close partnership against the Soviet bloc through economic assistance and military security arrangements. Within this international context, the people of West Germany were free to pursue their new democratic experiment.

West Germany Since 1949

Politics in the German Federal Republic have been characterized by continuity and change in attitudes and actions. The legal rules of a representative democracy have provided the framework, the dynamics of an advanced industrial society the ingredients.

The politics of the 1950s were those of reconstruction. Economic recovery was underway, but had not yet led to general affluence. A "provisional" state had been imposed on West Germany by the former occupation powers and had still to take root in the political culture. The politics of the 1960s were the politics of transition. Prosperity was no longer in doubt and came to include most West Germans. The constitutional order was more firmly established and authoritarian traditions were on the wane.

The politics of the 1970s carried the imprint of a different political climate and new policy concerns. The specters of the past were fading as a new political generation came to the fore. The broad political mood emphasized preservation of what had been achieved — prosperity and political stability at home, diplomatic, economic, and military stability abroad. Policy conflicts were more subdued than in the United States and Britain and less ideologically divisive than in France and Italy.

In the final analysis, however, the peculiarly German aspects of politics in the Federal Republic are less pronounced now than in its formative phase. In contrast to the situation then and under past regimes, political institutions and processes have become established and accepted, as have a more flexible political and administrative elite and a more involved citizenry. Major policy issues in the Federal Republic are now largely variations on themes common to other advanced industrial societies with capitalist systems and liberal democratic regimes. As the system has become increasingly institutionalized and economic growth has led to affluence at home and interdependence with other nations abroad, genuine satisfaction with the political status quo has become established among the majority of the population and the elites.

CONSTITUTIONAL ORGANIZATION

The Federal Republic and its Basic Law (*Grundgesetz*) are the products of the defeat of Germany in World War II and the inability of the conquerors to agree on the form of the nation's political reconstruction. The leaders of the four powers that assumed control over German territory in 1945 in separate American, British, French, and Russian zones initially pledged to collaborate in establishing a democratic regime for all of Germany. Their ideas of what this meant and how it might be attained, however, proved irreconcilable. The three Western zones became the Federal Republic of Germany, the Soviet zone the German Democratic Republic.

The Basic Law of 1949 was to provide a constitutional framework for a temporary state, pending reunification. It was drafted by the representatives of the three Western powers and West German leaders acceptable to them in the name of the entire German people — including those living in the area controlled by the Soviet Union. According to Article 145 of the Basic Law, it was to "cease to be in force on the day on which a constitution adopted by a free decision of the German people comes into force."

At the same time, the new instrument of government was designed to ensure long-range political stability in West Germany. Its framers were largely guided by their vivid recollection of events that had allowed Hitler to destroy an earlier democratic system in Germany. They therefore established very precise formal rules to guide West Germans in the difficult transition from an authoritarian past to a firmly established democratic order in a pluralist society. The constitution has been amended more often in thirty years than the American one has been in two hundred, but its original provisions remain the framework for the political system.

Rulers and Ruled

The roles assigned to those governing West Germany provide for a democratic state ruled by law and under law. Roles assigned to the governed reflect the founders' belief that too much direct democracy could lead to the destruction of their design. They conceived legal norms and formal structures to be more important guides and restraints on leaders than popular participation. The average citizen was allowed only an intermittent and indirect part in policy making, primarily as a voter in the election of local, state, and national legislators.

The rules of responsible citizenship oblige the governed to obey the legitimate decisions of public officials and to oppose illegitimate ones. The principles of responsible government, in turn, oblige the governors to observe and uphold the formal rules for their selection, their conduct, and the scope of their authority.

The Basic Law also provides a foundation of human and civil rights. Anyone living within the Federal Republic is entitled to the human rights of liberty, legal equality and redress, and freedom of religion and speech. Citizens are granted the civic rights of assembly, association, and travel within and out of the country.

Federalism

West Germany is the only major European country with a federal rather than a centralized form of government. Much as in the United States, legislative, executive, and judicial authority is dispersed among various geographic units. The essential jurisdictional division is between the organs of the federation (*Bund*) and those of the states (*Länder*). (See Figure 11.1 and Table 11.1.)

As in every other federation, the regional entities are subject to national rules. The Basic Law makes it the responsibility of the central government to see that they are observed. Federal law has preeminence over state law, the human and civil rights set forth in the Basic Law must be respected by state authorities, and the states must conform to the constitutional principles of "republican, democratic, and social government based on the rule of law."

At the same time, the geographic division of public authority entails a particular West German brand of federalism. The states wield broad powers specifically granted to them in the Basic Law, most importantly in education and cultural policies. The Federation has sole authority over a limited number of policy areas, notably defense and foreign policy. In most respects, policy making is shared by the executive and legislative authorities of the states and the Federation. Policy implementation rests largely with the states, through their control over the public administration, the police, radio and television stations, and public funds used by local authorities.

To balance the obligations of the member states toward the Federation and the limitations on their autonomy, the Basic Law assigns to their elected representatives key positions in national politics. They participate in the selection of the federal president and the justices of the principal federal courts, and, more importantly, they have a significant voice in

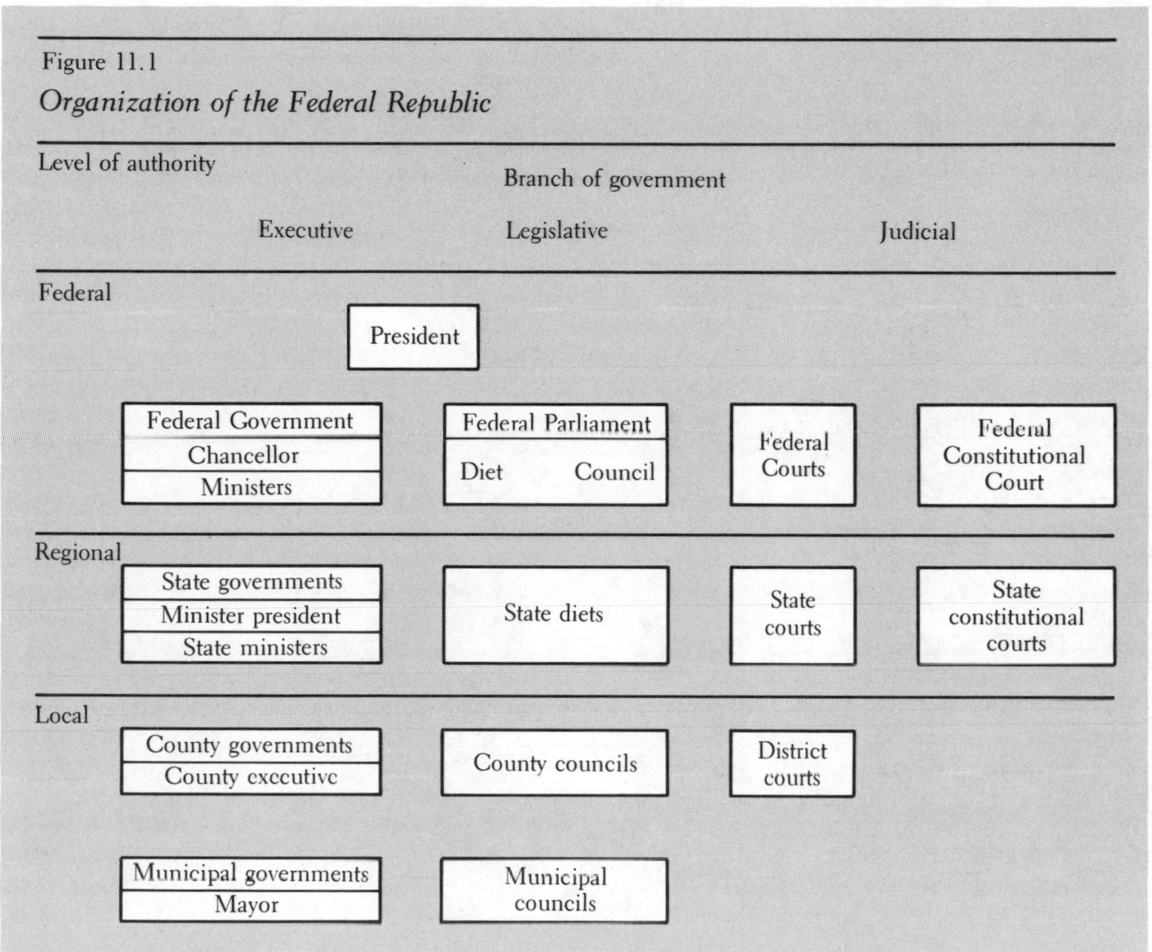

Figure 11.1
Organization of the Federal Republic

making and implementing federal policies through the Federal Council (*Bundesrat*).

In contrast to the United States Senate, the Federal Council is not directly elected and the states are not equally represented. The forty-one seats are allocated roughly on the basis of population, and vary from five for the most populous state to three for the least. The votes of each state are cast in a unit according to instruction of state governments chosen by and responsible to popularly elected state diets.

Federal officials may not bypass or overrule state authorities on matters subject to state prerogatives without the approval of a majority in the Federal Council. The federal government is required to submit all of its legislative drafts to the upper house before they go to the lower — the *Bundestag*, or Federal Diet — and most bills passed by the latter need the consent of the former. All ordinances of the federal executive must be approved by a Federal Council majority, as must executive decrees in the event of a "constitutional emergency."

The Federal President

Under the American division of power, executive authority rests in a single office, but West Germany's

Table 11.1
Area and Population of States in 1974

	Area (percent of total)	Population density (per sq. km.)	Percent of total population	Change in population size 1961–1974
Federal Republic[a]	100% (248,000 sq. km)	260	100% 60 million	+10.0%
North				
Schleswig-Holstein	6.3	159	4.3	+11.5
Hamburg	0.2	2,571	2.9	− 4.9
Bremen	0.1	1,750	1.2	+ 3.0
Lower Saxony	17.2	149	12.1	+ 9.4
Central				
North Rhine-Westphalia	13.6	496	28.7	+ 8.4
Hesse	8.5	255	9.3	+16.0
Saar	1.0	423	1.8	+ 3.3
Rhineland-Palatinate	7.9	184	6.1	+ 8.2
South				
Baden-Württemberg	14.4	248	15.4	+19.1
Bavaria	28.4	148	18.1	+14.0

[a] Not including West Berlin.

Source: Statistisches Jahrbuch für die Bundesrepublik Deutschland, 1975, pp. 49–50. Reprinted by permission of Statistisches Bundesamt, Wiesbaden.

Basic Law provides for a dual executive. The president of the republic (*Bundespräsident*) is the chief of state, but not the head of the federal government. As in most countries with a parliamentary government, the chief of state has no significant policy-making responsibilities — at least normally. He is not allowed to engage in partisan activities, he is generally bound to accept the decisions of the federal government, Parliament, and courts, and he is largely restricted to the symbolic exercise of ceremonial functions.

In contrast to the hereditary chiefs of state of parliamentary monarchies, who serve for life, the federal president holds an elective office for a fixed period. He is selected for a five-year term by the Federal Convention, composed of the deputies of the lower house of the Federal Parliament and an equal number of delegates elected by the state legislatures on the basis of proportional party representation.

The Federal Government

Executive authority is vested in the federal chancellor (*Bundeskanzler*) and his Cabinet. The chancellor is elected by a majority of the lower house of Parliament. He alone is accountable to it (hence indirectly to the voters of West Germany) for the conduct of the federal government. In this way, constitutional checks and balances call for a fusion as well as a separation of executive and legislative authority.

The intent of the framers of the Basic Law was to legitimate and restrict majority rule. West German leaders are less dependent on the constant support of a legislative majority than leaders in a pure parliamentary system, but more than an American-type presidential system. Between elections the chancellor need not resign when he loses the support of the lower house, unless its deputies elect a successor. But for all practical purposes his authority rests on the support of a majority of its members.

Once in office, a chancellor cannot be impeached, nor can he be forced to resign unless an absolute majority of the federal diet elects a successor under a unique constitutional provision requiring a "positive vote of no confidence." Should a majority refuse to give him a vote of confidence, but at the same time be unable to agree on a replacement, he may either ask the federal president to order new elections, or continue to govern up to six months if he has the support of the federal council and president. However, these rights lapse as soon as the lower chamber elects a new chancellor.

The exclusive constitutional responsibility of the chief of the federal government is formally matched by exclusive powers that give him primary authority over the formulation of governmental policies and over the activities of his associates in the federal government. Neither the president nor parliament can legally compel the chancellor to include anyone in his cabinet or to dismiss any of his ministers or advisers; the decision is officially his own. He may appoint them or remove them as he sees fit.

The federal ministers are formally not the chancellor's peers but his subordinates, and are responsible to him rather than to the Federal Parliament. They are appointed and dismissed by the president on the chancellor's recommendation; their terms of office end automatically with the death, resignation, or replacement of the chancellor, and they can neither be censured nor singled out for special vote of confidence by the legislature. The number of ministers and their specific field of responsibility is left to the chancellor's discretion by the Basic Law.

Under the constitution and the standing rules of the Federal Government, its ministers have four primary policymaking responsibilities. First, as members of the cabinet, they may participate in formulating decisions which the chancellor has the formal right to accept or reject. Second, they may individually advise the chancellor on policy matters, but he is entitled to ignore or overrule their recommendations. Third, they are charged with supervising and planning policy within their departments if they are not ministers without specific portfolios. Fourth, ministers have the formal authority to supervise the implementation of federal policies by subordinate officials, including state officials responsible for administering federal laws and deriving ministerial regulations.

The Federal Diet

The formal powers of the states and of the federal government are balanced by those bestowed on the only directly elected national body, the lower house of the Federal Parliament. The Federal Diet (*Bundestag*) is the primary legislative organ of the country and the principal organ of popular control over the federal government.

Federal deputies have an equal voice with the representatives of the states in the selection of the federal president and chief justices of the federal judiciary, and exclusive control over the selection of the chancellor. Constitutional amendments and bills concerned with shared state and federal rights require the consent of both upper and lower houses, but legislation within the jurisdiction of the federal government does not. International treaties, for instance, must only be ratified in the lower chamber. Under the Basic Law a conference committee of the two houses resolves differences on legislation requiring the consent of both. Direct or indirect approval of a majority of the members of the Diet is needed to give legitimacy to federal policy under all conditions but emergencies.

The Judiciary

Under the constitutional checks and balances, the adjudication of rules is vested in a system of independent courts. Courts are divided horizontally into a number of functional hierarchies, each one closely integrated vertically through an interlocking network of local, state, and federal courts (see Figure 11.2).

Violations of the criminal code are handled by the regular courts, while administrative courts deal with

Figure 11.2
Organization of the Courts

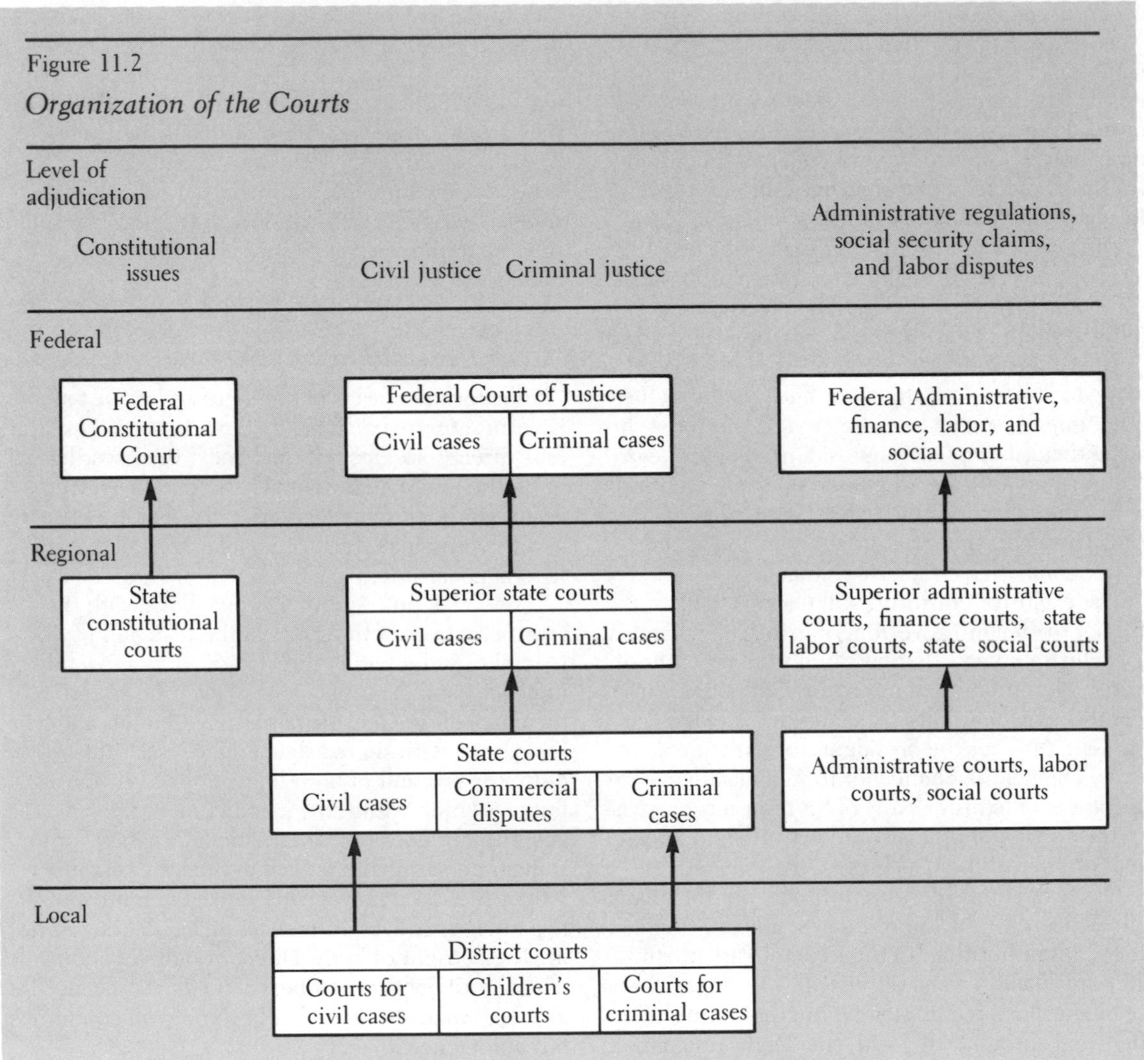

citizens' complaints against public officials. A West German may ask such a court to rule whether a policeman had the right to make a particular arrest, or whether a teacher followed correct procedures in punishing an unruly pupil. Government officials and agencies can also challenge the decisions of superior authorities in the administrative courts, on the grounds that actions violated regulations.

Other segments of the judiciary deal with special issues of public and private law that are considered by regular courts in the United States. Industrial disputes, for instance, are dealt with by the Federal Labor Courts, usually composed of an equal number of employer and employee representatives plus a professional specialist. Disputes over unemployment benefits, social security payments, and workmen's compensation claims fall under the jurisdiction of the Social Courts.

The Federal Constitutional Court is modelled after the American Supreme Court, but is not the court of final appeal on nonconstitutional issues. The sixteen judges of its two chambers are bound only by the Basic Law and may set aside the verdict of any other court — including the state constitutional courts — if they find it to conflict with the spirit or letter of the Basic Law. The court has original jurisdiction in constitutional disputes between the federal and state governments, between the federal executive and Parliament, and between different states. It may also consider complaints by individuals and organizations who assert their constitutional rights have been violated by public authorities.

Public Policy Administration

Responsibility for the implementation of national government policy is shared by central, regional, and local authorities. The state governments, however, exercise preeminent authority over the implementation of most domestic policies directly affecting average citizens. In addition to seeing to the enforcement of laws and regulations within their exclusive jurisdictions, the state ministries and their bureaucracies occupy strategic intervening positions between federal and local authorities in the application of federal legislation and ordinances (see Figure 11.3).

Whereas the administrative system is decentralized for the country as a whole, it is highly centralized within the ten states. Lines of authority run from the state governments — especially their ministries of Interior and Culture — through district administrations to local governments. In the last analysis, most laws are implemented by local officials accountable to state ministries. Whereas the federal government has relatively few local agents, the state ministries employ many (see Table 11.2). The collection of most direct taxes rests in the hands of the state governments, and most local administrative functions are strictly supervised by them.

THE POLICY ENVIRONMENT

The Domestic Setting

Unlike Britain, France, and Japan, and much like the United States, the Federal Republic has no single center of political, socioeconomic, and cultural affairs. Activity is dispersed among twenty-four metropolitan clusters, extending from the Hamburg area on the North Sea to the Munich area near the foothills of the Alps (see Figure 11.4). Bonn, the federal capital, is the seat of the central government and Parliament, and the focus of foreign relations. Other key federal agencies, such as the central bank and the top courts, however, are located in other cities. Most public administration and much domestic policy making are dispersed among the state capitals. Nongovernmental activities are also directed from centers scattered throughout the Federal Republic. For instance, the headquarters of the great industrial and commercial empires and of the principal mass media are not in Bonn but in Frankfurt, Hamburg, Munich, Cologne, and other metropolitan centers. These polycentric patterns support the division of governmental authority. At the same time, however, the relative smallness of the Federal Republic and the excellence of its communications facilitate the operation of countrywide networks of formal and informal relationships, especially among leaders in various sectors of public life.

The geographic distribution and mobility of the population lends significance to the interregional and rural-urban distinctions. By 1985, it is estimated three-fourths of the population will be urbanized and a much larger proportion than now will reside in the south. In that event, political alignments identified with urban and suburban interests and with southern regional interests may well assume increasing importance.

Generational differences in outlook and behavior are of some importance in the geography of German politics: younger Germans tend to move while older ones stay put. According to a 1972 survey, young adults without children were going to the major cities to further their educational or occupational objectives or to join a spouse. Young families with children, on the other hand, were moving from inner-city apartments to suburban homes. Older people were more firmly rooted and preferred to keep their established homes, especially in small towns and rural villages. Geographic mobility thus not only widened the gap in the relative size of the urban and rural populations, but the imbalance in their age structures as well.

In the urban centers beats the rapid pulse of an

Figure 11.3

Organization for Policy Implementation

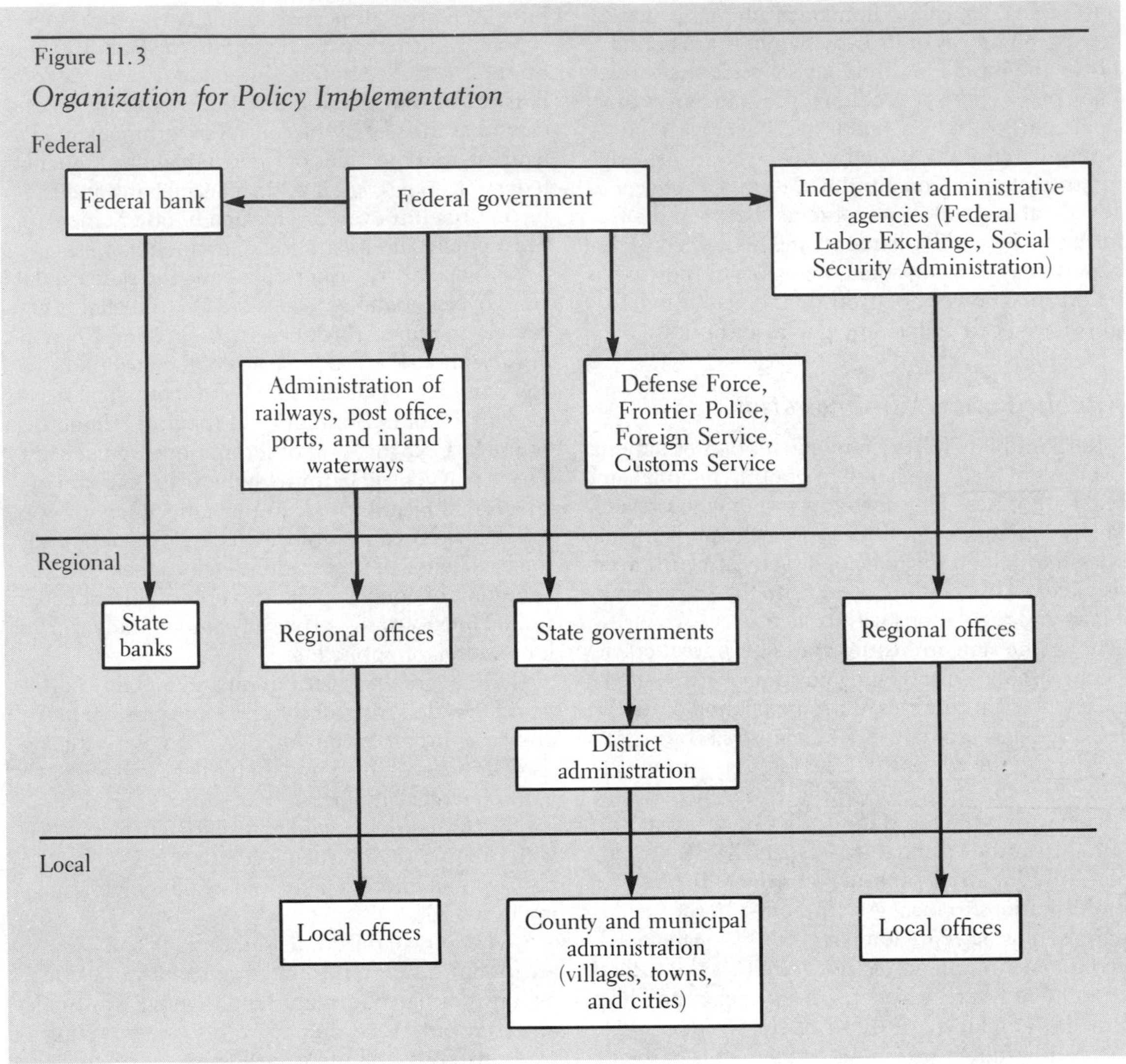

advanced industrial society. There, too, one encounters the conditions that have pushed urban affairs to the forefront in domestic politics. These issues are the fruits of the vast but poorly coordinated postwar reconstruction. To judge by the evidence of opinion polls, public concern with urban problems is on the increase. As long as city noise, congestion, pollution, and the like seemed unavoidable byproducts of a quantitative increase in homes, jobs, and private cars, people apparently felt they had to be tolerated. Of late, however, proposals for improving the quality of urban life have gained wide support.

POLITICAL ECONOMY The Federal Republic is one of the world's leading economic powers. Technological developments and changes in the pat-

Table 11.2

Public Administration Personnel in 1974

	Civil servants and judges	*Salaried employees*	*Wage earners*	*Total*
Federal[a]	3.4%	3.9%	4.4%	11.7%
State[b]	32.2	17.5	6.2	55.9
Local	5.3	16.9	10.2	32.4
Total	40.9	38.3	20.8	100.0%
N = 2,551,925				

[a] Not including about one million employed by public enterprises (federal railways and postal, telegraph, and telephone service) or members of the armed forces.

[b] Including teachers and university professors (43.1 percent of state personnel and 24.1 percent of all public administration personnel in West Germany).

Source: Statistisches Jahrbuch für die Bundesrepublik Deutschland, 1975, pp. 412–413. Reprinted by permission of Statistisches Bundesamt, Wiesbaden.

terns of production and consumption are producing shifts in its economy that are of increasing political significance. Industrial production is still the most important sector, especially the manufacture of steel and steel products, chemical goods, and electrical and technical products. The relative size of the service sectors — both public and private — has been growing rapidly, and that of the agricultural sector declining.

As in other non-Communist industrial countries, the economy is a mixed one dominated by big private and public enterprises. The private sector takes in a larger proportion of key enterprises than in Britain, France, and Italy, but a smaller one than in the United States and Japan. On the whole, the trend in West Germany has been toward a tightening of the interdependence between the public and private.

German big business has adapted to and survived a number of drastic changes in the political order — including the rise and fall of the Nazi regime — and played a major role in the process of economic reconstruction after World War II. Rapid recovery was the order of the day, and that was associated by policy makers with free-enterprise capitalism rather than government planning and state ownership of the means of production. Under Chancellor Konrad Adenauer (1949–1963), and with the active support of the United States, the government supported the growth of private business firms in the belief that the new regime had to rest on a solid material foundation. West German and foreign entrepreneurs were largely responsible for bringing unprecedented affluence to an impoverished, war-devastated country.

The fact that the present regime got its start during an explosion of individual and collective prosperity had a lasting impact on attitudes and relationships. The new political order became identified with a thriving capitalist economy that might be tempered, but not greatly tampered with; popular expectations of even more resources for mass consumption were tied to the steady expansion of production and foreign trade. Close cooperation between government agencies, big business, and trade unions was of the essence. The structural switches had been thrown and policy choices locked into courses of action that promised to keep the capitalist economic train on the track at maximum safe speed.

In this context other political issues involving economics have developed, for instance, over how to reconcile greater economic democracy with free-

Figure 11.4
The States and Major Urban Centers

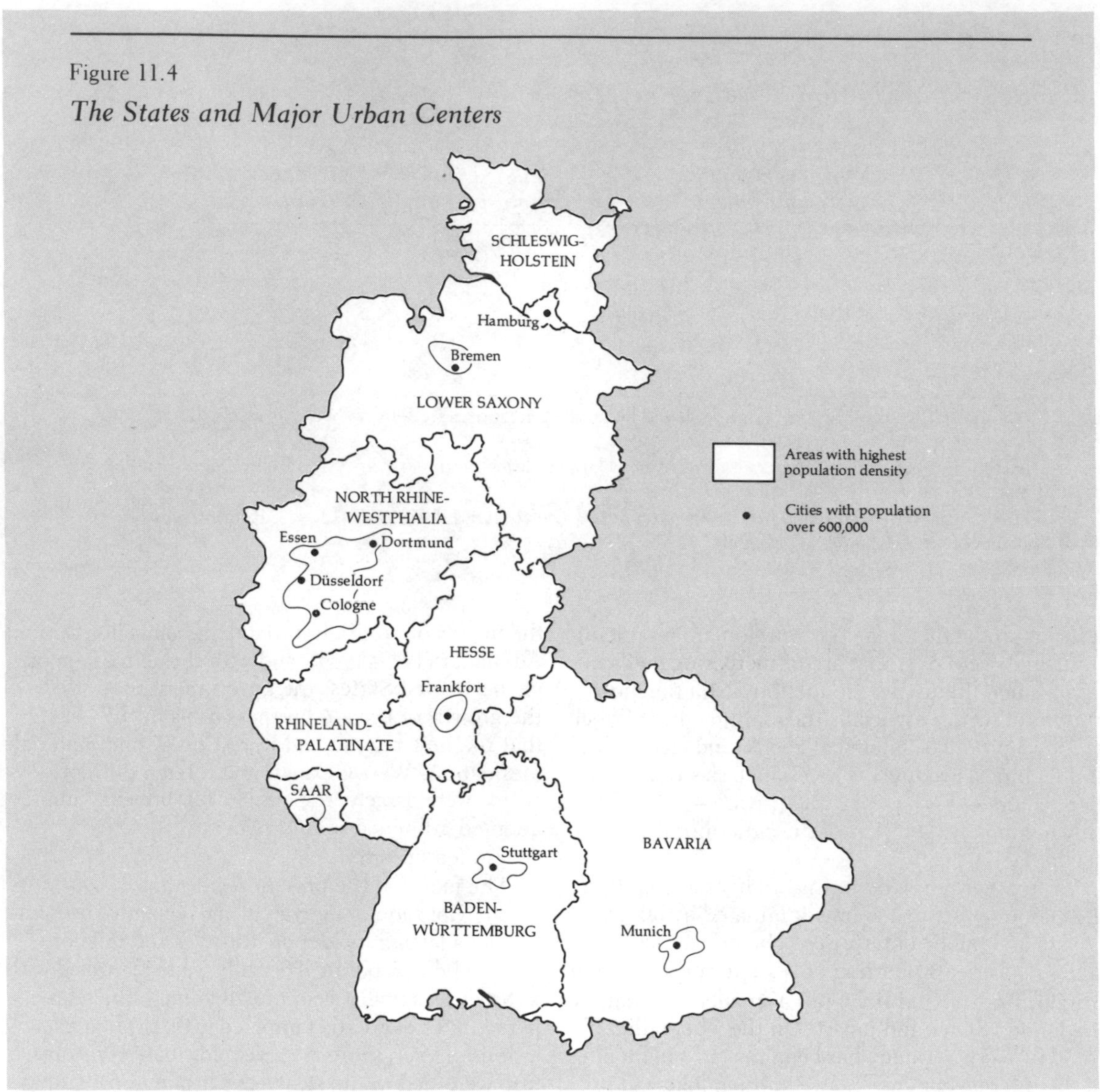

enterprise capitalism, the gains of technological advancement with its ecological and human costs, and military security considerations with the expansion of foreign trade. And in this context, too, political differences over the proper distribution of the fruits of a thriving economy have arisen among voters, parties, and interest groups, as well as policy makers.

OCCUPATIONAL AND INCOME PATTERNS

In the early years of the Federal Republic it seemed that profound changes in the political order were being accompanied by basic changes in the social order. Three decades later, it appears that while social differences are less pronounced the change has been neither as far nor as fast as seemed likely.

Fewer than half of the people work for a living, and most of the rest depend on those who do. The general characteristics of the working population are much like those in other advanced industrial countries. Two interconnected trends that accompanied the evolution of the regime are of particular political significance: a decline in family enterprises and self-employment, and a growth of employment in white-collar service occupations.

Between 1950 and 1971 the proportion of the working population engaged in agricultural production and related activities dropped from 22 percent to 8 percent. In the same period, employment in the service sector increased from 33 to 44 percent. The percentage of persons who derive their principal income from the operation of small farms has been declining, as has the proportion of self-employed businessmen and small family enterprises. Moreover, migration to the cities by young people who prefer blue-collar or white-collar jobs indicates that many remaining self-employed or family workers are older people whose children are unlikely to follow in their footsteps.

These aging "petty bourgeois" have traditionally constituted the mass of the most conservative elements in Germany. The growth of employment in private and public service occupations, especially in clerical and administrative jobs, has thus had a political impact. The younger people in these occupations, as well as industrial workers, give disproportionate support to the proponents of government-directed change in West German society.

As in the United States, personal income is derived primarily from employment, pensions, and profits. On the average, the West German people are more prosperous today than those in most other countries, and all income groups are appreciably better off than in the early years of the present regime. The trend has been toward a broad middle income stratum, rather than a polarization of rich and poor.

Averages, however, do not tell the whole story, for they obscure the persistent relative deprivation of different groups. Inequality in the distribution of wealth and income has not changed much over the last half century: a very small minority of the population has the most. To radical critics of the present order, these disparities testify to the social injustices inherent in capitalism. To its more conservative supporters, they merely reflect variations in monetary rewards for different levels of achievement in an open, competitive society.

EDUCATION The West German educational system is not just generally less egalitarian than the American, but contains a much stronger built-in bias against late bloomers and children from lower social strata. From primary school to university, educational competition and selection based on ostensibly objective criteria places even the brightest students from lower social strata at a distinct disadvantage. After four years of elementary school, students are sent to one of three types of secondary education on the basis of their past performance and apparent promise. Those judged qualified and capable are permitted to enter a university preparatory course at an academic high school, the more prestigious and more generously financed of the secondary schools. Those considered less capable at this early age — the vast majority — are dispatched to prevocational secondary schools. Some of these students go into an advanced vocational track, opening the possibility of a middle-range white-collar job. The majority, however, are relegated to the less promising track. Because of rigid divisions, it is exceedingly difficult for a child to switch from the vocational track to the academic one, once the choice has been made (see Figure 11.5).

Who makes it to the top of the educational ladder, into a university or professional school? Essentially a relatively small portion of university-age youth are able to get the education needed for the most prestigious white-collar jobs. In the late 1970s most of the students at institutions of higher learning were the children of university-educated civil servants, salaried employees, and self-employed professionals. Only one in eight came from a blue-collar family — compared to one in two in the United States, one in three in Britain, and one in five in France. This underrepresentation seems due more to the selective nature of the preparatory system than to lack of money. There are no tuition charges and in 1976 the state provided for the living expenses of four out of ten students.

THE STATUS OF WOMEN Public policy has been directed toward the complete emancipation of women from their traditionally inferior position. A

Figure 11.5
Organization of Educational System

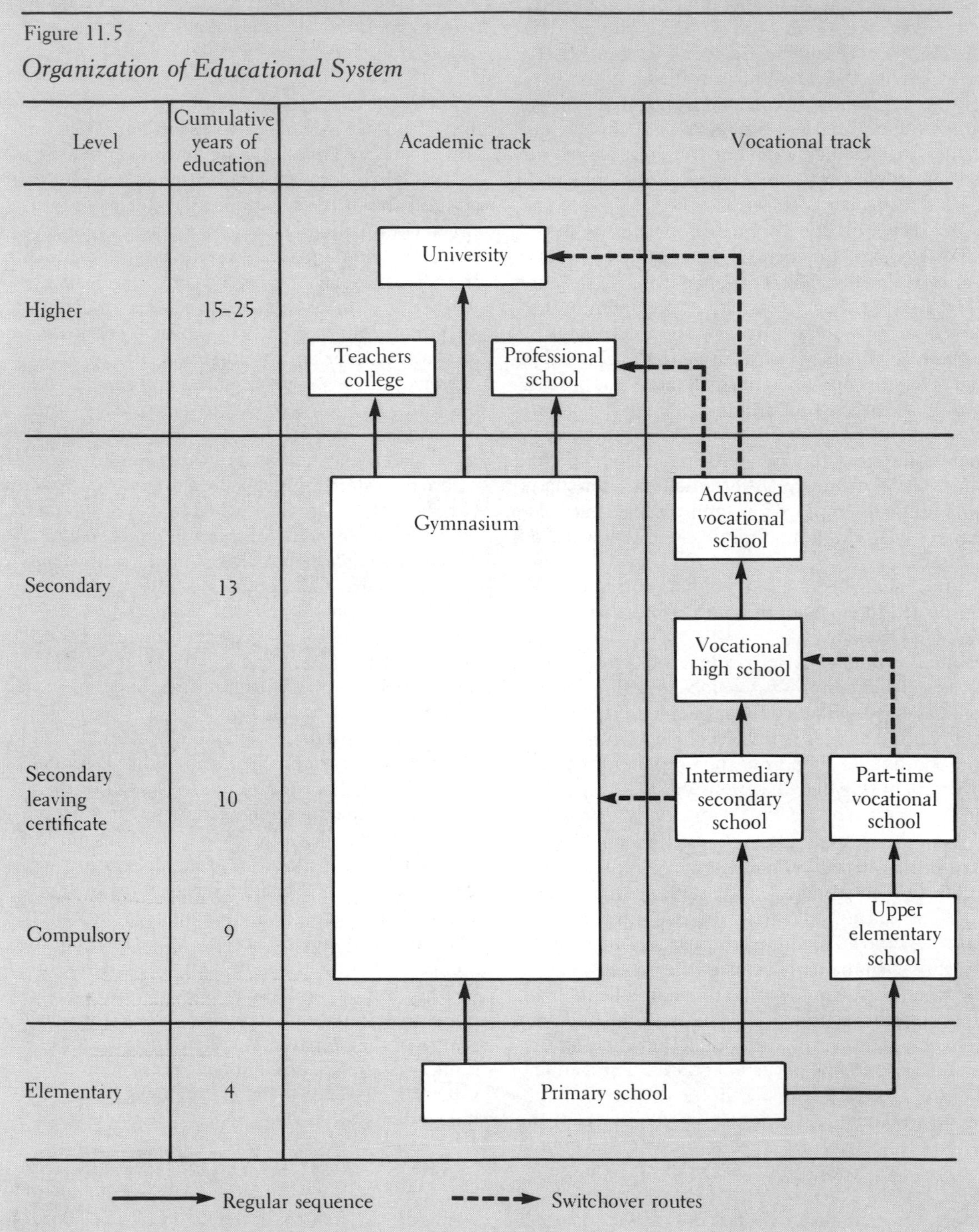

vast number of laws have sought to eradicate all sex discrimination in fact as well as in form. Old patterns of discrimination, however, are yielding slowly to governmental pressure for change. By and large West German men still take the traditional view that women belong in the home as housewives and mothers and do not need schooling for a lifelong career. To the distress of West German feminists, women tend to accept these roles with varying degrees of enthusiasm or resignation. While local women's organizations proliferated in the early 1970s, no national associations were formed, as in the United States.

THE ALIEN UNDERCLASS A controversy has, in recent times, focused on the integration into German society of 2 million foreign workers and their families. Continued growth in the 1960s required a constant supply of new labor. Demand exceeded the supply of native workers; for every person seeking a job there were on the average four to five vacancies, mostly in menial occupations shunned by West Germans. The consequence was a massive influx of foreign workers organized by public and private agencies. By the end of the 1970s, foreign workers made up more than 11 percent of the work force. In some urban areas, especially in the south, one of five workers was not German.

To a certain extent, it proved a mutually beneficial arrangement. Migrants were eager to work for West German wages, a good deal higher than what they could earn at home, and their native countries benefited from the substantial amounts of German currency these workers sent home. The tax payments of the foreign workers provided money for West German public expenditures, and their contributions to the social security system subsidized pension and welfare benefits. But most of the foreign workers and their dependents spoke little or no German, and lived in crowded guest worker ghettos. Many West Germans considered the migrants a necessary evil, economically useful, but socially undesirable. In cities with particularly large concentrations of migrants, many resented them as a growing burden on strained public services such as schools, hospitals, and transportation systems. Feelings grew worse with the economic downturn of the mid-seventies, and the government began restricting the number of workers entering and trying to induce those in Germany to go home.

The External Setting

Since the end of World War II, the two Germanies have been focal points in the shifting patterns of Soviet-American relations. Nowhere else have the two superpowers confronted each other as immediately and continuously over the last three decades, and nowhere else has there been as massive a concentration of foreign military power. The Federal Republic has become the focus of the American-dominated NATO alliance; the German Democratic Republic that of the Soviet-controlled Warsaw Pact. Both superpowers consider their defense bound up with the military security of their respective German ally.

In this context, West German policy makers have been limited in their options and restrained in their maneuverability. Their opportunities for pursuing independent action have been particularly restricted in periods of high tension in East-West relations, and relatively greater in times of lowered tension. High tension prevailed during the early years of the Federal Republic in the era of the Cold War. The failure of the United States and the Soviet Union to find a mutually acceptable solution to the German problem and the increasing friction between them elsewhere led to the rearmament of their two German clients. American demands for a German military contribution to the defense of the West overrode the objections of a substantial minority in West Germany: the Federal Republic was locked into NATO, and German reunification became, in effect, a dead issue.

The easing of East-West tensions from the mid-1960s onwards allowed a new set of West German policy makers to seek an accommodation with the Communist states of Eastern Europe. As a first step, they met Soviet demands for the Federal Republic's adherence to the Nuclear Test Ban and Nuclear Non-Proliferation treaties; compliance reaffirmed West Germany's status as a minor military power. This opened the way for a series of treaties in the early 1970s geared to the normalization of relations with the Russians and their allies. In essence, the West German leaders accepted the long contested political and territorial arrangements in Central Europe that had emerged in the wake of World War II, particularly the division of Germany and the annexation of former German territories by Russia and Poland. Public opinion turned with the tide. Opponents of the new Eastern policy were overwhelmed in the federal elections of 1972 and its proponents were strongly endorsed.

INTERNATIONAL ECONOMICS AND THE NEED FOR TRADE Another side of foreign relations has been the Federal Republic's leading position in world trade, a measure of its economic strength and its vulnerability. For while this position testifies to West Germany's key role in international commerce and finance, it also indicates the country's susceptibility to external political and economic developments that might undercut vital trade ties.

The Federal Republic ranks second only to the United States in its share of the world's exports and imports. But whereas exports represent a relatively small share of the American gross national product, they constitute about a fifth of West Germany's. Moreover, the Federal Republic — like Japan and the United Kingdom — needs to sell industrial goods in foreign markets more than does the United States. Whereas worldwide demand for agricultural products accounts for a large part of American exports, West German exports consist mostly of industrial items, which are in relatively smaller demand and larger supply.

Imports also play a far more crucial role in the West German economy than in that of the United States. The Federal Republic depends on foreign raw materials, such as copper and iron, and on foreign energy resources, notably oil, natural gas, and uranium. Like most other advanced industrial countries, it is far less self-sufficient in this regard than the United States, and is likely to become even more so over the coming decade. And interdependence comes not just from trade. The West German economy is linked to that of other nations in that a substantial portion of industry is either partly or wholly owned by American and multinational corporations.

The most extensive and intensive trade ties are those with the Federal Republic's partners in the European Economic Community. The proportion of trade with the other founding members of the Common Market increased vastly between 1962 and the present, in part because of the abolition of internal custom barriers and the introduction of a common tariff on goods from outside the member countries, in part because West Germans were cut off by the Cold War from former markets and suppliers in East Germany and Eastern Europe. These ties have reinforced the impact of the European Community policies on the West German economy and politics and have stimulated a growing German leadership role in the affairs of the European Community.

THE PROBLEM OF THE OTHER GERMANY The notion that some day, somehow, Germany might be reunified has been a constant theme in West German politics. The Basic Law calls upon "the entire German people . . . to achieve in free self-determination the unity and freedom of Germany." By all present indications, however, reunification is not even a remote possibility. It may be that time will heal all wounds, however, provided they are allowed to heal.

West German policy toward East Germany is overshadowed by factors of world and European politics militating against reunification. The 1972 Basic Treaty with the German Democratic Republic (GDR) represents a basic ingredient of West Germany's efforts to normalize relations with the Russians and the European Communist bloc. With this treaty, the government of Chancellor Willy Brandt abandoned the claim of its predecessors that the Federal Republic was the only legitimate German state and formally recognized a regime previously repudiated as an illegal instrument of Soviet control. Still denying East Germany recognition as an independent, sovereign nation, the West Germans acknowledged only the existence of a second German state within one German nation. West German policy had already emphasized closer cultural and trade associations with the GDR in intra-German rather than international relations.

East German leaders, to the contrary, maintain that theirs is a separate country whose people are first and foremost citizens of a sovereign socialist state, rather than the brethren of the Germans in the Federal Republic. Hard-line Communists in the Democratic Republic, like militant anti-Communists in the

Federal Republic, consider the very existence of the other political system a threat to their own, and believe that German reunification will only be possible if one or the other is overthrown.

The East German regime has shown its hostility to the Federal Republic in many ways. It has turned the border into an impenetrable no-man's-land, which refugees from the GDR occasionally attempt to cross at the risk of their lives. It subsidizes some of the radical groups in West Germany that are intent on the transformation of the Federal Republic into a socialist state. And it has sought to restrict the contacts of its citizens with the increasing numbers of West Germans traveling to East Germany in the 1970s.

None of these factors is insurmountable. In time, the present or a new East German leadership may become more relaxed about relations with West Germany, particularly if the relations of the Federal Republic with the Soviet Union and other East European countries continues to improve. Toward this end, West German policy makers have sought to bring the economic strength of the Federal Republic into play, and hold out the lure of trade and financial benefits to the East Germans and their Communist allies.

POLITICAL CULTURE AND POLITICAL SOCIALIZATION

Political change in West Germany has been marked by the institutionalization of the regime established in 1949. Leading and supporting political actors accept the legitimacy of the constitutional order. There is a high degree of congruence between the way the game of politics is played and the way the law says it should be played.

The Legacy of the Past

West Germans appear to have broken the ties to their autocratic past. In part this is attributable to the passage of time and the death of many who experienced the Hitler regime, be it as victims, opponents, or supporters. Much of what in the first two decades loomed as the problem of an unresolved Nazi legacy was resolved simply as years went by. In part too, divisive sentiments at home and abroad waned due to West German domestic and foreign policies designed to displace the legacy of Nazi persecution and aggression.

For most West Germans, the Hitler era and earlier history is evidently useful as a negative example on political rules, but offering few useful guidelines for specific policies. References to former conditions are usually considered of little relevance to current problems, and evocations of the past as more of a hindrance than a help in dealing with the here and now. The question that concerns citizens now, particularly young people, is not whether the present is better or worse than the past, but whether the future will be better than the present. Some less conscious attitudes, however, toward the state and its officials and perceptions of the role of the ordinary citizen indicate that although perceptual links to the past have frayed, they have not been entirely broken.

Sense of Political Community

A basic measure of the institutionalization of a state is the extent to which its citizens share a collective political identity. When the Federal Republic was carved out of the former German Reich, and for some time thereafter, most West Germans did not consider themselves members of a new political community except in a purely formal sense. West Germany was perceived as a geographic expression or an economic system, and its status as a distinct political entity was widely believed to be temporary, pending the reunification of the entire German nation. In 1959, according to a survey, relatively few West Germans held their political processes in esteem, whereas most Americans and English did. Instead they took pride in nonpolitical characteristics they associated with Germans as a whole: cleanliness, diligence, efficiency, and frugality.[1]

Now, however, it seems that political acculturation has gradually produced a greater degree of collective identification with the Federal Republic. With the integration of millions of refugees from Eastern Europe, the waning of prospects for reunification, and the absorption of new experiences,

[1] Gabriel A. Almond and Sidney Verba, *The Civic Culture* (Boston: Little, Brown, 1963), pp. 64–65, passim.

more and more West Germans have come to associate Germany with the Federal Republic, rather than the territory of the former Reich. Moreover, divergent developments in their respective political cultures have increasingly drawn West and East Germans apart. Geography and official references to intra-German ties notwithstanding, most West Germans perceive the Democratic Republic as a foreign land.

Conspicuously absent from this emerging sense of a West German political community are affective loyalties toward the Federal Republic, that is, love for the country. West Germans may root for their country in international athletic competitions, but few conceive of the Federal Republic as their fatherland in patriotic terms. It appears that neither identification with the Federal Republic nor the image of a single German nation is commonly held.

Concepts of the State

Political reconstruction in the early years of the Federal Republic, like economic reconstruction, was not so much an entirely new beginning as a reorganization and, to some extent, a restoration. The new leadership considered it necessary to provide for orderly legal procedures. The shattering of earlier authority patterns and a favorable climate of opinion promoted the institutionalization of a new *Rechtstaat*, a state governed under law rather than by rulers who considered themselves above the law. What facilitated political reconstruction was the fact that in German political culture the rule of law had been identified with legal principles that accentuated formalized authority relationships and explicit, comprehensive codes of political conduct.

The incorporation of these notions into constitutional theory and practice has greatly facilitated the acculturation of West Germans to the new aspects of the Federal Republic. For example, the liberal democratic norms of the Basic Law deemphasize state control over the citizenry and call for public policies that are the product of peacful bargaining and compromise among law-abiding members of a pluralist society. At the same time, however, the Basic Law accommodates the belief that the state is more than its parts and that its interests are broader and more enduring than those of particular parties, interest groups, or individuals. In this sense public authorities are responsible for the collective welfare of present and future citizens of the Federal Republic, and must safeguard societal harmony and stability.

Both concepts of the state have been accommodated in the political culture. West Germans have learned to see and evaluate the operation of their government in terms of the liberal democratic norms of the Basic Law. They consider the choice of policies and policy makers as largely the outcome of an interplay between a collection of elites, parties, interest groups, and voters. But West Germans still look beyond these groups to the state as the supreme guardian of law and order and ultimate judge of socioeconomic conflicts.

The state is conceived as something like a giant impersonal corporation with its managers (government), supervisory board of directors (Parliament), and administrative staff (civil service). The average citizen appears as a rather poorly informed small stockholder who may elect the directors but does not control management, who may or may not get efficient corporate services, and who gets whatever share of the profit management considers his due. Policy processes are evaluated, therefore, essentially in economic terms, with the state distributing goods and services in exchange for payments rendered — such as taxes and other citizenship duties — and some people getting more and some paying more.

PERCEPTIONS OF POLITICAL AUTHORITY

Unlike their forebearers, contemporary West Germans do not consider it their civic duty to be deferential, passive, and quiescent subjects. The days are past when German leaders could command obedience merely by virtue of their position.

But West Germans broadly trust their public officials to do what is right and proper, and accept the legitimacy of the existing patterns of political authority. Standards for evaluating the propriety and competence of rulers continue to change, and they vary a good deal among different socioeconomic strata, age groups, and political alignments. However, at no time since the regime's establishment have the dynamics of change in the political culture and of shifting subcultural cleavages led to widespread disaffection or to mass civil disobedience. Quite to the contrary, the longer the regime has been in existence, the more firmly have its organizational principles come to define legitimate authority patterns.

Policy making in the Federal Republic involves conflicts, bargaining, and compromise among leadership groups inside and outside government. The mass of the people are largely excluded from these processes. From their perspective, the political system manifests itself principally in terms of its policy outputs, specifically in what the outputs do to them and for them. Political authority is first and foremost represented by government agents who implement policy. Thus most West Germans are more inclined to place their trust in the state's executive and judicial agents than in their legislative representatives.

West Germans make a qualitative distinction between functionaries of the state and those of political parties and interest groups. The statesman and administrator enjoy high prestige by virtue of their association with legitimate public authority. The party politician and interest group spokesman, in contrast, are widely associated with behavior that at best does little to advance the public interest, and at worst injures it. Such perceptions of the wielders of public authority impose restraints on the conduct of political leaders. Elected and appointed officials seek to be known as statesmen and public servants and shun the labels of politicians and interest group representatives.

PERCEPTIONS OF THE CITIZEN'S ROLE

To most West Germans the formal rules of the political system define the roles an ordinary citizen can and should play in public affairs. In this regard traditional stress on the need for law and order in state and society has continued.

As we observed earlier, the founders of the Federal Republic formulated constitutional rules by which citizens were to play only intermittent and indirect roles in the choice of government policies and policy makers. By now, most West Germans have learned to accept the legitimacy of these roles, though many feel they should have a greater voice in public affairs. In a 1973 poll, for example, two out of three adults wanted more direct democracy than provided for by the Basic Law. Significantly, the higher the educational level of the respondent the more content they were with existing arrangements. Those most favored by present patterns of socio-economic stratification and those closest to the top of the political pyramid were also most inclined to maintain the status quo.

West Germans seem on the whole to be exceptionally interested in politics, according to various cross-national surveys — more so than Americans, English, and Italians for instance. Why this should be so, in light of their relatively limited political roles, is a puzzle. West German politics have been singularly devoid of the intense ideological conflicts and mass turmoil that are often associated with a high degree of political interest. And according to many political theories, the fact that most contemporary West Germans have received comparatively little formal education should make them less interested in politics than Americans.

One reason for the apparent gap between a large politically attentive public and a small politically active public may be the relatively extensive political content of the mass media. But there seem to be more basic reasons. Ordinary citizens may be poorly motivated to enter politics, but they generally want to be attentive to politics. German culture has traditionally valued the possession of knowledge, and over the past three decades this has increasingly come to include political knowledge. All Germans, but particularly younger people who grew up after the founding of the Federal Republic, have been told by civic educators that in former regimes mass political ignorance led to mass political impotence, and that a democratically competent citizen is a politically informed one. Closer examination of public opinion poll data indicates, however, that most West Germans are no better informed than most Americans about particular aspects of their political order, and find it no less difficult to comprehend the intricacies of policy processes.

Electoral turnout in West Germany has been exceptionally high over the years, compared to other liberal democratic regimes. Whereas in the United States only half of the eligible voters cast their ballots in national elections, West German federal elections have consistently drawn around 90 percent of the qualified electorate. On the face of it then, voting would again seem to indicate a singularly high sense of popular political involvement, independent of changing issues and candidates. But here, too, we find a gap between purely formal adherence to the

Although the Berlin Wall and the divisions that created it remain important elements of the political setting, tensions between East and West Germany have eased in recent years.

constitutional norms of democratic citizenship on the one hand and the way most West Germans perceive their role on the other. The turnout in federal elections has apparently been high not so much because West Germans believe that their votes determine policies, but because they consider voting their civic duty.

In summary, an electorate believing that voting has no decisive impact on policy has been extensively but not intensively involved in elections. The crucial factor appears to be the widely accepted legitimacy of the regime. Popular dissatisfaction with specific political leaders may produce some shifts in electoral support between two or three major parties; but usually such shifts have reflected protest votes against particular actors, rather than against the regime or the operation of the political system.

Political Socialization

Political man is primarily a child of nurture rather than nature. West Germans were, at first, simply issued new political birth certificates declaring them members of a "democratic and social" German state. In contemporary West Germany both the proponents and the critics of the prevailing political order believe that political socialization will determine whether it will endure. Who should learn what about politics, from whom and how, has been and promises to remain a major policy issue.

FAMILY AND SCHOOL Socialization begins at home, but there is very little hard evidence of the family's influence on West German political orientations. Relevant social norms that West German parents impress on their children have changed in recent times. They evidently still stress orderliness and diligence, but many now place greater emphasis on teaching children self-reliance, independence, and tolerance, and less on obedience, conformity, and devoutness. Whether this new emphasis will significantly affect on future political behavior remains to be seen.

Continuity in a family's party identification over several generations has not been nearly as common in the Federal Republic as in England and the United States. The sharp political discontinuities of the past and the relative blandness of contemporary partisanship have worked against the development of strongly rooted family loyalties to a particular party.

The primary focus of current controversies over political socialization is the educational system. When a West German child starts nursery and primary school, political socialization takes on a new dimension. The youngster passes from the exclusive, private sphere of family socialization and is exposed to new experiences shaped by public agents. Teachers are civil servants and the state educational ministries tell them what to teach. Political socialization in the West German schools is less diversified than in the United States, but more so than in countries with a more highly centralized system, such as France and Britain. Heterogeneity results from the different political complexion of the state governments, the party affiliations and policies of the educational administrators, the strength of regional traditions, and the relative power of various nongovernmental groups that endeavor to influence educational policies.

As we have noted, West German schoolchildren are segregated into separate educational programs early, largely on the basis of factors influenced by family background. Therefore, there is likely to be high congruence between their home environments and those of their peers, and continuing differentiation by class in their training for future political roles. Schooling appears in this regard to have a multiplier effect. Children from the upper strata tend to go to academic high schools, providing them with formal training for entering the uppermost occupations. Also, their interpersonal contacts are likely to be confined to teachers and students from a similar social background. Both factors interact with continuing family socialization to provide these children with social skills that enhance their opportunities for taking an active part in politics in adulthood. Children from the lower strata, on the other hand, are for the most part restricted to contact with youth from similar backgrounds inside as well as outside their vocational schools.

West German leaders consider explicit political socialization in the schools a key element of civic education. In the early years of the Federal Republic, such education for democracy was essentially indoctrination and adhered rather closely to traditional concepts of the state as the supreme source of political authority. By the late 1960s, it had become apparent to West German policy makers that this program did not provide a particularly effective training for democratic citizens. They were alarmed by an unexpected upsurge of right-wing, and especially left-wing, radicalism among the young. They also took note of an emerging youth subculture that learned more about politics from radio and television programs than from classroom instruction. Furthermore, the growing distance from the Nazi past and the waning of Cold War tensions made it no longer possible to rely heavily on anti-Nazi and anti-Communist indoctrination. Finally, studies indicated that while civic education reinforced the tendency for participation some youngsters got at home, it failed to overcome the political apathy and indifference of most.

All this led to policy changes. Civic education was made a required subject for ninth and tenth grade students in most West German states. It was redesigned to deemphasize teaching youngsters about a need for social and political harmony, and emphasize a critical examination of individual and group conflicts and their resolution. Less stress was to be placed on the description of political institutions and more on learning analytical skills that would enable adults to comprehend and cope with their political environment.

What effect these changes will have remains to be seen. Yet there are indications that socialization in adulthood is far more important than those who strive to control childhood civic education assume.

POLITICAL LEARNING IN ADULTHOOD

As West Germans near and enter adulthood, the sources of political learning proliferate and current information becomes more decisive in shaping their outlook. Insofar as the average citizen is interested in public affairs, he or she relies as a rule on information and interpretations provided by trusted sources — eminent journalists, civic leaders, professors, and high public officials.

The strategic role of the mass media in providing political information for West Germans, and consequently shaping their perceptions of and reactions to developments, is beyond dispute. For that reason, who does and who should control the media, and for what purpose and to what effect, has been a matter of considerable controversy.

There is no truly national press in the Federal Republic, in contrast to France and Britain. But in the 1970s just about every West German home had a television set and at least one radio; in fact, there were more of both per capita than in any other country except the United States. Radio and television are for most people the most frequent and trusted sources of political information. All the broadcasting networks are run by the public sector. They are organized as nonpartisan corporations under the jurisdiction of the states and are supervised by boards appointed to represent the major political parties, religious associations, and socioeconomic interest groups.

These public mass media offer their audiences rich and variegated political fare. Important debates in the Federal Diet are usually televised; opposing viewpoints on key political issues are presented in frequent panel discussions; and many programs present a critical and often highly controversial examination of particular aspects of the political system. Opinion makers who endeavor to shape political attitudes and influence preferences rely on these media to get their messages to the public.

In comparison with the public media, the socializing impact of privately owned publications appears neither as great as some observers wish, nor as powerful as others fear. There are about 500 newspapers; according to survey data, 83 percent of West Germans over sixteen read at least one daily. But the press serves more to entertain than to analyze politics, and the political content of most newspapers focuses on local and regional concerns, not national and international developments.

Journals devoted primarily to political subjects do not have a mass readership, but more than three-fourths of West German adults read one or more of the illustrated weeklies, which contain some political material. Competition between these publications is intense. Each tries to scoop the others with sensational political items to increase sales and advertising. They feature titillating revelations, interviews, and commentaries that focus on the more exciting aspects of politics such as factional fights and bribery scandals, rather than on more mundane aspects, like policy making.

Politically interested West Germans are informed more extensively through other printed media, books as well as newspapers and periodicals. But these interested people are a minority. One in ten West Germans, at most, consistently reads one or more of the few national dailies that specifically address the politically attentive and involved. These papers, and a few political weeklies and monthlies, are read by participants in public affairs and provide a forum for interelite communication over policy issues.

The Incoming Generation

Recent polls and election returns indicate certain generational differences in West German political opinions. Traditional, parochial, and law-and-order orientations are most prevalent among the oldest, those born before 1925. The middle-aged tend to be less steeped in the past and less orthodox than their seniors, but are still more conservative than their juniors. Young people born and raised in the Federal Republic are on the whole more strongly committed to the principles of the present order than their elders. Many, however, are quite critical of what they take to be its shortcomings. In their view, the Federal Republic is democratic and social more in constitutional form than in actual fact. They think far-reaching reforms and more direct democracy are needed to make the political system more egalitarian and more responsive to the needs of plain citizens.

Young West Germans are now far more individualistic than their forebearers. They show little interest in the collective ideologies of the past, such as romantic nationalism, and are inclined to be skeptical, if not cynical, about the efficacy of collective action for common goals. The young are usually more concerned with their private affairs than with what their would-be leaders call the public interest, except where the two appear to coincide.

According to a 1973 survey, young West Germans were less likely to consider their elders conservative than their age peers in other advanced industrial democracies. They were more prone to believe that family background determined a person's future station in life, but were exceptionally satisfied with the way they were governed. Notwithstanding socioeconomic and political opportunity inequalities, most young West Germans were not alienated from their political system.[2]

For that reason the supposed political restlessness and discontent of university students in the early 1970s pleased some of their elders and alarmed more. Both reactions, however, appeared in the late-1970s to rest on a rather distorted image of young West Germans in general and university students in particular. For one, the demands for drastic socioeconomic and political changes have come largely from a small, highly fractionalized minority concentrated at the universities. Secondly, the efforts of left-wing radicals to mobilize the support of people in the lower strata appear to have been rather unsuccessful.

Political Institutionalization and Change

The efforts of policy makers to achieve their objectives depend on a stable climate of supportive mass opinion, especially if other conditions are unstable. The durability of a political regime calls for organizational arrangements to be sufficiently institutionalized to provide for continuity even in the face of challenge. Secondly, durability requires enough flexibility to accommodate political change and adaptation.

[2] *Gallup Opinion Index*, Report No. 100 (October 1973), pp. 28–29.

Compared to the destabilizing divisions that prevail in many other countries, the West German regime appears to have popular support. The institutionalization of the present regime and the authority of its policy makers has been promoted by the fact that the extensive innovations introduced when it began have accommodated persistent as well as changing cultural values. The way West Germans perceive and evaluate their political system, and the degree to which they share an understanding of who is to do what and how, is colored both by a longstanding adherence to legal procedures and by the flexible norms of an advanced industrial and mass consumption society.

The institutionalization of the Federal Republic has been promoted by numerous factors. To begin with, the break with the past was not complete; traditional values were incorporated. Secondly, it was promoted by favorable environmental developments, particularly the rapid economic success and the integrative effect of strong anti-Communism during the Cold War. Thirdly, the new political arrangements came to be associated by the public with satisfactory government performance.

Though the regime's chances of survival appear to have increased, survival seems by no means assured. The ambivalence and paradoxes in contemporary political attitudes reflect unresolved contradictions and tensions in a changing political culture. More conservative policy makers believe that the necessary political authority of the state is in danger of being seriously undermined by an excessive emphasis on individual rights and by the loss of collective solidarity. In their view, the preservation of political stability and social harmony in the years ahead is threatened by the waning of traditional civic virtues. More reform-minded leaders agree with the conservatives that excessively high expectations for satisfactory performance combined with low emotional attachments to community, state, and society provide a rather weak basis for maintaining the system in the event of a major crisis. However, they take the position that this points to the need for progressive policies that will accommodate and anticipate changing norms in the political culture, harness existing demands, and stimulate more responsible citizen involvement.

PARTICIPATION AND RECRUITMENT

While the West German political system encompasses a variety of participant roles, these roles involve comparatively few actors (see Table 11.3). The premium placed on political know-how and legitimate forms of participation has enhanced the authority of those in leadership positions and inhibited the development of enduring grass-roots support for nonprofessional civic action groups, particularly when these are identified with radical opposition.

The Electorate

Three out of every four years regular local, state, and federal elections offer West Germans formal opportunities to participate in politics. But while voting gives West Germans a chance to express their preferences for policies and policy makers, it has limited impact on the actual recruitment of government leaders.

Particularly in state and federal elections, the ordinary voter has only an indirect voice in selection. Candidates are nominated through internal party processes; there are no open primaries as in the United States. In most West German elections, the voter may cast a ballot for a party slate but not for a particular candidate. In elections to the federal diet, however, he or she may vote for a constituency candidate as well as for a party. Accordingly, one half of the federal deputies owe their seats to a direct choice of most voters in single-member districts, as in the United States, England, and France. The rest owe them to having obtained a high enough position on their party's list of nominees in one of the ten states to win election to the national legislature through a complex system of proportional representation.

Another restriction on voting as an influence on policy is the so-called 5 percent clause. In all federal and most state elections, parties that fail to secure at least 5 percent of the entire vote or, alternatively, at least three constituencies get no seats. All those who voted for them thus have no voice whatever in decid-

Table 11.3

Involvement in National Politics

Political stratum	*Proportion of adult citizens (18 years and over)*	*Degree of participation and influence*
Political public		
Top-level participants (national elites)	0.001%	High
State and federal legislators	0.03	Medium high
Members of local and district councils	0.4	Medium
Functionaries of organizations in politics	0.5	Medium
Active party members	1.0	Medium
Inactive party members	4.0	Medium low
Members of organizations in politics	15.0	Medium low
Mass public		
Voters in local elections	70.0	Low
Voters in state elections	80.0	Low
Voters in federal elections	90.0	Low
Eligible voters	100.0	—

Source: Calculated from survey data, membership data, election statistics, and various studies on political participation and influence.

ing who is to govern. Finally, under the parliamentary form of government, the choice of legislative and executive leaders rests with the elected deputies, not the voters, though it usually falls on leaders of the parliamentary majority.

Voter turnout has nonetheless been very high in the Federal Republic. At least eighty percent of the eligible voters usually participate in state elections, and around 90 percent in federal elections. Various studies have indicated that this consistently high rate of participation provides two important elements for the stable operation of the political system. First, there is no sizable reservoir of electors who ordinarily do not vote but might be activated by dramatic events or leaders. Though the direction of voters' preferences may change, the high level of participation rules out any heavy impact from newly active voters. Second, present attitudes and voting patterns suggest that participation is generally not a function of either intense political engagement or socioeconomic class. People with pressing policy demands are prone to rely more heavily on other forms of interest articulation, such as using interest groups with direct access to governmental authorities.

Middle-Range Participants

Middle-range participants in local, state, and national politics link the mass public to the top policy makers, mostly through the media and formal organizations. They constitute about one-tenth of the citizenry and a good part of the well-informed and attentive political public. Such individuals may be leaders or members of radical student groups who want to change the political system; they may belong to ad hoc civic action groups, which have recently proliferated or be functionaries in the political parties. But most are only intermittently recruited into active political roles on specific issues through their occupation or organizational affiliations.

By far the largest proportion of middle-range participants are dues-paying members of associational interest groups, organized primarily for nonpolitical purposes but sporadically involved in political activities. In most instances, these are occupational associations, and middle-range participants are recruited largely from the most extensively organized occupational groups — businessmen, farmers, skilled workers, and professionals such as doctors, lawyers, and teachers. They are almost always men, preponderantly middle-aged, and, except for trade unionists, usually belong to the better educated, higher income, white-collar strata.

These political actors exert little direct influence on policy making. For the most part they represent the largely inactive reserves of the parties and interest groups; on occasion they are mobilized by leaders to lend numerical support to the groups' policy demands.

A small minority of upper middle-range participants plays more active and, sometimes, more influential roles. These subelites usually hold one or more governmental or nongovernmental positions that involve them in the articulation or aggregation of policy demands or in the recruitment of top decision makers. They may be party officials or civil servants whose tasks include such activities, but they may also be interest group functionaries, members of the clergy, or journalists who devote themselves primarily to nonpolitical matters. Essentially they play intervening roles linking leaders to followers and balancing demands from below with control from above.

This insulating pattern allows elite policy makers a large degree of autonomy in the everyday conduct of public affairs; but it also points to a source of potential weakness in the present system. Responsible and responsive leadership at the top requires sensitive communication from below that extends beneath the middle-range participants of the political public to the mass public.

Leading Participants

A few thousand elected and appointed, coopted and anointed leaders form the top layer in the hierarchy of political influence and participation. As national and subnational decision makers they not only have a great deal more specific knowledge about the operation of the political system than other citizens, but they can do a great deal more to shape popular demands and supports, as well as policy outcomes.

The members of this top stratum can be divided into two types. First, there are *manifest political leaders* occupying influential positions that involve continuous participation in policy processes. Second, there are *latent political leaders* holding positions calling for only intermittent participation, but involving considerable potential influence.

Manifest leaders belong to the policy-making stratum on the strength of holding key constitutional and paraconstitutional positions of authority. They comprise the leaders of the federal and state governments and members of the Federal Diet. They also include top civil servants; most decrees and laws promulgated by government decision makers are in fact drafted by appointed rather than elected officials, and the implementation of these rules involves interpretive decisions by leading public administrators and judges. Last, but by no means least, manifest leaders include the top functionaries of the major parties. The Basic Law makes parties paraconstitutional organizations that "participate in the formation of the political will of the people." Party officials hold strategic positions as mediators between key administrative officials on the one hand, and the political and mass publics on the other.

Latent leaders are less obviously and less constantly involved in public affairs. They include industrialists and bankers, employers and labor leaders, interest group leaders, mass media personalities, and intellectuals. Mass support, financial resources, professional expertise, or a generally recognized status of moral or intellectual authority provide them with access to and varying amounts of influence over the manifest leaders.

Elite Recruitment

While the Basic Law declares that "every German shall be equally eligible for any public office," it qualifies this right by specifying that he or she must also have the necessary "aptitude, qualifications, and professional achievements." When it comes to the selection of manifest and latent political leaders, such restrictive criteria are translated into rather exclusive standards.

In the Federal Republic, as in other countries, the structural opportunities for getting to the top favor university-educated males from the upper social strata. Also as in other countries, the structure of opportunities discriminates against young people. Even more than in the United States, and much as in England, France, and Japan, individuals must bide their time if they want to make it to the top. West German leaders usually arrive there in their late forties and early fifties and are likely to stay put for a decade or more.

The accumulation of experience has become more important as room at the top has opened up more slowly. Ambitious but relatively inexperienced young people were able to make their way to the top rather quickly during the initial years of the Federal Republic. The chances for zooming to the top now are far more limited. Relatively stable and increasingly institutionalized structures of leadership recruitment impede, if not actually block, the political ambitions of younger Germans.

In contrast to the general public, leading participants are always members of at least one and, usually several, nongovernmental organizations involved in policy making, some manifestly political and partisan and others not. They usually belong to a political party, an occupational association, and several civic organizations. In the highly organized and tightly structured West German political system, the aspiring leader with few or no specific technical skills requires the mass or elite support provided by such formal ties. His ascent and influence are measured by the size of such political capital. He may be able to do without mass support — particularly if he holds a nonelective position — but rare is the leader who makes it to the apex of the political pyramid without sponsorship from members of the organizational elites.

Elite Homogeneity and Heterogeneity

The most pronounced differences between the Federal Republic and earlier German regimes are found in the top layer of active participants. No influential group of key participants rejects the existing constitutional order as in the past. Contemporary elite relations are marked by an unprecedented degree of mutual trust and cooperation. Leadership elements formerly alienated from the prevailing political system identify with the regime.

Every major leadership group has a share in policy making today, and the norms of the elite political culture allow all key actors some influence — as long as they observe the rules of the game. Spokesmen for organized labor are no longer excluded from the ruling establishment. High civil servants and military leaders can no longer ignore or bypass the authority of elected officials but must reconcile their demands with those of elected representatives. The federal structure of the regime prevents the national government from riding roughshod over regional interests and compels it to negotiate with the state governments on most matters of domestic policy.

These more inclusive patterns of leadership participation have led various elites to place a high premium on present arrangements regulating their conflicts without involving the mass public. By law they may not, and for practical reasons they can not, ignore other key participants whose interests are likely to be affected by their policy decisions. No matter how great their mass support among the voters may be, governing elites must win the consent of other key actors involved to assure effective implementation of their policies.

Elite interaction in making policy is structured by the delegation of authority and limitations on mass participation. Legislative policy choices flow from negotiations among politicians, civil servants, and interest group functionaries. These conegotiators include not only the leaders of the governing parties but those of the major opposition parties as well. Formal decisions are normally the products of complex but stable bargaining among key participants at the local, state, and federal levels. Policy tends to be compromise solutions based on the issues involved, the alignment and strength of contending forces, and the feasible options.

This interdependence among elites is promoted by elaborate formal and informal relationships. In large part these are regulated by law. They are facilitated by interelite communications through the newspapers and periodicals of the political public, as well as by direct personal contacts. Above all, a net of organizational ties and multiple offices among and within different elite groups links government and nongovernment leaders and, through them, subordinates and clienteles.

Nationally, this organizational net centers on the manifest political leaders; apart from the legislature, it encompasses an enormous number of formal planning, coordinating, and advisory bodies of the executive. Broader groups, however, that are specialized deliberative bodies, exist in practically every area covered by public policy — for instance, committees for coordinating economic affairs periodically bring together key ministers and civil servants with leaders of the major economic interest groups.

The Coming Changing of the Guard

Some observers of contemporary West German politics believe that a conflict of generations is developing that will eventually shatter the present patterns of elite collaboration. They see a new "age cohort" of political activists coming to the fore; these activists place less emphasis on social harmony and political stability than the present leadership and are more deeply committed to divisive ideologies.

What is the basis for such a view? We noted some differences in the beliefs and values of West Germans who grew up before and after the establishment of the Federal Republic. But we also observed that such generational differences have evidently not given rise to major political cleavages between older and younger people, and have been far less pronounced than under earlier German regimes and in other countries.

What seems to hold for the youthful mass public, however, appears not as valid for younger political activists. Particularly in recent years, the politically most interested and engaged young people in the universities and the major parties — the pool for the leadership of the 1980s and 1990s — have made it clear that they are not simply going to follow in their elders' footsteps and that they have rather different ideas about the purposes and responsibilities of political leadership. While left-wing radicals have been the most vocal, young liberals and conservatives also appear unwilling to follow the conventions of the present top leaders.

The men who now rule the Federal Republic see themselves as highly pragmatic policy makers who have no use for wooly romanticism and doctrinaire ideologies. They are tough, highly skilled managers who prefer to focus their attention and energies on solving immediate rather than long-range problems. They favor modest socioeconomic and political reforms instead of major changes in domestic or foreign policy. Unavoidable adjustments to changing circumstances are to be made as gradually as possible, to avoid unsettling present patterns.

But will the elite consensus supporting the present regime outlast these leaders? The present rulers have sought to ensure the regime's continuity by grooming persons who essentially share their basic attachment to the prevailing political system. At the same time they have endeavored to block the rise of young political activists who seem to them ideologues and extremists. Whether such measures will suffice to overcome friction between members of the now dominant and the incoming generation of leaders, rather than exacerbate them, remains to be seen.

Political Participation and Political Stability

The prevailing patterns of participation seem well embedded in the West German political system. More than thirty years of elite-controlled institutionalization has yielded orderly relationships between the rulers and the ruled under a representative, liberal democracy.

As we have noted, the participation structure rests on role perceptions and assignments that leave a wide gap between the political and mass publics. If deteriorating economic conditions or other developments were to cause mass and elite outlooks to diverge more sharply than they do now, key participants identified with the present regime might find popular opinion turning against them and supporting leaders intent on its abolition or drastic transformation.

The Federal Republic has not yet experienced a severe test of its political system. If it came to that, the crucial question would be whether the unity and determination of the West German elites would be great enough to enable the existing regime to respond adequately to such a test. The rules of the game must be flexible enough to accommodate the values and interests of diverse elites and their clienteles. They must also be adaptable to dynamic conditions in domestic and international policy developments. Finally, they must be sufficiently acceptable to the incoming generation of leaders to maintain basic political agreement among present and future policy makers.

Though the prevailing recruitment and participation patterns have seemed well able to maintain political tranquility, they include a conservative bias that has excluded from the top stratum individuals and groups who significantly differ in their experiences from those now dominant. Elites essentially committed to the preservation of the status quo are not receptive to major innovations or to aspiring leaders who deviate from their own beliefs and values. In the years to come, however, the dynamics of domestic and foreign developments may confront West German policy makers with the need for decisions that would strain elite consensus. Ideological cleavages and recruitment processes that bar ambitious political activists from leading positions because they lack the proper qualifications and outlook may alienate key groups. The regime needs the support of the incoming generation to survive without fundamental structural changes.

INTEREST GROUP POLITICS

West German interest groups are more inclusive, more tightly organized, and occupy a more privileged position in policy processes than their American counterparts. Some of the most important associations date back to before the founding of the present regime and constitute elements of socioeconomic and cultural continuity in a country marked by sharp political discontinuities.

Some West German interest organizations are specifically established by law, in accordance with principles that go back to the Middle Ages, to represent certain common interests. Prime examples are the occupational "chambers," which have their roots in the corporate guilds of former times. Unlike the American chambers of commerce, these are semigovernmental organizations of public law that have jurisdiction over their members and are supposed to link key sectors of the economy to the state. Most private producers engaged in agriculture, commerce, and manufacturing, as well as members of the so-called free professions — such as self-employed physicians and lawyers — must belong to appropriate local chambers, which determine and enforce occupational standards and conduct. The leading functionaries of these chambers not only represent their members in politics, but exercise a semipublic authority over them. These multiple economic and political functions give considerable weight to policy demands put forward on behalf of the chambers.

Other groups of political relevance may be more freely organized, joined, and disbanded. These include traditional institutional groups explicitly endorsed and supported by the state, particularly the major churches, as well as a host of voluntary associations formed to promote symbolic causes and material interests.

The greatest and most extensive political influence rests with the official and unofficial spokesmen of the large national organizations. Formal and informal interelite channels permit them to exert direct pressure on leading party and government functionaries; at the same time, the major interest group elites can apply indirect pressure through influential opinion leaders and mass support.

Functional Representation

While American public officials pay attention to interest group demands if they wish, West German officials in many cases are legally bound to. As in most European countries, rules for the functional representation of many interests allow pressure groups to bypass the political parties and inject themselves directly into policy making.

Numerous laws and regulations formally sanction and encourage the long-established practice of direct contacts between organized interest associations and agencies of the state. The practical consequences of these arrangements are twofold. First, they encourage bargaining and accomodation between interest group spokesmen and key public officials. Such institutionalized practices are favored by both sides on the grounds that direct negotiations among policy specialists facilitate the orderly processing of interest group demands outside the public arena of partisan controversy.

Second, these procedures induce the rank and file of organized interest associations to depend on their representatives to obtain satisfaction for their policy demands, and compel the organizations comprising the peak associations, or major interest groups (see pages 290–293), to rely on elites who have direct access to policy makers. The formal justification for such arrangements is that they provide for the efficient and stable transmission of policy inputs from a pluralist society to the organs of the state. The intention is to prevent the inundation of federal agencies by individual and group demands and to allow specific collective interests to be aggregated and adapted before and while issues of concern are considered by executive, legislative, or judicial bodies. These formal arrangements for the representation of interests increase the power of federated groups and thus have a major effect on the structure of organized interests.

Political Representation

In electoral politics, large interest associations carry less weight today than in the early years of the Federal Republic. They can no longer persuade politicians that they can deliver their members' votes; even the largest and most active organizations have evidently been unable to induce significant numbers of voters to support their friends and punish their enemies. Moreover, laws now provide public funds for campaign expenses and sharply restrict contributions from private sources which reduces the importance of financial support from such organizations. Other means for exerting influence on political leaders have become more important to West German interest groups. On national issues the major means is effective representation by members of the federal government, the Federal Council, and the Federal Diet. In this respect traditional patterns of functional representation that bypass political parties have been complemented by the marked increase in collaborative interelite relations.

The principal organized interest groups have been particularly successful in placing their spokesmen in decision-making bodies. Key officials in federal ministries dealing with matters of concern to specific peak organizations have frequently been recruited from corresponding interest groups and returned to them after leaving office. For instance, leading members of the Ministry of Labor usually come from the trade unions and those of the Ministry of Agriculture from the farmers' organizations.

Even when the bonds are not all that close, federal ministers and their principal subordinates tend to act as the spokesmen of their interest group clients in the formulation of public policies.

Such relationships are considered to be mutually advantageous, and West German government leaders welcome and encourage them. First, they are thought to furnish public officials with expert advice and special information not available through other sources, such as information on the secret flow of foreign funds into and out of the private sector and on plans for business investments at home and abroad. Second, these contacts are believed to provide policy makers with opportunities for hearing and considering group demands and complaints put forward out of the public view by trusted colleagues. This is said to be most helpful in weighing the pros and cons of contemplated measures designed to influence the patterns of wages, prices, and profits. Finally, the representation of private interests in the executive branch is thought to be particularly useful for facilitating interelite negotiations prior to making a policy decision and for obtaining the cooperation of the affected interest groups in policy implementation.

Lobbying by associational interest groups is at least as prevalent in West Germany as in the United States. Several hundred national organizations maintain offices in Bonn for close contacts with government and party agencies. Negotiations on issues involving the major interest associations almost always reach into the top echelons of those groups and focus on direct links between corresponding elites.

West German interest group leaders concentrate their influence efforts first and foremost on the executive branch because it is the source of crucial administration regulations and most legislation. Bills introduced by the executive normally become law, whereas bills that originate in the legislature and legislative amendments opposed by the government usually do not.

In the Federal Parliament the representation of vested interests is particularly pronounced in the committees of the Diet, where most of the policy actions of the lower house take shape. This should not lead us to overestimate the impact of interest group politics in the legislature. Groups must not only contend with the tighter party control that the government normally exercises over the Diet than the American executive does over Congress, but also with constitutional limits on the policy-making powers of the Parliament. For instance, neither of its two chambers can compel the government to increase its budget. Under these conditions, interest groups tend to turn to Parliament only if they cannot get satisfaction from the executive branch.

Key Peak Organizations

ORGANIZED BUSINESS The collective interests of the business community are formally represented by employer associations organized along geographic and functional lines. Every employer of more than two or three workers is a member of local and state chambers of industry and trade, as well as of specific occupational associations, which in turn are organized into federated groups. Nationally these organizations are united in various peak associations — such as the Federal Association of German Bankers — that employ full-time staffs to look after the interests of their members. At the top of all of these groups are three peak associations whose leaders serve as the formal spokesmen for the political demands of the business community as a whole: the Diet of German Industry and Commerce, the Federation of German Employers' Associations, and the Federation of German Industry (BDI), the most important. This last encompasses thirty-nine federations representing all branches of German industry and, through them, includes 98 percent of all German industrial concerns. The leaders of these three top business associations frequently collaborate in national politics. Cooperation is facilitated by overlapping memberships in top organs and by a broad interelite consensus on the political interests of business. However, due to the heterogeneity of business interests in a pluralist society, these three associations lack the internal solidarity of smaller promotional groups. Furthermore, election returns indicate that the peak business associations do not command sufficient popular support to mobilize substantial voting power on behalf of their policy demands.

While their constituent organizations employ contacts with political and administrative elites to promote or block specific policies, the three peak associations have largely confined their joint efforts to more general objectives. They have opposed the expansion of public economic enterprises and the extension of state controls over the exchange of goods and services in the private sector. They have lobbied against anti-trust legislation and regulations designed to curb the power of big business in setting prices and allocating markets. And they have fought codetermination laws providing for employee participation in the direction of private enterprises.

Business associations, like other interest groups, use various routes of access to authoritative policy-makers. One is through the Federal Parliament. Relatively few business leaders have sought to get into the legislature, but business groups have not lacked friends there, especially among members of key economic committees and party study groups. Another, more effective, approach is for business groups to present their demands directly to the chancellor or his closest advisors and key ministers.

By no means, however, do leaders of big business organizations constitute a dominant or even homogeneous elite. Not only are countervailing domestic and foreign factors too strong to make this possible, but the contemporary business elite lacks the necessary attributes. In comparison with earlier regimes, it is more divided into various economic subgroups with different and often competing policy interests on specific issues. Secondly, the business elite is on the whole more international in outlook than formerly, and less disposed to identify its own interests with the national interests of the German state.

Finally, with the replacement of the traditional, patriarchical owner-entrepreneurs, such as the Krupps, by the executives of national and multinational corporations, a new political outlook has emerged. It rests on pragmatic calculations of costs and benefits of domestic and foreign economic policy. On the one hand, there is a far greater readiness than formerly to bargain with employee representatives without involving public authorities. On the other, there is more reliance on elected government and party leaders promoting policies to safeguard business and its interests.

ORGANIZED LABOR In comparison with their counterparts in other non-Communist and industrially advanced countries, West German labor leaders have by and large been able to depend on a high degree of rank-and-file support. The trade unions are democratically structured and their elected leaders have generally been responsive and responsible to the membership. At the same time, the trade union elite exercises a good deal of autonomy when it comes to defining and representing labor's interests on specific issues.

The preeminent peak association of organized labor is the German Confederation of Trade Unions (DGB). Its predominantly male membership takes in about one of every three employees and nine out of ten trade unionists. Practically all organized industrial workers, two-thirds of organized white-collar employees, and one half of organized civil servants belong to the DGB. The DGB is neither divided into a large number of amalgamated occupational unions, like the British Trade Union Congress, nor split into industrial and craft unions, like the American AFL-CIO. It is made up of seventeen federated national unions that are tightly organized by economic sectors, and its serves primarily as their representative in federal politics.

Extensive functional and political representation of organized labor gives its leaders many opportunities to promote their clients' interests out of the public view. In addition to their participation in numerous governmental and semigovernmental bodies, labor leaders have direct and indirect access to political leaders through the major parties. Relations between the DGB and leaders of the Social Democratic party are especially close due to a large overlap in the organizations' membership and objectives. In the mid-1970s almost half of the deputies in the Federal Diet were trade union members, and most of these belonged to the Social Democratic party. However, for labor leaders, as for other interest group elites, the primary target is not the legislative branch, but the executive, especially the Ministry of Labor.

The moderate course pursued by the trade unions since the establishment of the Federal Republic has led foreign observers and West German political leaders to give organized labor much of the credit for the exceptionally high degree of political stability. Some left-wingers inside and outside the labor movement contend that tranquility has been maintained at the expense of working-class interests and for the benefit of big business. But most union members loyally support their moderate leaders. Older trade unionists in particular are relatively con-

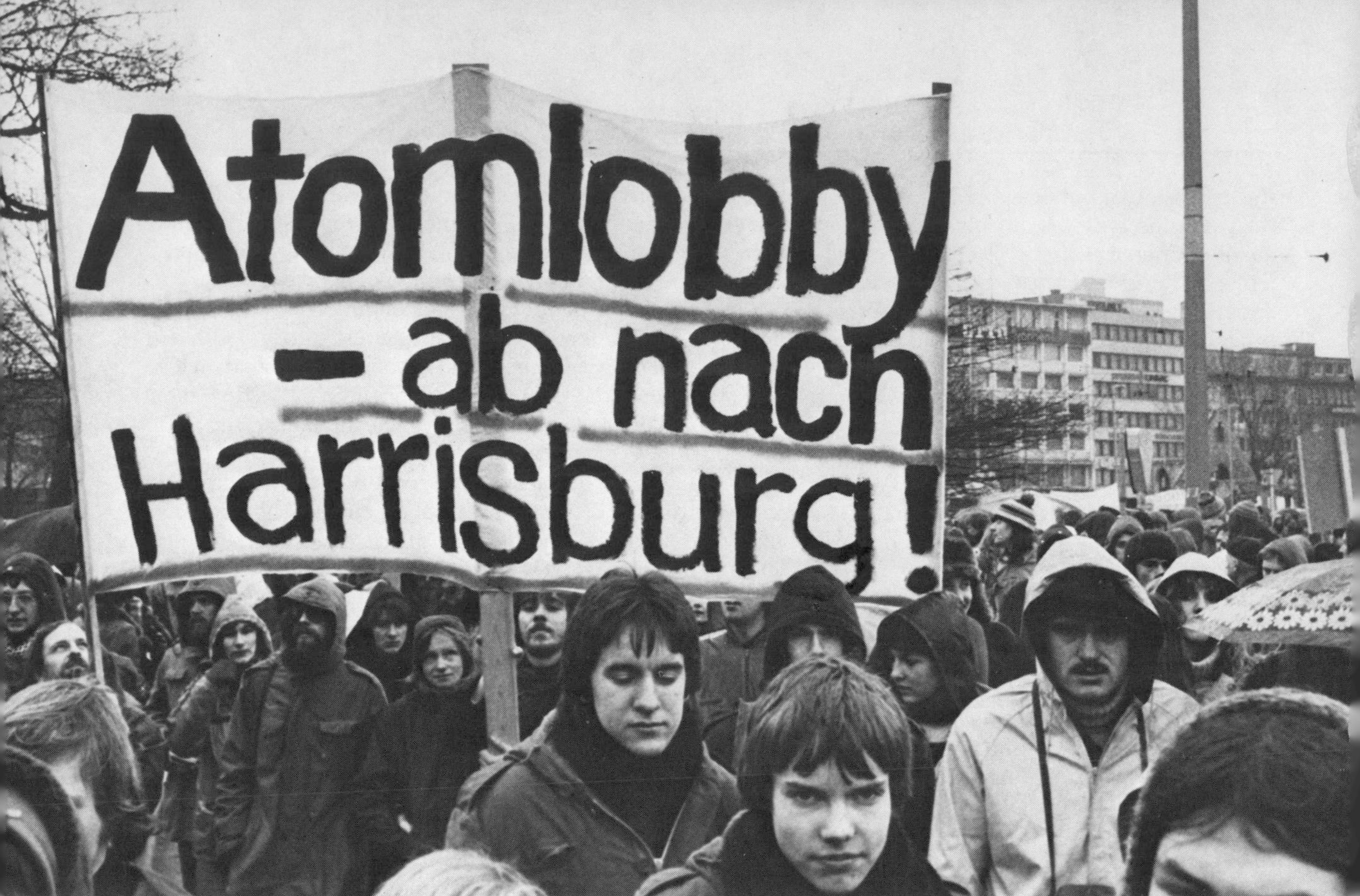

Nuclear power has become a major issue in West Germany, too; here, antinuclear protesters warn against a repetition of the dangerous accident at the American nuclear plant near Harrisburg.

servative and have little use for radicals who often share neither their background nor their outlook. Foreign workers and younger trade unionists, less content with their lot, have been more susceptible to left-wing agitation.

The labor leadership has either sought to tame the radicals or to expel them, for they represent a challenge not only to the performance of the trade union elite but to its conception of labor's role in state and society. First, labor leaders consider the unions integral components of a democratic and pluralist system of competing interest groups. Second, they believe that mass and elite differences on specific issues should not be carried to the point of disrupting a more fundamental consensus on the principles and rules of the system.

Like their American counterparts, West German labor leaders believe that the political activities of the unions should focus primarily on bread-and-butter issues and steer clear of doctrinal commitment to state ownership, income equalization, and similar socialist principles. They are more concerned with tax policies, budget allotments, and vocational training programs than in furthering class-conscious labor unity, and they prefer bargaining amicably with their business adversaries to fighting them.

Labor leaders direct extensive operations and participate in the management of both private and public enterprises. They are no less interested in keeping an essentially capitalist economy on track at maximum safe speed than their managerial counterparts. The policies advocated by union leaders may not always correspond to those favored by employer groups, but basically they are founded on the same argument as given by business in favor of sustained growth — the bigger the pie, the greater will be labor's share.

ORGANIZED AGRICULTURE West German farmers, unlike those in the United States, are represented in governmental and quasi-governmental bodies by spokesmen for complementary rather than rival agricultural groups. By law, farmers must belong to the League of Agricultural Chambers and most are also voluntary members of the League of German Farmers. These organizations collaborate closely in the so-called green front for the political promotion of agricultural interests. The agricultural lobby wielded great influence in the early Federal Republic, but its power has notably declined in recent times. Over the last 30 years the farming population has dropped from 5 million to less than 1 million, and government policies have promoted a flight from the land.

Indications are that the green front will find it a great deal more difficult than in the past to wring concessions from policy makers. Inflationary pressures have intensified the unwillingness of business and labor to absorb the cost of farm subsidies. The largely export-oriented patterns of the economy do not favor the claims of agricultural interests, since these tend to threaten the competitive prices of industry. Thus, if current trends continue, the agricultural lobby may increasingly be forced to fight a rearguard battle to save what can be saved.

RELIGIOUS ORGANIZATIONS Nine out of ten West Germans are either Protestants or Roman Catholics, in roughly equal proportions. Most of these attend religious services only infrequently, if ever. But all are required to pay a surcharge of 10 percent or more of their income taxes, which the government turns over to their respective churches — unless they opt out of the church officially, which is relatively rare. The churches also receive a good deal of tax-exempt income from extensive property holdings.

At both the federal and state levels, constitutional provisions and laws call for clerical participation in the formulation and implementation of social and cultural policies, such as representation on the boards of radio and television networks.

Three interrelated factors account for the still prominent role of religious elites in an otherwise increasingly secular society. One is the authority attributed to religious leaders on political matters touching on public faith and morals. Another is the belief of political leaders that organized religion is a major stabilizing element in West Germany.

A third and less conspicuous factor is the ties between the clerical hierarchy and high party functionaries and public officials. These interpersonal relations are facilitated by an interlocking network of religious interest groups and nonpartisan institutes affiliated with one of the major churches.

The formal representation of religious interests in public affairs provides for absolute parity between Catholics and Protestants. The leadership of organized Catholicism, however, has been by far the more active and militant in interest group politics, primarily because it has been more united in its political objectives and more determined in their pursuit. Catholicism has generally been a conservative element in West German politics. Until recently, the clerical hierarchy directed the faithful to vote for candidates embracing the church's Christian principles. The practice has not ceased altogether in Catholic strongholds, but it has become less common as governing social Democratic leaders have sought to collaborate more closely with the church hierarchy.

Interest Groups and Public Policy

In summary, organized interest groups are now less closely allied to the state than formerly, less intimately associated with political parties, and more flexible in their strategies and tactics. For the most part they are no longer identified with sharply segmented subcultures, and group differences tend to involve particular issues rather than more profound doctrinal disputes. And as the ideological camps of the past have gradually dissolved, tenuous and transitory coalitions formed over specific issues have become far more common.

A major feature of contemporary interest group politics is that they exclude most West Germans and involve primarily interelite relations at the policy-making level. The rules and operation of the regime have institutionalized mutually advantageous relationships between key interest group functionaries, party leaders, and public officials.

But though interest group elites may command extensive means for influencing public policies, they are constrained in their demands and their methods. They are limited by the formal and informal rules of legitimate interest group politics. They are constrained by cultural norms that place the interests of state and society above those of special interests and establish public officials as arbitrators of competing group demands. And there are cross-cutting mass and elite allegiances that may override identifications with nonpartisan groups and induce participants to disregard such identifications for the sake of partisan objectives or party discipline. Finally, the pluralism of competing elites involved in policy processes disperses rather than concentrates the power of organized interests.

PARTY POLITICS

A competitive party system and party government are at the heart of representative democracy in the Federal Republic. To an extent unprecedented in German history, political parties control the recruitment of elected and appointed public officials and coordinate diverse policy preferences held by members of the political and mass publics. In contrast to the situation in former times and in other countries, West German parties are by and large not the instruments of specific cultural and socioeconomic groups, but more general structues linking the state and society. As broadly based electoral organizations, they give legitimacy to constitutional principles of responsive and responsible democratic government; as narrowly constituted membership organizations, they integrate partisan activists into the political system.

The West German party system is essentially bifurcated into two major camps controlled by elites who support the regime and furnish its principal policy makers. The so-called union parties — the Christian Democratic Union (CDU) and its Bavarian affiliate, the Christian Social Union (CSU) — barely outdistanced the Social Democratic party (SPD) in the first federal election of 1949. Thereafter the CDU/CSU took a commanding lead; in 1953 it became the first party in German history to win an absolute parliamentary majority in a free national election, and in 1957 it became the first to win a majority of the popular votes. The SPD advanced more gradually in federal elections and did not score a popular plurality until 1972. The combined vote for the CDU/CSU and the SPD increased from 60 percent in 1949 to 91 percent in 1976, and their share of the seats in the Federal Diet from 67 to 92 percent (see Figure 11.6 and Figure 11.7). Of the seven minor parties in the first Bundestag, only one, the Free Democratic party (FDP), is still represented. It has survived largely as a junior coalition partner of one major party or the other because each has usually needed its support to form a parliamentary majority.

To Them That Have Shall Be Given

The Christian and Social Democratic party elites have over the years been able to expand and consolidate their position in West German politics on the basis of Article 21 of the Basic Law. This holds that political parties are essential intermediaries between the voters and their government in a democratic polity, but limits this function to parties supporting the existing regime. In effect, this modification of the principles of representative democracy has enabled the leaders of the major parties to make their organizations the primary contestants for electoral choice. It has also allowed them to impose far-reaching restrictions on alternative opportunities for political participation and the expression of policy demands.

The first advantage enjoyed by the major parties, therefore, has been legal, set forth in numerous laws, regulations, and judicial decisions. In the 1950s, for example, the Federal Constitutional Court sustained the contention of a government led by Christian Democrats that a right-wing party and an earlier version of the present Communist party should be outlawed as antidemocratic. Such rulings have served to warn political organizations opposed to the present system that they risked a similar fate if they overstepped the boundaries of legitimate opposition.

A second advantage for the major party elites is that they have far greater access to the mass media, public and private, than the leaders of other political

Figure 11.6

Popular Vote in Elections for the Federal Diet

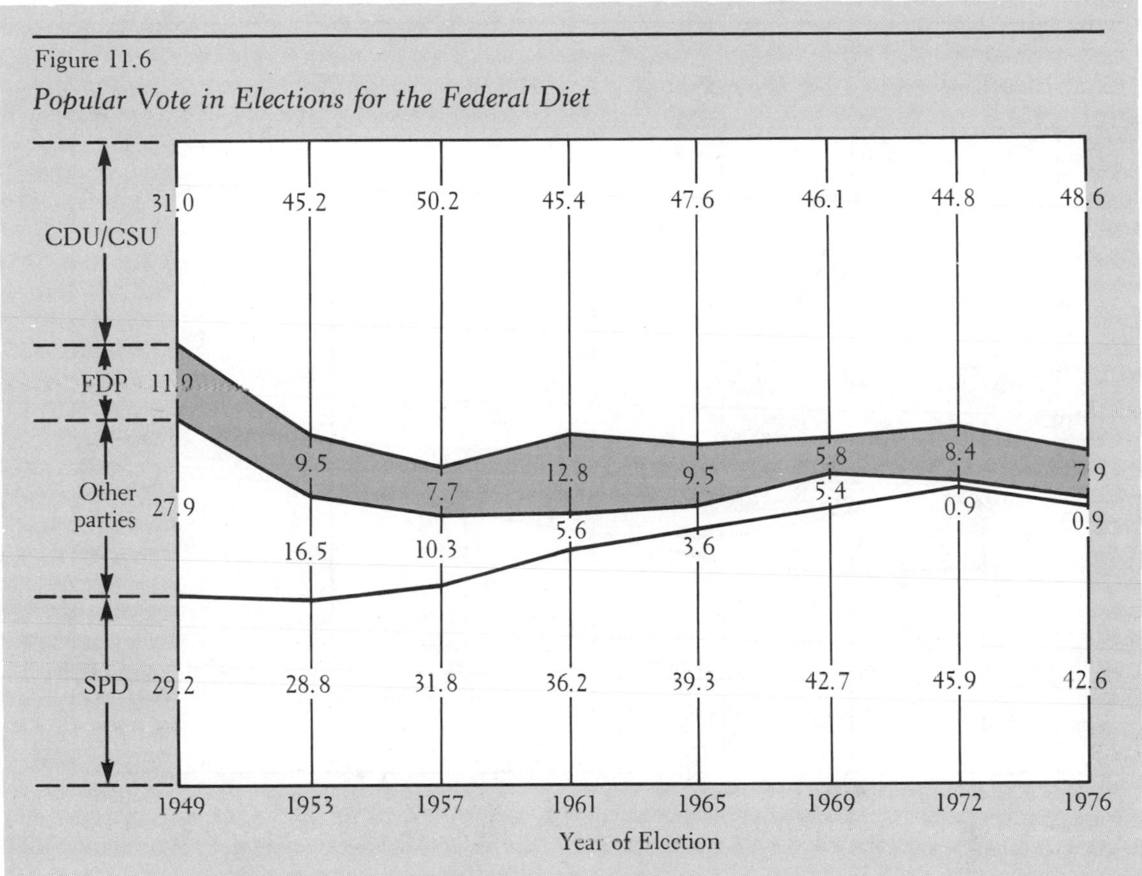

organizations. As spokesmen for the governing or major opposition parties, they make frequent appearances on television and get the lion's share of the free time allocated to the parties during election campaigns.

A third advantage is financial. All West German parties derive their income from membership dues, private contributions, and public funds. The major parties, however, get most of this money, allowing them to support organizational and promotional activities that are beyond the means of the smaller parties.

The complex regulations for the nomination and election of parliamentary deputies provide the major parties with a fourth advantage. A candidate must first be nominated in accordance with the electoral laws; this practically prevents persons who are not sponsored by a legitimate political party from entering the race, and greatly complicates the establishment of new parties. The system for federal elections then permits an individual to run as a constituency candidate, on a party-state list or both. But the constituency candidate with the most votes in a single-member district will not get its seat unless his or her party has won at least 5 percent of the national list vote, or at least two additional constituencies. And no list candidate will get a seat if his or her party fails to meet these stipulations. These rules restrain citizens from voting for parties that appear unlikely to gain the required minimal representation.

Figure 11.7

Party Representation in the Federal Diet

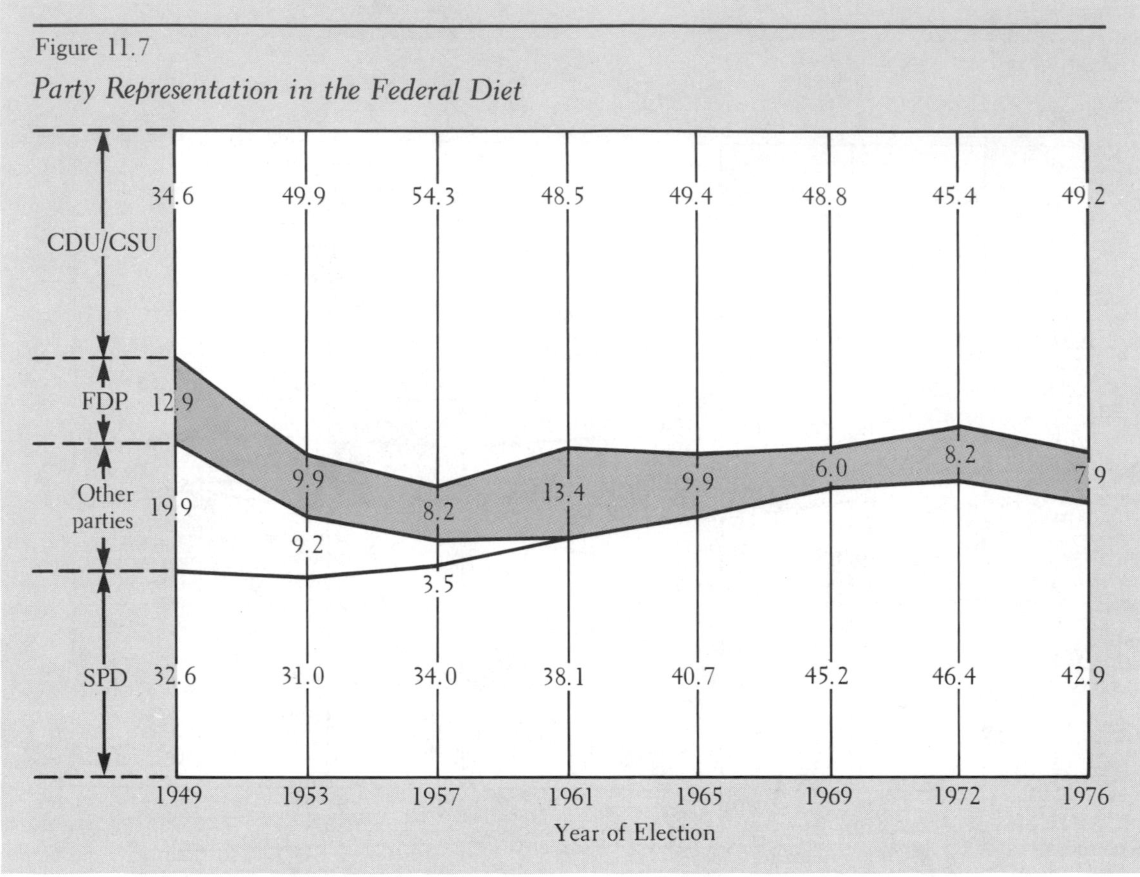

A fifth advantage enjoyed by the major parties — and more particularly by their leaders — is derived from parliamentary organization and procedures. In the Federal Diet all key legislative posts and all committee assignments are reserved for members of properly constituted parliamentary parties, and distributed by the legislative leadership in proportion to each party's strength in the chamber. A deputy will thus be excluded from the most important positions in the legislature if his party's delegation constitutes less than 5 percent of the Diet membership, the minimum size for parliamentary party status. He may also be impeded if he is out of favor with his party leadership. Such arrangements discourage interest groups from supporting minor party or independent candidates and consolidate discipline and cohesion within the existing parliamentary parties.

Parties and Voters

The rules of the political system limit the opportunities of voters to elect whom they please when they please. Except in some local elections, the voters do not pick their leaders directly. They are chosen by elected representatives. But voters also have only partial influence over the election of representatives. They can only accept or reject individuals chosen by a small number of active party members and functionaries. In summary, the electorate is induced to vote for or against the candidates of the major parties competing for the right to form a government. Voters know that ballots for minor parties are likely to be wasted.

The major competitive parties, however, have only offered voters general and limited alternatives in policies and policy makers. The CDU/CSU and the SPD are first and foremost electoral organizations for the broadest possible alignment of supporters; their appeals have accordingly been pitched to widely held preferences.

The most loyal supporters of the major parties have been middle-aged and older voters raised in a distinctive proletarian or Christian setting, and living and working in a corresponding, relatively encapsulated subculture. The SPD has been most consistently supported by skilled industrial workers in the urban areas of the northern and central parts of the country. Many come from a politically leftist home, most belong to a trade union, and their closest associates tend to be people who share their working-class background, life-style, and organizational ties. The most consistent supporters of the more conservative CDU/CSU, on the other hand, look on the SPD as a red menace. They may be devout Protestants and owners of large business enterprises; most often they are observant Roman Catholics who own shops and farms in the small towns and rural areas of the south, particularly in Bavaria.

In years past, the Christian and Social Democratic parties could count on loyal voters for most of their support. But these partisans have come to constitute an ever smaller proportion of the electorate as traditional political differences based on distinctions of sex, religion, and socioeconomic class have waned. As in other Western democracies, there has been an increasing number of independent voters. In West Germany, moreover, independents may split their ballots between the constituency candidates and electoral lists of different parties. Party competition has come to focus on winning their support.

The party preferences of floating voters are more closely linked to current issues than those of party loyalists, and thus are more sensitive to short-term changes. Their choice is largely determined by their sense of ongoing developments and their evaluation of what the different parties might do once in power. The Christian Democrats, for example, have been particularly identified with the preservation of law and order, and military security: when these are the preeminent issues for independents, they favor the CDU/CSU. The Social Democrats, on the other hand, have been more closely associated with social welfare measures and educational reforms; when these coincide with the wishes of independents, they are more likely to lean toward the SPD.

As the two major parties have moved toward balance in their electoral strengths, their strategies and tactics for winning votes without losing past supporters have assumed increasing importance. A small shift in votes may decide which party will form a government, whether it can rule alone or will need a coalition partner, and whether the party or parties dominating the Federal Diet will also control the Federal Council.

Similarities and differences in electoral strategy and tactics have been most evident in campaign programs. Phrased in general terms, these have come to resemble each other so closely that independents find it difficult to discover any significant differences.

The more indifferent people have been to such general appeals, the greater has been the inclination of particular campaigners to rely on divisive slogans and rhetoric. The danger in such tactics is that their impact might transcend campaigning and undermine the basic agreement on the form and rules of the political game. Maintenance of this consensus could prove difficult, if not impossible, if adverse socioeconomic developments should intensify interparty conflicts. Firebrands among CDU/CSU and SPD activists are willing to take that chance. Many maintain that a more sharply defined competitive party system would enhance democratic processes by providing the voters with more meaningful and therefore more effective choices. Moderate leaders want above all to preserve the consensual basis of representative government by party elites.

Rule by Party Elites

The preeminence of party elites in West German politics has become an accepted fact. The structure and dynamics of West German politics have accentuated interelite bargaining within and between the major parties. Negotiations among coalition partners and among the leaders of the government and the opposition further support this condition.

The constitutional division of powers between executive and legislative branches and between the federal and state governments provides the leaders of a strong and united opposition with considerable opportunity for influencing national policy. Thus when one of the major parties has controlled the federal executive, the other has been able to modify or block legislation with a large representation in the Federal Diet or a majority in the Federal Council, or both. Much as in the American two-party system, regional party leaders, without positions in national executive and legislative bodies, have frequently played key roles in the formulation of national policies.

At election time, the major party elites fight against each other and accentuate their differences; between elections they are impelled by their joint desire to make the system work to seek compromise solutions to partisan conflicts. This has been particularly evident in the passage of constitutional amendments to the Basic Law, which require a two-thirds majority in both houses of the Federal Parliament. But it has also applied to a good deal of bargaining over ordinary legislation.

A large number of laws passed by the federal as well as the state parliaments have been the product of informal arrangements between leaders of ostensibly opposing parties. Such conflict resolutions have been especially important when public opinion disagrees with the proposed policies of a governing party or parties. For instance, a 1965 law extending the statute of limitations on the prosecution of Nazi crimes could not have been passed without a de facto coalition between the leaders of the governing CDU/CSU and the opposition SPD.

Party Organization

Two factors are important for understanding variations in the nature of internal party affairs in the Federal Republic. The first is a party's proximity to power. The greater the real or prospective influence of leaders on public policy, the greater their influence within their party. A second factor bearing on intraparty relations is the dual character of thc major parties. On the one hand, they are, like American parties, electoral organizations for the direct or indirect recruitment of leading public officials; on the other hand, they are to a greater or lesser degree mass membership organizations, like most European parties. The greater the ratio between a party's voters and its active members, and the less closely it is identified with narrow objectives, the greater the autonomy of its leaders.

These two interdependent factors have recently had a pronounced impact on intraparty relations. The leaders of the FDP, the smallest governing party in terms of electoral support and membership, have remained the most flexible in their electoral strategy and coalition tactics. Those of the two major parties, the CDU/CSU and the SPD, have clearly been affected by a reciprocal process of imitation and adaptation.

As competing parties, the CDU/CSU and the SPD endeavor to aggregate a wide range of values, sentiments, and policy demands and seek to unite the largest possible alignment of voters. As membership parties, however, they are committed to particular ideologies and programs that may not appeal to outsiders. All the party elites have had to contend with intraparty tensions arising from conflicts between their organizations' internal and external relations and from efforts to reconcile the purposes of an ideologically diffuse electoral party with those of an ideologically cohesive membership party. On the whole they have managed to deal with such problems through compromise where necessary and party discipline where possible.

A democratic framework for intraparty relations is stipulated by public law and party statutes, and corresponds closely to the structure of the state. The regular party organizations are composed of interlocking local, regional, or state, and national components. Representative leadership at the top rests nominally on delegated authority from below, but in fact largely on oligarchic control by party elites.

As a rule, local party chapters provide the rank and file with its only opportunity to participate directly in party deliberations, since all higher party organs are representative bodies. Local party meetings, however, are usually poorly attended and dominated by a few active members. For party leaders in state and federal politics, local chapters are principally a source of grass-roots support; for the party organization they are a reservoir for unpaid campaign workers.

The regional district organizations of the SPD and state associations of the CDU/CSU are key arenas for intraparty relations. At this level the functions of the electoral party and the membership party intersect most significantly and middle-range activists play a particularly important role. This is true first because at this level intraparty alignments and the influence of interest groups enter most actively into the choice of candidates and platforms for the electoral party and into the deliberations on ideologically acceptable programs for the membership party. Second, this is the key organizational level for the conduct of the most intense campaign activities — canvassing, mass meetings, and the like. Third, at this level incumbent leaders maintain — and aspiring leaders seek to obtain — a strong power base on which to build prominent roles in state and federal politics. Members and likely members of the top party elites usually command the support of one or more large state or regional organizations.

National party conventions in West Germany are usually pretty dull affairs. The proceedings are dominated by national leaders and the leaders of the strongest state parties, and votes reflect subnational party alignments. Nonetheless these conventions serve two important functions. One is focused on the external relations of the electoral party. National conventions are usually held close to a federal or state election and are designed to draw public attention to candidates and platforms. Before a federal election, they dramatize the selection of a candidate for chancellor and demonstrate the party's solidarity behind its choice. The other function is to help integrate the membership party. They legitimate the authority of the party leadership through the election of national officers. Also, they may adopt a basic party program designed to establish policy guidelines for the membership party and its elected representatives.

Between conventions, a national executive committee and an even more select Presidium constitute the top decision-making bodies for the membership party at the federal level. Effective control over the national organizations of the major parties, however, ultimately rests with intraparty elites consisting of the top federal and state government leaders, legislative leaders, and party functionaries.

Parties and Representative Democracy

According to the majoritarian principles of the West German parliamentary system, competing parties propose candidates and the voters decide who is to make authoritative policy decisions. But as in other representative democracies, including the United States, the choice of the voters is to a considerable extent preempted by the choice of a small minority of political activists.

Almost all West German voters cast their two ballots in federal elections as a single vote for or against a party and its designated leaders. A constituency candidate's personal attractiveness to the voters is of secondary importance for his prospects of election. It matters not so much who he is as what party he is running with. Who then gets into the Federal Diet? A candidate who secures a place at the top of a state list, or is nominated in one of a party's constituency strongholds, is virtually assured a seat. Who gets to run in a safe or a marginal district, and who gets on the state lists and how close to the top, is decided by middle-range activists in the regional and state organizations, and only indirectly by the rank and file or the membership party. The national party headquarters in Bonn coordinate federal election campaigns in the states; they have, however, little or no influence on the selection of parliamentary candidates.

In short, formal arrangements and political developments have combined to make the major parties the principal structures for the elective recruitment of top West German policy makers.

POLICY MAKING

Who makes or should make public policy decisions, for what purposes, in what manner, and with what effect, are the crucial questions of West German politics. Controversies over these issues range from ideological cleavages between conservative proponents and radical critics of the prevailing regime, to procedural disputes among and within agencies of the state. They divide voters, parties, and interest groups, as well as members and would-be members of the policy-making elites.

A good many disputes are confined to the policy makers, and are waged and settled out of the public view in party councils, government agencies, and legislative committees. This is all the more likely when policy issues concern complex or sensitive matters, and when efforts to achieve compromise solutions involve relatively few decision makers. In these cases differences are only prone to surface when some or all of the participants feel that they have more to gain than to lose by calling them to the attention of the political public or the mass public.

The Context for Policy Making

Under the terms of the Basic Law, the federal executive and bicameral Parliament are responsible for translating the policy intentions of the government into rules. Administrative and judicial agencies are charged with the interpretation and application of general rules (see Figure 11.8).

A substantial part of national policy making involves more or less automatic procedures and concerns relatively mundane issues that arouse little or no public controversy. Quite a few governmental measures are routinely designed by civil servants and approved by their superiors, and if necessary by the Federal Cabinet, the chancellor, and Parliament. Much legislation turned out by the Federal Diet and the Federal Council deals with noncontroversial governmental bills passed with the support of the opposition as well as that of the ruling parties. Organized interest groups are likely to fare best under these circumstances and to find it more difficult to influence policy when they become embroiled in controversies and jurisdictional disputes.

Still, some key policy issues are divisive and not readily disposed of. In these instances, the ability of decision makers to resolve interelite conflicts and achieve a consensus becomes a crucial prerequisite for effective policy implementation.

The Executive Arena

Parliamentary government has made for greater coordination of executive and legislative policy in West Germany than in the United States, but pluralism inside the federal government has been far more pronounced. All governments have been coalitions with more or less significant factional cleavages within and between the parties. Also, the persistence of time-honored departmental prerogatives has accentuated the fragmentation of the executive branch and complicated the coordination of interrelated policy-making tasks.

Precise regulations define the responsibilities of government departments and assign to a dozen or more ministries exclusive jurisdiction over policy areas. For instance, the Ministry of Economics has the authority to deal with some aspects of foreign trade, but others come under the aegis of the Ministry of Economic Cooperation, while the preparation of the budget is the business of the Ministry of Finance.

Consequently, overlapping partisan and bureaucratic politics can delay or prevent decisive action. The partisan dimension is defined by the shifting complexion of political alignments and the degree of consensus in party governments. The bureaucratic dimension is determined by the range of policy differences among civil servants in autonomous departments. Both dimensions for potential disputes over ends and means reflect the checks and balances in the West German policy-making stratum in general and in the executive arena in particular. The management of national policy by the federal government depends on the cohesiveness of its top political officials — chancellor, ministers, and key division chiefs — and on the support of the career civil servants.

Effective policy making calls first for more or less broad agreement among the executive and legislative leaders of the ruling parties on what needs to be done and how. These understandings usually provide top government officials and their advisors with fairly general policy guidelines, allowing for flexibility. Specific policy options are formulated by the staff of appropriate ministries and submitted to the Federal Cabinet by way of intra- and interdepartmental screening processes.

Coalition politics and the departmentalization of the federal government underscore the coordinating roles of the chancellor and his chief assistants in the Chancellor's Office. At the same time, coalition poli-

Figure 11.8
Formal Federal Rule-Making Procedures

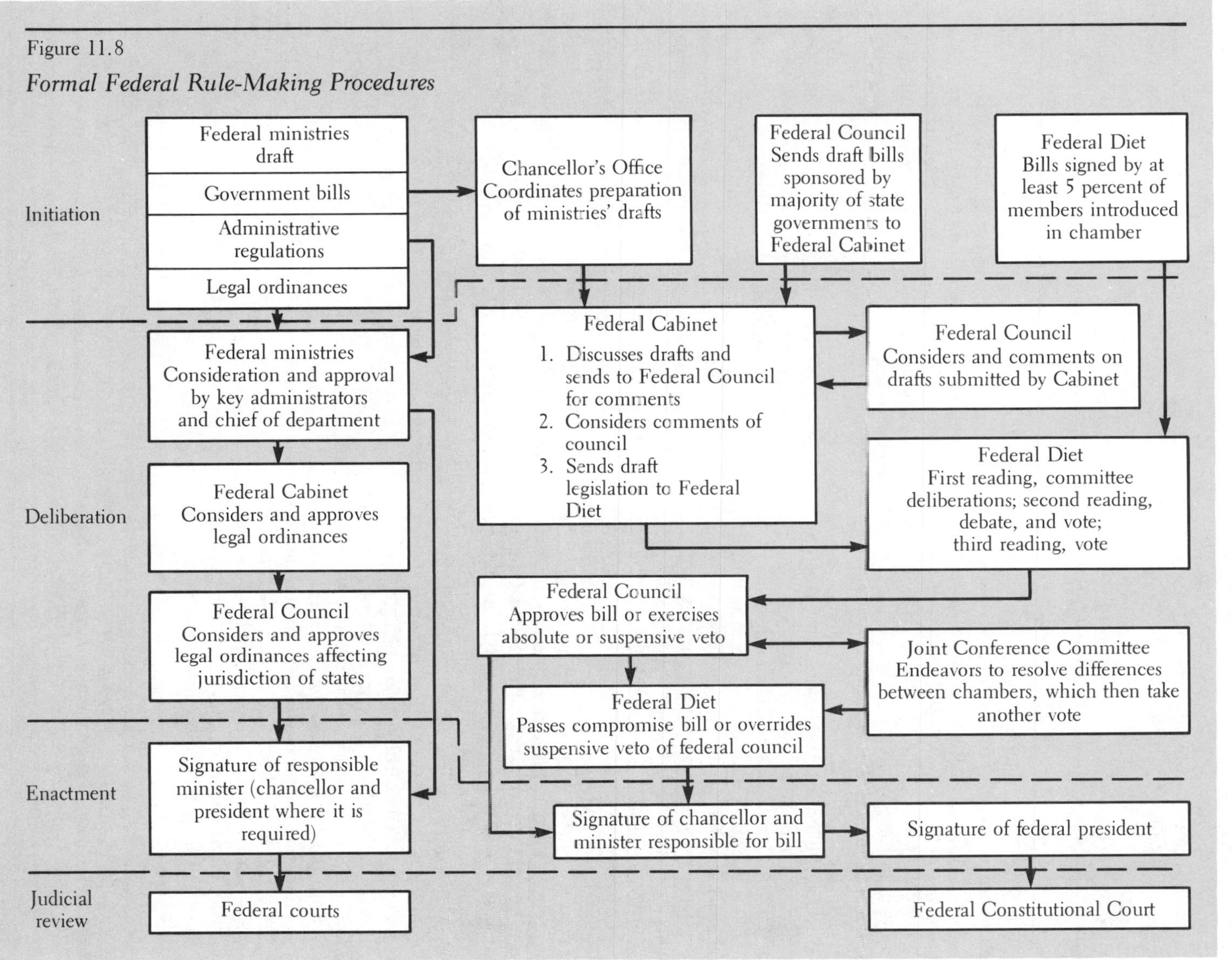

tics provide the most obvious constraints on the chancellor's control over ministers. The number and allocation of cabinet portfolios are crucial factors in the formation of governing coalitions; disputes on that score have sometimes required weeks of preliminary bargaining among party and interest group elites.[3]

Once a government is in place, the jurisdictions of its members limit the chancellor's control over policy formation. Ministers' partisan and personal interests combine with the special policy concerns of their departments to reduce the chancellor's freedom of choice and complicate the development of cohesive government policies. Ministers represent the concerns of their departments in relations with the chancellor, other government leaders, legislators, and the public. At the same time, they must pursue the common political objectives of the Federal Cabinet in relations with their subordinates and the interest group clients of their departments. By and large ministers identify themselves more with their departmental than their Cabinet functions, all the more so the longer they stay with one department.

The policies of the government have always been the products of collegial decision making, although this was less true in Adenauer's days than now. The chancellor, unlike the American president, does not have the right to disregard or overrule the Cabinet on major issues, and ministers need the approval of the chancellor and a majority of their peers for their proposals and their senior appointments. By the rules of the government, the Cabinet must approve the budget and all executive drafts of legislation and legal ordinances before they can be submitted to the Federal Parliament. It is also the ultimate authority for settling policy disputes in the executive. A minister will therefore not normally seek Cabinet approval for a policy unless he knows he can get it, and he will seek to resolve policy differences with the chancellor and other ministers before they reach the Cabinet.

Insofar as these formal provisions enable a chancellor to promote or block policy making, they tend to strengthen his authority as its chief executive; insofar as they compel him to base his own policies on a ministerial consensus, they tend to weaken it.

Policy disputes in the executive are most likely to become enmeshed in bureaucratic politics when they involve departments with competing interest group clienteles. Officials of the ministries of Agriculture and Finance may lock horns over the size of subsidy payments to farmers; those of the ministries of Economics and Labor may disagree over measures affecting wages and prices. The executive policy making system is designed to prevent such controversies or, if that is not possible, to resolve them before they reach the Cabinet. Negotiations between senior officials normally lead to compromise solutions at the subcabinet level. The Federal Cabinet has therefore been more a deliberative than a decision-making body. Perfunctory approval of a particular course of action or inaction at one of its weekly meetings usually follows from preliminary understandings among top officials of the government.

The Legislative Arena of the Federal Diet

For most West Germans, the popularly elected lower house of the Federal Parliament is the most conspicuous arena of national policy making. Its public plenary (meeting as a whole) and committee sessions are covered by the mass media, major floor debates are usually televised, and schoolchildren from all over the country are taken to watch proceedings from the visitors' gallery. But what the ordinary citizen reads, sees, and hears provides a limited and not particularly impressive picture of the policy-making functions of the Diet.

Nominally the Federal Diet has extensive constitutional powers, since all laws and treaties require its approval. In actual fact, however, the chamber wields only limited influence over policy choices.

The initiation, formulation, and enactment of legislation is generally controlled by the government and its legislative managers. Almost all bills passed by the Diet originate in the executive branch. Most deputies on both sides of the aisle confine their efforts to shape policy to focusing on specific details on

[3] See Renate Mayntz and Fritz W. Scharpf, *Policy-Making in the German Federal Bureaucracy* (New York: Elsevier, 1975), and Neville Johnson, *Government in the Federal Republic: The Executive at Work* (Oxford: Pergamon, 1973).

domestic legislation, usually on behalf of particular party or interest group concerns.

One major reason for the predominance of executive authority in the legislature is that the directly elected representatives of the people labor under the same handicap as lawmakers in other advanced industrial countries. The vast scope and complexity of policy making in a dynamic context inhibits the effective participation of deputies lacking the expertise, information, and supportive services available to executive leaders. Recent measures have somewhat improved that situation by providing the Diet and its parties with more office space and a larger staff. In this respect West German deputies are now better off than members of the British House of Commons, but still far less so than American members of Congress. Nor do they have as much power over the purse as the latter. The Diet not only has to share legislative supervisory authority with the Federal Council, it does not have the power to increase or shift allocations in the budget without the consent of the finance minister. The Diet's fiscal powers have also been restricted by the adoption of long-range development programs that commit the chamber to fixed annual expenditures in such key areas of national policy as the promotion of scientific research.

A second and related reason for executive predominance is that the constitutional authority of the Diet has been profoundly affected by the evolution of party government and party alignments. The authors of the Basic Law did not anticipate that both executive and legislative branches would be controlled by the leaders of just one or two parties. They also did not foresee that party government would penetrate deeply into the executive bureaucracy and reduce the autonomy of the direct representatives of the electorate.

While major controversies may on occasion surface in the mass media — especially at election time — policy conflicts and bargaining in the Diet are confined almost entirely to nonpublic meetings of its committees and party caucuses. Plenary meetings of the chamber are usually ritualistic public performances for the legitimation of policy decisions that have already been made.

Committee meetings take up a large part of the Diet's activities. Most deputies are unwilling to approve general laws that would give the government wide leeway in interpretation and application, and consider it their duty to submit bills to meticulous scrutiny in committee. In part this outlook is a legacy of German parliamentary tradition, which conceives of explicit legislative codification as the principal means of popular control over the executive. In part too, it is based on the deputies' belief that the input of pluralist interest demands in the Diet can be most adequately and efficiently processed through committees. Committee assignments, moreover, provide deputies with opportunities to look after the needs of their interest group clients and their local constituencies.

How much influence Diet committees have on policy making is a matter of considerable dispute. Some observers argue that the Diet "has disintegrated into a conglomerate of incoherent, highly specialized committees and working groups which are coordinated only by the leaders of the Parliamentary Parties, and whose horizons remain limited to narrowly defined areas of specialization."[4] In this view, the committees are far too dependent on guidance from the executive departments and are too bureaucratic in their working patterns. Others maintain that "an elaborate committee structure with the most influential parliamentarians of all parties as chairmen of the important committees will assure the West German parliament of a degree of substantive influence in policy processes that is not found in the classical parliamentary systems."[5] In this view, the Diet, through its committees, is closer in power to the American Congress than to legislatures in other representative democracies.

Judging by past experience, the degree of influence exercised by the committees depends on their jurisdiction and on particular circumstances. Those that deal with key areas of policy making — such as the Foreign Affairs, Defense, and Budget committees — are most closely guided by cues from the executive branch; highly specialized committees — such as the Agriculture Committee, the Committee

[4] Joachim Hirsch, "Scientific-Technical Progress and the Political System," in Klaus von Beyme (ed.), *German Political Studies*, Vol. 1 (Beverly Hills, Calif.: Sage Publications, 1974), p. 119.

[5] Mayntz and Scharpf, *Policy-Making in the German Federal Bureaucracy*, p. 36.

for Urban Affairs and Home Construction, and the Committee for Labor and Social Affairs — are more autonomous and more amenable to pressure from interest groups. Deputies who are primarily concerned with attending to constituent needs are likely to prefer a seat on the latter committees, whereas those more interested in broader issues opt for the former.

The Arena of Federalism

The governments of the ten constituent states of the Federal Republic play major roles in national policy making. This is noteworthy in light of current efforts in other advanced industrial countries, including the United States, to curb the concentration of public authority by decentralizing. The territorial dispersion of decision making is thought to extend the opportunities for democratic participation and control. It is also said to promote harmony by allowing for a more effective expression and accommodation of sectional interests than is thc case in a centralized state. And it is supposed to increase the efficiency of public administration and its responsiveness to popular needs and demands at the grass-roots level.

Observers are divided over how far these claims have been sustained in the Federal Republic, and whether they have been for better or for worse. Some laud the principles and practices of West German federalism for enhancing democratic pluralism, as well as political stability and government efficiency. Others maintain that federalist practices make it difficult for the central government to cope with pressing national problems, or that they unduly strengthen the executive authority of both federal and state leaders.

Patterns of conflict management in West German federalism are conditioned by formal rules for the integration of national and subnational institutions. The Basic Law fuses and divides the constitutional powers of federal and state authorities, and interposes state authority between federal and local government. This arrangement is reflected in the electoral system and in the organization of government bodies, political parties, and interest groups. Key agencies for countrywide policy coordination are: (1) intergovernmental committees (among state and federal agencies); (2) the Federal Council; and (3) the top echelons of the major parties and organized interest groups. Principal mechanisms for resolving policy conflicts are: (1) negotiations among officials of the federal and state governments; (2) bargaining among federal and state party leaders; and (3) adjudication by the Federal Constituitonal Court.

Beyond these formal features, we should take account of three interrelated developments. First, the effective autonomy of the states has diminished over the years as the scope of federal regulations has increased. Second, the progressive nationalization of problems has eroded the authority of the state parliaments while accentuating the role of the state governments in formulating national policy in the Federal Council and intergovernmental committees. And, third, policy disputes in the federal arena have come to focus largely on issues related to differences in the political economies of the states, as sectional religious and cultural distinctions have become less important.

The state governments are empowered to develop common policies without the participation of federal organs in two areas. One covers issues that fall under the exclusive jurisdiction of the states, principally control of broadcasting, education, law enforcement, and local administration. The other concerns the relatively few matters that remain subject to the authority of the states because federal organs have not exercised their overlapping legislative powers.

In both areas interstate negotiations resemble international negotiations between sovereign nations: No state government can be compelled by the others to follow a particular action. State officials deal with each other in regular ministerial conferences and special joint commissions. As the spokesmen for their state governments, they have similar, but not always identical interests. For example, diverse regional concerns and traditions have complicated efforts to coordinate local government operations, and sharp ideological differences between state leaders have surfaced in disputes over the contents of a standard school curriculum. Policy conflicts on such issues can only be settled by mutual agreement. Even then, there is no assurance that the settlement will be implemented in all the states. State officials may lack sufficient authority to deliver what they agreed to. In any event, the mutual understandings

Political parties are preeminent in West German politics; the most conspicuous area for their activity is the popularly elected lower house of the Federal Parliament — the Bundestag.

are usually in general terms and the more precise implementation varies a good deal from state to state.

Compromise efforts towards a greater degree of cooperative federalism have led to a proliferation of interministerial planning committees of executive officials from the federal and state governments. These bureaucratic organs develop national programs for urban and regional economic development, for scientific research and educational projects, for coordinated federal and state budgets, and for federal assistance to the states.

Since the establishment of the Federal Republic, the major parties have waged a continuous battle for a decisive majority of the state votes in the Federal Council. Because the state governments play a greater and more direct role in national policy making than in the United States, interstate party alignments are more important in West Germany. But neither governing nor opposition parties in the Diet have ever been able to count on a durable plurality, or better yet, two-thirds majority, in the upper house. Not only have parliamentary elections and changing coalitions in the states led to realignments in the Federal Council, but party affiliation does not carry as much weight there as in the Federal Diet.

Policy disputes are prone to transcend party ties when they involve issues related to differences in the states' economies. For example, the heavily industrialized states do not share the problems of states where agriculture remains important. Or take recent controversy over a national energy program. The states with an interest in using native and foreign coal have opposed those with an economic stake in using imported oil and natural gas. Above all, persistent intergovernmental conflicts over the distribution of national tax revenues among the states have involved cross-party alliances. Under the prevailing formula, the four richest states subsidize public services and economic development projects in the other six. Their governments seek to recapture as much as possible for their own use. On the other hand, the states with large populations demand a more equitable per capita distribution, while relatively small and poor states want both more than they contribute and more than they can claim on the basis of population.

The state governments, like the deputies of the Federal Diet, take most of their policy cues from the federal government. While they have the collective authority to introduce federal legislation through the Federal Council, they have seldom done so and then only on minor, uncontroversial matters. Policy conflicts in the federal arena are therefore usually prompted by actions of the national executive — either directly or by way of the Federal Diet — and the management of disputes rests principally with officials and legislative agents of the federal government. How they are dealt with in intra- and interparty bargaining in each chamber and between the two is complex. Should a bill requiring state approval be defeated in the Federal Council after passage in the lower house, a compromise solution may emerge from deliberations in the standing conference committee. Of some forty-two bills that the Federal Council vetoed between 1969 and 1976, all but two were ultimately approved in an amended form.

POLICY PERFORMANCE AND CONSEQUENCES

The vast scope of public policies in the Federal Republic means that they have wide-ranging ramifications, as one thing leads to another. Indeed, broadly conceived, their repercussions just about defy close analysis. We may attribute socioeconomic and cultural changes to particular policies, but more often than not, it is extremely difficult to establish a clear cause and effect. Frequently there is simply not enough evidence to warrant such conclusions, or the case all too easily leads to distorted or spurious findings.

A further problem is that policy performance may involve intangible sources and results. Take, for example, such elusive factors as the investment mood of the West German business community or the good will of opinion abroad. Both may influence demands on and support for policy makers, but they are not readily captured for an impact analysis.

We shall therefore confine ourselves in the following sections to discussing a relatively narrow range of direct policy outcomes. If socioeconomic matters loom particularly large, it is because they have been — and are likely to remain — in the forefront of domestic and international political issues.

Public Finance

The authority of elected officials to raise and spend money is a key policy instrument at every level of government in the Federal Republic. The allocation of the costs and benefits of public expenditures affects citizens and noncitizens, elites and nonelites, and enters into most disputes among parties and interest groups. Budgetary issues, therefore, attract a high degree of public attention and receive much exposure in the mass media.

TAXATION Who pays what in general taxes is as much as perennial issue in West German as in American politics. There, too, taxpayers resent apparent inequities in the distribution of the burdens and complain that they have to pay too much for what they receive in goods and services. And political leaders are no less sensitive to such sentiments, especially around election time. If they are out of office, they will do their best to exploit them to get in. Governing policy makers, on the other hand, are cautious about introducing tax measures likely to prove unpopular. Apart from these tactical, short-run factors, tax policies have shown a high degree of constancy since the establishment of the Federal Republic and have not been substantially affected by changes in ruling decision makers.

Personal and corporate income tax policies are designed to encourage productive private investments. They have neither sought nor produced a significant redistribution of wealth. Some attention has been directed to achieving a fair distribution of tax burdens. A good many West Germans, for example, are exempted from paying any income tax be-

Table 11.4

Changes in the Distribution of Federal, State, and Local Expenditures, 1950–1972[a]

	1950	1961	1972
Total appropriations (in billions of DM)	28.1	95.3	251.3
General government services	17.7%	23.8%	25.2%
Police and judiciary	4.0	3.9	4.1
Military	16.7	13.8	9.9
Transportation and communications	4.5	7.2	8.3
Health and social welfare	30.6	27.2	25.9
Education, research, and culture	7.4	9.5	15.8
Subsidies to economic enterprises	19.1	14.6	10.8
Total	100.0	100.0	100.0

[a] Debt payments are included.

Source: Calculated from data in *Statistisches Jahrbuch für die Bundesrepublik Deutschland* (1975), p. 398. Reprinted by permission of Statistisches Bundesamt, Wiesbaden.

cause they earn too little. In the 1970s this exemption included about a fourth of all wage and salary employees. High incomes are subject to a graduated tax, with those who earn more meant to pay proportionally more. In West Germany such direct assessments have been more progressive than in the United States and France, but less so than in Britain. In the end, however, the structure of direct taxation favors the richest and the poorest over those in between.[6]

Economic as well as political considerations have led West German lawmakers to rely more heavily on indirect consumption taxes than on direct income taxes when it comes to raising general revenues. The most widespread and lucrative is the Value Added Tax (VAT), which West Germany shares with other members of the European Community. It is a so-called turnover tax, by which a new levy is added at every stage that increases the cost of goods or services on their way tothe final customer. West German tax policies have strengthened the hand of government administrators; heavy reliance on indirect taxation has increased the flexibility of policy makers over the economic system. Relatively stable income tax patterns have made it easier to obtain political support for the most visible burdens of taxation.

SPENDING From the 1950s to the 1970s — a period of rapidly rising prosperity and relatively little inflation — the size of the West German federal budget grew more than tenfold, and that of all public expenditures (including state and local spending) increased by almost as much. Tables 11.4 and 11.5 give us some idea of where it went, and allow a comparison of federal spending patterns with those of all government levels combined.

Table 11.4 shows that the proportion allocated by federal, state, and local governments to general services was almost 10 percent more in the early 1970s than two decades earlier, though only slightly higher than one decade before. Most of that increase can be

[6] See Arnold H. Heidenheimer, Hugh Heclo, and Carolyn T. Adams, *Comparative Public Policy* (New York: St. Martin's Press, 1975), pp. 231, 241–245.

Table 11.5

Changes in the Distribution of Federal Government Expenditures, 1950–1975[a]

	1950	1961	1975
Total appropriations (in billions of DM)	11.6	39.7	155.3
General government services	9.9%	14.9%	25.4%
Police and judiciary	0.1	0.7	0.7
Military	36.7	32.6	20.5
Transportation and communication	3.3	4.2	7.2
Health and social welfare	38.4	32.0	35.6
Education, research, and culture	0.4	4.2	5.5
Subsidies to economic enterprises	11.2	9.8	5.1
Total	100.0	100.0	100.0

[a] Debt payments are included.

Source: Calculated from data derived from the following volumes of the *Statistisches Jahrbuch für die Bundesrepublik Deutschland* (1955), p. 398; (1963), p. 430; (1975), p. 399. Reprinted by permission of Statistisches Bundesamt, Wiesbaden.

attributed to more administrative services and higher personnel costs for state and federal governments. By now, one out of ten employed persons is working for a public agency or enterprise. A look at Table 11.5 shows that the proportion allocated to general government services in the federal budget more than doubled over twenty-five years. This disproportionate growth in federal expenditures is reflected in the growth of the total federal budget relative to all public expenditures. In 1950, it amounted to close to one third of total spending. By 1961, it had increased to almost one half, and by the early seventies, it was over the half-way mark.

Military expenditures — including substantial payments for allied forces stationed in the Federal Republic — have been treated as essential items by West German policy makers, no matter which parties have formed the government. However, their share in the total federal allocations has gone down with the expansion of the budget. The same has held true for subsidies to economic enterprises, particularly assistance payments to agriculture.

The budgetary consequences of a major policy change in the late sixties and early seventies show up in the substantial proportionate increases for education, research, and cultural activities. In this period government, especially state governments, put large sums into the expansion of higher education. A similar priority is evident in the increased allocations for transportation and communications. Health and welfare expenditures were especially high in the early years of social dislocation after World War II and then declined somewhat. The subsequent increase in federal expenditures in this category resulted from the expansion of national welfare programs in the late 1960s and early 1970s.

By way of comparison, general government services accounted in the mid-1970s for a larger portion of the West German national budget than in any other major Western democracy. The percentage for military expenditures was second only to that in the United States. Health and social welfare took up a larger share than in any of these countries except Japan, where it was only a bit higher. On the other hand, in comparison with those of Britain, France, and Japan, the West German government — like that of the United States — put relatively little into cash subsidies to economic enterprises. These figures reflect to some degree structural differences between these countries, but they also indicate variations in the priorities of their leaders.

By and large, however, the allocation of revenues in the Federal Republic is not that different from that in other industrially advanced Western countries. The trend is toward an expanding public service sector and increasing government expenditures for steady economic growth.

Social Welfare

Social welfare policies have generated far less political controversy in the Federal Republic than in many other countries. For one thing, there has been widespread agreement that the state should assure all citizens a decent existence; for another there have been sufficient resources to meet the demand for benefits.

As in other Western democracies, social welfare measures take in both public and private institutions. The former are usually autonomous agencies of the state run by public officials. The latter are regulated by the state and usually supported by government subsidies; the social services provided by the major religious organizations are, for example, aided by tax exemptions and tax funds.

SOCIAL INSURANCE West Germany has one of the most comprehensive social security systems in the world. The roots reach back a century to the social insurance laws of Imperial Germany that served as models for subsequent legislation in other societies. As in the United States and other countries, contributions are made through mandatory payroll deductions. In West Germany, employees are required by law to pay up to 18 percent of their income towards health, maternity, work injury, and retirement and survivors insurance.

All of the components of the social security system are designed to be self-sustaining. That is, contributions to the various funds are supposed to exceed or at least match payments and administrative expenses. Disbursements are met through transfer payments from those who pay social security taxes, rather than from general government revenues. Unearned income from sales, investments, rents, and savings are not subject to social security taxes. In effect, then, these measures place a proportionately heavier burden on lower than higher income groups. Increasing expenditures could lead to political conflicts over contributions required from the working population.

UNEMPLOYMENT COMPENSATION

Policies for the existing unemployment insurance system were established in an era of full employment, stable prices, and sustained growth in national and personal income. Far more money flowed into the insurance fund through mandatory deductions than was taken out in transfer payments. These conditions favored legislation that now provides the recipients of unemployment compensation with more generous payments than in any other major Western country.

When the Federal Republic was suddenly caught up in a worldwide recession in the mid-1970s and faced rising prices and mounting unemployment, the cash reserves of the unemployment fund were threatened. The federal government was required by law to make up shortages from general revenues, at the same time seeking to help along recovery by cutting down on nonessential expenditures. On the whole, it relied on measures designed to raise the levels of productive employment and reduce the costs of unemployment compensation. It refrained from raising income taxes and imposing wage and price controls. Mandatory employee contributions to the unemployment insurance fund, however, were substantially increased. Persistent inflation and unemployment in the future could give rise to policy disputes over new and perhaps less generous arrangements for the jobless.

OLD AGE SECURITY Not long ago, a young woman was overheard in an argument with a much older one at a political demonstration. She told her senior that she bitterly resented having to pay for the latter's old-age benefits. West German pension policies rest on the principle that old people should live out their days in comfort and dignity and share in the economic gains of the working population. Insurance benefits for the aged are now far more generous than ever before, but their costs are also greater and promise to mount with an aging population and continuing inflation.

Practically all West German adults are covered by old age insurance for themselves and their survivors. As in the United States, benefits are based on the highest achieved level of earning and not on the total of an individual's contributions to the retirement fund. Old age benefits almost doubled between 1969 and 1975.

West Germany has some 10 million pensioners — about one-sixth of its citizens — who absorb roughly one-tenth of its GNP. Moreover, pensioners can vote and constitute a significant block of about a fourth of the electorate. On all these counts, the needs and demands of the aged have carried considerable weight in West German politics, and are likely to be even more significant in the future. The increasing cost of the insurance paid for by working Germans and the increasing proportion of the older population suggest that a new social conflict along age lines may lie ahead. This would appear all the more likely if stalled or diminished growth made it more difficult to meet present pension commitments entirely through transfer payments. In that event, policy makers might have to fall back on public assistance for the elderly.

PUBLIC ASSISTANCE Public assistance, unlike social insurance, is based on need rather than right and comes out of budgetary appropriations from general tax revenues. Public assistance, again, has been far less controversial in the Federal Republic than in the United States. Most West Germans subscribe to the notion that public assistance to the needy is neither charity nor a subsidy for free loaders supported by taxpayers.

Up to now, relatively few persons have been poor enough to qualify for public assistance. They must either have no income or, as is more often the case, require a supplementary income to maintain an adequate standard of living. Of course, West Germans have found it easier to endorse public assistance since the outlays have thus far been relatively small.

All the forms of social welfare policy we have considered are highly susceptible to variations in economic conditions. The aim of these policies is to provide cushions against hardship of various sorts. They are tied to economic expansion, however, and require steady growth to maintain political stability. Under less favorable economic conditions, the popularity of programs based on transfer payments would be undermined and the demand for public assistance and its cost might go up without a commensurate growth in public revenues. A West German government would then be confronted with a choice between increasing general taxes or cutting down on non-essential expenditures. By current indications, the chances are that it would avoid raising income taxes and reduce outlays for public assistance before it would make cuts in defense appropriations, debt payments, and tax benefits for powerful groups.

Economic Concentration

Government policies in support of economic growth through private enterprise have furthered the expansion of large-scale businesses and the prominence of big business in West German public affairs. Legislation designed to stem the trend toward ever larger corporate bodies has been on the books but has not been particularly effective. Established business practices and government policies have supported the postwar trend towards concentration in all sectors of the economy.

A major portion of all West German capital and investments, for example, flows through just three private banks. A 1967 law intended to produce more competition among financial institutions failed to halt the elimination of smaller banks. In manufacturing, 1 percent of all West German industrial enterprises accounts for 40 percent of the total national product. Antitrust legislation appears not to have had much of an impact.

Government agricultural policies — in consonance with those of the European Community — have promoted the consolidation of farm holdings. Large proprietors have been the principal beneficiaries of subsidies for agricultural development. Consolidation in the private mass media has led to the rapid decline of independent newspapers and periodicals as small publications are strained by the increasing gap between their revenues and rising publishing costs. Huge supermarket and department store empires have increasingly forced small family stores out of the retail trade, in spite of legislation meant to assure the survival of the latter. The steady decline in the number of self-employed Germans reflects this trend.

Economic Democracy

West German and foreign observers have attributed much of the success of economic growth policies to exceptionally harmonious relations between employers and employees. They have singled out their country's co-determination laws as examples for other countries. The institutionalization of these measures, long pushed by the trade unions, led big labor to be more receptive to the trend toward economic concentration favored by big business.

Economic democracy through co-determination legislation rests on the general principle that West German employers and employees are basically social partners, rather than adversaries, in the production of goods and services. It is supposed to supplement collective bargaining for labor contracts and provides that both organized and unorganized workers have a say in the operation of the establishments where they work through representative participation.

One form this takes is neither new nor unusual. In every productive and service enterprise with more than five employees, including government offices, employees are entitled to elect a workers' or personnel council, to deal with management on their behalf. The council has the legal right to negotiate working conditions, and management must ordinarily obtain its consent on such matters as changes in working shifts and hours, leaves, rest periods, and paydays. However, the laws do not allow the council to block managerial decisions leading to layoffs, employee reorganization, technological innovations, mergers, and shutdowns justified by economic necessity. In effect, key decisions affecting employment and working conditions are still made by the owners or the managerial representatives, and are not subject to control by the employee council.

A far more innovative and significant form of economic democracy is worker representation on the supervisory boards of West German companies. The Co-Determination Law of 1951 provides that in the iron, steel, and coal industries, five out of eleven board members are elected by a company's employees, five by its stockholders, and that the eleventh, the board chairman, should be a neutral member chosen by the others and empowered to break tie votes. The Co-Determination Law of 1976 extended the principle of equal representation for employers and employees to the supervisory boards of all other companies with more than 2,000 employees — some 650 companies, with about one-sixth of the national labor force. However, other than in the coal, iron, and steel industries, one of the ten employee spokesmen on these boards must be a member of top management chosen by the white-collar staff from a slate nominated by senior company officers. Moreover, the board chairman, whose vote is decisive in case of a deadlock is not neutral but is representative of the shareholders. Capital and management thus retain joint control.

How far these changes will extend economic democracy is uncertain. Their impact, if any, will not be evident until the 1980s. A great deal will depend on the stakes then at issue in economic affairs in general and labor-management relations in particular. If co-determination continues to serve consensual policy making in economic enterprises, it may be adopted in other countries as an alternative to state ownership of the means of production. If it founders in industrial conflict, it may come to be viewed as an experiment that was doomed to fail in times of economic trouble.

European Integration

When the Federal Republic became a founding member of the European Economic Community (EEC) through the Treaty of Rome in 1956, some Germans feared the disappearance of the nation-state, and others were convinced the Common Market would make little difference to politics in the Federal Republic. While neither extreme outcome ensued, the scope of the EEC's policy coordinating functions expanded over the years, and West German leaders played major roles in promoting it.

The interlocking trade and monetary ties to fellow members of the European Community became major factors in the export-dependent West German industry. Common EEC taxes, customs tariffs, and economic regulations came to have a significant bearing on price and income levels in the Federal

Republic. Confirmation of the division of Germany made ties to and through the Community more important.

The bonds with the community have been forged primarily along two lines. One has been essentially technocratic and has featured specialized, interbureaucratic relations among the High Commission in Brussels and government agencies in other EEC countries. The other has been a more general international dimension, involving negotiations between government leaders of the member states.

The technocratic ties developed most rapidly during the community's great leap forward in the 1960s. In this period the High Commission, staffed by so-called Eurocrats, became its principal organ for joint policy planning and administrative coordination. A particularly important development was that the High Commission acquired the authority to maintain a common pricing system for agricultural products through subsidy payments and marketing regulations. For West Germany this had three major consequences. First, its government lost direct control over most policy decisions in this sphere. Second, the Federal Republic assumed the largest share of the financial burden for farm price supports that benefited French agriculture. Third, since West Germany depends heavily on agricultural imports, these measures for the protection of producers in the community have kept consumer prices at artificially high levels. West German leaders reluctantly acceded to French demands on this score; they considered the costs for their country steep, but necessary for continuing European economic cooperation.

In the seventies West German ties to the European Community were affected by a pronounced leveling off in the movement toward European integration. There was a less intensive forward movement along technocratic lines and more of a sideways development on the diplomatic dimension. The High Commission and its Eurocrats were not as much involved in establishing common policies as in the sixties, and the locus of joint decision making shifted to meetings of government leaders. With this, and with the inclusion of Britain, Denmark, and Ireland in the European Community policy agreements had to accommodate a wider range of diverse interests. Further political changes may follow the first election of the European Parliament by the voters and no longer the national legislatures of the member countries in 1979. The elections may enhance the influence of communitywide and sectional interest groups, but it could also prove to be no more than a symbolic gesture toward greater popular participation.

The prospects for the 1980s are uncertain. Thanks to its economic strength, the Federal Republic is likely to remain for the foreseeable future the foremost industrial, commercial, and financial power in the community. It contributes the lion's share to EC funds, not only those that go into transfer payments to French farmers, but also those that support regional development and other projects in other member countries. By all indications, West German leaders will do their best to use these resources to nudge, push, and even shove their European Community partners toward closer cooperation, especially in monetary policy.

Armament

Years of intense domestic and international controversy preceded the vote of the West German Diet in 1955 for membership in NATO and a substantial military contribution to the Western alliance against the Soviet bloc. Since then an armed West Germany has become an accepted fact in international politics, and its military establishment is viewed neither as a threat to world peace nor as a danger to the democratic order of the Federal Republic.

Extreme care was taken to assure firm civilian control over the military as a source of policy decisions and political pressure. The present Federal Defense Force bears very little resemblance to past German military establishments and appears to be well integrated into the society and polity. The political influence of the military is not only much lower than in former times in Germany, but evidently is a great deal smaller than in the United States. About half of the roughly 450,000 men in the armed forces are short-term draftees. Sharp differences that once divided the ranks no longer prevail; the proportion of workers' sons in the officer corps is now not only greater than at any time before, but larger than the proportion of working-class students in universities. Particularly younger career officers, commissioned and noncommissioned, have little use for traditional German military principles. They see themselves as public employees with specific job assignments in a defense establishment that requires hierarchy and discipline if it is to operate efficiently.

While armament has not given rise to a new military-industrial complex, one byproduct has been a relatively modest arms production and export industry. By all indications the Federal Republic has honored its treaty commitments not to manufacture or acquire weapons for atomic, biological, and chemical warfare, or any other offensive armament. It has not made use of its nuclear capability; it and Japan remain significant exceptions among major countries in this respect. Moreover, much of the military hardware for the West German army, navy, and air force has been and continues to be bought from allied countries — especially the United States — and neither economic nor political leaders have thus far expressed any desire for expanding West German arms production substantially.

In international politics West German armament may well have strengthened the external security of the Federal Republic by helping to stabilize the military standoff in Central Europe. It apparently has not become a matter of great anxiety for West Germany's communist neighbors and it has led other NATO countries to rely on a West German military contribution for their own defense.

West German troops have become the mainstay of NATO's conventional military forces in Europe and their potential fighting capability is rated rather high by Western military experts. But all German combat units are under direct NATO command and not equipped with nuclear weapons, in contrast to American, British, and French forces. Questions concerning their disposition, training, logistics, and equipment must be settled by agreement with allied leaders. And though West German officers have a voice in the Nuclear Planning Council and other NATO military organs for the defense of their country, it is by no means a dominant one among the fifteen members of the alliance. Now as before, West German policy makers depend on the protection of an American nuclear umbrella and on American leadership of NATO.

Unanticipated Consequences

The policy outcomes we have discussed so far have all been more or less consonant with the intentions of policy makers. But decision making is always something of a gamble, for policy outcomes are never entirely predictable. Let us take one example.

In the late 1960s and early 1970s the governing policy makers moved to extend university education to larger sections of the West German population. As we noted earlier, the proportion of university students and graduates in the population had been appreciably lower than in other advanced industrial countries, and opportunities for upward mobility correspondingly more limited.

Federal and state authorities introduced massive, expensive new programs for university expansion. Unanticipated developments produced unexpected results. On the one hand the release of previously pent-up demands for higher education swamped not only the universities, but also the preparatory schools. On the other, an unforeseen downturn in the country's economy reduced both government funds for higher education and the demand for university graduates in the job market. This combination of unexpected factors led West German policy makers to abandon open admissions and to introduce tighter performance criteria for entry and study in higher education.

Economic growth has been associated with numerous unanticipated problems, including urban congestion, industrial pollution, and social tensions created by the mass importation of foreign workers. At the same time, not only income and profits, but also the extensive patterns of West Germany's social welfare and development policies remain dependent on sustained growth. Given this far-reaching orientation to continued expansion, explosive charges presently concealed in the domestic and foreign environments could go off and cause unanticipated consequences in any of the policy fields just discussed.

PROBLEMS AND PROSPECTS

While we may expect political changes in West Germany in the years to come, we cannot forecast their precise nature, direction, and magnitude. What we can do is pinpoint certain interrelated policy problems likely to loom large in the coming years.

Military Security and Peace

We can expect defense problems to remain leading policy items as long as key West German decision makers consider the threat and use of force by other states a distinct possibility. Further advances in weapons technology will require increasing expenditures. It seems unlikely that the Federal Republic will acquire an independent nuclear deterrent force in the 1980s, but it may obtain more influence over those of Britain and France through tighter European integration. Even then, West Germans will probably continue to rely ultimately on American security guarantees.

These speculations assume that a combination of basic factors in the external environment of the Federal Republic will remain constant, including the Soviet-American military standoff, the predominant Soviet role in Eastern Europe and especially in East Germany, and the United States commitment to defend West Berlin and the Federal Republic.

In any event, external security will have a major effect on socioeconomic policy. West Germans have not yet had to choose between guns and butter, thanks to an almost uninterrupted expansion of national income. Whether this will continue to be the case depends not just on the scope of military security demands, but on economic developments.

Economic Security and Growth

The public in West Germany can be expected to push for steady growth as long as most citizens define the good life in terms of economic security and abundant goods and services. Perhaps such materialistic values will in time give way to more idealistic standards for the general welfare and personal self-fulfillment, but such change will come only slowly.

It is highly doubtful, however, that the circumstances that supported West German economic growth will persist. The era of spectacular expansion, ensured full employment, and rapidly rising affluence is evidently over. As in other rich, non-Communist states, rulers and ruled in the Federal Republic now confront unavoidable decisions on just how much and what sort of growth is necessary, desirable, and feasible.

These issues may contain the seeds for bitter domestic and international disputes over the mobilization and allocation of scarce resources. At home they involve such controversial questions as deciding the best trade-off between technological progress and resulting unemployment, the costs and benefits of pollution control, the use or conservation of natural resources, and the consumption or reinvestment of economic products. In foreign affairs policy makers differ on the right mix of economic competition and cooperation between industrially advanced countries and on how much and what kind of aid should be given to less developed nations.

These problems are not unique to West Germany, but a number of factors underscore their significance for politics in the Federal Republic. One is that the existing democratic order is associated by most West Germans and their leaders with a high level of prosperity. If there should be less to go around, social and political stability might give way to new and intense socioeconomic conflicts. Demands for decisive action by the political executive might increase correspondingly.

A second factor is that West Germans are not united by strong bonds of national community that transcend socioeconomic and political cleavages, as in the United States and other countries. Public officials find it harder to invoke patriotic feelings to obtain compliance with unpopular austerity measures.

A third factor is that the heavily trade-dependent West German economy is highly vulnerable to protectionist policies of other countries and to unfavorable international conditions of demand and supply. There is growing pressure from allies, but economically competing countries for far reaching concessions from West Germany. At the same time there is increasing insistence from less prosperous countries for more generous financial assistance and trade agreements. In both cases, West German policy makers risk strong internal opposition if they accede to these demands. However, future international conditions inside and outside the European Community may leave them no other choice.

Internal Security and Civil Liberties

The possibility that conflicts on these issues might seriously strain and even tear the political fabric accentuates a recently highlighted and perhaps decisive question for the future of the West German regime. The principles of the Basic Law of the Federal Republic call for as much personal freedom as possible and as much collective internal security as necessary. What balance should be struck between the two has been a sticky political issue, and may prove even more so in the future.

By some accounts there is a clear and present danger that aspiring Communist and militant socialist counterelites will abuse their civil liberties to undermine the constitutional order from below, ostensibly to achieve more participatory democracy, but in fact to create a leftist dictatorship. According to other accounts West German democracy is threatened by the gradual erosion of civil liberties through autocratic measures from above, ostensibly for the good of all, but in fact to maintain the power of the ruling few. The former view stresses the pressing need for effective internal security by public officials, the latter the urgent necessity for more adequate popular control over public officials. A major illustration of these tensions has been the sustained controversy over a 1972 decree of the federal government and all state governments barring subversives from public employment. More recently the terrorist acts of small anarchist groups led public authorities to curb some civil liberties. Such restrictions might become more extensive if outright opposition to the present regime increases substantially.

As matters stand now, however, West Germans do not appear very close to losing their liberties to either a capitalist or a socialist police state. They may be more attached to law and order and less to maximum freedom for all citizens than people in countries with older libertarian traditions, but the warning examples of Nazi and East German autocracy, and pronounced individualism, have made West Germans, particularly young West Germans, all the more resistant to the notion that personal freedom and privacy must be limited to ensure internal security.

KEY TERMS

Weimar Republic
Basic Law (Grundgesetz)
Federal Diet (Bundestag)
foreign workers ("guest workers")
German Democratic Republic (DDR)
economic democracy (codetermination)
Führer
Federal Council (Bundesrat)
Federal Chancellor (Bundeskanzler)
Eastern Policy (Ostpolitik)
coalition policies

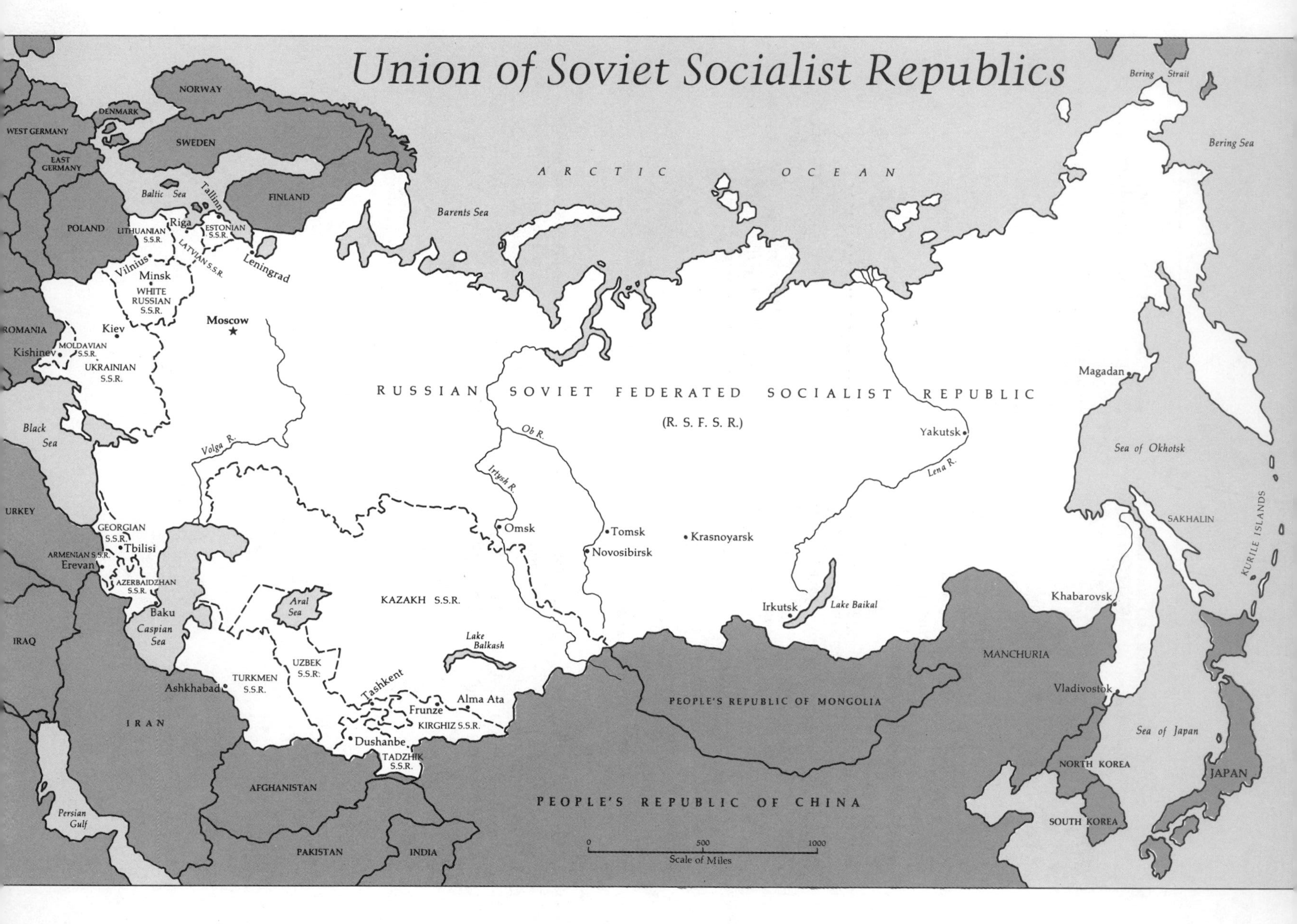
Union of Soviet Socialist Republics
ARCTIC OCEAN
Barents Sea
Bering Strait
Bering Sea
NORWAY
SWEDEN
FINLAND
DENMARK
WEST GERMANY
EAST GERMANY
POLAND
ROMANIA
Baltic Sea
Tallinn
ESTONIAN S.S.R.
Riga
LATVIAN S.S.R.
LITHUANIAN S.S.R.
Vilnius
Minsk
WHITE RUSSIAN S.S.R.
Leningrad
Moscow
Kiev
Kishinev
MOLDAVIAN S.S.R.
UKRAINIAN S.S.R.
Black Sea
URKEY
GEORGIAN S.S.R.
Tbilisi
ARMENIAN S.S.R.
Erevan
AZERBAIDZHAN S.S.R.
Baku
Caspian Sea
IRAQ
IRAN
Persian Gulf
Volga R.
RUSSIAN SOVIET FEDERATED SOCIALIST REPUBLIC
(R. S. F. S. R.)
Ob R.
Irtysh R.
Omsk
Tomsk
Novosibirsk
Krasnoyarsk
Yakutsk
Lena R.
Irkutsk
Lake Baikal
Magadan
Sea of Okhotsk
SAKHALIN
KURILE ISLANDS
Khabarovsk
Vladivostok
Sea of Japan
JAPAN
MANCHURIA
NORTH KOREA
SOUTH KOREA
KAZAKH S.S.R.
Aral Sea
Lake Balkash
UZBEK S.S.R.
TURKMEN S.S.R.
Ashkhabad
Tashkent
Frunze
Alma Ata
KIRGHIZ S.S.R.
Dushanbe
TADZHIK S.S.R.
AFGHANISTAN
PAKISTAN
INDIA
PEOPLE'S REPUBLIC OF MONGOLIA
PEOPLE'S REPUBLIC OF CHINA
0
500
1000
Scale of Miles

CHAPTER TWELVE

FREDERICK C. BARGHOORN

Politics in the U.S.S.R.

THE SIGNIFICANCE OF THE RUSSIAN REVOLUTION

The impact of a revolution on human societies might be likened to that of an earthquake on the natural environment, or as Crane Brinton argued in *The Anatomy of Revolution*, to the effect of acute but not mortal illness on a human being.[1] Such events unleash forces that, if sustained long enough at full power, bring total transformation or destruction.

However, catastrophes and crises are succeeded sooner or later by a new equilibrium. Organisms, species, and communities survive. The postrevolutionary state of affairs, in the case of political and social systems, represents a combination of elements and influences carried over from the prerevolutionary order and changes wrought by the forces that upset the old equilibrium. Thus, in both the French Revolution of the eighteenth century and the Russian in the twentieth, bureaucratic centralism seems to have survived stronger than ever. If the country experiencing revolution was relatively backward, the outcome of the revolution, after the inevitable partial return to prerevolutionary patterns, is likely to disappoint many, especially in advanced countries. This is the case with the Russian Revolution. However, many people in underdeveloped countries perceive the progress in industry and technology of the new Russian regime more positively than do most westerners. Clearly the meanings of revolutions differ, depending on the interests, biases, and temperaments of observers and on whether those affected by them are actual or would-be beneficiaries or victims, winners or losers. More than any other political experience, revolutions engage the emotions of men and women, kindling commitment and hope for a bright future in some, fear and loathing in others. These observations apply with particular force to the irreconcilable, intransigent challenge to established authority and political culture not only of Russia but of the whole capitalist world posed by the Bolsheviks, led by Lenin (real name Vladimir Ilyich Ulyanov), when they seized power on November 6, 1917 (October 25, old style calendar).

The ambitions of the Bolsheviks were seemingly boundless. Their program demanded the abolition of

[1] Crane Brinton, *The Anatomy of Revolution*, rev. ed. (New York: Vintage, 1965).

private property and even of a money economy, the smashing of the bourgeois state and its replacement first by the dictatorship of the proletariat and ultimately by a stateless, classless, coercionless society. They even went further, calling for the transformation of human beings into new, socialist men and women, purged of all the defects and weaknesses produced by feudalism and capitalism.

The Bolsheviks brought to their task of transforming Russia and the world the unique organizational weapon of the elite vanguard political party.[2] If Bolshevism's "goal culture" — to borrow a term coined by the anthropologist Anthony Wallace — was utopian, its "transfer culture," prescribing the means by which goals were to be achieved, was Machiavellian, pragmatic. As a result — to simplify somewhat — means obscured ends, just as state swallowed society. Political strategy, tactics, propaganda, and organization — above all, organization — were Lenin's major concerns and were, increasingly, to be those who have ruled Russia in his name since his death. The vanguard, Leninist hegemonic party embodied the organizational and strategic know-how Lenin distilled from his experience as a revolutionary conspirator and political prisoner in Russia and as an exile and polemicist in Europe. However, there was much diversity of outlook among the Bolsheviks and Lenin had to draw heavily on his astuteness and strength of will to guide the party, which came to power disastrously lacking a consensus on specific programs.

Although Lenin's "party of a new type" was designed to destroy the autocracy of the tsars, it absorbed from the authoritarian politics and environment in which it had struggled an authoritarian-bureaucratic spirit. This autocratic-hierarchical strain coexisted with other elements, including veneration for technology and utopian militant outlook, derived both from Marxism and from Russian radicals, such as Nicholas Chernyshevski. Lenin, Leon Trotski, Joseph Stalin, and Nicholas Bukharin, with other Bolsheviks, fashioned an autocracy more repressive than the one they overthrew — though perhaps Lenin and certainly Bukharin wished to offer an alternative evolutionary, gradualist model of development that might have saved Russia and the world much grief if it had been adopted instead of Stalin's terrorist "revolution from above."[3]

Of course, the new regime brought many changes, and it is the changes, rather than the resemblances to the tsars' regime, that Soviet leaders emphasize, although less vigorously since the consolidation of Stalin's dictatorship in the late 1930s than before. Despite the two regimes' similar authoritarianism, the Bolshevik elite, recruited on the basis of performance (including loyalty) rather than inheritance, differed enormously from the hereditary nobility and the rising middle classes who dominated the political and social life of the empire. Even today, the Soviet regime at least pays lip service to egalitarian, plebian, and populist values absent from the tsarist political culture. On the other hand, the Soviet political culture, heavily reliant on ritualistic conformity to authority, bears a striking resemblance to that of tsarist Russia.

Obviously the Soviet regime has been more successful than the empire in generating military power and projecting it abroad. Here the centralized political machine created by Lenin and perfected by Stalin has been invaluable. Also, the Bolsheviks' enthusiasm for economic development, science, and technology — expressed in recent years primarily in the movement to effect the scientific-technological revolution — has fed economic and military muscle. Bolshevik foreign policy also benefited from their opportunity as leaders of the first socialist state, and therefore as the apparent friend of oppressed classes and nations, to turn to their advantage social and national tensions in a world in which western modernization is increasingly undermining established structures and values.

The new regime carried forward more ruthlessly and singlemindedly developmental trends already inaugurated by some of the ablest of the imperial

[2] The Bolsheviks were one faction of the Russian Social Democratic Labor Party, which, after the Bolshevik seizure of power in Russia suppressed their Menshevik opponents and later took the names Russian Communist Party (1918), All-Union Communist Party (of Bolsheviks) (1925) and since 1952 has been known officially as the Communist Party of the Soviet Union (CPSU).

[3] See Stephen Cohen, *Bukharin and the Bolshevik Revolution* (New York: Knopf, 1973).

civil servants. Its achievements are considerable, though often overrated; certainly they have been costly in human life and freedom. Living standards for the majority of the population are now about a quarter or a third as high as those in Italy, France, and Britain. The Soviet record has been fairly good — but again often overrated — in such fields as mass access to social services, public health, and education. But it must be kept in mind that since the 1930s persons of high bureaucratic or professional status and city dwellers have been heavily favored over workers, and the latter over peasants. Moreover, as far as many peasant families are concerned, the discrimination, harassment, and persecution practiced by the regime against religious believers has been a major source of suffering, though the regime regards its militant atheist propaganda as one of its most important services to its subjects.

But of course the developments described above — even the achievements — have little in common with the just, classless, coercionless society that, in the enthusiastic early years of the revolution, was believed by some Russians to be near at hand. Many evils that Lenin denounced — such as ethnic discrimination, official corruption, persecution of dissenters, and restriction of emigration and travel — are present, some in aggravated forms.

Is it possible to explain the limited success of the Russian Revolution? The following suggestions may be useful in seeking an answer to this difficult question.

1. The Bolshevik political culture was, at its core, highly authoritarian and pragmatic. When choices had to be made between ends and means, expedience got priority — sometimes, to be sure, only just in time to avert disaster.
2. The attempt to impose the ambitious Leninist program of institutional, ideological, economic, and cultural development and transformation on the largely tradition-bound population generated fierce resistance. The new leaders felt that suppression of resistance and maintenance of the regime's power, not to mention the prosaic but vital tasks of economic administration, required rapid construction of a centralized state machine, equipped with a massive coercive capability.
3. Although pressure on the labor force was intense during the civil war (1918–1921), the previous point applies more to the large-scale, forced-draft industrialization and collectivization drives inaugurated by Stalin in 1929, Stalin's "revolution from above." In this period — even more than during the civil war, when the new regime defeated its counterrevolutionary and foreign enemies — the administrative methods and attitudes underlying contemporary Soviet policy took shape. The Soviet regime survived the civil war of 1918–1921 partly because it expropriated the lands of the crown, nobility, and bourgeoisie, and transferred them to the peasants. Stalin's virtual reenserfment of the peasants by collectivization and deportation of millions of recalcitrant or suspect peasants to forced labor camps was a major factor in the ballooning of the ranks of the secret police, a major feature of his rule.
4. The Bolsheviks' zeal to extend their system beyond Soviet borders and the hostility of foreign governments to the new regime, partly but not solely a response to revolutionary expansionism, spurred and justified militarization of the Soviet economy and a militaristic mentality.
5. Despite its dictatorial character, the Soviet regime could not completely ignore public opinion, especially that of party members, many of whom were of peasant origin. This was particularly true during the struggle with Nazi Germany, when in the interests of survival Stalin tapped the deep currents of Russian nationalism and even made concessions to the Russian Orthodox church. The increased role of Russian nationalism in Soviet politics and culture has had mixed effects, but probably has strengthened authoritarian attitudes, since the Russian peasants, whose support it was intended to gain, were generally authoritarian, premodern and even primitive in outlook.
6. Leninist ideology, especially its downplaying of the role of law in favor of arbitrary coercion as an instrument of social control, and the enduring habit of justifying expedient actions in the name of noble goals, made it difficult to face up to problems regarded as the heart of politics in the west: limiting the powers of the state vis-à-vis individuals and establishing accountability of political leaders to the citizenry.

7. Political authorities in Russia not only have the powers possessed by capitalist governments but also control the economy — and thus control employment and the life chances of the population, which militates against individual and group freedom.

In pondering future development of the U.S.S.R., which will be covered at the end of this chapter, it is well to remember that the influence of the authoritarian heritage of the Russian and Soviet past weighs heavily on contemporary political life. Liberalization and democratization will not come easily, but they are not impossible. It may turn out that, imperfect as it has been, Soviet economic, technical, and scientific development, in combination with such factors as revulsion against Stalin's inhumanity, has created prerequisites for positive change.

Historical Background

Soviet power was forged and acquired enduring characteristics in the crucible of revolution and civil war. Beginning with the abdication of Tsar Nicholas II in February 1917, the Russian empire rapidly disintegrated. A society already savagely battered by the German offensives of World War I faced four years of civil war. In an inexperienced Provisional Government, power passed from bourgeois liberals to the moderate socialist Alexander Kerenski, but by November 1917 the Bolshevik faction of the Marxist Social Democrats, headed by Lenin, Trotski, Stalin, Gregory Zinovev, Lev Kamenev, Bukharin, and other seasoned revolutionaries, was able to seize power. Thus began the most profound and radical social revolution of our century. The ideals of equality and justice proclaimed by Lenin remain unrealized, but all Soviet leaders since Lenin have claimed legitimacy in his name and in the name of the official creed, formulated under Stalin, of Marxism-Leninism.

While the revolution's roots lie deep in Russia's past, its catalyst was catastrophic defeat in World War I. The earlier humiliating defeat in the Russo-Japanese war of 1904–1905 had produced a crisis viewed by Lenin as a dress rehearsal for the great revolution to come. But it was Russia's enormous losses in World War I that broke the back of the old regime. The war at first had popular support, but disastrous mismanagement of the fight with Germany led to disillusionment. Most of the tsar's subjects, including eventually the military, turned against the war; the Bolsheviks' promise to end Russia's participation in it was a major factor in their victory.

An unpopular war was not the only reason for Lenin's stunning conquest. Bolshevik land-reform slogans fanned a peasant uprising; many peasant-soldiers deserted the army and came home to seize their share of the land. In the cities there were food shortages that brought to the boiling point simmering antagonism between workers and employers. Another factor was the dissatisfaction of the non-Russian nationalities that formed half of the population. Pressures mounted in 1917 as diverse elements — radicalized soldiers, peasants, workers, and national minorities — were mobilized by the Bolsheviks, by far the best organized and most skillfully led of the revolutionary parties, into a force that brought a new form of government into the world, dedicated to abolishing capitalism and building socialism.

Bolshevik rule was consolidated and partly legitimized by victory in the bitter civil war (1918–1920), in which moderate socialist parties, such as the Mensheviks and the Socialist Revolutionaries, and all nonsocialists were eliminated from contention. Battle lines were drawn between the "Reds" (Bolsheviks) and the "Whites" (forces loyal to the deposed Tsar Nicholas). Halfhearted, bungling intervention by France and Britain, in which the United States and Japan also took part, probably helped rather than hurt the communists, casting them as defenders of the homeland against foreign foes.

In 1921, in an effort to facilitate economic recovery, the communists permitted a limited return to private enterprise. Actually, the leaders of the revolution had few illusions about the difficulties of speedily transforming Russia into a socialist society. Neither Lenin nor Trotski, his chief lieutenant, believed it possible to build real socialism in backward Russia alone. They expected their revolution to be aided by working-class regimes in more advanced countries, notably Germany. The revolution in

Western Europe was aborted, however, and Russia — its economy seriously damaged after years of warfare — was isolated in a capitalist world recovering from war, in no position to seriously threaten the proud but poor society, yet not disposed to help it either.

The Communist party, which had greatly expanded its membership after assuming rule, now attracted power-hungry careerists without the principled convictions of the original Bolsheviks. After Lenin's death in 1924, bitter conflicts surfaced among the leaders, the most important being an increasingly angry quarrel between Stalin and Trotski. Trotski was determined to preserve the internationalist goals and faith in the masses that had characterized the party under Lenin; but Stalin, through his position as party secretary, overwhelmed Trotski by creating a bureaucratic elite loyal to him and eager to advance their own careers in the new institutions of power. After crushing the rightist faction led by Bukharin and the leftists led by Trotski, Stalin achieved dominance. Stalin then rewrote the history of the revolution. In Stalin's scenario, he, not Trotski, figured as Lenin's logical heir.

As he solidified his control, Stalin gradually fashioned the official creed, which he called Marxism-Leninism, and established himself as its interpreter. He propounded the doctrine of socialism in one country and argued that Russia could build a socialist society without immediate worldwide revolution. To accomplish his goals, Stalin mobilized patriotic sentiment; offered money incentives for executive and professional work; ruthlessly collectivized agriculture, a process that involved exiling or killing millions of *kulaks* (peasants whose possession of somewhat greater wealth than their fellows rendered them suspect); and later imprisoned, exiled, or executed hundreds of thousands of party, government, and military officials and other "enemies of the people" in the Great Purges of 1936–1938. His ruthless dictatorship drastically limited participation in decision making and established rigid censorship and a terroristic political police, creating a pattern of rule that has lasted, in modified form, to the present.

Today the Soviet political system seems one of the most stable in the world. Its stability, however, like that of regimes everywhere in this era of unsettling change, may be more apparent than real.

Since the mid-1960s, the official political culture of the U.S.S.R. has been challenged by the small but determined democratic movement. Although by no means homogeneous in composition, this loosely organized dissident movement represents sectors of the population that are well educated and have contacts with foreign scientists, writers, and other professionals. Running through much of their criticism of traditional Soviet doctrines and policies is a belief that the Stalinist system, though it has important scientific and economic achievements to its credit, has become more of a liability than an asset. The dissenters, however, do not agree on a program of reform; some apparently wish to borrow capitalist techniques, especially in economics, while others want a return to revolutionary ideals. But most agree that the rule of law must replace police coercion.

The official political culture of the U.S.S.R. represents a rationalization of the political monopoly enjoyed by the bureaucratic elite. Its defenders present it as the repository of universal truth and wisdom, but they have falsified Soviet history and excluded alien influences in order to give the official culture a semblance of logical consistency. As we analyze the different features of the Soviet political system, we shall see how the post-Stalin leaders have preserved the myths and institutions that legitimize their rule, while adapting policies and propaganda to the requirements of a society more difficult to control than Stalin's because it is economically more advanced, technologically more complex, better educated, and less isolated. In fact, lacking Stalin's stature, his successors seem even more dependent for legitimacy on the more irrelevant but still indispensable doctrines of Marxism-Leninism.[4]

Society and Economy

With nearly 9 million square miles, stretching from the Baltic Sea to the Pacific Ocean, the Union

[4] For fuller treatment of Russian and Soviet political culture see this author's *Politics in the U.S.S.R.*, 2nd ed. (Boston: Little, Brown, 1972); John S. Reshetar, *The Soviet Polity* (New York: Dodd, Mead, 1971); and Stephen White, "U.S.S.R.: Autocracy and Industrialism," in Archie Brown and Jack Gray (eds.), *Political Culture and Political Change in Communist States* (New York: Holmes and Meier, 1977).

of Soviet Socialist Republics (U.S.S.R.) is by far the largest country in the world. Its population in 1979 was about 260 million. Comprising most of Northern Asia and Eastern Europe, the U.S.S.R. is endowed with diverse human and natural resources. Despite considerable progress in economic development under the tsars and the intensive modernization drive of the Soviet regime, there are still wide differences in levels of economic and cultural development, especially between the European and Asian areas. There are almost two hundred different ethnic groups, most speaking their own languages or dialects as well as Russian, the most common language, unifying this polyglot realm. The highest percentage of the population is Slavic, and among the Slavs the Great Russians predominate, with Ukrainians next. Great Russians, in fact, make up just about 50 percent of the population of the U.S.S.R., though their birthrate is much lower than that of the Asiatic non-Russian peoples and a few others, such as the Armenians.[5]

From a primarily agricultural economy at the time of the 1917 revolution, the Soviet Union has developed into the world's second strongest industrial power (the United States is first). While much of its success in economic development can be attributed to its wealth of resources and population, and to the industrialization already begun under the tsarist regime, the extraordinary pace of economic modernization in Russia since 1929 was largely the consequence of the social mobilization and priority given to heavy industry over light industry and agriculture in the centralized Soviet economy. Since the 1950s, Soviet economic growth, though respectable, has been gradually slowing and if, as most Western specialists predict, this slackening continues, many problems will result.

The Achilles' heel of the Soviet economy remains agriculture. In spite of attempts to overcome this weakness through the forced reorganization of farms into collectives and other innovations, agriculture is still the main economic worry of the Soviet leaders. In 1959, approximately 34 percent of the Soviet male labor force was engaged in agriculture, compared with 8 percent (in 1965) for the United States.[6] However, according to official Soviet statistics, the percentage of the total labor force engaged in agriculture had dropped by 1974 to 24.

In sharp contrast to the large proportion of the Soviet labor force working in agriculture, less than 3 percent of the total employed American labor force (of more than 84 million) was working in agriculture. The Soviet Union needs a large agricultural force because it still has to devote a larger proportion of its resources to feeding its population than does the United States.

Governmental Characteristics

The Constitution of the U.S.S.R., both the Stalinist version of 1936 and its 1977 replacement, specifies the functions of the formal institutions of government. In reality these institutions are controlled by the higher organs of the monolithic Communist party of the Soviet Union (CPSU). On paper, Soviet government structures resemble those of many Western democracies. The Constitution provides for a central legislature, the Supreme Soviet. Its two chambers are the Soviet of the Union and the Soviet of Nationalities, where the territorial ethnic groups are represented. Between meetings of the Supreme Soviet, state power is formally held by its

[5] For demographic, educational, and other politically relevant data, see Ellen P. Mickiewicz (ed.), *Handbook of Soviet Social Science Data* (New York: Free Press, 1973). Since publication of her book, the population balance has swung against the Slavs largely due to very rapid increases among the Turkic peoples and the continued low birthrate of the three Slavic peoples, the Russians, Ukrainians and Belorussians. A census was taken in January 1979; its final results will not be available until the end of 1981.

[6] See Charles L. Taylor and Michael Hudson, *World Handbook of Political and Social Indicators*, 2nd ed. (New Haven, Conn.: Yale University Press, 1972). See also *Narodnoe Khozyaistve S.S.R.R.* [The National Economy of the U.S.S.R., 1974] (Moscow, 1975), pp. 7, 547, 559 for Soviet data for 1974 and 1975; and *The U.S. Factbook* (New York: Grosset and Dunlap, 1975), pp. 18, 350. This is the statistical abstract prepared by the Bureau of the Census. The Soviet gross national product in 1969 was 395 billion dollars. In 1976 it was 857 billion. U.S. GNP rose from about 700 billion in 1960 to close to two trillion dollars in 1977. For trends in Soviet GNP to 1969 see Ellen P. Mickiewicz (ed.), *Handbook of Soviet Social Science Data* (New York: Free Press, 1973), p. 93. For latest available Soviet and U.S. GNP, see *The Hammond Almanac* (Maplewood, N.J.: Hammond Almanac, Inc., 1979), pp. 682, 689.

Politburo (called, from the Nineteenth to the Twenty-third Party Congresses, the Presidium), a smaller group elected by members of both legislative chambers.[7]

Executive power is vested in a Council of Ministers corresponding to the cabinet in parliamentary democracies. Ministers are appointed by and responsible to the Supreme Soviet and the Politburo, but in practice overlapping membership in the council and executive organs of the party subjects all ministers to party control. Like their counterparts in the Western democracies, ministers are responsible for execution of national economic policy, maintenance of public order, conduct of foreign policy, and so forth. The Supreme Soviet also appoints a Supreme Court of the U.S.S.R., with each court appointee serving five years.

According to the Soviet constitution the U.S.S.R. is a federation, which grants extensive political rights to minority nationalities. The U.S.S.R. consists of fifteen union republics, which differ from the American states in that each tends to be composed of or named after a different ethnic group. In several, such as the Latvian, Turkmen, and Tadzhik, only a little more than half of the republic's population is accounted for by the eponymous nationality, and in Kirghizia and Kazakhstan non-Kirghiz and non-Kazakh elements constitute well over half of the population. Heavy Slavic immigration, especially since 1939, is a major reason for this situation, which has generated tension between the indigenous population and the migrants, who dominate industry and public administration. The largest republic, the Russian Soviet Federal Socialist Republic (R.S.F.S.R.), contains over half the population of the U.S.S.R., although this republic includes a number of diverse ethnic units. The other union republics are the Ukrainian, Belorussian (White Russian), Georgian, Armenian, Uzbek, Kazakh, Tadzhik, Kirghiz, Turkmen, Azerbaidzhanian, Moldavian, Lithuanian, Latvian, and Estonian. There are also autonomous regions (*oblasti*, singular *oblast*), and national areas (*kraya*, singular *krai*), mostly located in the R.S.F.S.R. Theoretically, the sovereign republics have greater powers than American states, including the right to secede from the U.S.S.R. Actually, federalism in the U.S.S.R., although it accords a measure of autonomy to non-Russians in such matters as the use of their native languages in education and the arts, is severely limited by the control exercised by the Moscow-centered national government and above all by the CPSU. According to Article 6 of the new 1977 Constitution, the communist party is the "nucleus" of the Soviet political system and all state and "public" organizations, the activities of which are directed by groups and party members.[8]

The CPSU is of course not a political party as citizens of Western democracies understand the term. It is the only legitimate, functioning political organization in the U.S.S.R. It guides, controls, integrates, and coordinates the activities of all government, economic, social, and cultural agencies in the land. The CPSU recruits, trains, and supplies executive personnel for all government and other social organizations, gives them guidance, systematically checks up on how its directions are carried out, and mobilizes citizens for mass participation in carrying out policy. Not only the *soviets* (the government institutions) but also the courts, police, security service, military, trade unions, professional associations, and mass media are controlled by party units, reporting to higher echelons of the party command.

[7] For an English translation of the 1936 Constitution, see John N. Hazard, *The Soviet System of Government*, 4th ed. (Chicago: University of Chicago Press, 1968). After more than twenty years of promises of a new constitution, a new one was unanimously and hastily adopted by the Supreme Soviet in 1977. During the well-organized discussion of its draft version, Leonid Brezhnev took over Nikolai Podgorny's job as formal chief of state; this lent credence to speculation that adoption of the new fundamental law was a ploy by Brezhnev to enhance his already great powers. The new charter brought no essential changes. Increased references in it to citizen rights are more than balanced by stress on the duty of all to "strengthen and develop the socialist system." More explicitly than the 1936 Constitution, that of 1977 identifies the CPSU as the "guiding force" of Soviet society. For an English translation of the new constitution see *Constitution (Fundamental Law) of the Union of Soviet Socialist Republics* (Moscow: Novosti Press Agency, 1977). There is a good discussion of the latest constitution in Robert Sharlet (ed.), *The New Soviet Constitution of 1977* (Brunswick, Ohio: King's Court Communications, 1978).

[8] On Russian-non-Russian relations and the workings of Soviet federalism, see Zev Katz, Rosemarie Rogers and Frederic Harned (eds.), *Handbook of Major Soviet Nationalities* (New York: The Free Press, 1975).

Among Soviet government institutions, only the military and security police have ever presented even a potential danger to party control, but they have thus far been kept in check by periodic changes in their leadership.

Unlike the state, the party is not even federal in form. It theoretically operates according to Lenin's principle of democratic centralism: all members may freely express their views and make proposals, but once an issue is decided, all must support and help carry out policy even if they disagree with it. In fact, the democratic aspect of the principle has all but vanished since Lenin's death, and only the centralism remains in force.

In theory, the Party Congress of 5,000 delegates that gathers every five years is the most powerful body in the CPSU. It elects the Central Committee (see Figure 12.1), which chooses the Politburo and the Secretariat. In practice, however, the lines of control operate in reverse. The congress, meeting rarely and briefly, ratifies policies made by the party leaders in the Politburo and the Secretariat. As a rule the Central Committee, like the Party Congress, is mainly a forum for the announcement and approval of policies previously set by the CPSU's Politburo, with the assistance of the Secretariat and also of the Council of Ministers. The Central Committee elected by the Twenty Fifth CPSU Congress in 1976 had 287 full, or voting, members, and 137 non-voting ("candidates") members. The Central Committee "represents" the party apparatus elite (consisting largely of oblast and republic committee party organization, first secretaries and heads of central committee secretariate departments) and the other main segments of the political economic elite, including the top state, police and military leaders. It

Election poster tells workers: "Work Harder." The poster illustrates the mobilizing role of Communist no-contest elections.

Figure 12.1

CPSU Central Committee Apparatus, November 23, 1971

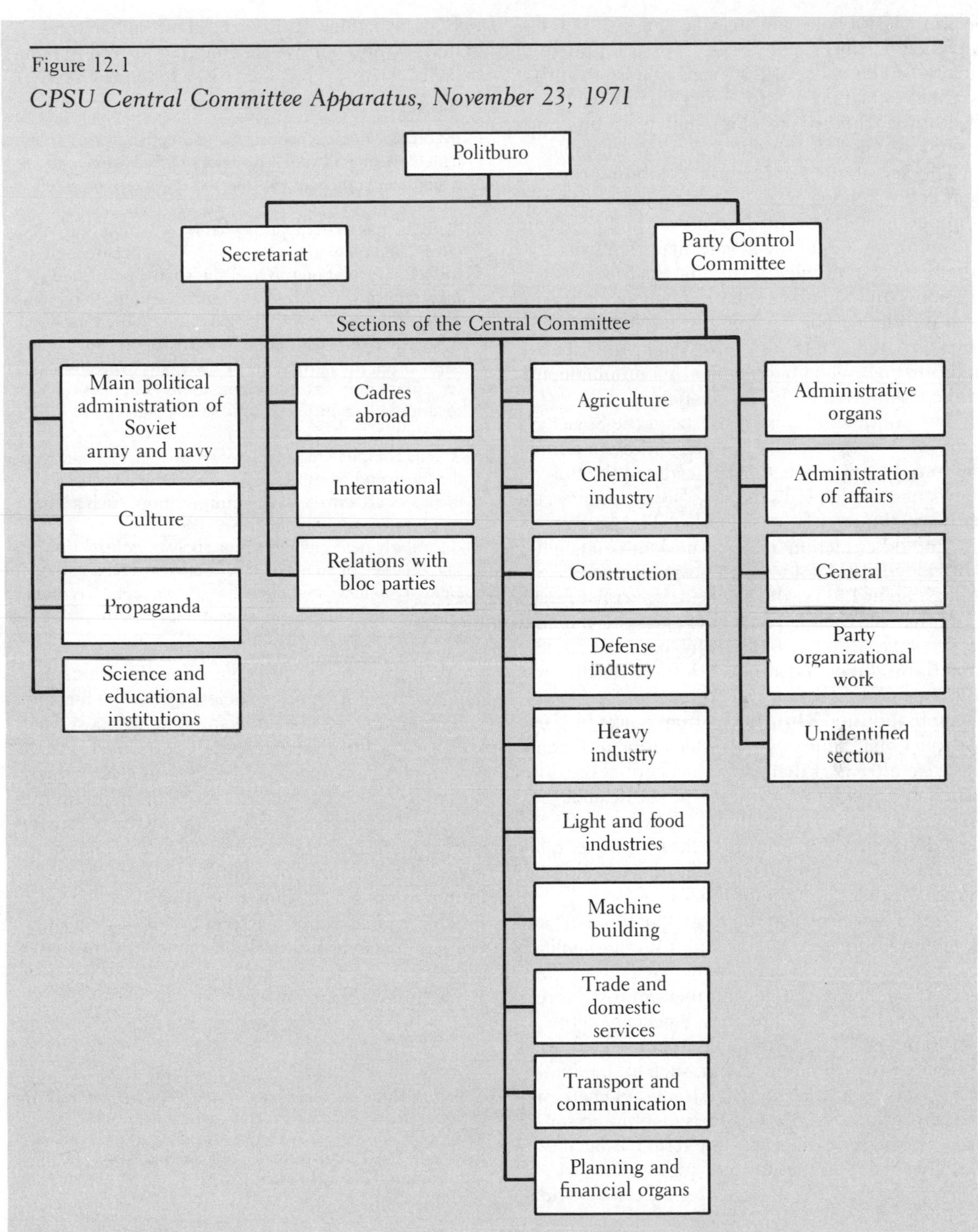

seldom plays a policymaking role, but in 1957 it intervened on Khrushchev's side — or as his instrument — in his successful struggle against an anti-Krushchev faction that for a time dominated the Politburo. Whether or not it might in a future crisis again assert itself is intriguing but unpredictable.

The Secretariat serves as the Politburo's expert staff and watchdog agency. Its departments, now numbering about twenty, coordinate and check on the performances of the government ministries which are responsible for running the Soviet economy and the other spheres of public policy and administration. The most powerful Politburo members, as a rule, are those — like Stalin, Khrushchev and Brezhnev who hold membership simultaneously in the Politburo and the Secretariat.

One conspicuous characteristic of the Soviet system is its concentration of power. Although Lenin, the founder and unchallenged leader of the Bolshevik party, tolerated a degree of loyal dissent in the party, Stalin, after he had quashed Trotski, Bukharin, and other faction leaders, ruled autocratically. Khrushchev held a dominant position after 1957, though he had to heed his colleagues' wishes far more than did Stalin. The tendency has been for collective leadership by an oligarchy to prevail for a brief transition period after the death of the dictator, until one man fights his way to superiority. The group that ousted Khrushchev from power in 1964 has so far maintained its oligarchic form, although it was clear after 1971 that party chief Leonid Brezhnev dominated Aleksei Kosygin, the titular head of the Soviet government, though not of the state. This reflected the party's superiority to the government, but perhaps also Kosygin's deteriorating health, although Brezhnev's health was poor too.

Until a few years ago the terms "totalitarian" and "totalitarianism" were used by most Western political scientists to refer to systems of the Soviet type. Those terms are still widely used, but they confuse more than they clarify Soviet politics, especially in the post-Stalin era. The term totalitarian has been used to signify many different things, such as domination of a society by a single party, extremes of coercion and terror, interference of government in personal matters, and so forth. Often the term has been used as if it were a synonym for monstrous evil.

To make the notion more precise, Carl J. Friedrich and Zbigniew K. Brzezinski offered an integrated, comprehensive scheme that proved influential. According to their analysis, a totalitarian system possesses six characteristics:

1. An official ideology, consisting of an official body of doctrine covering all vital aspects of man's existence to which everyone living in that society is supposed to adhere.
2. A single mass party typically led by one man, the "dictator," and consisting of a relatively small percentage of the total population (up to 10%), such a party being hierarchically organized and either superior to or completely intertwined with the government organization.
3. A system of terroristic police control supporting but also supervising the party for its leaders, and typically directed not only against demonstrable "enemies" of the regime, but against arbitrarily selected classes of the population.
4. A near complete monopoly of control, in the hands of the party and its subservient [member/workers], of all means of effective mass communication, such as the press, radio, motion pictures.
5. A similarly near complete monopoly of control (in the same hands) of all means of effective armed combat.
6. Central control and direction of the entire economy, typically including most associations and group activities.[9]

Even with this careful definition, the concepts and analytical schemes associated with the term are not adequate tools for understanding the post-Stalin U.S.S.R. or the East European communist systems. The totalitarian model has defects, such as exaggeration of the role of coercion, failure to shed much light on the interrelationships among the characteristics it identifies, and — most serious — failure to allow for possibilities of significant change in communist systems. Totalitarianism describes not so much a type of political system as a historical situation, in which a dictator unifies and wins the active support of a society beset by a crisis so intense as to threaten its destruction.

For the time being, perhaps, we must choose dif-

[9] Reprinted by permission from Carl J. Friedrich and Zbigniew K. Brzezinski, *Totalitarian Dictatorship and Autocracy* (Cambridge, Mass.: Harvard University Press, 1956), p. 9. Brzezinski subsequently gave up the term totalitarian. See Zbigniew K. Brzezinski and Samuel P. Huntington, *Political Power: U.S.A./U.S.S.R.* (New York: Vintage, 1964).

ferent terms to apply to different aspects of communist countries. The regime of the Soviet Union, and perhaps of other communist political systems, might be described as an *inclusive hegemony*, a polity in which open and legal opposition is, insofar as possible, suppressed, but extensive participation, initiated by the leadership and supervised by the party, exists.

THE DOMINANT POLITICAL CULTURE

In studying Soviet political culture it is impossible to use the survey and interview methods so helpful in studying the cultures of less secretive systems. Students of Soviet political culture must depend on the controlled Soviet media of communication, supplemented by foreigners' reports of contacts with Soviet citizens and an increasing flow to the West of unauthorized publications by Soviet dissidents. We can, however, learn much from official Soviet sources, including surveys made under party control that are sometimes, especially for a few relatively free years in the 1960s, quite revealing.

The dominant political culture is essentially the culture of the CPSU, especially its elite members. Its style can best be described as ideological, partisan, elitist, and subject-participatory. Characterizing it as ideological reflects the persistent claim that Soviet political life is guided by the precepts of Marxism-Leninism. The Leninist path is extolled as a blueprint of mankind's future. There is no place in the official creed for partial, selective, or qualified commitment to its goals. Doctrine and authority are closely associated. Power and ideology legitimize one another. This pattern is a source of strength, but it also creates problems. Because it endows rulers with a mystique based on ideological correctness, their errors go unchallenged.

From this ideological conception of the nature of political obligation flow demands for loyalty to the party, or partisanship (*partiinost*), as well as for principledness, intellectual conviction, and other evidences of whole-hearted commitment to Marxism-Leninism. Militant partisanship is basic to the political culture. Hence all Soviet leaders, from Lenin to Brezhnev, have rejected the concept of the coexistence of ideologies, though they frequently acknowledge the value of "coexistence of states with different social systems" for practical purposes, such as trade with capitalist countries.

The elitist aspect of the political culture refers both to the leading role of the CPSU in Soviet society and to the staffing of the party's middle and upper ranks by paid, full-time bureaucrats, designated on three levels: functionaries, cadres, and leading cadres.

The term subject-participatory refers to the subordination of Soviet citizens to superiors in one or more bureaucratic chain of command and to every citizen's obligation to participate in the work of the collective or organization to which he or she belongs. Soviet leaders attribute great value to the participatory and collective aspects of political life. Brezhnev at the Twenty-fourth Party Congress proudly reported on the activities of the 25 million "dedicated voluntary assistants" who backstop the 2 million deputies of soviets, mostly local government bodies, in the performance of their administrative duties. He also spoke of a need for "broader participation of the people in economic management," which, he made clear, must be carefully guided by the party.

It would be a mistake to classify Soviet political culture as simply bureaucratic and authoritarian. But it is clear that participation occurs within a framework of values, directives, and controls emanating from a vast national bureaucracy that is subject to the commands of the party Politburo.

Ideological Themes

The official ideology expresses utopian and idealistic as well as realistic and pragmatic goals. It promises a golden age of human development and fulfillment; it warns that the path to the classless, coercionless utopia is rocky and dangerous. Salvation can be gained only through hard work, discipline, and sacrifice.

The utopian perspectives of the official political culture were set forth systematically in the three party programs adopted in 1903, 1919, and 1961. These documents proclaim party and national goals. The current program was adopted by the Twenty-second Party Congress in 1961; it is more conservative than earlier programs, concerned mainly with how the people of the U.S.S.R. may within the foreseeable future achieve a reasonable level of material prosperity, provided that they respond to Kremlin commands.[10]

The program predicts the ultimate achievement of a classless society. It reiterates the intention of the CPSU to build a communist society in which the governing rule will be "from each according to his ability, to each according to his needs." In defining rewards and incentives for the present, however, the program follows the precept "from each according to his abilities, to each according to his *work*." For the time being, the distribution of rewards will be governed by the principle of material interest, until a "new Soviet man" is created who works unselfishly for the benefit of the collective. The program also declares that "the main economic task of the Party and Soviet people is to create the material and technical basis of communism within two decades." This statement expresses the industrial thrust of Soviet ideology, which has borrowed from early capitalism its work ethic and industrial virtues.

Leadership and Changing Political Culture

Lenin was the CPSU's founder. His mission was social revolution, in the pursuit of which he developed his conception of the party of professional revolutionaries, set forth most fully in his tract *What Is To Be Done?*[11] Lenin was a charismatic leader of a special type — a secular revolutionary ideologue. Mao Zedong in China and Fidel Castro in Cuba may be regarded as similar. Lenin abhorred adulation from his followers, and although he was an ideological and political autocrat, it can be argued that he regarded the rigid hierarchical relationships necessary for seizure of power by the "vanguard of the proletariat" as temporary expedients, to be gradually replaced by socialist democracy as the new social order acquired stability and support.

Lenin, the prophet, hero, exemplar, teacher, and fountainhead of authority for the U.S.S.R., achieved a stature and influence rarely enjoyed by political leaders. He made at least three major contributions to the communist cause. First, he was an innovative theorist, especially in regard to party organization. Second, his strategic genius and driving will led the party to victory in 1917. Finally, Lenin laid the institutional foundations of the Soviet system: the single-party democracy, the state-directed economy, and so forth. Lenin's political heirs, and the Soviet leadership as a whole, based their claim to be the rightful rulers of Russia on their custody of Lenin's ideological legacy.

When Lenin died, the only Soviet leader of comparable stature and intellectual force was Leon Trotski, the coleader of the 1917 revolution and founder of the Red Army. Probably because of Trotski's unquestionable theoretical agility and political skills (he was a better writer and speaker than Lenin), all other contenders for Lenin's leadership formed a coalition against him. Once Trotski was forced out of the running, the remaining contenders fought among themselves until Stalin, who excelled in manipulative shrewdness, won out.

Although Stalin's stature has substantially diminished during the more than twenty-five years since his death, leadership in that period has been exercised by men whom Stalin, not Lenin, trained. Some of them, particularly Khrushchev, bitterly resented the caprice and brutality of Stalin's rule. None, however, seems to have objected strongly to some of the most essential features of Stalinism. For example, they kept tight concentration of policy making in the party Politburo, leaving the Central Committee, which under Lenin had been the scene of lively debate, with only ratification and ceremonial roles. Moreover, Stalin's successors continued the practice, foreign to Lenin's methods, of party intervention in the arts and intellectual life.

However, the Brezhnev-Kosygin-Podgorny-Suslov leadership team,[12] in some respects more ra-

[10] For a translation, with commentary, of the 1919 and 1961 party programs and the 1952 and 1961 CPSU rules, see Jan F. Triska (ed.), *Soviet Communism: Programs and Rules* (San Francisco: Chandler, 1962).

[11] Vladimir Ilyich Lenin, *What Is To Be Done?* (New York: International Publishers, 1929). See Robert C. Tucker (ed.), *The Lenin Anthology* (New York: Norton, 1975) for translations of Lenin's main works.

[12] When they assumed rule in 1964, the four held the following positions: Brezhnev was party first secretary, Kosygin was chairman of the Presidium, and Podgorny was

tional and pragmatic than Khrushchev's, granted considerable autonomy and a consulting role to experts, especially natural scientists, provided that they refrained from expressing opinions the Politburo regarded as politically dangerous. Brezhnev's leadership style is oligarchic, with all power concentrated in the hands of a single leader or a small group of leaders, while Khrushchev's was more populist, with the first secretary of the party (Khrushchev) forming an alliance with the people against the bureaucracy. This alarmed other members of the leadership elite. Khrushchev coupled with his populism a tendency, denounced by his successors, to place himself above the collective leadership. The fact that Khrushchev was simply forced into retirement, not executed, and that Brezhnev, despite a burgeoning cult, has not yet instituted one-man rule reflects a certain political development of the Soviet system. The leadership doctrines and practices after Khrushchev's ouster represent a provisional consensus on the rules of the game in Soviet elite politics. However, the durability of these rules — a product of many factors, not the least being the fact that older men control the Politburo — remains unpredictable.

SOCIAL STRUCTURE AND POLITICAL SUBCULTURES

Official Soviet doctrine holds that Soviet society consists of two friendly classes, workers and collective farmers, plus a stratum formed by the working intelligentsia (those who earn their living by mental or nonmanual labor), but a number of subgroups or subcultures also take part in the making of public policy. Their demands sometimes shape alternative policy proposals through what remains a disguised, never officially recognized, political process.

Any examination of subcultures in the U.S.S.R. should reflect the very rapid increase in the attainments of the population. Mostly because of rapid industralization, the occupations of Soviet citizens are now significantly different from what they were even twenty or thirty years ago. Corresponding changes have occurred in patterns of residence and education. According to Soviet census figures, in 1970 urban population exceeded rural for the first time. Of a total population of 241.7 million, urban residents in 1970 numbered 136 million, or 56 percent, and rural population was 105.7 million. The estimated figures for 1971 were 139 million and 104.9 million, respectively (see Table 12.1).[13] The urban population now significantly exceeds the rural component, and the total population is now about 260 million.

Education figures also show substantial changes (see Tables 12.2 and 12.3). In 1939, almost 1.2 million Soviet citizens had received higher education in some form. By 1959 the number had grown to near 3.8 million and by 1970 to over 8.2 million. Many of these, especially in the 1960s, had graduated from evening or correspondence schools. Khrushchev had encouraged such programs in his hope to make the educational system more democratic by expanding opportunities for youths from outside the intelligentsia. After his ouster, the importance of these programs declined. Although the number of students entering higher educational institutions continued to grow in the 1960s, the rate of growth began to slow. Today, about 80 percent of Soviet young people receive a secondary school education, or ten years of formal schooling.[14]

Every year more and more educated citizens enter Soviet society and are drawn into the intelligentsia. By 1959, it numbered almost 13 million; by 1967 it had grown to 27 million.

It is easy, but incorrect, to regard the intelligentsia as the establishment or new class of Soviet society. True, the intelligentsia enjoys a great many material advantages, and its members, especially the stars of science and art, are the most respected citizens in the land. However, the intelligentsia is also suspect in the eyes of the rulers, and produces far more than its share of dissenters.

chairman of the Supreme Soviet. Suslov was the senior member of the Secretariat. The party's leading ideological specialist, he had been entrusted with many responsible tasks, such as rebutting Chinese criticism of Soviet policy.

[13] *Izvestiya*, April 17, 1971; and Roger Clarke, *Soviet Economic Facts, 1917–1970* (London: Macmillan, 1972), p. 4.

[14] Leonid Brezhnev, *Report of the Central Committee of the Communist Party of the Soviet Union* (Moscow: State Political Publishing House, 1971).

Table 12.1

Population of the U.S.S.R., 1870–1975 (in millions)

Year	*Urban*	*Rural*	*Total*
1870	9.5	76.8	86.3
1897[a]	18.4	106.2	124.6
1914[a]	24.7	114.6	139.3
1920	20.8	110.1	130.9
1923[a]	21.6	111.9	133.5
1924[a]	—	—	137.6
1925[a]	—	—	140.6
1926	26.3	120.7	147.0
1929	27.6	126.7	154.3
1931[a]	33.6	128.5	162.1
1933[a]	40.3	125.4	165.7
1939[a]	60.4	130.3	190.7
1940[a]	63.1	131.0	194.1
1950	69.4	109.1	178.5
1952	76.8	108.0	184.8
1954	83.6	107.4	191.0
1956	88.2	109.7	197.9
1958	95.6	109.3	204.9
1960[a]	103.6	108.0	212.4
1962	111.2	108.8	220.0
1964	117.7	109.0	226.7
1966	123.7	108.5	232.2
1968	129.8	107.4	237.2
1970	136.0	105.7	241.7
1972	—	—	246.3

[a] Estimate.

Source: Adapted by permission of Macmillan, London and Basingstoke, and Halsted Press, a Division of John Wiley and Sons, Inc., from Roger Clarke, *Soviet Economic Facts*, 1917–1970 (London: Macmillan, 1972), pp. 3–4.

The top levels of the party bureaucracy, together with the state bureaucracy, the military, and the security police, still constitute the power elite, as contrasted with the prestige elite heading the scientific and cultural intelligentsia. It is no accident that more party members than professionals are employed in the military services, the police, the courts, and generally in the government and other bureaucracies.

Groups and Strata in the Communist Party

The basic activity of the Communist party is control of Soviet society. The keystone of this effort is to include in the disciplined party adequate numbers of the administrative and professional elites. As the society becomes more complex and the level of education rises, party control is reinforced by party workers specially trained to deal successfully with the tasks they are to supervise. In 1961, more than 55,000 CPSU members held candidate or doctor of sciences degrees, roughly equivalent to the M.A. and the Ph.D. A high proportion of the CPSU leadership holds engineering degrees. By 1967, 16.5 percent of party members had higher education and 31.5 percent had secondary education (see Table 12.4).

Party members fall into three main categories. In the highest ranks of the party command structure are the full-time, paid professional functionaries, including party secretaries, deputy secretaries, department and section chiefs, and instructors of party committees. They are divided into levels, in descending order from central, regional, to local. These professionals are often referred to as *apparatchiki* — men of the apparatus.

The second category of command within the party consists of secretaries of the lowest level, the primary party organizations, numbering 370,000 in 1966 and 394,000 in 1977. Most of these secretaries are not full-time, paid workers, but more than 350,000 volunteers furnish valuable assistance to the full-time functionaries.

The full-time apparatchiki, together with other activists who can always be counted on to perform unpaid chores, constitute the backbone of the political system. However, there is another important category, party members in groups important for decision making or opinion formation or enjoying high actual or potential prestige. The party sees to it that there is a nucleus of members in such groups who can keep close to the party line and offset any tendency to develop leadership alternatives to the party. Although they are pressed to give their primary loyalty to the party, members of this category, often highly trained specialists, sometimes develop perspectives different from those of the party functionaries.

Table 12.2

Growth of Literacy in the U.S.S.R. Among Population Aged 9–49, 1926–1959

	Both sexes			*Male*			*Female*		
Territory	*1926*	*1939*	*1959*	*1926*	*1939*	*1959*	*1926*	*1939*	*1959*
U.S.S.R.	56.6%	87.4%	98.5%	71.5%	93.5%	99.3%	42.7%	81.6%	97.8%
Armenia	38.7	83.9	98.4	53.7	92.7	99.2	22.7	74.7	97.6
Azerbaidzhan	28.2	82.8	97.3	36.1	88.8	98.8	19.2	76.1	96.0
Belorussia	59.7	80.8	99.0	79.1	90.7	99.5	41.3	71.4	98.6
Estonia	—	98.6	99.6	—	98.9	99.7	—	98.3	99.5
Georgia	53.0	89.3	99.0	61.2	93.4	99.4	44.6	85.2	98.6
Kazakhstan	25.2	83.6	96.9	35.4	90.3	98.8	14.5	75.8	95.1
Kirgizia	16.5	79.8	98.0	23.9	84.9	99.0	8.4	74.4	97.0
Latvia	—	92.7	99.0	—	94.6	99.4	—	91.0	98.8
Lithuania	—	76.7	98.5	—	78.7	98.9	—	75.0	98.1
Moldavia	—	45.9	97.8	—	59.0	99.1	—	33.1	96.6
R.S.F.S.R.	60.9	89.7	98.5	77.1	96.0	99.3	46.4	83.9	97.7
Tadzhikistan	3.8	82.8	96.2	6.4	87.4	98.0	0.9	77.5	94.6
Turkmenia	14.0	77.7	95.4	18.3	83.0	97.7	8.8	71.9	93.4
Ukraine	63.6	88.2	99.1	81.1	93.9	99.6	47.2	82.9	98.8
Uzbekistan	11.6	78.7	98.1	15.3	83.6	99.0	7.3	73.3	97.3

Source: Reprinted by permission of Macmillan Publishing Co., Inc., from Ellen P. Mickiewicz (ed.) *Handbook of Soviet Social Science Data*. Copyright © 1973 by The Free Press, a Division of Macmillan Publishing Co., Inc.

Estimates of the numbers of full-time functionaries range from a hundred thousand up to about a quarter of a million. There seems to have been some contraction in the size of the apparatus as a result of the post-Stalin drive to replace paid functionaries with volunteers. This contraction occurred in spite of the growth of total party membership (see Table 12.5).

At the bottom of the party pyramid, yet still much more influential than nonparty people, are rank-and-file members without specialist training or status. They are members neither of the dominant, cadre stratum of the party nor of the prestigious intelligentsia. But these "privates" are expected to furnish a pool for recruits to the upper levels, transmit the party's policies to nonparty citizens, supply information to local party organizations (acting as an intelligence network), and set an example to the nonparty masses of superior performance in all spheres of public activity and private life.

It is interesting that both Khrushchev and Brezhnev encouraged recruitment of workers into the party. During the Stalin era, distinct preference had been given to technical, managerial, and administrative personnel. However, in terms of both recruitment rate and current party membership, workers were still underrepresented in proportion to their share of the population, though less so than farmers. Brezhnev stated that the party composition was 40.1 percent workers, 15.1 percent collective farmers, and 44.8 percent office workers.[15]

[15] Brezhnev, *Report of the Central Committee*, p. 109. For a comparison of Stalin and post-Stalin recruitment policy, see T. Harry Rigby, *Communist Party Membership in the U.S.S.R., 1917–1967* (Princeton, N.J.: Princeton University Press, 1966).

Table 12.3

Growth of Higher Education in the U.S.S.R., 1914–1969 (in thousands of students)

Year	*U.S.S.R.*	*Armenia*	*Azerbaidzhan*	*Belorussia*	*Estonia*	*Georgia*	*Kazakhstan*	*Kirgizia*	*Latvia*	*Lithuania*	*Moldavia*	*R.S.F.S.R.*	*Tadzhikistan*	*Turkmenia*	*Ukraine*	*Uzbekistan*
1914–1915	127.4	0	0	0	3.3	0.3	0	0	2.1	0	0	86.5	0	0	35.2	0
1927–1928	168.5	1.6	4.5	4.6	—	10.5	0.1	0	—	—	0	114.2	0	0	29.1	3.9
1940–1941	811.7	11.1	14.6	21.5	4.8	28.5	10.4	3.1	9.9	6.0	2.5	478.1	2.3	3.0	196.8	17.1
1950–1951	1,247.4	15.1	28.6	31.6	8.8	35.0	31.2	8.6	14.2	11.4	8.7	796.7	7.1	6.6	201.6	42.2
1955–1956	1,867.0	19.4	34.7	50.5	11.9	38.0	49.2	13.6	15.7	22.7	17.2	1,176.1	14.4	12.2	325.9	65.5
1956–1957	2,001.0	20.2	34.6	52.3	11.9	39.9	55.2	14.8	16.2	24.0	17.8	1,266.7	16.3	13.0	346.6	71.5
1957–1958	2,099.1	20.4	34.0	54.8	12.0	41.7	58.8	15.1	18.2	24.6	17.0	1,326.5	17.1	13.4	367.2	78.3
1958–1959	2,178.9	19.6	36.0	57.0	12.1	48.2	65.2	15.8	18.3	24.4	16.2	1,365.7	18.2	12.9	381.1	88.2
1959–1960	2,267.0	19.1	34.6	56.8	12.9	51.1	70.2	17.1	18.9	25.4	18.0	1,417.3	18.9	12.8	401.6	92.3
1960–1961	2,396.1	20.2	36.0	59.3	13.5	56.3	77.1	17.4	21.6	26.7	19.2	1,496.7	20.0	13.1	417.7	101.3
1961–1962	2,639.9	22.1	39.0	66.2	15.1	60.1	86.1	19.7	24.7	29.8	21.6	1,645.5	21.2	14.0	460.6	114.2
1962–1963	2,943.7	25.9	45.1	75.7	16.6	65.9	98.0	23.1	27.4	33.3	24.8	1,827.0	22.0	14.8	517.6	126.5
1963–1964	3,260.7	29.1	53.0	86.3	17.9	69.8	113.3	25.1	29.2	38.0	28.8	2,013.6	23.6	17.0	576.8	139.2
1964–1965	3,608.4	33.7	58.7	96.3	19.9	74.8	132.0	29.0	31.4	42.8	33.4	2,212.9	26.9	18.5	643.8	154.3
1965–1966	3,860.5	38.9	67.0	104.0	21.4	76.6	144.7	32.2	33.1	46.4	36.3	2,353.9	30.4	19.8	690.0	165.8
1966–1967	4,123.2	43.3	78.3	115.9	21.9	81.4	163.1	36.7	36.0	50.7	40.6	2,470.5	34.7	22.7	739.1	188.3
1967–1968	4,310.9	48.5	87.4	124.8	22.7	86.0	176.1	40.5	38.8	53.4	43.1	2,555.5	37.9	24.6	766.9	204.7
1968–1969	4,469.7	51.8	95.0	131.5	22.8	89.3	188.4	43.9	40.1	54.5	45.4	2,622.5	40.9	27.3	792.2	224.1

Source: Reprinted by permission of Macmillan Publishing Co., Inc., from Ellen P. Mickiewicz (ed.), *Handbook of Soviet Social Science Data*.

Table 12.4
Education of CPSU Secretaries, 1947–1967

	In republic, oblast, and krai organizations			*In okrug, city, and district organizations*			*In primary party organizations*		
Education	*1947*	*1957*	*1967*	*1947*	*1957*	*1967*	*1947*	*1957*	*1967*
Higher	41.3%	86.8%	97.6%	12.7%	39.6%	91.1%	8.8%	12.5%	30.1%
Unfinished higher	10.3	6.8	1.4	7.2	46.4	6.3	0	8.0	6.0
Secondary	29.3	5.6	1.0	33.4	11.7	2.6	26.2	26.2	43.8
Unfinished secondary	9.8	0.8	0	25.0	2.3	0	24.0	29.7	16.7
Primary	9.3	0	0	21.7	0	0	41.0	18.8	3.4

Note: In 1971 and 1976, virtually all republic, oblast, and krai secretaries had higher education. By January 1976 47.8 percent of secretaries even of primary party organizations (the lowest level) reportedly had completed higher education. Hardly any had only primary schooling.

Source: Adapted by permission of Macmillan Publishing Co., Inc., from Ellen P. Mickiewicz (ed.), *Handbook of Soviet Social Science Data*. Copyright © 1973 by The Free Press, a Division of Macmillan Publishing Co., Inc. Data for 1971 and 1976 are taken from *Partiinaya zhizn* [Party Life] No. 10 (May 1976), p. 22.

Soviet pluralistic politics, in which several groups compete for political influence, takes two forms. On one level, the party must still cope with attitudes and customs inherited from prerevolutionary tsarist society. Nationalism, religion, and other survivals of capitalism are among the remnants of traditional society against which, even today, the party struggles. On another level, the regime is also increasingly confronted with serious new challenges posed by the aspirations of social strata that — though basically loyal to the socialist ideology that nurtured them — are critical of the leadership's interpretation and implementation of this ideology.

Group differentiation in Soviet society is increasingly recognized, but the regime insists on the right to forbid the expression of group interests if they clash with its criteria of what is permissible in a socialist society.

Privileges and Problems of the Intelligentsia

The situation of the intelligentsia is paradoxical. On the one hand, intellectuals, especially outstanding scientists and artists, are the most privileged members of Soviet society, except for upper-level party apparatchiki and state officials. Intellectuals have superior access to information, travel, and contact with foreign colleagues, as well as the prestige arising from education and professional status. Moreover, the children of this elite have a better chance of getting into the best institutions of higher learning than do the children of ordinary people.

In return for these privileges, however, political authorities demand not only good professional performance but ideological orthodoxy and political fidelity. Some members of the intelligentsia feel that they cannot comply with the regime's ideological and organizational demands without compromising their personal and professional integrity. Some have even resorted to opposition, including open demands for abolition of political controls over the creative process, criticism of officials, withdrawal from literary or scientific activity, protest petitions to the authorities, street demonstrations, and appeals to foreign public opinion.

A growing trend in the late 1960s toward solidarity among dissenting intellectuals undoubtedly caused

Table 12.5
CPSU Membership, 1917–1976

Year	*Members*	*Candidates*	*Total*
1917	24,000	0	24,000
1918	350,000	0	350,000
1919	390,000	0	390,000
1920	611,978	0	611,978
1926	639,652	440,162	1,079,814
1927	786,288	426,217	1,212,505
1928	914,307	391,547	1,305,854
1929	1,090,508	444,854	1,535,362
1930	1,184,651	493,259	1,667,910
1940	1,982,743	1,417,232	3,339,975
1950	5,510,787	829,396	6,340,183
1953	6,067,027	830,197	6,897,224
1954	6,402,284	462,579	6,864,863
1955	6,610,238	346,867	6,957,105
1956	6,767,644	405,877	7,173,521
1957	7,001,114	493,459	6,340,183
1958	7,296,559	546,637	7,843,196
1959	7,662,356	616,775	8,239,131
1960	8,017,249	691,418	8,708,667
1961	8,472,396	803,430	9,275,826
1962	9,051,934	839,134	9,891,068
1963	9,581,149	806,047	10,387,196
1964	10,182,916	839,453	11,022,369
1965	10,811,443	946,726	11,758,169
1966	11,546,287	809,021	12,357,308
1967	12,135,103	549,030	12,684,133
1968	13,640,000	681,600	14,321,600
1969	13,395,253	616,531	14,011,784
1971	13,810,089	645,232	14,455,321
1976	15,058,017	636,170	15,694,187

Source: Reprinted by permission of Macmillan Publishing Co., Inc., from Ellen P. Mickiewicz (ed.), *Handbook of Soviet Social Science Data*. Copyright © 1973 by The Free Press, a Division of Macmillan Publishing Co., Inc. For the 1972 and 1976 figures above, see *Partiinaya zhizn* [Party Life], No. 101 (May 1976), pp. 13–22. According to the official *Ezhegodnik* [Yearbook] for 1977, as of January 1 of that year party members numbered 15,365,000, and candidates 628,876. There were 394,000 primary party organizations. See *Ezhegodnik bolshoi sovetskoi entsiklopedii* [Yearbook of the Great Soviet Encyclopedia] (Moscow: Soviet Encyclopedia Publishing House, 1977), p. 16.

official uneasiness. There has, however, been no significant evidence of support among ordinary workers and peasants for this rebelliousness among the intelligentsia. Since the regime fears, more than anything, an alliance between subversive intellectuals and the masses, it will likely do all it can to remove from society the intellectual rebels who might lead such a movement.

Among the occupational groups discernible within the intelligentsia, the economic intelligentsia is the largest (its members form about one-third of the party) and politically the most conservative. Its members direct the main branches of Soviet industry, the planning centers, and that large section of the state apparatus devoted to economic affairs. They are generally far more conformist than, for instance, the writers.

The natural scientists, even under Stalin, enjoyed great prestige and a superior standard of living, especially at the exalted level of the U.S.S.R. Academy of Sciences. Its members had high salaries, summer homes, and government drivers. Relations between the party and natural scientists, especially physicists, whose work had obvious military applications, were less affected by ideological considerations than those between the regime and writers and artists. Demands among scientists for professional autonomy and even for a voice in making decisions that affect their interests were largely granted, but in return these privileged strata were expected to refrain from unauthorized political or ideological communication or activity.

On balance, Khrushchev's successors, concerned as they were about economic and military development, probably pursued policies more acceptable to scientists than did Khrushchev. Doubtless pleasing to the scientific world were the celebration in 1966 of the sixtieth anniversary of Einstein's theory of relativity, denounced in the Stalin era as idealistic, bourgeois, and alien to the proletariat, and the publication of an article asserting that Lenin welcomed both the relativity theory and classical genetics.

However, there have been indications of rising concern among Soviet scientists over various policies. Many scientists shared the general alarm in intellectual circles over the end of de-Stalinization and the resumption of police methods for suppressing dissent, and many signed petitions protesting arrests and trials of nonconformist intellectuals. Hundreds contributed to the underground publication *Chronicle of Current Events*, which has been reaching the West since 1968. And a considerable number of scientists, most of them relatively unknown and of junior status, were arrested, apparently for protest. By 1979, a number of distinguished physicists, mathematicians, and computer specialists were in prison, unemployed, or in exile in the West. The leading dissident scientist, Andre Sakharov, though free, has been severely harassed.

Social scientists — historians, legal scholars, psychologists, and others — have enjoyed much less favor than natural scientists. Many fields, such as Freudian psychology, are still taboo. Moreover, social scientists must work within strict ideological guidelines. But if a social scientist does not stray from the ideological path and can make a good case for the practical value of a project (such as improvement of labor productivity, economic planning, or management), he or she will find it increasingly easy to obtain needed support for her research.

Tolerance for intellectual freedom, however, is not abundant in the field of history. The patriotic and by no means liberal historian A. M. Nekrich was fiercely condemned in 1967 and expelled from the party because his *June 22, 1941*, ran afoul of the post-Khrushchev leadership's effort to restore Stalin to respectability. He is now in emigration.

Among writers and artists the struggle is most acute: the party wants to control creative autonomy and the artist wants to use it as he sees fit. Nonrepresentational, abstract art is not allowed, and artists who want to paint in abstract ways keep their work hidden. Musicians who intrude into political controversies may be corrected and punished.

Some writers, like the poet Evgeni Evtushenko, have taken at face value the promise of utopian Leninist gospel and have expressed their disappointment at what has evolved in Soviet society. Others, like the late poet Anna Akhmatova, want to express their own vision of life. Some are satirists, like Mikhail Zoshchenko, who openly presented the seamy side of Soviet reality. Others, like Vladimir Dudintsev, author of *Not by Bread Alone*, dare to criticize the way the Soviet order was working, though not the essential tenets of Marxism-Leninism. Boris Pasternak, a Nobel Prize winner and author of *Doctor Zhivago*, was alone among major Soviet writers in openly rejecting the Bolshevik revolution and its consequences. All have been punished either by criticism, withdrawal of privileges, maltreatment of persons close to them, or imprisonment.

Creative autonomy is disturbing to party bureaucrats. So is the open demand made by some Soviet intellectuals, especially Nobel Prize winner Alexander

Solzhenitsyn, that administrative controls over aesthetic expression be eliminated. The 1966 trial of writers Andrei Sinyavski and Yuli Daniel, who had published abroad works critical of the regime, marked the beginning of a new phase in relations between the party and the intelligentsia. It signified a shift in emphasis from Khrushchev's reliance on persuasion and social pressure to a policy of intimidation and selective repression of rebellious writers and other intellectual dissenters.

The Status of Workers

Although official mythology holds that the industrial worker forms the leading class of Soviet society, the greatest rewards of the society are actually reserved for others. The worker lives under constant pressure to increase his production and live the life of a Soviet citizen. She has few opportunities to express whatever discontent she may feel as a worker or as a consumer. This gulf between the worker's theoretical and real position is apparent in a number of ways.

As we have pointed out, the CPSU is far from a proletarian party, although it seems in recent years to have stepped up recruitment of the better-paid, most-skilled workers, because this stratum seems more supportive and reliable than intellectuals.

Almost all wage-earners and salaried employees belong to a network of industrial unions known as the All-Union Central Council of Trade Unions (AUCCTU). The head of the organization is usually at least a middle level party official (its present leader is Alexander I. Shibaev, a youngish party executive), who primarily conveys the policies of the regime to the workers and urges increased production.

In addition to its main function, stimulating production, the AUCCTU performs welfare functions like administering social insurance and operates social and cultural agencies such as clubs, houses of culture, and people's universities. However, the emphasis in all relations between workers and the party or trade unions remains increased production. The worker must be as productive and achievement oriented as possible. This pressure continues both on the job and in the worker's free time.

The official doctrine, of course, is that the U.S.S.R. has no class conflict; hence workers are not allowed to strike. Nevertheless, in recent years a number of ad hoc strikes and riots have taken place, and *Trud*, the official trade union newspaper, has occasionally reported cautiously on minor work stoppages.

A Soviet worker has to work proportionately much longer to buy food or clothing than his American or West European counterpart. His wages average about one-quarter as much as those of American, West German or Swedish workers, so far as can be determined from Soviet and United States official statistics and from accounts by responsible Western reporters. Housing is inexpensive but of low quality. The average worker cannot support his family without the help of another working member in the family. And, of course, the Soviet system makes no formal provision for the expression of consumer interests.

It would be a serious error, however, to imagine that the Soviet worker is seething with discontent. He is better off materially than at any other time in Russian history. The factories and trade unions have achieved modest success in their prescribed function as schools of communism. Certainly the worker in the Soviet Union feels superior to the farmer. Also, particularly in the highest-paid, skilled categories, he is materially better off than lower-level members of the intelligentsia, not to mention clerical workers. Furthermore, the life-style of the worker apparently differs less from that of the bosses than it does in most capitalist countries. Workers of the U.S.S.R. may also feel less social distance from their bosses because of widespread participation in common cultural activities, such as theater, opera, and ballet. However, they resent the privileges of bosses and officials. In 1977 and 1978 some workers expressed their resentment by forming a union independent of the official, party-controlled trade union organization. Though they had slim prospects of achieving impact, their action may have been a harbinger of serious future problems.

The Collective Farmers

Contrasts between the workers and the collective farm peasantry, or *kolkhozniki*, are striking. The peasantry form the section of the population that is the most underprivileged and most poorly represented in the party and government. They have no organization and belong to no trade unions. They are kept under close supervision by rural party organizations and a network of police informers. But in spite of their lack of organization, the collective farm peasantry has proven to be one of the most difficult social forces for the party to control. Indeed, it could be argued that the collective farmers and the creative writers are the two social groups that have offered the most effective resistance to party strictures and influence.

Industrialization, education, and the penetration of the village by motion pictures, radio, and television have already transformed ways of life and thought. Still, cultural differences persist between the peasant and the city worker, especially the higher-educated city dweller; and the differences are much greater than those that distinguish the American farmer from her counterpart in the city. The gap is compounded by ethnic difference when the peasant belongs to a minority nationality.

In recent years, the Soviet leadership has sought to deal with peasant discontent by granting better material conditions and other organizational or procedural concessions. Concessions granted in 1965 include higher prices for farm products and a promise that prices would remain stable. They also included a pledge of more and better machinery and other aids to farming and, perhaps most important, a loosening of restrictions on the freedom of collective farmers to operate and sell produce from their small but precious private plots. One of the first results of the 1965 reform was a boom in the sale of food in Moscow. Soviet leaders still attach enormous importance both to increasing agricultural productivity and to providing the farmers with an increasing share of the material benefits of economic progress. Perhaps the best proof of this was the unprecedented decision, taken in 1967, to provide collective farmers with a guaranteed wage.

Ethnic Pluralism and Its Political Consequences

Soviet ethnic problems are significant because about half of the population does not belong to the Great Russian stock, which from the sixteenth to the nineteenth centuries built a vast multinational empire by colonization and conquest. According to the 1970 census, twelve non-Russian nationalities number more than 2 million persons each; another nine have more than a million. Ukrainians are 40 million strong. The several Muslim Turkic peoples of Central Asia and the Caucasus are increasing in numbers more rapidly than the Slavic Great Russians, Ukrainians, and Belorussians.

Especially in the Caucasus, Central Asia, and the Baltic area, national differences are accompanied by extreme differences of cultural and social background. There is evidence to support Brzezinski's view that non-Russian nationalism in the U.S.S.R. could become "a political issue of even greater proportions than that posed by the current racial crisis in the United States."[16] The consensus, however, seems to be that, barring unforeseeable circumstances such as war, the regime can probably continue to cope with ethnic discontent for a long time.

The Soviet government is federal in form. Each of its fifteen union republics, nineteen autonomous republics, five autonomous oblasti (regions), and ten national *okrugs* (territories) has an assigned number of votes in the Soviet of Nationalities. In addition to the constitutional provisions, complex legal, administrative, educational, and cultural arrangements guarantee some expression of national and ethnic values. At the same time, Soviet federalism has always been severely limited. The economy of the U.S.S.R. is administered according to central rather than federal principles.

Prior to Stalin's exploitation of anti-Semitism (which Lenin despised) as an instrument of state policy, Jews who were committed to Soviet goals were, together with Armenians and Georgians, prime beneficiaries of the increased social mobility fostered by the revolution. However, in the 1940s and early 1950s, and again after a brief let-up following Stalin's death, Jews were pressured to renounce their heritage. Jewish cultural institutions such as the Moscow

[16] Zbigniew K. Brzezinski (ed.), *Dilemmas of Change in Soviet Politics* (New York: Columbia University Press, 1969), p. 161. For a wealth of up-to-date information on ethnic problems in the U.S.S.R., see Zev Katz et al. (eds.), *Handbook of Major Soviet Nationalities* (New York: Free Press, 1975). For a broad comparison of Russia and America see Paul Hollander, *Soviet and American Society* (New York: Oxford, 1973).

Jewish Theater were closed. Jews continued to play a role in the professions and in intellectual life out of proportion to their percentage of the population, but they were excluded from sensitive fields such as diplomacy and the intelligence services, and they found it increasingly hard to obtain admission to the best institutions of higher education.

One response by Soviet Jews to the gradual deterioration of their situation in the U.S.S.R. has been emigration to Israel, and increasingly, in recent years, to the United States. By 1979 perhaps as many as 150,000 had been permitted to leave, often after intense harassment and long delays, especially in cases of persons especially valuable to the Soviet economy.[17]

Organized religions, indeed all religious sentiment and practice, are regarded, together with ethnic sensitivities as objectionable survivals of capitalism. In their policy against organized religion, the post-Stalin regimes — especially Khrushchev's — have been far more rigorous than Stalin had been. They resumed antireligious propaganda and harassment of religious bodies, a policy abandoned by Stalin in 1941 in an effort to foster national unity during the struggle with Germany.[18]

POLITICAL SOCIALIZATION

The high priority assigned by Soviet leaders to the formation of desired attitudes and values is reflected in the size and scope of socialization. Determined to transform a backward society into the model for mankind's future, the leaders sought to inculcate in new generations devotion to the agencies of revolutionary transformation, especially the CPSU. The party has initiated, proclaimed, and supervised the fulfillment of all major decisions in education. It has set in motion one of the most systematic political indoctrination programs to which any population has ever been subjected, exceeded perhaps only by that instituted by the communists of China.

The Schools

The most important instrument of political socialization in the Soviet Union has always been a tightly woven network of educational institutions, from the primary school through the university. After the consolidation of communist power in about 1921, and especially after the start of rapid industrialization and agricultural collectivization in the late 1920s, Soviet educational institutions embarked on an elaborate effort to impart traits such as orderliness, punctuality, and discipline to a population that was (and to some extent still is, especially in Asiatic Russia) preindustrial in outlook. Millions of village children were made conscious of national and international political events and issues. Simultaneously, Soviet educators provided Marxist-Leninist training in history, philosophy, and political economy for the few who went all the way through secondary and higher education.[19]

In the primary and secondary schools the history of political socialization breaks down into three main phases. The first phase took place in the confused but hopeful years following the revolution, when some teachers experimented with American-style progressive education and with a polytechnical approach designed to acquaint their pupils with the underlying principles of modern industry.

The second phase extended from about 1929 until 1958. The inculcation of loyalty and support for the polity, the party, its leaders; and their policies remained the central tasks of political socialization. However, the methods, spirit, and content changed drastically. Belief in the moral superiority of socialism over capitalism and in the historically inevitable triumph of the former over the latter continued as a prominent element. It was increasingly overshadowed, however, by two other themes, reflecting Stalin's pessimistic view of the ever more threatening international situation and his ideas

[17] For background, see Leonard Schroeter, *The Last Exodus* (New York: Universe Books, 1974).

[18] See David E. Powell, *Anti-Religious Propaganda in the Soviet Union* (Cambridge, Mass.: MIT Press, 1975).

[19] See George Z. F. Bereday and Jaan Pennar (eds.), *The Politics of Soviet Education* (London: Stevens, 1960); George Z. F. Bereday et al., *The Changing Soviet School* (London: Constable, 1960); and Jeremy R. Azrael, "The Soviet Union," in James S. Coleman (ed.), *Education and Political Development* (Princeton, N.J.: Princeton University Press, 1965).

about coercive industrialization. One theme expressed itself in emotionally charged calls for vigilance, military preparation, and patriotism to counter a mortal threat to the socialist motherland. The other took the form of Stalin's demand — reiterated by Khrushchev and Brezhnev — that Soviet citizens, from school days on, be imbued with a spirit of disciplined initiative in the service of collective goals and be capable of an "independent search for the best way to fulfill a command."

In his effort to rally the Soviet people against encirclement, Stalin called for a revival of pride in Russian military tradition. History texts exalted the heroism of Russian troops in battles against Tatars, Swedes, French, and Germans. All citizens were asked to take pride in prerevolutionary and Soviet achievement, in all spheres of endeavor. Prerevolutionary and Soviet heroes were held up as models to school children. Symbols of rank, status, and success reminiscent of the tsarist era were reintroduced on a broad scale. Many Soviet people felt, as did Trotski, that these measures constituted a betrayal of the 1917 Revolution in favor of a new elite of party, state, military, economic, and cultural bureaucrats.[20]

Stalin's program left his successors with some difficult problems. The classical content of education, with its expectation that secondary-school graduates would automatically go on to universities, had resulted in a contempt for manual labor that was unacceptable to Khrushchev and his colleagues. Furthermore, the children of the privileged groups (officials and intelligentsia) were filling from 60 to 70 percent of university classes. A kind of careerism had developed that seemed to emphasize personal advancement and downgrade commitment to the tasks of the community, deepening the psychological gulf between the intelligentsia and other groups and producing various forms of political apathy and disaffection.

The educational reforms of 1958 had two main aspects of political significance: the introduction of a system of boarding schools (700,000 enrollees by 1961–1962), and the reintroduction into the primary and secondary systems of a modified version of the polytechnical emphasis eliminated by Stalin. Under Khrushchev, vocational instruction was added to academics in the lower grades, while the upper secondary grades had to spend one-third of their time working in agriculture or industry. Probably the most important feature of this revival of the polytechnical principle was the decision that 80 percent of the students in institutions of higher education would be secondary-school graduates with at least two years of work experience after graduation. (This was not to apply to the most gifted students in mathematics and the physical sciences.)

Thus regular secondary-school graduates would no longer think they had an automatic right to higher education, while the chances of higher education for workers' children, who completed secondary education in evening schools, would be increased. The introduction of boarding schools was to lessen family influence. Before Khrushchev's fall, it seemed likely, as authorities proclaimed, that "the boarding schools will become the new schools of communist society."

After Khrushchev's ouster in 1964, his educational reforms were widely criticized. It had been apparent long before that Khrushchev's attempt to add a heavy dose of labor training and actual factory and farm work to the secondary-school curriculum was adversely affecting the quality of education. Beginning with the school year 1964–1965, the length of time required for a complete secondary education was reduced from eleven to ten years, cutting back on the time spent by students in nonacademic activity. Khrushchev's boarding school innovation was also criticized, and increased stress was placed on the family's importance in the moral upbringing of children.

There was no reason to believe, however, that these changes presaged a return to the crudities of the Stalin era. Rather, in the post-Khrushchev period an educational pattern appeared that attempted to combine ideological orthodoxy with increased rationality by presenting ideological concepts clearly and systematically, and by substituting, for rote learning, increased use of seminars, discussion, and individual instruction.

The avowed intent of Soviet educational policy has always been to develop a communist morality. But Soviet moral training is strikingly conservative, for example, in its exaltation of obedience, respect

[20] Leon Trotski, *The Revolution Betrayed* (New York: Doubleday, 1937).

for authority, and the value of hard work. Although Lenin was an internationalist, Soviet teaching after his time has emphasized patriotism as the most prominent feature of communist morality. In Stalin's time it was usually described as Soviet patriotism; in more recent times it has been called socialist patriotism. As presented in the current party program, the first principle in the "moral code of the builder of communism" is "devotion to the communist cause, love of the socialist motherland and of the other socialist countries."

The teaching of history, in the U.S.S.R. the most political of academic disciplines, was affected by high-level conflicts over Stalin and Stalinism. Khrushchev's revision of Soviet history led to a shift of emphasis from the figure of Stalin to the people, acclaimed as the creator of history. The scope of Khrushchev's de-Stalinization was limited — his political opponents, such as Bukharin and Trotski, were not rehabilitated. But some historians, made bold by Khrushchev's revelations, demanded that the party open its archives to scholars and permit them to write objective and critical history. Khrushchev, having stimulated expectations that might have undermined the legitimacy of a regime already shaken by his "secret speech" exposing Stalin's crimes, quickly cracked down on the historians.

Khrushchev's fitful de-Stalinization was followed by his own more thorough obliteration from public attention and by a cautious restoration of Stalin to an honorable, but far from commanding, place in Soviet history. Khrushchev's victorious opponents might have honored Stalin's memory more enthusiastically had it not been for their realization that doing so would alarm the ranks of the intelligentsia, whose productive efforts are necessary for maximizing national power.

Despite the revival of social science, there is almost no teaching in Soviet schools and universities of empirical political science or sociology. However, there is a good deal of indoctrination for citizenship. In 1962 a course on fundamentals of political knowledge was added to the secondary-school curriculum. The compendium *Fundamentals of Marxism-Leninsim* was published in 1959 for university students.[21] Through such measures, Stalin's successors substituted for Stalin worship a program of systematic political instruction, broken down into segments suitable for each educational level. But the new program, like the one it replaced, was dogmatic and authoritarian. It preserved the essentials of Stalinism without Stalin.

The Komsomol and Its Affiliates

The pervasive Soviet effort at political socialization requires that "schools of communism" be deployed throughout the society. These socialization agencies include such varied organizations as collective farms and factories, trade unions, the armed services, the courts, and the official and sole youth organization, the All-Union Lenin-Communist League of Youth (Komsomol), founded in 1918. The Komsomol is officially characterized as the reserve and helper of the party. Efforts are apparently being made to give to Komsomol leaders and members an increasing sense of the significance of their role in working together with the party. Brezhnev reported at the Twenty-fourth Party Congress that the party was turning over to the Komsomol more and more tasks in the areas of labor, education, recreation, and the everyday life of youth. At the same time, he expressed satisfaction that since the Twenty-third Congress 1.35 million Komsomol members had become members of the party — 45 percent of all new party members. He was also pleased to report that the number of CPSU members working in the Komsomol had more than doubled, thus tightening links between the party and the Komsomol.[22]

At all levels of the educational system the Komsomol and its junior affiliates, the Pioneers and the Octobrists, reinforce the efforts of other agencies engaged in moral education. The three helpers also assist the party, through the schools, in the functions of social control, discipline, and instrumentation. The ages of membership in the Pioneers are seven through nine, in the Octobrists ten through thirteen, and in the Komsomol fourteen through twenty-eight (although party members working within the Komsomol may be older).

The enormous membership of these bodies by the mid-1960s caused one author to predict that "before

[21] *Fundamentals of Marxism-Leninism*, 2nd rev. ed. (Moscow: Foreign Languages Publishing House, 1963).

[22] Brezhnev, *Report of the Central Committee*, pp. 93–94.

Organized spontaneous unity as revealed in Red Square parade posters with portraits of Lenin and Politburo members.

many years virtually every Soviet subject over the age of six will be an active member or graduate of the youth program."[23] Almost all school pupils are or have been Pioneers. And although Komsomol membership is sparser, especially in rural and non-Russian areas, virtually all university-level students belong.

Some Pioneer activities, such as hiking and camping trips, resemble activities of the Boy Scouts of America. But the Pioneer organization's subordination to the CPSU, the political militancy that pervades its messages, and its characteristic emphasis upon collectivism distinguish it sharply from the Boy Scouts. Among other things, the Pioneers mobilize school children for revolutionary holidays, assist in patriotic drives, organized "Lenin corners" for propaganda work among children, and correspond with children's groups in foreign countries. Many Soviet schoolchildren, especially from larger cities, spend several weeks each summer in Pioneer camps. Under the guidance of teachers and Komsomol workers, both paid and volunteer, the Pioneers also operate a wide range of hobby groups and study circles.

The Komsomol is one of the agencies (the party and the trade unions are others) empowered to provide a university applicant with the required character reference. One of the major Komsomol activities at the university level is organization of circles and seminars for study and discussion of Marxism-Leninism. Moreover, students as well as professors are encouraged to participate in mass educational work. Komsomol activists also give special lectures on political subjects such as international problems, sponsor radio broadcasts, and post newspapers like the *Komsomolskaya Pravda* on bulletin boards.

[23] Allen Kassof, *The Soviet Youth Program* (Cambridge, Mass.: Harvard University Press, 1965).

The Komsomol, an important auxiliary agent of social mobilization and political recruitment, also assists in the conduct of programs of physical culture, sports, and military training. It played an important part in persuading, or pressuring, Soviet youths to volunteer for such campaigns as the 1954 plan for settling virgin lands of Kazakhstan and Siberia, and for the many subsequent shock brigade construction projects, which are group competitions between young workers, and student construction detachments.

The Komsomol makes an important contribution to the early stages of recruitment into the Soviet political elite. It assists the party in identifying and training activists, persons who distinguish themselves in such community activities as propaganda, welfare, or recreational programs, and who often also keep an eye on fellow students.

The Komsomol's success in mobilization, political recruitment, and promoting outward conformity far exceeds its ability to inculcate ideological conviction. It is expected to help in shaping the "new Soviet man," unselfishly dedicated to community goals. In fact, millions of Soviet youths display aversion to manual labor, evade the work assignments they are expected to perform in return for their education, or slide into alcoholism, delinquency, or crime.[24]

The Role of the Family

The family, although potentially threatened by Khrushchev's plan for boarding-school education, has had a relatively stable role ever since the upheavals of the 1920s died down. As the regime became more conservative, it relied more on the family to help maintain social stability.

However, there is evidence that the influence of parents and grandparents also works to frustrate the regime's socialization efforts. The family reinforces pluralistic tendencies generated by occupational and economic status or shaped by ethnic and religious background. Among the most significant family influences at variance with official ideology is the tendency of parents among the intelligentsia to wish to ensure for their children the advantages they had achieved in vigorous competitive struggle.

Among non-Russians, especially among Muslim peasants, many parents interfere both consciously and unwittingly with the regime's efforts to eliminate resistance to the obligatory adoption of the dominant urban, industrial, Russian communist culture. A study of the so far unsuccessful campaign against various religious sects suggests that their survival attests to the continued vitality of the family in shaping attitudes and beliefs.[25]

Even more difficult than assessing the Soviet family's influence in political socialization is evaluating the overall success of this gigantic effort to create a "Soviet man." Certainly it has not been fully successful, or criticism of the work of indoctrination and complaints against so many persisting survivals of capitalism would not be as prominent as they still are in the Soviet press. At the same time, and despite its serious shortcomings, political socialization in the U.S.S.R. has many formidable achievements to its credit. Objective Western scholars generally agree that although it has not created a universal political culture, it has created a fairly high level of popular consensus. While only a few Soviet youths have a profound knowledge of Marxist-Leninist doctrine, the youths shaped by the agencies described here, especially the student activists who are future leaders, are imbued with the peculiar mixture of anticapitalism and nationalism known as Soviet patriotism.

Adult Political Socialization

For more than five decades the CPSU has conducted a large-scale program of adult, after-work political instruction and training.[26] This vast adult socialization program, staffed mainly by unpaid activists who worked to fulfill a part of their obligation to the party, has several objectives: to encourage,

[24] See Joel Schwartz, "The Elusive New Soviet Man," *Problems of Communism* 22:5 (September–October 1973), pp. 39–50.

[25] Ethel Dunn and Stephen P. Dunn, "Religion as an Instrument of Culture Change: The Problem of the Sects in the Soviet Union," *Slavic Review*, 23:3 (September 1964) pp. 473–478.

[26] See Ellen P. Mickiewicz, *Soviet Political Schools* (New Haven, Conn.: Yale University Press, 1967).

reinforce, and, when necessary, modify political beliefs and attitudes, and, along with other channels of political communication, to increase support for current policies.

The scope, organization, and content of this program have undergone drastic changes, reflecting shifts in leadership and policy. Its development may be divided into four main stages: the period from 1917 until the consolidation of Stalin's dictatorship; the years of the Stalin "cult," 1938–1953; the era of Khrushchev's leadership; and the post-Khrushchev period.

In the earlier period of Stalin's leadership, about half of the political indoctrination students were not even party members. Many were worker-activists. After 1938, emphasis on ordinary workers was condemned. Stress during the last 15 years of Stalin's rule was on intensive training of bureaucrats and skilled specialists. The publication in 1938 of the *Short Course* in party history provided a bible of ideological orthodoxy, though ritualistic explanations of the text and rote memorization characterized political studies during this period.

To bridge the gulf between the elite and the rest of society that had widened during Stalin's dictatorship Khrushchev urged a Marxist education for all citizens.

The Brezhnev-Kosygin team, unlike Stalin, did not restrict political studies to upper-level party members, but did substantially exclude nonmembers from the program. They cut enrollment in the program drastically, but it remained far larger than under Stalin. As before its trainees were mainly urban party members. Distinctly different from the practices of both Stalin and Khrushchev, moreover, was their effort to set up a systematic and efficient program of Marxist-Leninist education. For the first time, propagandists for party schools were carefully recruited and trained, and their work objectively evaluated. Despite this trend toward professionalism, however, propagandists continued to be part-time volunteers, working under the direction of full-time party functionaries specializing in ideology and political communication.

Despite significant differences between the policies of Khrushchev and his successors, political indoctrination throughout the post-Stalin era has differed markedly from Stalin's pattern. Lacking Stalin's stature, and ruling an increasingly educated people, his successors turned away from command and decree and sought to achieve their ends through persuasion. They recommended a different approach for each occupational, ethnic, and educational group enrolled in institutions of political training, and, as political education became increasingly complex, developed new textbooks on party history and other subjects. Adult socialization occurs on four levels for those who have not graduated from secondary school, for those who have, for training propagandists, and for training cadres.

The elementary political schools for those who have not graduated from secondary schools are intended to accustom communists to the systematic reading of political literature, including periodicals and a minimum of Lenin's works. At this level theory is not broken down into components but is treated as a unified subject. The basic teaching method is informal discussion. School work is supplemented by practical tasks designed to illustrate theoretical ideas and by systematic discussion of current CPSU policy.

At the Marxism-Leninism schools for second-level students, the approach is more analytical. Students study one or more subjects, such as CPSU history and political economy, chiefly through lectures. The practical tasks assigned at this level include carrying out economic reform or political work in collective farms.

Evening universities are the principal agency of instruction at the third level of party education. Their main function now appears to be the training of propagandists, 250,000 of whom were enrolled in 1970. The evening universities also train party, government, trade union, and Komsomol functionaries. Students in the evening universities study for two years if they have higher education and for three if they have only secondary education.

At this third level, instruction includes lectures, seminars, and theoretical conferences. At this level, a participant is considered sufficiently mature, with the help of her party organization, to choose among available programs of instruction, with the understanding that every party member must master Marxist-Leninist theory and fight bourgeois ideology.

The highest level of adult political socialization is

the training of the party functionaries or cadres, who attend special schools, and constitute a select group.

All programs in these institutions include basic political subjects, such as the history of the CPSU, dialectical and historical materialism, political economy, the history of the international labor and national liberation movements, as well as the history of the U.S.S.R. and Soviet construction. In addition, each program requires technical and practical subjects, ranging from law, economics, and planning the national economy through bookkeeping, statistics, and production practices. Roughly one-third of the curriculum in the higher party schools consists of political and ideological subjects; the remaining subjects have to do with general and technical education.

New subjects, such as cybernetics and social development, Marxist-Leninist sociology and empirical sociological research, and current problems of social psychology, have recently been added to the curriculum, reflecting the efforts of the Brezhnev-Kosygin regime to increase the relevance and credibility of ideology by aligning it with scientific data.

On September 7, 1978 a new institution for training leaders of the CPSU opened in Moscow. Amalgamating the existing Academy of Social Sciences and the Higher Party School, both under the CPSU Central Committee, the new agency seemed to be intended to give party workers improved understanding of the increasingly complex social, political, economic and international environment in which they must operate.[27]

Although the basic theme of all material for the political courses remains the struggle between socialism and capitalism, official perceptions of the struggle and the language used to describe it have changed since Stalin. Compare, for example, the *Short Course* used in the Stalin era with basic post-Stalin political texts.

The *Short Course* was essentially a chronicle — extremely biased and full of calculated distortions — of Lenin's contributions to communism as interpreted by Stalin and, above all, of Stalin's struggles against and victories over his enemies. Apart from praise of Lenin and Stalin, the principal feature of the *Short Course* is its harsh criticism of "spies," "monsters," and "dregs of humanity" — Trotski, Bukharin, Kamenev, Zinovev, and others either murdered or removed from office during Stalin's control of Soviet political power.

The elementary text *Foundations of Political Knowledge* (1959 and 1963), although still containing historical oversimplifications and polemic, seems rational, sober, and well balanced in comparison with the *Short Course*. The post-Stalin text is organized according to topics rather than chronologically, beginning with a chapter on the class struggle and the socialist revolution. There follow chapters on "socialism, the first phase of communism," the victory of socialism in the U.S.S.R., and so forth. The third section begins with a chapter on "communism — the future of mankind," which is followed by chapters on "the international liberation movement," "peaceful coexistence and the struggle for peace," and a final chapter, "the Communist Party — the leader of the Soviet people." Stalin is ignored in this work, which gives Lenin all credit for the concepts upon which the Soviet state and party are built.

Post-Khrushchev works used at the upper level of the party training program, such as the still unfinished, multivolume *History of the Communist Party of the Soviet Union*, projected a more positive image of Stalin than was approved under Khrushchev. As in the past, political developments powerfully influence the agenda of the political training program.

Stalin's methods had several strengths, including sharpness of tone, intensity of mood, and simplicity of presentation; his successors sought relevance, timeliness, and concreteness for propaganda programs, but not at the cost of ideological orthodoxy. Khrushchev's innovations, however, seemed to threaten a watering down of official doctrine.

The expansion of adult socialization, especially under Khrushchev, relied much more on nonprofessional volunteers than either Stalin or Brezhnev did. This deprofessionalization of the system sought to enhance its appeal and generate new vitality, but it had the grave disadvantage from the viewpoint of Khrushchev's conservative opponents of reducing

[27] Sergei Vorotnytsyn, "New Academy of Social Sciences to Serve as Center for Training Top Party Managers," *Radio Liberty Research Bulletin*, No. 227/78, October 17, 1978, 2pp.

the homogeneity and authority that had characterized Stalinist indoctrination.

POLITICAL COMMUNICATION

Nowhere is the contrast between Soviet and American politics more striking than in their patterns of political communication, which is one reason why citizens of either society feel uneasy about the other. Russians are shocked by the sensationalism and commercialism of the Western press. Americans are appalled by the massive effort made to ensure that citizens see the world as rulers want them to. American society confronts citizens with a free choice among many sometimes contradictory facts and interpretations; the Soviet system bombards them with messages bent on reforming them and meant to reinforce official versions of truth.

In both the United States and the Soviet Union, access to communication channels is easiest for groups and individuals of high status. And in both, the cards are stacked against information or opinions that elite groups see as subversive. Obviously, however, the range of permissible disclosure and advocacy is vastly broader in the United States and other Western democracies.

Criticism of the monotony and staleness of news supplied by Soviet press, radio, and television is increasing. And in some cases, Soviet radio and television have been permitted to release kinds of information not previously published in the press.[28] Soviet television is, however, still dull in content and weak in impact, and it is also surprisingly undeveloped, considering the regime's interest in the propaganda potential of communications technology. The press, still dominant in the communications system, has been prodded to provide fresher news and has even been encouraged to present a more realistic and less consistently positive picture of Soviet life.

In the U.S.S.R., all agencies that inform the public are supervised by party functionaries and internal party units. The top policy-making agency for political communication is the Section for Propaganda, a part of the CPSU Central Committee. Its control extends down through party agencies to primary party organizations.

Directives from the Section for Propaganda of the Central Party headquarters go out to state organs, such as the State Commission on Radio and Television and the State Commission on Cinematography, to public organizations such as the Union of Soviet Writers and the Union of Soviet Artists, and to an organization known as Znanie ("Knowledge"), which has over one million members drawn from the intelligentsia, workers, and farmers. These agencies mobilize opinion and help the party to establish and maintain links with the masses. Members of Znanie, for example, reportedly delivered 17 million lectures in 1968.

The primary party organizations are at the base of the party pyramid. They send out the party's directives and receive citizens' complaints and reactions, which they pass on up the pyramid. They must make certain that all patterns and instruments of communication are coordinated and attuned to current policy. They are expected to organize voluntary lecture groups, to publish local papers, and select workers in factories to serve as editors of wall newspapers, radio news, and the like. They also see that clubs and other cultural groups function properly and that the propaganda and agitation of the mass media are reaching their targets.

In performing these functions, the primary party organizations draw on a large number of volunteers. Some are unpaid volunteer workers or village correspondents (*rabselkory*), whose history reaches back to the 1920s. Originally intended as contributors to a people's press, the rabselkory fell under bureaucratic control during the Stalin period but were revived on a vast scale by Khrushchev. By 1960 they numbered about 5 million, including both party members and nonmembers. They participated in major opinion mobilization drives, discovered how party directives were actually being carried out (by raiding on factories and farms), and conveyed to newspapers, radio, and television information about workers performance, morale, and complaints. The shortage of data on the rabselkory since Khrushchev's fall seems to indicate that they are not as important to Soviet

[28] Mark W. Hopkins, *Mass Media in the Soviet Union* (New York: Pegasus, 1970), pp. 242–245.

journalism as they were in the era of the populist Khrushchev.

Oral Agitation

A distinctively Soviet technique of political communication is personal oral agitation. Russian communists pioneered in using organized word of mouth to shape public opinion. Unlike journalists, oral agitators operate face-to-face with their audiences and are able to observe and report to their superiors on public attitudes and moods.

The massive development of oral agitation was in large part a result of economic and social underdevelopment. Where literacy and educational and technological levels were low, it was an effective way of getting word of the party to the masses, particularly in places of work. Oral agitation conveyed urgent political messages better than the press could, and it provided a two-way line of communication between ordinary people and the local party organizations.

During World War II the principal task of the agitators was to enlist every citizen's full energies to the war effort. In peacetime, oral agitation traditionally reaches its most massive proportions during elections to village, town, republic, oblast, and U.S.S.R. soviets. From the standpoint of Western democracies, of course, the one-party, one-candidate Soviet elections are not elections. But in Soviet doctrine, unanimity among voters is a test of the unity between society and the party, one of the themes that agitators emphasize at election time.

The Brezhnev-Kosygin leadership did not abandon oral agitation as an instrument of mass pressure, but it did attempt to make it more sophisticated and effective.[29] A new type of agitator, the political communicator (*politinformator*), appeared. Political communicators, each a skilled defender of party policy, speak or lead discussions in a variety of locations, not just in a single factory or mine, as was the case with agitators. There is also evidence that the focus of oral agitation has shifted to the city block or the apartment house, perhaps as a reflection of the decrease in time spent at work places.

The Press

All Soviet newspapers are published by the party and its organs. *Pravda (Truth)*, the most important Soviet newspaper, is published by the Central Committee. *Izvestiya (News)*, the second-ranking daily, is the organ of the Supreme Soviet. The fifteen republics also have newspapers, produced jointly by party headquarters and the republican government, with most editorials reprinted from *Pravda*. The armed forces, trade unions, Komsomol, and other organizations also publish their own newspapers and periodicals. At times, local publications make it possible for liberal authors to publish works that Moscow would have censored. But in general, access to these newspapers is tightly controlled by the party.

The Soviet press might be described as the largest journalistic operation in the world under one management. The exceptionally uniform perspective and approach that party control ensures is reinforced by the special place that the major Moscow newspapers, especially *Pravda*, occupy in the total press system. In 1969 *Pravda* had a circulation of 8.4 million, *Izvestiya* 8.3 million, and *Komsomolskaya Pravda* 7.1 million (see Table 12.6).[30]

Except for strictly local news, much of the information published in Soviet newspapers comes from the central news agency, TASS. Because all Soviet citizens are active builders of communism bound together by common goals, the regional press must supply its readers with the same information about national and international events that readers of the central press receive.

[29] Jerry F. Hough, *The Soviet Prefects* (Cambridge, Mass.: Harvard University Press, 1969), p. 133. As of 1974, there were more than one and a half million political communicators, according to N. A. Shipeleva, et al., *Politicheskaya informatsiya* [Political Information] Moscow: Mysl (Thought) Publishing House, 1974. This book provides evidence of dissatisfaction of Soviet audiences with the far from fresh or interesting news supplied to them and also with the leadership's concern over loss of influence on the public and determination to use polling and other techniques to remedy defects in the mass communication system. It asserts that the party's function is to explain to the masses what their true needs and interests are.

[30] *Pechat v sssr* [The Press in the U.S.S.R.], an official Soviet publication, annually provides data on numbers and circulation of Soviet newspapers. Above data were in its 1970 issue.

Table 12.6

Growth of Newspaper Circulation in the U.S.S.R., 1950–1968

Administrative level	*1950*	*1958*	*1963*	*1968*
National				
Number of papers	23	24	23	26
Copies printed per issue (in thousands)	18,906	19,984	33,433	55,977
Republic				
Number of papers	137	176	148	157
Copies printed per issue (in thousands)	4,819	10,581	15,492	21,097
Krai, oblast, okrug				
Number of papers	310	324	282	289
Copies printed per issue (in thousands)	7,349	10,703	12,754	16,295
Autonomous *oblast* and *okrug*				
Number of papers	71	107	92	96
Copies printed per issue (in thousands)	838	1,607	1,884	2,819
City				
Number of papers	346	460	421	597
Copies printed per issue (in thousands)	1,493	3,109	4,265	9,329
Production administrations of collective and state farms				
Number of papers	—	—	1,751	—
Copies printed per issue (in thousands)	—	—	10,773	—
Raion (district)				
Number of papers	4,193	4,148	20	2,793
Copies printed per issue (in thousands)	6,903	7,927	34	13,417
Lower press (house organs)				
Number of papers	2,751	2,447	2,430	3,349
Copies printed per issue (in thousands)	5,139	4,862	4,434	6,519
Individual collective farms				
Number of papers	—	2,777	1,624	1,447
Copies printed per issue (in thousands)	—	1,628	1,151	1,000
Total				
Number of papers	7,831	10,733	6,791	8,754
Copies printed per issue (in thousands)	35,964	59,323	84,220	126,453

Source: From *Soviet Political Indoctrination: Development in Mass Media and Propaganda Since Stalin* by Gayle Durham Hollander. Copyright © 1972 by Praeger Publishers, Inc. Reprinted by permission of Holt, Rinehart and Winston. According to the newspaper *Sovetskaya Rossiya* for May 6, 1978, there were 7,985 newspapers in 56 languages, and the total print had reached 170 million copies. The editorial making the above assertions also stated that there were 4,726 periodicals in the country.

Increasingly, journalists are trained in the universities and higher party schools, where they encounter a steady flow of party resolutions and officially written articles. According to a director of TASS, newspaper material must not only be timely and truthful; it must also contain information that is organized, instructive, and didactic.

Since the death of Stalin, the agencies of communication, like other aspects of the political system, have tended to be more responsive than before to consumer frustration and other reader interests. Under Khrushchev, open conflict over literary and artistic questions flourished. The post-Stalin years saw extensive use of a pre-Stalinist technique — public discussion of policies. Although basic policies had already been formulated by the party, an effort was made to elicit informed expert opinion and to mobilize all possible public support.

In the 1960s, the regime began again (for the first time since the 1920s) to use opinion polls, surveys, and other social science techniques to analyze group attitudes and to shape a satisfactory consensus. One of the regime's responses to the increased sophistication of media audiences was to institute large-scale audience surveys, including major studies of *Izvestiya* and other papers. Among other things, these studies indicated that readers were not interested in heavy articles on economics but wanted more human interest stories and information on foreign affairs. Even so, the familiar technique of discrediting opinion deemed damaging to public morale by labeling it imperialist propaganda or espionage has been resorted to more and more frequently since Krushchev's ouster. Furthermore, tight surveillance continued to be exercised over the media by doctrinal, administrative, and legal controls. Formal censorship is exercised by the Chief Administration for the Affairs of Literature and Publishing Houses (Glavlit). A control over communication more important than that of Glavlit is the indirect censorship effected by party organizations in their day-to-day operations, through party members selected as editors and journalists.

Unauthorized Communication: Dissent and Repression

In the mid-1960s an underground literature began to be circulated in the U.S.S.R. and smuggled abroad. The expansion of such *samizdat* ("self-published") writing, which bypassed the censorship agencies, was one of the most important aspects of a new phenomenon: the appearance of an unorthodox, though not necessarily anti-Marxist, current of public opinion. Since April 1968 Soviet civil rights advocates have been compiling, disseminating, and sending abroad a *Chronicle of Current Events*, containing protest petitions, reports of arrests, trials, sentences of dissenters, and related materials. Dissent in the U.S.S.R. can be viewed as the harbinger of a nascent counter-regime political culture, antipodal to the "monolithic" official political culture. Its articulators reject authoritarianism in doctrine and conformity in behavior. They protest against official norms and policies as individuals or as members of loosely organized groups. Their views vary widely, ranging from revisionist Marxism through Western-oriented liberalism to a neo-Slavophilism inspired by nostalgia for Russian Orthodox religious values — and, even further to the "right," all the way to neo-Fascist Russian nationalism. Many non-Russian dissidents are motivated primarily by indignation over what they regard as Moscow's violation of ethnic and national values ostensibly protected by Soviet law. Thus the roots of dissent are very diverse.

However, there has over the years been close cooperation — as well as some friction — between representatives of the Soviet civil rights, or "democratic" dissenters, and other dissident tendencies. This cooperation grew especially close after Yuri Orlov, a physicist, organized in May 1976 the Moscow Public Group to Promote the Fulfillment of the Helsinki Accords. This group coordinated its activities with a number of other small groups, some organized on a territorial basis. They included a Commission to Investigate Abuses of Psychiatry, the Christian Committee for the Defense of Believers' Rights, etc. All of these groups — often referred to collectively as Helsinki monitoring groups, shared the purpose of generating pressure, mainly by gaining support abroad, to persuade the Soviet authorities to fulfill the human rights pledges contained in the Final Acts of the Conference on Security and Cooperation in Europe (concluded July 31, 1975). Academician Andrei Sakharov, since the late 1960s the most powerful proponent of human rights in the U.S.S.R., strongly supported Orlov's movement, and Elena Bonner, Sakharov's wife, was one of its organizers.

The Soviet Helsinki movement undoubtedly achieved a more powerful impact on world public opinion than any previous effort made by Soviet advocates of human rights and "democratization." Doubtless much of this impact resulted from President Carter's espousal of human rights as a major theme of United States foreign policy, and his statements and actions expressing support for the Soviet human rights movement.

Perhaps the impact of the Helsinki campaign inside the U.S.S.R. was, potentially, even more important than its effects abroad. There is evidence that the campaign of exposure of violations by Soviet officials of individual and group rights conducted by the Helsinki groups was beginning to mobilize segments of the Soviet public that had previously not been affected by dissident communications. Perhaps particularly important were the links that began to develop between the Helsinki groups and a number of Soviet workers who sought to form a "true labor union," independent of the official All Union Council of Trade Unions. Visitors from all parts of the U.S.S.R. reportedly showed up at Orlov's apartment in Moscow.

By the spring of 1979 the Soviet authorities had sentenced to prison camps, or permitted (or forced), to emigrate not only almost all of the sixty odd active participants in the Helsinki Moritorium Movement (besides Orlov's Moscow group there were affiliated groups in Kiev, capitol of the Ukraine and in the capitals of the Lithuanian, Armenian and Georgian republics) — one member of the Ukranian group had apparently died after torture, which had not, however, forced him to recant — but also most of the remaining veteran dissident activists who had begun to agitate for human rights in the mid-1960s. It seemed likely that for a time there would be a pause in the human rights campaign, while new forces gathered to resume the struggle. However, academician Andrei Sakharov, since 1968 the central figure in the human rights campaign, continued to protest to the Soviet authorities and to world opinion what he regarded as official Soviet violations of the human rights provisions of the Soviet constitution and laws, and of international pacts signed by the U.S.S.R. Moreover, a tradition of self-sacrificing struggle, by peaceful means, for basic rights and liberties had grown up. Its creators had demonstrated impressive tenacity in support of their convictions. Undoubtedly the Soviet advocates of "democratization," though a small minority even among Soviet intellectuals, articulated the opinions of growing circles of Soviet society most members of which were not yet ready to run the awesome risks involved in openly demanding freedom of speech, inviolability of correspondence, freedom to reside and move wherever they wished inside their country, or to leave it and return to it freely, and other rights and liberties taken for granted in Western democracies. The Kremlin harshly repressed the proponents of civil and human rights, including champions of freedom of religion and those who spoke out for rights of non-Russian ethnic groups ostensibly granted by the Soviet laws and constitution. It also moved swiftly to nip in the bud Vladinin Klebanov's (an ex-coal miner) attempt in 1977–1978 to organize a labor union outside the CPSU-controlled official labor movement. But it is significant that many workers — as well as other citizens — got in touch with Klebanov, or journeyed to Moscow to see Orlov, or in other ways responded to the impetus of the Helsinki monitoring groups.

The persistence of dissent since 1965 — when a group of Soviet citizens demonstrated in Moscow, carrying banners demanding that the Soviet government respect the Soviet constitution — impels us to take seriously a proposition set forth by Peter Reddaway, perhaps the leading authority in the West on Soviet dissent. According to Reddaway, "dissent in the Soviet Union is endemic and spreading, because the regime is not alleviating its root cause — the suppression of civil, political, cultural and religious freedom."[31]

[31] Peter B. Reddaway, "Notes from Underground," *The Times Literary Supplement*, June 16, 1978. On Klebanov's "free labor union," see Valeri Chalidze, ed., *SSSR — Rabochee drizhenie?* [U.S.S.R. — A Labor Movement?] (New York: Chronicle Press, 1978); on the attractive force of Orlov's movement for workers and others, see Ludmilla Alexeeva, in *Novoe Russkoe Slovo* [*New Russian Word*] (New York), March 27, 1977; also *Documents of Helsinki Dissent from the Soviet Union and Eastern Europe*, compiled by the staff of the Commission on Security and Cooperation in Europe (Washington, D.C., 1978). For background, see Rudolf L. Tokes, ed., *Dissent in the U.S.S.R.* (Baltimore: Johns Hopkins University Press, 1975), and Frederick C. Barghoorn, *Detente and the Democratic Movement in the U.S.S.R.* (New York: Free Press, 1976).

POLITICAL PARTICIPATION AND RECRUITMENT

The Recruitment of the Elites

Although Soviet leaders and theorists do not claim that equality exists in Soviet society, they deny the existence of an elite of any kind. They assert that Soviet socialism offers talented and public-spirited citizens greater equality of opportunity for advancement to society's highest political, economic, and cultural positions than exists in capitalist societies.

In fact, however, elite recruitment in the U.S.S.R. is only partially determined by equality of opportunity. In the Soviet Union, as elsewhere, those in positions of power and influence tend to obstruct the entry of newcomers into the establishment, especially newcomers whose perspectives differ from their own.

The tightly centralized Soviet recruitment system tends to protect the mediocre and exclude much talent from participation in public life. Nevertheless, from the Kremlin's point of view the recruitment system has advantages, the most important being that it tends to ensure the filling of all strategic posts by politically reliable personnel.

The Soviet personnel system is controlled by the top leadership of the CPSU, working through the central party and state administrative organs. It is not surprising therefore that recruitment is planned and supervised by the executives who control the party's central organs and that the top leader devotes a good deal of time to this task.

In the Central Committee, a powerful secretary usually acts as the leader's deputy in what are referred to as organizational matters, including the selection of top-level personnel. Such a person — for example, Georgi M. Malenkov in Stalin's time or Andrei I. Kirichenko and Frol R. Kozlov at different times under Khrushchev — is likely to be the second-ranking man in the political hierarchy, although no such post is explicitly identified. In the post-Khrushchev era, however, control over top-level personnel seems to be exercised collectively; presumably the leaders jointly play the major role. Usually a specialist, V. N. Titov under Khrushchev or I. V. Kapitonov under Brezhnev, operates the administrative mechanism of upper-level leadership selection. Since 1966, Kapitonov has headed the Central Committee section for party organs, consistently the most powerful of the Central Committee staff agencies.

A system of *rekommendatsiya* ("recommendation") for high political positions is used by the top leadership of the CPSU. Direct intervention by the party leaders in high-level leadership selection is not openly acknowledged, but the rapid rise of certain protégés of top men indicates the persistence of this procedure.[32]

The day-to-day business of elite recruitment is handled through the *nomenklatura* ("nomenclature") system, which refers to key job categories and descriptions that a specific party committee or a governmental or other agency is responsible for filling.

There seems to be no provision for the nomenclature system in Soviet law. Once an official is on a nomenclature list, he is apparently assured of tenure for life, barring serious incompetence, flagrant political errors or close involvement with a fallen leader. Through this system the party leadership largely determines the life chances of skilled professionals, whether or not they are party members. Because access to command posts in Soviet society is controlled by the top executives of the major bureaucracies, it follows that success depends partly on such factors as personal and organizational relationships with rising and falling leaders. Political earthquakes in the leadership structure can thus have a shattering effect on careers, even at the periphery. Under Brezhnev's leadership, security of tenure was much greater than under Stalin or Khrushchev.

RECRUITMENT TRENDS WITHIN THE APPARATUS When the economy was still underdeveloped and the political system not yet consolidated, the party could make do with cadres who were for the most part Bolshevik apparatchiki, highly committed ideologically but often poorly educated and lacking professional skills. With industrialization, however, it became necessary to bring into the party leadership more and more specialists. The

[32] See Frederick C. Barghoorn, "Trends in Top Political Leadership in the U.S.S.R.," in R. Barry Farrell (ed.), *Political Leadership in Eastern Europe and the Soviet Union* (Chicago: Aldine, 1970), p. 62. On tenure under Brezhnev, see Jerry F. Hough and Merle Fainsod, *How the Soviet Union is Governed* (Harvard University Press: Cambridge, Mass., 1979), pp. 260–264.

problem for the party was how to harness the precious skills of these people without allowing them to acquire influence that might alter the direction and structure of the emerging socialist system.

Stalin's answer was compulsion laced with terror, material incentives, and a measure of autonomy for the state and managerial bureaucracies. Khrushchev, because he did not use terror as Stalin had, was less willing to grant bureaucratic autonomy. He sought to cope with the problem by providing attractive opportunities for specialists within the party leadership. Although at first Khrushchev curbed the technocrats on whom Stalin had conferred vast administrative powers his recruitment policy seemed to create conditions that would allow industrial managers and other production specialists to gain unprecedented influence within the party. This prospect aroused resentment and opposition among the less specialized apparatchiki who feared for their own influence. The Brezhnev-Kosygin leadership has professed to show greater favor to the traditional party members, to the professional propagandists and to the police, intelligence units, and military.

THE ROLE AND INFLUENCE OF THE APPARATCHIK Even in the Stalin era, when great insecurity was the lot of party cadres, positions in the party were eagerly sought because of their power and prestige. In lists of officials printed by the Soviet press, the names of party secretaries always precede those of the highest-ranking government officials. In every city and town, the best buildings are reserved for party headquarters and offices. In important national celebrations, party officials have the positions of honor.

Apparatchiki continue to dominate the political elite, but new criteria increasingly influence the selection of these political executives. George Fischer notes the emergence between 1958 and 1962 of a dual executive trend in recruitment, meaning that an increasing proportion of party executives had done "extensive work of two kinds within the economy, technical work and party work, prior to getting a top party post."[33] Frederic J. Fleron, Jr., applies the term "co-opted officials" to "those who entered the political elite in mid or late career and who had probably established very close professional-vocational ties outside the political elite."[34] He points out that between 1952 and 1965 the proportion of CPSU Central Committee members from the scientific, economic, cultural, and technical intelligentsia increased significantly, while the number of professional politicians decreased. Despite these trends, the largest group on the Central Committee and in the political elite are general utility officials, promoted after lengthy hours at lower levels.

A common characteristic of the modern-day party executive is his improved educational background, particularly in engineering and other technical fields. Many Soviet engineers who become political leaders either do not practice their profession after graduation from technical school or do so for only a short time. Often they have already, as students, devoted much time to Komsomol or party activity and were tapped for political careers while very young. Still, more and more apparatchiki have had technical educations. Many have graduated from other types of institutions, such as the higher party school, where the curriculum features industrial administration and technology. A good many were also educated as agricultural specialists, school teachers, journalists, and so forth.

The supremacy of party over state can be seen in the careers of the men who have risen to the top of the Soviet power pyramid. Lenin created the party organization and then became head of state. Stalin won power as head of the party apparatus he himself had fashioned. Malenkov and Khrushchev were party leaders, and Brezhnev and Kosygin had important party experience before assuming top leadership posts in the Soviet political system.

ACCESS TO ELITE MEMBERSHIP For some large social groups — women, youth, farmers, and workers — opportunity to enter the party elite, and especially executive party bodies, is quite limited. Men, middle-aged functionaries with seniority, city dwellers, and politically reliable members of the intelligentsia enjoy preference.

[33] George Fischer, *The Soviet System and Modern Society* (New York: Atherton, 1969), pp. 39, 47–64.

[34] Frederic J. Fleron, Jr., "Representation of Career Types in Soviet Political Leadership," in Farrell (ed.), *Political Leadership in Eastern Europe and the Soviet Union*, pp. 108–139.

Since the mid-1930s, when a trend favoring the recruitment of women abruptly ended, a man's chances of becoming a party member has been about five times greater than a woman's. Though women's chances grew slightly in the 1960s, there were only a handful of women on the CPSU Central Committees elected in 1971 and 1976. It is worth noting, however, that a very high percentage of Soviet physicians, lawyers, engineers, and other professionals are women. They do not, as a rule, achieve professional eminance or administrative authority.[35]

Non-Russian and especially some non-Slavic ethnic minorities are also underrepresented in CPSU membership, and despite efforts to recruit more ordinary workers and collective farm peasants, they continue to be poorly represented in the party, and still more so in the leadership.

Directed Political Participation

Running the national economy is the Soviet elite's most important role, at least in terms of the proportion of party leadership cadres assigned to it. Other roles include overseeing national security policy, maintaining order, supervising education, culture, and communications, and directing the activities of public organizations. These organizations include the CPSU, the trade unions, and the Komsomol, as well as work collectives and meetings of soldiers. These organizations are hierarchies controlled from Moscow. Their structures and processes conform to the regime's interpretation of the Leninist principle of democratic centralism. Even if the Moscow leadership made the utmost effort to ensure that they functioned in accordance with the principle of socialist democracy, such enormous bureaucracies — the CPSU has more than 16 million members, the party-dominated All-Union Central Council of Trade Unions has more than 100 million — could hardly provide anything but a largely mandatory, routinized participation for their rank and file. In fact, participation in the activities of these bodies consists not in influencing policy making, but in rendering various services to the state and demonstrating support and allegiance for the regime's doctrines and policies. Thus "mass participation," as these activities are called, has little in common with political participation in Western democracies.

In keeping with the guided, mobilizational style of Soviet mass participation, the officials who direct it are assigned to their jobs by the CPSU. As a rule, political careers are not made by rising to high rank in public organizations; rather, individuals who have already made a name for themselves in the party are assigned to high rank in the organizations. However, as was indicated earlier, individuals — for example, former Komsomol head Eugene Tyazhelnikov, now CPSU secretary for propaganda — who display leadership qualities in Komsomol work sometimes become important party apparatchiki.

In *On Socialist Democracy*, a remarkably objective, well-informed analysis written from a reformist Marxist perspective, dissident Roy Medvedev has argued that the quality of political and social participation in the U.S.S.R. falls far below the levels set both by Marxist ideals and by contemporary Western bourgeois practices. According to him, except to some extent at the lowest level, elections to party, soviet, trade union, and other offices are rigged by higher ranking units. Rank-and-file members have neither the information nor — given the rewards for conformity and the penalties for dissent — the inclination to protest or resist policies and directives handed down.[36]

However, from the point of view of the regime, Soviet-style political participation is useful. Like the massive political socialization programs, which in some ways it supplements and reinforces, organized mass participation keeps the masses busy and out of mischief. It also, by involving them in regime-directed routines and rituals, fosters habits of compliance in people and instills a perception of the omnipotence of the leadership.

Even for the Soviet masses, directed participation may to some extent be a source of psychological satisfaction. For one thing, its changeless routines may create a reassuring sense of stability, though this may be offset for some by boredom with official ritu-

[35] On the limited role of women in the political life of the U.S.S.R. and other communist countries, see Barbara Wolfe Jancar, *Women Under Communism* (Baltimore, Maryland: Johns Hopkins University Press, 1978), Chapter 5.

[36] Roy A. Medvedev, *On Socialist Democracy* (New York: Knopf, 1975), ch. 6–9.

als and slogans and for others by anger at pressure to step up compliance with regime demands. However, pressures are mitigated, or so recent emigrants say, by the tendency of those in charge of Soviet organizations to be satisfied with minimal levels of conformity, provided it is not accompanied by open protest, or what is considered intolerable, organized, collective protest. It should be borne in mind, too, that for docile members the mass organizations provide coveted benefits, such as cheap, all-expense-paid travel to vacation resorts.

It would be unrealistic to expect Soviet citizens — except perhaps those of Jewish or Baltic origin, who have a less authoritarian tradition than others under Soviet rule, especially the Russians — to be as irked by controlled, single candidate elections as we fancy we would be. Political pluralism as it has been known in Western democracies for a century or more existed in Russsia only briefly between the 1905 revolution and the breakdown of the tsarist regime in 1917, and was in a severely circumscribed form at that. It did not sink its roots deep enough, or last long enough, to transform the traditional authoritarian Russian political culture into one resembling what Gabriel Almond and Sidney Verba called the civic culture, or to generate, to use Robert Dahl's term, the institutions and beliefs appropriate to polyarchy.[37]

Bureaucracy — as manifested in Soviet public organizations and in the system as a whole — has attained its most elephantine dimensions in this socialist society whose founders thought they could abolish it. But the phenomena discussed here must to some extent be regarded as an extreme of characteristics common to modern industrial societies, where economic development has provided governments with organizational and communications facilities capable of mobilizing and socializing unprecedently large numbers. However, comparison between Soviet and advanced industrial societies should not be pushed too far. In the latter there is no centralized, coordinated system of political mobilization even remotely comparable to the hypertrophied bureaucratic mechanism of directed political participation, Soviet style.

[37] See Gabriel A. Almond and Sidney Verba, *The Civic Culture* (Princeton, N.J.: Princeton University Press, 1963); Robert A. Dahl, *Polyarchy: Participation and Opposition* (New Haven, Conn.: Yale University Press, 1971).

POWER STRUGGLES AND POLICY MAKING

The obscurity that shrouds all aspects of Soviet politics hangs heaviest around the policy-making process. To be sure, Soviet sources provide us with voluminous justifications of Kremlin decisions and attacks on the decisions of other governments, but the lavishness of their propaganda contrasts sharply with the unwillingness of Soviet spokesmen to speak frankly about who initiates and sponsors policy, policy discussion and deliberation, deciding on resource allocation, methods of implementing policy, and other essential information. However, careful study of the Soviet press and periodical literature in the light of what is known from other sources (including Soviet actions) can reveal much about the actors in the Soviet political process and their ideological perspectives, political strategies, and personal interactions.

Only a tiny minority of experienced leaders who have worked their way to the innermost agencies of political power — the Secretariat and Politburo of the CPSU and the highest government body, the Council of Ministers — normally participate in national policy making. However, persons at lower levels of party, scientific, state, police, military, and other bureaucracies often play important supportive or implementing roles.

The Khrushchev and post-Khrushchev administrations differed more from Stalin's practices than from one another. Both post-Stalin regimes renounced terror, though not repression against dissidents. Both, especially the post-Khrushchev leadership, were oligarchical or collective in practice and in principle. Under both regimes, policies were hammered out laboriously through extensive debate and discussion — mainly in the Politburo — that culminated in votes legitimizing final decisions. And the top leader in both regimes has at times had to alter policy in response to opposition from other Politburo members. Khrushchev had to treat his conservative opponents in the antiparty group more leniently than he wished to. He was defeated in his effort to reverse the traditional economic priority of development rather than consumption, and he had to renounce favorite projects such as the establishment of unions and collective farms. The conservative Brezhnev, though more successful than Khrushchev in building consensus at the highest levels, has had considerable difficulty balancing between opposing opinion groups on issues such as the official attitude toward Stalin, the respective roles to be played in the Soviet system by party and state cultural policy, and resource allocation.

Group Interests and Policy Making

Until recently scholars agreed that effective participation in Soviet policy making and implementation was confined to the top leaders and persons they consulted. In the last few years, however, other scholars have argued that professional groups, including economists, jurists, and natural scientists, as well as members of bureaucracies such as the police, army, and groups with shared opinions on issues of concern to them influence policymaking, at least on some issues.[38] A good example was the decision in 1964 to abandon one of Khrushchev's favorite policies, the inclusion in school curricula of vocational training and work experience. Philip Stewart concluded from the success of an informal coalition of educational officials and scientists in changing this policy favored by Khrushchev that "the norms of Soviet policy making do not exclude interest groupings, in this case middle rank officials and experts and some distinguished scientists, from all stages of the policy process.[39]

In the post-Khrushchev period, well-informed observers agree, a wide range of interests assert themselves in the published media. However, it has become more difficult since Khrushchev's day to bring about innovation. The post-Khrushchev leadership has encouraged the articulation of conservative, nationalist opinions; this trend is supported by the political administration of the armed forces and the security agencies. Advocates of democratization have openly protested such trends. They linked freedom of expression to technical and economic progress, denying the possibility of the latter if the former is curtailed.[40]

Succession Crises

Stalin ruled with overwhelming power achieved in a number of ways. He ruthlessly demolished opposition, whether real or suspected, and did not hesitate to exile to remote regions whole classes and populations or to liquidate respected leaders, such as Nikolai Bukharin, who opposed his terror.

During World War II, Stalin took over a number of top government posts in addition to his position as general secretary of the CPSU. He became head of the government, then chairman of the State Defense Committee (a cabinet that supervised all policies involved in waging war) and commissar of defense. He later named himself commander-in-chief of the armed forces and, finally, generalissimo.

Stalin was keenly sensitive to power machinations in his entourage. He organized the duties of his Politburo lieutenants so that he knew what they were doing at all times, even if they were kept guessing about their standing with him.[41] The struggle to succeed him, however, persisted all the while, particularly as Stalin grew older. During most of the period from 1939 to Stalin's death in 1953, Georgi M. Malenkov was the leading contender, with Andrei A. Zhdanov, Nikita S. Khrushchev, and Laurenti P. Beria also vying for the dictator's favor.

Malenkov, whose education included training as an engineer, was a Kremlin insider, a political worker in the Red Army during the Civil War who then began a period of long service in the Central Committee apparatus. By 1939 he was a member of the party Secretariat, and in 1946 he became a member of the Politburo, where he was outranked by

[38] See H. Gordon Skilling and Franklyn Griffiths (eds.) *Interest Groups in Soviet Politics* (Princeton, N.J.: Princeton University Press, 1971).

[39] Philip D. Stewart, "Soviet Interest Groups and the Policy Process: The Repeal of Production Education," *World Politics*, 22:5 (October 1969), pp. 29–50.

[40] See especially "Manifesto II," by Andrei Sakharov, Valentine Turchin and Roy Medvedev in *Sakharov Speaks* (New York: Vintage Books, 1974), pp. 116–134.

[41] Howard R. Swearer, *The Politics of Succession in the U.S.S.R.* (Boston: Little, Brown, 1964), p. 11.

Zhdanov and Khrushchev, whose memberships went back to 1939. Malenkov's activities and statements indicate that he valued organizational and industrial production efficiency more than ideological zeal. From 1948 on, Malenkov belonged to the three main Soviet executive bodies — the Politburo, Secretariat, and Council of Ministers — a position of interlocking influence equaled only by Stalin.

Until his death, Zhdanov, rather than Khrushchev, was Malenkov's main rival. A veteran functionary like Malenkov, Zhdanov held important party posts in Leningrad and Moscow and represented those in the apparatus who gave highest priority to strict ideological orthodoxy. Zhdanov supported Marshal Tito of Yugoslavia, then pressing for vigorous communist expansion, but the Soviet-Yugoslav split in June 1948 dashed the hopes of his supporters, and at the end of August of that year Zhdanov died.[42] During the following months his close associates were purged, and Malenkov's associates began to occupy the vacated posts.

By late 1948, there were three survivors of the Kremlin power struggle: Malenkov, Beria, and Khrushchev. Beria entered the party in 1917 and took part in the Civil War. In 1921 he entered the Cheka, or secret police, where he made good progress. In 1938 he became head of the NKVD, as the secret police were then called. In 1946 he became a member of the Politburo.

Khrushchev joined the party in 1918. A coal miner without formal education, he was sent to party training institutions and did party work in his native Ukraine. In 1934 he became second secretary of the Moscow party organization and in 1938 first secretary of the Ukrainian party. In 1939 he became a member of the Politburo, and in 1949 Khrushchev returned to Moscow, as first secretary of the Moscow party organization and as one of the secretaries of the Central Committee.

Thus, at Stalin's death in 1953, there were three contenders for the succession: Malenkov, a party specialist with experience at the center; Beria, a party and secret police leader; and Khrushchev, a party leader with experience in the Ukraine and at the center.

Khrushchev won the struggle despite Beria's and Malenkov's important sources of power. His personality and skills, his career associations, and his political programs helped him — after the elimination of Beria, who so threatened the other top leaders that they united against him — to mobilize an effective majority of the top and middle party apparatus in the Politburo, especially in the Central Committee. Malenkov's greatest liability was his lack of experience and contacts outside of Moscow. Unlike Khrushchev, who had been head of the important Ukrainian party organization, he was unable to build a large following among territorial party secretaries. And Khrushchev, because he had been absent from Moscow during the terror of 1936–1938, was relatively free of the stigma attached to those closely associated with Stalin's rule.

Formally elected first secretary of the Central Committee in 1953, Khrushchev proceeded to expand the Secretariat, to which he appointed many followers. In his drive for power during the first period of his rule (1953–1957), Khrushchev relied mainly on support from his old associates in the Ukrainian party apparatus, on the territorial apparatus generally, and on the armed forces.

By mid-1957 Khrushchev was ready to deal with his opponents, including conservatives like Molotov and Kaganovich, who had spent many years in the state and economic bureaucracy, in addition to the ever-ambitious Malenkov. Khrushchev exploded his bombshell in July 1957. The Central Committee made public a resolution "Concerning the Anti-Party Group of Malenkov, G. M. Kaganovich, L. M. Molotov, V. M." accusing them of having taken a "conservative attitude" toward many urgently needed reforms and especially of obstructing measures "for the purpose of relaxing international tension."

Two threads run through the resolution's criticisms of the antiparty group. First, its members were accused of Khrushchev's obstructing policies, such as de-Stalinization and industrial reorganization. Second, and probably more serious, they had allegedly engaged in un-Leninist, conspiratorial methods of political struggle. These changes were later spelled out in vivid detail.

[42] Robert Conquest, *Power and Policy in the U.S.S.R.: The Struggle for Stalin's Succession, 1945–1950* (New York: St. Martin's Press, 1960), p. 95.

Despite the consolidation of Khrushchev's power in 1957, factional, bureaucratic, and policy struggles continued throughout the second period of his rule, from 1957 to his fall in 1964. It was clear from various top-level personnel shifts as well as from contradictions and omissions in newspapers and other media that affairs of state continued to be dominated by a struggle among powerful competing interests, clashing behind closed doors.

Throughout his tenure, except for a series of fatal blunders near the end, Khrushchev kept a watchful eye on the maneuvering of his rivals. He kept the top executive posts for himself, including the vital position of party first secretary. A. I. Kerechenko, who, like many of the prominent leaders in the Khrushchev and post-Khrushchev political machines, had made his mark in the Ukrainian party organization, was Khrushchev's first lieutenant in the party apparatus. In January 1960 he was dismissed from the Secretariat, probably because of his failure to oppose with sufficient vigor nationalist tendencies in the non-Russian republics. Frol R. Kozlov became the ranking secretary.

Kozlov had served the party apparatus for many years, chiefly in Leningrad. Unlike Kerechenko, Brezhnev, and other top leaders of the late Khrushchev era, Kozlov had not risen through personal links with Khrushchev. He soon became a conspicuous leader of the conservative opposition to Khrushchev, particularly in economic matters. After three years' absence, Brezhnev returned to the Secretariat in 1963. Also appointed was Podgorny, who, like Kirichenko and Brezhnev, was a product of the Ukrainian republic party organization. Brezhnev's and Podgorny's arrivals made it clear that Kozlov's incumbency as second in command was over.

In July 1964, when Brezhnev resigned the ceremonial post of chairman of the Presidium of the Supreme Soviet (head of state in title only), it seemed that his power would increase now that he had more time for his work on the Secretariat. The speculation was not idle. In October 1964, while Khrushchev was vacationing in Georgia, a group of his colleagues called a meeting of the Central Committee plenum and successfully demanded his resignation. Brezhnev was then installed as chief executive of the CPSU.

Khrushchev's successors, under the leadership of Brezhnev, Kosygin, Suslov, Podgorny, and others, have sought the safety and security of familiar routines. Even the most reform-minded among the new leadership felt that Khrushchev had moved too fast, into too many areas, and too inconsistently.

Ironically, Khrushchev had paved the way for his own downfall by providing an atmosphere of relative personal security for his lieutenants, which allowed them to learn to work together. When, in the last few years of his regime, Khrushchev began to pack Central Committee meetings with his supporters, his lieutenants became anxious. When Khrushchev began to make important decisions without consultation and to take what appeared to be anti-Leninist positions, irritation and anxiety turned to alarm. Added to all this was dissatisfaction with Khrushchev's policies in agriculture, science (notably his support of Lysenko's discredited genetic theories), and party organization, with his attitude toward the military, and with his foreign policy. In the end, practically all the top leadership ganged up on Khrushchev. Though the military did not join with his opponents, neither did they make any effort to save their deposed leader.[43]

For several years power seems to have been shared by Leonid Ilyich Brezhnev and Aleksei Nikolaevich Kosygin, though Brezhnev from the beginning overshadowed Kosygin and in recent years his predominance has been overwhelming. Brezhnev, born in an industrial region of the Ukraine, worked in agriculture as a young man and then graduated from a metallurgical institute. In 1937, during the purge of the Ukrainian party, he began a rapid rise in the party apparatus, under Khrushchev's direction. After several party secretaryships in republics, he became a member of the Secretariat in 1956 and of the Presidium in 1957. After Khrushchev was ousted, Brezhnev became first secretary of the party; in 1966 he followed Stalin's pattern and was named general secretary.

Kosygin became chairman of the U.S.S.R.

[43] For accounts of how Khrushchev was deposed, see Michel Tatu, *Power in the Kremlin* (Baltimore: Johns Hopkins University Press, 1966); and Carl Linden, *Khrushchev and the Soviet Leadership* (Baltimore: Johns Hopkins University Press, 1966). See also Myron Rush, "The Khrushchev Succession Crisis," *World Politics*, 15:2 (January 1962), pp. 859–882.

Council of Ministers, that is, head of the government (as opposed to head of the party). Although he had not served in the Secretariat, he had held important party posts. His career included impressive managerial and governmental administrative experience. He was a factory director, a deputy head of the State Planning Committee (Gosplan), and head of the ministries of textiles, light industry, consumer goods, and finance.

Also in the top leadership were Mikhail A. Suslov, Andrei P. Kirilenko, Nikolai V. Podgorny, and, at least until the abolition in 1965 of the Party-State Control Committee, which he headed, Alexander N. Shelepin. The first three, together with Brezhnev and Kosygin, constituted until May 1977 the inner core of Soviet political leadership. In May 1977, as already noted, Podgorny lost all political stature when Brezhnev took over his functions as chief of state.

In 1966, to emphasize the repudiation of Khrushchev, the Presidium was renamed the Politburo, as it had been called originally under Lenin. This change in language, accompanied by reduction of overlap in the membership of the Secretariat and the Politburo, seemed to emphasize the primacy of the Politburo over the Secretariat. Other moves, reassuring to the new bureaucratic oligarchy of party and state, included revocation of Khrushchev's rule requiring a regular 25 percent turnover in Central Committee membership and an end to the 1962 division of party organizations into industrial and agricultrual sections.

The political chieftains who toppled Khrushchev obviously had much in common, or they could not have worked together so successfully in their dangerous enterprise. However, the new leaders also represented powerful lobbies, with divergent goals and perspectives. The two most powerful lobbies,

Molding Soviet man: a scene in the Young Pioneers room of a school.

neither a cohesive interest group, were the party cadres, led by Brezhnev, and the economic bureaucracy, led by Kosygin.

The policies of the post-Khrushchev leadership, given to compromise and eager to avoid internal discord, tended to drift and to adhere to routine. Hoping to keep the peace among themselves, the post-Khrushchev team generally postponed difficult decisions if they appeared to threaten the interests of some segment of top leadership.

The most conspicuous policy was the apparent agreement that the two most important Soviet political positions — first secretary of the Central Committee (Brezhnev) and chairman of the Council of Ministers (Kosygin) — should not again be held by the same man. Moreover, responsibility for making national policy was distributed with remarkable equity among members of the Politburo, the Secretariat, and the Council of Ministers.

The Late Brezhnev Era: Gerontocracy, Consensus, and A Looming Succession Problem

The years between the 24th CPSU Congress in 1971 and May 1977 witnessed few changes in top political leadership. Brezhnev's apparent authority grew steadily, though his health and vigor obviously diminished. Nevertheless, he seems to have prevailed against challengers of his policies, and in terms of symbolic recognition of his primacy he far outshone Khrushchev — though unlike the latter Brezhnev was not made Chairman of the Council of Ministers. The removal of Petro Shelest from the Politburo in May 1972 and from leadership of the Ukrainian party organization in April 1973 seems to have reflected the anger of the Politburo majority over Shelest's failure to take prompt action against representatives of Ukrainian ethnic assertiveness such as Ivan Dzyuba and Valentyn Moroz. Shelest's Politburo seat, as well as the first secretaryship of the Ukrainian party organization, were given to Brezhnev's close associate, Volodymyr Shcherbitzki, like Shelest a Ukrainian, but one who was more prepared than Shelest to suppress any manifestation of Ukrainian nationalism.

Politburo member Alexander Shelepin completed his slow but inexorable slide to political oblivion with the loss in 1975 of leadership of the trade union organization and of membership in the Politburo. Dimitri Polyanski, like Shelepin a young Politburo member (both were under sixty), lost his party and his government position as minister of agriculture in the 1976 congress. Shortly thereafter vacancies opened in the Politburo and the leadership of the Ministry of Defense with the death of Marshall Andrei Grechko, who was replaced by a civilian, Dmitri F. Ustinov. Some analysts thought that replacing a military leader with a civilian signified accommodative tendencies in Soviet foreign policy, a view possibly supported by the Lenin Day speech of Politburo member and KGB chief Yuri Andropov, which criticized domestic opponents of detente. On the other hand, some experts on civil-military relations emphasized that Ustinov had headed the Soviet war production machine for forty-four years, and said that the military had suffered no loss of influence. Interesting in this connection were reports that Ustinov was unfavorable to détente and the fact that Soviet military aid to several African states and revolutionary movements was increased in 1977 and 1978.

Probably intended by Brezhnev to facilitate conduct of his detente with West Germany and the United States, and also to bolster his position against any internal elite criticism of detente were the appointments, simultaneous with Grechko's, of the veteran Minister of Foreign Affairs, Andrei Gromyko, and the top security officer, Chairman of the Committee of State Security (KGB) Yuri Andropov, to the Politburo as full members. Andropov Leonein, a veteran party executive, and former head of the CPSU Central Committee department in charge of relations with ruling communist parties, as noted, delivered the Lenin birthday anniversary address in 1976, perhaps indicative of his influence as one of Brezhnev's closest associates, of growing KGB status, of political tensions in Soviet ruling circles, or of all three.

The Twenty-fifth Party Congress in 1976 named Ustinov and Gregory Romanov, the first secretary of the important Leningrad oblast party committee, to full Politburo membership. Romanov, young at fifty-three in a body rich in septuagenarians seemed to be one of the ascendant party leaders with a fair chance to one day succeed Brezhnev as supreme CPSU leader. His elevation also signaled enhanced status for the Leningrad party organization, for some time not represented in the Politburo.

Until his death at age 60 in 1978, Fedor Kulakov, a full Politburo member since 1971, and the Central Committee's agricultural specialist, seemed to some Western analysts to be one of the strongest prospects to eventually replace Brezhnev as top party leader. Kulakov's passing left Romanov, Shcherbitski, perhaps KGB head Andropov, and also Vladimir Dolgikh with some reasonable prospects for achieving supreme leadership. Since 1972, Dolgikh, in his fifties, has been the Secretariat's heavy industry expert. Another possible contender, Konstantin Katushev, with experience both in party work in industry and in relations between the CPSU and the East European party leadership, went into eclipse by 1978. A strange situation, very difficult to analyze, existed. Even though some of the younger, more visible possible replacements for Brezhnev had good qualifications, some, perhaps all, were disqualified. Andropov's KGB connections might rule him out, as might Shcherbitski's non-Russian ethnic origin. Romanov had had little experience in Moscow. Dolgikh was not a member of the Politburo. It seemed likely that if Brezhnev were replaced within a relatively short time, his interim successor would be either his frequent stand-in, Andrei Kirilenko, or the senior secretary, Mikhail Suslov, both older than Brezhnev.

At the 1976 congress, the CPSU Secretariat, praised by Brezhnev and other speakers, gained in status and membership. It was already, next to the Politburo, the most powerful organ of the Soviet body politic. Most of the superstars of Soviet politics, including Brezhnev, Kirilenko, and Suslov were both full (voting, as distinguished from alternate) members of the Politburo and the Secretariat. After the congress, the Secretariat numbered eleven members, an increase of two, accounted for by the newcomers Konstantin Chernenko and Mikhail Zimyanin. As of April 1979, it had nine members.

Policy Issues: Khrushchev and Brezhnev

Throughout Soviet history, the most important problems confronting the leadership have revolved around the allocation of resources — the dilemmas of investment versus consumption, agriculture versus industry, guns versus butter. The more Soviet leaders said about improving the standard of living of the ordinary citizen, the more citizens' expectations were raised. Under Khrushchev, industrial workers were helped by the repeal of some restrictive laws and by the improved position of trade unions (at least on paper), but these measures did not resolve increasing worker frustration or prevent the growth of labor unrest. Workers began to leave their jobs and go on strike. Nor did the position of the peasantry improve: dissatisfaction continued and increased in this most stubborn and unorganized segment of society.

Nevertheless, Khrushchev's efforts brought the Soviet Union to the earliest stages of a mass consumption economy. And the progress was sufficient to call into question a good many traditional theories and methods. For example, if the Soviet Union wanted to satisfy consumer needs, it would have to increase industrial productivity. But this would require more flexibility in economic planning and an increase in the responsibility and operational autonomy of managers of industrial enterprises.

Khrushchev's economic reforms had been mainly administrative. From the point of view of the party apparatus, an economy based on price and profit could, in spite of advantages resulting from increased consumer production, be disadvantageous if it gave too much power to the economic elite.

A consumer-oriented economy would require a shift from production for national power to production for general welfare. Such a shift might undercut ideological militancy, encourage advocates of diplomacy with the West, and threaten the vested interests of the military (as well as of the conservative apparatchiki, the secret police, and the managers of heavy industry). Some military leaders were clearly disturbed by reductions in Soviet armed forces made from 1955 to 1959 and by Khrushchev's partially implemented 1960 plan for additional demobilization. Soviet military leaders were also afraid that the Nuclear Test Ban Treaty of July 1963 might create illusions about the extent of Soviet friendliness toward the West.[44]

Khrushchev also alarmed his would-be successors

[44] See Thomas W. Wolfe, *Soviet Strategy at the Crossroads* (Cambridge, Mass.: Harvard University Press, 1964).

by too rapidly relaxing controls over intellectual and cultural contact with the West and by bringing the intelligentsia into a kind of junior partnership with the regime. Conservatives believed these policies could undermine ideological purity and give the intelligentsia too inflated a view of its rights.

Brezhnev was the most powerful individual of the new leaders, though during the first year or two of the new regime Kosygin enjoyed greater prestige. After the Soviet invasion of Czechoslovakia in 1968, which Brezhnev planned and executed despite the apparent opposition of some of his colleagues, Brezhnev's prestige increased. The trend was encouraged by increasing agreement among top Soviet leaders in favor of a traditional economic policy stressing centralism and heavy industry. This economic shift reduced the influence of Kosygin, whose name was associated with the economic reforms begun in 1965.

Toward the end of 1969, a Brezhnev cult suddenly blossomed. The press credited him with having written a book, and the related publicity made him even more prominent than before. Most important, Brezhnev seemed to be injecting himself more into economic affairs (Kosygin's preserve) and into relations with the military. The publication in 1970 of a two-volume collection of Brezhnev's speeches and articles was an indication of his enhanced prestige. He could now claim the authority, aspired to by all previous party chiefs, to interpret official doctrine.

Soon he had published a spate of books. Other oligarchs also published, but their works received less publicity than Brezhnev's. His primacy was highlighted by numerous honors in 1976, notably his designation as a marshal of the army after Grechko's death. This reminded the military of the party's supremacy but honored them by associating them with top party leadership. Another evidence of Brezhnev's stature and of CPSU dominance was the frequency with which Brezhnev, though he had no executive post in the government, performed the functions of head of state, such as signing treaties and conferring honorary titles. (As previously mentioned, Brezhnev became the official chief of state in 1977.) Enormous publicity greeted his autobiography, published with the assistance of a team of experts from the U.S.S.R. Academy of Sciences in 1978.

In his first years as party leader, Brezhnev had allied himself with the military and hard-liners in the party command who favored an expanded heavy industry and increased expenditures for defense. By 1968, he began to urge more spending on food and consumer goods and apparently went along with a Politburo majority favoring Strategic Arms Limitation Talks (SALT) with the United States, which began in November 1969.

In his report to the Twenty-fourth Party Congress in 1971, Brezhnev announced modest new welfare proposals, such as money allowances for low-income families — the latest in a series of small but beneficial reforms since 1965. He proclaimed that a "substantial rise of the standard of living of the working people" was to be the "main task" of the Ninth Five-Year Plan. This promise was difficult, perhaps impossible, to fulfill, given the constraints imposed by the structure of the Soviet political system and by policies the leadership has usually considered necessary for maintaining the system. Since the early 1960s the Soviet leaders have been attempting to spur an increasingly sluggish economy to a level of performance adequate to support ambitious foreign policy goals and to satisfy the expectations of the public for a quality of life appropriate to the developed socialist society that the leadership asserts has been established.

There are good reasons to doubt that the trend of the 1960s and early 1970s toward a substantial rise in living standards, including a considerable increase in consumption of meat, can be sustained. This judgment seems logical from analysis of the results of the Ninth Five-Year Plan (1971–1975) and references made at the Twenty-fifth Party Congress to the tenth (1976–1980). Of course it should be understood that the prognosis of Western experts is for diminishing growth for the Soviet economy, not no growth. There is wide agreement that the Soviet economy will continue to grow at a rate sufficient to generate formidable military power and a slowly rising standard of living. However, the crop failures of 1963, 1965, 1967, 1972, and the particularly disastrous one of 1975 and a poor harvest in 1979 — which have impelled Soviet authorities to allocate to agriculture an increasing share of capital — as well as such other factors as a rapid decline in the productivity of labor, a growing scarcity of labor, and other problems, "ensure that the Soviet leadership will be faced with many difficult choices of both a political and an economic nature."[45]

Among potential domestic political consequences of the economic difficulties that seem likely in coming years, one deserves especially close attention. This is the possibility that disappointment over failure of living standards to rise as rapidly as desired might lead to violent protests, such as those that erupted in Poland in December 1970 and June 1976. Few questions are closer to the attention of Soviet policy makers. Indeed, the increased emphasis on widened distribution of material and social benefits and stepped-up recruitment of workers into the CPSU, may have been responses to Polish worker's discontent of a few months earlier. On a still more speculative level, one may ask whether the severe repression of even mild dissent partly reflected fear that a partnership might develop between masses demanding more material goods and intellectuals seeking freedom and justice. Such a potential coalition — similar to the one that took shape in Czechoslovakia in 1968 — could pose enormous problems for the leadership.

It seems almost certain that Moscow's pursuit of détente with the West since 1970 was motivated to some degree by calculation that it could relieve internal economic pressures confronting the Politburo. Détente was accompanied by Soviet efforts to normalize economic relations and thus, it was clearly hoped, facilitate access to Western scientific and technological know-how. It would distort reality to attribute the adoption of détente by Brezhnev and his colleagues solely to Soviet economic needs. Fundamental were the shared concerns of Moscow and Washington over the threat of nuclear holocaust, and of course Politburo anxiety regarding Maoist China. The way was paved by American withdrawal from Vietnam, in connection with which Soviet diplomacy seems to have provided some lubrication. Indicative of the high priority accorded by the Soviet Politburo to trade with the United States was the prominence in the Soviet press of reports on United States-Soviet trade talks at a time of intensified bombardment of Hanoi and Haiphong. Many Western economists and political analysts think the expansion of Soviet trade and contacts with the West signified recognition by the Kremlin that it was less dangerous to attempt to rejuvenate the Soviet economy by massive infusions of foreign technology than by bold internal reforms. These observers pointed out that since the limited economic reform of 1965, the effort to enhance market factors in shaping Soviet economic life and to downgrade the role of traditional administrative controls had faltered. It seems certain that fundamental economic reform in systems of the Soviet type poses difficult political problems, though Hungary's ability to combine political stability with far more liberal economic policies raises intriguing questions. In any case, the Soviet political elite has been skittish about experiments in sensitive areas, such as the economy or intellectual and cultural life; the artistic doctrine of socialist realism, which seemed for a while defunct, has since Khrushchev's ouster received a new lease on life.

Soviet domestic difficulties deserve scrutiny, but it would be a serious error to underestimate the survival power of the vast and growing Soviet economic organism. Particularly important are the massive efforts under way to harness to the political, economic, and ideological goals of the regime the fruits of the contemporary worldwide scientific-technical revolution. According to Soviet doctrine, only under a socialist system can the results of this revolution be fully and beneficially used. To be sure, the campaign to spur innovation and increased efficiency — to which cyberneticists, computer scientists, and other specialists respond enthusiastically — has been considerably hampered by bureaucratic rigidity. How-

[45] See Gregory Grossman, "An Economy at Middle Age," *Problems of Communism*, 25:2 (March–April 1976), pp. 18–33. See also Jerry F. Hough, "The Man and the System" *Problems of Communism*, 25:2 (March–April 1976), pp. 1–17. Hough takes a more positive view than Grossman about recent improvements in Soviet living standards and the possibility of a continuation of such improvement, but without placing this trend within a framework of rigorous economic analysis, such as Grossman provided. Hough also makes interesting claims regarding egalitarian trends in Soviet income policy, but these are difficult to take at face value, in view of the many secret privileges enjoyed by members of the Soviet elite, which have been exposed, to some extent, in the writings of Andrei Sakharov and other dissidents.

An area of deterioration in welfare worth mentioning is the current rise in infant mortality rates and decline in life expectancy. See Christopher Davis and Murray Feshbach, "Life Expectancy in the Soviet Union," *Wall Street Journal*, June 20, 1978.

ever, vast sums are being allocated to these fields of research and development. There is every reason to believe that an energetic effort will be made to unshackle the initiative of Soviet scientific and managerial talent, insofar as this is compatible with maintenance of strong central controls. This will be accompanied by voracious borrowing of Western science and technology. The Soviet leaders are aware that such borrowing involves the risk of exposing increasing numbers of Soviet citizens to subversive foreign influences, but they regard it as essential in their endless struggle to overtake and surpass the bourgeois West.

Keen competitiveness pervades the Soviet approach to international politics, from ideological struggle to culture, sports, diplomacy, space exploration, and — most conspicuously — arms race. Détente has not been accompanied by any disposition to accord ideological legitimacy to capitalist regimes, movements, or parties, or even "revisionist" socialist ones. To be sure, Moscow has vociferously demanded relaxation of international tensions, but to the extent that it acknowledged that relaxation had occurred, it attributed the trend almost exclusively to its own efforts and those of its peaceloving, progressive supporters. In the meantime Soviet diplomacy bargained tenaciously and skillfully for arms control, though to some extent this effort seemed at times to be overshadowed by demagogic propaganda for immediate general and complete disarmament, reminiscent of the Stalin-era Stockholm Appeal campaign to ban the bomb. On July 31 1975, the U.S.S.R. and thirty-four other nations, including the United States, agreed, in the Final Act of the Helsinki Conference on Security and Cooperation in Europe, to promote human contact, increase the exchange of information, and foster peace and security in Europe. Numerous Soviet actions, such as the refusal to permit the noted scientist and humanitarian, Andrei Sakharov, to go to Stockholm to accept the Nobel Peace Prize, cast doubt on the sincerity with which Leonid Brezhnev signed the Final Act. The defensive tone of much official comment on human rights in the U.S.S.R. indicated concern over foreign — and perhaps internal — opinion regarding performance in this field. But at the same time, Soviet words and actions, such as the successful proxy war waged by Soviet-equipped Cubans in Angola and other pressure in African, underscored the limits of détente, Soviet-style.

POLICY IMPLEMENTATION

In previous sections we have considered the critically important role of the CPSU's policy-making organs and leaders in generating and controlling political influence and power. Analysis of the Soviet system would be incomplete without giving attention to government institutions through which the party command translates its decisions into the directives, rules, and regulations that control citizens' daily lives.

The party coordinates and controls a complex and interlocking network of governmental and bureaucratic structures, with duplication, or proliferation, of lines of command. There are several hierarchies of organizations with headquarters in Moscow and agencies in the field. There is also a powerful corps of "prefects," as Hough describes the party secretaries at middle levels, who "ride herd" on the field representatives of most other bureaucracies.[46] They serve as Moscow's eyes, ears, and guiding hand in the field.

The formal structure of government, despite its relative powerlessness, performs functions indispensable to the fulfillment of the party's purposes. The bureaucracy's functions are to legitimize policies passed down by party leaders and to implement these policies through elected officials, civil service bureaucrats, and other experts. Helping both unpaid elected officials and paid functionaries are millions of nonstaff volunteers.

Soviet terminology divides all organizations into two main categories: public, mass, voluntary organizations (sometimes characterized in Soviet legal and social science literature as "representative"); and state organizations. The party, the trade unions, the Komsomol, and (though only partially) the Soviets belong to the first category. State organizations include ministries, military and police, and state committees and commissions. Official doctrine makes a distinction between the structure and legal status of the two types of organizations. Leaders of state organizations and their personnel are generally ap-

[46] Hough, *Soviet Prefects*.

pointed and have the lawful power to enforce their commands. Leaders of public organizations, by contrast, have no legal powers of compulsion over their members.

The Structure of the Soviets

The soviets, which are organized in descending order from the national Supreme Soviet to village soviets, are the backbone of the government structure. The elected soviets and their inner core of executive committee bureaucrats have some of the characteristics of both public and state organizations. Deputies to the soviets at all levels, from village to Supreme Soviet, are elected by all voting citizens. All soviets are invested with legal powers. In fact, the U.S.S.R. Constitution vests in the Supreme Soviet the exclusive power of national legislation and designates it as the U.S.S.R.'s "supreme organ of state power."

The Supreme Soviet is bicameral. Its two legislative chambers are the Soviet of the Union and the Soviet of Nationalities. The latter provides symbolic representation for ethnic minorities clustered in a geographic area. The Supreme Soviet normally meets for a few days twice a year. Legislation is passed unanimously, but standing commissions, which engage in "consultation with the public" and also draft legislation, have played an increasingly important role in Soviet lawmaking since Stalin.

The intermeshing of the soviet and party networks can be demonstrated in several ways (see Figure 12.2). The Constitution states that the party "is the leading core of all organizations of the working people, both public and state." Although party guidance of the soviet's work is generally affected indirectly and unobtrusively by leading party members, party organizations frequently interfere directly, even at times in purely administrative functions such as street cleaning.

Through the principle of dual subordination, many operations of the soviets are controlled by the agencies of appropriate ministries. According to this principle, the administrative subdivisions of local soviets are accountable both to the executive committees of the local soviet and to the section of the ministries (education, health, culture, finance) in that territory.

Limited as the powers of the soviets are, it would be a mistake to underestimate their significance as agents of socialization and legitimation. They offer opportunities to millions of people for limited participation in political life that generates support for the state. Party domination of the political process is hidden behind a facade of mass representation.

Whatever democratic aura the soviets project is perhaps most convincingly manifested during elections of their deputies. Elections at the all-union and republic levels are held every four years, at the lower levels every two years. The candidates designated by the party usually receive over 99 percent of the vote. The Soviet voter is expected to vote for the party-selected candidate by dropping her ballot in a box outside the polling booth. Her alternative is to enter the polling booth, cross out the candidate's name, and then drop the ballot in the box — thus attracting attention to herself. Even riskier than this is failure to vote at all, which can be construed as enmity toward the regime.[47]

The structure of the soviets largely parallels or duplicates that of the party. Below the level of the national Supreme Soviet are the supreme soviets of each of the fifteen constituent republics of the U.S.S.R. Below the republic level are the local organs of state power, consisting of soviets in oblasti, kraya, urban and rural districts, and villages. However, there are no counterparts in the hierarchy of soviets to party organizations in factories, scientific and educational institutions, government agencies, and the like.

Each soviet, at whatever level, is headed by an executive body. At the top levels, this body is called the presidium. From the regional level down, it is called the "executive committee." The chairmen of executive committees dominate the soviets. The majority of soviet deputies work full time at nonpolitical jobs; because of this and because the soviets meet infrequently and briefly, ordinary deputies have little political power.

Politically subordinate though they are, the soviets, especially at lower levels, perform a number of administrative tasks. Local soviets supply goods and services like food supplies, social security pay-

[47] Max E. Mote, *Soviet Local and Republic Elections* (Stanford, Calif.: Stanford University Press, 1965), p. 78.

Figure 12.2

Hierarchical Structure of Government and Party Organs

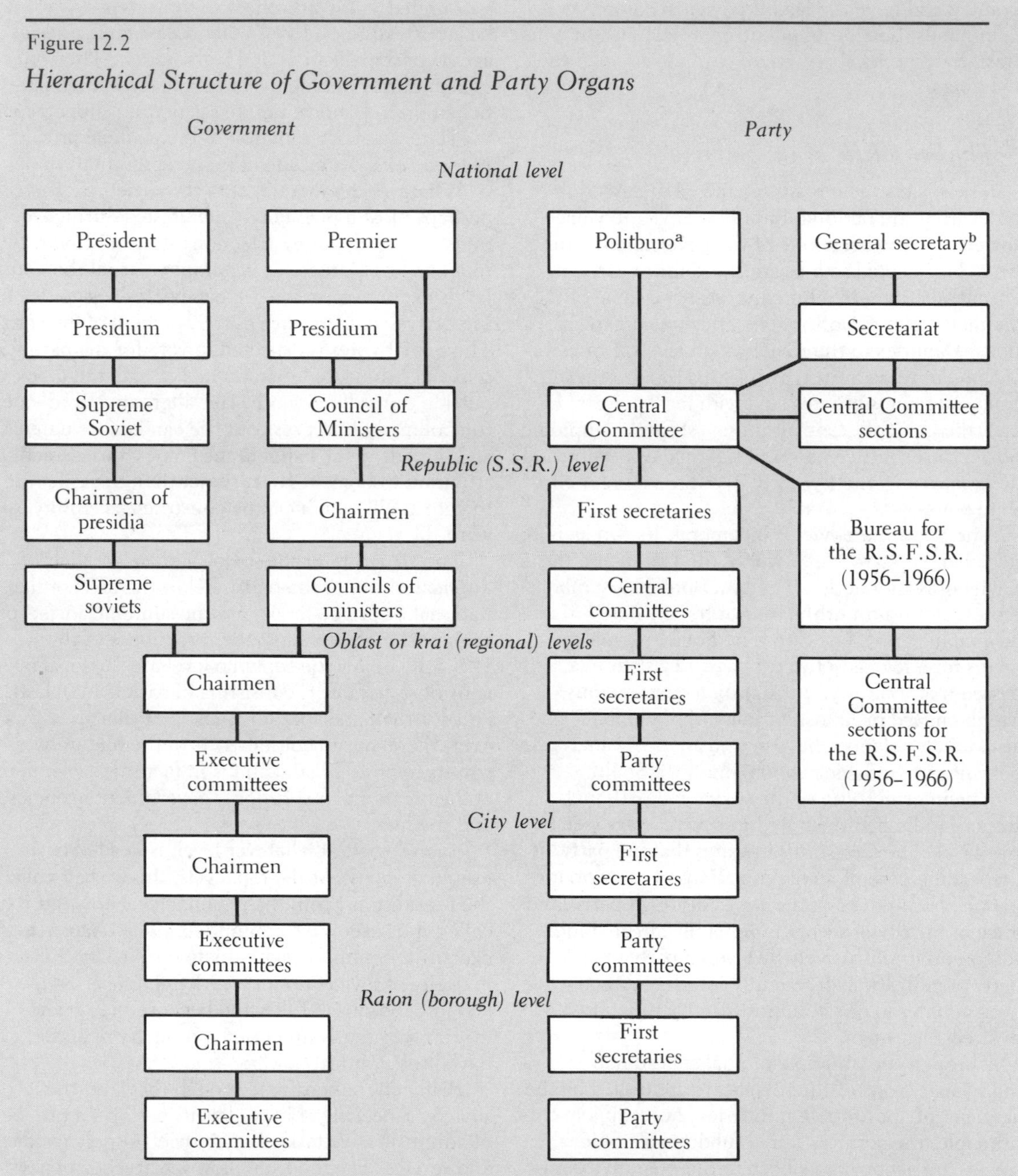

[a] Until 1966, this was named the Presidium.

[b] Until 1966, the title first secretary was used.

Source: Adapted by permission from Werner G. Hahn, *The Politics of Soviet Agriculture, 1960–1970* (Baltimore: Johns Hopkins University Press, 1972), p. xiv.

ments, housing, and roads and transportation, as well as laundries, motion picture theaters, libraries, and clubs.

The state bureaucracy includes three types of ministries: all-union, union-republic, and republic, in descending order of centralization of structure and jurisdiction. All-union ministries are in sole charge of one sphere of administration such as defense, coal, or iron, and are not accountable to any of the republic governments. Union-republic ministries have a central office in Moscow, but function through ministries located in each republic capital. Republic ministries are the lowest rung of the ladder, responsible solely to the government of the republic in which they are located. The republic ministries handle two kinds of business — matters affected by the linguistic and ethnic composition of their republics (such as education, public health, and justice), and local economic activities using locally obtainable raw materials, labor, etc. In comparison to all-union ministries, the republic ministries have small budgets and staffs.

The ministerial hierarchy leads up to the Council of Ministers of the U.S.S.R. (see Figure 12.3). The Council of Ministers is headed by a chairman whose functions roughly correspond to those of a premier or prime minister in parliamentary systems — but with the vital difference that he carries out policies determined by the permanently ruling CPSU. Subordinate to the chairman of the Council of Ministers are first deputy chairmen and deputy chairmen, chairmen of state committees, the State Bank, and others. The numerous state committees, such as the State Committee for Science and Technology, the State Planning Committee (Gosplan), and the Committee of State Security (KGB), are probably more powerful than all but a few ministries, such as the Defense Ministry.

The State Bureaucracy

The most obvious and striking characteristic of bureaucracy in the U.S.S.R. is its vastness and its pervasive influence on the daily life of the citizen. The functions of the government are broad, ranging from national defense to regulation of economic and cultural life. When we add to the functions of public administration the responsibilities of ideological indoctrination and social transformation, it is not surprising that the administrative organs of the Soviet Union not only are ubiquitous but also have very large staffs.

A characteristic that distinguishes Soviet public administration from that of the West is the practice of investing even minor governmental acts with ideological sacredness. Official statements relate the process of government directly to Marxist-Leninist doctrine. Institutions like the soviets, the courts, and the army are frequently referred to as schools of communism. Even authors of scholarly studies on economic, social, and political topics consider it appropriate — or expedient — to pad their works with lengthy propagandistic sections praising Soviet practices and institutions and criticizing bourgeois counterparts.

Another much publicized feature of Soviet public administration is the effort to accommodate ethnic and cultural differences. Local languages are used in educational, law-enforcement, judicial, and other institutions in political units with a predominantly non-Russian population. However, official Soviet theory regards concessions to the national sentiments of non-Russian peoples as temporary expedients to be used until the fusion of the peoples has been achieved. Especially since 1972 — when Brezhnev proclaimed the doctrine that a new community, the "Soviet people," had been created — Russification of non-Russian cultures has been intensified.

Party Control of the Bureaucracy

Though both in theory and in practice the Soviet system assigns separate spheres of competence to the CPSU and the state organs, the distinction has been fluid and shifting. Generally speaking, party executives exercise leadership (*rukovodstvo*), and government officials engage in administration (*upravlenie*). Decision, particularly critical and innovative decision, is the prerogative of the party; implementation and routine supervision are the jobs of the soviets and ministries, though the party keeps a watchful eye on how implementation is carried out. Direct party involvement in administration increases during periods of innovation (such as Stalin's collectivization of 1929–1931), when the survival of the system is at stake (as during the Nazi invasion), and when revitalization is needed (as in Khrushchev's agricul-

Figure 12.3
Organization of the U.S.S.R. Council of Ministers, December, 1978

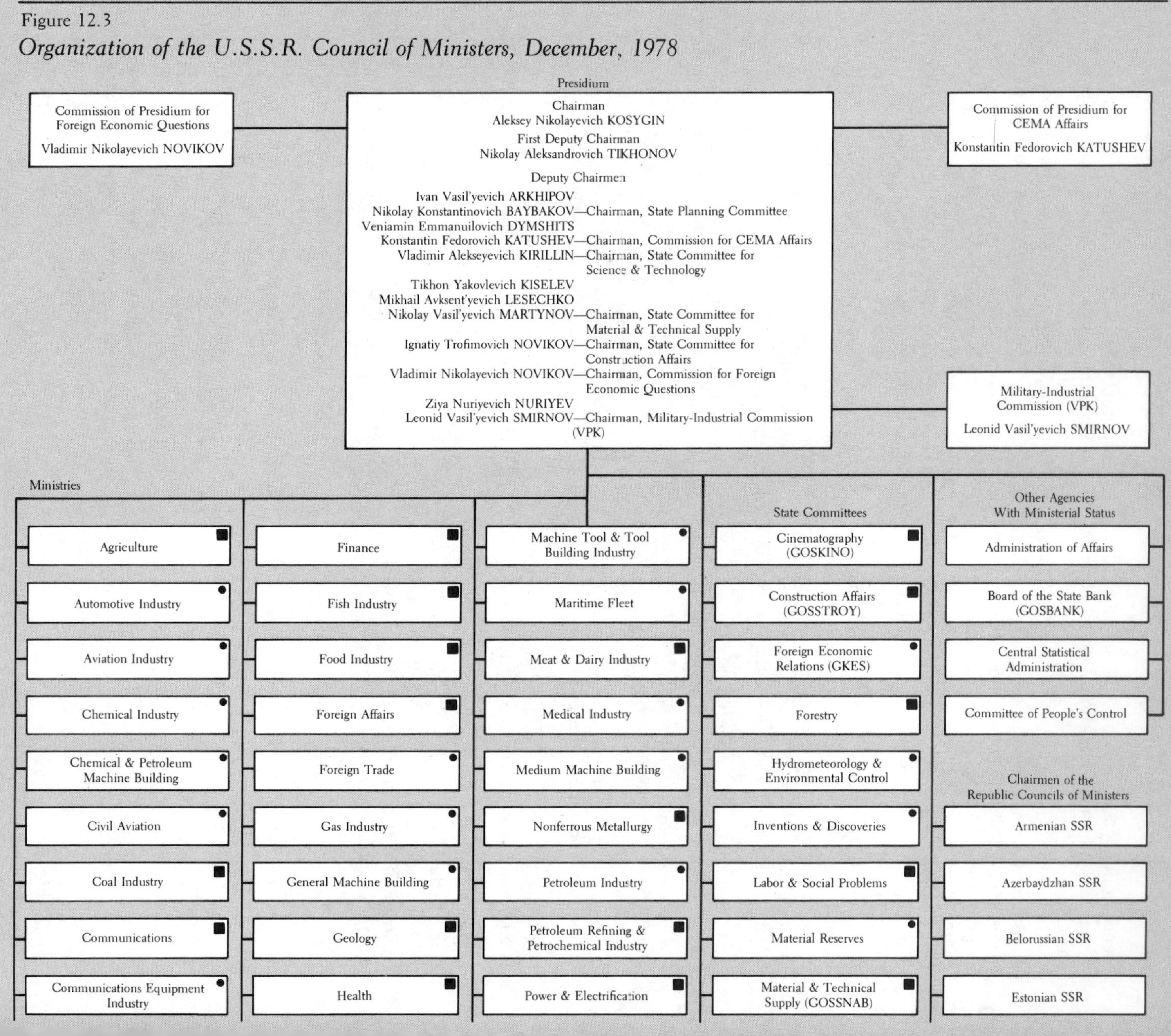
Presidium
Chairman
Aleksey Nikolayevich KOSYGIN
First Deputy Chairman
Nikolay Aleksandrovich TIKHONOV
Deputy Chairmen
Ivan Vasil'yevich ARKHIPOV
Nikolay Konstantinovich BAYBAKOV—Chairman, State Planning Committee
Veniamin Emmanuilovich DYMSHITS
Konstantin Fedorovich KATUSHEV—Chairman, Commission for CEMA Affairs
Vladimir Alekseyevich KIRILLIN—Chairman, State Committee for Science & Technology
Tikhon Yakovlevich KISELEV
Mikhail Avksent'yevich LESECHKO
Nikolay Vasil'yevich MARTYNOV—Chairman, State Committee for Material & Technical Supply
Ignatiy Trofimovich NOVIKOV—Chairman, State Committee for Construction Affairs
Vladimir Nikolayevich NOVIKOV—Chairman, Commission for Foreign Economic Questions
Ziya Nuriyevich NURIYEV
Leonid Vasil'yevich SMIRNOV—Chairman, Military-Industrial Commission (VPK)
Commission of Presidium for Foreign Economic Questions
Vladimir Nikolayevich NOVIKOV
Commission of Presidium for CEMA Affairs
Konstantin Fedorovich KATUSHEV
Military-Industrial Commission (VPK)
Leonid Vasil'yevich SMIRNOV
Ministries
Agriculture
Automotive Industry
Aviation Industry
Chemical Industry
Chemical & Petroleum Machine Building
Civil Aviation
Coal Industry
Communications
Communications Equipment Industry
Finance
Fish Industry
Food Industry
Foreign Affairs
Foreign Trade
Gas Industry
General Machine Building
Geology
Health
Machine Tool & Tool Building Industry
Maritime Fleet
Meat & Dairy Industry
Medical Industry
Medium Machine Building
Nonferrous Metallurgy
Petroleum Industry
Petroleum Refining & Petrochemical Industry
Power & Electrification
State Committees
Cinematography (GOSKINO)
Construction Affairs (GOSSTROY)
Foreign Economic Relations (GKES)
Forestry
Hydrometeorology & Environmental Control
Inventions & Discoveries
Labor & Social Problems
Material Reserves
Material & Technical Supply (GOSSNAB)
Other Agencies With Ministerial Status
Administration of Affairs
Board of the State Bank (GOSBANK)
Central Statistical Administration
Committee of People's Control
Chairmen of the Republic Councils of Ministers
Armenian SSR
Azerbaydzhan SSR
Belorussian SSR
Estonian SSR

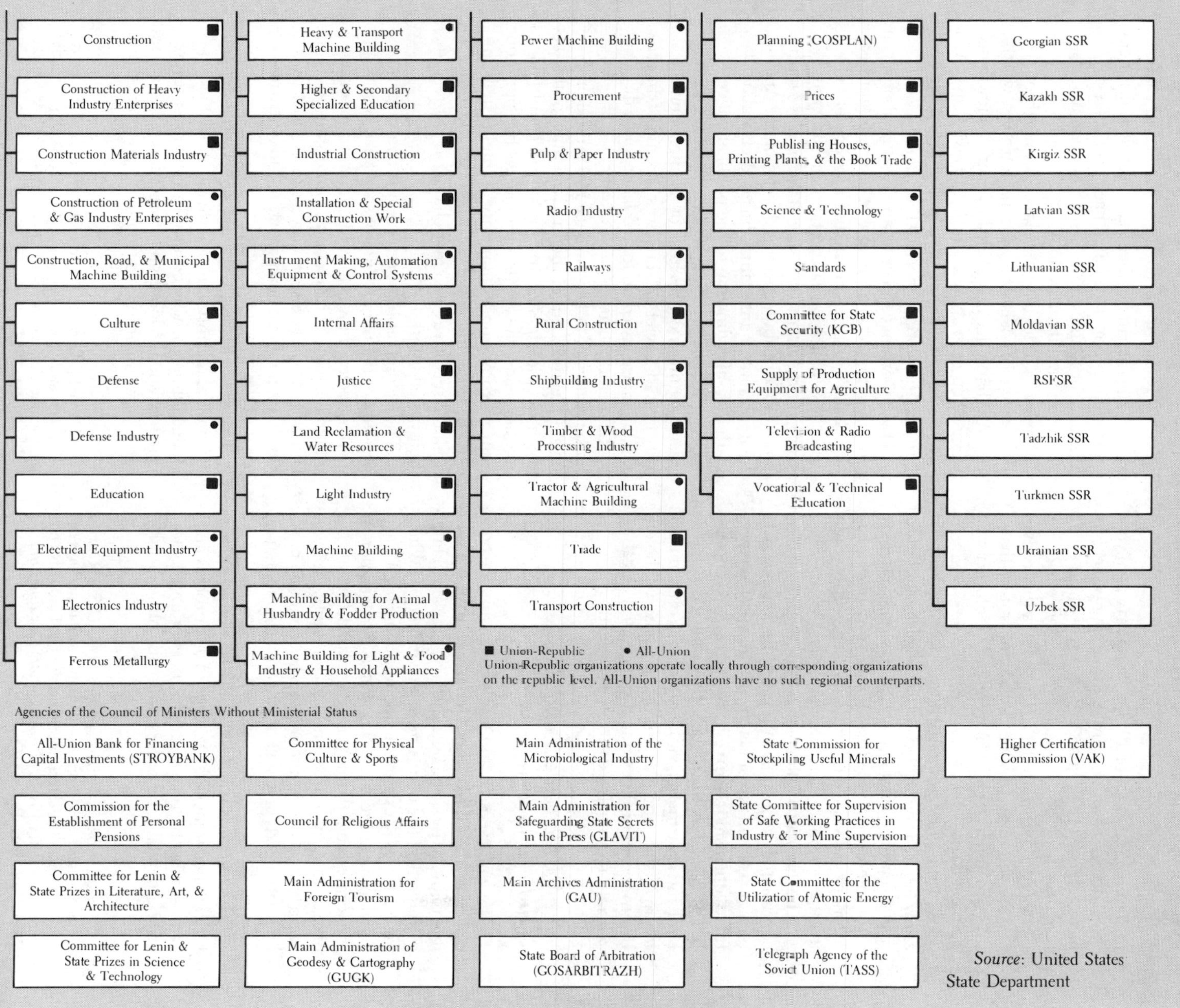

Source: United States State Department

tural reorganization of 1953–1958). Party involvement decreases when party-led campaigns seem to have achieved their goals or are provoking antiparty resentments, when party cadres are needed elsewhere, and when the Kremlin fears that cadres may be getting so involved in administration that they are in danger of losing sight of ideological and political goals.

A prime source of party power over the bureaucracy lies in its control over the assignment of executive and professional personnel. Although it seems most interested in the top 15 or 20 percent of government posts the party does not necessarily confine its supervision to these high reaches.

The party also influences administrators through control and inspection. Although the Stalinist pattern of rampant terror is a thing of the past, a powerful mechanism for surveillance persists. Agencies have been set up to combat bribery, illegal disposal of land and apartments, violation of rules on admission to universities and granting of diplomas, withholding by farmers of produce due the state, and illegal relaxation of quality controls by industry.

Law Enforcement and the Judicial Process

Law enforcement and legal scholarship are controlled by the CPSU, though party control is less direct than it is over the bureaucracy. Law and adjudication reflect the party line of a given period. When, for example, Khrushchev's populist approach was developing in the late 1950s, public participation in the legal system dramatically increased, though often in an amateurish and vigilante style. At the same time, a campaign to increase economic productivity led to new severity against "economic crimes."[48]

Khrushchev's successors have tended to redress the balance somewhat in favor of due process and against mass participation. But in their anxiety to strengthen law and order and to discipline drunkards, hooligans, and embezzlers, as well as dissident intellectuals, they have fallen back on tactics reminiscent of Stalinist terror, such as detaining dissenters in mental institutions.

The party influences judicial decisions through the doctrine of socialist legal consciousness, which requires that judges be guided by party policy in deciding whether to apply a statute to a given case. As a result, a defendant's fate may be decided on the basis of the political preferences of the regime.

The importance of law as an instrument of social control increased and the role of terror diminished after Stalin's death. Khrushchev's speech of February 1956, which revealed Stalin's arbitrary and cruel actions, almost accusing Stalin of grave misuse of power, contributed to this development. Among the important changes introduced after Stalin's death was subordination of the political police — once a principal instrument of party rule. Of even greater significance, because of its impact on the daily lives of Soviet citizens, was the end of an economic empire based on forced labor, once directed by the secret police.

Reformers of Soviet law face two critical problems. One arises out of the fundamental conflict between any dictatorship and the rule of law. In law as in other fields, the Soviet system feels two pulls, one from a reform-minded minority of intellectuals, including some influential legal scholars, the other from conservatives who fear change as a threat to their vested interests.[49]

The second problem rests on the communist position that crime is a product of society. If that is so, then as society moves toward communism, crime should decrease. The fact that crime statistics in the U.S.S.R. are a state secret seems to indicate that crime has not been decreasing, to the embarrassment of the regime.

Under Soviet law, the range of activities defined as criminal is enormous. Murder and theft are included among private crimes. But the most severe penalties and the loosest interpretation of law are reserved for numerous and frequently committed pub-

[48] See Harold J. Berman, *Justice in the U.S.S.R.* (New York: Vintage, 1968), pp. 81–88. This work is perhaps the most significant Western monograph in its field. Also outstanding is Peter Juviler, *Revolutionary Law and Order* (New York: Free Press, 1976).

[49] Harold J. Berman, "The Dilemma of Soviet Law Reform," *Harvard Law Review*, 76:5 (March 1963), p. 950. See also George Feifer, *Justice in Moscow* (New York: Simon and Schuster, 1964).

lic crimes, crimes against the state, such as production of poor quality, failure to supply certain products according to plan, inefficiency, and poor performance. Even more harshly treated are political crimes, such as anti-Soviet agitation, of which dissidents are often accused.

The distinction between ordinary poor performance and criminal poor performance is subtle. In Stalin's time it was virtually impossible to conduct an industrial or collective enterprise without running afoul of the criminal laws. Accounts of criminal proceedings against workers, farmers, and managers continue today. So do calls for increased efficiency, dedication, and ardor in the daily tasks of building the economy and state.

The Legal Profession: Judges, Advocates, Procurators

The legal profession is almost completely under the control of the party, although in a few cases defense attorneys for dissidents have resisted party guidance. Its main components are judges, who conduct court proceedings, advocates, or lawyers, and procurators, the enforcing arm of the government and one of its legal watchdogs.

Although elected by popular vote at the lowest level and by the soviets at higher levels, Soviet judges are essentially civil servants, promoted from lower to higher courts on the basis of ability. Virtually all judges have some higher legal education. The U.S.S.R. Constitution states that "judges are independent and subject only to law"; direct interference by party organizations in particular cases is condemned. Even so, almost all Soviet judges are CPSU members and hence subject to party discipline (and, under Stalin, to control by terror).

The scope of the judicial function is narrower in the Soviet Union than in polyarchies. Soviet judges cannot refuse to enforce statutes on constitutional grounds, and they lack jurisdiction over major economic disputes. Few Soviets judges are politically prominent. In ability and prestige, it appears, the judge in the U.S.S.R. is outranked by the procurator.

The position of the advocate, or trial lawyer, is ambiguous. In most cases he is better off financially than both judges and procurators, and more than half of all advocates are members of the party. On the other hand, advocates seem able to get more than the official fee for their services, a practice that casts a bourgeois shadow on their public image.

Like everyone else, advocates are subject to party and government control. The 1962 statute concerning them gave the government control over the enforcement of professional standards and the schedule of fees and conditions for gratuitous service.[50] At the same time, the statute provided for colleges of advocates; the duly trained and qualified attorneys of a given area were to elect a governing board to manage their own affairs — subject, of course, to state supervision. The colleges are given jurisdiction over organizational rights, duties, and compensation. Consultation offices working out of these colleges offer legal advice to the public, assist people in filling out petitions, and perform similar services.

Advocates, like judges and procurators, have been subjected to periodic social-pressure campaigns to punish criminals more severely. As a result, when advocates defend their clients in the courtroom, they often play a subdued role. The defense lawyer may not marshal all resources for the defense that are provided for in the law. Her concluding statement may be more a recitation of mitigating circumstances than a denial of guilt or a presentation of purely legal arguments.[51] She may, however, file an appeal to the higher courts.

Procurators outshine judges and advocates in training, organization, and power. In the application and interpretation of the law, procurators are second only to the national police (KGB) in real power, and even the KGB cannot start an investigation or make an arrest without written permission from the appropriate officer of the procuracy.

The procuracy is a kind of bureaucratic and legal hydra. Its most important administrative function is to fight graft and corruption in the economy. In its legal aspect, the procuracy seeks to ensure that policy is carried out and that officials of middle and low rank do not exercise power arbitrarily. For this pur-

[50] See Lawrence M. Friedman and Zigurds L. Zile, "Soviet Legal Profession," *Wisconsin Law Review*, 1:1 (1964) pp. 32–77.

[51] Feifer, *Justice in Moscow*, p. 239.

pose it has departments charged with general supervision of the legality of all governmental operations, including the courts (except the U.S.S.R. Supreme Court) and other administrative and economic agencies. The Council of Ministers of the U.S.S.R. and the CPSU are not included under its supervision. Procuracy officers conduct pretrial investigations in criminal cases, leaving the political cases to the KGB. They act as government prosecutors in court. Though they sometimes defend the accused in court and sometimes defend ordinary citizens whose rights have been violated by public officials, their principal work is to defend the interests of the party, both directly as criminal investigators and prosecutors and indirectly as watchdogs over judges, advocates, and administrators.

Pretrial investigations may last months. They are strictly controlled by the procuracy or, in political crimes, the KGB. Prisoners are kept isolated and helpless. They may be told that failure to answer questions will result in imprisonment and that false answers will be punished by the imposition of a prison sentence. The accused is at a considerable disadvantage during this process because Soviet criminal law does not give the accused the right to counsel until after the preliminary investigation has ended.

Because of its formidable role, efforts have been made to keep the procuracy free of local party and government links that might entangle it. The general procurator of the U.S.S.R. is, in accordance with the Constitution, appointed by the Supreme Soviet of the U.S.S.R. for a term of seven years. He appoints the procurators of the union republics for five-year terms. They in turn appoint procurators for the administrative regions within their republics (see Figure 12.4).

The procuracy provides its officials with the professional training necessary to guarantee zeal for the defense of party and government values and to ensure the status and authority needed to inspire awe in potential and actual law breakers. Outstanding graduates of the law faculties are often attracted into the procuracy.

The Court System

THE REGULAR COURTS The regular courts exist at four levels. People's courts (numbering about 3,500) have original jurisdiction over almost all cases, both civil and criminal. City and oblast courts (numbering 147) have original jurisdiction over cases such as murder with aggravating circumstances, counterfeiting, and desertion. Supreme courts of the fifteen republics can review decisions of the intermediate courts. The Supreme Court of the U.S.S.R., the only all-union court, has original jurisdiction over certain important political cases and the power to reverse cases appealed from decisions of republic supreme courts.

The vast majority of both civil and criminal cases are settled in the people's courts, although appeal to higher courts is always possible. People's courts have one elected judge, assisted by two lay assessors elected from factories and nearby residential areas. Higher courts have three judges, who, though formally elected by the soviets, are in effect appointed, and there are no lay assessors.

COMRADES' COURTS Comrades' courts, staffed by volunteers, rely on persuasive rather than coercive sanctions. Although comrades' courts may impose small fines and recommend eviction from an apartment or other penalties, they do not operate in terms of conventional legal terminology. A person charged with an offense is not the accused but a "person brought before the comrades court." The hearings are informal and usually held in the social room of a factory, apartment house, neighborhood, or collective farm. Lawyers do not usually participate in the argument, and the judges are not civil servants but neighbors or fellow-workers, perhaps with elementary legal training. The members of the comrades' courts are formally elected by open ballot at meetings called by trade-union committees, the boards of collective farms, or the executive committees of local soviets.

Comrades' courts consider a variety of cases, including violators of labor discipline, unwarranted personal use of state or collective farm property, petty hooliganism; petty speculation; petty theft of state or social property, if committed for the first time; drunkenness in public places or at work; and many other infractions or offenses against public order.[52]

[52] Harold J. Berman and James W. Spindler, *Soviet Law and Procedure* (Cambridge, Mass.: Harvard University Press, 1966) pp. 863–865. See also the second edition of the

Figure 12.4

Organization of the Procuracy of the U.S.S.R.

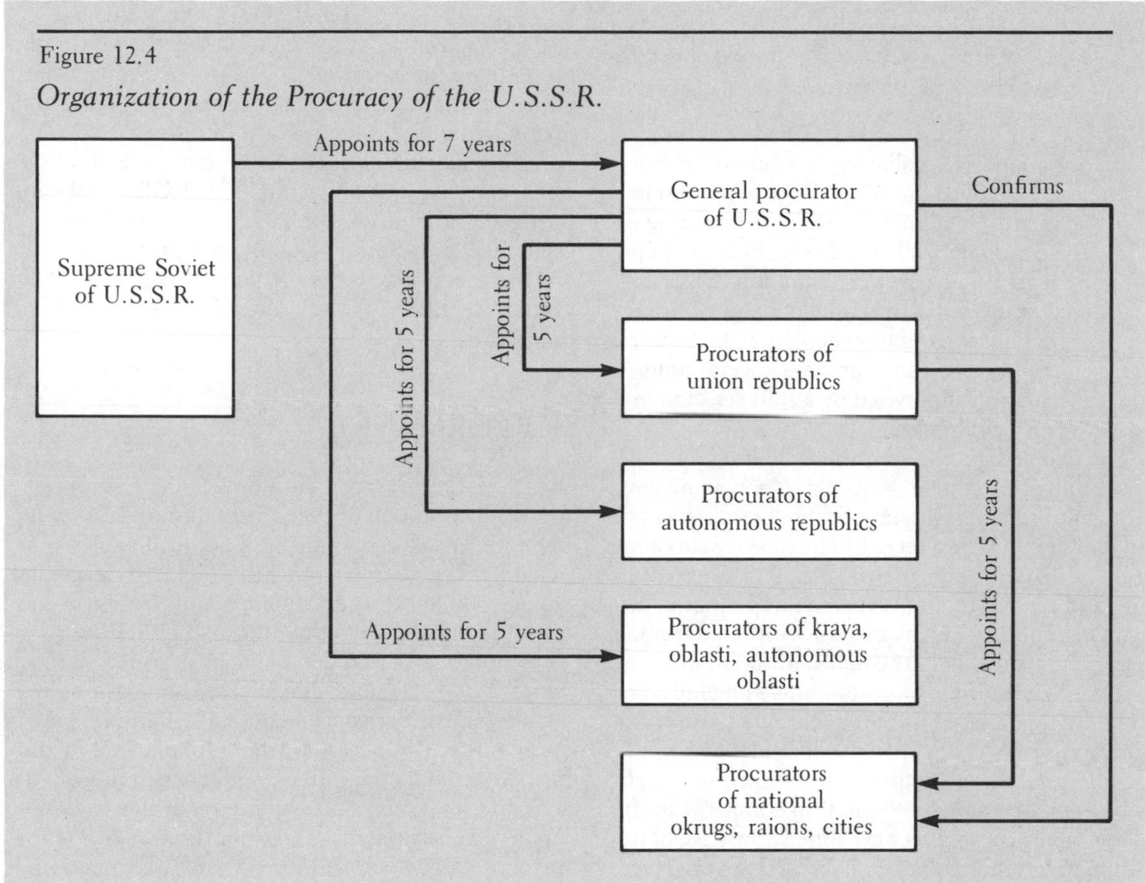

Cases may be brought before comrades' courts by people's guard units, trade-union committees, executive committees of local societies, state agencies — including courts and the procuracy — and at the initiative of the comrades' court itself. The court may reprimand and fine. If it is convinced of the necessity of holding the offender criminally responsible, it may turn a case over to the appropriate state agencies.

Police Agencies

THE MILITIA The militia, or regular police, is semimilitary in its training, organization, and ranks. It is under strict party and government control, and is directed by the Ministry of Internal Affairs. Its work includes traffic direction, maintaining public order, and apprehending criminals. At the same time, both its functions and its organization have some peculiarities. For example, the militia administers crucial instruments of social control, such as the Soviet internal passport system. All citizens who have reached the age of sixteen and who reside in specified categories of urban communities must have an internal passport and must, upon demand, present it to the militia and other authorities.

In addition, the militia administers many other controls, including procedures for obtaining permission to have and use printing, mimeographing, typewriting, and other reproduction and communication equipment, as well as photographic equip-

same book (1972), which contains texts of new laws against "especially dangerous state crimes" adopted in the late 1960s.

ment, guns, and explosives. Such police controls over communication reinforce other controls over the press and literature.

THE PEOPLE'S GUARDS The people's guards are a kind of auxiliary police, intended to assist the regular police or militia. First organized in 1958, the guards' total membership by the spring of 1963 was 5.5 million, well over 2 percent of the population; early in 1972 there were 7 million. Units are established at the initiative of the party or of Komsomol or trade-union organizations. Each unit works under a commander who supervises several units. The units are also supervised by a staff selected by the local party committee.

The people's guards are unpaid volunteers who must be at least eighteen years old. Upon admission, each guard receives an identification card, lapel pin, and handbook. When on patrol he or she wears a red armband. Guard units may be found in places of work and residence, in universities and other educational institutions, and even in the restricted frontier areas. The patrols help the police in traffic work, in discouraging disorders in restaurants and clubs, and in conducting raids to uncover shortchanging of customers in stores. They may demand identifying documents and even detain or arrest citizens, a right that has on occasion led them into conflict with the militia. Since the guards have little knowledge of the law, relatively limited police skills, and are unarmed, they have met with some popular resistance.

THE KGB More formidable than the Ministry of Internal Affairs and the regular police force is the Committee for State Security (KGB), the national political police.

Despite its sinister heritage and the danger that it might revert to earlier practices, the present position of the KGB differs significantly from that of the past. The special boards, which had been responsible for the summary exile of millions to labor camps, have been abolished. The security agencies, although given a role in the investigation of state crimes, are subjected to the same supervision in their investigations as the regular police.

The KGB is still a terrifying instrument of political control but, unlike Stalin's and Beria's police, it is not used to instill terror among Soviet citizens. Even so, the political and quasi judicial powers of the KGB remain formidable. It has the power of preliminary investigation in cases concerning state crimes. It often assumes leadership in detecting and investigating persons suspected of crimes such as currency speculation, large-scale embezzlement of state property, and smuggling. The KGB arrests, interrogates, and otherwise handles cases involving espionage, anti-Soviet agitation and propaganda, and other sensitive areas. Because these crimes are vaguely defined in the law, the KGB has vast discretion.

PERFORMANCE

Soviet secrecy deprives both Soviet citizens and foreigners of much of the information necessary for in-depth social, economic, and political analysis, making it considerably more difficult to describe, let alone evaluate, the performance and success of the Soviet political system than those of either the advanced industrialized democracies or much of the Third World. Data are defective or nonexistent in such significant areas as income distribution and crime rates. Matters are further complicated by the rarity of candid communication between Soviet citizens and foreigners. Obstacles to communication include the sealing off of most of the U.S.S.R. to travel by foreigners, and the controls placed on information necessary for full comparison of the Soviet with other political systems. However, a good deal is known about various aspects of Soviet political performance, and what follows will attempt to summarize scholarly opinion on some vital matters.

We shall discuss Soviet performance with respect to the extraction of resources and services from the population, the regulation and control by the political regime of the activities of the citizenry, and the distribution of goods to the people of the U.S.S.R. Some attention will also be paid to symbolic performance. In a flood of propagandistic exhortations and commands in mass media and by way of agitation, indoctrination, and mass political rituals, symbolic performance plays a peculiarly conspicuous, pervasive role in Soviet type polities. Of course, it should be kept in mind that the outputs and outcomes of performance capabilities are interrelated and interdependent; comparatively high development of one capability and its outcomes and goods may result in a relatively low level of other outcomes. For example, hypertrophy of the regulative capacity, a characteristic of the Soviet system, results in curtailment of personal and group initiative and liberty for all but a small fraction of the population, and may even render the ruling class prisoners of the immense bureaucracies.

Extractive Performance

In extraction of resources from the population, the Soviet regime is effective, though as in all fields except perhaps police controls and military power, its efficiency is not outstanding. Through the centralized bureaucracy, penetrated and under surveillance of the party and the KGB, and more specifically, by means of the well-known turnover tax on most goods, particularly consumer goods, the government derives enormous revenues. They are supplemented by other forms of taxation, which are relatively unimportant, and by the profits of state-operated enterprises. Members of the CPSU, the trade unions, and the other public organizations — and Soviet citizens are virtually required to belong to at least one — also pay dues. These, together with revenues from organization newspapers and other enterprises constitute important sources of income for these organizations.

The Soviet state extracts labor in many ways other than in the operation of the state-run economy. The mass organizations require their members, as part of their obligation as citizens of a socialist society, to perform a myriad of unpaid tasks, such as assistance in child-care centers, auxiliary police work, agitation for getting out the vote in elections, and, in the case of scientists and other professionals, delivering public lectures. A characteristic type of voluntary public service in the U.S.S.R., especially for industrial workers, consists of unpaid labor in an effort to fulfill or exceed the economic plans. This practice has apparently expanded in recent years. One of its aspects is the *subbotniki* (from the Russian word for Saturday), involving labor donated to the state on weekends and holidays by workers whose efforts are praised as manifestations of Leninist public spirit. Sometimes even top-flight scientists are mobilized to plant potatoes and students spend part of their summers helping to harvest grain or raise vegetables, which are often in very short supply.

Military service in the U.S.S.R. is compulsory. By the time a Soviet youngster reaches the age of military service, he or she has already acquired a good deal of military training, some of it rather advanced. This training is received in school and in the Young Pioneers, the Komsomol, and the para-military program of DOSAAF (Voluntary Society for Assistance to the Army, Air Force, and Navy).

A type of extraction of services that seems peculiar to socialist systems is forced labor in corrective labor colonies. According to the authoritative estimates of Amnesty International, there are at present at least 1 million Soviet citizens in Soviet labor camps. This figure is minuscule in comparison with the dimensions of forced labor under Stalin, when Beria's slave empire was a significant component of the Soviet national economy, but it is still not negligible. Also, this estimate is far lower than that alleged by informed Soviet dissidents.

The foregoing suggests the vastness of the extractive performance of the Soviet system. While to some extent the activities it entails may be a source of satisfaction to Soviet people — and of course that is how they are portrayed in the Soviet mass media — there can be little doubt that one of the outcomes of the Soviet system's formidable extractive performance is poverty for many millions of citizens, especially unskilled workers and collective farmers. This is because a disproportionate share of the resources extracted, especially from the turnover tax, does not produce food and consumer goods, but is invested in capital goods, armaments, and military aid to national liberation movements abroad. The economic outcome of this aspect of Soviet policy performance could undoubtedly be reduced if the economy were less inefficient, but achievement of greater efficiency would probably require less reliance on command methods of economic administration and a greater role for market mechanisms. The mediocre record of attempted economic reforms to date, however, strongly indicates that the political leadership fears that reliance on market and price mechanisms would undermine the processes, political culture, and power relationships they identify with and are determined to preserve.

It is clear that the extractive performance of the U.S.S.R. together with the regulative performance underpinning it, distorts and stunts political participation. Under such conditions, participation is drained of much of its meaning, and tends to become a chore, to be evaded if possible, and performed, when it must be, perfunctorily.

Regulative Performance

Let us turn now to regulative performance, the output of the party, the economic, cultural, and ideological bureaucracies, and the order maintenance agencies, such as the police, courts, and their mass auxiliaries. Behind the police, of course, stand the military forces, which would have to be relied on to suppress large-scale disturbances of public order, and were indeed called upon to put down the serious labor unrest that broke out in Novocherkassk in 1962, an episode described brilliantly by Alexander Solzhenitsyn in the third volume of his *Gulag Archipelago*. Detailed discussion of the international aspects of regulative performance in the U.S.S.R. would take us far afield, but we should note that the Soviet leadership sees its task of order maintenance as extending beyond the borders of the U.S.S.R., as the Soviet-led military intervention by the Warsaw Pact in Czechoslovakia in 1968 demonstrated. This action was justified by the Brezhnev doctrine — that all members of the socialist commonwealth are obliged to defend and preserve the achievements of socialism whenever they are, in the opinion of Soviet leaders, threatened by subversive forces in any Warsaw Pact state. The policy reflects concern that liberalization in any East European state might inspire or incite parallel efforts in the U.S.S.R. itself.

Quite apart from its international dimension, the scope of regulative performance is immense. The largest component of CPSU membership and of party leadership consists of persons directing and regulating the country's scientific, technological, and economic life. High-ranking party members, holding posts in the Council of Ministers or as heads of economic ministries or committees are deployed throughout the command posts of the economy. In the economy, as in culture, ideology, propaganda, and communications — all of which are controlled by party leaders — there are also representatives of the KGB, whose duty it is to prevent infiltration of alien ideas into Soviet media and also into textbooks and other materials used in the educational and socialization process.

Efforts at economic, scientific, and cultural regulation are somewhat less successful than one might expect, in view of the enormous resources allocated to them. Perhaps this is because overregulation stunts initiative. However, the increasing use of incremental, experimental approaches to decision making in the economy, science, and technology may eventually ameliorate the negative effects of hypertrophied regulation. Also, it must be borne in mind that for certain fields, such as scientific research and development, the U.S.S.R. allocates some three times the proportion of its gross national product that the United States does. This enormous effort, even if not as efficient as the corresponding American one, nevertheless pays off impressively, especially in terms of military power. Also, more than 1 million Soviet citizens engaged in scientific work have psychic satisfactions that offset the alienating effects of bureaucratic regulation. One of the CPSU's major preoccupations in recent years has been to structure the party organizations that supervise scientific work in such a way as to achieve the best mix of political control and quality of scientific output.

In some areas of the economy, particularly agriculture, the party continues to forego complete regulation to promote material productivity. Continued dependence on the collective farmers' private plots as the source of a large proportion of fruits and vegetables, eggs, meat, and dairy products requires reluctant toleration of a limited private — or, as it is called in official terminology, cooperative — component of the economy.

But there are gaps in the regulative performance of the Soviet system that are perhaps more worrisome to the Soviet leaders than the exception reluctantly made in favor of the collective farmers' private plots. There is in the U.S.S.R. a large, semilegal or totally illegal, complex of economic activity often referred to as the "second economy." This is a kind of underground market economy, which enjoys intermittent tolerance on the part of the authorities. At its best, this constitutes a gray market, its existence imparting a precious, probably indispensable flexibility to an economy that would strangle in red tape if its rigidity were not offset by channels that enable plant managers, for example, to obtain raw materials and personnel outside of official channels. At its worst, the second economy is rife with bribery, theft, embezzlement, and fraud. At times, as in the scandals that rocked the Georgian republic in the early 1970s, Moscow feels it must intervene, removing high officials from leadership posts and even prosecuting them. If private enterprise, Soviet style, was not thus occasionally repressed, it might become a major threat to the integrity of the Soviet system, the economic morality of which is at low ebb, according to the testimony of Soviet dissidents and recent emigrants.

Turning to the evasion of cultural, ideological, and communications regulation, there is much more to report than we can mention. The enormous and continuing output of samizdat constitutes a challenge to the official political culture and to the legitimacy of the Soviet leaders. Closely related to the democratic movement and other causes that have found expression in samizdat are the persistent demands for the right to emigrate put forward by thousands of Soviet Jews, Germans, and members of various religious groups, especially Evangelical Christian Baptists and Pentecostalists. Less immediately threatening to the system's regulation capabilities, but potentially perhaps even more threatening, is widespread crime, alcoholism, and declining labor morale.

Soviet leaders have dealt with these problems with repression, exhortation, including nationalist and chauvinist propaganda, and efforts to deflect domestic discontent onto the alleged iniquities of the imperialists, especially the United States and its accomplices in Israel and South Africa.

Distributive Performance

Distributive performance in recent years has been adversely affected by a decline in the growth rate of the Soviet economy. This does not mean that the pie to be divided among Soviet consumers has shrunk. On the contrary, it has continued to grow at a respectable rate. The Soviet standard of living is slowly improving, especially in household applicances and to a lesser degree in housing and clothing; automobiles are still only a dream for the majority. Nevertheless, the standard is low for an industrial society; a generous estimate would be an income equivalent to about two hundred dollars a month for the average industrial worker. Although collective farmers make even less, they may be better off because of easier access to foodstuffs, especially in agriculturally rich areas. They are still substantially worse off in terms of access to cultural facilities and their children have a smaller probability of a higher education. The rural population of the U.S.S.R., still about a third of the total, bulks larger than in the advanced market economy countries. If a youngster is both of peasant stock and a member of a non-Russian ethnic group, the probability that she will not receive higher education rises. This often happens because of poor quality of Russian language instruction in rural areas; applicants do not necessarily achieve a command of Russian satisfactory to the examiners. Even if a person is Russian, Ukrainian, or Belorussian, he is likely to be discriminated against educationally if it is known that his parents are religious. Soviet Jews suffer educational and other forms of discrimination, begun first in the late Stalin era and increased since the upsurge of Jewish national consciousness after the Six-Day War of 1967.

On the more positive side, upward mobility can be achieved by loyal and conformist citizens of ability and talent, especially children of urban officials and professionals, but even of workers. Those who graduate from the universities and technical institutes are sure of a job. Because they know that any serious ideological blot on their record means expulsion from the university, Soviet students thus far have been conformist politically.

The implicit principle of Soviet distributive policy is the career open to talents. There is great inequality of reward for successful job performance, especially in industry, but also in the arts and sciences and other fields. There are no data on the percentage of national income going to the various percentiles of the population, and there are no studies of the opinions, life-styles, income levels, or other aspects of the lives of party and government officials. These facts are among many indirect indications that there is a high degree of distributive inequality. This cannot be adequately documented, but numerous samizdat documents, have presented impressive evidence on the semicovert, informal system of certificate rubles, which have vastly higher purchasing power than money received by ordinary citizens, on special stores stocked with goods not available to the general public, and on numerous other perquisites of the elite.

There is increasing evidence that inequality of distribution and the real poverty of unskilled workers, especially those with large families, is generating significant discontent. But discontent has thus far been held in check, not only by fear of repression but also by the policy of subsidizing cheap bread and other basic foodstuffs, perhaps partly to prevent Soviet workers from following the Polish examples of 1956, 1970, and 1976 and rioting and striking to exert economic and political pressure. However, there is increasing reason to doubt the capability of the Soviet system — barring fundamental economic reform, which at present is not on the horizon — to continue to improve popular welfare, at least at a rate sufficient to stave off disaffection. An important fact in this regard is that since the early 1970s the infant mortality rate has risen, while life expectancy, especially for males, has fallen.[53]

According to official doctrine, a developed socialist society now flourishes in the U.S.S.R. In view of what is known about the performance of the Soviet polity, the official claim seems a bit exaggerated, especially if socialism means high scores on such criteria as material abundance, distributive equality, meaningful, uninhibited political participation, and security from crime and arbitrary government. It would be more accurate to appraise Soviet performance as appropriate for a system occupying a position toward the middle of a scale from advanced to backward, and a system showing increasing signs of malaise, although by no means an incurable sickness. Although it is probably slowly declining, the considerable equality of opportunity still available to Soviet citizens, may permit us to say that distributive performance is the greatest strength of the Soviet system. The respectable level in this sector is dearly paid for, however, in terms of the extraordinary extractive and regulative pressures to which Soviet citizens are subjected.

ALTERNATIVE PATHS OF DEVELOPMENT

The following speculations on the Soviet future assume that the fate of the people of the U.S.S.R. and to some extent of mankind in general, is contingent upon the Soviet regime's response to issues that have recently become increasingly troublesome. Space is available for discussion of only a few of these vital questions. Selectivity precludes detailed examination of some very important matters, such as the much discussed problem of political succession, which is part of the larger problem of replacing the present aged, unrepresentative, political leadership.[54] Our speculation about the future will focus mainly on the following issues: scientific-technological modernization (usually discussed in Soviet sources as the problem of the scientific-technological revolution); democratization; nationality problems; and détente.

In recent years the Kremlin has made appreciable progress only in connection with the first of these problems. Progress in resolving the numerous crucial issues posed by the scientific-technological revolution has obviously been less than what the leadership hoped, but it has been considerable, especially in fields with military applications, such as weaponry and space. There has even been borrowing of West-

[53] Christopher Davis and Murray Feshbach, "Life Expectancy in the Soviet Union," *Wall Street Journal*, June 20, 1978.

[54] See Grey Hodnett, "Soviet Succession Contingencies," *Problems of Communism*, 24:2 (March–April, 1975) pp. 1–21, for a model of informed analysis and forecasting of probable developments in this field. On the problems of recruiting competent personnel to cope with problems posed by the new trends in administration of science and technology, see T. H. Rigby and Robert F. Miller, "Political and Administrative Aspects of the Scientific and Technical Revolution in the U.S.S.R.," Occasional Paper No. 11, Department of Political Science, Australian National University (Canberra, Australia, 1976), pp. 35–38. Interesting in this connection is the establishment in recent years of several specialized institutions for training high-level managers and administrators, the most recent being the Academy of the National Economy of the U.S.S.R., established in May 1978. See *Radio Liberty Research*, 123:78 (May 30, 1978).

ern techniques in applied social science, such as the use of social experiments to improve decision making, and judging by published official encouragement for such efforts, the regime is determined to develop them further, provided it in no way undermines CPSU control over the economy or threatens the power and privileges of the establishment. Apparently bureaucratic resistance based on cost calculations, and on the pervasive conservatism characteristic of the post-Khrushchev leadership, explains the virtual failure of the economic reform of 1965, and the quiet shelving of other innovative policies, such as Brezhnev's abortive attempt to adopt long-range (twenty-year) economic plans, in place of short-term plans.[55]

For about ten years some of the most knowledgeable and thoughful Soviet dissidents have been advancing the thesis that resolving the problems posed by Soviet competition with the West in economic, scientific, and technological development depends on democratization of Soviet political and cultural life. Lending significance to the dissident's demands is evidence that their views reflect those of a great many of Russia's best-trained and most talented citizens who see their rulers as routine-minded careerists, clinging to power and privileges rather than developing the capabilities of modern science in the interests of public welfare. Hopes stirred by Khrushchev's de-Stalinization efforts remain unfulfilled, leaving many professionals bitter and apprehensive about the future.

The most important achievements of the Communist party have been making and consolidating a drastic social revolution and then industrializing an underdeveloped society. Now that these tasks are largely completed and are giving way to the more ordinary, but perhaps more difficult, problems of managing and coordinating a complex postrevolutionary society, there is decreasing justification for a high level of ideological mobilization and coercion.

There is good reason to believe that pressures and demands from writers, scientists, and newer groups such as computer scientists and space technologists will increase in range, scope, and intensity. The Soviet intelligentsia has its share of material values and respect, but still lacks political power. The history of revolutionary change indicates that groups with a high sense of their worth and capabilities eventually achieve a full share of all the values at the disposal of society. That the defenders of official orthodoxy fear the potentially disruptive effects of such demands is indicated by numerous criticisms of groupism and professionalism, and by severe penalties meted out to the dissidents who openly voice the aspirations of many colleagues who fear to speak out.

This is not to argue that the socialist economy is likely to be repudiated. It is certain, however, that a decentralized socialism and a revisionist, or "Bukharinist," Marxism stripped of myth are far more appealing to many Soviet intellectuals and specialists than are the present command society and the regime's increasingly obsolete orthodoxy. As Stephen Cohen has written, "Many Soviet analysts will probably conclude that some form of Bukharinism would have been . . . preferable — that while Stalin's course produced spectacular achievements at spectacular costs, Bukharin's, producing neither, would have been more successful."[56]

Of course, many, if not most, Soviet advocates of democratization have pushed for vastly increased freedom, discussion, and participation in policy making not only because they regard such goals as vital to the economy, but also because they consider freedom, under law, an indispensable attribute of civilized human life. That such arguments are persuasive and such values dear to many, even if only a small fraction, of Soviet scientists and other specialists and intellectuals is clear from the persistence of dissent. But the regime, although presumably not indifferent to the domestic and foreign costs

[55] Perhaps the best analysis of the large issues posed by the scientific-technological revolution in the U.S.S.R. is Paul Cocks' chapter, "The Scientific-Technological Revolution and Bureaucratic Politics," in Paul Cocks, Robert V. Daniels, Nancy W. Heer (eds.), *The Dynamics of Soviet Politics* (Cambridge, Mass.: Harvard University Press, 1976), pp. 156–178.

[56] Stephen F. Cohen, *Bukharin and the Bolshevik Revolution* (New York: Knopf, 1973), p. 316. See also Moshe Lewin, "Political Undercurrents of Soviet Economic Debates" (Princeton, N.J.: Princeton University Press, 1974). Lewin's book interestingly links post-Stalin aspirations for political economic liberalization with the heritage of "Bukharinism."

of its suppression of dissent, acts as though the benefits, in maintaining the Soviet system, are greater. Intensification of repression since early 1977, particularly against well-known dissidents, such as Anatoli Shcharanski, Alexander Ginzburg, and Yuri Orlov who protested Soviet violation of the human rights provisions of the Helsinki Accords, indicated that repressive, rather than responsive behavior, would continue to be the Kremlin's policy toward efforts of Soviet citizens to effect peaceful reform of the Soviet system.

Those who dominate Soviet political life evidently will continue to act as if they regard the costs of repression necessary for maintaining their power. They have already paid a high price — though of course a small one compared to that paid by their victims — in the loss of hundreds of the best qualified, most talented citizens to concentration camps, psychiatric hospitals, and forced exile. There is every reason to believe that censorship, arbitrary law enforcement, and suppression of individual and group rights will continue.

In respect to nationality, and probably also religion, the struggle for civil and political rights will probably widen and deepen. After a brief interlude under Khrushchev of greater accommodation of the aspirations of non-Russian nationalities, the regime has recently reverted to Stalinist policies of Russification and appeals to Russian chauvinism. Opposition to these policies has intensified among non-Russians, particularly in the Baltic area, the Ukraine, the Caucasus, and among Soviet Jews. Opposition has been articulated by intellectuals, often with the support of the Moscow-based democrats, such as Andrei Sakharov, Yuri Orlov, and others. In 1972 the top leadership promulgated a doctrine more assimilationist even than Stalin's, saying that the Soviet people constituted a new human community. The implementation of this policy will sharpen tensions in ethnic relations in the future.

Finally, we turn to détente, and more generally to the sphere of foreign relations. There is, and has been for several years, much evidence that the Moscow ruling group has decided that world conditions, especially the disarray, disunity, and even disintegration of the West, favor to Soviet foreign policy not of détente but of rapid, worldwide projection of Soviet military-political influence. Such a policy is psychologically appealing to the Soviet elite, to some in terms of Marxist missionary zeal, but probably more widely and deeply in terms of Russian nationalism. It also may appear useful as a means of distracting attention from intractable domestic problems including, besides those already mentioned, widespread alcoholism, increasing dissatisfaction among Soviet workers (at least the unskilled ones) over subsistence living standards, crime, and juvenile delinquency. In the long run, the people of the U.S.S.R. and the world will suffer if the satisfactions derived from chauvinism and jingoism are substituted for those that could be obtained by heeding the advice of the the real Soviet patriots, who for years have pleaded with their leaders to arrest internal decay by liberalizing and democratizing political institutions more relevant to dismantling the tsarist autocracy than to governing a mature socialist society. However, not only the recent opportunistic course of Soviet foreign policy, especially in Africa, but the inclusion in the new Constitution of a foreign policy chapter incorporating expansionist goals threatens world tranquility.

To sum up, the course of Soviet political development appears to be set in the direction of a limited technocracy, at the service of CPSU hegemony, and of opportunistic Soviet expansionism rather than democratization. While these trends promised short-term rewards for the regime, they boded ill for the future. However, in view of the durability of the Soviet system, it hardly seems realistic or prudent to assign anything but a very low probability to the disintegration or collapse of the regime in the imaginable future. More likely is the prospect of the non-Soviet world having to exert vast effort to cope with increasing Soviet power and expansionism.

However, the somewhat somber implications of the foregoing must not be regarded as predictions of doom. These tentative predictions are *essentially* speculations, short-term projections of trends that call for thoughtful analysis and attention. People of intelligence, good will and good sense everywhere must work for a future less compatible with the values of Stalin and Brezhnev and more consonant with the ideals of Sakharov and Orlov.

KEY TERMS

Vladimir Lenin
Leon Trotski
Joseph Stalin
Bolshevism
vanguard party
revolution from above
Marxism-Leninism
socialism in one country
kulak
Great Purges
Communist Party of the Soviet Union (CPSU)
Supreme Soviet
Politburo
Party Congress
Presidium
Council of Ministers
democratic centralism
Central Committee
Secretariat
Leonid Brezhnev
Aleksei Kosygin
People's courts
Nikita Khrushchev
totalitarianism
inclusive hegemony
apparatchiki
All-Union Central Council of Trade Unions
Komsomol
Young Pioneers
Octobrists
agitation
Pravda
Izvestiya
primary organizations
TASS
nomenklatura system
Helsinki accord
dual subordination
socialist legal consciousness
KGB (Committee for State Security)
advocate
procurator
Comrade's courts
Samizdat (self-published tracts)

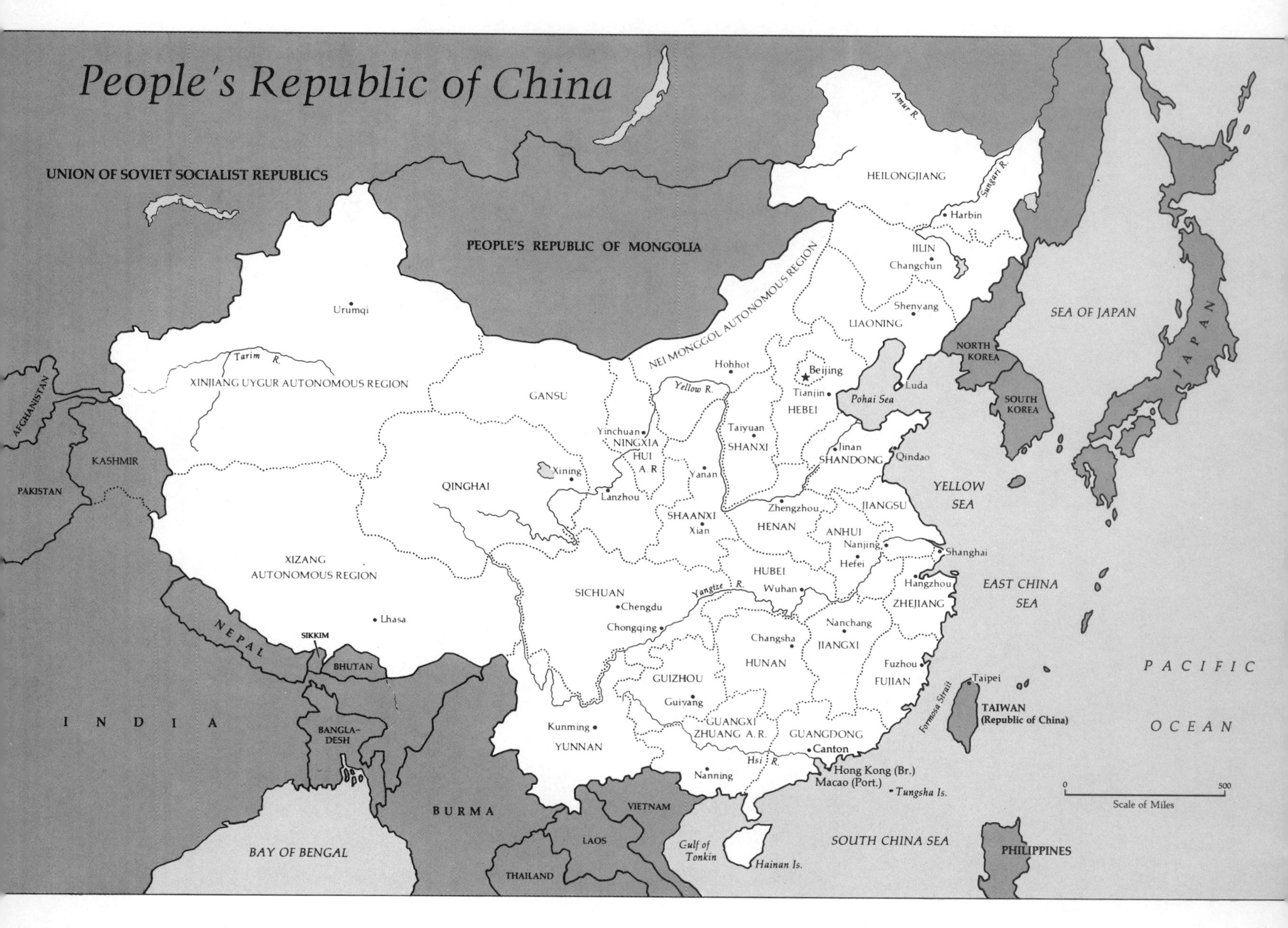

People's Republic of China
UNION OF SOVIET SOCIALIST REPUBLICS
PEOPLE'S REPUBLIC OF MONGOLIA
Amur R.
HEILONGJIANG
Sungari R.
Harbin
JILIN
Changchun
Shenyang
LIAONING
SEA OF JAPAN
JAPAN
NORTH KOREA
SOUTH KOREA
Luda
Pohai Sea
Beijing
Tianjin
HEBEI
NEI MONGGOL AUTONOMOUS REGION
Hohhot
Yellow R.
Urumqi
Tarim R.
XINJIANG UYGUR AUTONOMOUS REGION
AFGHANISTAN
KASHMIR
PAKISTAN
GANSU
Yinchuan
NINGXIA HUI A.R
Taiyuan
SHANXI
Jinan
SHANDONG
Qindao
YELLOW SEA
Xining
QINGHAI
Lanzhou
Yanan
Zhengzhou
JIANGSU
SHAANXI
Xian
HENAN
ANHUI
Nanjing
Shanghai
Hefei
XIZANG AUTONOMOUS REGION
HUBEI
Hangzhou
EAST CHINA SEA
SICHUAN
Yangtze R.
Wuhan
ZHEJIANG
Chengdu
Lhasa
Chongqing
Nanchang
NEPAL
SIKKIM
Changsha
JIANGXI
BHUTAN
HUNAN
Fuzhou
PACIFIC OCEAN
GUIZHOU
FUJIAN
Taipei
Guiyang
Formosa Strait
INDIA
BANGLA-DESH
Kunming
GUANGXI ZHUANG A.R.
GUANGDONG
TAIWAN (Republic of China)
YUNNAN
Canton
Hsi R.
Hong Kong (Br.)
Nanning
Macao (Port.)
Tungsha Is.
0
500
Scale of Miles
BURMA
VIETNAM
LAOS
BAY OF BENGAL
Gulf of Tonkin
Hainan Is.
SOUTH CHINA SEA
PHILIPPINES
THAILAND

CHAPTER THIRTEEN

JAMES R. TOWNSEND

Politics in China

INTRODUCTION

Politics in China is the product of a prolonged revolutionary era, lasting from 1911 to 1949 and including three forceful overthrows of the political system. The first revolution, in 1911, displaced an imperial system that had endured for centuries. The second, culminating in 1928 with the establishment of a new central government under the control of the Guomindang (KMT),[1] replaced the disunited warlord rule of early republican China with a more vigorous, organized, and centralized system of single-party domination. The third revolution of 1949 brought the Chinese Communist party (CCP) to power, and led to the creation of the present communist system.

The establishment of the People's Republic of China (P.R.C.) in 1949 did not end the revolutionary era, however. A series of mass mobilization campaigns — of which the Great Proletarian Cultural Revolution of 1966–1969 was the most powerful — kept revolutionary symbols, themes, and conflicts alive and countered trends toward institutionalization. The death in September 1976 of Mao Zedong, who had led the CCP since the mid-1930s and had been the chief promoter of continuing the revolution, may have marked the P.R.C.'s transition to a genuinely postrevolutionary period. Nonetheless, Chinese politics from 1949 to 1976 are best seen as a continuation of, rather than a departure from, China's long revolutionary era.

Three themes have dominated China's revolutionary era. The first is the nationalistic drive to recapture China's strength and power, to claim a secure and influential place in the global order. Before 1949, this drive centered on the eradication of foreign control over portions of China's territory, economy, and culture. Since 1949, it has concentrated on maintaining national security in a threatening international environment and establishing an independent posture. China is the world's third largest state, with an area of about 3.7 million square miles. Its population — estimated at 950 million in

[1] Chinese names are transliterated in the *pinyin* system now standard in the P.R.C. The Guomindang is referred to hereafter as the KMT. Confucius and Chiang Kai-shek are not rendered in *pinyin*.

1976 — is approximately one-fifth of the world's total and exceeds by far that of any other country. Sharing borders with the Soviet Union, India, Pakistan, Southeast Asia, and Korea, and in regional proximity to Japan, the P.R.C. occupies a strategic position in a region of utmost significance. Although not yet a superpower like the United States or the Soviet Union, China is rapidly emerging as one of the world's leading actors.

The second theme is the effort to establish a new political community in the wake of the old imperial system. Initially the revolutionary forces demanded reunification of the country, an end to the divisions that followed the collapse of the empire and made a mockery of national government. As the revolution gathered momentum, however, it became clear that China needed a new kind of political community, one that would not simply unify rival regions and movements but also integrate the population across class and ethnic lines, into a system in which political authority came to bear on every citizen and was the object of popular support and loyalty.

At issue here has been the question of models, or as the Chinese say, roads. The CCP victory of 1949 settled the choice between the bourgeois democratic and socialist roads, inaugurating a period in which the Soviet Union was adopted as the model for Chinese socialism. Soon, however, Mao began to pull the CCP away from the Soviet model, initiating a second struggle, between the Maoist road and the Soviet revisionist road that he saw leading back to capitalism. With Mao's death, his successors began to edge away from the more radical version of the Maoist road, while claiming continued hostility toward the Soviet road. The Chinese see post-1949 politics as a struggle between two lines, with the Maoist or proletarian line representing the correct Marxist-Leninist position on the left, and the KMT, the Soviet revisionists, and all Chinese opponents of Maoism representing the bourgeois, capitalist-roading position on the right. While this is a highly simplified gloss, which does not acknowledge post-1976 deviations from Maoism, it is important to note that most political issues in China have been highly polarized and conflictual, presented as sharp choices between fundamentally different systems; in that perspective, political conflict has had a revolutionary aura.

The third theme is socioeconomic development, which initially aimed at relieving the oppression of traditional society and improving the obviously backward preindustrial economy. Social oppression and economic misery were the sources of much of the revolution's momentum. After 1949, as economic development got underway and old social patterns gave way before radical reforms, new issues came to the fore. Problems of economic planning and balance, of population growth and food production, of urban and rural development, of institutions or mass mobilization as agents of development — all these and many others complicated policies for development and required hard choices. Inevitably, these choices fueled the fires of the two-line struggle, leading to extreme postures among policy makers.

These three themes become almost inseparable within the Chinese political process. The split with the Soviet Union brought greater security concerns; mass mobilization has sometimes compromised national planning; emphasis on higher education and bureaucratic efficiency has menaced populist values; rapprochement with the United States and the search for Western technology compromise claims to ideological purity. Issues blend together as part of the political calculus that Chinese leaders must master. In this chapter, we will give primary attention to the two-line struggle, which has been the central theme in China's search for its own developmental model and which offers a way of generalizing about the other two themes. However, the historical survey in the next section should assist the reader in understanding the national and socioeconomic revolutions that have accompanied the evolution of the P.R.C.'s political system.

HISTORY, SOCIETY, ECONOMY, INTERNATIONAL ENVIRONMENT

In Chinese perspective, the P.R.C. is a new political system. The old imperial order, which ended in 1911 with the overthrow of the Qing (Manchu) dynasty, had endured for over two thousand years. This political tradition, with its remarkable power and longevity, continues to influence Chinese political thought and institutions. Historical orientations, analogies, and comparisons remain common in political discourse. One obvious comparison is that the present system has governed for only a fraction of the span of several of the great dynasties.

Personal experience reinforces the closeness and relevance of tradition. Most of the leaders who governed the P.R.C. until recently were born before the fall of the Qing dynasty. Mao and his colleagues knew imperial society firsthand and were educated at least partly in the style followed by Chinese intellectuals for centuries. Only in the 1970s has leadership begun to shift to younger figures without direct experience of the imperial past, but even they are aware of traditional ideas and social patterns that survived after 1911. And all the post-1949 leaders were recruited into politics in the midst of the revolutionary upheavals of 1911–1949. It is important, therefore, to take a closer look at the political tradition and revolutionary setting from which the CCP emerged. This will be followed by an overview of post-1949 political history, emphasizing changes in China's society, economy, and international environment.

The Chinese Political Tradition

In structuring political authority, the imperial political system sharply distinguished ruler and subject, official and citizen, both in theory and practice. The result was a two-class social order of elite and masses. The elite included officials of the imperial bureaucracy and the degree-holding scholars or gentry from whose ranks officials were chosen.

Supplementing this distinction was a hierarchical structure of authority throughout society, an intricate network of superior-inferior relationships. Within the political elite, the emperor stood alone at the top of the hierarchy, with absolute power over all his officials and subjects. The bureaucracy was divided by ranks and grades, with each official's position fixed in a hierarchy descending from the emperor. Beneath the officials came degree holders not selected for official position, ranked according to the degree they held.

Ordinary subjects, who constituted most of the population, did not fall into this political hierarchy. But where the political hierarchy left off, a highly complex structuring of social relationships took over, with profound implications for the political system. Authority within a family or larger kinship group was held by the eldest male within generational lines; the older generation held sway over younger ones, and elder males were superior to females and younger males of the same generation. Of course, the family head was subordinate to the hierarchy extending downward from the emperor, and thereby brought those beneath him into an ordered relationship with political authority. Therefore, the pattern of hierarchical authority was dominant at both elite and popular levels; any kind of social action, political or not, had to take place within its framework. As a result, the rupture of authority that came with the collapse of the old political system had a traumatic effect on all social relations, and Chinese attempts to reconstruct their political system have usually involved elitist and hierarchical authority structures.

The authority structure of traditional China gave the political system supreme power, since the emperor and the bureaucracy — the political leaders — sat at the top of the social hierarchy. Equally significant was the political system's relative independence from external influence or restraint. Theoretically, the imperial system had an organic relationship with Chinese society; supposedly modeled on the family, it was to serve society by maintaining order, performing religious functions, and preserving the virtues of the past. However, there developed over time a set of institutions and attitudes that reduced the system's ability to recognize any legitimate external influence on its actions. It was a law unto itself, self-perpetuating and self-regulating, entering into its relationships with domestic and foreign entities assuming its own superiority.

One important aspect of the system's self-governing status was its handling of political recruitment and advancement. Individuals could prepare for a political career by acquiring knowledge or wealth, but formal certification came only from the government. Once there, an officeholder had no constituency that might dilute service to the emperor. Political representation was an unknown concept, although a quota system in the examinations encouraged a distribution of degree holders among the provinces.

Just as it denied external claims to influence or to membership, the regime acknowledged no legal or institutional limitations on its actions. The government could initiate, manage, regulate, adjudicate, or repress as it saw fit. Elites admitted a moral obligation to provide just and responsive government, but enforcement of that obligation depended on recruitment, which allegedly chose only men of superior virtue, or on the bureaucracy's own mechanisms of control and supervision. That is, the obligation was enforceable only by elite self-regulation.

The ideal of government by a disinterested, educated elite, chosen through examinations without reference to class or wealth, had a profound impact on traditional China, but it was never an unqualified reality. Wealth mattered, since officials and official status could be bought. Personal obligations and loyalties to family could erode an official's impartiality, as could those to the same clan, locality, or school. The system tolerated these discrepancies within bounds because it had little choice; but it never granted them legal or moral acceptance, and it frequently punished pronounced partisan activity.

Like its imperial predecessor, the Communist elite has rejected claims to representation or recognition of partisan interests within the government. Competing political organizations are firmly discouraged in favor of the monolithic authority of the party. Factionalism within the ruling structure is anathema now, as it was under the emperor, although disapproval has failed in both cases to prevent the evil. In contrast to the past, the present system has extended its authority directly to the mass level, reducing sharply the limited local autonomy allowed under the Manchus. At the same time, by enlarging the size and responsibilities of the bureaucracy and by encouraging mass political mobilization, it has made the governmental process more complex and more open to societal pressures and demands.

The Chinese tradition contained from ancient times a number of philosophical-religious schools of thought, but Confucianism became the official ideology of the imperial system. Government officials were appointed mainly on the basis of superior performance in examinations that tested their knowledge of the Confucian classics. The legitimacy of political authority rested on observance of this moral doctrine, and Confucian ideology thus became an integrative force that justified political rule, defined the purposes of the state, provided the values of the elite, and harmonized diverse interests in society. To the extent that it was widely accepted, it would bring society and officialdom together in common loyalty to rightful imperial authority.

The indispensability of official ideology, carefully defined and studied, is also central to the Communist government, although the substance of contemporary ideology differs significantly. Indeed, the CCP has gone far beyond the imperial elite in exploiting the integrative benefits of ideology, using it with the masses as well. The Confucian ethic exerted the greatest influence on the elite alone, while subjects had little to do with the political elite and its ideology. The Communists, on the other hand, engage in intensive political education of the population as a whole. Although they are concerned about possible deviations from their ideology, their vigorous propagation of it encourages a consciousness of popular membership in the political system. Moreover, the current ideology stresses the virtues of the common people and their role in society, making it significantly more populist than the Confucian ethic.

The Revolutionary Setting

In the introduction, we emphasized that the P.R.C. is part of a revolutionary era dominated by three major themes. Since the revolution had been in progress for decades before the CCP became a significant force in Chinese politics, a sense of how these themes merged with the history of the party is essential to understanding of the present system.

The first theme, nationalism, has been at the forefront throughout the revolution. Perhaps its clearest manifestation was the desire for independence from foreign influence and control. From 1900 to about 1925, virtually all political movements with significant popular support — the anti-Manchu struggles, the frequent boycotts of foreign goods and enterprises, the strikes and demonstrations of May Fourth (1919) and May Thirtieth (1925) — appealed directly to popular resentment of foreign involvement in Chinese affairs. Independence remained a prominent issue in the Nationalist Revolution of 1926–1928 and in the early years of the KMT government, and with the Japanese invasion of 1937 it again became the paramount national objective. Although China largely regained its independent status in the postwar years, its conflicts with the United States and the Soviet Union have continued the legacy of earlier anti-imperialist struggles.

China was never a full-fledged colony, but both Chinese and foreigners recognized that Chinese independence was only nominal. Although imperialism never had a direct impact on most areas of Chinese life, its effects were highly visible to urbanized laborers, intellectuals, and businessmen who were influential in defining national political issues. Most politically conscious Chinese believed that foreign economic activities had damaged Chinese development, and virtually all Chinese exposed to the foreign presence resented its forced and privileged penetration of their country. The leaders of the CCP absorbed the anti-imperialist attitudes, used them in their rise to power, and have continued to nourish them since 1949.

A second theme of the Chinese revolution has been national unification under a central authority. After the Revolution of 1911, the basic form of Chinese government was warlordism. This term refers specifically to the years between 1916 and 1928, when control of the central government shifted frequently from one military leader to another. It also refers in a broader sense to the chronic political and military disunity that prevailed until 1949.

Military unification alone could not fully replace the imperial political system. Reunification required a new political structure, sensitive to the demands of a modern nation-state. In administrative terms, reunification required a new system of political recruitment and an expanded range of governmental activities at all levels. In ideological terms, it called for a new doctrine that would not only justify the exercise of political authority but also seek the allegiance of ordinary citizens and integrate them into the political system.

Finally, no discussion of the Chinese revolution is complete without reference to socioeconomic conditions and demands for radical change in them. China's economic situation in the first half of the twentieth century imposed harsh burdens on a troubled and rebellious populace. High rates of tenancy and the presence of a few large landowners were obvious sources of peasant dissatisfaction and obvious targets for reformers and revolutionaries, although neither condition was typical of all China. High rents and taxes, usurious credit, small and fragmented farms, traditional farming methods, low productivity, illiteracy, and external disturbances all contributed to the poverty and vulnerability of most of the rural population. The cities afforded better opportunities for a small but growing industrial proletariat, but living conditions were scarcely an improvement. Low wages, long hours, unsafe working conditions, inadequate housing, high rates of female and child labor, and large pools of unemployed or irregular workers were the rule in China's emerging factory cities.

By the 1920s, the banner of socioeconomic reform had passed from scattered intellectuals to organized political parties, with increasing evidence that it could be the basis for a popular movement. The Nationalist Revolution of 1928 clung to the proven appeal of national independence and unification, but at least briefly from 1925 to 1927, its radical wing (which included the Communists) was able to organize a worker-peasant movement that brought class struggle to the fore. From that point on, social and economic reform was an unavoidable issue. It was also the most divisive of the three main revolutionary themes. The KMT did more to advance it than any previous government had, but persistently gave it lower priority than independence and unification. The CCP, on the other hand, saw social and economic change as central to its program, inseparable from its nationalist objectives, and it was more successful than the KMT in tapping this vein of potential popular support.

Soviet Communism

There can be no simple explanation of the historical relationship between the Russian and Chinese comrades or Soviet communism's influence on the political system developed in China after 1949. It is undeniable, however, that the Soviet Union has had a powerful influence on Chinese Communist politics for half a century.

From the founding of the CCP in July 1921 (the date of the party's First Congress) to the early 1930s, the Soviet Communist party controlled the official line and leadership of the CCP. Through Russian advisers, the Soviet elite drafted the CCP's major policy statements and chose its highest officials. This

Chinese soldiers and militiamen of a minority nationality guard a cold northeastern frontier, representing P.R.C. unity in its conflict with the Soviet Union. Sino-Soviet differences have been a major issue in Chinese politics ever since the late 1950s.

control began to slip following the 1927 rupture of the first KMT-CCP alliance. Soviet leadership became increasingly concerned with European affairs, and the anticommunist stance of the new KMT government made communications with and support of the CCP more difficult. Most important, the bulk of CCP activity shifted after 1927 to the countryside, to the scattered rural soviets of south-central China, where the demands of survival and the autonomy derived from geographic isolation and military strength encouraged local leaders to differ at times with the party center.

In late 1934 KMT military pressure compelled the Communists to evacuate their principal stronghold in southern Jiangxi province and embark on the Long March, which relocated their major forces in the northwestern province of Shaanxi. Early in the course of this march, at the Zunyi Conference in January 1935, Mao Zedong successfully challenged the leadership installed by Moscow and became the leading figure within the CCP. Thereafter, Moscow did not control Chinese Communist affairs.

Soviet influence — as distinguished from control — is more difficult to analyze. The influence of Soviet communism, largely through the propagation of Marxism-Leninism, became an integral part of Chinese communism and remained long after Moscow's control of CCP affairs had ended. During the founding years of the party, most Chinese Communists shared a revolutionary commitment that overshadowed their commitment to Marxism-Leninism; that is, they identified more with the Bolshevik Revolution's general message of radical change than with the specifics of its ideology. Anti-imperialism was perhaps the strongest element in this message; the insistence that foreign oppression must and would be overthrown made Marxism-Leninism an immediately relevant explanation of a crucial fact of Chinese political life.

Some Chinese, seeking a revolutionary transformation that would propel their country into the modern era on a basis of full equality with the West, found inspiration and guidance in Marxism-Leninism. The doctrine not only asserted the inevitability of progress in altering China's inferior international status, but did so with a claim to science and modernity, which had previously seemed the monopoly of capitalism. Particularly important was the Leninist notion that a small intellectual elite could, by organized intervention in the historical process, accelerate and guide the transformation; to Chinese intellectuals aware of their society's inertia and their own traditional role of political leadership, this idea held a special appeal.

In addition, during the first KMT-CCP United Front of 1923–1927, the U.S.S.R. was a source of organizational and military aid to Chinese Communists and Nationalists, when both needed support and were unlikely to secure it elsewhere. As in the realm of ideas, Soviet communism had something to offer that supported and reinforced, but did not alter, the shape of the Chinese revolution.

Most fundamentally, the CCP came to accept the Soviet Union as a model and the Soviet Communist party as the most advanced and authoritative among all communist parties. The influence of this model has been particularly prominent in the CCP's organization and its conception of its political role. China has had only two significant mass-based political parties, the KMT and the CCP, and both owe their basic organizational structure to Russian advisers who guided their development during the 1920s. The guidelines came from the Soviet Communist party — a hierarchical, disciplined organization that concentrated authority in the hands of a small elite.

Soviet communism's impact on CCP ideology is even more difficult to assess. The CCP's long revolutionary experience encouraged adaptation of the doctrine to the Chinese political context, but the Soviet version of Marxism-Leninism was the ideological point of departure.

Foremost among the ideas that came with the acceptance of Marxism-Leninism were the concepts of class struggle, class analysis, and the leadership role of the proletariat. The Marxist vision of a classless society, populated by a new socialist man and based on collective ownership and organization, has also had a profound impact. Through its claim to universality, the doctrine broadened the revolutionary struggle to include not only China but all other societies as well. This has given the present Chinese regime a sense of intimate, reciprocal involvement in the international system, an attitude not characteristic of China in the past.

Soviet communism also suggested guidelines for the reconstruction of China that were not necessarily called for by national traditions or conditions. When the CCP came to power, it simply assumed that socialist construction required such policies as rapid industrialization, centralized economic planning and administration, and the collectivization of agriculture. It decided, in short, to follow the Soviet model, despite the fact that China's economic conditions were quite different from those in Russia.

CCP History

Two years after its First Congress in 1921, the CCP entered into an alliance with the KMT to hasten the conclusion of the national revolution against imperialism and the northern warlords. The decision to enter this alliance was imposed on the CCP by Soviet advisers, who were also working with the KMT. This first United Front was a period of major growth and expansion for both the KMT and the CCP (see Table 13.1.) It ended in 1927 when the KMT expelled the Communists and broke off its contacts with Soviet advisers.

The rupture of the first United Front left the CCP a fragmented, outlaw party. Small bands of armed and mobile Communists survived in relatively isolated rural areas. Gradually these forces acquired loose territorial bases referred to as soviets. The most prominent soviet was in the mountains of Jiangxi, where Mao Zedong was a leading political figure. In late 1933, KMT leader Chiang Kai-shek launched the fifth in a series of campaigns against the Jiangxi soviet, and by the latter part of 1934 this campaign had forced the Communists to abandon their stronghold and set out on the Long March.

While the Communists were on the way to Shaanxi, which their first units reached in October

Table 13.1

Growth of the Chinese Communist Party, 1921–1977

Period and year	*Number of members*	*Years covered*	*Average annual increase*
First Revolutionary Civil War			
1921 (First Congress)	57	—	—
1922 (Second Congress)	123	1	66
1923 (Third Congress)	432	1	309
1925 (Fourth Congress)	950	2	259
1927 (Fifth Congress)	57,967	2	28,508
1927 (after KMT-CCP rupture)	10,000	—	—
Second Revolutionary Civil War			
1928 (Sixth Congress)	40,000	1	30,000
1930	122,318	2	41,159
1933	300,000	3	59,227
1937 (after the Long March)	40,000	4	−65,000
Anti-Japanese War			
1940	800,000	3	253,333
1941	763,447	1	−36,553
1942	736,151	1	−27,296
1944	853,420	2	58,635
1945 (Seventh Congress)	1,211,128	1	357,708
Third Revolutionary Civil War			
1946	1,348,320	1	137,192
1947	2,759,456	1	1,411,136
1948	3,065,533	1	306,077
1949	4,488,080	1	1,422,547
People's Republic of China			
1950	5,821,604	1	1,333,524
1951	5,762,293	1	−59,311
1952	6,001,698	1	239,405
1953	6,612,254	1	610,556
1954	7,859,473	1	1,247,219
1955	9,393,394	1	1,533,921
1956 (Eighth Congress)	10,734,384	1	1,340,990
1957	12,720,000	1	1,985,616
1959	13,960,000	2	620,000
1961	17,000,000	2	1,520,000
1973 (Tenth Congress)	28,000,000	12	916,666
1977 (Eleventh Congress)	35,000,000+	4	1,750,000

Sources: The figures for 1921 to 1961 are from John W. Lewis, *Leadership in Communist China* (Ithaca, N.Y.: Cornell University Press, 1963); the 1973 figure from Zhou Enlai's "Report" in *The Tenth National Congress of the Communist Party of China (Documents)* (Peking: Foreign Languages Press, 1973), p. 8; and the 1977 figure from *Peking Review*, 35 (August 26, 1977), p. 6.

1935 in greatly weakened condition, a second United Front with the KMT was taking shape in response to growing military pressure from the Japanese. With the beginning of full-scale war between China and Japan in 1937, the second United Front became a reality. This alliance was significantly different from the first, however, being essentially an armed truce in the interests of anti-Japanese unity. There was little cooperation between the two parties, aside from a loosely observed understanding that they would avoid open war on each other, and that Communist-controlled territories and forces would retain de facto independence.

CCP strength grew remarkably during the second United Front, which lasted until Japan's defeat in 1945. From headquarters in Yanan, Mao Zedong consolidated his position as party leader and established his thought as the CCP's guide for the application of Marxism-Leninism to China. The focus of the movement became national rather than class struggle, and the Communists entered the postwar period as genuine competitors for national political power.

After the Japanese surrender in August 1945, the two major contenders for power briefly negotiated, with American mediation, for a peaceful solution to their conflict. The American role was compromised from the first, however, by its support for the Nationalist government, while the profound suspicion and hostility between the KMT and CCP made a workable agreement unlikely. By 1946, a civil war had begun. The Nationalist armies had superior numbers and weapons and scored some initial successes, but the Communists soon demonstrated their superiority in the field. The tide had turned by 1948, and within a year the Nationalist forces were defeated. The KMT retreated to the island of Taiwan and the CCP established its new government on the mainland.

The CCP came to power with a conviction that mobilization and struggle are the essence of politics. Military virtues — enthusiasm, heroism, sacrifice, and collective effort — acquired great value. To the CCP elite, politics was not simply peaceful competition or management of material resources, but mobilizing and activating human resources in a crisis.

Closely related to these themes is the party's mass line, a principle that originated in the circumstances the CCP faced on the road to power. The mass line, a basic element of Maoism, is perhaps the most complicated and pervasive concept in CCP doctrine. In one dimension, it is a recognition of the fact that the movement cannot be sustained by party members alone, but depends on the support, intelligence, food supplies, new recruits, and even administrative skills of nonparty masses. In a second dimension, the mass line has a control function with respect to bureaucrats and intellectuals. By insisting that officials interact with the masses, the CCP hopes to uncover abuses and foster a new type of bureaucrat; by entrusting many administrative duties to popular groups, it hopes to reduce or dilute the bureaucratic structure. Finally, with its exhortations to "eat, live, work and consult with the masses," the mass line is an expression of identification with and commitment to the welfare of the people. Developed during the soviet period, the mass line carries a strong orientation toward the peasants, simply because the Chinese Communists could not talk about their popular base or obligations without talking about the peasantry.

Self-reliance is a third element of the CCP's political style that draws strength from historical experience. The conditions encouraging it were the relative geographic, economic, and political isolation of the Communists' bases from 1927 on. Each soviet was largely on its own, depending for survival on military and economic self-sufficiency. The principle of self-reliance has both national and international implications. Nationally, it has fostered a preference for local units that are relatively self-sufficient. Internationally, the Chinese Communists remain sensitive to the way a foreign presence can lead to foreign interference and control. Although they welcome international support and will offer it themselves to other countries and movements with which they sympathize, they still insist that each must rely on its own resources to accomplish its goals.

The most difficult doctrinal problem the Chinese Communists have faced has been to create a socialist revolution and build a socialist society in an agrarian country close to its feudal past. How could this goal be reached in the absence of a proletarian base? The answer is that proletarian ideology can be created by education rather than by objective economic conditions. But the Maoists have never assumed that this road to ideological purity would be easy, and they have warned repeatedly that powerful nonproletarian influences in their society can corrupt even those who seem to have been converted.

There was another necessary ingredient, at least in the thought of Mao Zedong: human will. For Mao, human will and effort can be the decisive factor in any given situation; they should be guided by ideological understanding, but first having the will to act is crucial, and permits education to work, through the testing and application of ideas. The entire history of the CCP, with its struggle and ultimate victory under adverse conditions, reinforced this conviction.

Political History of the P.R.C.

In terms of the "two-line struggle," P.R.C. history falls into three periods. The first, from 1949 to 1957, witnessed China's early efforts to establish a socialist system along the lines of the Soviet model. The second, from 1958 to 1976, marked the ascendancy of the Maoist model as an alternative; it was a period of acute conflict, with turbulent mass mobilization campaigns and complicated struggles and purges within the CCP. The third, which began after Mao's death in September 1976, has brought some significant modifications of the Maoist model, although Mao's authority and ideas are used to legitimize the new policies.

THE SOVIET MODEL: RECONSTRUCTION AND THE FIRST FIVE-YEAR PLAN, 1949–1957

In January 1950, the P.R.C. concluded a treaty of friendship and alliance with the Soviet Union. In the Cold War climate, soon to be worsened by Sino-American military confrontation in Korea, Mao saw the treaty as China's best hope for national security and economic assistance. Despite previous conflicts between Chinese and Russian Communists, and obvious differences between the two societies in economic development and revolutionary history, the Soviet model seemed the best, indeed the only, guide for socialist development.

To reconstruct the economy, devastated by decades of war and disorder, was the first task. It was completed by 1952, with production restored to prewar highs, national finances stabilized, and the way prepared for socialization of the economy. The CCP was also consolidating its control over the administrative structure and extending its organizational apparatus to the mass level. Both efforts moved forward in conjunction with mass campaigns that served as vehicles both for party penetration of the villages and implementation of policy. Land reform (1949–1952) took land from large holders and gave it to small holders, tenants, and agricultural laborers, thereby breaking the power of the landlords and leveling the rural economy and society. The marriage law campaign proclaimed the legal equality of women and initiated (although far from completed) important changes in kinship organization, social values, and sex roles. Suppression of counterrevolutionaries eradicated KMT supporters and other opponents of the new order, removing any doubts about the new government's willingness and capacity to deal harshly with its enemies. With its political authority consolidated, major social reforms underway, and the economy restored to an even keel, the CCP was ready to begin the transition to socialism.

The First Five-Year Plan, for 1953–1957, was a comprehensive program of planned economic development closely modelled on Soviet practice and emphasizing investment in heavy industry. Soviet aid provided many key industrial facilities and supplies. Russian advisers and engineers were instrumental in drafting and implementing the plan. Socialization of the economy proceeded rapidly, as all but the smallest enterprises were brought under state control. In the countryside, collectivization began with mutual aid teams that encouraged informal cooperation among small groups of peasant households, moved on to lower agricultural producers' cooperatives that collectivized production but left some ownership rights intact, and then — in a "high tide" proclaimed by Mao in 1955 — pushed ahead to the fully socialist higher agricultural producers' cooperatives, or collectives (see Table 13.2). By 1956, China's economy was basically socialized, with no private control of any significant assets or means of production.

The plan brought rapid industrialization and urbanization. The power and complexity of the central government kept pace, with a top-heavy bureaucracy emerging as the controlling force in Chinese society. Signs of institutionalization were evident in the

Table 13.2
Development of Collectivized Agriculture

	Household	*Small village or village section (20–40 households)*	*Large village or village cluster (100–300 households)*	*Rural marketing area*
1949–1952	Land reform ends large holdings and tenancy, destroys old rural			
1952–1955		Mutual aid teams of 4–10 households lead into lower agricultural producers' cooperatives which become BAU.[a]		
1955–1957	Households retain small private plots.	Early coops become production teams within higher coops.	Higher agricultural producers' cooperatives emerge, become BAU, full collectivization begins.	
1958–1959	Private plots absorbed by communes.	Become production teams within communes.	Become production brigades within commune.	People's communes formed and become BAU; early total of 25,000 large-scale communes, many exceeding marketing area in extent.
	Experimentation with highly collectivized communities; large-scale rural labor mobilization for water conservation and other construction projects.			
1960–1962	Private plots returned to households.	Production team becomes BAU.		Communes reduced in size to total of 75,000 probably based on marketing areas.
	"Agriculture as the foundation" policy adopted; increased emphasis on rural mechanization, agricultural technology, use of chemical fertilizers.			
1963–1978	Private plots retained despite some radical pressure to return them to collective.	Most production teams remain BAU, despite some pressure to move to higher level.	A few production brigades serve as BAU.	Communes grow slowly in size, due to population increase and some unit combinations, with total of 50,000 in mid-1970s. Most remain coterminous with marketing areas, which are also expanding, due to modernization of countryside.
	"Agriculture as the foundation" policy continued, with increasing modernization and diversification of rural economy; great emphasis on developing small-scale rural industry and social services after Cultural Revolution.			

[a] BAU = basic accounting unit. This is the unit responsible for making work assignments, organizing agricultural production, and collecting and distributing the agricultural product; it handles its own accounting and is responsible for its own profits and losses; hence, an important indicator of the level of collectivization.

CCP, in the state structure established in the Constitution of 1954, and in the panoply of mass organizations for youth, women, workers, and various professions. But a combination of factors diverted this modernization from its conventional course.

Sino-Soviet relations began to cool with Khrushchev's de-Stalinization speech in 1956 and the related disorders in Poland and Hungary, which the Chinese saw as symptoms of Russian irresponsibility at home and disregard of "fraternal" parties abroad. Soviet overtures to the United States and lack of enthusiasm for providing military backing or nuclear development aid to the P.R.C. revealed increasingly divergent international interests between the two socialist powers. Domestically, Mao was concerned about the centralization, urbanization, and bureaucratization accompanying the plan. Agricultural production was barely keeping pace with population growth, while rural areas seemed to be falling further behind urban centers. An outburst of criticism from intellectuals in the spring of 1957, in the course of the Hundred Flowers Campaign, persuaded many Chinese leaders that it was no time to relax their guard against the "bourgeois" intellectuals, specialists, and technicians favored by modernization.[2] These complicated issues were debated at length between 1956 and 1958, but by late 1957 Mao had led his colleagues to reject the Soviet model and adopt a new approach to development.

THE MAOIST MODEL: GREAT LEAP AND CULTURAL REVOLUTION, 1958–1976 The Maoist model emerged gradually from the debates of the mid-1950s, but its characteristics became clear only in the Great Leap Forward of 1958–1960. The Great Leap was the pivotal issue in Chinese politics between 1958 and 1966, and the general principles it advanced held the political initiative until Mao's death in 1976. The Great Leap pulled China sharply away from the Soviet model, embarking the country on policies more in keeping with the CCP's revolutionary tradition and Mao's perception of China's priorities. The difficulties it soon encountered led to a retreat from some of its features. The result was an increasingly tense debate between Maoists and the moderates or revisionists, which erupted in the Cultural Revolution and continued throughout the next decade.

Four principles — drawn from a combination of Mao's thought, CCP experience, and dissatisfaction with the five-year plan — underlay the Great Leap. First was the idea of all-around development, that China could accelerate development on all fronts without leaving any sectors behind. Industry retained priority, but agricultural production, and the rural sector in general, were to catch up with it. The people's commune, which emerged in the summer of 1958, was the institution for promoting the Great Leap in the countryside. In 1958 the communes, a larger and more collectivized unit, replaced the cooperatives and simultaneously became the unit of local government in rural areas (see Table 13.2). They were to facilitate large-scale labor mobilization and projects, encourage mechanization and rural industrialization, and generally accelerate output in rural areas without diverting central funds from heavy industry. Mass mobilization, the second principle, indicated the resource base for the developmental surge. Greater utilization of manpower — through harder work, better motivation, larger organization, and mobilization of the unemployed — made China's population an asset to be substituted for scarce investment funds.

The third principle — that politics takes command — brought much greater emphasis on political unanimity and zeal, partly a reaction against the rightist criticism of 1956–1957, and shifted decision-making power away from state ministries toward party committees. Political cadres (party workers), not bureaucrats and experts, were to guide the process. Bureaucrats and intellectuals were pressured to mend their bureaucratic ways and engage in manual labor at the mass level. The fourth factor, decentralization, loosened central control and encouraged lower-level units to exercise greater initiative. Decentralization also reflected the heavy stress on mass line and populist themes that characterized the rhetoric of the period.

The Great Leap achieved some production increases at first, but a crisis soon developed. Bad weather, the withdrawal of Russian aid and technicians in 1960 as the Sino-Soviet conflict intensified,

[2] The Hundred Flowers campaign was a brief period of liberalization, in which competing views were allowed. Its name comes from Mao's slogan "Let a hundred flowers bloom, a hundred schools of thought contend." It was ended when the criticism got out of hand.

and problems in the leap itself combined to produce a downward economic trend and growing disenchantment. Flaws in the early leap strategy included the weakening of planning and statistical controls, the initiation of ill-conceived projects, the overworking of the labor force, and the general disruption of established work, marketing, and administrative patterns; the last was particularly acute, as the communes amalgamated units that had not previously worked together. Agricultural output declined in 1959, with industrial decline soon following, leading to declining per capita GNP from 1959 to 1961 (see Table 13.3).

In 1961, the CCP moderated the Great Leap.

Table 13.3

Per Capita Indicators of Consumer Welfare

	GNP[a] *(1976 US $)*	*Grain output*[b] *(kg)*	*Cotton cloth output (Linear m)*	*Consumer goods output (index 1957 = 100)*
1949	96	206	3.5	33
1950	116	237	4.6	42
1951	132	253	5.5	55
1952	153	283	6.7	67
1953	159	281	8.0	80
1954	162	278	8.8	88
1955	173	295	7.1	85
1956	183	302	9.2	96
1957	190	298	7.9	100
1958	221	315	8.7	115
1959	205	256	9.1	125
1960	196	229	7.2	107
1961	152	242	4.8	74
1962	167	255	5.0	75
1963	183	264	6.4	97
1964	202	264	6.9	117
1965	220	259	8.5	156
1966	241	280	8.7	172
1967	227	287	7.0	161
1968	223	262	7.5	176
1969	242	262	8.0	182
1970	275	289	8.9	208
1971	287	286	8.4	203
1972	294	273	8.3	215
1973	325	297	8.5	239
1974	330	300	8.3	243
1975	346	304	8.1	252
1976	340	300	—	—

[a] Derived from unrounded data.

[b] Including soybeans.

Source: CIA, National Foreign Assessment Center, *China: Economic Indicators* (ER 77–10508, October 1977), p. 43.

Political mobilization gave way to a cautious orientation toward restoring production. Planners, managers, technicians, and experts regained some of their lost status. Commune policy shifted in three fundamental ways (see Table 13.2). First, the basic accounting unit (the unit with prime responsibility for planning, collecting, and distributing the agricultural production), which had been raised from the higher cooperatives to the commune in 1958, was moved back, first to the production brigade and then to the production team, the lowest level of organization. The effect was a decollectivization of rural accounting back to the mid-1950s level, although many more centralized features of commune life remained. Second, private plots — the small patches of land left for private cultivation — were returned to peasant households. Third, communes were made smaller, the number increasing from 25,000 in 1958 to 75,000 in the early 1960s. Finally, the CCP adopted a new slogan, "agriculture as the foundation," committing the government for the first time to the principle that investment, mechanization, and industrialization policies must serve the needs of the agricultural sector.

These reforms had widespread support; in the main, they have endured down to the present. Politically however, they became controversial. For one thing, some moderates wanted to go further, to experiment with even more "capitalistic" formulas. Moreover, the leap had touched off debates questioning not only Mao's policies but also his leadership. Increasingly the issue seemed not simply how to adjust the Great Leap, but whether the CCP was to remain committed to the Maoist model. The issue escalated to more general and potentially factional grounds, feeding on the tensions generated by now open Sino-Soviet hostility. As the Maoists saw the Soviet Union as both hostile and an "incorrect" model, they looked more closely at domestic opponents for signs of similar tendencies. They found enough evidence to persuade them that their fears of capitalist restoration were justified. Meanwhile, American escalation in Vietnam revived Chinese fears of this old "number one enemy," even as the Soviet Union loomed more threateningly. For Mao, the danger to his image of the revolution was real and immediate.

The Cultural Revolution was the second great effort to implement the Maoist model. Like the Great Leap, it began by asserting the model in dramatic, and sometimes extreme, terms, moved into a period of consolidation of central control, and ended with a debate over how much of the initial movement to retain. Unlike the Great Leap, the Cultural Revolution was not primarily an economic campaign — the post–Great Leap economic adjustments remained, despite some criticism — nor did it produce economic difficulties as severe as those of 1959–1961. It was far more violent and disruptive, however, and it posed far more sharply the question of how, and at what level, the Maoist model should be institutionalized.

The campaign began in the fall of 1965 with written criticism of some of Mao's lesser critics. In spring 1966, the attack shifted to some high party leaders, charging that capitalist roaders trying to install a revisionist system were opposing Mao. Simultaneously, it demanded thorough reform of culture — thought, attitudes, and behavior — to implant the Maoist ethic of struggle, mass line, collectivism, egalitarianism, and unstinting service to society. Soon students in Red Guard groups were carrying the struggle to the streets with fearless criticism of and sometimes violent action against those believed to be opposing Mao or representing bourgeois culture. The Cultural Revolution was thus at once a purge of the political elite, a drive for cultural reform in the broadest sense, and a mobilization of mass action that invited spontaneous organization and criticism. Of course, the Maoists in Beijing sought to control the movement, but their encouragement or at least tolerance of Red Guard activities — which included publication of uncensored newspapers, formation of federations among the mass organizations, and direct action against rival groups and individuals — gave the campaign a degree of spontaneity unique in the history of communist systems.

Between the summers of 1966 and 1967, the P.R.C. slipped close to anarchy. Party and state offices were paralyzed, schools were closed, cadres at all levels were vulnerable to disgrace or dismissal, and mass organizations brought work stoppages, disrupted transportation and communications, and, in many cases, engaged in full-scale street fighting among rival groups, some of them armed. When the disorder began to involve units of the People's Liberation Army (PLA), the Maoists pulled back. From the fall of 1967 on, order was restored. The PLA assumed control of much of the administrative apparatus, mass organizations were disbanded, economic functions were reemphasized, and the reconstruction of party and state offices began. The Ninth Party Congress in April 1969 proclaimed defeat of the capitalist roaders and initiation of new policies in accord with Chairman Mao's directives. Roughly one-half of the party leadership was gone; the two highest victims were Liu Shaoqi (second to Mao in pre-1966 party rankings) and Deng Xiaoping (perhaps fourth in power, after Mao, Liu, and Premier Zhou Enlai, and who later was to make two dramatic returns to prominence). Replacing these old revolutionary cadres were a large number of PLA commanders, radical party figures, and some new mass representatives who had achieved prominence in the course of the campaign. Of course, there was also a substantial contingent of experienced leaders who had passed the test of the Cultural Revolution and remained in office.

The post-1969 leadership was a coalition of three groupings: the most ardent Maoists, or radicals, who drew strength from close association with the Chairman and their manipulation of his directives (Jiang Qing, Mao's wife, was perhaps most representative of this group); military figures who, though not united, benefitted from Defense Minister Lin Biao's designation as second-in-command and Mao's chosen successor; and veteran administrators, led by Zhou Enlai, who represented what was left of the moderates.

This coalition proved unstable. Lin Biao's purge in 1971, for allegedly plotting a coup against Mao, was followed by a reduction of PLA influence — a tendency fostered, too, by the policy of returning to normalcy. The radicals and moderates were left in uneasy balance, with mounting tension as Mao's health failed and Zhou sponsored the restoration of many old cadres purged in the Cultural Revolution. Deng Xiaoping was the most prominent example. His return to power triggered an intense dispute, forced into the open in January 1976 when Zhou died, leaving Deng as his most likely successor as premier. Instead, the Maoists engineered Deng's second purge, with the premiership going to a relative newcomer and compromise choice, Hua Guofeng. But when Mao died in September, the tables were turned. Hua Guofeng arrested the Gang of Four — the epithet chosen for Jiang Qing and the three other leading radicals — and unleashed a vitriolic campaign against them for distorting Mao's thought, sabotaging the government and economy with factionalism, and generally following a right-wing line under the guise of radicalism.

The death of Mao and purge of the Gang opened the way for a reassessment of the Maoist model. The Cultural Revolution had clearly called for changes that would promote not only the Maoist model of development but also the Maoist image of man. Between 1967 and 1971, new policies to implement these goals began to emerge. Educational reforms emphasized enrollment in primary school, political education, applied and practical studies, manual labor experience, and service to society for all citizens; higher education, academic grades and examinations, theoretical study, and pure research were deemphasized. Intellectuals and bureaucrats were to spend substantial periods outside their offices in various work-study programs. Cultural policy promoted art with simple revolutionary themes in a rigid populist style; Jiang Qing and her associates sharply limited the range of permissible forms of cultural expression. Revolutionary committees, which brought mass representatives into decision-making bodies, replaced most old administrative organs. Generally, people were pressured to conform to the mass line and to egalitarian behavior and relationships.

These reforms fit the rhetoric of the Cultural Revolution and were launched with much fanfare, but they encountered problems in the 1970s. Some people, especially professionals and bureaucrats, resisted the extreme demands. Continuing factionalism and purges tarnished the image of what the Cultural Revolution had produced. Many cadres bitterly resented abuse they received in its course. Sharp border clashes with the Soviet Union in 1969, coupled with the beginnings of American withdrawal from Vietnam, made Mao and Zhou more receptive to rapprochement with the United States, which was consummated with President Richard Nixon's visit and the Shanghai Communique in early 1972. Once this step had been taken, the logic of trade and cooperation with capitalist countries — to serve China's trade, technology, and security needs — was unmistakable. The radicals resisted this notion, as well as any diminution of post–Cultural Revolution reforms, but the latter were already slipping or becoming routinized. The factional struggle sharpened, with labor disputes, intraenterprise feuds, and lowered labor morale. An economic slowdown occurred in 1974–1976 (see Table 13.4), caused by many factors but providing good ammunition for those who disliked the Maoist emphasis on struggle. Thus, when Mao died his model was secure in CCP ideology and official rhetoric, but was far from having a firm institutional base or unqualified support for the radical interpretation.

THE POST-MAO PERIOD, 1976–1979
Following Mao's death and the purge of the Gang of Four, the new administration under Hua Guofeng moved rapidly to consolidate its authority. A long campaign criticized the Gang as sham leftists, but as rightists in reality, who were responsible for all of China's problems over the preceding decade. Initially this was done in Mao's name, as Hua made heavy use of Maoist symbols to legitimize his position, and with no significant policy changes.

The Eleventh Party Congress in August 1977 was a major turning point. Hua emphasized that the P.R.C. had entered a new period in which the main task was to achieve the "four modernizations" (of agriculture, industry, national defense and science and technology) by the year 2000. Equally important was the reinstatement of Deng Xiaoping as CCP vice-chairman and later vice-premier of the government (Hua remained CCP chairman and premier of the government). Deng quickly elipsed Hua in political prominence and became the spokesman for new policies designed to realize the four modernizations.

The new line on modernization brought changes in four areas. First, it openly repudiated the Cultural Revolution, rehabilitating almost all its victims, and sharply diminished Mao's image of infallibility. Maoism remained a legitimating theme, but it was linked to Mao's most conservative statements rather than his radical Cultural Revolution phase. Second, the new line emphasized academic standards in education, rapid development of science and technology, and a freer atmosphere for intellectual discussion. A new hundred flowers atmosphere developed, bringing an outburst of public debate and demonstrations in the winter of 1978–1979. A third change was concentration on economic goals and incentives, accompanied by calls for order, observance of regulations, and strengthening of the socialist legal system. New party and state constitutions (adopted in August 1977 and March 1978 respectively) revived many institutional features of the 1950s, underscoring this more legalistic approach. Finally, the new period initiated substantial growth in foreign trade, credits, investment and tourism as China set out to acquire the advanced technology, capital equipment and foreign exchange needed to support the four modernizations. A key indicator of the opening to capitalist countries, which were the main partners in the upsurge of foreign contacts, was establishment of diplomatic relations with the United States at the beginning of 1979.

These changes modified the Maoist model by accommodating it to accelerated economic development in closer cooperation with capitalist countries. Yet they retained some Maoist symbolism and even some Maoist policies, such as decentralization and emphasis on agricultural development. Events in the spring of 1979 demonstrated the need for caution in characterizing the new period. The Chinese invasion of Vietnam in February was followed by a cutback in some of the most ambitious economic goals, by a more restrained attitude toward foreign contacts, and by tighter controls on public debate and criticism. Although the repudiation of the Cultural Revolution appeared irreversible, these events showed that some aspects of the four modernizations were controversial and that the pace of change might be slowed.

Socioeconomic Change

We conclude this survey of post-1949 history with a few general observations on the social and economic transformation that has accompanied the three decades of CCP rule. In society, the most obvious change has been in class structure, with the elimination or neutralization of some social strata and the expansion of others. The civil war and early campaigns not only destroyed the KMT governmental elite and its warlord allies, but also dispossessed landlords, merchants, industrialists, and other local political leaders. The new political elite, defined al-

Table 13.4

Selected Economic Indicators

	1952	*1957*	*1965*	*1970*	*1971*	*1972*	*1973*	*1974*	*1975*	*1976*	*1977*	*1978* [1]
GNP (billion 1977 US $)	92	128	172	244	261	273	308	320	342	342	370	407
Population, midyear (million persons)	570	640	754	847	867	886	906	924	943	962	983	1004
Per capita GNP (1977 US $)	162	201	228	288	301	308	341	346	363	355	377	407
Agricultural production index (1957 = 100)	84	100	101	126	130	126	142	146	148	148	146	151
Industrial production index (1957 = 100)	48	100	199	316	349	385	436	455	502	502	572	646
Producer goods index (1957 = 100)	39	100	211	350	407	452	513	536	602	...	...	...
Machinery index (1957 = 100)	33	100	257	586	711	795	930	992	1156	...	...	...
Other producer goods index (1957 = 100)	41	100	200	294	336	371	415	429	472	...	...	...
Consumer goods index (1957 = 100)	60	100	183	272	272	295	334	347	368	...	...	...
Foreign trade (billion current US $)	1.9	3.1	3.9	4.3	4.8	6.0	10.3	14.1	14.6	13.3	15.1	20.8

[1] Preliminary.

Source: CIA, *China: Economic Indicators* (ER 78–10750, December 1978), p. 1.

most solely by CCP membership, differs significantly in ideology, political experience, and social origin. A new intermediate stratum of moderately privileged groups has emerged, consisting of skilled industrial workers, college and middle-school graduates, and professional, scientific, and technical workers. While peasants remain by far the largest class — perhaps 85 percent of the population live in rural areas, although not necessarily engaging in agriculture — they are now better educated and more secure economically; as members of collectives and as participants in rural mechanization and industrialization, fewer and fewer of them fit the traditional peasant stereotype.

The nuclear family remains the basic residential and kinship unit, and continues to be a key economic unit for income and expenditures, but many of its former functions have passed to the state or collective. The larger kinship groups (lineages and clans) have lost the power they once held. Within the family, the domination of older males has weakened, with much greater opportunity and mobility for women and young people. Clear differences remain in sex roles, but the change from traditional patterns has been great.

Finally, there has been a major shift in the relationship between government and society, centering on expansion of the government's resources, personnel, operations, claims, and power. Although old indicators of economic and social status still have some relevance, increasingly it is government action that determines the citizen's social and economic role and defines favored and disfavored status. This concentration of power in the hands of party-state-army bureaucracies has had a great leveling effect on Chinese society, particularly in conjunction with the egalitarianism of the Maoist ethic. At the same time, the expanded scope and responsibilities of government have made the political process more receptive to claims from society, to competition for social and economic rewards. In short, the new government is both more powerful and more responsive, in relation to society, than its predecessors.

Tables 13.3 and 13.4 summarize economic development in post-1949 China. Despite recessions in 1959–1961, 1967–1968, and 1974–1976, economic growth has been impressive. The average annual growth rate of GNP for 1952–1977 was about 6 percent (in constant dollars), with per capita gains of about 4 percent. Industrial growth averaged about 10 percent annually, agricultural growth probably only 2 percent — about the same as the rate of population increase. These crude figures compare favorably to those for other large underdeveloped countries. P.R.C. economic performance has been particularly strong in mobilizing investment with relatively little reliance on foreign aid or loans.

As the low agricultural growth rate suggests, China continues to face the centuries-old task of feeding its immense population. Although birth control programs in the 1960s and 1970s reduced the annual rate of population increase, possibly below 2 percent, the margin of agricultural increase over population increase is nil or very small. The basic problem is illustrated in Figures 13.1 and 13.2. Virtually all of China's population and productive land is concentrated in the eastern half of the country. The P.R.C. must support over one-fifth of the world's population with less than 7 percent of its cultivated land; its cultivated land is only 70 percent of the United States', which has about one-fourth China's population. The message is clear: increasing agricultural production through technological revolution is a necessity for China's future economic growth and well being.

These broad social and economic parameters are politically significant in two respects. First, they suggest the extent of revolutionary transformation in modern China and the political system's performance in guiding that transformation. Second, they underscore the social and economic logic of the new policies emerging after Mao's death. The P.R.C. of the 1980s will be vastly different from that of the 1950s, let alone of the 1930s, when Maoism took shape. Now a budding international power — possessing nuclear weapons and space technology, deeply involved in global politics, and seeking foreign trade and technology — the P.R.C. cannot sustain the earlier isolationist policy of self-reliance. Domestically, the increasing complexity and sophistication of Chinese society, and the dependence of economic growth on an accelerated technical and scientific revolution, also point to modification of Mao's emphasis on mass mobilization and struggle and his distrust of intellectuals and technicians. How far these modifications will go cannot be predicted, but some movement in their direction seems appropriate for China's new stage of development, a stage so clearly

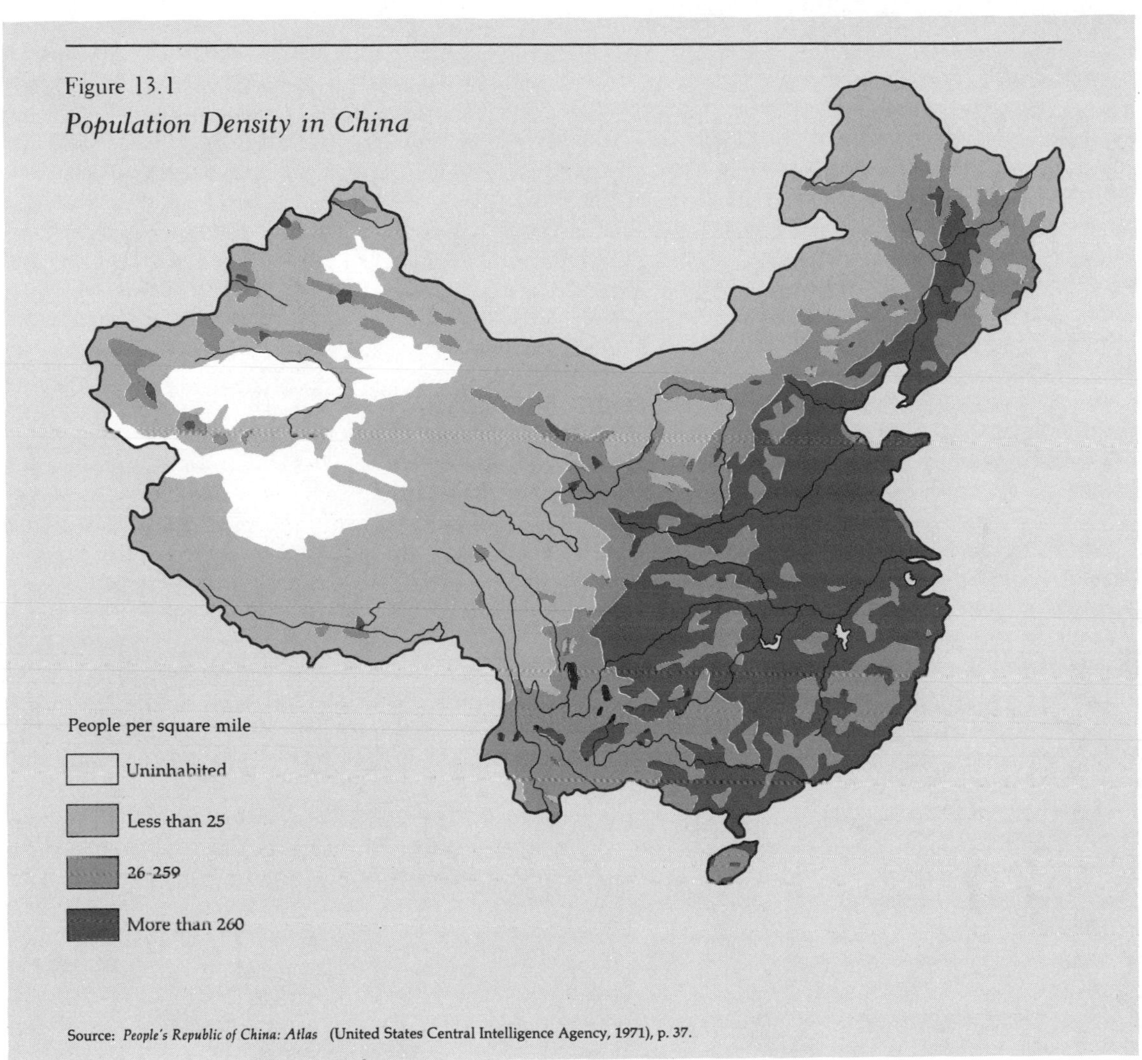

Figure 13.1
Population Density in China

Source: *People's Republic of China: Atlas* (United States Central Intelligence Agency, 1971), p. 37.

different from the past that one suspects Mao would have recognized and acted on it, too.

CONSTITUTION AND POLITICAL STRUCTURE

The political structure of the P.R.C. consists of three major organizational hierarchies — the state, the party, and the army — plus a variety of mass organizations that provide additional links between these hierarchies and the citizenry. All these institutions have undergone significant changes since 1949, both internally and in relationship to each other. Party organization dominates politically and state organization defines the formal government structure, but it is not easy to generalize further. In the Maoist era, politics took command of institutions, creating considerable uncertainty and fluidity in the political structure.

Figure 13.2
Agriculture in China

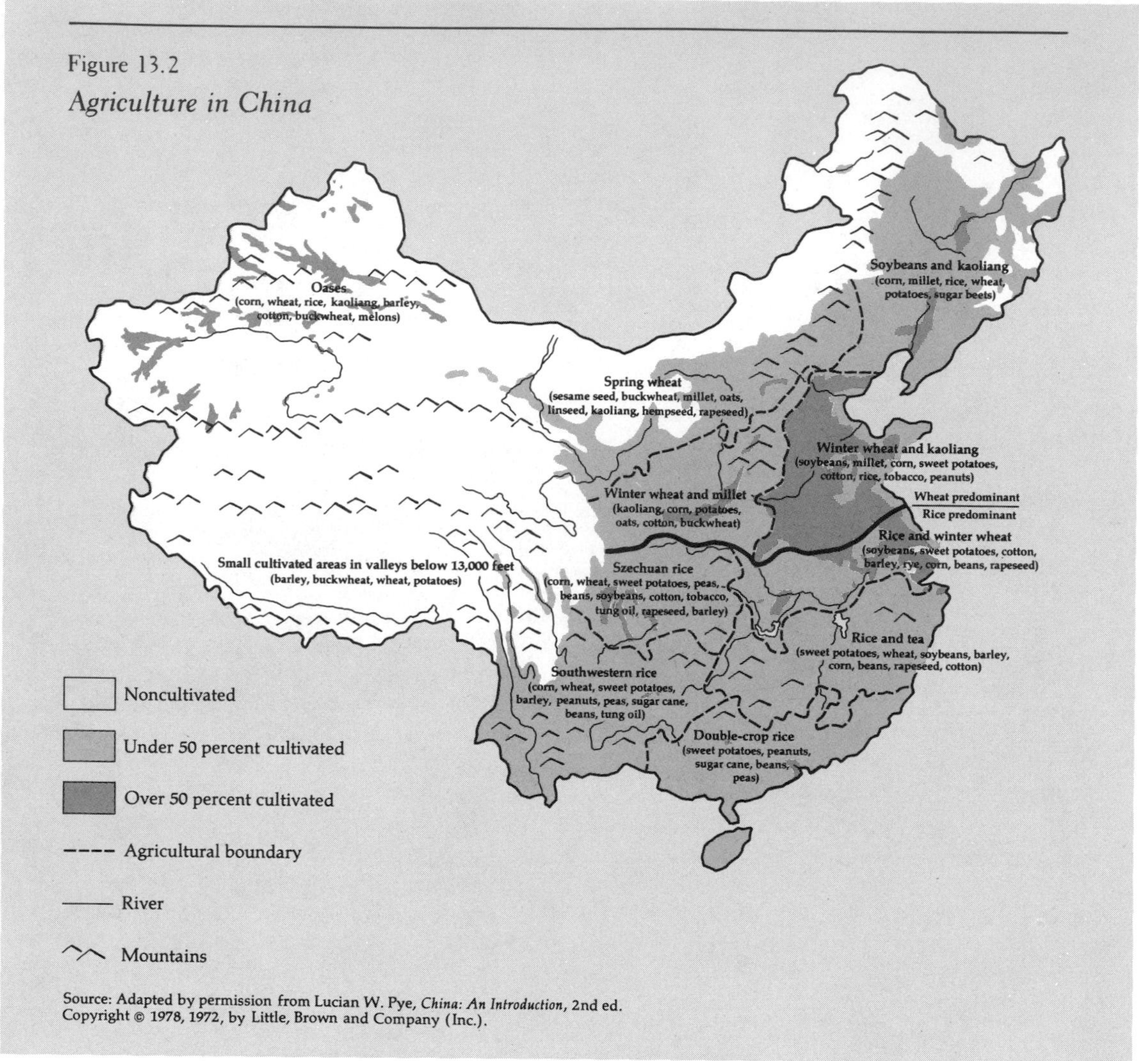

Source: Adapted by permission from Lucian W. Pye, *China: An Introduction*, 2nd ed. Copyright © 1978, 1972, by Little, Brown and Company (Inc.).

State

The P.R.C.'s initial state structure, from 1949 to 1954, was a temporary administrative system that relied heavily on regional military units to oversee reconstruction and early reforms. A constitution was adopted in 1954, establishing a centralized government to administer the transition to socialism. Soon, however, the Great Leap brought important changes, as decentralization and CCP assertiveness weakened central state organs, while the communes created new patterns of local administration. The Cultural Revolution further unsettled the 1954 system and, in effect, abolished the constitution. State structure remained in limbo, without formal guidelines, until a second constitution was adopted in 1975. The 1975 Constitution incorporated many principles of the Cultural Revolution, significantly altering the previous structure. However, in March 1978 another new constitution was adopted, which was somewhat closer to the 1954 model. The discussion describes the 1978 Constitution (see Figure 13.3).

According to the Constitution, the National

Figure 13.3

Structure of the State, 1978 Constitution

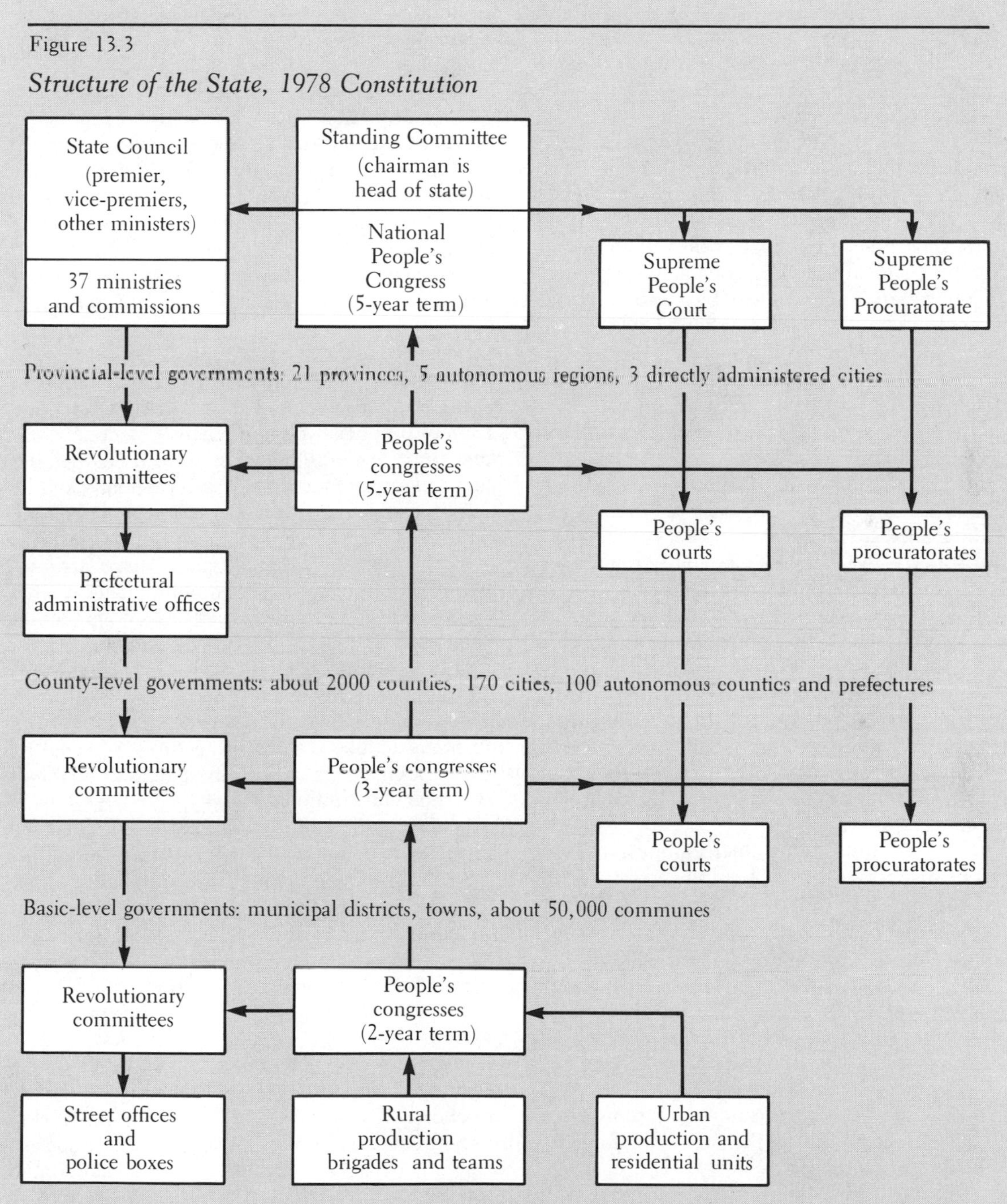

Source: The Constitution of the People's Republic of China, adopted March 5, 1978, by the First Session of the Fifth National People's Congress, text in *Peking Review,* 11 (March 11, 1978), pp. 5–14.

People's Congress (NPC) is the highest organ of state power. It is a large (3,459 deputies for the March 1978 session) representative body, consisting of deputies elected by provincial congresses and army units. It meets once a year for five years. However, the Constitution allows NPC meetings to be advanced or postponed, which happens frequently; there was no meeting of the NPC between February 1965 and January 1975, for example. In any case, NPC meetings are short and ceremonial, as deputies hear and then ratify major reports and documents presented to them by party leaders. The NPC symbolizes the regime's legitimacy and popular base, publicizes major events, and honors the politically favored deputies elected to it, but is not in practice the highest organ of power. That power resides in the CCP — even the state constitution acknowledges party leadership over the state.

The NPC's extensive formal powers of legislation, amendment, and so forth are exercised in fact by its Standing Committee, a much smaller permanent body. But even the Standing Committee remains essentially a clearinghouse for the ratification of state decisions. The chairman of the Standing Committee serves as the P.R.C.'s ceremonial head of state. The 1954 Constitution had a chairman of the government as a whole, a position held by Mao (1954–1959) and then Liu Shaoqi (1959–1966), both men using it as part of their power base. But both post–Cultural Revolution constitutions have omitted it, presumably to avoid any possible challenge to the chairmanship of the CCP.

The State Countil is the chief administrative organ of government. It includes the premier (Zhou Enlai from 1954–1976, Hua Guofeng since 1976), several vice-premiers, and the ministers who head the ministries and commissions of the central government. The State Council consists almost entirely of high-ranking party members. As translator of party decisions into state decrees, with administrative control over government action at all levels, it is the true center of state power.

The Constitution entrusts judicial authority to a Supreme People's Court at the central level and to unspecified local and special people's court. All courts are formally responsible to the congresses (to the Standing Committee in the case of the Supreme People's Court) at their respective levels. The procuratorates, also formally responsible to congresses at each level, are supervisory and investigative bodies set up to ensure observance of the Constitution and the law. These organs were an important part of the legal system of the 1950s, but were not mentioned in the 1975 Constitution. Their restoration in the 1978 Constitution, which had expanded sections on the court system as well, coincides with the renewed interest in legality that has marked the post-Mao period. Even so, the actual operation of the P.R.C.'s formal legal organs is obscure and they appear to be firmly controlled by the political-administrative hierarchy.

Local government consists of three formal levels — provincial, county, and basic — plus a variety of other units between and beneath them. Each government unit has two main organs: a people's congress and a revolutionary committee. Like the NPC, local congresses meet briefly and irregularly and have little real power. It is the revolutionary committees (called people's councils in the 1954 Constitution), like the State Council, that manage government affairs. Revolutionary committees are elected by congresses, but that election and all their actions are subject to approval by the next higher government, and ultimately by the State Council. The prefectures shown on Figure 11.3 are administrative subdivisions of provincial government. The word *autonomous* denotes regions, prefectures, and counties heavily populated by non-Chinese minorities; it indicates their constitutional right to preserve certain aspects of minority culture, but they do not differ significantly in administrative terms from other units.

From the citizen's point of view, the most important units are beneath the basic level. These include production brigades and production teams in the rural communes; and urban districts, residential units, factories, schools, and so forth in the cities. All of these are political as well as production or residential units. They elect deputies to basic-level congresses — the only direct elections in which all citizens participate, since deputies to higher congresses are chosen by congresses of the next lower level (both direct and indirect elections generally consist of approval of a slate of candidates worked out under party leadership). These units have some kind of organization for managing their internal affairs and giving citizens opportunities for discussing matters relating to daily work and living. Moreover, the citizen is most likely to encounter the government directly in the administrative offices and police stations established by basic-level governments within rural villages and urban neighborhoods.

Party

The CCP Constitution adopted at the Eleventh Party Congress in August 1977 sets forth an organization roughly parallel to that of the state (see Figure 13.4). Positioning some form of party organization alongside most state organs strengthens CCP leadership of the state, by encouraging party supervision and the assignment of party members to roles in both hierarchies. Whatever formal powers a state organ holds, the party organ at the corresponding level has the authoritative voice. The party Constitution stipulates that all state organs, army units, and other organizations must accept the absolute leadership of the party.

The 1977 party Constitution, like its state counterpart, defines the representative congresses or general members' meetings as the leading bodies at their respective levels. But as in the state system, the committees elected by these congresses — or the standing committees and secretaries elected by the full committees — are the true seat of party power at their respective levels. The Constitution states that the National Party Congress shall be convened every five years, and that it may be convened early or postponed. This provision is realistic, historically speaking, since party congresses have been rare and irregular; the Seventh Party Congress met in 1945, the eighth in 1956, the ninth in 1969 and the tenth in 1973. Despite their infrequency, party congresses are important. Each of the last five has produced a new constitution and elected a significantly altered Central Committee.

The Central Committee (CC) acts for the Congress and is the most important representative body in the P.R.C. It is identified by the number of the congress that elected it, and its full meetings are known as *plenums*. Thus, the first full meeting of the CC elected by the Eleventh Congress was the first plenum of the eleventh CC. Plenums meet irregularly, perhaps once a year on the average, although four years have elapsed between some. However, because most CC members are high-ranking officials who hold important positions in Peking or provincial capitals, many partial or informal meetings occur. Through plenums and other meetings, the CC provides a forum for discussing and ratifying important policies, if not actually initiating or deciding them.

The CC's most important function is electing the party's top leadership, namely the Politburo, its Standing Committee, and the chairman and vice-chairmen of the CC. The Politburo elected at the first plenum of the eleventh CC, in August 1977, had twenty-three regular and three alternate members, and was headed by a Standing Committee of five (Chairman Hua Guofeng plus the four vice-chairmen). The Politburo and its Standing Committee exercise all functions and powers of the CC between plenums and constitute the supreme political elite of China. They are headed by the chairman, a position held by Mao Zedong from the 1930s until his death in September 1976, when he was succeeded by Hua.

Under the 1956 Constitution, a staff agency known as the Secretariat supervised all the central party departments and committees responsible for particular lines of state and party work. The 1973 and 1977 constitutions omitted reference to the Secretariat, the latter only stating that: "Party committees at all levels should set up their working bodies in accordance with the principles of close ties with the masses and of structural simplicity and efficiency." Despite this virtual silence, the CCP clearly retains its powerful central bureaucracy, although it may be more compact and flexible than in the past. Through it, the Politburo supervises the execution of its decisions by the secretaries and standing committees that carry on day-to-day party work, from the provincial level down to the primary party units.

The organizational principle of the entire party structure, according to all the constitutions, is democratic centralism. Democracy requires that all bodies be elected by their members or congresses, report to those members and congresses, and listen to their opinions and criticisms. Centralism requires unified discipline within the whole party. "The individual is subordinate to the organization, the minority is subordinate to the majority, the lower level is subordinate to the higher level, and the entire Party is subordinate to the Central Committee." Cen-

Figure 13.4

Structure of the CCP, 1977 Constitution

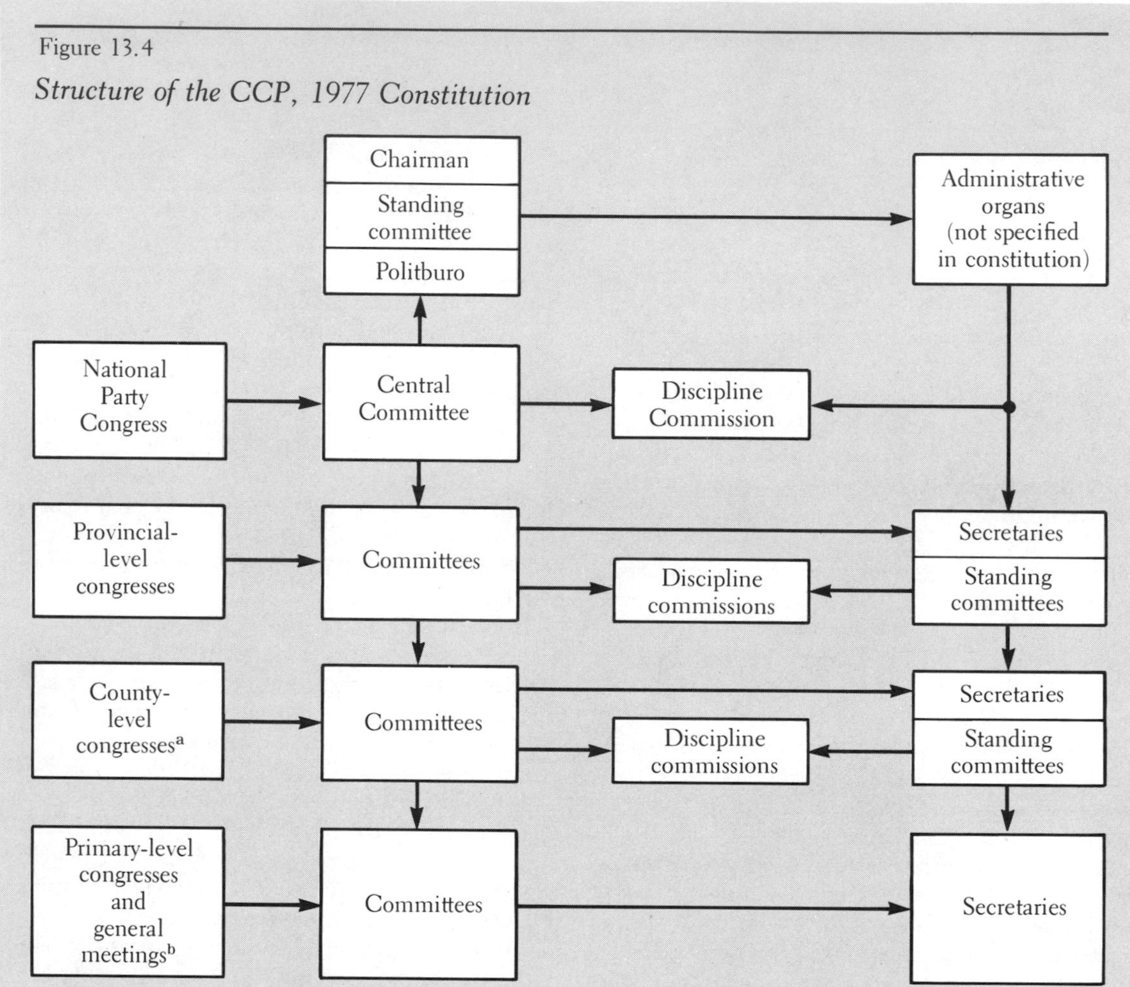

[a] County-level organizations include congresses and committees at the regimental level and above in the PLA.
[b] Primary-level organizations include branches, general branches, or committees set up in factories, mines, and other enterprises, communes, offices, schools, shops, neighborhoods, PLA companies, and other such units.

Source: The Constitution adopted by the Eleventh Party Congress on August 18, 1977, text in *Peking Review*, 36 (September 2, 1977), pp. 16–22.

tralism is also evident in the provision that congresses are convened by their committees, and that the convening of all local congresses and committees must be approved by higher party organizations.

The 1977 Constitution contains strong language on the necessity of maintaining party discipline, and its supporting documents were full of criticism of the factional activities of the Gang of Four. The most concrete constitutional sign of this urge to eradicate the factionalism exposed by the Cultural Revolution is the establishment of commissions for inspecting discipline at all levels of party organization from the county on up. The commissions are to educate members about discipline, check on its observance, and punish violations of it. Formal election is by party committees at the particular level, but one may assume that the commissions will be an integral and potent part of the central organs of the CCP.

Army

The People's Liberation Army (PLA) is the third major arm of the national political structure. From its founding in the late 1920s until 1949, the PLA organization was virtually inseparable from party organization, and the army held major government responsibilities in the areas under CCP control. Since 1949, the PLA has continued to perform a variety of nonmilitary functions, including party recruitment and training, economic construction, and education. During the early reconstruction years and the Cultural Revolution it also assumed important administrative powers. Moreover, the salience of internal and external security issues in Chinese politics has placed the PLA, willingly or not, close to the center of many national policy debates.

The PLA is subordinate to the Ministry of National Defense within the State Council. However, the 1978 state Constitution asserts that the PLA (including field armies, regional forces, and militia) is led by the CCP and that the chairman of the CC is the commander of the armed forces. Party leadership of the PLA rests mainly on two structures: the Military Affairs Committee of the CC and the system of political departments within the PLA. The Military Affairs Committee has always been one of the most important of the party's central organs; like others, it is not mentioned by name in the 1977 party Constitution, but has held general responsibility for military policy throughout the history of the P.R.C.

Political departments, headed by commisars, are a regular part of each PLA unit's general headquarters down to the division level; below that, they are represented by a political office in the regiment, and by political officers in battalions, companies, and platoons. Thus a commissar (or political officer at lower levels) works alongside the commanding officer of every army headquarters or unit, and is responsible for implementing CCP policies and carrying out political education among the troops. Political departments and their commissars are not subordinate to the military commanders in their military units, but to the next-highest functionary in the CCP organization. Their chain of command within the army ascends through higher political departments to the General Political Department and the Military Affairs Committee. At the same time, each is responsible to the CCP committee in its own military unit.

Mass Organizations

Chinese political institutions also include many mass organizations that mobilize ordinary citizens, supplementing and supporting the three dominant institutions. In general, mass organizations are national in scale and have a hierarchy of units extending downward to a mass membership defined by a common social or economic characteristic, for example, youth, students, women, workers, or other occupational groups. These organizations play a key role in implementing the party's mass line, "coming from the masses and going to the masses." They provide a sounding board for popular opinion, channel representatives into the state and party structure, and mobilize support for CCP policies from different segments of the population. In some cases, they perform administrative and service functions for the groups they represent.

The most important mass organization before the Cultural Revolution was the Communist Youth League (CYL). During the 1950s and early 1960s, the CYL was responsible for leadership of all youth activities and other youth organizations, was a major source of new recruits for the CCP, and generally assisted in the implementation of all policies at the basic level. Other important mass organizations before the Cultural Revolution included the Young Pioneers, for children aged nine to fifteen; the All-China Women's Federation; the All-China Federation of Trade Unions; and a variety of associations for occupational and professional groups. Closely related were the democratic parties, a collective term for eight minor parties that cooperated with the Communist-led United Front of the late 1940s and continued to operate after 1949, in a sharply limited way, by virtue of their acceptance of the CCP's national leadership.

All of these mass organizations were suspended

during the Cultural Revolution. They were replaced by the Red Guards (mainly student organizations) and "revolutionary rebels" (mainly organizations of workers and peasants), localized popular organizations that played a vigorous, militant, and sometimes independent role in the Cultural Revolution. Despite their early prominence, their evident urban strength, and their close ties with some Maoist leaders, Red Guards and rebels never established themselves as national organizations and were disbanded in the later stages of the Cultural Revolution.

The mass organizations began to revive after 1969. By the early 1970s, the CYL, Women's Federation, Trade Union Federation, and Young Pioneers were reorganizing, as were some professional associations. Rebuilding was slow, however, suggesting that these forms of association remained controversial. Following the fall of the Gang, which was blamed for wreaking havoc on mass organizations, reactivation accelerated. National congresses of the CYL, Women's Federation, and Trade Union Federation were held in late 1978. The professional associations became prominent again and even the democratic parties — which had been portrayed in the Cultural Revolution as strongholds for China's "bourgeois intellectuals" — reappeared. The revival of these organizations is one of the clearest signs that the post-Mao leadership favors a more highly institutionalized structure than that associated with the Cultural Revolution.

POLITICAL CULTURE AND POLITICAL SOCIALIZATION

The Maoist prescription for Chinese political culture calls for a redefinition of the social units to which primary loyalties are due and from which authority flows. In traditional China, the dominant social institution was typically a kinship unit; individuals geared their actions to its maintenance and prosperity, and accepted its leaders' authority over their social behavior. Individual loyalties and responsibilities arose largely out of personal experience, creating a web of obligations that protected and benefited insiders at the expense of outsiders. In the Maoist ethic, collective experience determines loyalty and authority. Political authority, at whatever level, is superior to the claims of any elements within the community; loyalties belong to the collective regardless of personal associations and ties. As slogans like "serve the people" and "fight self-interest" suggest, Maoist principles require dedication to the public cause and conscious suppression of selfish concerns.

The traditional order emphasized the maintenance of harmony in social relations. People were to be well-ordered and peaceful, avoiding or suppressing antagonism. Today, official doctrine portrays society as torn by constant class struggle, both as a consequence of exploitation and as a condition of social progress. Citizens are expected to participate actively and voluntarily in this struggle, sharpening its features and challenging openly those whose positions or actions stand in the way of socialism.

Traditional authoritarianism, and the strictures against challenging its harmonious ordering of society, led to heavy dependence on those holding positions of authority. Self-reliance, the Maoist principle, insists that human efforts can overcome all obstacles and urges people to employ their own initiative and capacities, both individual and collective, to accomplish the tasks that face them. The proper outlook now is that people need not and should not expect paternalistic protection and assistance from any source, including the government.

Hierarchical relationships were viewed as natural and necessary in traditional Chinese society. The principles governing the social hierarchy were complex, involving age, generation, kinship, sex, wealth, scholarly attainment, and official status. Nonetheless, individuals knew who their superiors and subordinates were in various settings, so that authority and status were clear in most social relationships. The Maoist view of social distinctions is much more open ended. Though recognizing the existence of classes, the inevitability of some division of labor, and the necessity of maintaining political authority, it is hostile to the elaboration and reinforcement of hierarchy. Within the inescapable political and administrative hierarchy, it is hostile toward privileges, symbols, and economic differences that set the elite apart as a special group and give its members an aura of superiority extending beyond their specific political roles.

Both Maoist and traditional systems rely on elite defined models of the most valued life-style, but the style differs greatly. The ideal life-style in traditional society was that of the scholar-official, whereas in the Maoist ethic it is that of the common man. The former placed the burden of attainment on the people, allowing members of the elite to perpetuate their way of life; the latter places a burden of change on elite members, who are expected to pursue a life traditionally considered beneath them. The former admired intellectual and bureaucratic achievement; the latter respects physically active and productive lives.

Although these brief remarks greatly simplify the comparison of traditional and Maoist values, they suggest why political socialization has such a prominent place in Chinese politics. At issue is not simply transferring allegiance to a new regime, but creating a new political community, with all individuals transforming their images of public life and finding their roles within it. The Maoist prescriptions indicate the general direction of desired change and the magnitude of the task. They also help explain why the CCP has tried to expand the scope of socialization to include adults as well as children, elites as well as masses, and to establish political control over all agents of socialization.

Agents of Socialization

THE FAMILY The Chinese Communists have looked on the traditional kinship hierarchy — including the immediate family and the larger lineages or clans so influential in parts of China — as a citadel of oppression, reactionary values, and potential opposition to socialism. Accordingly, they have tried to reform the family system, which has produced tension and resistance. Some features of the old system have been marked for destruction: the organizational power of the lineage; traditional marriage practices, which helped perpetuate the subordination of women and youth to family elders; and those values that made kinship obligations superior to all others within social relationships. But aside from destroying the lineage hierarchy that encompassed several families and even whole villages, Communist policy with respect to basic kinship structure has not been particularly radical. The officially approved family unit is the nuclear family (parents and children), frequently joined by one or more grandparents — the unit that was the most common form of family organization in pre-Communist China, and that is close to the pattern prevailing in industrialized Western societies.

Communist policy has sought to secure compliance within the family to the norms of socialization established by political authority. The most important step was adoption of the marriage law in 1950, which established legal equality of the sexes and made illegal many traditional marital and kinship arrangements. Reforms associated with the development of communes during the Great Leap Forward temporarily endangered the nuclear family, but they were dropped before their effects were widely felt. With retrenchment, the CCP decided that the family and village could become positive agents of socialization, reinforcing state policy by encouraging production skills, hard work, community service, and respect for authority.

This moderation of policy toward the family mirrored the basic dilemma of Chinese politics in the 1960s — how to reconcile the need for authority and stability with the uncertainties of continued revolution — and was questioned in the Cultural Revolution. Nonetheless, the policy that gradually emerged in the Cultural Revolution was not radically different from the one that preceded it. What did change was the previous period's tolerance of some disfavored traditional practices. There was no room in the Cultural Revolution for compromise. The family was not a target of hostility but neither was it immune from revolutionary struggle; it had to revolutionize itself, fearlessly rooting out any evil tendencies persisting or arising within it. That the family was no longer treated with hostility suggests that Communist social and economic reforms had greatly reduced its once dominant role in Chinese society. The post-1976 emphasis on social stability seemed to remove the family from the field of revolutionary struggle.

PUBLIC EDUCATION The system of public education is one of the state's most effective agents for altering Chinese political attitudes. Unlike the family, which affects everyone at an impressionable age but is difficult for the state to penetrate, schools provide an easily controlled mechanism for universal, sustained, and structured contact with all school-age citizens.

The educational system includes five major branches: preschool programs, primary schools, middle schools (including junior and senior levels, plus a variety of vocational and technical schools), institutions of higher education, and various part-time and spare-time schools that overlap in level with the full-time schools. Although the system is controlled by central ministries that establish national standards for administration and content, variations within the system are common. Universal education is the system's basic objective. To shift the burden of socialization toward the public realm, and to establish the mass literacy needed for political education and involvement, the schools are expected to approach near-total enrollment for those of school age.

Under Communist leadership, the school system greatly expanded educational opportunities during the 1950s but then began to lose its momentum (see Table 13.5). At best, it was providing a few years of primary education for most children, three years of junior middle school for a select minority, and higher education (senior middle school and college) for a tiny fraction of the population. By the late 1950s, some Chinese leaders were seriously concerned. The system was seen as giving relatively advanced and prolonged education to the few, encouraging hopes for a purely academic or cadre career, while limiting its benefit for rural areas and the working population. Two major lines of reform were proposed, as part of the Great Leap Forward. One was reform of the regular system, reducing the years of study, deemphasizing specialization, and injecting working or production experience into the school schedule. The other reform was to expand spare-time and part-time schools.

These efforts failed to restructure the educational system. The collapse of the Great Leap, the economic crisis and retrenchment policies that followed, and the general inertia or resistance of many within the school system prevented radical departures from established patterns. The spare-time and part-time schools survived, continuing to serve at least some of their intended functions, bringing political and practical education to millions excluded from the regular schools, but they remained inferior to the regular schools in academic quality and social prestige. A frontal assault on the educational establishment was postponed until the Cultural Revolution.

Despite Maoist rejection of the educational system in the late 1960s, largely on the grounds that it was not performing its political mission, the schools have been a powerful agent of socialization in post-1949 China. Certain political themes have been an inescapable part of the school experience. One is patriotism, the attempt to transmit basic information about China, its accomplishments and resources, and to instill love, loyalty, and respect for the motherland. Another is support for the Communist system, encouraged through a review of the history and achievements of the CCP and its leaders, particularly Mao Zedong, and the portrayal of the party — and, again, Mao himself — as the benevolent and righteous leader of the country. Coupled with this is criticism of negative political models, such as the old feudal system, the KMT, and American and Soviet imperialism. Finally, political education has emphasized the qualities of the model citizen: hard work, sacrifice, and discipline for the sake of society and the collective.

THE COMMUNICATIONS NETWORK The Chinese communications network, like that in other societies, includes an immense variety and volume of messages. The most fundamental fact about the network is that it is almost exclusively an official state or party operation, controlled in content and management. The public is told what the political elite wants it to know; competing or contradictory messages have no organized means for winning a hearing.

A second characteristic of political communications in China is the dominance of ideology and its special vocabulary. Most messages are cast in the language of the official ideology, which provides a unifying mechanism for those who speak it and a screen for those who do not. As a result, the most authoritative and thorough communications are generally directed toward the elite or subelite, who understand ideological discourse; it is their responsibility to transmit it, with appropriate explanation and reference to local circumstances, to the general

Table 13.5

Enrollments and Graduates by Level of School (in thousands)

	Primary schools		*Middle schools*		*Universities*	
Year	*Enrollment*	*Graduates*	*Enrollment*	*Graduates*	*Enrollment*	*Graduates*
Peak year prior to 1949	23,683	4,633	1,879	399	155	25
1949	24,391	2,387	1,268	352	117	21
1952	51,100	5,942	3,126	289	191	32
1958	86,400	16,225	9,990	1,504	660	72
1960					955	135
1965	116,000		14,418		674	170
Cultural Revolution: All schools closed for at least two years, with primary schools the first to reopen, universities last. The closures produced a noticeable lag in graduates from middle schools and universities. No complete figures on post–Cultural Revolution enrollments are available, but the following estimates indicate the main trends. University enrollments for 1978 were expected to increase by as much as 200,000 over 1977 due to new priorities.						
1967				690		10
1970				1,266		40
1975	130,000		34,000		400	
1977	150,000		59,079		584	

Sources: Figures for the years down to 1958 are from John Phillip Emerson, "Employment in Mainland China," U.S. Congress, Joint Economic Committee, *An Economic Profile of Mainland China* (Washington, D.C.: U.S. Government Printing Office, 1967), pp. 424–425. The 1960 university enrollment is from Emerson, "Manpower Training and Utilization of Specialized Cadres, 1949–68," in John Lewis (ed.), *The City in Communist China* (Stanford, Calif.: Stanford University Press, 1971), p. 200. Enrollments for 1965 are from *Peking Review*, 5 (February 3, 1978), p. 17. Enrollments for 1975 are from *The United States and China: A Report to the Senate Foreign Relations Committee and the House International Relations Committee*, U.S. Congress (Washington, D.C.: U.S. Government Printing Office, 1975), p. 21. Graduates for 1960, 1965, 1967, and 1970 are from Leo Orleans, "China's Science and Technology," in U.S. Congress, Joint Economic Committee, *People's Republic of China: An Economic Assessment* (Washington, D.C.: U.S. Government Printing Office, 1972), pp. 218–219. Enrollments for 1977 are from Suzanne Pepper, "An Interview on Changes in Chinese Education After the 'Gang of Four,' " *China Quarterly*, 72 (December 1977), pp. 815–816.

population. Mass media also use the ideological language but rely heavily on slogans to simplify the message for the general public.

Finally, the style of communications is pedagogical. As a Great Leap slogan put it, "the whole nation is a classroom," and the communications system plays a vital part in the education or reeducation of the nation's population.

Political communications in China vary in their intended audience, the medium employed, and the intensity of the exchange. At the apex of the elite media — aimed at the most literate and politically involved citizens — is *Renmin Ribao* (*People's Daily*), the Central Committee's official newspaper.

The mass media are aimed at the ordinary citizen, with radio the most important of them. Capable of bridging the literacy barrier (although not always linguistic barriers), amenable to extension into remote areas, and capable of immediate and simultaneous transmission of messages to large audiences, radio is government's best instrument for mass communication. Newspapers for the masses include local newspapers (normally published by provincial and municipal party committees): rural editions of the local press, designed to serve the surrounding countryside; newsletters or papers put out by units, enterprises, and schools for their own clientele; and a variety of general reading matter suitable for hand-outs or posting. Other mass media include films, live dramatic performances, and television, but these are less important because of the difficulty of bringing them to rural areas.

One of the communications network's most important and distinctive forms is face-to-face contact in meetings or small-group encounters, via an army of political cadres and activists who penetrate every working or residential collective in China. These low-level cadres and activists are expected to grasp political issues revealed in the formal media and call them to popular attention, explaining and persuading to secure mass support. They may do this through regular discussion and study groups that review current news and issues, through special meetings called for problems of urgency, or simply through daily conversation.

Virtually all Chinese citizens are exposed regularly to the messages of at least some formal media, and all messages have high political content. This

Mao's picture, quotations, and "little red book" guide study preparations for a meeting of a country committee during the Cultural Revolution. Although reliance on Mao's works and authority has diminished since 1976, organized political study remains an important means of political socialization in the PRC.

exposure has probably increased general knowledge about political personalities and affairs, created a greater sense of identification with the political system, and encouraged greater receptivity to the demands and values of the political elite. The intensity of communications is heightened considerably — and in a way that guarantees some citizen response — by the encouragement of discussion and study under the guidance of the cadre.

The most intense political communications occur in rectification, struggle, and thought reform. Particular individuals or groups are criticized in a highly structured setting that allows no escape from confrontation with prescribed norms. Rectification campaigns aim at various levels or sectors of the elite, especially CCP members. The goal is for the individual to acknowledge errors and renew commitment to the correct line or standpoint. Those found seriously deficient will suffer demotion, purge, or more hostile struggle. Struggle and thought reform are the extremes of political education, brought to bear on individuals whose political guilt is already established, whether through rectification or another way. It must be remembered that relatively few Chinese have been on the receiving end of these techniques, at least since the early postliberation years, when whole social groups, such as landlords or intellectuals, were designated for struggle and reform.

In summary, the communications system is most effective in expanding knowledge about politics and heightening sensitivity to political issues. Its role in changing deeply felt attitudes is more uncertain, but political discussion groups have probably encouraged a greater willingness among the general population to take an active part in national and local politics.

POLITICAL AND SOCIAL EXPERIENCE

One of the CCP's most ambitious goals has been to involve every Chinese citizen in regular, organized political activity at the basic level, largely through mass movements, representation in basic-level government, membership in mass organizations, and participation in the management of primary production and residential units. In most cases, real initiative and control rests with higher authorities, and no doubt some participants perform assignments for which they have little understanding or enthusiasm. Even so, the participant is learning something about the governmental process, the possibilities of political association, and her relationship to politics.

Mass campaigns, the most intense political activity, have probably increased the impact of politics for all, generated an enthusiasm for collective action for some, and led to genuine political activism by others. On the negative side, however, most Chinese have seen their lives disrupted by one or more of these campaigns, or know of people who have suffered heavily from them.

The elite and subelite have participated more heavily than the masses in these activities, and have been the target of measures designed to reduce their status and privilege. Some of these measures have been explicitly egalitarian, such as the abolition of rank insignia and titles in the PLA in 1965 and the reduction of wage differentials during the Cultural Revolution. By far the most ambitious, however, has been the practice of *xia fang* (assignment to lower levels), which gives those holding or aspiring to official positions a taste of manual labor. This is meant to overcome any notion they may have that educational or political credentials exempt them from discomfort and hard work, and to persuade the masses that the elite cannot isolate itself from the realities of life.

Socialization and the Cultural Revolution

Political socialization became a prime target for reform in the Cultural Revolution. Dissatisfaction with the established pattern of political socialization focused on the educational system and the general quality of public life. Hostility toward the schools rested on the Maoist conviction that "revisionists" had erected a two-track system; one track of less prestigious schools provided token or inferior mass education, the other track, leading to the best higher schools, catered to an academically and career-oriented elite. These better schools, although providing ritualistic political education and labor experience for students, were turning out graduates whose skills and ambitions were largely professional or bureaucratic, and hence at odds with the Maoist ethic and the practical work many would do. The Maoists perceived the educational system as cultivating successors who were not sufficiently revolutionary in either social background or outlook.

Concern over the quality of social experience was less clearly formulated. In simplest terms, the Maoists argued that revisionists were structuring mass participation and organization to serve their own bureaucratic requirements, rather than to increase popular political activity and bring cadres and citizens closer together. Liu Shaoqi, identified as the principal example of this tendency, was charged with wanting people to serve as "docile tools" and "stainless screws," and with supporting the idea of "joining the Party to become an official."

The upheavals of 1966–1967 drastically affected most of the institutions for political socialization. Schools closed in the summer of 1966, not to reopen for formal instruction for two or three years. Cadres at every level came under mass criticism, frequently leading to public humiliation and dismissal. The old mass organizations fell into disarray or inactivity, while new associations of Red Guards and rebel groups sprang into action, sometimes forming citywide federations and commanding real power. As the communications system ceased to provide authoritative direction, these groups began to develop their own information, platforms, and publications in the midst of a barrage of competing political messages. This exercise in spontaneous mass action did not continue for long. Alarmed by the threat of anarchy and civil war, and torn by factional disputes within its own ranks, the Maoist coalition sought an institutional basis for its reformist mood.

Educational reform was the Cultural Revolution's most visible contribution to a new socialization process. The number of primary, middle, and part-time schools was increased in a renewed effort to broaden basic education. As Table 13.5 indicates, these efforts were successful; by 1977 primary enrollments were close to universal for the age group, while middle school enrollments were greatly expanded, although far from universal. University enrollments fell sharply, however, and the length of the university education was reduced. Political criteria took precedence over academic standards in admission and promotion. Advanced study and theoretical research suffered under pressures for a more practical curriculum and more vocational training. Students at all levels spent more time outside the classroom in manual labor or in on-the-spot instruction in fields and factories. No one was permitted to apply for college without two to three years of work experience.

These reforms were in place by the early 1970s, but they were not firmly established. Deviations began to appear, with considerable debate over the precise weight to be attached to examinations, academic questions, advanced and theoretical work, and so forth. As in many other areas, the purge of the Gang of Four brought modification of education policies. The drive for universality of primary and middle school education was reaffirmed, as was the general importance of political influence in the educational process, but many policies on higher education were reversed. Examinations became the primary means for evaluating students, courses of study were lengthened, and the requirement for work experience before college was relaxed. Officials now underscored the need to encourage theoretical and technical research, with guaranteed work time (meaning fewer political distractions), better facilities, more recognition of individual achievement, and more active recruitment of bright youngsters for training in special schools. In short, a distinct shift toward more academic, professional standards had occurred.

The radicals had pushed Maoist policies to the extreme in culture and education, so it is not surprising that the post-Mao reaction was most evident there. Hua Guofeng's administration seems committed to less politicized cultural and educational forms, to encourage more variety, more development of individual talent, and more interaction with international influences. Nonetheless, the Cultural Revolution had a real impact on socialization. The event itself was unforgettable, demonstrating the possibilities for mass action and criticism as well as the dangers of civil violence and factionalism. It led to greater pre-college educational opportunities and to greater interaction between schools and society. It encouraged more egalitarian relationships in society and more popular participation in community affairs. Officially, at least, the new leaders remain committed to these principles. It is quite possible that the educational shifts of 1977–1978 will foster greater stratification in Chinese society, but such a trend is likely to encounter resistance from other elements in the Maoist ethic that have yet to be repudiated.

POLITICAL PARTICIPATION AND RECRUITMENT

Political participation and recruitment are inseparable from the articulation and aggregation of interests, the demands individuals bring with them as they enter politics. This section initiates discussion of the Chinese political process by identifying general patterns of participation and recruitment. The two subsequent sections, on interest articulation and aggregation, will deal more concretely with the substance of conflicting interests.

Participation

There is a basic distinction in China, as in all political systems, between specialized and nonspecialized political roles, between elites, who have acquired special political responsibilities and power, and the ordinary citizens, who have not. Analysis of recruitment reveals how elites are chosen, and study of interest conflicts focuses on the organized activities of those recruited. Participation, however, is open to elites and masses. The CCP's political ideals, especially in the Maoist formulation, demand intense participation from all citizens. They project a highly politicized society in which everyone participates fully, to the limits of her potential role.

The participatory style of the elite requires little elaboration. Although idealized expectations are never wholly fulfilled, Chinese activists, cadres, and party members lead lives of intense political commitment and responsibility. For them, the model of participatory behavior is at least an approximation of reality. But what about ordinary citizens? To what extent do they participate politically, and how significant are the allegedly political acts in which they engage? These are controversial questions, especially given Western democratic assumptions about participation and how those assumptions are altered in an authoritarian communist system.

The P.R.C. is a single-party system that does not legitimate organized political opposition. The CCP dominates state, army, communications media, schools — all organized groups and activities of any size. Simply put, there is little place in the system for participation that does not conform to party expectations about what participation ought to be. On the other hand, these expectations took shape over decades of mass-line practice, in revolutionary struggle, political campaigns, and movements for socioeconomic development. This development means they include a certain tolerance for the contradictions that necessarily appear when the party solicits mass opinions and supportive action. Moreover, the Maoist reliance on decentralization and mass movements, in a society so large and complex, has frequently opened the way for local initiative. In short, although most participation in China is solicited, some is not; some that is solicited is expected to differ from the party line; and some that is solicited will produce unexpected deviations and conflict.

Political participation may perform many functions. It influences decisions or decision makers, either by controlling the process or injecting demands into it; it helps implement policies; it socializes the participant, influencing future political acts and attitudes; and it symbolizes support for or identification with the community. Participation may also take different forms, ranging from conventional acts like voting, discussion of issues, support for favored policies or candidates, and communication with elites, to unconventional acts, like violence or illegality. Finally, participation may fall into different modes, the characteristic settings in which a kind of participation most frequently occurs. We will note the most important modes of participation in China, with brief comments on their functions and form.

The first mode is participation in the formal institutions of the state structure, essentially the election of deputies to rural commune and urban district congresses (recall that higher-level congresses are elected indirectly). This mode is widespread but largely symbolic, because basic-level congresses have little power, and the election itself is usually a matter of ratifying an officially approved candidate list. Participation in mass campaigns is a much more significant mode, offering some opportunity for all the functions mentioned above. It calls for implementation when mass participation is required to overcome human or natural resistance; has important socializing and symbolic functions; and allows for some influence on local decisions or decision makers, through the criticism of cadres and the experimentation that are part of many campaigns.

Political study and discussion is one of the most distinctive modes of mass participation in China. It occurs most regularly and formally in small groups organized at the work place or residence, but intensifies and moves into larger, more informal groups in the midst of the struggle campaigns just discussed. Socialization is the primary function of discussion, which uses the study of documents and current affairs and criticism and self-criticism sessions analyzing individual attitudes and behavior. It may also lead to the expression of unorthodox opinions, either within the group or through letters and *dazibao* ("big character posters" for public display).

A fourth mode is participation in the internal affairs of primary units beneath the basic level of government, such as production brigades and teams, urban neighborhood organizations, schools, factories, and other units. This mode produces the most regular and significant forms of participation: the masses have greater say in the elections of unit leaders, they have more regular and influential contact with these leaders, and they are able to discuss issues that bear directly on their daily lives. Local units also recruit people into activist roles, or lead them to serve the community by accepting assignments that contribute to collective welfare.

In summary, mass political participation in China has little to do with decision making, except within primary units that have little leverage against the system, but it plays an important role in policy implementation, political socialization, and symbolic expression. As noted in the discussion of socialization, Chinese modes of participation have produced tension, hardship, and alienation for some citizens. The participant may be compelled to implement unpopular policies, to criticize self and others in cynical or destructive ways, to spend dreary hours in the study of materials that have little personal meaning. The general pattern weakens or routinizes some conventional forms of participation (voting, for example), while encouraging unconventional forms that may bring psychological and physical violence (seen most clearly in the Cultural Revolution). Yet the pattern has also developed regularized features — particularly within primary units —that link citizens closely to the political system and appear to enhance their sense of efficacy in community affairs.

Recruitment

Three important political roles — activist, cadre, and party member — dominate the staffing of the Chinese political system. Activists are ordinary citizens, not holding full-time official positions, who acquire special interest, initiative, or responsibility in public affairs. Cadres are those who hold a leadership position in an organization, normally as a full-time post. Party members, of course, are just that.

Becoming an activist is generally the first step in political recruitment, and it is from the ranks of activists that most new cadres and CCP members are drawn. Local party organizations keep track of activists within their jurisdiction, turning to them when political campaigns and recruitment are underway. In practice, activists are designated on the basis of self-selection, personal ability, and group support, with local officials watching closely to veto undesirables and to select the most promising for more important roles.

Recruitment to cadre status is different. State cadres, who staff state, party, and mass organization hierarchies above the primary level and who receive their salaries from the government, are appointed from within the bureaucracies, through the personnel sections of the state and the departments of the CCP. The most serious problem in cadre recruitment is tension between the dissimilar criteria of professional skills and political orthodoxy. In practice, there has been a tendency to accept the priority of expert qualifications in the recruitment of nonparty cadres, and orthodoxy with party cadres.

Admission to the CCP is the decisive act of political recruitment. Party membership alone provides entrance into a political career with significant opportunities for advancement and power. The party member is always in a position of relative political prominence. If an ordinary worker, the member is a prime candidate for the activist role; among activists, members are the most likely to be selected as cadres; and among cadres, members have superior political status and opportunities.

From the late 1920s to the late 1940s, most party members were politically committed recruits. Party members did not join the Communist movement for security, material, or opportunistic reasons. Hardship, danger, and the threat of execution by the Nationalists were risks faced by party members and followers alike, and there was little assurance of ultimate victory until very late. A second pattern began to emerge in the late 1940s and lasted through 1953. This was the period when CCP military power spread rapidly over all of China, when a new political structure was needed to begin reconstruction, and when a great many recruits for activist, cadre, and party roles were needed. The CCP recognized that the new circumstances made it easier for opportunists, careerists, and even "class enemies" to acquire political status and was relatively cautious in recruitment.

The need for activists and cadres could not be postponed, however. The great campaigns of 1949–1952 demanded and produced millions of new activists, primarily from oppressed and outcast groups in the countryside, with large numbers of students also answering the call. Intensive efforts raised the number of state cadres from 720,000 in 1949 to over 3.3 million in 1952, almost 5.3 million in 1955, and nearly 8 million in 1958. The CCP could take satisfaction in having met the problem of numbers, but it was acutely aware of problems arising from the necessarily loose standards. Party strength was still insufficient to supervise thoroughly the work of all offices, many filled with cadres of questionable "redness," and most activists and low-level cadres had few cultural and technical skills — many were illiterate and totally untrained for administrative work.

To rectify this situation, the CCP after 1954 institutionalized the recruitment process through two organizations, the People's Liberation Army and the Communist Youth League. The PLA has always been a major supplier and employer of CCP members. Demobilized and transferred soldiers have been prime candidates for activist, cadre, and party-member status. Their service gives them disciplined organizational experience, regular political education, minimal literacy, and sometimes technical skills. Moreover, the PLA's conscripts are an elite group to begin with, since only a fraction of those who reach the conscription age of eighteen are taken. Many are from peasant families, which gives them the added advantage of a favored class background, but they are the pick of China's rural youth.

The CYL's importance in recruitment is obvious; until 1966 it was officially recognized as the most appropriate organization in which youth might acquire advanced political qualifications. The league's growth in the 1950s was impressive. Starting from scratch in 1949, it matched the CCP in size by 1952 and was nearly twice the CCP's size by 1956. The league became the leading source of new party members in about 1954, when the CCP began its own major growth period. The CCP, seeking candidates both "red" and expert, logically focused its search on the CYL, its own auxiliary and second only to the party in the political activism and purity of its membership.

This institutionalized recruitment pattern gave weight to seniority and made upward mobility difficult for the post-1954 recruit. Central leadership remained closed to all but the oldest. By 1965, the CCP was an organization of recent recruits lacking revolutionary experience, with most responsible positions held by a small stratum of old revolutionary cadres.

Table 13.6 summarizes the preceding discussion, emphasizing changes in party organization between 1945 and 1965. Maoists recognized the shift from a revolutionary to a bureaucratic party and tried to combat it. There were attempts to reduce cadre members in the mid-1950s; initiation of xia fang, movements to recruit more peasant CCP and CYL members, and repoliticalization of the PLA in the late 1950s; socialist education and cultivation of revolutionary successor campaigns in the early 1960s; and a new CYL recruitment drive to add worker-peasant members and rejuvenate league organization in 1964–1965. These measures checked the institutionalization of recruitment but did not reverse it. With the exception of the PLA, where Lin Biao's revival of the revolutionary political style had a marked impact, none of the institutions involved turned decisively away from the post-1953 pattern.

The Cultural Revolution produced many real and

Table 13.6

Contrasts in the Chinese Communist Party of 1945 and 1965

	1945	*1965*
Membership	1,211,128	Over 17,000,000
Age of top leaders	Forties	Sixties
Social background of members		
Percentage rural	Near 100	Over 60
Percentage urban	Near 0	Over 30
Primary work	Peasant or soldier	Cadre or office work
Style of political work	Generalist: mass mobilization and face-to-face relationships	Specialist: administrative in a bureaucratic setting
Remuneration	Nonsalaried	Salaried
Upward mobility	Open	Closed
Recruitment	Self-recruitment, screened by performance in revolutionary action	Competitive selection, screened by admission to feeder institutions (PLA, Youth League)

rhetorical attacks on the established recruitment process, and as the campaign shifted to its consolidation phase, a more open and vigorous recruitment policy seemed to appear, guided by a quotation from Mao:

> A human being has arteries and veins through which the heart makes the blood circulate, and he breathes with his lungs, exhaling carbon dioxide and inhaling fresh oxygen, that is, getting rid of the stale and taking in the fresh. A proletarian party must also get rid of the stale and take in the fresh for only thus can it be full of vitality. Without eliminating waste matter and absorbing fresh blood the Party has no vigor.[3]

The CCP proceeded to take in fresh blood, but how well it was absorbed is another matter. With an apparent loosening of admission standards, the party swelled to over 35 million members in 1977 (see Table 13.1); nearly half the total membership had joined since the Cultural Revolution. High turnover occurred as well, since numerous purges and other departures accompanied the Cultural Revolution. The campaign also loosened the grip of the Long March generation on the CCP's top leadership. From 1935 to the early 1970s, the top elite came almost exclusively from those who had joined the party before the 1934–1935 Long March. The Central Committee elected at the Ninth Congress in 1969 was the first serious break in this pattern, with only 19 percent of its members drawn from the preceding Central Committee (see Table 13.7). Subsequent deaths and purges further depleted old guard strength, so that by the late 1970s top leadership was passing to a second generation whose formative political experience centered on the late 1930s and 1940s.

The problem with this fresh blood was that so much of it reflected Cultural Revolution tensions, in particular the influence of the Gang of Four. Speak-

[3] "Absorb Fresh Blood from the Proletariat — An Important Question in Party Consolidation," *Peking Review*, 43 (October 25, 1968), pp. 4–7.

ers at the Eleventh Congress claimed that the Gang's indiscriminate recruitment efforts, to strengthen their faction, had led to "impurities" of ideology and organizational work; discipline commissions and tighter regulations on admission were added to the 1977 party Constitution to respond to this concern. The return to the Tenth and Eleventh Central Committees of many old cadres purged in the Cultural Revolution (see Table 13.7) also reflected a desire to minimize the loss of experienced leadership.

By 1978, a new recruitment pattern appeared to be taking shape. Stricter admission policies and the reactivation of the CYL suggested an institutionalized system reminiscent of the 1950s, while the new emphasis on development of science and technology suggested that more highly educated recruits would be favored. Whatever the exact pattern, the CCP has undergone a fundamental change. The old revolutionary elite is all but gone; the rank and file is almost entirely post-1949 recruits. The CCP is no longer a revolutionary party in the experience of its members, but rather an organization of 35 million members, drawn from post-1949 society, that must adapt itself to the increasingly technological problems of China's future development. If this organization is to maintain the discipline and skills needed to lead China's drive for modernization, it probably has to accept a relatively high degree of bureaucratization and institutionalization of recruitment, even though that trend pulls it away from the Maoist organizational ideal.

INTEREST ARTICULATION

The central process in every political system is the conversion of demands, representing the interests, goals, and desires of individuals or groups within the society, into political decisions that are then applied and enforced by the government. The CCP's idea of how this process ought to work is contained in the mass line, stated in a directive written for the Central Committee in June 1943 by Mao Zedong:

> In all the practical work of our Party, all correct leadership is necessarily "from the masses, to the masses." This means: Take the ideas of the masses (scattered and unsystematic ideas) and concentrate them (through study turn them into concentrated and systematic ideas), then go to the masses and propagate and explain these ideas until the masses embrace them as their own, hold fast to them and translate them into action, and test the correctness of these ideas in such action. Then once again concentrate ideas from the masses and once again go to the masses so that the ideas are persevered in and carried through. And so on, over and over again in an endless spiral, with the ideas becoming more correct, more vital and richer each time.[4]

Masses articulate interests (express their "scattered and unsystematic ideas"), while the party — and only the party — aggregates them (turns them into "concentrated and systematic ideas" that can become policy alternatives). There are, of course, organizations other than the CCP that have the capacity, in membership and scale, to pull together and synthesize the demands of particular groups in Chinese society. But these organizations are not autonomous. Their leadership is dominated by party members whose job is to protect the CCP's favored position in the formulation of policy proposals and to discourage demands that conflict with the CCP's general line.

The CCP's willingness to encourage political claims from the populace conflicts with its fear of organized competition or opposition. The result is that many such claims are put forward in unorganized, fragmented fashion.

Popular demands are most frequently and effectively expressed within basic-level government, especially within primary production and residential units. The smallest groups — production teams in the countryside, work teams in factories, and residents' groups in cities — have frequent meetings and choose their own group leadership. The masses also have a direct voice in more inclusive groups — production brigades, factorywide organizations, and residents' committees — through selection of representatives to managing committees or meetings of the entire constituency. Selection of leaders and representatives may stem from discussion and consensus rather than from contested elections, and individuals unacceptable to higher cadres are not likely to be

[4] "Some Questions Concerning Methods of Leadership," *Selected Works of Mao Tse-tung* (Peking: Foreign Languages Press, 1965), vol. 3, p. 119.

Table 13.7

Changes in Composition of CCP Central Committees

	Eighth (1956–1958)	*Ninth (1969)*	*Tenth (1973)*	*Eleventh (1977)*
Number of members				
Full	97	170	195	201
Alternate	96[a]	109	124	132
Total	193	279	319	333
Background of members[b]				
Holdovers from previous CC	40%	19%	64%	56%
Newcomers	60	81	31	38
Returnees[c]	0	0	5	6
Occupational background[b]				
Civilian	81	55	63	71
Military	19	45	32	29
Unknown	0	0	5	0
Occupational level[b]				
National	62	33	33	35
Provincial	38	67	62	65
Unknown	0	0	5	0
Average age of full members at election[d]	56.4	61.4	62.1	64.6

[a] Twenty-five alternate members were added to the Eighth Central Committee at its second plenary session in 1958.

[b] Figures represent percentages of total (full and alternate) membership.

[c] Returnees are those full and alternate members who were not elected to the immediately previous committee but who were members of an earlier committee.

[d] Data for 1969 based on 162 of 170 full members; data for 1977 based on 163 of 201 full members.

Sources: Who's Who in Communist China (Hong Kong: Union Research Institute, 1966), pp. 703–707; Donald W. Klein and Lois B. Hager, "The Ninth Central Committee," *China Quarterly*, 45 (January-February 1971), pp. 37–56; Malcolm Lamb, *Directory of Central Officials in the People's Republic of China, 1968–1975* (Canberra: Australian National University, 1976), pp. 5–16; K'ung Te-liang, "An Analysis of the CCP's 10th National Congress," *Issues and Studies*, 10: 1 (October 1973), pp. 17–30; *China: A Look at the 11th Central Committee* (Washington, D.C.: Central Intelligence Agency, October 1977), 7 p.; Jurgen Domes, "The Ninth CCP Central Committee in Statistical Perspective," *Current Scene*, 9: 2 (February 7, 1971), pp. 5–14; and Jurgen Domes, "China in 1977: A Reversal of the Verdict," *Asian Survey*, 18: 1 (January 1978), pp. 6–9.

chosen. The leaders chosen are in constant association with the mass membership, however; they are ordinary citizens serving in unpaid leadership posts, not cadres assigned to manage these units in the interests of the bureaucracy. In this context, popular interests can and do make themselves heard.

There are other means of expressing individualized or deviant demands. The writing of dazibao is a common means of placing one's views before the unit as a whole. Letters to communications media and personal visits to higher-level cadres and offices are encouraged. In rectification campaigns, the masses have a special opportunity to review and criticize the performance of the local elite. All of these add to the scope of unorganized articulation. For a brief period in the Cultural Revolution, they overshadowed the regular channels of participation within primary units.

Finally, popular demands make themselves known through acts of noncompliance or resistance, such as being absent from work, slowing work down, secretly violating regulations, and taking advantage of loopholes or ambiguities in policy. This method has its limitations, of course. Unless so widespread and spontaneous that it seems to signal incipient rebellion, thereby forcing elite accommodation, it can be disregarded or overcome.

Organized articulation occurs when the group making the demand has members drawn from many units or localities and some means of communicating with its members and the larger public. The most powerful and enduring organizations of this kind have been elite political structures — the state bureaucracies, the CCP, the PLA, and the Youth League — but other more popular organizations, such as the Women's Federation, the trade unions, and the democratic parties, have also played a role in organized interest articulation.

The Women's Federation has probably been the most outspoken and effective articulator of group interests. It alone among the mass organizations has consistently criticized the social position of its membership and demanded improvements. The CCP has generally endorsed these demands, agreeing that women have not yet won the equality that was promised. Although the political vigor of the women's movement has depended on the backing of the national elite, this movement has carried the main burden of promoting equality between the sexes.

The All-China Federation of Trade Unions (ACFTU) offers a different example of the possibilities for organized articulation. Three times since 1949 an independent stand has provoked elite retaliation. The first two times (1951 and 1957), the CCP removed the offending leaders from their ACFTU positions and reasserted the primacy of its policies as a guide for union action. The third instance occurred in the winter of 1966–1967, when some workers resisted an extension of the Cultural Revolution into the factories. As a result, the ACFTU was dissolved, its publications suspended, and its policies denounced as "economism" in the service of Liu Shaogi's line. This experience suggests the dilemma that confronts organizations whose demands deviate from CCP policy. If the top leadership says these demands represent a narrow, selfish interest contrary to the collective interest, the organization has little choice but to give in or to advance a different version of the collective interest, thereby confronting party authority directly.

Something like this happened in the Cultural Revolution, which again provides instructive examples of the limits of Chinese political processes. The Cultural Revolution began with intraelite debate, opened up to the Red Guard stage that permitted a mixture of spontaneous unorganized articulation and support of the official line, and then moved into a period of vigorous organized articulation, as newly formed mass organizations began to present lists of demands to local authorities and play coalition politics with each other in an effort to maximize their influence. Throughout 1967, party and PLA elites had to negotiate and compromise with such groups — many organized into citywide federations — to form municipal and provincial revolutionary committees. Some groups were remarkably persistent in their definition of which individuals and policy positions were "revolutionary" and which were not. Faced with increasingly overt challenges to its authority, Beijing suppressed the Red Guard and rebel federations.

The 1966–1969 campaign left behind a confused situation, in which unorganized articulation was more vigorous than before. Sporadic popular criticism of cadres and policies continued, and in 1974–1976 there was a groundswell of unrest and work stoppages in many industrial areas. Some of this was solicited by rival elite factions, but some appeared to represent a more spontaneous expression of concern over wages, factory management, and other issues.

The unrest of 1974–1976 culminated in the Tienanmen Incident in Beijing in April 1976. Initially a peaceful demonstration commemorating the death of Zhou Enlai, the gathering turned into an unruly political rally supporting Deng Xiaoping and opposing the Gang of Four's policies. Beijing authorities suppressed the demonstration, called it counterrevolutionary, and used it as ammunition in purging Deng. In the fall of 1978, after Deng had returned to power, the Tienanmen Incident was redefined as a correct mass revolutionary action. Emboldened by this and other signs of liberalization, many citizens participated in a rash of public debates and demonstration in several cities during the winter of 1978–1979. Once again the activities were a mixture of support for the current official line and pointed criticism of cadres and regime policies. In *dazibao*, street discussions and marches, and some near riots, participants debated sensitive issues such as the state of democracy and human rights in China, violations of legal procedures, and the strengths and weaknesses of Mao's leadership of the country. The CCP cracked down in March 1979, arresting some of the most outspoken critics, restricting the scope of permissible debate, and reminding citizens that socialist democracy must be used to support the socialist system and party leadership.

In summary, popular articulation of interests tends to limit itself to unorganized expression of demands within the primary unit. Organized articulation is risky, and likely to occur only when in conformity with official policy or when the group has high-level bureaucratic support; in such cases, it is difficult to tell whether the demand starts below and receives elite support or whether it appears only after elites solicit it as a weapon in higher-level debate. In either case, elite allies are normally essential for wider dissemination of the demand and for any hopes of favorable response. The episodes in which popular demands have exceeded elite guidelines are significant exceptions to these generalizations, but, as we have noted, each episode brought suppression of dissidents and reaffirmation of the party's right to define the limits of popular political activity.

INTEREST AGGREGATION AND ELITE CONFLICT

In theory the CCP is the only organization that shapes diverse interests and demands into policy alternatives, monopolizing interest aggregation in a unified way that does not acknowledge the legitimacy of competition once central decisions are made. In practice, as we have seen, interest articulation sometimes becomes aggregation, especially in the Maoist open-ended campaign style, and the notion of unified aggregation has been a myth. Conflict between radicals (associated with a literal or extreme interpretation of Maoist revolutionary themes, emphasizing mass movements and egalitarianism) and moderates (associated with a more bureaucratic or revisionist version of Maoism, emphasizing institutionalized procedures and economic priorities) suggests a pattern of ongoing struggle between two or more elite groups.

The official description of this conflict as a struggle between two lines invariably labels one as correct and the other as incorrect, protecting the claim of the unity of the revolutionary line. Nonetheless, the 1949–1976 period saw conflictual aggregation become the rule rather than the exception in Chinese politics. Although ideology precluded recognition of a legitimate opposition, let alone a second party, intraparty factions became strong and relatively well organized. Moreover, all laid claim to the authority of Marxism-Leninism-Maoism, so it was by no means clear — to outsiders or participants — which was revolutionary or counterrevolutionary. We will concentrate in this section on the emergence and development of factionalism within the CCP central leadership.

Franz Schurmann's distinction between "opinion groups" and "factions" within the CCP provides a useful point of departure.[5] An opinion group is an "aggregate of individuals" who have in common a "likeness of individual opinions" but no organizational basis. The CCP tends to tolerate such groups

[5] Franz Schurmann, *Ideology and Organization in Communist China*, 2nd ed. (Berkeley: University of California Press, 1968), pp. 55–56.

so long as they accept majority decisions and avoid the temptation to organize. A faction is an "opinion group with organized force behind it"; it has resources for action that can split the party along fixed lines, and it is viewed as an illegitimate form of intraparty conflict. During the 1950s the CCP contained intraorganizational conflict by practicing opinion-group politics and restraining factionalism.

Two exceptions to this pattern demonstrated the party elite's ability to enforce its distaste for factional conflict without splitting the party. Politburo member Gao Gang and the director of the Central Committee's Organization Department, Rao Shushi, were purged in 1954 for attempting to capture control of the central party apparatus. In 1959, Minister of Defense Peng Dehuai, also a member of the Politburo, and some of his associates, were purged in a case involving Peng's disagreement with Great Leap policies. In both cases, the party elite kept the conflict closed until after it had made its decision, and then supported with apparent unanimity the decision rendered.

The image of unanimity disappeared in the 1960s with the Cultural Revolution, which opened to public view the bitter conflicts that eventually led to sweeping purges. Factions grew stronger in the 1960s, protecting their members and forming coalitions. Behind this shift lay an intensification of conflict over fundamental issues, represented by the struggle between two lines of the two most powerful leaders, Mao Zedong and Liu Shaoqi.

The fascinating question is why their conflict, contained in the 1950s, acquired sufficient virulence to split the party openly in the 1960s. The change was due partly to a natural hardening of views with age and experience. As both men grew older, and Liu's likely succession more apparent, the need to settle the struggle became more urgent. Moreover, Mao had become less and less a factor in decision making. During the 1950s, his vigor and prestige were usually sufficient to build a consensus on major decisions. But by the early 1960s, Mao had lost his decisive authority within the top leadership, although his public stature was as high as ever. This loss of authority encouraged a growth of factionalism in which Mao himself participated.

By the time of the Cultural Revolution, factions or potential factions were too numerous to be isolated and repressed. A power vacuum existed, and those seeking power needed the backing of several united forces, which invited coalition tactics. Mao reestablished his leadership only by forging a coalition and mobilizing mass support for a public attack on his entrenched opponents. For the first time since 1949, a purge was initiated and made public before the Central Committee had worked out its own consensus decision.

The intricate factional maneuverings that characterized elite behavior between 1965 and 1969 are difficult to describe with any precision. In simplest terms, Mao defeated the Liu revisionists by seizing the initiative in forming a coalition and then maneuvering it with great skill. This coalition was held together by personal commitment to Mao's leadership, but it consisted of at least three factions. The most distinct was the radical faction, which favored the emphatic Maoist position spelled out early in the Cultural Revolution. Its leadership included Mao's wife, his reputed son-in-law, and several intimate associates. It had a powerful regional base in Shanghai and established a mass base in the Red Guards, who looked to coalition members for authoritative indications of Mao's wishes. It held the initiative during the early part of the Cultural Revolution.

The second faction was associated with Lin Biao, whose strength rested on the PLA and his designation in the summer of 1966 as Mao's "closest comrade-in-arms" and heir apparent. Lin's post as defense minister gave his faction tremendous leverage within the organization that became the de facto government during much of the Cultural Revolution. Premier Zhou Enlai headed the third group, high-level cadres who survived the first year's purges. The weakest and least distinct of the three, this was a faction by default, a residual group of leaders who held on because of Zhou's protection and the need for continuity in administrative leadership.

The Maoist coalition emerged from the Cultural Revolution as an uneasy balance of forces. The Lin faction was strengthened not only by Lin's position as Mao's successor, but also by solid PLA representation in new state and party organs (see the increase in military members of the Central Committee in Table 13.7). The radical faction had strength in the Politburo and was still the faction most personally identified with Mao, but its programs and mass base had weakened during the consolidation phase of the campaign. Zhou Enlai was more prominent than ever, assuming leadership of governmental operations as Mao once again withdrew from public life and glorification of the chairman began to recede.

The pattern of elite conflict in 1969–1976 combined elements of both earlier periods. Conflict was again contained, in the sense that purge decisions were secret, without appeals for mass support or public revelations about personalities until after the elite had acted. But despite this return to the guarded style of the 1950s, factional politics continued to divide the top leadership.

Chen Boda, elected to the Standing Committee of the Politburo at the Ninth Congress and the highest-ranking radical, disappeared from view in August 1970. Later, in July 1972, Mao Zedong told foreign visitors that Lin Biao had died in an airplane crash (in Mongolia on September 13, 1971) after he had conspired to assassinate Mao and establish a military dictatorship. At the same time, Chinese officials linked Lin's downfall with Chen's claiming the two had worked together to seize power for themselves. Once established as Mao's apparent successor and facing resistance from other leaders, the story went, Lin had begun to plan a military coup. His plans had become known, and matters came to a head in September 1971. When Lin died, reportedly attempting to escape, his faction was eliminated. Disappearing with him — not necessarily in the crash — were five Politburo members and several other members of the Central Committee and provincial organs.

Factional politics provide the simplest explanation of the Lin Biao incident. From this perspective, the purge of Chen Boda was a defeat for the radicals, who then mobilized their remaining leaders, plus Mao and Zhou, to curb Lin's power. Anticipating his likely downfall, Lin decided to attempt a military coup, to settle the matter once and for all. It is possible, on the other hand, that new issues and perspectives had recast the factions and that the explanation of Lin's downfall is quite different. Lin apparently opposed the Sino-American rapprochement, a position that would have aligned him with some of the radicals. Or he may have chosen the drastic alternative of a coup to stop the gradual reassertion of party control over the PLA that took shape in 1971–1972.

The fall of Chen and Lin, coupled with declining military influence (see the decrease of the military on the Central Committee in Table 13.7), cleared the decks for a second stage of post–Cultural Revolution factionalism. From 1972 to 1976, as Mao's vigor waned, radical and moderate forces struggled for position. (Remember that these labels are loose; neither group had a sharply defined membership and neither conformed exactly to earlier radical and moderate positions on the Chinese political spectrum.) The striking feature of this conflict was the extent to which the tactics employed led to something like two competing organizations within the CCP (for discussion of the main issues in debate, see pages 395–396). Unlike the 1950s, when elite conflict was relatively well contained, or the Cultural Revolution, when factionalism was most evident among mass organizations, the 1972–1976 rivalry extended the split across several dimensions of party life.

Personnel administration was one dimension, as moderates tried to protect senior cadres and rehabilitate victims of the Cultural Revolution, whereas radicals attacked many senior figures and tried to expand their base among the millions of recruits joining the party. Symbol differentiation sharpened, each group developing its own key words, themes, and slogans to identify its position and assault the opposition. For example, in the "criticize Lin and Confucius" campaign that followed Lin Biao's purge, moderates concentrated on Lin's conservative (Confucian) errors, whereas radicals implied that there was a contemporary Confucius (Zhou Enlai) who should be criticized along with Lin. The struggle over symbols — esoteric phrases and their interpretation, cultural forms, and models — was unmistakable because of a third dimension of the conflict, namely, the emergence of competing communications systems. Not satisfied with their generally strong communications base, the radicals began to publish their own theoretical journal in Shanghai, in competition with the Beijing-based organ of the Central Committee; they also used pen names and academic journals to identify and advance their policy statements. The radicals had a stronghold in Shanghai, retained enough influence among workers and students to make factories and universities a frequent battleground, and even tried to acquire an armed organizational base by controlling a new urban militia.

The extent and variety of these factional activities lends credibility to charges that the Gang of Four forged or misrepresented some of Mao's directives and were planning a coup against Hua Guofeng when he struck against them. However that may be, there is no doubt that factionalism had gotten out of hand, and that the new leadership was determined to restore tighter discipline. For almost two years after the purge of the Gang, Mao's successors avoided open factionalism, maintaining a loose consensus on the four modernizations policies and the need to rebuild party unity and discipline. There were differences between Hua Guofeng and Deng Xiaoping, however, with Hua sticking closer to Maoist themes and Deng pushing for more substantial revision of Mao's legacy.

The late 1978 redefinition of the Tienanmen Incident as revolutionary rather than counterrevolutionary was a victory for Deng, who had been purged as a result of the incident, and a defeat for Hua, who had criticized Deng and secured the premiership after the incident. Deng's ascendancy over his nominal superior was confirmed at a CC plenum in December, which demoted some of Hua's supporters (although not Hua himself) and added Deng supporters to the Politburo. The struggle was more restrained than those of the 1966–1976 decade, but it plainly involved disputes that went beyond revision of the Tienanmen decision. There were signs of disagreement in early 1979 on the Chinese invasion of Vietnam, the pace of economic development and expansion of foreign contacts, and the proper response to the popular movement discussed above. It will not be easy for Mao's successors to avoid renewal of open factional conflict.

POLICY MAKING AND POLICY IMPLEMENTATION

The primary decision maker in the Chinese system is the CCP, which shapes policy on the basis of alternatives made known to it. The decision-making structure is therefore narrow, based on party committees acting in closed session. There is no open legislative process and relatively little issuance of public laws. Decisions take the form of general statements on policy or doctrine, or emerge as administrative directives and regulations.

In Mao's formulation, the mass line acts as a dynamic pattern of reciprocal communication between party members and citizens. It assigns the masses a continuous role in presenting their ideas to the party and carrying out decisions rendered from above. Even in its most idealized form, the mass-line principle reserves actual decision-making power for the party, and national institutions provide few opportunities for popular influence on political decisions, although influence does exist on the basic level. However, the mass line significantly broadens policy implementation by encouraging citizen participation.

The mass line's influence on policy making is reinforced by the CCP's willingness to decentralize management in many areas. When decentralization extends to primary units that include member participation, encouraging them to embark on projects of their own and to assist in the operation of schools, health facilities, and other social services, it provides the institutional opportunity for practice of the mass line's basic tenet — that the people must accept party policies as their own and demonstrate this in political action. In Mao's view, the transferral of responsibilities to the lowest feasible level is directly linked to the mass line's emphasis on direct popular action rather than bureaucratic administration.

Although the government issues legal-sounding rules, implying implementation at a specific time and procedures to enforce compliance, its decisions on many important issues have a tentative and experimental quality. They are cast in the form of general statements, indicating models to be followed or goals to be attained but not specifying exact procedures, forms, and relationships. The meaning of such a decision emerges only in practice, as lower levels begin to develop concrete responses to the tasks demanded of them. In the midst of this practice, higher levels review and investigate the early results. They may decide to accelerate or decelerate the process, publicize new models, or even issue new directives that alter the initial thrust of the policy. Members of the party elite seem to regard the attendant shifts and variations as necessary for the development of viable policies. It is their way of practicing the mass line, of refining their views through practical experience.

Decision Making

Supreme decision-making power resides in the CCP Politburo and its Standing Committee. Politburo members conduct all major CCP meetings, and there is no regular mechanism by which other organs can overrule the Politburo's decisions. This small group has broadened policy making by convening frequent and rather loosely structured meetings with other party, state, and military elites that have informed, refined, supported, and criticized its proposals. Although the Politburo controls the agenda and representation for such meetings, they prove to be vigorous working sessions that play an important role in policy formulation. Central Committee plenums have sometimes been called to review and ratify the results, but they have not figured prominently in policy making. Translation of Politburo decisions into actual directives has been the responsibility of the State Council, the central party headquarters, and the Military Affairs Committee.

Mao Zedong was long the central figure in Chinese decision making, initiating, approving, and legitimating many of the most important CCP policies. His knowledge of personalities and issues, his self-confidence and determination, his ability to persuade, and his sensitivity to tactics and strategy made him a formidable politician. As party chairman, he had ample power to shape the procedural and institutional context of elite politics. Above all, he held unique authority and prestige. His politics were occasionally criticized, resisted, or altered, but direct challenges to his leadership were doomed to failure.

For several reasons, however, it is a mistake to look on decision making under Mao as a dictatorial process. Although Mao's influence was greater than that of any other leader, his changing perceptions of priorities and his own personal style led him to exercise it unevenly. His authority over senior colleagues weakened at times, the years just before the Cultural Revolution being the best example. After the Cultural Revolution, declining vigor removed him from an active role in administration. He continued to play a decisive role in some key decisions — for example, the rapproachement with the United States, the purge of Lin Biao, and the 1976 demotion of Deng Xiaoping — but his domination of central politics was coming to a close well before his death. Mao's departure did not leave quite so large a gap in decision making as his career might suggest, which may partly explain how his successors have seemed to consolidate their control so quickly.

Moreover, other restraints limit the power of any central leaders to control the government. Decentralization allows local units to draft some of their own rules, or at least to interpret central directives flexibly; hence, central decision making is not the last word in decision making. Limitations of human and natural resources also circumscribe central decision makers' options. With the economy still depending heavily on the harvest and with popular compliance essential for the success of mass campaigns of social change, central plans may come up against unexpected and immaleable obstacles. The Great Leap Forward is probably the best example of what may happen when elites defy the uncertainties of weather, harvests, and popular morale.

Another set of questions about Chinese decision making concerns its capacity to assess rationally a significant range of policy alternatives and their possible consequences. Some observers argue that the concentration of power in a small group of party elites, combined with the insistence on unswerving loyalty to the thought of Chairman Mao, closes the process to needed unorthodox or nonparty views. But although there is ample evidence of dogmatism, the process as a whole has not excluded consideration of a wide range of alternatives. The debates and conflicts discussed earlier indicate the contrary. The real problem seems to be the hazards associated with sponsoring a rejected alternative; these hazards lead to caution in taking a stand on an issue not yet decided. The curious and frustrating language of Chinese political debate is best understood as a function of this desire to argue a position without appearing to deviate from orthodoxy.

The insistence that politics takes command, with its implied mistrust of experts and professionals, is also relevant here, and again the evidence is mixed. At times the preference of orthodoxy to expertise has contributed to poorly conceived or executed policies. Several aspects of the Great Leap reflected an absence or disregard of expert opinion; radical prejudice against professionals and technicians in the post–Cultural Revolution period stunted the growth

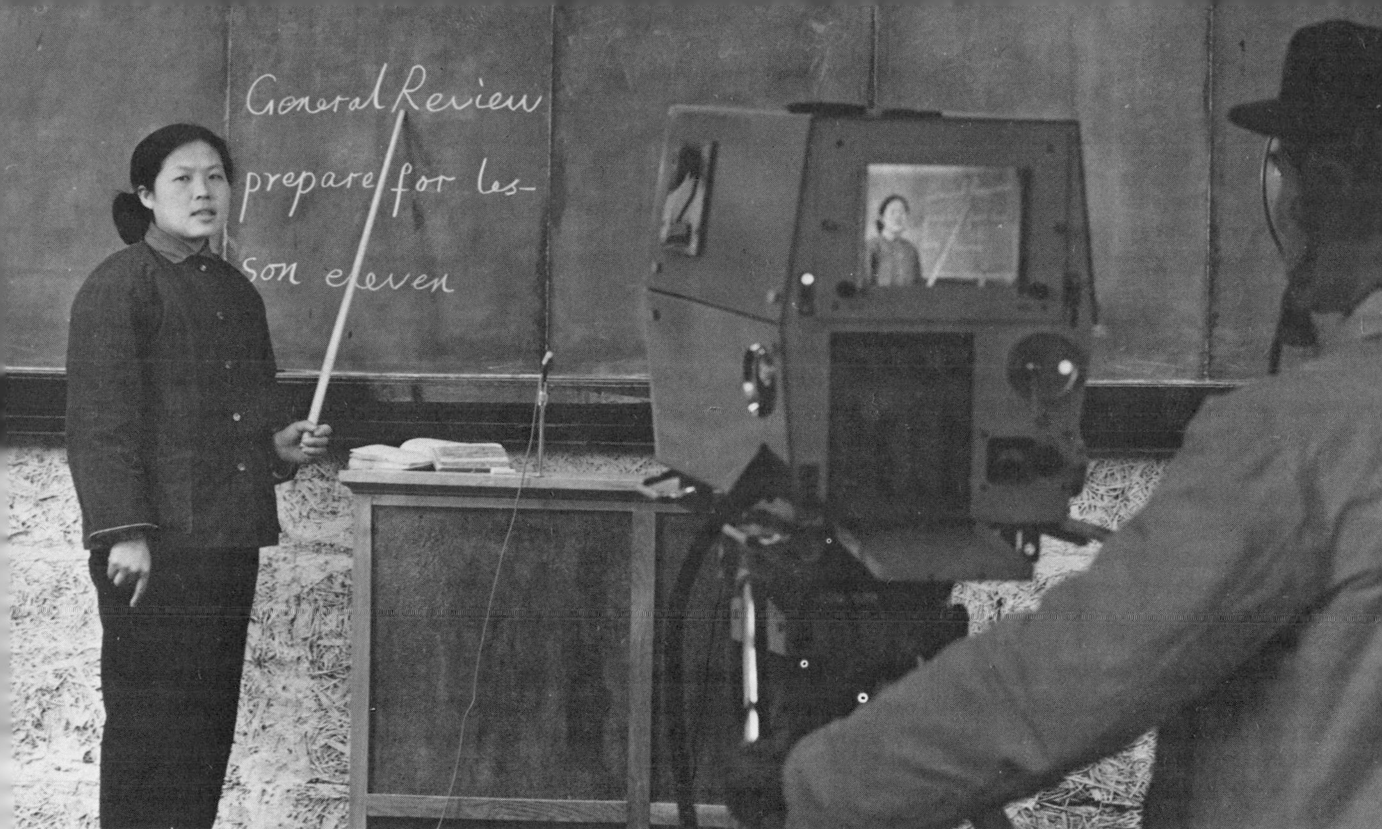

English classes on television symbolize several features of the post–1976 "four modernizations" policy: foreign language study to facilitate learning from abroad; expansion of adult education; and scientific and technological advance. All figure prominently in China's effort to modernize by the year 2000.

of Chinese technology. But in the main, Chinese elites have had access to expert opinion in their policy deliberations. The Maoist position has not been to exclude it, but to ensure that politicians rather than experts make the decisions on basic goals and priorities. Although experts have been frequent targets of abuse since 1949, the P.R.C.'s overall developmental record suggests that their services have not been renounced.

Finally, one might ask if the weakness of popular representation above the basic level and of independent political communications restricts policy makers' understanding of how decisions will be received. The answer must be yes, since the central elite relies on cadre reports filtered up through the bureaucracy for its impressions of popular mood. As in all bureaucracies, such reports reflect what bureaucrats think their superiors want to see as well as what is actually happening. However, elites have some ways of guarding against serious miscalculations of popular response. One is the combination of mass line and decentralization that leaves implementation to units better informed of local conditions. Another is the experimental approach that permits alteration of initial policies on the basis of early results.

Administration

The Chinese political system entrusts the application of its rules to a variety of structures, including state, party, and army bureaucracies and the communications systems they control; the management organs of primary units; and a multitude of popular committees, organizations, and meetings that mobilize the population for direct action on government programs. The Chinese Communists have made remarkable efforts to restrain the exercise of bureaucratic power. Although they accept the necessity of centrally directed organizational hierarchies, they have tried to ensure bureaucracy's responsiveness to political controls and to keep its structure simple and efficient. As a result, the history of bureaucracy in post-1949 China has been one of recurring tendencies to expand its role matched by counterpressures to limit it.

The Chinese Communists' mistrust of bureaucracy involves two basic principles. One accepts some degree of bureaucratization as inevitable but relies on political guidance to ensure the bureaucracy's subordination to the political leadership and its acceptance of a mass-line style. This check on the bureaucracy is simplified by the high proportion of party members serving in state organs. The drive for political control has also involved direct pressure on cadres to follow political standards of conduct, to work in a mass-line style instead of in the elitist, authoritarian style associated with bureaucracy. The techniques employed have included political study and self-criticism for cadres, the practice of xia fang, and the creation of opportunities for popular supervision and criticism of their leaders.

The other principle involved in the Chinese Communists' mistrust of bureaucracy is the view that bureaucracy is a nonproductive superstructure divorced from the front line of political struggle. As a result, the party seeks to reduce the scope of bureaucracy by transferring administrative powers to the lowest feasible level, thereby giving local units the chance to develop their own resources. Underlying this view is the conviction that creating a new political culture requires creating opportunities for local action that cannot be realized under a highly centralized system.

Control of bureaucracy is not the only rationale for decentralization. More pragmatic considerations include the desire to rationalize the economic system by encouraging diversification and regional growth, cutting transportation and distribution costs, and reducing the red tape and expense of a centralized planning apparatus. The size of the country and its uneven economic development provide powerful arguments for decentralization. Decentralization may also be a response to pressure from subnational elites, or at least a product of bargaining between central and local authorities. Finally, decentralization promotes regional self-sufficiency and economic diversification, which strengthen national capacity to withstand a war.

Decentralization is a mixed blessing. It increases the possibility of real local autonomy, of the emergence of independent kingdoms from which subnational elites defy the authority of the center. Decentralization also creates problems for national planning and data collection. China's failure since the late 1950s to articulate a detailed economic plan or publish comprehensive economic statistics is partly due to the fact that much economic activity takes place outside the center's authority. Although this does not seem to be a serious limitation on economic development now, it may become so as development proceeds. Finally, decentralization may limit the central government's capacity to control economic performance and direction. Since a large proportion of state revenue is collected and distributed by subnational governments, and since defense-related expenditures constitute a large fixed claim on central resources, the central government does not have much flexibility in its allocation of investment funds.

Despite their sensitivity to these problems, members of the Chinese elite apparently remain committed to their pattern of diffuse administration. This pattern has served as a check on bureaucratic expansionism, prepared the country for resistance to foreign attack, and compiled a creditable record of economic growth. Most significantly, perhaps, it has created an administrative system that is sensitive to the growth potential of localities and encourages them to maximize their resources. This aspect of decentralization, in combination with the mass-line style of work, supports political mobilization and community involvement among the population.

Rule Enforcement and Adjudication

Examination of how the political system enforces and adjudicates its rules begins with the formal legal system. In China, the institutions concerned are the courts, whose function is to try cases, render verdicts, and assign sentences; the procuracy, which investigates and prosecutes possible violations of law; public security or police organs; and the CCP, which is deeply involved in the entire legal process. The structure and activity of these institutions, and their relationships, set the tone of law enforcement in China. However, it is also important to note that the formal legal system plays a relatively modest role in social control. The CCP approach to law enforcement and adjudication is not highly legalistic, in the sense of reliance on statutes and institutionalized procedures for their application and interpretation. Rather, the party views social control from the perspectives of its ideology and the Chinese legal tradition, which weaken legal formalities and shift legal functions away from the structures designed to perform them.

The party has little sympathy, for example, for the idea of judicial independence. Although the 1954 Constitution stated that the courts should be independent in their administration of justice, there was little in Chinese legal history or previous Communist experience to support this principle. According to one scholar, "Law and legal institutions still serve principally as instruments for enhancing the power of the state and for disciplining the people to perform its bidding."[6] The CCP has provided few safeguards against the potential arbitrariness of the legal system. Regulatory acts often emerge as administrative edicts, subject to change and interpretation by cadres; a comprehensive criminal code, proposed in the mid-1950s, was not adopted. The right to legal defense in a public trial, cited in the 1954 Constitution, has not been regularly observed. Determination of guilt and sanctions by police and procurators or by extralegal bodies has been common.

Underlying these practices is a more fundamental emphasis on control of the person, not his or her performance. Compliance flows from the person's acceptance of rules rather than from external pressures or sanctions that enforce standards of behavior. The burden of control falls on the socializing effect of political and ideological work; if this process takes hold, the formal legal system becomes a secondary aspect of social control, necessary for dealing with recalcitrant members of society but required only in special cases that have not responded to nonlegal methods of control.

Rule enforcement in China is designed to prevent violations, ideally through voluntary compliance rather than through formal legal action. The effort to avoid legal action is evident in the relatively minor roles assigned the procuracy and the courts. However, neither the effort to prevent offenses nor the desire to minimize formal legal proceedings completely eliminates the need for coercive instruments and action.

China's coercive apparatus is extensive. It centers on the state public security system, which is tightly controlled by the CCP and particularly influential within local governments. Public security organs are resourceful and powerful. They include administrative cadres, police, and secret police; they maintain extensive files, based on both regular police reports and the numerous activities over which they have some supervisory powers (such as rationing, census, travel, and the work of popular security and mediation committees); and they have the power to arrest, investigate, adjudicate, and sentence in many cases that never reach the courts or that are subject to only nominal review and ratification by other legal arms. The police presence is not oppressive, in terms of numbers or display of force and arms, but it is backed by the militia and the PLA, which leaves little doubt about its capacity to employ force when it chooses.

The coercive apparatus also includes certain structures of a quasi-legal or extralegal nature, which have acted occasionally but with telling effect. The most prominent of these were the struggle and speak bitterness meetings, people's tribunals and mass trials of the reconstruction era, which meted out revolutionary justice to landlords, counter-revolutionaries, and other enemies of the new regime. The ad hoc measures of 1950–1952 have not been repeated on a comparable scale, but mass struggle meetings in campaigns have continued the policy of allowing extralegal institutions to bring real or threatened force to bear on political deviants.

As noted earlier, the 1978 state constitution and its supporting documents revived interest in the formal legal system, which had been neglected, if not disregarded, throughout the 1958–1976 ascendancy of the Maoist model. There was discussion of moving ahead on long-postponed civil and criminal codes, of

[6] Jerome Alan Cohen, "The Criminal Process in China," in Donald W. Treadgold (ed.), *Soviet and Chinese Communism: Similarities and Differences* (Seattle: University of Washington Press, 1967), p. 109.

closer observance of legal procedures, and of renewed study of law as an academic field. Taken with other recent trends — new policies on science and technology, efforts to modernize management systems, greater emphasis on central planning and coordination, and a general moderation of Maoist rhetoric — this legalist stance indicates that Mao's successors are embarking on a course that will, in the long run, modify the policy making and implementation described in this section. The overall process will be harder to change than specific policies, however, resting as it does on such a complex mixture of political behavior, values, and institutions. It will be a long time before the systemic consequences of recent reforms can be assessed with confidence.

PUBLIC POLICY: PERFORMANCE AND EVALUATION

This concluding section evaluates China's public policies. Ideally, evaluation would assemble statistics that quantified government performance, facilitating comparison with other systems. Tables 13.3 and 13.4 present a few relevant indicators, but statistics on the P.R.C. are relatively thin and must be used with care, especially for purposes of comparison. Accordingly, the discussion here will be a general commentary on government performance, including the system's capabilities, the outcome of its policies, and a brief evaluation of that performance.

Performance Capabilities

A system's capabilities include its capacity to extract resources, distribute goods and services, regulate behavior, and symbolize goals in ways that enhance other capabilities. In general, the P.R.C. has markedly increased all four capabilities over those of previous Chinese governments, and has thereby laid the groundwork for strengthened government performance. This expansion has been uneven, however, largely due to competition for the limited resources of what was, in 1949, a very poor and disorganized society.

The P.R.C.'s first decade brought a great increase in extractive and regulatory capability, essential for the Soviet developmental model, and more modest growth in distributive and symbolic capability. The central government rapidly acquired greater control over national resources, initially by confiscating some foreign and domestic assets but mainly by socializing the economy, which transformed profits into state revenues. More systematic tax collection also added to extractive capability. The key regulatory mechanism was, of course, the First Five-Year Plan, backed by other measures adopted in the early 1950s — rationing, wage and price controls, residential registration and occupational placement, military conscription, and so forth. Land reform was testimony to the new regime's distributive capability; it was followed by declining status for former elite groups and rising status, with modest economic gains, for the working population. Generally, however, the emerging pattern of distribution was uneven; it favored the state sector and urban groups associated with it at the expense of the rural population. Symbolic capability expanded with the development of education, communications, and the propaganda network, but was restrained by adherence to the Soviet model.

The Great Leap was an effort to increase extraction by heightened labor mobilization, but it was soon apparent that the system had overreached itself. The government simply did not have the regulatory power to control the progress and effects of the movement or to induce the peasants to continue their efforts. Symbolic appeals were called upon to fill the gap, contributing to the early momentum of the campaign, but proved to be no help for rural areas so close to the margin of survival that economic difficulties produced immediate threats of malnutrition and disaffection. In effect, the extractive thrust of the Great Leap fell victim to the relative weakness of other capabilities.

The chain of events following the economic crisis of 1959–1961 was complex, and includes the trauma of the Cultural Revolution, but generally the period from 1961 to 1976 brought pronounced emphasis on the development of distributive and symbolic capability. Under the slogan of agriculture first and with the rural-oriented policies of the Cultural Revolution, the countryside began to experience substantial gains. Material and human resources were shifted to rural units, which began to use more of their production for stockpiling, reinvestment, and distribution to commune members. The egalitarian ethic fostered by the Cultural Revolution also contributed to some leveling in society, evidenced in expanded educational opportunities for peasants and reduced differences in wages, symbols of status, and consumption patterns. Development of the symbolic capability centered on the unifying theme of Maoism, including both the personal authority of the chairman and the content of his ideas, which gave the P.R.C.'s self-image a clarity and autonomy lacking in the 1950s. The idea of a self-reliant China, leading the world revolution in opposition to the two superpowers while building a truly socialist society on the basis of collectivist ideals and self-sacrifice, was a potent tool for the mobilization of national resources.

In many ways, this expansion in distributive and symbolic capability reinforced the earlier extractive and regulatory development. Emphasis on rural areas strengthened the economic foundation, while egalitarian controls on income and consumption freed more resources for collective use. The Maoist ethic gave society a sense of purpose and collective effort that supplemented bureaucratic controls. Nonetheless, the Cultural Revolution and the factionalism of 1971–1976 exposed important contradictions in the Maoist model. Although the economy grew over this period, the slumps of 1966–1968 and 1974–1976 were cause for concern. Recurring civil disorder and violence indicated that mass mobilization actually weakened regulatory controls at times. By the mid-1970s, Maoist symbolism may have weakened, too, due to abuses committed in its name and the contradictory implications of moves like the rapprochement with the United States.

If early indicators are an accurate guide, the post-Mao leadership will strike a balance between the trends of the 1950s and the Maoist period. It is committed to a new surge of economic development that will modernize the country by the year 2000. The state will accelerate expansion of extractive capability, relying heavily on scientific and technical development (including foreign trade and technology) to serve the defense, industrial, and energy requirements of this growth. It will extend its regulatory controls to ensure adherence to a fuller and more formalized planning system. It will refine distributive capability, continuing to emphasize rural development but granting more benefits to the groups that lead modernization. It will want to retain the symbolic power generated by the Maoist model while shifting its content away from revolutionary themes that encourage political struggle toward modernizing themes that channel energies into economic development. In education, culture, and communications, it will focus more on improving quality and material facilities than on ideological purity. And if hard choices have to be made among these competing priorities, it is likely to favor extraction and regulation over distribution and symbolism.

Performance Outcomes

The preceding comments emphasized the general expansion of government capabilities and changes in their balance. The next question concerns the actual outcomes flowing from these shifting capabilities. Since general trends in Chinese economy, society, and polity were discussed previously, particularly in the survey of post-1949 history, a summary will suffice.

Economic growth has been one major product of CCP rule, transforming the weak and intermittent development of pre-1949 years into rapid, long-term industrialization. Overall growth rates have been strong, more than quadrupling GNP between 1952 and 1978 (see Table 13.4). Industrial growth has been particularly impressive, as has the rise of state investment. Gains in per capita income have been solid, though much below those in GNP, while agricultural growth has been modest. It is instructive to note that the government emphasis on agriculture after 1961 did not achieve a major breakthrough. Grain output per capita in 1976 remained roughly at the 1956–1958 level (see Table 13.3) even though population growth slowed in the 1960s and 1970s. In short, agricultural productivity remains a problem; outcomes do not yet reflect the extent of governmental energies devoted to it.

Distribution policies of the Chinese government have enhanced the per capita gains shown in aggregate data. The P.R.C. is by no means a fully egalitarian society. There are significant differences in income between the high-level cadres and professionals at the top of the pay scale and the peasants and unskilled workers at the bottom; unequal status and privilege accompany these income differentials. This is another area in which outcomes fall short of what might be expected, particularly given the symbolic efforts devoted to attainment of Maoist egalitarianism. Nonetheless, China is a relatively egalitarian society. Extreme wealth and poverty (by Chinese standards) have been eliminated, the number of people receiving higher incomes is small, and the bulk of the population has experienced important welfare gains. While incomes have risen slowly, prices have been stable and taxes have declined as a percentage of income; prices on essentials (rent, food, clothing), are quite low, those on luxury consumer goods high. A major accomplishment of policy since the late 1950s has been to keep rural areas from falling further behind advanced urban areas, although rural incomes generally remain lower than urban ones. Primary school attendance is now virtually universal, middle school attendance greatly enlarged. Distributive policies have extended such social services as health care, occupational training, maternity leave, and retirement programs. Opportunities for higher education remain very limited, however, and most Chinese citizens cannot expect much upward mobility. Distributive policies, in other words, have established low but adequate incomes and basic social services for China's vast population, while sharply restricting opportunities for greater affluence.

Security and order outcomes are difficult to assess, since so much depends on what China is compared to. In comparison to pre-1949 China, the P.R.C. appears relatively secure and orderly. The depredations of warlords, bandits, and corrupt officials are gone, as is the threat of ruin or famine that faced the lower classes during much of the revolutionary era. Public services and institutions function well in what is basically an orderly society with little crime or social unrest. Internationally, the P.R.C. is free of imperialists, has regained most of the territory that slipped from Chinese control in the preceding century, has successfully defended its frontiers against threats of foreign incursions, and has reestablished China's international influence and independence. Both domestically and internationally, the P.R.C. is far more secure than its predecessors. This is the comparison that the CCP stresses most, and there is no reason to doubt that most Chinese believe it valid.

At the same time, new security and order problems have arisen since 1949. Domestically, the most prominent have been associated with the campaign periods of 1949–1952, 1958–1960, 1966–1969, and, to a lesser extent, 1974–1976, which have destabilized Chinese society. Civil violence, personal insecurity, and economic decline have occurred in some or all of these periods, producing a pattern of recurring upheavals interspersed with longer periods of stability. The most severe effects of these campaigns have been limited to particular social groups or localities, but most Chinese have probably experienced some uncertainty from them and see this uncertainty as a direct outcome of government action. Their view might plausibly be that life is more secure than in the past but still less secure than it could be.

New international insecurities stem mainly from relations with the United States and the Soviet Union. Problems were most acute during the 1960s when China was vulnerable to attack from both of the nuclear superpowers. Rapprochement with the United States eased the situation, but relations with the U.S.S.R. worsened after the 1969 border conflict. China's continued stress on war preparedness stems from fear of Soviet attack. Its risky invasion of Vietnam in early 1979 was mainly a reaction to Vietnamese expansion, which the Chinese saw as a vehicle for Soviet encirclement of China. P.R.C. territorial claims — principally with regard to Taiwan, Hong Kong, Macao, and various island groups to the east and south — are also issues that might produce confrontations in the future. Generally, the P.R.C. is secure as an independent state, but must now accept the risks and costs of possible nuclear conflict. As a relatively weak military power in nuclear terms, it will have profound national security concerns for the foreseeable future.

Finally, government policies have strengthened the Chinese national identity and, to some extent, pushed it in new directions. Unification of the country, successful economic development, and growing international status — including the acquisition of nuclear and space technology — provide tangible signs of national regeneration. Expansion of education and communications facilities, leading to greatly increased literacy and use of the national spoken language, promotes national integration. Popular participation gives ordinary citizens greater information about their country and some sense of personal involvement in its affairs. China has always had a strong sense of a common history and tradition, but in the past the tradition in question was mainly that of the Confucian elite, which the masses did not wholly share. In broadening material and cultural linkages among all the people, the CCP has injected populism into national identity, made the people more forward looking, and tied them to global processes of revolution, industrialization, and modernization. The historical and cultural tradition is by no means rejected, since it establishes links with past greatness, but its central role in shaping Chinese identity is giving way to new images of what it means to be Chinese.

Chinese national identity is not wholly homogeneous, of course. The non-Chinese minorities who constitute about 6 percent of the population do not share fully the Chinese identity and will not be easily assimilated. If experience elsewhere is a guide, neither the Chinese nor the minorities have yet come to terms with what integration requires of them. There are divisions among the Chinese, too, in the commitment to traditional symbols of identity (there is still ambivalence on how to deal with Confucius and the written literary tradition) and to Maoist images of the future. Despite the purge of the Gang of Four, many Chinese undoubtedly cling to more nativist and populist images of China's future, looking with suspicion on the current drive to modernize, with its implications of foreign contacts and techniques. Thus, the increasing integration of Chinese society, with widespread recognition of national accomplishments, does not mean that national identity is fixed or no longer an element in cultural, social, and political conflict.

Evaluation

This chapter has revolved around three major themes of China's revolutionary era: restoration of national status and power; creation of a new political community that adapts socialist institutions to the Chinese setting; and attainment of socioeconomic development. The P.R.C. has made significant progress in all three areas. Indeed, the passing of Mao suggests that the revolutionary era has ended and that China is entering a new stage, in which goals will reflect the different circumstances and assumptions of a postrevolutionary era. This is a way of saying that the Maoist model successfully negotiated the transition from the revolutionary to the postrevolutionary era. This final section will go a step further, with a brief evaluation not linked so specifically to the uniqueness of the Chinese revolution, to identify relative strengths and weaknesses of China on issues of more universal concern in political analysis.

One such issue is the balance between stability and adaptation, with the Chinese system favoring the latter. There have been elements of stability since 1949. The prolonged leadership of a small group of senior party elites was one; continuity in many local economic and residential units is another. There have also been periods of stronger concern for stable, institutionalized growth, as in the mid-1950s and the immediate post-1976 period. In the main, however, the early revolutionary campaigns and the subsequent ascendancy of the Maoist model emphasized change and experimentation and were suspicious of institutionalization. As a result, the system has responded well to pressures for adaptation in both domestic and international arenas, while resisting or undercutting arguments for stabilization.

Another general issue concerns the quality of participation in politics, including compliance with and trust in the process as well as direct acts of participation. The Chinese citizen receives high demands for compliance and support, which are legitimized by national goals and collective interest as well as by explicit assertions about the correctness of party leadership. Much of what appears as participation is compliance with elite directives in which citizens have had little say. The process offers few guarantees of procedural justice or consistency. It portrays politics as largely a struggle between two wholly contradictory lines, in which incorrect positions must be eradicated without legal or procedural encumbrances. The process is frequently subjective and erratic, participation inherently hazardous. The point should not be overstated, however. Citizens learn which issues carry some guarantees and which are most vulnerable to intervention; they can participate with greater assurance than foreign observers might think. But the fact remains that guarantees at one time prove unreliable at another, positions or leaders once correct are later incorrect, and the authorized scope of citizen political activity shifts from one campaign period to another. Popular participation is highly valued and actively solicited, but reflects this mixture of high demands for compliance and low predictability of consequences. It is very weak as a mechanism for advancing interests or influencing decisions above the basic level. On the other hand, it contributes to interest articulation and decision making in primary units and serves as an important mode of citizen identification with and commitment to the political community.

A final issue concerns benefits derived from the government. The Chinese system emphatically places state and collective interests above those of individuals, so it is no surprise to observe that the state is the primary beneficiary of government distribution or that strengthened national security and economic development have priority over increased individual income. Over most of the post-1949 period, however, government resources have been sufficient to provide benefits for both state and society. The general pattern of distribution has emphasized a relatively egalitarian income structure and a broad dispersal of social services that provide low-level income and welfare benefits for the population as a whole; it has guaranteed minimal economic security for all with few frills for anyone, except a small elite, and even that is not exceptionally privileged. The system offers little mobility or choice to most citizens. Wages, prices, educational opportunities, job assignments, residence, and many economic options are subject to varying degrees of state regulation. Equality and security take precedence over liberty.

As China entered the post-Mao era, its leaders acknowledged the need for new policies to accommodate the new stage. Their statements explicitly referred to more stability, more procedural or legal equity and consistency, and, at least intellectually and culturally, more liberty. They were even more assertive, however, in their commitment to continuing rapid industrial growth, to raising the rate of agricultural growth, and to meeting a host of new national goals in energy development and advanced scientific and technical development. Whether or not the Chinese political system can develop its capacities fast enough to meet both sets of goals remains to be seen.

KEY TERMS

Maoism
Guomindang (KMT)
mass line
Cultural Revolution
capitalist roader
Politburo
People's Liberation Army (PLA)
Chinese communist party (CCP)
dazibao (wall posters)
warlord
Long March
Great Leap Forward
Gang of Four
National People's Congress
democratic centralism
cadre
Mao Zedong
Zhou Enlai
Hua Guofeng
Deng Xiaoping

Mexico
UNITED STATES
Gulf of Mexico
Gulf of Campeche
Caribbean Sea
PACIFIC OCEAN
Gulf of California
Gulf of Tehuantepec
Tiajuana
Mexicali
Juárez
BAJA CALIFORNIA NORTE
BAJA CALIFORNIA SUR
SONORA
Yaqui R.
CHIHUAHUA
Chihuahua
Conchos R.
Bravo del Norte R.
COAHUILA
NUEVO LEÓN
Monterrey
SINALOA
DURANGO
ZACATECAS
TAMAULIPAS
SAN LUIS POTOSÍ
Tampico
Pánuco R.
NAYARIT
AGUAS-CALIENTES
GUANAJUATO
León
JALISCO
Guadalajara
Querétaro
QUERÉTARO
HIDALGO
Santiago R.
MÉXICO
FEDERAL DISTRICT
TLAXCALA
Puebla
MORELOS
PUEBLA
COLIMA
MICHOACÁN
Balsas R.
GUERRERO
OAXACA
VERACRUZ
Veracruz
TABASCO
CHIAPAS
Mezcalapa R.
CAMPECHE
YUCATÁN
Mérida
QUINTANA ROO
BELIZE
GUATEMALA
HONDURAS
0
400
Scale of Miles

CHAPTER FOURTEEN

ROBERT E. SCOTT

Politics in Mexico

THE MEXICAN MIRACLE

Mexico is the world's most populous Spanish-speaking country, with 72 million inhabitants in 1980 and growing almost 3 percent each year, about twice the rate of the United States or Canada. Mexico has more people than any Western European state and in Latin America is second only to huge Brazil in population and gross national product. During the 1970s Mexico was economically in the middle range, not on a par with the advanced industrialized states but one of the higher income industrializing, non-oil exporting countries, well above most Asian and African nations and over the average for Latin America. Discovery of large petroleum and natural gas reserves late in the decade markedly increased the country's economic potential.

Many leaders of emerging states see Mexico's political system as a model adaptable to their own needs for social and political structures capable of handling the multiple difficulties accompanying speedy economic development. Like Mexico earlier in this century, most developing nations face problems of regionalism, unbalanced growth, disputes among disparate interests, and the confrontation of modern with traditional values, exacerbated usually by rapidly rising popular expectations and frequently by exploding populations.

Beleaguered politicians search for mechanisms that can contain tensions arising from frequently irreconcilable claims on government. They seek ways of involving the citizenry in politics and also concentrating authority, to ensure national integration. They must distribute material benefits widely through a mass consumption economy and simultaneously channel resources toward investment in transportation, communications, and industry. Sad experience makes such leaders despair of achieving the slow, incremental evolution that produced integrated, representative, and responsible government in Western Europe and North America. Instead, they see their situations as analogous to Mexico's modernizing experience, though they are at an earlier stage because their countries began development much later.

Long before modernization disrupted most other Third World peoples, pressures engendered by change shattered Mexico's traditional order. In the wake of the Revolution of 1910, new factions entered the national arena. For twenty years near chaos reigned, as emerging interests contended among themselves and with more established interests. By the early 1930s a coherent and organized political system began to establish constructive and complementary relationships among the competing interests. The system was based on a relatively consistent approach to development and on the resolution of political and social conflicts through the operations of mutually reinforcing political structures. A strong presidency, bolstered by a dominant official party servicing a Revolutionary elite, focused and stabilized government efforts to encourage economic growth and social progress. An effective national integrating mechanism was at work.

In the quarter century after 1940 newly independent or recently revitalized states all over the world were struggling to organize viable political systems which could handle the multiple problems accompanying development. During this period, Mexico was demonstrating the impressive dividends paid by an orderly decision making process based on effective political structures. Considering the country's social and economic levels of fifty or even twenty-five years earlier, today's indicators of its development — improvement in literacy, urbanization, industrialization, and a shift from subsistence farming toward commercial food and fiber production — suggest a remarkable record of achievement, especially in light of the burdens imposed by rapid population growth. No wonder politicians around the world are tempted to adopt similar arrangements, in hopes of duplicating the "Mexican Miracle."

Of course, Mexico's experience over a half century provides no magic formula for instant modernization, nor any pat solutions for governance problems elsewhere. The country's development process began before the rate and range of change accelerated in most of the emerging world, preceding the explosions in communications and education that forced simultaneous crises in material distribution and political participation on so many other governments. Mexico's leaders enjoyed the luxury of time. From the 1930s until the 1950s, they had relatively few internal or external pressures, while the present political arrangements could evolve and become institutionalized, legitimized by the symbols of the 1910 Revolution.

During the formation of the present political system, the emerging Revolutionary elites were able to impose their own political and developmental criteria on the tractable Mexican masses, accustomed to accepting direction from above and not yet sensing the possibility of self-determination. The system worked precisely because its political structures operated in accordance with long established and widely held understandings about the power and political relationships of a subject political culture.

The subject-oriented structures that perform important functions in Mexico's political system are not modern, but more efficient versions of traditional semiauthoritarian mechanisms. Technology enables them to penetrate once isolated regions and to permeate once insulated minds as they perform centralized control operations, whether the control is physical, by road or airplane; mental, by mass media or near universal primary education; or political, by drawing more people into the national society and economy at the same time that expanding bureaucratized government services and regulations make that sector of society ever more dependent on the regime. Two pervasive factors influence these carryovers from the earlier era. One is the dominant leader-passive follower dependency relationship, personified in the paternalistic role of the President of the Republic. The other is the representation of interests not through individual citizen action but through collective units particularly in the functionally organized government party, the Partido Revolucionario Institucional (PRI).

Third World leaders involved in a more modern development phase cannot count on either the time or the tradition that enabled the Mexican political system to evolve, so merely copying governmental organization will not serve, as Brazil, Peru, and other states have learned. Furthermore, recent breaks in the facade of stable and orderly Mexican politics suggest that congruence between the operating political structures and the political culture no longer may be complete. Since 1965 long-deferred demands for material distribution and political participation have increasingly disrupted the political system. The stability that permitted economic development and social progress produces new conditions that generate different attitudes toward the government's responsibility for the general welfare and the citizens' right to share in policy making. Greater awareness, reinforced by involvement in national life and the money economy, leads an expanding minority of Mexicans to question the legitimacy of the existing subject-oriented system and to seek more democratic, participant politics.

The 1968 university student Olympic riots, the 1976 agricultural invasions, and continuing urban as well as rural unrest during the rest of the decade all evidence the frustrations felt by emerging elements who challenge persistent traditional values and the political action patterns they spark. Some Mexican leaders recognize the need to update the political process, but their efforts to do so are hampered by the defense tactics of other *políticos* (politicians), who control the functional organizations representing vested interests that are embedded deeply in the existing governmental system. Not even the immense authority of the president himself can change that system easily.

Third World leaders should look to the Mexican experience not as a model of integration but to reach an understanding of the problems inherent in the transition from traditional to modern government. Like most Third World countries, Mexico faces a dual set of pressures — one traditional, semi-authoritarian, corporative, and rigid; the other more nearly modern, calling for flexible, representative, responsible constitutional government. The traditional system served effectively as a national integrating mechanism because it reflected dominant subject political culture values that saw the best "politics of scarcity" as a scarcity of politics. But the success of this arrangement caused new conditions to evolve, and they call for a shift to a modern political mechanism that can respond to the expectations of an increasingly informed citizenry and balance a multiplicity of interests resulting from functional specialization.

To comprehend the complexity of the task facing the political reform attempting to convert one governmental system into another, we must consider in detail the setting in which this transformation is taking place.

THE GENERAL SETTING

Historical Perspective

Considering Mexico's present degree of integration, it is hard to believe that until a very few years ago nearly every geographic, economic, and social fact seemed to conspire against uniting its distinct regions and social groups. The land is splintered into a multitude of tiny sections and a few larger regions, all separated by rugged mountains, deep valleys, and almost impassable deserts. Mexico's few rivers were unsuitable for easy transportation and, for the most part, were poorly located to supply irrigation water for farming. A great arid section had once isolated vast northern territories from the more densely settled intermountain basins around Mexico City, so that much of what now is Texas, California, Arizona, and adjacent regions was lost to the United States. The subtropical Isthmus of Tehuantepec split the core area from the south, leaving the present-day states of Chiapas, Campeche, Yucatán, and Quintana Roo nearly independent from the center.

During the colonial era and into the post-1821 independence period, those natives who managed to keep control of their lands and escape subjugation by Europeans clustered in villages around a parish church. The inhabitants of these *pueblos* gradually developed a sense of isolation, inwardness, and suspicion of others as they struggled over land claims and water rights with neighbors, nearby localities, or encroaching *hacendados* (large landowners). For their part, those running the *haciendas* ("ranches" or "plantations") had few local ties and did little to strengthen a regional or national economy. They produced mainly for their own consumption or for export outside the locality. The terrain impeded easy shipment of goods and inhibited frequent movement of people or the spread of common ideas. Localism and mistrust of strangers were far stronger than nationalism or a sense of common interest and general welfare.

Indians spoke a bewildering array of languages, observed different social customs, and had no cross-regional economic ties to bring them together. The one thing they shared was fear and mistrust of their Spanish or *criollo* (Mexican-born) rulers. The European-oriented aristocracy looked on the Indians as savages permitted to exist simply because they could be exploited, almost like beasts of burden. Even after the first vestiges of a nonracial class system appeared in the nineteenth century, most cultural Indians and *mestizos* (persons of mixed Indian-European culture) were groups apart, separate from each other and from any sense of the nation. There were exceptions, like Benito Juárez, a full-blooded Zapotec Indian from the state of Oaxaca and a successful lawyer who became Mexico's greatest president when he led a national liberation movement against the French during the 1860s. But for every Juárez there were a hundred thousand mestizos and a million Indians still thinking in localistic terms. Despite some mobility into the ruling elites, not even the 1910 Revolution put an end to the stratified class system, because divisive elements in the environment remained too powerful.

For four hundred years the vast majority of Mexicans have been Roman Catholics of sorts, with beliefs ranging from orthodoxy to a Christian-pagan cult of the saints, but as a social institution the church has often been more disruptive than unifying. During the colonial period the religious hierarchy identified strongly with the aristocracy, though two priests, fathers Miguel Hidalgo and José Morelos, sounded the first cries for separation from Spain, identifying independence with social justice for the popular masses. After independence, the church remained a principal landowner until presidents Juárez and Sebastian Lerdo de Tejada stripped it of its holdings in the 1860s. Under President Porfirio Díaz these lands were taken over by lay *latifundistas* (landholders); even so, most clergy identified with the large landholders and other conservatives during the early days of the 1910 Revolution. They continued to do so during the 1926–1929 Cristero Rebellion, which opposed President Plutarco Elías Calles's rigorous application of the anticlerical provisions of the 1917 Constitution. Today for the most part the church plays a reduced role in national politics, partly because it has learned to separate religious from secular concerns and partly because it has little access for making its concerns felt in decision making.

Historically, then, divisiveness in land and institutions made integration of the country's people and politics virtually impossible. Only the strongest centralized authority could overcome such barriers, and then only for a time. Prior to 1910, Mexico was caught in a recurring cycle of overconcentrated power followed by near anarchy. Periodically, fragmented and antagonistic local units would be bound together by a centralizing power that tried to counteract separatist influences, only to see its efforts fail and coordination turn into chaos. The inability of regional and social groups to pool their resources and act as a single unit permitted the Spanish conquerors to defeat the Aztecs in the sixteenth century, helped the criollos win independence from Spain in 1821, and eased the way for North American and French invaders during the nineteenth century. Some Mexicans today say that lack of national focus still encourages foreign cultural and economic imperialism.

In the 1870s, the dictatorship of General Porfirio Díaz achieved political stability and material progress through centralized control. His regime lasted nearly forty years, and introduced industrialism, though at terrible human cost to the laborers who toiled on the haciendas, slaved in the mines, and built the railroads. Many of President Díaz's Cabinet ministers espoused the supposedly scientific philosophy of positivism as a justification for exploiting "inferior" Indian and mestizo workers. To officials accepting such ideas, popular misery was a reasonable price to pay for economic growth, for human labor was simply one more factor in production.

Positivism, a highly materialistic doctrine that applies a simplified version of the "survival of the fittest" evolutionary concept to human beings in economic situations, offers a rationalization for elitist authoritarian social attitudes that permits a tiny ruling group to take ruthless advantage of an uneducated, disorganized, and submissive lower class. The effect of positivism carries over to present-day Mexico in the condescension toward the common people of the *patrón* (the paternalistic authoritarian leader), the technocratic government official, and the functional group leader, all of whom are lineal heirs of the *científicos* (as General Díaz's Cabinet members were known, because they followed "scientific" social theories). It also contributes to the lingering mistrust of authority exhibited by the popular masses, who see their relationship to government as a contest between "us" and "them."

After the Díaz regime fell in 1910, Francisco Madero, the liberal reformist lawyer who became president, was unable to organize a workable constitutional government. In 1913 he was murdered by General Victoriano Huerta, after which power was seized by regional caudillos, military chieftains like Emiliano Zapata, Pancho Villa, Álvaro Obregón, or Plutarco Elías Calles. These "generals" led local uprisings throughout the country, usually in search of land distribution, social justice, and personal influ-

Mexico's isolated southeast produces a petroleum boom, but like this torch burning off unused natural gas, it leaves little for the inhabitants of rural Tabasco except uncontrolled inflation.

ence, often with a touch of antiforeign nationalism as well. Once again the cycle had turned and confusion reigned.

The 1910 Revolution had no formal ideology to give it shape. Not even the 1917 Constitution, which contained an extensive list of social, economic, and political aspirations, provided a program around which regional leaders could rally, because most of the reforms it called for required an effective national government and therefore were not possible under existing conditions. Between 1910 and 1925 the population declined, as nearly a million Mexicans were shot or starved to death. Around the mid-1920s the situation began to stabilize, as most military politicians perceived that the needs of their followers as well as their personal advantage lay in an end to chaos. The two most powerful caudillos contested for dominance but the stronger, General Obregón, was assassinated, leaving General Calles in supreme power. He consolidated his authority in 1929 by setting up the National Revolutionary party.

At first, political initiative was shared by regional party leaders and General Calles, especially during the five years that he used the party to control the three puppet presidents who succeeded him. In 1934, however, General Lázaro Cárdenas became president and recaptured political ascendancy for the incumbent chief executive, reorganizing the party into the functional sector pattern that still exists. He also began to make the various subunits of the Revolutionary coalition dependent on the presidency, enormously strengthening the office but leading directly to the trap of concentrating all principal political functions in one person.

In the beginning the official party's function in the political system shifted to accommodate new conditions, but it has done so less during the past several decades, when authority has been centralized. The party originated as a loose confederation of local political bosses and military strong men, but as power slowly moved toward the center the political system became more formally structured and its participating interest groups more interdependent. Existing functional associations like labor unions were absorbed into its machinery or new ones set up — *ejido* (communal) farmers' leagues, government bureaucratic organizations, or schoolteachers' unions, for example. These units became part of the party's labor, agrarian, or popular (middle class) sectors, dependent on the national party and undermining the support base of local políticos. In time, as the party could not adequately aggregate increasingly competitive interests within the system, the president assumed the balancing function, providing a nucleus around which power could focus.

Since its inception the government party has borne three names. Until 1937 it was called the National Revolutionary Party (Partido Nacional Revolucionario, or PNR); between 1937 and 1945 it was the Party of the Mexican Revolution (Partido de la Revolución Mexicana, or PRM); since 1945 it has been the Institutional Revolutionary Party (Partido Revolucionario Institucional, or PRI). Note the legitimizing reference to the Revolution in each name, though some Mexicans assert that the party today is more concerned with perpetuating status quo "institutions" than with encouraging "Revolutionary" change.

How is it that the Mexican Revolution did not engender an entirely new political system? The response is simple. Unless it is written on a completely clean slate, with all previous experience and social values wiped out, no revolution can be all pervading. Mexico's was not. Like the French and Russian revolutions, Mexico's upheaval in 1910 was a true revolution; it shattered many institutional and individual relationships. It ended, reduced, or challenged the stultifying influence of such entrenched power groups as the aristocratic latifundistas, foreign-dominated mining, utility, and large business interests, and the conservative hierarchy of the Roman Catholic church. The political process was taken over by a Revolutionary coalition of regional military politicians who gradually shared their power with certain middle-class elements, notably leaders of interest organizations grouping labor or small-scale agriculture, lawyers, engineers, and other professionals, as well as Mexican industrial and commercial entrepreneurs. But the exchange of elites did not immediately alter the semiauthoritarian relationship between a clique of select leaders and the popular masses, for most citizens were not yet prepared to take independent political initiative.

As in the French and Soviet experiments, the reforms introduced by Mexico's Revolution were not as pervasive as first suggested by the rallying cries of change, especially in the political realm. The 1917 Constitution that replaced the 1857 document carried over formal provisions concerning government organization which had been copied almost verbatim from the United States Constitution. Equally important, many traditional values and practices were unaffected by the two decades of violence and confusion after 1910. Despite Revolutionary stress on social justice and a need for improving the condition of the masses, for example, prevailing norms did not encourage direct individual participation in national political life.

By the 1930s most regional *caudillos* (military chiefs) and *caciques* (local political bosses) recognized that their personal ambition and reformist aspirations would best be served by submitting to a stabilizing and centralizing national political organization. The mechanism that evolved was a dominant party controlled by an all-powerful President of the Republic, an arrangement not unlike that prior to 1910. How could it be otherwise? A subject political culture still conditioned the values and actions of most Mexicans, both leaders and followers.

Once national integration structures acted to restore calm, deeply-rooted traditional political attitudes and the relationships they evoked reasserted themselves. Even as each succeeding president advocated greater political involvement for all the people, he and his collaborators acted to revive Mexico's long-standing patrón-client arrangement, with the chieftain assuming a paternalistic stance, imposing his own judgments rather than encouraging mass input or responding to citizen demands. Popular political initiative was rare anyway, for elite control occurred naturally when most members of the lower classes accepted a submissive role. The great majority of Mexicans lacked sufficient political knowledge or skills to influence local or national policy, and as they were predominantly subsistence farmers or marginal city workers with no immediate stake in government programs, they had little incentive to learn how to.

Opportunities for individual participation in politics actually diminished after 1940. Seeking to build a broad power base and at the same time rationalize the conflicts of proliferating social and economic interests, the regime moved away from rudimentary participatory political mobilization toward Hispanic-style corporative representation through functional units manipulated by their leaders. This disciplinary mobilization gradually became institutionalized, as the evolving political system coopted existing groups and even formed new ones to capture emerging elements. Some were brought into the government party's three sectors, while others operated outside the organization but enjoyed access to the policy process through contacts with the president and government departments. These nonparty groupings with quasi-legal entry to government included Chambers of Commerce and of Industry, bankers and insurance associations, employer groups, "colleges" of engineers, lawyers, and other professionals, and bodies representing many other socioeconomic elements.[1]

Nearly exclusive collective representation of interests through associations inside and out of the official party which dealt directly with the president or an executive department, attenuated the influence of political or legal structures the average citizen might use to exercise influence. Because individual voters had no real voice in selecting congressional candidates, or influence over their actions once they were seated, elections became formalistic rituals to which it has become harder to attract voters, particularly as the legislature has delegated its independent policy-making function to the executive.

The opportunity for mass participation decreased in direct proportion to the expansion of group intervention, which had a chilling effect on the system's elasticity. Growing economic and social complexity bred functional specialization, which produced new interests seeking accommodation. But the natural tendency of those groups already in the power structure was to freeze out challengers to protect their own positions. This reduced the possibility of updating the political system to meet changing conditions, which resulted in the systemic crises of the late 1960s and 1970s.

Sensing the necessity for basic change, President Luis Echeverría (1970–1976) sought quick solutions to the crises in participation and distribution early in his administration. He tried to ease central control over the official party so that popular pressure could force wider disbursement of public benefits among the hungry masses. But the system protected its own. The president's influence over policy moved down only as far as the heads of the organized interest groups making up the PRI's three functional sectors, rather than to the rank-and-file members or to the majority of citizens outside the party. Once it became clear that the in-group leadership had no intention of sharing political initiative or material advantage with challengers in or out of the "Revolutionary Family," the president reconcentrated political power in a new PRI central hierarchy that would work with him at least to compel short-term economic assistance programs for the desperately needy, increasingly vocal masses.

The remaining two years of Echeverría's term were insufficient to implement his distributive policies, much less to establish mechanisms for greater popular participation in decision making. To counter foot dragging by government bureaucrats who share the protectionist attitudes of their clientele groups in the Revolutionary party's functional organizations, he reverted to the traditional authoritarian stance of the all-powerful President of the Republic who imposes his own policy with a minimum of consultation with contending forces.

Part of Echeverría's difficulty in satisfying demands for participation and distribution resulted from the worldwide recession, fueled in Mexico by rampant inflation reflecting too fast an explosion of government service agencies and programs. But his major problem was the inability of the established political machinery to accommodate changing conditions affecting large portions of the population.

[1] A tendency toward corporative grouping is widespread throughout Latin America. In Mexico the pattern is more structured than elsewhere because of the formalized relationships among functional groups in the government party's three sectors and the acceptance of quasi-legal roles for many interest organizations in the governmental process. For a discussion of the general phenomenon of such private governments, see Robert E. Scott, "Political Elites and Political Modernization," in Seymour Martin Lipset and Aldo Solari (eds.), *Elites in Latin America* (New York: Oxford University Press, 1967).

On taking office in 1976, President José López Portillo (1976–1982) inherited a political system under siege, with entrenched groups defending their vested interests against emerging elements who see more access to decision making as ensuring a fairer share of government benefits. His first response to the systemic crisis was economic. To gain time for long-term solutions he sought to stabilize conditions and reduce inflation through an Alliance for Production, not unlike former British Prime Minister Callaghan's Social Contract. In rural areas, landless peasant invasions of private holdings that were productive were discouraged while land allocation policy was reexamined and agro-industrial growth pushed. In the cities consumer price rises were controlled and wage increases limited, to encourage private investment that could increase employment and expand production.

During the first half of López Portillo's term, government austerity and the announcement of the discovery of vast oil resources, coupled with an improved balance of trade, reduced inflation to a more manageable level and eased immediate economic pressures. But the underlying causes of the pressures remain — a rapidly growing population, insufficient arable land inefficiently worked, unbalanced industrial and commercial development, serious unemployment, internal mass migration sparking an urban explosion, and rapidly expanding popular expectations. Such problems can be addressed effectively only if the political system becomes flexible enough to handle proliferating claims on government from outside as well as within the established Revolutionary coalition.

President López Portillo therefore inaugurated a major political reform. The principal announced aims were to inculcate a sense of political efficacy in the average Mexican and to encourage popular input into policy making. This would return government to the more participant pattern long proclaimed in the Constitution and by Revolutionary rhetoric but diverted after 1929 by the emergence of the party system. Learning from his predecessor's frustrations, López Portillo moved carefully. He started his reform from the bottom, retaining the president's authority so that the changes could be enforced against recalcitrant vested interests, but removing some barriers to popular political activity and attempting to provide a pluralistic setting in which citizens espousing all shades of opinion could play a role in policy making.

Under the leadership of the Secretary of Gobernación, Lic. Jesús Reyes Heroles, a commission on political reform held extensive hearings and presented a comprehensive but varied set of proposals for change. To some extent, this well publicized attempt to legislate reform created a false sense of popular expectations, for not all of the recommendations were adopted and those that were could not always alter long established patterns of political action. In a few cases — such as the suggestions to allow the citizens of the national capital to elect their own Regent (mayor) or at least to influence municipal policy through an initiative and referendum procedure — the proposals were permitted to languish and opposition political parties took them up as campaign issues during the 1979 congressional election.

Late in 1977 a new Law of Political Organizations and Electoral Processes (LOPPE) eased requirements for registration of political parties, providing them with public financing of campaigns and with free radio and television time. A constitutional amendment doubled the size of the national Chamber of Deputies to 400 members, of whom at least a hundred would be assigned to opposition parties by proportional representation. It also required minority party representation in state and local legislatures. Another amendment assigned exclusive oversight responsibility in foreign affairs to the Senate and in finance and decentralized government agency operations to the Chamber.

During 1978 a political amnesty freed many dissidents who had acted against the established governmental system; some of these "joined" the system, participating in the following year's elections. In August, 1978, the PRI's ninth General Assembly amended its statutes to permit somewhat greater rank-and-file participation in party activities and in the nomination process but the degree to which these changes were implemented in practice was slight. Finally, three new national political parties were registered legally, making a total of seven for the 1979 mid-term elections to the national Chamber of Deputies.[2]

[2] In addition to the PRI, previously recognized parties included the conservative National Action party (Partido de Acción Nacional, or PAN), the Marxist-intellectual Popular Socialist party (Partido Popular Socialista, or PPS), and

Implementation of change has proved as difficult for José López Portillo as for Luìs Echeverría, however, because the existing corporatively organized and elitist system works against legitimatizing opposition movements or welcoming mass involvement in politics. Probably no political reform could hope to accomplish such goals by simple fiat, for statutory enactment or redrafting of party rules do not erase long established patterns of paternalistic leadership or organized group control around which a political system has operated for a half century. Pluralism — accepting the right of differing interests or points of view to exist and compete politically — was not legislated into being with the Political Organizations Law and the registration of new parties. Organized opposition groups will gain legitimacy only as suspicion against them eases. That can occur only by working within the "Revolutionary" system. No amnesty will incorporate the urban guerrillas who use kidnapping and assassination as political gestures of their rejection of the system.

Given its corporative structure, operating inside the system requires the acceptance of group rather than individual politics. Generally the political reforms implemented during the late 1970s have done nothing to weaken the in-group's monopoly of power and little to permit entry of challenging emergent interests. In fact, many changes have reinforced the existing arrangements, which interfere with the emergence of more flexible structures that might encourage greater citizen activity. In terms of being elected or sitting in PRI councils, participation has become easier for leaders of newly recognized parties and for a few (but not all) challenging labor or farm groups. But it is not easier for rank-and-file members or for the great majority of Mexicans, whose unorganized needs and aspirations are unable to force access to the decision-making process. Nor does the average voter sense much likelihood of influencing public policy through party militancy, much less through active support of PRI or opposition party candidates who are already committed to the groups they lead. For this reason, many citizens are unmoved by election campaigns and are apathetic toward voting.

The PRI's 1978 General Assembly explains why. For all the talk of change, it failed to restructure itself to end the in-group functional representation pattern and open the party to new interests and popular influences. Offering membership to individuals and emerging functional groups is not attractive because the new members or the new group must affiliate with an existing party organization that dominates the sector's share of nominations to elective office and monopolizes clientele relationships with the executive departments. In effect, the new recruits are absorbed into the party machinery that defends the status quo.

Few other reforms are apt to satisfy growing popular expectations for a voice in politics. Doubling the size of the Chamber of Deputies, ensuring opposition parties minority membership in legislatures, even granting policy review authority to Congress, means little to the increasingly sophisticated citizen who sees that elected legislators cannot influence policy significantly as long as initiative remains with the chief executive. Similarly, minority members in a state legislature manipulated by the governor, or (if it should ever come to pass) an elected council for the Federal District dominated by a presidentially appointed "Regent" can do little to resolve local problems, especially while most fiscal resources remain under the control of the central government.

Despite President López Portillo's attempt to increase the number of political parties and encourage the rank and file's involvement, low public interest in nominations and election campaigns, culminating in low voter turnout, suggests that a growing number of Mexicans believe that party activities do not provide them with any real leverage to affect public policy.

The 1978–1979 municipal elections are a case in point. In selecting candidates for *presidente municipal* (mayor) and *regidores* (councilmen) for almost 1000 *municipios* (city-council governments) in sixteen states, the PRI tried to apply *democrácia transparente* ("showcase democracy"). Assemblies of local party members used secret ballots to elect delegates to municipal nominating conventions, which then named candidates in open session. The general public showed little interest in the selection process and less in the elections that followed.

a spinoff of the PRI, the Authentic Revolutionary party (Partido Auténtico de la Revolución Mexicana, or PARM). New parties recognized in 1978 were the Communists (Partido Comunista Mexicano, or PCM), the Socialist Workers party (Partido Socialista de los Trabajadores, or PST), part of whose members spun off from the PPS, and the rightist, Sinarquista-inspired Mexican Democratic party (Partido Demócrata Mexicano, or PDM).

The local election experience in the state of Mexico illustrates how strongly the established político reacted against the reform and how little the average citizen cared. The Revolutionary party's formal nomination process was impressive: 1.5 million *priístas* (members of the PRI) selected some 35,000 delegates to conventions in 121 municipios. In smaller, more isolated cities the PRI's indirect selection process worked smoothly, sometimes because the caciques accepted the decisions of the delegates, but usually because the convention named candidates already approved by the state governor and the local leaders. Significantly, in larger and more politically sophisticated cities like Nezahualcóyotl, Ecetepec, or Cuautitlán, and in some smaller towns as well, traditional bosses resented delegate independence, seeking a return to *dedazo* selection (literally, "fingering" nominees, or naming them in the state capital or even Mexico City) and instigating riots to negate the convention's decisions. Although the delegate selection process was upheld by the national PRI hierarchy, most party members and other citizens did not feel that the actions of either delegates or caciques represented popular interests, so they did not become involved in the controversy — or in the campaign and election that followed.

Nor could competition from the opposition generate much electoral enthusiasm. The PAN very nearly refused to participate and, like the remaining parties, had difficulty finding candidates at all, without going through a representative selection process. In the end, the PRI's nominees were contested in only twenty-nine of the 121 municipios of the state of Mexico. Is it surprising that few citizens felt involved in the elections here, or elsewhere throughout the country during this period?

Some aspects of the July 1979 midterm elections for the national Chamber of Deputies, as well as for seven state governors and legislators and a few city administrators, were spirited, but mainly for insiders haggling over the spoils. Doubling the Chamber's size and assuring minority parties proportional representation merely increased competition among ambitious PRI functional association leaders or sparked power struggles within both existing and newly registered opposition groups. While new totals for state deputy delegations were assigned, electoral district boundaries redrawn, and party slates prepared from which to select minority deputies according to each party's share of popular votes, the *políticos* scrambled for the pay and perquisites of a deputy and sought to maximize their own PRI sector's share of seats or to undermine the opposition parties' ability to capture popular votes.

The ideal of rank-and-file Revolutionary party member participation in nominations and later in congressional campaigns was largely ignored. For their part, opposition parties were less concerned with assuring a popular role in selecting candidates than with finding warm bodies to contest districts almost certain to be won by the official party. But finding candidates was necessary for the party to garner enough votes to share in the nondistrict, proportionally-assigned minority seats. As it was, neither the PARM nor the PDM could find candidates for all 300 districts, and the PPS supported the PRI gubernatorial candidates in Sonora, Colima, and San Luis Potosí, as did the PARM in Colima.

Many citizens tended to view the 1979 elections as the acid test of the government's intention to implement real political change, forgetting the reforms that already had been carried out. During the campaign, the president missed several opportunities to convince the ever-skeptical Mexicans of his sincerity, opting in each case for a short-term, politically expedient policy favoring the existing "Revolutionary" system over a decision that might support a more participatory and pluralistic political situation. We have seen that the PRI's ninth Assembly did not restructure the party to eliminate the restrictive sector organization. Then, despite loudly heralded plans for individual party member influence on the selection of official party candidates, disruptive battles among rival functional leaders for congressional nominations and at the state level for control of local organizations forced the central authorities to impose their handpicked PRI candidates more ruthlessly than ever.

As the election approached, many of the local Revolutionary politicians demonstrated their unwillingness to allow minority candidates to campaign freely. Disruption of meetings, arrest or roughing up of speakers, and defacing opposition posters — all became commonplace. Nor did the minority parties use cleaner tactics. Not only did the right launch a vicious anti-Communist campaign against the left, but the two conservative parties reserved their strongest terms for each other. And the leftists did the same for their ideological brethren. An increasingly bitter political atmosphere was not improved when the president removed the government official who had led the political reform and enjoyed a reputation for evenhanded application of the law. Two months before the elections Lic. Jesús Reyes Heroles was replaced as Secretary of Gobernación by an individual identified with traditional PRI politics.

Significantly, this infighting among party leaders did little to rouse popular interest in the elections. The most politically aware citizens showed little desire to involve themselves in selecting candidates for a Chamber of Deputies that is little more than a rubber stamp for approving initiatives of laws prepared by an all-power executive. Their feeling was enhanced by the negative reception given a proposal offered by one of the more able PRI candidates who suggested a stronger lawmaking role for Congress to reduce "presidentialistic" government. Not only did the national Revolutionary leadership downplay the idea, but a new Organic Law of the Congress adopted at this time reinforced government political control mechanisms over the members of both chambers.

Having been excluded from the nominating process and being increasingly conscious that the makeup of a legislature subservient to the executive matters little in regard to the representation of interests, many citizens perceived the 1979 elections less as a contest than as a bore. Voter registration lagged, rallies for candidates of all parties were sparsely attended, and the final results indicate a minimum of popular involvement.

Voter turnout was the lowest in recent years and, for the most part, electoral success reflected traditional PRI dominance. In spite of an intensive and expensive voter registration drive, including a house by house canvass by some 4000 Federal Election Commission employees, 15 percent of eligible citizens were never enrolled. Again, despite the strongest turn-out-the-vote campaign I have ever witnessed anywhere, over 50 percent of those who did register failed to exercise their franchise. In specific figures, of 30.6 million adult Mexicans, 27.9 million registered and 13.8 million voted. About 8 percent of the ballots cast were invalid, some because of voter error but more because of deliberate attempts to indicate rejection of the political system.

To suggest how the tendency toward abstention counteracted the attempt of the political reform to encourage popular participation, let us compare recent elections. Considering abstention to be the percentage of registered voters who fail to vote, the record is as follows:

1961 — 31.5% (Deputy elections)
1964 — 33.3 (Presidential election)
1967 — 34.7 (Deputy elections)
1970 — 35.0 (Presidential election)
1973 — 36.2 (Deputy elections)
1976 — 38.1 (Presidential election)
1979 — 50.5 (Deputy elections)

If we consider the total potential voters (adult Mexicans) who failed to vote, the 1979 rate of abstention rises to 56.8 percent. That means that less than 44 percent of eligible Mexicans voted.

In the congressional portion of the election, the PRI's share was 9.4 million, or about 69 percent of the votes cast. But this was only 37 percent of the potential vote. The PAN captured 12.9 percent of the actual vote and the Communist party 4.87 percent. The other parties trailed, with the PPS getting 3.08 percent, the PST 2.02 percent, the PARM 2.36 percent, and the PDM 2.04 percent.

The final results for the Chamber of Deputies gave the PRI 296 of the 300 election district seats and the PAN four, though five Revolutionary party victories were annulled by the post-election review because of campaign and polling irregularities. The 100 proportional representation seats reserved for minority parties were alloted as follows: PAN, 39; PCM, 18; PARM, 12; PPS, 11; PST, 10; and PDM, 10. One significant change from previous congressional election results was the relatively strong showing of the Communist party, which had just been registered after being off the ballot for thirty years. Voter support made it the third strongest political force, after the PRI and the PAN. The weaker showing of the other parties — old and new — reflects their respective influence in the political arena.

In local elections, the PRI won all seven governor's races although victory in Nuevo Leon was announced by the state legislature with what one high government official called "indecent haste," before all the ballots were counted. The losing PAN candidate alleged improprieties and complained unsuccessfully to the Federal Election Commission and the U.N. Human Rights Commission. The PAN did win control of four city governments and two state legislative posts in the state of Sonora.

Clearly, if its primary aim was to ease pressures on the political system by making the government more responsive to the proliferating needs and expectations of the public, the political reform enacted is so far cosmetic. Tinkering with parties and electoral procedures cannot produce responsible government as long as the ongoing political action patterns impede popular control over selection of decision makers and prevents political reprisals against those who fail to represent constituents' interests. Paradoxically, the one change that could break the pattern cannot be implemented as a single step, but must be carried out over time.

The existing political system rests on an authority principle that vests ultimate power in the President of the Republic. Both the Constitution and Revolutionary myth indicate that political power be shared with other popularly responsible units — the national Congress, state and local governments, democratic political parties — and that the nomination and election of the chief executive reflect much public input. If this were the case, not only would routes of access to the decision-making process increase and diversify, but the average voter could enforce political responsibility through mass participation in electing officials.

Unfortunately, the Revolutionary concept of No Reelection reinforces practices that deter effective suffrage, and the need to update the system precludes transferring real power from the presidency to other political agencies. Luis Echeverría's experience showed José López Portillo that the president must retain his absolute authority if he is to impose any political reform on recalcitrant vested interests. But only as subordinate government agencies and functional interest groups assume a more flexible and responsible stance can the executive gradually share political power with them.

To be effective, political reform must go beyond legislative enactments opening up the present subject-oriented corporative structures to a few challenging interests willing to work within the existing system. It must seek out and remove legal and informal impediments to the more malleable, participant political relationships and action patterns that reflect shifting socioeconomic conditions. Growing popular political awareness and unbearable frustration caused the unrest and physical violence that produced political reform in the first place. As barriers to popular action disappear and as citizens clearly understand the need for better access to government, they can force presently subservient agencies to exercise more responsibility and assume more power. By attrition, therefore, presidential authority gradually will be divided among a variety of political units that the average citizen can influence.

This is not to suggest that Mexico's subject-oriented system represents a plot devised by cynical políticos mouthing slogans about popular rule merely to exploit an innocent and uninformed populace. On the contrary, during and ever since the Revolution, most leaders have identified their political aspirations with an idealized concept of politics that accords high status to constitutional agencies and related political structures that assume individual citizen input into the political process. They carefully observe the forms of representative and responsible government, and in most cases are convinced that it really exists. For this reason the kind of participant political reform envisioned by President López Portillo stirs the imagination of some Mexicans.

In practice, however, applying participant political norms within a subject political culture has proved impossible. A second set of political structures has evolved, quite distinct from the constitutional patterns. These structures reflect the semi-authoritarian values of the society. In considering Mexican politics, therefore, we must differentiate between constitutional agencies, or mass participation mechanisms, and the operational traditional semi-authoritarian structures representing the subject political culture. If we do so, it is apparent that both structures are legitimate, but for different sections of the Mexican population. As the subject-oriented ones lose influence, the possibility of representative and responsible government increases.

Reading about Mexico's government in the free primary level textbooks distributed to every schoolchild, or studying the Constitution and statutes, leaves an impression of democratic political processes based on widely shared popular initiatives. These sources show an open system appropriate to a pluralistic environment, in which individuals and groups with conflicting views freely enjoy their right to participate politically. Exercise of authority is carefully limited by federalism, dividing government activities between state and national levels, as well as by a presidential system separating powers among executive, legislative, and judicial branches, which check each other's influence. In this idealized version of Mexican government legal units are further controlled by the informal activities of a competitive multiparty system, in which seven national parties contest elections and voters select president, governors, and legislators. But the realities of an unintegrated country, a stratified class system, and a pattern of uncompromising suspicion have produced quite different politics in real life.

Legal provisions and myths of individual involvement notwithstanding, Mexico's governmental system is highly centralized and more nearly authoritarian than broadly democratic. While the Constitution establishes federalism, political control of state units falls to the central authorities. The national government is not so much presidential as "presidentialistic." Despite formal separation of powers among three branches, the vast bulk of legal as well as political authority inheres in the person of the chief executive with legislature and judiciary doing little more than ratifying policies initiated by what some Mexicans term a "six-year emperor." The President of the Republic, nominally elected popularly for a single, never-repeatable term, is really selected by the outgoing predecessor, whose choice is legitimized by a referendum-like electoral formality orchestrated by the official party. Token competition for state and national elective offices is provided by a few legislative candidates, and perhaps by an innocuous presidential nominee presented by each of the six legally registered but mainly ineffectual opposition parties.

Perhaps the best indication of how established patterns persisted in influencing the system is not political but economic. Presidential political authority has always been strongly reinforced by the direction taken by Mexico's economy. The mercantilism of the colonial era, which concentrated economic controls in the government, lapsed somewhat after independence, but was revived in the 1917 Constitution and further implemented by the strategy for development pursued by most recent leaders. They favor a mixed economy, with the public sector not only exploiting mineral and petroleum resources but also performing many production and commercial activities carried out by the private sector under capitalism. Centralization is enhanced by modern industrialism, which requires that government accept a great deal of responsibility for managing both the public and the private sectors of the economy (see Table 7.3, p. 120). As a result, the presidential role reflects not simply traditional political power, but also the influence that inheres in the chief of the executive branch whose agencies regulate an expanding and more complex economy. This overlap of political and administrative functions makes today's president the most dominant central authority in Mexico's history.

Presidential influence is not merely regulatory; it includes patronage as well. For a variety of historical reasons, the state administers a large number of concerns, some as decentralized government agencies (wholly owned government corporations) and others as mixed corporations, with shared public and private ownership. The government controls the petroleum industry and railroads, taken over during the 1930s, and telephones, electric power, and other utilities, and it has majority stock in banking, mass communications facilities, steel mills, and various smaller enterprises. During the Echeverría administration government participation in the mixed economy jumped dramatically, reaching about 20 percent of gross national product.

If we lump employees of these government enterprises with state and national bureaucrats and teachers, the number of workers on public payrolls totals some 2 million, about 10 percent of the country's labor force. Exclude the chronic unemployed and underemployed, and over 15.3 percent of wage earners work for government, the most steadily employed and best organized groups in the country — and the most dependent on the chief executive for their jobs.

These public employees are not the only assured supporters of party leaders. Many private sector workers are organized into units controlled by leaders loyal to any incumbent president. Some 2 million union members in thirty-four federations are affiliated with the Congreso del Trabajo (Labor Congress) in the PRI's labor sector, and over twice as many *ejiditarios* (holders of farmlands under restrictive conditions) and *pequeño propietarios* (small farm-owners) are in the agrarian and popular sectors. Those belonging to functional associations, together with their families, make up the bulk of the government party's 15 million members, about half the total electorate. As long as they remain loyal to the Revolutionary movement and its candidates, the disorganized opposition has little hope of capturing political initiative from the president.

Economic and Social Change

The same industrialism that strengthened the chief executive is producing the changes that challenge the political system he heads. It provides the physical and social means of uniting the Mexican people, making possible a national, domestically oriented economic system that encourages regional interdependence by supplying raw materials and by offering internal markets for the country's products. It supports a web of railroads and highways that moves goods and people throughout the land. It supplies technology needed for mass communications, the spreading of ideas, and the sharing of values. Industry's need for trained manpower has led to organization of a mass education system. In short, industrialism has opened a whole new world for the general populace, and in the process has caused major social and economic transformations, with inevitable political consequences.

At the beginning of this century, the great majority of Mexicans involved in subsistence agriculture or working for starvation wages on haciendas were insulated from national affairs or ideas circulating elsewhere in the country. Even those with perspectives beyond the hacienda thought mainly in local or regional terms. Few people were part of the money economy, which depended largely on export agriculture and mining, and the tiny domestic market supported very little large-scale commerce or industry. No balanced, self-sustaining internal economy made the various regions interdependent by using their raw materials and meeting their needs for finished goods.

For all its excesses, the pre-Revolutionary regime of President Díaz did initiate change. Railroads and some roads were constructed, mining jobs and other salaried occupations increased, expanding the market for manufactured goods, and a growing middle class began to congregate in urban areas. By 1910 the number of politically aware and discontented people was sufficient to spark an uprising, led by frustrated middle-class elements. The Revolutionary governments then enjoyed a relatively long period to con-

Table 14.1

Occupational Structure of Mexican Work Force (in millions)

	1940		*1950*		*1960*		*1970*		*1980 (est.)*	
	No.	%	No.	%	No.	%	No.	%	No.	%
Agriculture, livestock, forest products	3.8	63.2	4.8	58.7	6.3	52.5	5.1	36.4	6.6	33.0
Industry	0.9	15.2	1.3	15.8	2.0	16.7	2.8	20.0	4.0	20.0
Services	1.3	21.8	2.1	25.5	3.7	30.8	6.1	43.6	9.4	47.0
Total population economically active	6.0	100.0	8.2	100.0	12.0	100.0	14.0	100.0	20.1	100.0

Source: All data comes from official Mexican government sources. See especially the Dirección General de Estadística.

solidate their authority and form a base for fundamental development by improving the infrastructure (highways, power dams, irrigation dams, popular education services, and the like).

Not until 1945 did Mexico achieve self-sustaining growth, with a domestic market capable of supporting a balanced industrial, commercial, and mechanized agricultural economy. Even then, development was uneven, with the countryside overworked to benefit the urban population and industrial expansion. Economic growth had been speeded up by large infusions of foreign investment and technology (especially from the United States), a situation that has begun to provoke a nationalistic reaction. Tables 14.1 and 14.2 indicate that the economy has been moving away from traditional unskilled and agricultural activities toward industrial, commercial, and service functions, all occupations in which government policies can have a direct effect on the interests of the workers.

Table 14.3

Population of Mexico, 1900–1980

Year	*Total (in thousands)*	*Percentage living in localities of 2,500+ inhabitants*
1900	13,607	29.0
1910	15,160	29.3
1921	14,335	31.2
1930	16,553	33.5
1940	19,654	35.1
1950	25,791	42.6
1960	34,626	50.7
1970	48,225	58.5
1980 (est.)	72,000	68.0

Source: All data comes from official Mexican government sources. See especially the Dirección General de Estadística.

Table 14.2

Employment of Mexican Population Aged 12 or Older, 1950 and 1970 (in percentages)

Area of employment	*1950*	*1970*
Agriculture, cattle, and related activities	58.3	39.5
Petroleum production	—	0.7
Mining industries	1.2	0.8
Refining industries	11.8	16.7
Construction	2.7	4.4
Electrical energy	0.3	0.4
Commerce	8.3	9.6
Transportation	2.5	2.8
Services	10.6	16.6
Government	—	3.1
Insufficiently specific	4.3	5.8
Total	100.0	100.0

Source: All data comes from official Mexican government sources. See especially the Dirección General de Estadística.

Between 1945 and 1975, Mexico's gross domestic product (GDP) increased about 6.4 percent a year, a remarkable achievement, but one that must be viewed within the context of a population increase of over 3.3 percent annually during the same period. Population growth cuts per capita GDP growth in half, just as the citizenry becomes more urbanized, aware, and demanding. Table 14.3 shows growth of total population and the proportion of city dwellers.

No one who knows Mexico would suggest that the people living in towns with 2,500 or even 5,000 inhabitants enjoy all the urban amenities or are likely to be linked tightly to national life. But growing concentrations of population in larger urban areas — where people hear about national policies and politics — and the shift toward economic activities affected by government have induced desire for direct participation in the political process. It also has produced a sense of frustration when informed citizens feel their political activities are ineffectual.

The highest political sophistication is found in larger cities and metropolitan areas, where growth has been significant in the past two decades. In 1960, 17.5 million people (50 percent of total population) lived in 145 cities with populations over 20,000; the total grew to 26.4 million (54.7 percent) in 1970.

Table 14.4

Growth of Population in Principal Mexican Cities and Corresponding Metropolitan Areas, 1960–1970

	1960 (in thousands)		*1970 (in thousands)*		*Percentage growth of city, 1960–1970*
	City	*Urban area*	*City*	*Urban area*	
Mexico (Federal District)	4,871	5,564	6,874	8,605	3.5
Guadalajara	737	875	1,194	1,445	4.9
Monterrey	597	750	858	1,167	3.7
Juárez	262	271	407	415	4.5
Puebla	289	763	402	990	3.4
León	210	249	365	427	5.7
Tiajuana	152	156	277	300	6.2
Mexicali	175	191	267	285	4.3
Chihuahua	150	175	257	265	5.5
Total	7,443	8,994	10,901	13,899	

Source: All data comes from official Mexican government sources. See especially the Dirección General de Estadística.

Table 14.4 shows that in 1970, 22.6 percent of all Mexicans lived in nine cities with populations in excess of 250,000; if their metropolitan areas are included, the large city population rises to 28.8 percent. By 1980, some 60 million Mexicans (about 83 percent of the 72 million national population) will live in cities with over 15,000 inhabitants, sixteen with over 500,000, and six with over 1 million people. Mexico City alone will top 13 million, and with its surrounding metropolitan area total over 15 million.

Another indicator of broad exposure to information that can expand political awareness is Mexico's fast rising literacy rate, especially in northern and central areas of the country, where isolated, closed Indian cultures are less influential (see Table 14.5 and Figure 14.1). Some of these new readers probably are functional illiterates who scarcely can write their own names. A majority of Mexicans now are able to read political news and act on the informa-

Table 14.5

Literacy of Mexicans Aged 10 or Older, 1910–1970

Year	*Percentage literate*
1910	28.42
1921	33.83
1930	39.39
1940	43.19
1950	56.82
1960	66.51
1970	76.19

Source: All data comes from official Mexican government sources. See especially the Dirección General de Estadística.

Figure 14.1
Mexican Illiterates, Aged 10 or Older, by State, 1970

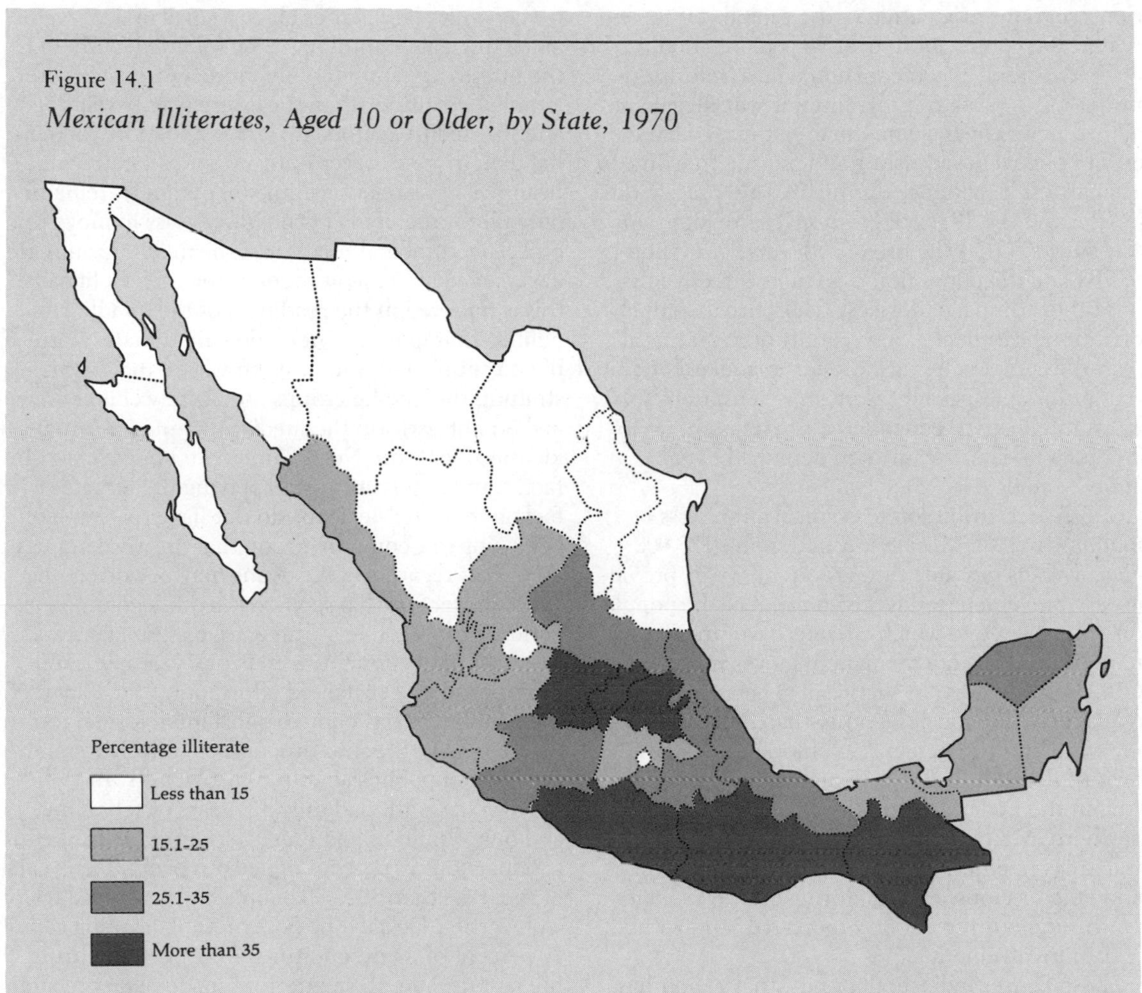

tion, but we shall see that they do not always do so.

Closely akin to literacy as an inducement to political activism is the opportunity to learn about potential policy through the mass media. Although most Mexican newspapers are careful not to print personal attacks on the president or other leading políticos, some of the better ones do comment on shortcomings of national, state, and local government programs. Mexico City alone has over twenty newspapers, some with excellent political coverage although, as elsewhere, others are more concerned with sex, sadism, and crime than with public policy. Several of the capital's papers circulate throughout the republic, but most major cities have several newspapers of their own. Numerous weekly and biweekly journals of political commentary representing all shades of opinion also appear.

The Mexico City metropolitan area is served by six television channels and some thirty radio stations; most of the rest of the country relies on local outlets or on programs originating in the capital. Of the estimated 1980 population, over 70 percent should have radios and 40 percent should have televisions. Prior to 1972, partisan programming was illegal and political news coverage minimal, but recent laws permit political broadcasting and provide free time to legal parties. Experience during the 1976 presidential election and the 1979 congressional campaign, however, suggests that the use of radio and television by the PRI and the opposition is no more effective than their other campaign devices. Lack of real competition among candidates and scarcity of meaningful policy differences among most parties makes for dull programming, especially as most presentations follow an intellectual, educational format about as exciting as a fly-killing campaign described over Chinese radio.

Another contribution to political awareness is mobility. By 1980 Mexico will have some 125,000 miles of roads passable throughout the year, providing easy movement for over 85 percent of the population. The degree to which citizens have broadened their outlook through permanent moves is suggested by 1970 census data. In that year 15 percent of the populace lived in localities other than those in which they were born; 10 percent had moved during the previous decade. Roughly 35 percent of the people living in the Federal District in 1970 were born elsewhere. Many of the moves were from isolated rural areas to cities, where socialization strengthens national consciousness. All during the 1970s migration throughout the country increased, and with it political involvement.

These figures indicate that industrialization has recently brought Mexicans into national life quickly and in large numbers, a pattern with significant political implications. Nonetheless, we must avoid letting a few indicators mislead us about the speed and depth of real change. Shifts in economic activity, literacy, and contact with the world transform political values and behavior, but slowly and unevenly. Culturally reinforced, deeply ingrained attitudes and behavior patterns tend to survive long after the physical or mental conditions that produced them disappear. This is the case in Mexico.

Despite the government's ambitious plans for social and economic reform, not even a revolution was able to wipe out the stratified class system. The pattern of a very large lower class, a small middle sector, and a tiny elite continues to be followed. Although the masses are considerably more aware and more national in outlook than they were twenty years ago, and the middle sectors are larger and more influential than in some other Latin American countries, historical class relationships still obtain. It remains difficult for members of the lower class to move up, especially rural marginals, and the middle groups are always ready to exploit them as they try. Politically, this is reflected in the readiness of the middle-class político to impose his views on subordinates, instead of consulting with them. Even within their own stratum, the middle groups are fiercely competitive and do not perform the mediating function usually identified with the North American middle class. In fact, some observers avoid applying the term *class*, feeling that the Mexicans do not have the sense of belonging to a common group that the word implies.

In that regard the Mexicans may be correct, because the factors that seem to provide a common experience may not be as integrative as first appears. Mexico's educational record is one example. After three decades of sustained effort, only a small part of the population has enough substantial formal training to prepare them to function effectively in modern life and politics as active participants. In 1977, the average adult had only 3.6 years of schooling, and only 3 million had more than nine years of education, about 10 percent of persons over fifteen years of age. Less than 300,000 people had graduated from a university. Despite the government devoting about 10 percent of its expenditures to education during the past decade, this pattern of inadequate preparation probably will not improve much in the immediate future for the half of the population under eighteen. The high birthrate produces so many children that it is hard to build schools or train teachers quickly enough to service them. Many who do begin the six-year primary cycle drop out before finishing, mostly for economic or social reasons, rather than intellectual ones.

Data for the 1978–1979 school year reflects recent improvements, but the pattern of incomplete primary training still exists. Of 15 million children of primary age, 13.7 million (91 percent) were in school, but only 60 percent of those were expected to finish. So nearly half of tomorrow's citizens will not have even six years of formal preparation for the complexities of modern life, or the sense of personal and political adequacy a more complete education instills.

Wide disparities in income are another indicator of incomplete national integration. Until the outbreak of double-digit inflation in 1973 (see Table 14.6), Mexico's per capita income had been rising about 3 percent each year, increasing from $70 in 1930 to nearly $700 in 1972. During the next few years, take-home pay almost doubled but real purchasing power actually fell slightly. In any case, even in the late 1970s two-thirds of the population earned less than $1500 a year, with figures slightly better in larger urban areas. Nor do these figures take into account serious structural unemployment, exacerbated by an exploding labor force that doubled between 1960 and 1980 and is expected to double again by the end of the century (see Table 14.7). In 1970 over 3 million workers (25.4 percent of the work force) suffered *equivalent unemployment*, either having no job or working well below their skill level. The growing labor supply and the post-1973 recession have expanded unemployment to at least 35 percent of the 1980 work force, 7 million persons out of 20 milliom.

Most seriously affected by inflation are the marginals — perhaps 6 million people, 30 percent of the labor force — rural people without land and unskilled city dwellers who do not work steadily enough to come under the minimum wage or collective bargaining contracts that have risen along with prices. For them, desperate competition for employment keeps sporadic income far beneath subsistence. Even these usually passive Mexicans have been driven by the struggle for survival into some sort of action — invading large landowners' arable land, moving to cities, or emigrating to the United States illegally — and more recently into political pressure on the government for some sort of relief.

If the entire population shared economic disadvantages the political implications of poverty might be less threatening. But the gulf between haves and have-nots is wide and expanding, and inflation has made it more evident. Despite ex-President Echeverría's redistribution programs, by the late 1970s some 10 percent of the population in the upper class enjoyed 50 percent of the national product, while the 50 percent in the lower class received only 15 percent.

For members of the lowest stratum, cultural and physical isolation and virtual exclusion from the money economy produce scattered groups living in poverty and political parochialism. Such existence is the lot of 10 percent of the total population. This includes 2 million Indians speaking dozens of local languages who, the government believes, still need special education and training assistance. The poverty pockets also include many mixed culture mestizos not fully attuned to national life. Some ejiditarios have failed to make the transition from

Table 14.6

Rise in Mexican Consumer Price Index, 1961–1979

1961–1965	1.9%	1974	22.5%
1966–1970	3.7	1975	16.8
		1976	27.0
1971	5.7	1977	20.0
1972	5.0	1978	16.2
1973	11.3	1979	20.0

Source: All data comes from official Mexican government sources. See especially the Dirección General de Estadística.

Table 14.7

Mexican Labor Force, 1960–2000, Real and Projected (in thousands)

1960	10,992	1985	23,934
1965	12,520	1990	28,316
1970	14,489	1995	33,650
1975	17,071	2000	39,663
1980	20,167		

Source: All data comes from official Mexican government sources. See especially the Dirección General de Estadística.

subsistence farming to market agriculture, and even in the cities surprisingly large numbers of persons remain marginal to modern society because of inadequate work skills or emotional resistance.

Some observers say there are two Mexicos — one urban, modern, and nationally involved, the other rural, traditional, and alienated from the larger community. In fact, there are many Mexicos, because divisions abound in the cities as well as the countryside. But it is true that the least integrated Mexicans are scattered in the 80,000 communities with less than 500 inhabitants. As in other countries, Japan and the Soviet Union for example, most of Mexico's rural population fared badly in modernization. Uneducated, dispersed, poorly organized, and worse led, they have been unable to exert effective pressures to protect themselves from central government policies shortchanging them while accumulating capital for industrial development. Despite symbolic land distribution programs and constant discussion of agrarian needs, until very recently Mexico invested little in farm credit facilities, marketing arrangements, or training in scientific agriculture. Population growth is especially high in rural areas, and neither allocations for ejidos nor distribution of privately owned irrigated plots has satisfied the land hunger of the rural masses. Hence the migration to the cities and the land violence of the mid-1970s.

Although almost half of Mexico's people still live in rural communities, agriculture's contribution to the economy is low. During 1960, half the labor force worked on farms to produce only 15.9 percent of Mexico's GDP, compared with 22.6 percent for manufacturing; by 1976, with about 35 percent of the workers in agriculture, the share had fallen to 9.1 percent, while manufacturing's share had risen to 28.2 percent. Although agricultural economists say that food production has kept pace with population growth, changing eating habits forced expensive imports during the late 1970s.

Recognizing the potential explosiveness of rural unrest and inefficiency, the government instituted a series of reforms in the 1970s. Increased amounts of credit and development funds were made available, and in 1972 an economic decentralization program was initiated to establish agro-industrial facilities in 150 sites. The new programs sought to dampen rural discontent by providing sources of income and to slow movement to the cities by making survival possible in the hinterland, while bringing in some of the conveniences of urban living. Change was not speedy enough to avoid the 1976 land invasions, however, or to ease rural pressures on the López Portillo administration. One by-product of the rural development program, however, has been greater popular awareness and a growing spirit of political competence among less integrated Mexicans, who previously left political initiative in the hands of the Revolutionary elites.

POLITICAL CULTURE AND SOCIALIZATION

Three Political Subcultures

Mexico's political system was not invented by the authors of the 1917 Constitution, or by the leaders who set up the official party in 1929. It developed over time, its broad outlines shaped by legally established government units and by informal structures like the interest groups and political parties. The patterned political activity that gives life to the system reflects values evolved by the country's inhabitants during centuries of adaptation to the pressures of violence, insecurity, and authority.

Over the years, Mexicans have learned to endure the harsh realities of an unfriendly physical environment. Most have also learned to endure the harsher human and material realities of an isolated and unsettled rural life. Weak or nonexistent links to the national society and economy have bred in them strong identification with their own small community (*localismo*) and deep mistrust of outsiders, who too often have proved to be land grabbers, tax collectors, or army recruiters. Their relations with neighbors have been marked by suspicion and envy; in the absence of effective police or an impartial judicial system, violence frequently has been the only available form of self-defense. In order to survive, the individual Mexican has learned to choose personal advantage over the general good and to trust only those persons bound to him by mutual interest. Distrust of others, combined with a lack of social institutions that might have enforced some broadly shared code of human conduct, has led most individuals to rely on relationships based on long and face-to-face contact. This is called *personalismo*.

Personalismo is founded on a dependency relationship between two individuals which is basic to Mexican politics. We shall see presently that most Mexicans tend to be submissive to authority and feel so insecure psychologically that they seek a submissive-dominant relationship with some other, usually more influential person. This patrón-client arrangement rests upon expectation of reciprocal advantages.

One political consequence of personalismo is that most people do not relate easily to abstract concepts or impersonal organizations but only to the individual who leads the movement or unit. This affects the kind of identification a citizen is likely to have with the interest associations or groups (electrical workers' union, farmers' collective, the church) that are potentially the most influential factors in politics. In many countries, the citizen supports or rejects a political party or candidate in terms of how their proposed programs will benefit or harm the groups with which he identifies most strongly. If a Mexican identifies with a single leader, that leader's unit becomes the follower's reference group. That is, he identifies almost entirely with the purposes and activities of that one group, adjusting his response to every political stimulus in terms of its effect on the reference group. For the follower this makes sense, because he would not identify with the leader if he did not receive or expect to receive a substantial emotional or material payoff.

This essentially self-centered viewpoint is enhanced by the way most Mexicans measure their personal worth. The Canadian or American generally sees himself as more like other people than different; human similarities are more basic than human differences and therefore every person is as good as the next. In contrast, the Mexican considers himself to be quite unlike any other individual and, as a distinct human entity, entitled to maximize his particular interest at everyone else's expense. Within this frame of reference personal aggrandizement, even public corruption, is not immoral but highly functional.

The Mexican's extreme individualism is reinforced by widespread mistrust and suspicion of the motives and actions of other persons. Politically, this means firm political alliances, for an individual is not likely to invest his personal resources or energies in political activities unless he follows a leader to whom he transfers some sense of identity and interest. This may arise out of blood kinship or, more commonly, from an expectation of the mutual exchange of benefits.

Given this outlook, it is difficult for a Mexican to imagine or accept the personal limitations or responsibilities implicit in concepts like the general welfare or the national interest. The reaction of most Mexicans depends on how abstract ideas — a political movement's internally consistent and all-inclusive program — translate into personal and immediate advantage. It also depends on whether the citizen identifies personally with the political leader who delivers the package.

Historically, until the material, social, and psychological changes wrought by technology began to make their impact felt, most traditional Mexicans shrank from competition with their environment and the people in it, adopting a fatalistic, even submissive approach to the world around them. They had little confidence in their ability to change material conditions by, say, applying scientific agricultural innovations or entering the market economy, and even less belief in the likelihood of success in altering their relations with the tiny ruling elite. Despite their rejection of outsiders, people tended to seek solutions to problems not through their own efforts but through the action of some external force, usually a patrón, be he the owner of a hacienda, a saint in heaven, or a político in government.

The situation today is complicated because not all Mexicans are changing at the same rate. Some are more isolated geographically and culturally, others labor outside the emerging national economy or do not speak the national language. A few are psychologically unable to accept the dislocations that accompany new conditions. And not all those who are changing have moved the same distance toward modernity. But enough citizens have become aware of their stake in national life so that pressure is building up for major changes in political structures. Not all citizens react the same way, however, so it becomes increasingly difficult to accommodate their diverse needs within a single set of political structures.

Mexico's inhabitants can be divided into three overlapping but distinct political subcultures, the members of which play different roles in national politics.[3]

1. *Parochials* are little involved in the national society and economy and largely uninformed about their country or its politics. Other than in a negative sense, they do not affect the national political system, until they move into the next group. They are members of the huge and shapeless lower sector and are among the least effective members of that sector.
2. *Subjects* are conscious of Mexico as a country and are aware of its government, but they generally make little effort to influence decision making. These are the passive Mexicans of whom we have spoken, inclined to let government act in their name and willing to support political leaders who ostensibly represent their interests. The great majority of citizens fall into this group, which continues to grow in proportion as well as in numbers because as parochials become aware they turn into subjects, while subjects become participants only with great difficulty. Most subjects are members of the more informed sections of the lower sector, but a few spill over into the lower middle sector, or even higher in the socioeconomic hierarchy.
3. *Participants*, by preparation, knowledge, occupation, and strategic location in urban areas, are able to imagine and to seek a direct role in the planning as well as the execution of public policy. Most national and many regional political leaders, challengers as well as PRI members, are participants. So are members of the top government and private-sector managerial elites. The participant group increases quite slowly because of psychological as well as political structural barriers to movement into this category. Most participants come from the middle middle sector, but they range up to the highest social levels.

[3] Robert E. Scott, "Mexico, the Established Revolution," in Lucien W. Pye and Sidney Verba (eds.), *Political Culture and Political Development* (Princeton: Princeton University Press, 1965), pp. 330–395.

A complicated formula involving socioeconomic characteristics, attitudinal factors, and behavioral data produces Table 14.8, which shows changes over time in the estimated number and proportion of Mexicans in each subculture. The table illustrates that both the absolute and relative number of parochials is declining as urbanization increases and education and communications reach out to the hinterland. It also illustrates that while the move from parochial to subject is nearly automatic as the nation becomes more unified, the shift from subject to participant is much slower. This reflects the tenacity of traditional values and the defense of the political structures, which interact to weaken the impact of disruptive new challenges upon the system.

Political Socialization

Mexicans view political events and react to government actions on the basis of understandings absorbed unconsciously by observing the actions and attitudes of parents, relatives, and peer groups in their daily existence. Growing up in a splintered and highly competitive environment, the first human contacts prepare the Mexican child to be suspicious of others, trusting only a few persons, and then only if they have earned confidence in face-to-face dealings. Family ties or reciprocal exchange of services between unrelated individuals ensure this relationship better than impersonal institutions or the enunciation of abstract ideals. The culture encourages a sense of personal ineffectualness suggesting that individuals can survive better by submitting to the world around them than by trying to change it. In this atmosphere, most women follow a role of resigned passivity, as do many men. But other males compensate for feelings of personal inadequacy by adopting aggressive behavior known as *machismo*. This behavior has social and political consequences, such as bullying and refusal to compromise as well as the sexual implications usually associated with the term.

Because they feel unable to cope alone, many Mexicans develop a dependency relationship with a patrón, identifying their own aspirations with his

Table 14.8

Mexicans in Three Political Subcultures, 1910–1980

	1910		1963		1980	
Subculture	*Number*	*Percentage of population*	*Number*	*Percentage of population*	*Number*	*Percentage of population*
Parochials	12,250,000	90	9,250,000	25	7,200,000	10
Subjects	1,090,000	8	24,050,000	65	51,800,000	72
Participants	275,000	2	3,500,000	10	13,000,000	18

Source: Constructed from data permitting informed estimates. The materials reviewed included:

1. Social factors: educational statistics; number of inhabitants in various-sized urban communities; rural occupations (subsistence farming, commercial farming, day-wage laborer, housewife); urban occupations (professional, including teachers, managerial, technical, clerical, artisan, unskilled labor); cultural (Indian, mestizo, European). Wherever possible membership in labor unions, farmers' leagues, and popular or professional associations was considered.
2. Economic factors: levels and sources of income; economic activity, by type; unemployed.
3. Attitudinal and behavioral factors: spotty survey material dealing with political attitudes; past and contemplated political performance; state and national election data.

For earlier periods both range and probable validity of data are reduced. But because these categories are rough approximations, the weakness is not fatal.

person rather than with an abstract cause. Or they seek an outside solution to their problems, perhaps relying on government rather than their own efforts. Although these norms are learned rather than inherent, they are assimilated so early and so well and reinforce each other so effectively that they become primitive values — the individual assumes they are endemic in himself or herself and society.

In a stable social and political environment, changing political norms is difficult, for the values underlying socializing structures are internally consistent and complementary. If family relations are formal, with parents acting as authority figures, and if the priest, the schoolteacher, and the employer all perform the same function, chances are that the farm group leader, the union chief, or the político will also be seen as a symbol of authority. This has been the pattern in Mexico. Although city dwellers exposed to modernizing influences are more likely to adopt new kinds of social and political behavior, even they are guided mainly by deeply rooted traditional values and their behavior patterns do not change very quickly.

In a very real sense, Mexicans share so many values that there is only one political culture, but enough pattern variations exist to divide it into the three political subcultures just discussed. The fact that each subculture calls for rather different sorts of political and governmental structures to perform the basic political functions explains some of the difficulties faced by the regimes of the past few years.

THE FAMILY The earliest and generally most effective socializer is, of course, the family. An infant's first experiences of love or rejection, privilege or punishment, condition the individual's response to other human beings for the rest of his or her life. So do a child's observations of family contacts with outsiders, be they neighbors, employers, police officers, or politicians. Parents and close family friends provide most people with the models upon which they pattern their own actions. If such persons are basically insecure, they will transmit their sense of inadequacy to the child, who in turn will be affected as an adult. In Mexico, social conflicts and highly stratified class differences, heightened by cultural, economic, and psychological elitism, combine with all the problems of a rapidly changing environment to make most citizens unsure of the norms for behavior, and therefore of their status. Because conditions shift so speedily, what was workable and constructive one day may prove detrimental the next. Even the most stable personality may not be able to adjust adequately to such pressures.

A young person imbued with such uncertainty moves out of the protected setting of the home into the world and discovers inconsistency and contradiction among the institutions he encounters. Almost automatically a young Mexican male assumes a defensive stance of aggressiveness or an unreal sense of personal competence. Later in life, his inability to live up to his exaggerated self-image further fuels his sense of ineffectualness, and the cycle begins anew. Almond and Verba's five-country study provides evidence of this trait as it operates in Mexican families and schools and is transferred to politics.[4] Respondents were asked how much influence they had on family decisions at age sixteen. Mexicans recalled having had more influence than Germans and Italians did, but when asked how freely they could and did complain about family decisions, the same Mexicans were at the bottom of the scale. Roughly the same pattern appeared among Mexicans estimating their ability to object to or influence government decisions. Most stated they felt competent to intervene but when asked how often they had done so, or when asked to suggest tactics for changing public policy, their responses indicated that they had seldom acted and possessed little understanding of how to do so.

Some important shifts in frequency of complaining and acting have occurred in both family and politics. The more schooling, the more likely an individual is to have complained and acted on that discontent. This is not to suggest that formal education as such makes the difference. Schooling relates closely to status, social class, economic influence, and other factors that could motivate a citizen to act but are harder to measure. In Mexico, even the person with consistent opportunities for social participation does not enter politics as frequently as counterparts in Germany or England. Apparently the Mexicans' deep mistrust and passivity inhibit them from performing an active political role.

[4] Gabriel A. Almond and Sidney Verba, *The Civic Culture* (Princeton, N.J.: Princeton University Press, 1963).

EDUCATION Another important socializing mechanism is public education, though it is not clear whether Mexican schools are supporters of tradition or modernization. One source of ambiguity is the difficulty schools have in deciding what their objective should be. In a transitional situation with shifting values, and a divisive society with strongly marked regional, rural-urban, class, and cultural differences, the educational system cannot be all things to all people, for needs are as varied as experiences and aspirations. Historically, education has transmitted established cultural and social values. In a changing environment it is expected to do so still but also to infuse modern attitudes.

The Mexican who has had some schooling must feel ambivalent about what his social and political role should be. According to lesson plans and the free primary school textbooks distributed by the government, all Mexicans are equal and entitled to fair and dignified treatment, every citizen is a thinking human being who must assume civic responsibilities and participate freely in local and national politics. In the classroom, however, the teacher often is a highly authoritarian figure enforcing rigid discipline. Relations between pupil and professor are generally formal, with a minimum of interchange and virtually no questioning. With overcrowded classrooms, double shifts, overwhelming teaching loads, and inadequate professional preparation, few instructors have the time, skill, or inclination to help students develop their reasoning. Those who try may do their students no favor, for centralized examinations aimed at enforcing minimum standards often require rote responses and rarely reward reasoning or personal initiative.

The educational reform initiated in 1973 recognized many of these problems and sought to restate teaching goals, with changes in subject matter and an upgrading of teachers to ensure a change in classroom atmosphere. Most observers feel that progress to date has been slight, for while texts can be changed the attitudes of teachers are less flexible, particularly under the pressures of numbers and inadequate facilities. Until the 1.3 million children of primary-school age who are not now registered can be enrolled, no educational influence can reach them; until the 40 percent of pupils who do not complete the six-year cycle can be retained, the schools' impact will be limited. For the remaining students, most teachers will be more concerned with controlling their pupils and imparting a few basics than with projecting a democratic image.

DAILY LIFE In adulthood Mexicans discover that each day's experiences are equally conflicting. Church, social group, work-place, labor union, professional association, political organization, all are caught up in the same transitional dilemma. Members do not share any set of values. Within each unit an unbridgeable generation gap of attitudes and understanding divides older and younger members, but differing perceptions of interest may also split the more informed rank and file from the leadership. With continuous, fundamental change occurring, it is difficult for individuals to agree on meaningful values for the moment; it is harder still to adopt permanent and universal values for an entire nation. Because new views are adopted by individuals sporadically and frequently cancel each other out, traditional norms continue to influence a majority of people, no matter how much they are exposed to modern conditions.

For the time being, therefore, most citizens will continue to share some or all of the traits listed by a Mexican psychologist, who characterized them as

> a childlike people, near adolescence, with few examples of maturity, or of productive character. Common attributes are receptivity, dependency, irresponsibility, scorn for human life, physical force, feminine conquest, mourning and death, armed aggression, and maternal reliance that seeks a miracle to resolve problems. Mexicans avoid reliance on their own resources, do not employ prolonged effort, constancy, and efficiency. They also like facilitation, improvisation, pull, nepotism, recommendation; [they] demand pardon from everybody else.[5]

[5] Ancieto Aramoni, *Psicoanálisis de la Dinámica de un Pueblo* (Mexico, D.F.: Universidad Nacional Autónoma de Mexico, 1961), p. 287.

POLITICAL RECRUITMENT

Recruitment to political activism may take very different forms from one political system to another, but it usually means more than voting or expressing individual indignation between elections. In Mexico, with a mainly passive citizenry and a corporative dominant party, whose nominees are selected with minimal popular influence, recruitment generally results from involvement with some group. This group may be a functional association in one of the PRI's sectors, an independent, quasi-legal interest group, or even an opposition political party.

Certainly, until very recently the great bulk of citizens seldom acted politically on their own initiative or sought individual membership in a party, except for the tiny, elitist opposition movements composed primarily of intellectuals. Instead, the ordinary Mexican was coopted into organized politics through membership in a farmers' league, a labor union, or some other social or occupational group. Often an individual became affiliated with a movement through the action of a functional organization leader, who engineered the alliance with little or no consultation among the membership; just as often the leader continued his paternalistic ways, speaking for his people in party councils and seeking to deliver their votes with a minimum of inquiry into their views or desires.

The organization of the Revolutionary party mirrors this pattern. Most of the other parties claim to oppose group affiliation on principle, but their short rosters and inability to deliver massive votes suggest that they do so because the PRI has preempted most popularly based organizations. The fact is that a large portion of Mexico's population is still not mobilized for any effective independent political participation, and the more informed voter is still unconvinced that acting in an elite-led party will influence public policy to his or her advantage.

We already have noted the major consequence of such attitudes, electoral apathy. The 1976 presidential election results underline the problem. With almost 30 million citizens eligible, only 26 million registered and about 18 million voted, 15.4 million for the PRI's nominee, the only candidate on the ballot. The PRI claimed about 10 million members, and the opposition parties claimed about a million and a half, leaving four million independent voters. In percentages, 59 percent of the potential voters cast ballots, 68 percent of those registered. In other words, although 86 percent of the actual votes were for José López Portillo, only 51 percent of all potential voters supported him, hardly a brilliant showing for the sole candidate listed. This is a judgment not on the individual, but on the existing system's ability to recruit politically, even at the level of voting.

Many educated and economically important Mexicans who are politically influential do not belong to any party. This does not mean that they operate as unorganized independents, for they channel their claims on government through quasi-legal interest associations such as the Chambers of Commerce or Industry, or the collective private governments. Increasingly, independent labor and farm groups unable to gain entry to or satisfaction from the PRI's functional organizations follow the same route. Generally, such nonsector units bypass the parties and the legislature, carrying their raw demands to the executive agencies or, if possible, directly to the president. The effectiveness of this sort of political recruitment through group operations is demonstrated by the multiplication of such units and the growth of their membership in recent years.

Political Leaders

The most obvious and important form of political recruitment is that of political leaders. In Mexico, with the exception of the leaders of independent groups just discussed, this means the middle- and upper-level party officials. With few exceptions, Mexican politicians spring from the educated, urban, middle sectors and act like patrones. This is true of PRI leaders, opposition party chiefs, and the leaders of the nonparty social or economic interest associations as well. They are all products of the same socializing conditions.

Unlike the Revolutionary political elite, the interest group and opposition party leaders are generally not full-time políticos and must earn their livelihood some other way. The representatives of the private governments often cap their financial success in business or industry by accepting a responsible post in a quasi-legal peak association like the Employers Association or the Chamber of Industries. Their political influence usually reflects their group's contribution to national life and to the president's program.

Some leaders are intellectuals, others are in business. Their organizations are neither wealthy enough to support them nor influential enough to ensure appointment to salaried public office, though a few do win seats in Congress or are named to government regulatory boards. Most young people who move into leadership roles in these parties and groups do so as a gesture of their rejection of the official party or because they see opposition politics as a way of promoting a particular ideology.

The Revolutionary party's younger leaders, by contrast, enjoy all the advantages of power. Moving back and forth between party posts and government jobs, they can devote their full energies to a career with the dominant political force in the country. With the exception of a few aging carryovers from an earlier era, in the agrarian and the labor sectors the educational and cultural gap between the rank and file and the leaders is so great that university-trained professionals are invariably tapped to speak for the mass membership. Almost by definition, leadership in the popular sector of the PRI is similar, for the bulk of members are middle-class professionals or well-informed, urban, middle- and lower-class types. Significantly, some candidates nominated by the popular sector in past elections have had little previous identification with the PRI and a few actually have been members of opposition political movements at one time. This coopting of potential competitive leaders is no longer possible, for in 1978 the party statutes were amended to require five years membership before nomination.

We cannot separate PRI leaders from members of the government bureaucracy or other public positions, for the more successful party politicians move in and out of state and national elective and appointive posts frequently. In 1971 the PRI formalized this arrangement, setting up in Mexico City a Political Training Institute (Instituto de Capatación Política, or ICAP). Within a few years, similar state level units were established in many sections of the country. Promising young male and female secondary and university graduates from outlying regions are brought in for training lasting up to a year, with all

Village Mexico's traditional patterns are increasingly affected by outside forces, national and international, commercial and political.

expenses paid. After training in applied sociology, economics, administration, political leadership, and propaganda, they return home assured of a government job and assigned to work with the local party organization.

Moving up the ladder has become the accepted way of recruiting top government and PRI leaders. An able and ambitious young person enters the Revolutionary coalition by establishing a dependency relationship with an established leader, who sponsors him for a series of jobs in government or the party. As he is assigned new tasks, the rising político expands his range of experience and gradually assumes greater responsibilities. If he balances success with loyalty to the system and to his sponsor, he eventually may become President of the Republic, as did José López Portillo in 1976.

President López Portillo's career is not a perfect model of this pattern, for he came to active politics relatively late, at age thirty-eight, and prior to his presidential campaign had never run for office and had held relatively few government posts. He was a professor of law and of political science at the National University until 1958, when he joined the campaign staff of the PRI's presidential candidate, Adolfo López Mateos. He then held increasingly important appointive posts in the secretariats of Public Education and National Patrimony, and became subsecretary of the presidency in 1968. Although he and Luis Echeverría were boyhood friends, López Portillo gave early support to another precandidate for nomination in 1970 and was temporarily shoved to the edge of the political ladder. He was named subsecretary of national patrimony, and later director of the Federal Electric Commission, but in 1973, having rehabilitated himself with President Echeverría he was appointed secretary of the treasury. His selection as the 1976 presidential candidate surprised most observers, but it has been suggested that Echeverría wanted a successor who had no personal political machine, so that he could act as the power behind the throne. If so, the ex-president must be disappointed, for the very nature of Mexico's political system has forced López Portillo to be a strong president in his own right.

The careers of most other recent presidents conform to the pattern more closely. For over thirty years every PRI presidential candidate has been a member of the Cabinet, and all but two were secretary of *Gobernación* (Government, the politically most influential post). Although experience as a state governor, national deputy, or high-ranking party officer is useful in moving up the ladder, it is the combination of broad-gauge administrative experience as head of a major department and close proximity to the kingmaker — the incumbent president — that wins the Revolutionary party's nomination.

How party leaders advance their careers affects how they perform as president. After twenty years in a political hierarchy, with success dependent on willingness to sublimate personal independence to the will of superiors, a rising young party-government bureaucrat develops extensive experience in applying administrative skills and a strong sense of loyalty to and discipline within the political system. The most effective leaders are capable, driving, dedicated workers who have demonstrated their ability to operate within the established arrangements. Their own rise to power convinces them that the present political system is valid and good, for it has recognized their worth and rewarded their contributions.

But this kind of experience does little to enhance the qualities that make a successful president under the present changing conditions. Apart from having skills as a bureaucrat, Mexico's present-day chief executive must be a statesman and politician in the best sense of the terms. The president must be prepared to question the basic tenets of the society, economy, and political community if he is to provide imaginative leadership for change where necessary. To accomplish this, a national leader must combine a high degree of personal initiative with a sensitivity for the feelings and aspirations of a heterogeneous population. A lifetime of being a good follower, suppressing one's own impulses, and accomplishing specific, limited objectives assigned from above, does not prepare an individual to confront, much less to act on, the problems challenging a political system in a rapidly shifting environment. Several recent presidents who rose by the traditional pattern proved unable or unwilling to encourage changes in the established political system, leading to a dangerous buildup of discontent among emerging interests.

Perhaps because he was more flexible, perhaps because of the accumulated pressures he inherited from President Díaz Ordaz, President Echeverría took steps to open the political system a bit and to shift the emphasis of public policy away from industrial and commercial development and toward distributive programs to meet the masses' rising expectations. As we have seen, negative reactions from PRI leaders forced him to recapture control of the government party to impose his populist reforms.

Some of the opposition and unrest he encountered near the end of his term, however, can be attributed to the eclectic experience he brought to the presidency. Service in many posts with different functions but relatively little political responsibility left Echeverría with a piecemeal approach to his presidential duties, so he found it difficult to formulate a coherent program. During his first years in office he opposed government participation in the economy; later he increased the number and role of "decentralized agencies" (publicly owned or controlled commercial, manufacturing, and service units). First he tried to democratize the official party; then he reasserted his control. The emphasis on redistribution did not take form until the second half of his term and its implementation was at times erratic.

The first half of President López Portillo's term indicates that he can perform more effectively. Experience with administrative planning in the Secretariat of the Presidency and with public finance in the Treasury gave him the ability to coordinate policies into a comprehensive program. During his first year in office López Portillo acted more to consolidate the disturbed political situation than to initiate new policies, but did so in a more structured and incremental way than his predecessor. He consolidated several Cabinet departments and set up Cabinet coordinating committees for finance, agricultural affairs, and other matters. He also reorganized and strengthened the planning functions of the old Secretariat of the Presidency, making it the Secretariat of Budget and Planning. The next year he inaugurated several programs, including the political reform discussed, and implemented further reorganization, especially administrative reorganization.

Considering the magnitude of the problems confronting the Mexican president, who has too many major administrative responsibilities and fundamental political functions, a period of in-service training for the position is an expensive luxury. Perhaps a different form of recruitment into public service, ultimately to the presidency, is called for. But this cannot take place until the political system — and its practitioners — undergoes reform. A closer look at the mechanics of that system will help us understand why.

CONSTITUTIONAL AND LEGAL NORMS

The Constitution of 1917 was modeled on earlier Mexican laws that copied the general contours of the United States Constitution. Relations between the national government and local governmental units are regulated by a federal division of powers between state units and the central government, with the legal rights and responsibilities of each level carefully defined. At the national level, formal authority is shared among three apparently coequal branches — legislative, executive, and judicial — each selected differently and empowered to perform specific duties, but each also acting as a restraint on the other two, in checks and balances paralleling the United States system.

The 1917 Constitution includes a comprehensive bill of rights, together with detailed comment on social and economic matters, a reflection of Revolutionary reform aspirations and strong nationalist tendencies. These policy statements establish such goals as agrarian reform and labor's right to collective bargaining and profit sharing, and assert the authority of the nation to control and exploit its own mineral and petroleum resources.

The ambitious social and economic goals written into the 1917 law might be called wishful thinking, for the country was neither psychologically nor financially ready to implement them. In fact, despite gradual and piecemeal action over the years, some of these constitutional requirements have not yet been carried out. But to educated Mexicans these reform provisions are important as a symbolic standard for future action.

The political arrangements established by the Constitution were similarly symbolic. Technically, the division of powers between central and local governments and the three-way separation of powers at the national level are carefully observed. So are the outward forms of most personal and political rights, including freedom of speech and assembly, membership in legal opposition parties, and voting in contested elections. But the fact of concentrated and nearly uncontrolled authority seems well beyond the reach of the limitations that constitutional government and democratic legislation are supposed to provide.

The Mexican Constitution provides for a separation of national government into executive, legislative, and judicial branches. In practice, however, the president comes close to being the personification of all government. A combination of historical, cultural, and legal factors make him the country's absolute administrative authority and also its dominant political power and personality, the supreme patrón.

The heads of the president's administrative departments (the *secretarías*) are fully subordinate to the chief executive, without the bargaining power enjoyed by cabinet members in other countries. To a large degree members of Congress and the judiciary are equally submissive. Most proposals for new or amended laws originate in the secretarías rather than with legislators, and all initiatives are carefully coordinated with the president's governmental program before being introduced. Once in the Chamber of Deputies or the Senate, executive-sponsored bills sail through with a minimum of serious amendment, though the content may be discussed extensively, to educate the citizenry about the reasons for adopting a given policy.

Like the PRI, to which the vast majority of legislators belong, the legislative chambers have delegated their aggregating and compromising — their political functions — to the president. Over the past thirty years, no piece of major legislation has been vetoed by the president, a good indicator of how little independence Congress has retained.

In the same way, Mexico's national court system has rarely questioned the president's constitutional or legal right to do what he wishes. This is not because it lacks formal power or jurisdiction, for Mexican law gives the judiciary wider scope in certain matters than the United States Constitution does. Mexican courts have simply carried to its ultimate logical conclusion the United States judicial practice of refusing to consider political questions. The judges refuse to attack presidential policies or reject important government programs. This avoidance of confrontation is made easier by Mexico's modified code-law system, which limits judicial initiative far more than the American common-law tradition does.

While legal forms of federalism are observed, in practice the states are little more than colonies governed by proconsuls whose nominations are approved by the president. Although the governors and the one-chamber state legislatures are popularly elected, victory usually goes to PRI candidates. A 1977 constitutional amendment ensured minority representation in state legislatures, but it is doubtful that this will ensure a broader electoral base for state officials to use to reduce presidential dominance at state and municipal levels.

A shift of power seems improbable, since the Constitution favors the central government at the expense of local government to a greater extent than does the United States model. Implementation of the document's broad social and economic provisions is assigned mainly to the national regime, and the list of limitations on local units is surprisingly long. The Constitution even empowers the national Senate to declare "disappearance of a state's powers," remove its elected officials, and invite the president to appoint more docile ones. Given the chief executive's political dominance, such drastic intervention in local affairs has tended not to be necessary recently. Instead, when a midterm shift in state leadership seems advisable — perhaps because a governor is administratively inept or because he or local legislators have been caught in blatant bribery — a convenient resignation "because of ill health" or an appointment to some other less sensitive post usually can be arranged.

Domination of the national government in making and implementing policy is not simply a matter of constitutional content or application of political clout. In practice, the central government determines which public programs will be stressed by assigning or withholding funds. Over the years, a series of national laws have preempted most of the really productive revenue sources for the national government. Some of this money returns to local authorities in the form of loans or grants for specific programs, but almost always to support activities that complement those being carried out by national agencies. Because this form of revenue sharing finances most state and local government service programs, national power to grant or refuse funds can be used to discipline uncooperative local officials with devastating effect.

In spite of the Constitution's formal provisions, neither true federalism nor effective separation of powers exists in Mexico. Political authority flows toward the center, to the president of the republic. This flow of power is channeled by an extralegal but semiofficial structure, the dominant Revolutionary Party. During the 1940s and 1950s, the party performed several political functions. By engaging the loyalty of the few existing interest associations, and by establishing new ones as citizens became aware of their emerging interests, the official party provided a means for coordinating reform efforts and beginning development. At the same time, the party forced compromise among claimants for public benefits before their requests reached the government. It could perform this informal but very helpful function effectively because only a few relatively uncomplicated groups were involved. The 1910 upheaval had broken the influence of many traditionally privileged social and economic interests (including the church hierarchy, large landholders, and mining syndicates), and the few old-style political parties based on regionalism or class that had operated under General Díaz had disappeared or lost their potency. Moreover, the vast number of narrow interest groups that accompany technological growth had not yet appeared.

In this earlier period Mexico's economy was still

quite simple, so the interests regarded as legitimate and entitled to representation in the Revolutionary party could be grouped in three broad categories, each represented by a party sector. The first was agriculture, represented primarily by ejiditarios, small farmers who had been allocated parcels of land under the agrarian reform but who, ostensibly for their protection, were not given title to that land. The agrarian sector organization, the National Farmers Federation (Confederación Nacional Campesina, or CNC), was led primarily by middle-class agronomists, lawyers, and the like. The second sector was labor, consisting of trade unions. Most were grouped together under the Mexican Federation of Labor (Confederación de Trabajadores Mexicanos, or CTM), though some smaller federations and independent unions also participated. While some labor leaders came from the working class, others were intellectuals or professionals, and virtually all soon began acting like patrones. The third group, the popular sector, was a catchall for middle-class interests — lawyers, engineers, and other professionals, small shopkeepers, clerical workers, and other more urbanized and aware Mexicans — organized into a National Federation of Popular Organizations (Confederación Nacional de Organizaciones Populares, or CNOP). Two other strong interests with associations — national government bureaucrats and schoolteachers — operated within the popular sector.

In all three sectors, the vast majority of party members were coopted, brought into the party as a group because the association to which they belonged — a peasants' league, a labor union, a taxicab cooperative — affiliated with one of the three sectors. Given the passivity of most Mexicans and the paternalism of their leaders, conflicting demands within each sector or among the several sectors could be handled within the party's machinery, allowing it to offer the president of the republic an integrated set of demands to use in preparing his national governmental program. The party also presented a single front in support of the chief executive's program in the national Congress.

During its formative years, the Revolutionary movement responded faithfully to the shifting needs of Mexico's political system. In spite of its monolithic hold on policy making, the party allowed emerging interests not included in the sectors to put their views before party leaders. As new major interests arose, the sectors either absorbed them or found some other way to bring them into the political process, even if outside party machinery. This flexibility was possible because neither the number nor the intensity of competing claims was great enough to endanger the vested positions of the various sector associations or their leaders. In fact, economic growth was so little hampered by disruptive conflict among interests, and popular desires for improved living standards were so effectively deferred or held to a minimum, that a high rate of capital accumulation resulted. This permitted large-scale public investment in programs such as road building, irrigation and power projects, and school construction. Political stability, coupled with Mexico's natural resources, encouraged private domestic and foreign investment in industry, commerce, and related activities. As a result, Mexico enjoyed remarkable though rather unbalanced social and economic progress.

Through the 1960s and 1970s, these advances affected a growing number of Mexicans, who have begun to press new and sometimes conflicting demands on the political system. Over more than a decade of rapid change and growing socioeconomic complexity, during which the proportion of informed citizens has greatly increased, the PRI has lagged in adjusting to the new situation. The harmonizing and compromising political functions it once performed have passed largely to the government, especially the president. That this aggregating role is performed by the chief executive rather than the legislature, where constitutional logic and the PRI's majority of seats might place it, suggests the party acts more as an electoral machine for sector leaders than as a participant in decision making.

This shift in the party's role is at least partially explained by the fact that pluralism does not exist in Mexico. The term is widely used in Mexico, but its meaning is distinct. Outside Mexico, the concept implies that a country's population shares so many political values and so much understanding about the proper functions of government that challenges to public policy or priorities are felt to be legitimate. In a country like Mexico — where speed of change and the class imbalance exacerbated by socioeconomic development have frustrated the development of broadly shared political norms — traditional, less permissive attitudes persist, and opposition is usually considered disloyal, even subversive.

To alter this viewpoint is extremely difficult, even for a leader who conceives of disagreement as potentially useful. Because they are unaccustomed to constructive opposition, his political opponents may see a more relaxed policy as a sign of weakness and an invitation to anarchy; because they are unwilling to share scarce benefits or compromise their personal importance, his followers may see flexibility as a violation of principle or a sellout to the enemy. When stable government requires a single set of arbitrary though consistent political values, rejection of the legitimacy of opposition may be a sound strategy. So in spite of the increase in the number and diversity of economic interests and social groups that accompanies development, a minimum of autonomy is encouraged for them.

These considerations explain the PRI's domination of the central and local governments and its control over the activities of the groups making up the three sectors. They also suggest why the other political parties are so careful to moderate their campaign rhetoric, confining their opposition to ringing generalities about how they could accomplish Revolutionary goals more effectively than the incumbent regime. In that sense they are a part of the Revolutionary political system.

This need to minimize divisiveness affects the reciprocal patrón-client arrangement between politician and follower. Because the leader feels he must fit his supporters into integrated national goals, even if it means restricting their freedom of action, he exploits their traditional tractability. Thus more power and initiative flow to the *político* than do benefits to his *militantes*, as his followers are called.

Because the Revolutionary movement did not tolerate real opposition, emerging groups were prevented from joining the PRI. The complexity of new demands, coupled with existing clientele relationships between the party sector organizations and government agencies, reduced outsiders' chances of access to the decision making through the executive secretarías. A crisis of competence had to occur, because the "political" aggregating functions once performed by the party had been shifted to the presidency at the same time that claims on the political system multiplied. President Echeverría's attempt to transfer some of this balancing responsibility back to the official party failed, so he was forced to reassume presidential dominance to impose his own solutions. Echeverría's distributive programs did not resolve the access problem, so President López Portillo sought a more long-term solution, attempting to open up the Revolutionary system with his political reform.

THE PRI — POLITICAL AGGREGATION AND POLICY MAKING

Political Mobilization

Most social scientists use *political mobilization* to describe the arousing to political consciousness and the organizing of citizens for continuous and effective political participation. In Mexico, however, mobilization has operated more as a control than as a stimulus to popular political involvement and influence.

The historical and psychological reasons for this pattern are clear. Industrial development and the Revolution of 1910 brought large numbers of previously isolated peoples into national life. The need to organize and rationalize the activities of the politically inexperienced masses was obvious; so was the need to reduce social disorder and maximize discipline. We have seen that Mexico's political culture produces in most citizens a dependence on elite leadership and works against individual action. This passive attitude made it relatively easy, after the National Revolutionary party was formed in 1929, to minimize individual participation, and to gain control of the labor unions, farm organizations, and other interest associations. Existing groups were absorbed by the party and new ones were created to manipulate contending groups, so that Revolutionary leadership could impose its own version of national development. This led naturally to the organization pattern still followed by the PRI.

This variant of political mobilization has recently been challenged by a growing minority. Many persons, including some PRI sector unit members, seek a more direct voice in politics, more direct participation in a bargaining process where contending interests compromise their claims within a framework of national interest — an approach to political action that contrasts with existing political practice.

Mexico's present political system is based on a petitioning pattern and not a bargaining process. Most Mexicans still see government as a dispenser of favors rather than as a mechanism that implements policy decisions reached after give-and-take among competing interests. Most party and government functionaries have the same view. But this petitioning approach cannot satisfy the expectations of citizens who seek more participation, especially those unable to win effective access to the decision-making process.

Pressures on the political system are multiplying because the PRI does not perform the harmonizing and compromising aggregation function as efficiently as before, and no other informal political structures have assumed the task. This means that diverse and competitive demands are carried directly to the executive branch, bypassing the Congress, which might have narrowed them down through compromise and selection. The result is that administrative officials, and ultimately the president, are swamped with demands. Why has the PRI allowed political initiative to slip away to such an extent? That question can be answered in several ways. Most party members are unaware of lost power. During the Revolutionary party's existence, the president has been its leader, so the transfer of authority to the president seems more a shift in emphasis than a net loss. And since almost every party member shares traditional dependence on a patrón, the changing role of president and party has seemed a natural evolution.

Until it reorganizes, there is little the PRI can do to reverse its loss of influence. Its three-sector structure is not well adapted to the new socioeconomic situation; worse, the associational arrangement actually impedes the party's adjustment to changing conditions. The exclusionist, protectionist attitude of most sector leaders has driven many recently emerging interests away from the PRI to directly petition the Government. As a result, the party includes fewer and fewer of the politically active and influential socioeconomic groups in the country. At the same time, the PRI dissipates energy in struggles among those groups for whom it does speak.

Internal conflict is likely for any large group, but particularly for one that seeks to coordinate and control the activities of a set of formally organized and potentially competitive groups with easily identifiable socioeconomic characteristics. As long as the conditions that brought the original group together remain unchanged, cooperation will continue. But when shifts in these conditions occur, the stability of the larger coordinating body will be threatened and its effectiveness curtailed. This is what is happening to the PRI. The party's three sectors, which originated as symbols for vague, abstract, and all-inclusive popular interests, now must represent a multitude of self-consciously different claimants who have frequently incompatible demands. Each sector's functional associations, which once controlled a pliant rank and file, are now torn by internal conflict among special groups actively defending their interests.

The party is less able to perform efficiently as an integrating and compromising structure because the separation of interest groups by sector is breaking down. Associations representing some aspect of a general occupational category — agriculture, for example — can now be found in each of the three sectors. This happens for a variety of reasons, mostly because of technical specialization. Some association leaders deny adequate representation to emerging interests, driving them to another sector or even outside the party. In other cases, sector membership competes with vocational loyalty, as when an agronomist, as a professional, belongs to the popular rather than to the agrarian sector. Similarly, recent government policies may blur long-established sector distinctions. Public employees are supposed to belong to the popular sector, but what about organized workers in enterprises whose majority stock interest has been purchased by the central authorities? Electrical workers belong to a CTM union in the labor sector; teachers' syndicates, affiliated formally with the popular sector, seek close cooperation with the Congress of Labor, which tries to coordinate the groups making up the labor sector.

In Mexico's transitional environment conflicting attitudes of rank-and-file members also complicate the sectors' coordinating function. Leaders who try to accomodate pressures from challenging interests face objections from the more traditional subjects, who see compromise with outsiders as a sellout. On the other hand, association members who are acquiring participant norms reject the patrón-client relationship and resist imposed decisions, whether for cooperation with other groups or exclusiveness. The internal stresses produced by these differences cannot help but weaken the PRI's role as an integrating mechanism, as a few specific examples of organizational problems will demonstrate.

Agriculture no longer can be considered a single monolithic interest centering in the ejido farmers and their association, the National Farmers Federation (CNC). Instead, new groups with specific interests represented by their own organizations have appeared. Different forms of landholding, different kinds of labor, particular kinds of foods and fiber production, food processing, marketing machinery, and a hundred other special interests cannot be lumped together under the term agriculture and represented by the CNC.

Because small farmowners were not welcomed by the agrarian sector, they set up their own group, the Pequeño Propietarios (Small Landowners), in the popular sector. Landless day-wage peons could not get fair representation in existing agriculture groups, and because of a deal with the agrarian leaders, the labor sector would not organize them. So a separate movement sprang up, the Independent Farmers (Centro Campesino Independiente, or CCI). The CCI then split into two groups, one operating within the agrarian sector, in competition with the CNC, and the other working outside the party.

As the agro-industrial decentralization program matures, chances are that the new food processing workers and farm machinery operators will be organized. Meanwhile, in 1978 both the CNC in the agrarian sector and the CTM in the labor sector announced plans to organize the day laborers on some of the larger ejidos' and small landowners' holdings. Because these laborers work in scattered areas and on a day-wage basis, this will be extremely difficult, and even if both organizing units follow their intentions the two resulting unions will tend to cancel each other out.

To complicate matters, distinct agricultural interests urge conflicting government policies. Those producing for export to the United States view tariff problems differently from those producing for the domestic market; cotton and hemp growers' credit needs are unlike those of food producers; corn and wheat farmers market differently than meat and milk producers. The CNC, speaking mainly for the least developed and most inefficient segment of Mexican agriculture, could scarcely pretend to represent all these complex interests, so it decided that if you can't lick them, join them, initiating the 1975 Pact of Ocampo. This alliance included the CNC, one faction of the CCI, and several smaller agrarian groups; a few months later part of the small farmers' federation was added. Other agriculturalists, including most of the larger and more efficient pequeño propietarios, formed their own organization and made informal arrangements with private-sector business and financial groups to defend their interests against President Echeverría's distributive policies from outside the party.

Similar problems arise within the other two official party sectors. Labor has set up the Labor Congress (Congreso del Trabajo) as a mechanism to settle conflicts among some thirty-four rival federations, but many workers believe that the Congress only protects the interests of established groups, especially the huge Mexican Labor Federation (CTM). Younger union leaders, and increasing numbers of the rank and file as well, feel that long-entrenched labor bosses must be replaced, both because of age and because they represent *charro* unionism, which sells out to management or to the government policy of deferred gratification. Some labor elements find they can accomplish their aims more effectively by operating outside the party sector. After they split off from the major group, Volkswagen workers doubled their real income. Other labor leaders, ambitious for personal power as well as to improve their followers' benefits, seek to capture control of unions within the dominant labor federations. Two factions of the electrical workers have engaged in a bitter and continuing struggle, despite government attempts to force agreement — an agreement that would favor the established leadership. Moreover, the PRI's labor sector is supposed to provide access to decision making for all workers, but it really represents the interests of organized union members, who make up less than a quarter of Mexico's nonagricultural work force. As unorganized laborers become increasingly sophisticated, they must find entry to the party or they will turn to nonparty tactics, as several independent unions already have done. Moreover, several of the newly recognized political parties may bid for their support, as already is happening.

With a middle-class rather than an occupational base, the popular sector has suffered from an identity crisis from its inception. The so-called popular organizations making up the National Federation of Popular Organizations (Confederación Nacional de Organizaciones Populares, or CNOP) include such disparate types as taxicab drivers, small shopkeepers and street vendors, members of cooperatives, and lawyers, physicians, or engineers. Also included in the popular sector as separate entities are the government bureaucrats and schoolteachers' unions.

Because of their strategic location in cities and greater political awareness, members of the groups in this sector have won from the government benefits far out of proportion to their numbers. But at the same time that claims on the public purse double and redouble, from the other sectors inside the party as well as more knowledgeable masses outside, internal competition among popular sector units multiplies. As a result, not only are nonparty commercial and industrial elements bypassing the party to deal directly with government, but some party components are too.

The feeling that the popular sector does not represent middle-class interests effectively is clearly reflected by electoral statistics in more affluent districts in the larger cities. PRI vote totals for both presidential and legislative candidates in these districts run below the national average of those from poorer districts. Some might argue that a Revolutionary party should be less concerned with middle-sector desires anyway, but in Mexico the middle groups are both aware and growing. If the PRI does not serve them they may abstain from political participation or look to other political movements for relief.

Political Aggregation

Because of apparent similarities in formal and some informal mechanisms, one might guess that as in the United States, aggregation in Mexico is performed by many structures. Perhaps it is achieved through interaction among competing groups in and out of the party system, leading to compromise in the legislative body. This simply is not the case. Fierce competition exists, but not free interplay in a variety of political structures. The true policy arena is the executive branch of the national government, particularly the Secretariat of Planning and Budget, with the president as judge of last resort.

Into the 1950s the government party to some degree did aggregate the interests within its three sectors, but since then it has gradually lost this function to the presidency and become mainly an election machine. The reversion to traditional presidential power occurred because the party could not aggregate adequately under shifting conditions, which multiplied the number of competing groups and made incorporating them into the existing sectors nearly impossible.

Despite the aspirations of President López Portillo's political reform, policy is not made in a pluralistic setting. Confrontation politics inherited from a national history shot through with deep divisions and mistrust intensified when political stability and economic growth dramatically increased the number of organized special interests, all demanding a greater share of available benefits but few willing to compromise. Neither the functionally structured party nor the legislature dominated by its members served as a brokering mechanism to balance conflicting claims. In fact, the party's sectors impeded the entry of some emerging and challenging groups, not only into the party but into the decision process, using their client relationship with executive agencies to do so. As a consequence, raw, unaggregated demands from groups inside and outside the party deluged the president, who was forced to accept responsibility for imposing a compromise. In doing so, he acted more in the historic role of patrón than in the constitutionally prescribed capacity as chief executive.

Does all this mean that while studying Mexico's politics we can safely ignore legal units of government or informal political structures? Definitely not. Recently these more participant mechanisms have ceased being mere symbols of an idealized democracy and have contributed to the structural crisis threatening the political system.

Paradoxically, this crisis is a product of the system's success, for it involves the inability of spokesmen for certain in-groups to accept changes in political roles caused by shifts in the socioeconomic environment produced by development. The mix of patrón leadership and corporative interest representation that worked so well in a subject political culture is proving too inelastic as more participatory values emerge. Economic progress during the 1950s and 1960s not only multiplied the number of special groups but also established conditions under which the traditional economic dependency and political inadequacy of their members could change, indeed had to change. A growing number of Mexicans — still a minority of the total population, but its most aware and potentially active portion — have entered national life and politics. And the remainder, the unorganized masses, are beginning to make their presence felt sufficiently to affect the comfortable in-house division of public benefits among the functional interests.

Some Mexicans continue to accept elite-dominated structures appropriate to a subject political culture. Others reject such nonparticipatory patterns and demand greater roles in government. This is especially true of those citizens whose psychological horizons have widened enough to question the patrón-client relationship. Some of these last continue to show a predilection for corporative representation, but reject the disciplined political mobilization that restricts their group's freedom to seek advantage while barring entry into the PRI. A growing number of potential participants, on the other hand, are not part of functional groups, either because their peculiar interests are not conducive to collective action or because they mistrust such ap-

Members of the newly recognized Communist party parading at Mexico City's monument to the 1910 Revolution in support of their own revolution.

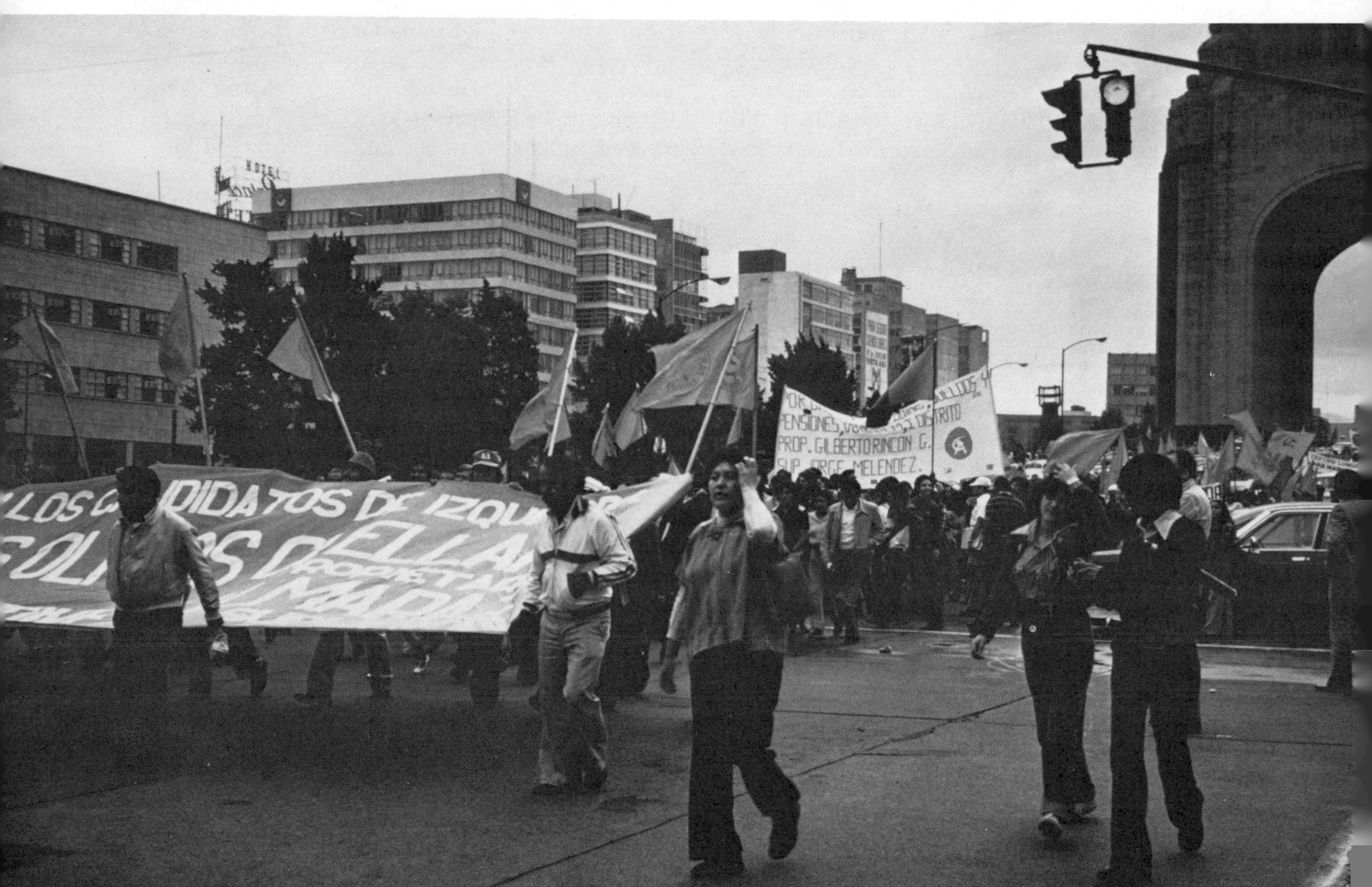

proaches. All of these outsiders have one thing in common — a need to change the system to permit them access.

These emerging forces know that they must have a stronger voice in determining policies that affect them, but they find entry blocked. For one thing, leaders of the established corporative organizations mistrust this new breed of independent and self-starting participants who might undermine the patrón's influence. For another, material benefits cannot be distributed to new claimants without adversely affecting privileged interests, for population growth and exploding popular expectations far surpass expanding production. Finally, the proliferation of functionally specific groupings seriously overloads the decision-making process.

The political machinery that evolved and gelled in the mold of an earlier and simpler era divided government benefits among a few broad, almost abstract areas of interest, with government party corporative organizations as spokesmen. Today, with functional specialization generating a multiplicity of distinct groupings, no one unit can pretend to represent adequately all types of "agricultural" interests, "labor" demands, or "middle class" aspirations, especially if emerging elements are excluded systematically from participating in the party organization's activities because its established leaders try to perpetuate their power monopoly by evading the claims of outsiders.

Most recent major upsets in Mexico's politics — conservative protests over the content of primary school texts, land seizures, small landholders' agricultural stoppages, disruptive splits in labor unions, and capital flight and investment strikes by private-sector entrepreneurs — result from the inability of divergent interests to get consideration of their vital claims because they cannot win effective access to the policy process. Such confrontations usually involve the actions of organized interests whose corporative form impedes the accommodation between the claims and counterclaims of "in" and "out" groups, overloading even a system specifically designed to handle this sort of collective representation.

Some time around the mid-1960s the cumulative influence of the outsiders, both organized and not, began to threaten the insiders. The Revolutionary coalition structured around the official party and the presidency is still the single most powerful political movement in Mexico, and the challengers are badly splintered. But the diffuse pressures they exert are growing and continuous, so much so that in order to keep the political system working the president has had to act on their demands.

President Gustavo Díaz Ordaz (1964–1970) had managed for the most part to ignore the changing situation, so the pressures accumulated. Luis Echeverría (1970–1976) was a populist, more sensitive to growing frustrations in the populace. He responded by attempting to democratize the party's candidate selection process, encouraging greater rank-and-file participation. The experiment did not work well. Erosion of the sector leaders' authority encouraged specialized interest dissidence within the sector organizations but did not weaken the determination of most party members (or of the government bureaucrats they were clients to) to protect their privileged positions against interlopers.

Echeverría reverted to the traditional Mexican presidential role of dominating authority figure, naming new national party officers who restored central control and imposed on the government coalition programs designed to share the country's limited wealth with the masses. For several years the president quarreled sporadically with the institutionalized forces of the Revolution, in turn characterizing labor leaders, bureaucrats, private-sector entrepreneurs, and small agriculturalists as counterrevolutionaries, or worse.

The precariously balanced system nearly tottered during 1976, as Echeverría's term moved to a close. Population pressures on jobs and resources combined with rising popular expectations just as uncertainties over distributive policies disrupted agriculture and industrial growth. Economic problems brought on two devaluations of the peso within three months. Rumors of a possible military coup were part of a campaign from within and outside the Revolutionary coalition to discredit Echeverría and his populist policies; they were wildly exaggerated, but all evidence proves that pressures on the political system were real enough.

During the first portion of his term, President López Portillo (1976–1982) sought to prescribe for the ills besetting the country. We have discussed his remedies, from the Alliance for Production to political reform, suggesting that the immediate crisis has eased but that the long-term prognosis is guarded. The immediate threat of systemic breakdown has diminished, but continuing confrontations among contending interests suggests that President López Portillo's medicine may treat symptoms rather than the disease itself.

This rather negative outlook for Mexico's political system results from an obvious structural weakness. Too many functions on both the input and the output sides of the political process have had to be assumed by the presidency or, given the country's personalistic politics, by the president of the republic himself. Since most new public policies originate in the executive departments in the name of the president, a large share of interest articulation takes place there. As we have seen, real aggregation occurs there, with minimal assistance from political structures usually associated with the input process. Similarly, despite careful observance of the forms of legislative review and approval, ultimate authoritative decision making is a presidential prerogative. Obviously, implementation of policy too is an executive responsibility. Finally, both because of roman (civil) law procedures and accepted political practice, policy adjudication lies mainly with the president and his secretarías.

Political arrangements which served well under a subject political culture, organized for disciplinary political mobilization on a corporative basis reflecting a less complex set of interests and led by an elite accustomed to a semi-authoritarian relationship with docile followers, became inadequate under development induced change. The president took over more and more of the principal political functions in order to avert overloading of the system. But it becomes increasingly evident of late that without new auxiliary political structures the executive alone cannot cope with multitudes of ever more specialized demands, and not merely because there are not enough resources to go around. The emerging more aware and participant elements in the population simply require more distinct and independent structures for access to the political process.

If the pressures of rapid change continue to accumulate faster than new balancing mechanisms to augment the president's efforts can evolve, the present system could break down and some form of military intervention be set up to provide authoritarian stabilization, as has happened in so many other parts of the emerging world. On the other hand, considering that some of the system's difficulties have been engendered by increasing emphasis on participation, we may see the gradual displacement of personalistic presidential power by a mix of constitutional structures or more responsible informal ones. This might mean the development of a brokering party system, a powerful, broadly representative legislature, an executive politically responsive to the needs of the whole citizenry, or some combination of them. So basic a shift in the political system might require more time than growing pressures permit, but long identification of Revolutionary aims with democracy and the careful observance of constitutional and participatory forms could ease the transition. This presupposes continuing socioeconomic change that encourages further movement away from confrontation politics toward compromise within a pluralistic environment.

Whether or not Mexican politics turns in either of these directions, unless major changes in the organization and functioning of the political system occur, a structural crisis remains a strong possibility. Let us now look more closely at the factors that will help or hinder such changes.

MEXICO'S POLITICAL FUTURE

The Clash of Political Cultures

For all its progress, Mexico is a country in transition. Certain mechanisms of the present political system are still appropriate for that part of the population just emerging from parochialism, isolation, ignorance, and subsistence agriculture, an existence that breeds a mentality of adaptation and submission to external forces. But this dependence is not attractive to urbanized, knowledgeable, middle-sector citizens working in an industrial economy and aware of how government decisions affect their personal interests. People of this sort challenge paternalistic leaders and seek personal involvement in the political process to influence the policies that affect them.

During the past decade the operations of the political system have been increasingly disturbed by the conflicting demands made by these two different groups and by those in between them, the majority of their fellow citizens. Unless the political system finds ways to reconcile these conflicting claims, the activities of its component structures will become more and more incongruent with each other as groups with incompatible political values capture control of them.

Expressions of popular discontent have multiplied, reflecting the difficulties the system faces in trying to satisfy increasingly divergent popular needs and expectations. As they grow more aware politically, and at times more desperate, some members of the lower class react to continuing inequities in the distribution of benefits with riots, land seizures, or other forms of direct protest. This is especially true of those in extreme poverty in rural areas. Challengers from the middle sector may not resort to violence, but they can withhold goods or services, refuse to invest in new production facilities, establish a rival group for a nonrepresentative one, or otherwise express their grievances in ways that force the government to consider their claims.

As it presently operates, the system does not offer the unorganized majority or the unofficial functional groups enough access to the policy process to ensure fair representation. While awareness was low and demands on government few, the "search for a miracle" based on a dependency relationship with some external force — a patrón — may have provided sufficient access, but this is no longer the case. Spokesmen for corporatively organized in-groups, who have client relationships, can deal more directly and effectively with decision makers and policy implementers in the executive. Furthermore, even a supreme patrón, like the president, may be unable to satisfy the outsiders' needs after they win his support. For one thing, there are not enough resources to go around, and established groups may have preempted so large a share that redistributive efforts are nearly meaningless. For another, the continuous and disciplined activities of organized in-groups can defeat the reform efforts even of an all-powerful president, simply by outwaiting him. Former President Echeverría attempted in the mid-1970s to set up a popular alliance to counterbalance the influence of what he called entrepreneurial profit-mongers, unfeeling bureaucrats, selfish functional interest associations, and others within the Revolutionary coalition. The attempt failed, partly because his alliance was incapable of focusing pressure on specific government agencies, but also because the president's term ran out. In such situations frustrated citizens may give up on the existing political system.

Political Abstention

Political abstention has many causes. Historically, the peasant in subsistence agriculture or working on a large hacienda was scarcely aware of formal government, much less of political parties and elections. Even today many Mexicans remain isolated from the mainstream of national life — by geography, lack of education, noninvolvement in the money economy, or other barriers. More worldly Mexicans may not participate because of culturally induced submissiveness.

Citizens who do seek an active political role may encounter obstructions to effective participation. Relatively few persons seeking political influence join one of the minor parties, either because they do not wish to conform to a narrow ideological approach or because such movements have little possibility of winning elections or influencing policy. For its part, the PRI has long recruited its members almost entirely from the functional interest organizations making up its three sectors. And the interest association leaders strongly discourage initiative by individual members or by groups of followers. Finally, many citizens abstain from voting because they view nomination by the PRI as equivalent to victory, due either to its overwhelming power or to manipulation of the election machinery.

A growing sense of frustration is felt by many Mexicans with newly developed interests. Because they cannot gain access to the policy process through the parties or through the national and state legislatures, they turn to the national government's executive departments. But for the most part these administrative agencies and their chiefs are poorly equipped to satisfy such raw demands, which rarely fit gracefully into current programs, no matter how valid the claims may be. After repeated rebuffs, many Mexicans simply stop trying to work through the political system, and instead operate as best they can outside it. The real danger to the party is that pressure on government by these proliferating interests may eventually be coordinated by some other political movement, one that can satisfy their aspirations.

Despite formal observance of the Revolutionary motto "Effective suffrage, no reelection," voting has been used more to legitimize the indirect control mechanisms than to select representative policy makers. To date, the PRI has not lost any major election; it is too well organized and the opposition parties too feeble. Over the past three decades, the party's presidential and congressional nominees, as well as state level contenders, have swamped their electoral opponents. In 1976, Lic. López Portillo[6] won 86 percent of the vote, and the PRI took every senate seat (sharing one with a candidate jointly nominated by the Popular Socialist party) and all but a handful of deputy posts.

If the Revolutionary party is so successful, why worry about election results? Because careful analysis of voting statistics over the past ten years shows slippage in the PRI's influence over strategic portions of the populace and foreshadows additional attrition for the future. The party has lost municipal elections in several larger cities, done poorly in others, and lost races for state legislatures. Similarly, the winning proportion of votes for all candidates from president to local officials often has been markedly lower in the Federal District and the more developed states. At the same time, large numbers of citizens do not bother to cast a ballot, despite compulsory voting laws with quite rigorous sanctions. As a result, the PRI shows weakness in urban areas and states where informed and independent middle-sector voters congregate. The problem, then, is that as the country becomes more integrated and industrialized and a higher proportion of citizens more knowledgeable, the pattern of ebbing government party influence and weakening popular support for the political system may continue.

While campaigning for the presidency in 1970, Luis Echeverría made the point that the greatest danger to the system is failure of many citizens to participate, especially by voting. Lack of a broad power base could lead to erosion of political authority and ultimately to defeat of the Revolutionary movement. But the more immediate disquieting fact about a refusal to perform this formal act of participation is that growing numbers of Mexicans are opting out of the existing political system.

The 1976 presidential election suggests the implications of the problem. Lic. López Portillo won 86 percent of the actual votes, but only 51 percent of the potential vote. Despite a frantic registration and get-out-the-vote campaign, 13 percent of adults failed to register and 31 percent of those who registered failed to vote, so that only 59 percent of the potential voters participated. In the Federal District, López Portillo captured only 52 percent of the potential votes, a poor showing for the sole candidate, particularly as the PARM and the PPS had named him as their nominee, and the PAN had been unable to agree on a candidate. Of the thirty-two national entities (thirty-one states and the Federal District), about a third cast less than the national average percentage vote for López Portillo. Significantly, many of these units are among the more economically and socially advanced and contain most of the larger cities in the country.

PRI políticos frequently complain, "We made the middle class, and now they reject us." This is not correct, for the Revolutionary leaders who dominate the functional organizations and protect their interests against the middle sector challengers come from the same stratum. They are merely defending established positions against other urban dissenters, whose expectations compete with the vested interests in the party and with those of the private governments outside the party that have worked out a comfortable accommodation with it.

Until the PRI provides access for these new elements, middle-class conflict with the system will increase rather than disappear. This struggle is compli-

[6] "Lic." is the abbreviation for *licenciado*, the formal title given persons satisfying academic and legal requirements for practicing a profession. In Mexico the great majority of *licenciados* are lawyers, though economists, sociologists, and even journalists may bear the title. Other professional persons may designate their specialties (*ingeniero*, *doctor*, *arquitecto*) and military officers may combine rank with a civilian title (as in Colonel y Lic. Juan Fulano). Widespread use of formal titles reflects continuing class distinctions as well as a sense of personal insecurity that seeks public recognition for individual status and accomplishment.

cated by the growing needs of the urban and rural masses. As more members of the popular classes become integrated into national life, they too will press for a meaningful role, both as individual citizens and as members of functional organizations. Inevitably, like it or not, contending interests in the middle sector will have to share status and material benefits with the emerging majority. Herein lies the structural crisis facing the political system, for its present mechanisms cannot accommodate these new interests.

We already have considered possible directions Mexico's political system might turn. Only time will tell which route the country takes. How soon the decision must be taken will depend on how pressing are the psychic and material needs of the citizens. To a large extent this depends on government performance, to which we now turn.

GOVERNMENT PERFORMANCE AND POLITICAL SYSTEM PERFORMANCE

At the beginning of this chapter we spoke about Third World states undergoing simultaneous crises in material distribution and political participation. By now it must be evident that Mexico faces its own version of these crises, despite its early start on modernization and the delay in the appearance of the crises, resulting from the development strategy followed by the Revolutionary regimes after 1930. We can view a political system as a mechanism for the resolution of such crises, that is, for managing the tensions between the creation and distribution of material benefits, or between the concentration of political authority and the sharing of it. In that case, our judgment of the success or failure of Mexico's development strategy and the political system it produced depends on the answers to two questions. Did the strategy create a strong, institutionalized political system and a viable, self-sustaining economy before the buildup of pressures to share power and welfare arose to challenge them? Is the political system adaptive enough to handle the stresses caused by the basic changes in the power structure that these pressures call for?

The answer to the first question is yes; the answer to the second awaits the verdict of history. To understand why, let us consider the quality of government performance over the past half century, and then turn to the reaction of the political system to the two crises.

Comparing the levels of government service and welfare of a few decades ago with the present suggests that Mexico's Revolutionary regime has accomplished a great deal, perhaps because the "authoritarian-technocratic-mobilization strategy"[7] it imposed was well suited to the subject political culture. This approach suspended competitive individual participation in the political process to ensure a high degree of stability, thus facilitating economic development. Given the responsibility for social reform and economic growth assumed by the government in the 1917 Constitution, it is not surprising that a mixed economy evolved. In the beginning, government played a positive but indirect role. It offered tax incentives and protective tariffs to attract foreign and domestic investment; it supported growth through inequity, deferring gratification of urban workers' demands while underpaying the farmer for his crops to keep urban prices low, attracting foreign investors and permitting domestic entrepreneurs to accumulate capital; it assigned scarce revenues to provide an infrastructure on which the economy could build. Later, government played a more direct role, taking control of many basic materials, production facilities, and service activities. It nationalized petroleum, the railroads, electric power, and other utilities; it built steel mills and engaged in industrial production; it expanded the number and scope of its decentralized agencies. By 1980 government's share of gross domestic product would be about 20 percent.

Almond and Powell speak of the Mexican approach as an arrested mobilization system, because the mobilized egalitarian pattern of the Cárdenas phase of the Revolution (mid-1930s to early 1940s) became largely symbolic as the dominant party "served as a cooptative, preemptive system, sharply restricting the activities of other political parties, re-

[7] Many of the terms and concepts used here are adopted from Gabriel A. Almond and G. Bingham Powell, *Comparative Politics: System, Process, Policy*, 2nd ed. (Boston: Little, Brown, 1978), ch. 13–14.

pressing dissent, and following policies primarily benefiting the privileged sectors of the population."[8] This freezing of participation became more marked as the official party, which had performed some representational functions, became only one structure among many used by the presidency. Reverting to a traditional Mexican pattern, control of most political initiative and domination of all major political functions passed to the incumbent President of the Republic, who operated through a technocratic bureaucracy.

Concentrated political authority and disciplinary mobilization of the citizenry, based on corporative organization of quasi-legal functional units, ensured a minimum of dissent. Economic growth fed on political stability and, for the time being, vice versa. As long as the president was willing and able to use his power to enforce the development strategy, institutionalized government and solidly based economic systems could operate. Threats to both arose during the 1960s, partly because of a shift in the norms against which government performance was measured.

To evaluate the quality of government performance, we must decide, performance for what or whom? Under a development strategy that was more concerned with economic growth than social justice or political participation, the record of material expansion was impressive. Highways, steel mills, electric power grids, and communications networks all contribute to the general economy. So do some welfare services that make the worker more efficient — education, health programs, or the like. But emphasis on such works assumes a docile population that does not demand more immediate benefits from government. It also assumes the regime is both willing and strong enough financially to supply both sorts of service. Mexico's Revolutionary regime is neither.

Despite government's acceptance of responsibility for material development, and its lip service to social justice, the regime's financial involvement in national life and the economy is relatively low. For example, if we consider 1978 figures, despite worldwide inflation, for central government revenues and expenditures as a percentage of gross domestic product, we find Mexico falling below other equally developed Latin American countries and nearer the less developed (see Table 14.9). This means that the proportion of resources extracted from the economy to finance government services is lower in Mexico than in many states facing equally complex and competing claims.

Table 14.9

1978 Central Government Revenues and Expenditures

Country	*Revenues (Percentage of GDP)*	*Expenditures (Percentage of GDP)*
Chile	23.1	24.0
Peru	15.4	20.6
Mexico	12.1	15.3
Colombia	9.2	8.7
Guatemala	11.4	13.1

Source: Inter-American Development Bank reports.

Not even the 20 percent of annual GNP produced by government decentralized agencies under Mexico's mixed economy alters this pattern. Most such units are so inefficient and badly managed that instead of providing revenues to support public services they require yearly subsidies from government. During 1979, for the first time in a decade Aeromexico announced proudly that it would not lose money. But necessary expansion in the electric power industry and the national petroleum monopoly — PEMEX — requires such high expenditures for construction and capital equipment that neither agency expects to reach a break-even point in its operations before 1985.

In 1978, with ex-President Echeverría's distributive program to improve the quality of life for the disadvantaged well under way, the share of central government expenditures allocated to three welfare programs remained low. Again, Mexico's record was closer to less developed states than to equally advanced ones (see Table 14.10). Even though Mexico is the only country with a federal system among

[8] Almond and Powell, *Comparative Politics*, p. 383.

Table 14.10

Percentage of 1978 Central Government Expenditures for Popular Welfare

	Education	*Public health*	*Housing*	*Per capita*[a] *(GDP 1978)*
Chile	17.8	7.1	3.1	1360.8
Peru	17.0	5.0	1.0	848.0
Mexico	8.4	10.1	0.7	1016.0
Colombia[b]	13.2	6.6	1.7	637.1
Guatemala	10.7	7.1	3.7	880.5

[a] Based on 1976 U.S. dollars.

[b] Figures on expenditures are for 1977.

Source: Inter-American Development Bank reports.

those compared, a substantial share of services is not financed by state governments. Of the programs considered, only education is partly a state and local responsibility; public health and housing are national programs. In any event, the Mexican system preempts nearly every major fiscal source for the national treasury; the few state programs in existence are financed almost entirely by grants from the central government.

These figures represent a development strategy in which public services were long restricted mainly to a small portion of the urban population, with little advantage to marginals in city or country. Education and health services are becoming more widespread but expansion has not only been uneven, especially in the countryside, but incremental, so that support has risen slowly, considering population growth. Housing expenditures for 1978 were relatively low because at that time the comprehensive programs were just beginning to take form. Since then public programs for urban and rural construction have grown markedly, financed largely by payroll taxes and employer contributions rather than by general tax income.

The government's performance in service to the general citizenry is not impressive. Such a standard goes beyond the frame of reference of the government's development strategy, but it is not unfair to apply it — the regime assumes responsibility for providing general welfare. The Constitution of 1917 promised benefits for all. Ever since, políticos have sought to outbid each other in promising government supplied housing, health services, educational facilities, land reform, and full employment.

As long as "all" consisted mainly of a small, privileged urban minority — the in-groups of the Revolutionary coalition — such talk presented no problems. But some of the consequences of political stability have set into motion forces over which the government has little control. Information, movement, and absorption into the national life and economy have multiplied the number of politically aware and potentially active citizens, upsetting the premise of a development strategy that assumed a continuing subject political culture with limited popular expectations.

To the uninvolved observer — who can take into account the implications of such national problems as the terrain, which isolates 80,000 localities of less than 500 inhabitants, or overfast population growth, which leaves over half of Mexicans under eighteen years old — government welfare accomplishments over the past fifty years may seem remarkable. To the marginal Mexican without a school for his children, inadequately housed, fed, and dressed, and unemployed or seriously underemployed, government performance must seem woefully inadequate.

Official programs to resolve many of these problems do exist, but most are so poorly administered and meagerly financed, considering the magnitude of the need, that they are more symbolic than significant. But their existence raises the expectations of the marginals, so that failure to provide solutions merely heightens the frustration.

The situation would not be so serious if development had not caused a shift toward more participatory political norms, and if the structures of the present system were flexible enough to permit adaptation to such values. However, the corporative structural pattern resists incorporation of challenging forces into the system. It has closed ranks against outsiders, just as disciplined mobilization is being replaced by dynamic activism.

Not even Luis Echeverría, the most powerful recent political figure, could impose distributive policies on the established structures within the Revolutionary coalition. The institutionalization of existing collective arrangements stands in the way of altering forms of representation and popular participation in the political process; it impedes updating the system, as we see suggested by the weak influence of President López Portillo's political reform upon the 1979 congressional election. Whether this corporative pattern has enough defenses to withstand the exploding popular pressures is something that is being tested every day. The battle is joined between two contending sets of values, which seek to direct Mexico's political system along opposite routes. Whether the participatory, inclusive, and democratic norms or the authoritarian, exclusionist, and elitist approach will prevail in Mexico is still uncertain.

KEY TERMS

José López Portillo
Partido Revolucionario Institutional (PRI)
patrón
caudillos
Luis Echeverría
Positivism
corporate representation
stratified class system
marginals
personalismo
secretarias
code-law system
National Farmers Federation
Mexican Federation of Labor
National Federation of Popular Organizations
political mobilization
confrontation politics

Tanzania

Tanzania
Scale of Miles
0
100
200
UGANDA
RWANDA
BURUNDI
ZAIRE
ZAMBIA
MALAWI
MOZAMBIQUE
KENYA
INDIAN OCEAN
Lake Victoria
Lake Tanganyika
Lake Nyasa
Lake Rukwa
Lake Eyasi
Lake Manyara
WEST LAKE
MWANZA
MARA
SHINYANGA
ARUSHA
KILIMANJARO
TANGA
KIGOMA
TABORA
SINGIDA
DODOMA
COAST
MOROGORO
IRINGA
MBEYA
MTWARA
RUVUMA
ZANZIBAR
Bukoba
Mwanza
Geita
Arusha
Moshi
Tanga
Ujiji
Tabora
Dodoma
Bagamoyo
Zanzibar
Dar es Salaam
Morogoro
Iringa
Kasanga
Mbeya
Mwaya
Kilwa Masoko
Lindi
Mtwara
Moyowosi R.
Wembere R.
Pangani R.
Ugalla R.
Rungwa R.
Njombe R.
Great Ruaha R.
Wami R.
Rufiji R.
Ruvuma R.

CHAPTER FIFTEEN

CHARLES W. GOSSETT

Politics in Tanzania

INTRODUCTION

Sub-Saharan Africa and the Tanzanian Case

Africa, until the late 1950s and early 1960s, was a continent of colonies. Only Ethiopia, Liberia, and South Africa, amongst the countries south of the Sahara Desert, were in any sense independent. France, Britain, Belgium, Portugal, and Spain controlled the rest of tropical Africa's inhabitants. But by the late 1950s, the rise of nationalist movements and the increasing costs of colonialism to European governments resulted in a widespread transfer of formal political power to a host of new African states. That economic power did not necessarily change hands at the same time is now clear. Charges by African nationalists of neocolonialism and neo-imperialism are, in part, expressions of their frustration at the realization that political power is circumscribed to the extent that it does not correspond to economic control.

Most transfers of power were relatively smooth, although events in the former Portuguese colonies, the Western Sahara, Guinea, and Kenya provide exceptions. Hurried attempts to establish democratic institutions in the colony were a feature of the last few years, or in some cases months, of colonial rule. Since the 1960s the fragility of the hastily constructed governments modeled on European patterns has been exposed. Unable to rule and unable to resist, a large number of African states have experienced the replacement of civilian governments by military rulers — Nigeria, Uganda, Zaire, and Upper Volta, for example. Others have seen civilian leaders invalidate or rewrite constitutions to prevent the electorate from exercising control. In Malawi, Hastings Kamuzu Banda had himself declared president-for-life; in Swaziland, King Sobhuza abolished the Parliament and the Constitution and reinstituted the monarchy; in Lesotho, Prime Minister Leabua Jonathon voided the 1970 election he lost.

To identify a typical African state is impossible. Tanzania is both like and unlike other African countries. Although slightly larger in area and population than most, the country is among the continent's least urbanized. It has been independent for less than two decades, as is the case with most of the continent.[1] Only one political party is allowed to exist, a situation characteristic of all but a few African states under civilian rule. But whereas many new states have either lapsed or been led into leadership resembling the patrimonialism of traditional societies, Tanzanian leaders have worked hard to transform parochial citizens into participants. Still, almost every project undertaken in the country has been strongly influenced by the ideals espoused by President Julius Nyerere, although this has not led to the personality cult that has developed around other African leaders, like Mobuto Sese Seko of Zaire.

Tanzania ranks as one of the world's twenty-five poorest nations. Growth of the gross national product (GNP) has been moderate by African standards, but since population growth has kept pace with economic growth, there has been little change in per capita GNP over the past few years. However, some redistribution of national wealth in favor of poorer and middle income groups has taken place, since wage and price controls became prominent government tools in 1967. In 1976, a strong economic recovery from the combined effects of a drought and world inflation in the mid-1970s suggested that Tanzania's economic leadership was more capable than that of some other countries. While the economic dependence of colonies has frequently continued unabated into independence, even in some cases been encouraged, Tanzania has continuously tried to create a self-reliant socialist state that can deal as an equal, not a dependent, with other countries.

Transforming the political, social, and economic character of a society is not easy. The environment in which Tanzania is attempting to change is such that the possibility of authoritarianism must constantly be kept in mind. Likewise, leaders want to avoid the development of vast inequalities of wealth. To discover how successfully Tanzania has managed to realize its goals, a brief discussion of its land, its people, and its history will be required.

[1] Tanzania, as a unique political entity, has existed since April 26, 1964. At that time Tanganyika and Zanzibar merged, to form the United Republic of Tanganyika and Zanzibar. A few months later, the name was changed to the United Republic of Tanzania. The mainland (Tanganyika) and the islands (Zanzibar) have not, despite the name, acted as a united republic in many matters. More closely coordinated activities began in 1977. Most of the information provided here refers to the mainland unless otherwise stated.

Land, People, History

LAND AND RESOURCES Tanzania is a part of East Africa. It is bordered on the north by Kenya and Uganda, on the west by Rwanda, Burundi, Zaire, on the southwest by Zambia and Malawi, and on the south by Mozambique. The coast, on the east, stretches for nearly 450 miles. The mainland has an area of slightly over 360,000 square miles, while the islands add about 1,200 square miles, making the country larger than France and Britain combined. The landscape ranges from coastal swamps to high mountains, and includes rain forests, savannas, and arid plateaus. Its position between the Equator and the Tropic of Capricorn means that the climate is basically tropical. However, rainfall is not evenly distributed and some sections are quite dry and difficult to farm.

The amount of arable land in Tanzania is steadily increasing as reclamation of flooded or insect-infested areas is completed, and as areas subject to periodic drought are irrigated. Still, much of the arable land is not cultivated. Low levels of agricultural technology, relatively low population density, and the concentration, until recently, of the internal transportation system in the north, contributed to the lack of cultivation of much of the arable land. The major export crops are coffee, cotton, sisal, cashews, and cloves. Important domestic crops include sugar, maize, rice, tea, and tobacco. Instability of agricultural prices on the world market has caused Tanzanian leaders to seek more diversification of crops. They hope to avoid financial problems similar to those resulting from the decline of sisal prices in the late 1950s and early 1960s. Cattle production is also important, but the ability to make full use of potential grazing lands is restricted by the infestation of tsetse flies in many areas. Fishing in lakes, rivers, and the ocean provides a large part of the local food supply.

Reliance on arable land and on fishing is responsible for the pattern of settlement in Tanzania. The population is distributed around the periphery of the

President Nyerere of Tanzania addressing a public meeting.

country, leaving the center sparsely inhabited (see Figure 15.1). Communication and transportation, therefore, are more difficult and expensive than they would be if the population were more concentrated. In an effort to improve communication links between all parts of the nation, the government is in the process of moving the capital from the coastal city of Dar es Salaam to Dodoma, which is closer to the country's geographical center.

Mining is not as important a source of revenue for Tanzania as it is for many other African countries. Diamonds are the most valuable mineral export. Tin, gold, other gems, and salt are also mined. Low-grade coal has been discovered, as has iron ore, but it will take several years before the mines can be opened.

Wild animals and impressive scenery provide another resource Tanzania might exploit. However, there have been serious debates as to the wisdom of relying on tourism as a basis for socialist economic development in the last few years. An international airport was constructed in the heart of the game park area near Arusha in the early 1970s, but attitudes toward tourism are ambivalent. Some leaders fear that the nonsocialist values introduced by tourists, the nonegalitarian relationship that easily develops between tourist and service personnel, the relatively few employment opportunities it would provide, and the necessity of importing luxury items (foods, liquors) to stock hotels and restaurants will constrain the ability to achieve other national goals.

PEOPLE Tanzania has an extremely heterogeneous population of over 15 million, which many observers feel has contributed to the country's political stability. People of European, Asian, and

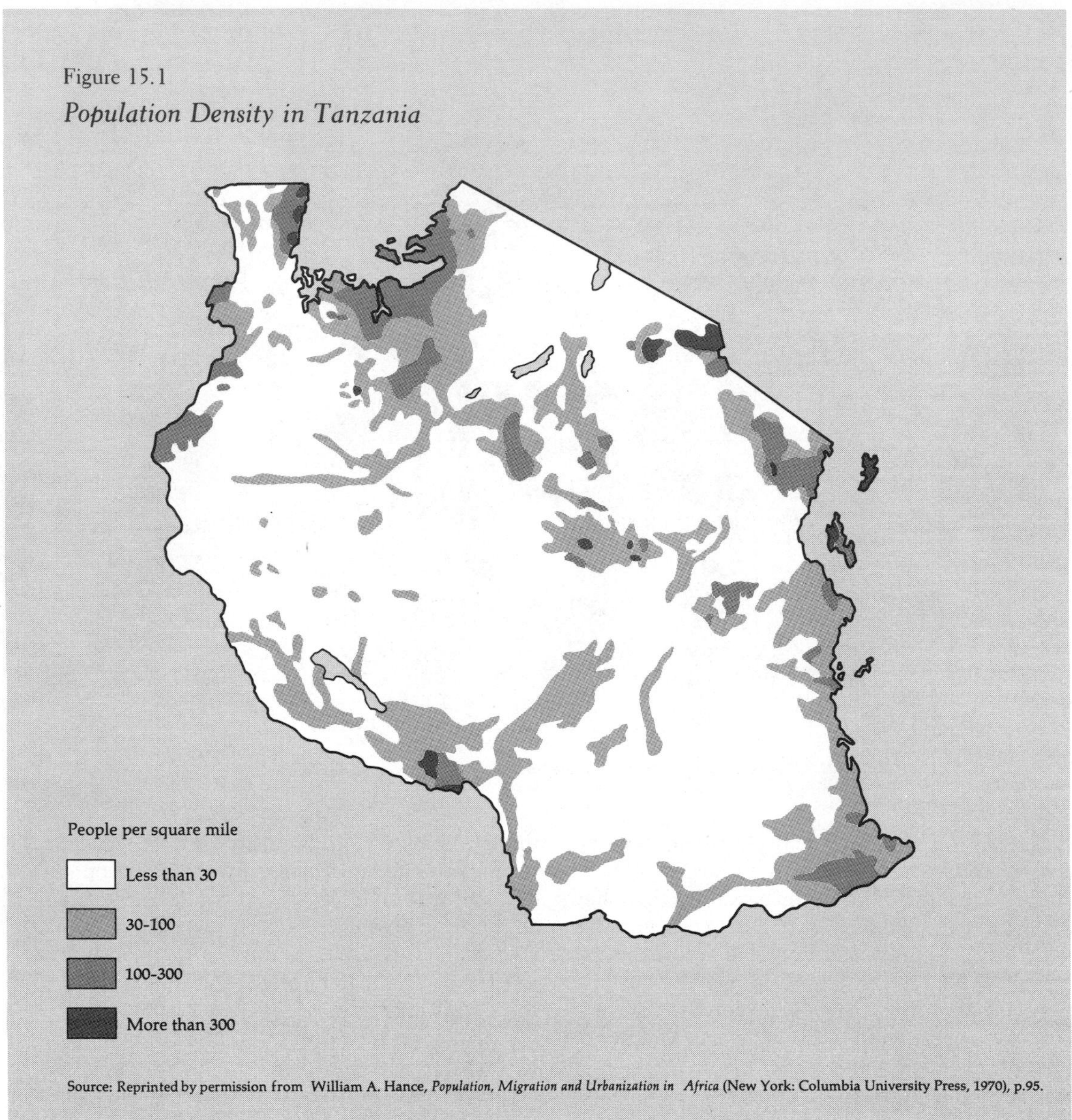

Figure 15.1
Population Density in Tanzania

Source: Reprinted by permission from William A. Hance, *Population, Migration and Urbanization in Africa* (New York: Columbia University Press, 1970), p.95.

Arab descent, as well as indigenous Africans, are citizens of Tanzania. Perhaps more importantly, Africans, who comprise about 98 percent of the population, are members of over 125 different ethnic groups (see Figure 15.2). The Sukuma, who form the largest group, make up only about 13 percent of the population, while the Nyamwezi, Makonde, Haya, and Chagga each represent about 4 percent of the total

Figure 15.2
Major Tribes on Mainland Tanzania

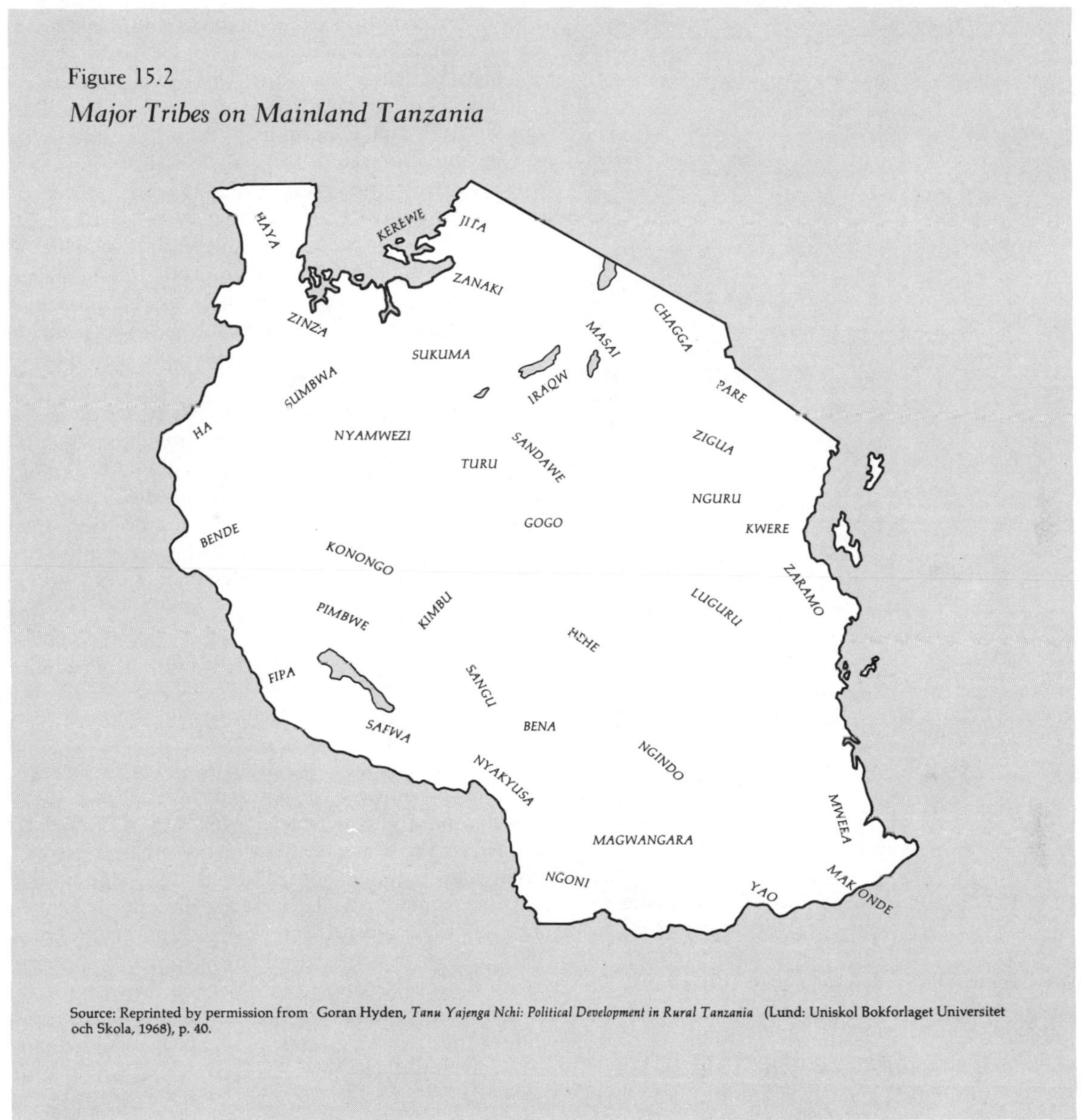

Source: Reprinted by permission from Goran Hyden, *Tanu Yajenga Nchi: Political Development in Rural Tanzania* (Lund: Uniskol Bokforlaget Universitet och Skola, 1968), p. 40.

(see Table 15.1). No particular ethnic group dominates political and social life as the Kikuyu do in neighboring Kenya, so tribalism plays only a minor role in domestic politics.

Traditional social organization varies widely between these many groups. Two examples will give some notion of the diversity. The Makonde in the southeastern corner of the country, for exam-

Table 15.1

Major Ethnic Groups in Mainland Tanzania, 1957

Tribe or race	*Percentage of total*
Sukuma	12.5
Nyamwezi	4.1
Makonde	3.8
Haya	3.7
Chagga	3.6
Gogo	3.4
Ha	3.3
Hehe	2.9
Nyakusa	2.5
Luguru	2.3
Bena	2.2
Turu	2.2
Sambaa	2.2
Zaramo	2.1
Other tribes	47.9
Asian	0.9
Arab	0.2
European	0.2

Source: Adapted from *Statistical Abstract, 1964* (Das es Salaam: Government Printer, 1965), pp. 22–23.

ple, did not develop a centralized political system.[2] Fear of raids by neighboring tribes and climatic and soil conditions that required fairly wide areas for cultivation kept the Makonde from settling in large villages. People who settled near each other formed a *chirambo* (village) which was usually headed by the area's first settler. This leader allocated land, acted as a judge, and performed some religious rites, but other responsibilities, such as distribution of inheritance and care for the aged, belonged to extended kin groups. Some communal functions were performed at the neighborhood level, including clearing fields, building houses, defending against wild animals, and helping new arrivals get settled.

Hierarchical relationships within a chirambo were simple. The leader's responsibilities did not result in significantly higher economic status than other residents and although descent was traced through female kin, women did not exercise equal power to men in political decision making. Non-Makonde residents could not participate fully in the social life of the community. Matrilineal kin were occasionally used as security against default on a debt, making such persons semislaves until the debt was paid. Slaves taken by force during battles also could be found in Makonde areas.

When a chirambo became too large to be supported by the land or when raids forced settlements to disperse, new *virambo* (plural of chirambo) would be created. Disputes between different virambo could not be appealed to any higher authority, since none existed. Serious disputes had to be negotiated by the leaders involved. If that failed, fighting broke out.

In the northwest corner of Tanzania, quite a different social system evolved. The Haya exhibit a great deal of social stratification and role specialization.[3] Three major clans make up this ethnic group — at the top was the Hinda royalty, then the Nfura clans which primarily herd cattle, and at the lowest non-slave level were the agricultural Iru clans. In patrimonial style, all property (cattle and land) was owned by the king. He allowed his subjects use of them and could collect tribute, thereby eliminating the necessity for royalty to engage directly in productive labor. As rewards for services rendered, a king would assign persons, whether royalty or commoners, control over parcels of land. Anyone living on that land became a tenant of the new owner. Sometimes one of these feudal estates, particularly those held by princes, would attempt to break away and form a new kingdom.

Three levels of political organization existed in a Haya kingdom. At the center was the king and his court of royal family members and commoners. Next were governors, usually commoners, who looked

[2] The discussion of the Makonde is based on J. Gus Liebenow, *Colonial Rule and Political Development in Tanzania: The Case of the Makonde* (Evanston, Ill.: Northwestern University Press, 1971), ch. 3.

[3] The discussion of the Haya is based on Audrey I. Richards (ed.), *East African Chiefs* (New York: Praeger, 1959), ch. 7.

after the political and economic interests of the king in the districts of the kingdom. Last were villages, ruled by princes who replicated the court society at a lower level. Decisions taken at either the district or village level could be appealed to the king.

The wide range of political traditions — exemplified by the differences between Makonde and Haya society — could, if there were not some common culture, be a major hindrance to national unity. Swahili culture, primarily a synthesis of Arab and African languages and customs, helps to unite the different racial and tribal groups in Tanzania. Swahili is the language of all primary-school and some secondary-school instruction, the language of parliamentary debate, and the language of trade. Serious efforts are made by the government to develop the language so that it can deal with today's increasingly complex technological world, rather than simply defaulting to European languages, as has happened in virtually every other African state.

Religious variations can also be found in Tanzania, although government efforts to depoliticize religious issues have largely succeeded. While nearly half the population adheres to traditional African religious practices, there are about 3 million Muslims and 4 million Christians (roughly evenly divided between Catholics and Protestants). In the colonial period, Christian Africans had better access to education than others. Currently Christians tend to dominate in occupations requiring high education and their children are overrepresented in schools above the primary level. This present advantage, however, is probably the result of class differences rather than of religious discrimination. Islam is closely associated with Swahili culture and appears to be a growing force among the people, while Christianity seems to be losing the influence it enjoyed during the colonial period.

EARLY HISTORY Remains of early humans dating from over 1.5 million years ago have been discovered in Tanzania's Olduvai Gorge. What little evidence there is suggests that stone-age life there was not much different from that in other places and that the progression from hunters and gatherers through settled food producers and herders was not unusual. As the diversity of the current population of Tanzania suggests, no single migratory wave of Africans is responsible for peopling the country. Entry into the area was from all directions and the combination and breakdown of ethnic or tribal groups have yielded the pattern one sees today.[4]

Similarly, there is no single way in which the various societies organized themselves. In some descent was patrilineal, in others it was matrilineal. Political units ranged in size from small chiefdoms with most political functions performed by a single chief or clan head, to fairly extensive kingdoms with specialized religious, administrative, military, and judicial functions. Naturally, these systems were not static. Changes were induced as they are in any society. Political ambition, natural disasters, and technological innovation, for example, forced modifications. Contact with outside groups, especially through trade and war, introduced new ideas that could be adapted to the needs of a group or, in the case of conquest, be forced upon it.

The coast of East Africa has a long history of contact with traders and explorers of the Indian Ocean. Phoenicians, Greeks, and Romans are all believed to have had some contact with the coastal and island areas of modern Tanzania. Written records of Arab activities in East Africa begin in the late seventh century. Kilwa, in Tanzania, was the site of Arab, Asian, and Persian settlement perhaps as early as the tenth century, and later became the commercial center of the coast. Chinese trade with East Africa possibly began as early as the thirteenth century.

European contact with Kilwa began in 1500 when the Portuguese attacked the city and set up a military outpost, which lasted for about seven years. Portuguese domination of the trade in this region led to a decline in Kilwa's importance and forced it to develop contacts with the hinterland in order to stay a trading center. Trade among the many noncoastal groups existed before Kilwa merchants turned inland, so contact with the coast should be viewed as an extension of this trade, not as a new phenomenon.

Beginning in the latter half of the seventeenth century, Arabs from Oman gradually took over control of the coast of East Africa from Portugal. Zan-

[4] For a good survey of Tanzania's past, see I. N. Kimambo and A. J. Tamu (eds.), *A History of Tanzania* (Nairobi: East African Publishing House, 1969).

zibar became the seat of Arab power in this area, and served as the capital of the Omani empire from 1840 when the sultan, Seyyid Said, moved his court there. This move resulted in increased trade in ivory, slaves, and cloves. Asian financiers furnished the credit Arab merchants needed to finance expeditions into the mainland. However, all slaves were not sent out of East Africa. Some were only relocated to coastal towns, like Dar es Salaam, Tanga, and Bagamoyo, and the islands, meaning that human ties between the interior and coast were established. Swahili culture was also spread as slavery was institutionalized. (Such historical ties may help explain why Zanzibar joined with Tanganyika after the descendants of these Arab rulers were overthrown in 1964.) Arab sultans made trade agreements not only with African rulers, but established commercial links with the United States, France, Great Britain, and Germany in the middle of the nineteenth century.

GERMAN RULE[5] Interest in East Africa on the part of German traders intensified during the 1870s. But Otto von Bismarck's government was somewhat reluctant to engage in the scramble for Africa at first, and not until 1885 were German adventurers able to secure official protection over what was called German East Africa. Gunboat diplomacy forced the sultan of Zanzibar's acquiescence to this new state of affairs, although a coastal strip remained under his control for three more years. Germany delegated administration of this territory to the German East African Company. However, the company's inability to contain simultaneous Arab and African rebellions in the coastal areas led to the importation of German troops (largely African mercenaries) and the establishment of rule by the German government itself. Nearly nine more years of sporadic, but intense, fighting with individual tribes was needed to pacify the territory.

The actual number of German administrators in the colony was small. Chiefs were employed as German agents and where no chiefs could be found, Arabs and Africans were hired as *akidas*, tax collectors and petty judicial officers directly responsible to the colonial administration. To offset the high cost of overseas administration, the Germans focused on ways of developing the colony's economy. Plantations, settler farms, and growing cash crops were all tried with varying degrees of success. Examples of each could be found at independence. Cash crops were introduced to provide Africans with a taxable income. Harsh implementation of cash cropping in the southern regions led to African resistance in what became known as the Maji-Maji Rebellion of 1905–1907.[6] For nearly eighteen months, Africans in the southern region engaged the Germans in a major military effort. Perhaps most importantly, this rebellion involved the coordination of several tribes' efforts, unlike previous resistance attempts. While the organization which evolved during Maji-Maji was unable to defeat the superior German technology, it has subsequently symbolized the Tanzanian desire for independence and national unity.

After the rebels were defeated, attention was turned to education and welfare — the Germans hoping to forestall further disturbances and the Africans hoping to improve their position in relation to the Germans. Central schools were established, attracting students from across the country. These students were then posted as akidas and clerks, another factor encouraging cross-tribal unity.

Some fighting occurred in German East Africa during World War I. British, Indian, and South African troops skirmished with the Germans, but no major battles were ever fought, compared with those fought in Europe, nor was the German commander captured. The end of the war in Europe signaled the end of the war in East Africa. As a condition of peace, Germany was required to give up all of its overseas colonies. Rather than award colonies to the victors as outright spoils of war, the League of Nations established a mandate system, by which ex-German colonies were to be administered on behalf of the international community by an allied power. Primarily this meant that trade and commerce were to be internationalized and that the mandated territory could not be used as a military staging ground by the administering country. Great Britain became the

[5] The discussion of this period of Tanganyikan history is based on John Iliffe, *Tanganyika under German Rule 1905–1915* (Cambridge: Cambridge University Press, 1969).

[6] *Maji*, in Swahili, means water. Before going into battle, warriors were sprinkled with water, which was believed to protect them against bullets.

mandated power for Tanganyika, while the far western part of the country came under the Belgian mandate of Ruanda-Urundi (later the two separate countries of Rwanda and Burundi).

BRITISH RULE Britain established a protectorate over Zanzibar in 1890. Britain first saw its role as providing support for the sultan, who continued to exercise a great deal of independent authority. Within a few years, however, the British replaced the reigning sultan with one more to their liking and began to create, via education and civil service employment, an Arab aristocracy that could handle routine administrative work. This arrangement continued up to independence.

Among the first actions taken by the British in Tanganyika was the redistribution of German-held land. Significantly, such land was not sold just to European farmers, as in Kenya. Asians and Africans were also allowed to purchase plantations and smaller plots of land. Thus, whenever a federation of the three East African colonies — Tanganiyka, Uganda, and Kenya — was proposed, it met with hostility from Asians and Africans in Tanganyika, who feared the restrictive land policies of Kenya would be extended to their territory.

Indirect rule was the administrative policy adopted by the British in Tanganyika. This meant that, as far as possible, rulers selected in the traditional manner, rather than agents appointed by the British, were responsible for some executive, judicial, and financial functions (see Figure 15.3). Responsibility for maintaining law and order, collecting taxes, and settling disputes between Africans belonged to tribal chiefs. All these activities, however, were subject to ultimate control by the British authorities. The latter determined whether order was adequately maintained, whether enough taxes were collected, and whether punishments were satisfactory. The British enforced these opinions by sustaining or removing particular chiefs, just as they would a low-ranking civil servant.

In comparison with the other British colonies in East Africa, relatively little was done to develop the economy of Tanganyika. Most of Britain's resources for development in this region were already committed to Kenya and Uganda. Since the meaning of being a League of Nations Mandated Territory was unclear, investment in Tanganyika was seen as more risky by both the British government and private investors alike. A few improvements in infrastructure were made, such as adding branch lines to the railway and road construction. Foreign exchange was derived primarily from the export of agricultural products. Manufacturing was almost nonexistent, investment came primarily from external sources, and there were no controls on the repatriation of profits by foreign investors.

In 1926, a Legislative Council (Legco), composed of five European and two Asian residents and fourteen British colonial officers, was formed. All of the members were appointed by the governor. The Legco's purpose was to advise the governor and the Executive Council of five high-ranking civil servants. The Legco also served to legitimate the policies adopted by the administration, at least in the eyes of the non-African community. British colonial policy, particularly after World War II, was guided by the principles of trusteeship as laid down in the United Nations Charter. Britain was required to prepare its colonial possessions for eventual self-rule. Changes in the representation of various groups in the Legco give some indication of the political development of the territory, both in terms of the political balance between racial groups and the relative strength of British and resident elements in the country (see Table 15.2). The transition from appointed to elected representatives is also illustrated by Legco changes.

Despite their lack of representation on the Legco until after World War II, Africans did influence policies adopted by the British rulers. Agitation for particular services, like education and health care, and reaction to attempts to change traditional agricultural practices and land tenure occasionally modified government behavior. Modern organization of Africans dates from the early 1920s, when the Tanganyika Territory African Civil Service Association was formed to represent African clerks employed by the government. In 1929, the Tanganyika African Association (TAA) was established to serve the social and welfare needs of city-dwelling Africans. Although this organization had no base in the general society, it provided an early opportunity for potential leaders to come together and identify themselves as Tanganyikans, rather than as people from different tribes.

Figure 15.3

Traditional and Colonial Patterns of Government in Tanzania

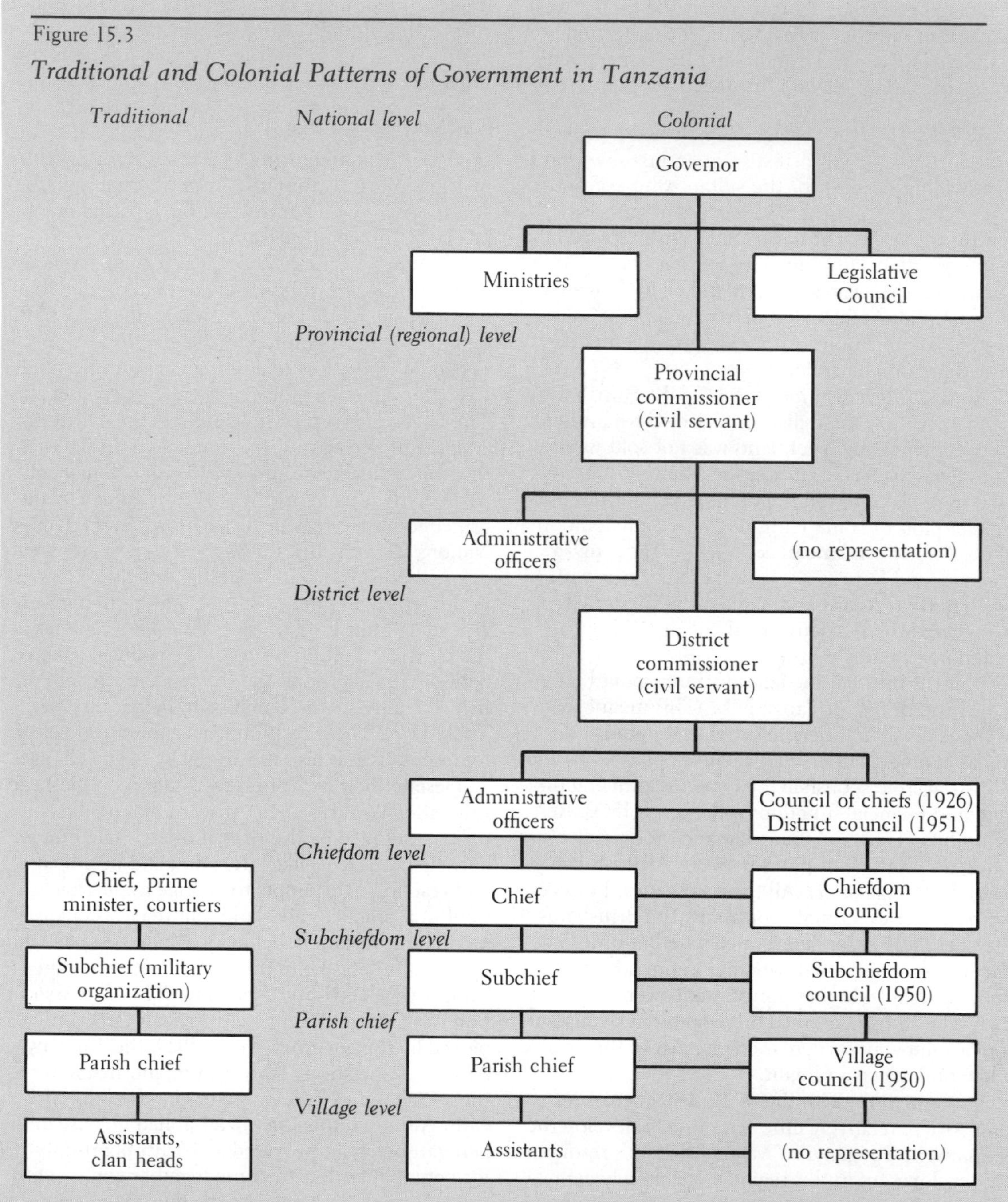

Source: Reprinted by permission from Goran Hyden, *Tanu Yajenga Nchi: Political Development in Rural Tanzania* (Lund: Uniskol, Bokforlaget Universitet och Skola, 1968), p. 138.

Table 15.2

Racial Composition of the Tanganyika Legislative Council

Year	Officials	Nonofficials: Europeans	Nonofficials: Asians	Nonofficials: Africans	Total
1926	13	5	2	0	20
1945	15	7	3	4	29
1955	31[a]	10	10	10	61
1957	34[b]	11	11	11	67
1959[c]	28	9	9	7	53
1960[d]	0	16	12	53	81

[a] Of these thirty-one officials, there were twenty-one Europeans, six Asians, and four Africans.

[b] Of these thirty-four officials, there were twenty Europeans, three Asians, and eleven Africans.

[c] All the unofficial members were elected, ten from each racial group. Five are included in the first column because they were appointed as ministers.

[d] Seventy-one of these members were elected; ten appointed. Ten of the elected seats were reserved for Europeans, eleven for Asians, fifty seats were open to all races. One of those counted as an African was of Arab descent.

Source: J. Clagett Taylor, *The Political Development of Tanganyika* (Stanford, Calif.: Stanford University Press, 1963), p. 78, 92, 155, 181, and 193; and Judith Listowell, *The Making of Tanganyika* (New York: London House and Maxwell, 1965), p. 79.

In 1953, Julius Kambarage Nyerere, a teacher at a secondary school outside Dar es Salaam, became president of the TAA, and began to transform what had been primarily a social club into a political movement.[7] Nyerere was, at that time, probably the best educated African in Tanganyika. He had attended local Catholic boarding schools, Makerere College in Uganda, and the University of Edinburgh, from which he received a masters degree in history and economics. He was the child of a Zanaki chief and one of his junior wives (the Zanaki are a small tribe located on the eastern shore of Lake Victoria). After twelve years of traditional upbringing, he began attending Catholic mission schools, converting to Catholicism eight years later. His six years at the elite Tabora secondary school and two years at Makerere College in Uganda enabled him to meet young men from all parts of East Africa. After a few years of teaching in Tanganyika, he went to Edinburgh. At this time he developed many of his ideas about racial equality, democracy, and socialism — he was greatly influenced by British Fabianism. His attempts to put these ideas into practice began almost immediately upon his return from Scotland in 1952.

The Tanganyika African National Union (TANU) was formed on July 7, 1954, now celebrated as "Saba Saba Day," the seventh day of the seventh month. It was formed under Nyerere's leadership by members of the TAA and leaders from various tribal-based organizations. Their ultimate goal was to end colonial rule. But first they focused activity on resisting the government's attempt to impose "multiracialism," a system that would accord equal representation in the district councils to each racial group, regardless of the relative size of those groups. Because of TANU's opposition, few multiracial district councils were established.

When the first elections for the Legislative Coun-

[7] Biographical information on Nyerere can be found in William E. Smith, *Nyerere of Tanzania* (London: Victor Gollancz Ltd., 1973).

cil were held in 1958, each district was allotted three seats — one to be held by an African, one by an Asian, and one by a European. Five districts were to hold elections in late 1958 and the remaining five in early 1959. Strict eligibility requirements based on educational and economic criteria limited the size of the African electorate, but they still made up a majority of the voters. Opposition to TANU came from the government-initiated, multiracial United Tanganyika Party (UTP). Since TANU had only African members, the UTP was expected to win all the European and Asian seats easily, and it was thought to be competitive in the African contests too. Unexpectedly, however, TANU endorsed independent European and Asian candidates who supported its position. As a result, all fifteen seats contested in the first election were won by TANU-backed candidates. In the second election, TANU again won all fifteen seats, although this time only three of the TANU candidates were challenged.

Widespread popular support for TANU, as evidenced by the election results, put Nyerere in a very strong bargaining position with the colonial government. He was able to convince the British that unless TANU's relatively moderate demands for African political advancement were met, violence might result. Persuaded, the British moved rapidly toward independence.

Responding to TANU's demands for new elections in which an unofficial majority would be elected and the practice of equal racial representation would be abandoned, the colonial government scheduled new elections for August 1960. This time seventy-one legislative seats were available — fifty "open seats," for which all races were eligible, and twenty-one "reserved seats," eleven for Asians and ten for Europeans. Seventy of the seventy-one seats were won by TANU-supported candidates. After this election, TANU was no longer an opposition, but a government. Of the twelve ministerial portfolios, nine were held by TANU members of Parliament (MPs) and only three were retained by British civil servants. Nyerere, himself, became the chief minister. Of course, being new at their jobs, many of these ministers had to rely heavily on advice from their predecessors, British colonial civil servants. But they began to gain experience in ruling Tanganyika as a modern nation-state. On December 9, 1961, formal independence was granted.

POLITICAL CULTURE AND SOCIALIZATION

The Traditional Colonial Mix

Tanzania, like post–World War II Germany, Cuba, and China, is attempting to transform its political culture. Unlike these other countries, however, the transformation process places a large emphasis on reclaiming traditions — in this case, precolonial traditions are being sought as a means of developing a new socialist personality. Deliberate efforts at cultural transformation tend to be dialectical processes, in which the values and behaviors that political leaders desire are counterpoised against already existing values and behaviors. Inasmuch as these values differ from one another and the holders of existing values often resist the new ones, the new must struggle for predominance.

Tanzania underwent this transformation twice. First was the juxtaposition of traditional tribal values against those of the colonial power, first the Germans and then the English. The second was the challenge posed by the independent government to the synthesized values created in the colonial era. This synthesis contained some values that were little changed from precolonial times, others that had been successfully implanted by colonial administrators, and some that represented a compromise. Because so many ethnic groups exist and the British penetrated the country to varying degrees, the post-independence rulers have had to find ways of getting a number of different political cultures to adopt their values. Reference to the Haya and the Makonde will again be used for illustrative purposes.

During the colonial period, several important changes took place in the Haya area. Both the Germans and the British reduced the Haya kings to civil servants who became responsible for implementing colonial policies and collecting taxes.[8] Many of the

[8] See Goran Hyden, "Political Engineering and Social Change," in Lionel Cliffe, et al. (eds.), *Government and Development in East Africa* (The Hague: Martinus Nijhoff, 1977), pp. 188–200.

policies changed traditional agricultural practices, which had evolved over many years within the region's ecological constraints and had taken on ritual and economic importance. As a result, the authority of the kings and princes increasingly had to be buttressed by the coercive power of the colonial state. Traditional land tenure arrangements were formalized by the British, who felt individual ownership of the land was essential for economic development. Thus, tenants now owed specific rents, and their freedom to secure farming land on the basis of personal negotiation for service or tribute to the landlord was removed. Status differences between tenants and landlords became more sharply defined. When the nationalist movement was criticizing the colonial rulers and their African collaborators in the 1950s, many Haya tenants eagerly supported it.

Traditional Makonde institutions were, like those of the Haya, eviscerated by colonialism.[9] What scholars have called a capricious administrative policy characterized British rule in Makonde areas. People did not know what to expect from colonial officials, who rarely remained in the area for any length of time. As a response to this unpredictable political environment, the Makonde adopted a passive, even supplicating, attitude toward these rulers imposed from the outside. In addition to this submissiveness, the isolation of the Makonde from the major centers of economic activity limited the region's growth. The rulers of newly independent Tanzania faced a Makonde population that was economically not much different from that which faced the colonial rulers fifty years earlier but, also, a population that was suspicious of rulers from outside the area.

Ideology

Tanzanian leaders rule a territory almost as heterogeneous as that ruled by the colonialists. But their approach to government is much more ideological than the colonial rulers' was, and more systematic than the approaches taken by leaders of other African countries. Knowledge of Tanzanian ideology is essential to understanding the actions taken by the government. In addition, the relative clarity with which the ideology has been articulated and its importance as a standard against which other African development strategies are often measured, justifies describing it at some length.

A philosophy of African socialism, known as *ujamaa* (Swahili for "familyhood"), has evolved through various speeches and activities of national leaders, most notably those of President Julius K. Nyerere.[10] The first detailed statement of this ideology was the Arusha Declaration of 1967. Ujamaa is based on three major assumptions about traditional life.[11] First, it is assumed that in traditional society "Each member of the family recognized the place and rights of the other members"; mutual respect among all people existed. Second, there is a belief that traditionally "all the basic goods were held in common, and shared among all members of the unit. . . . Inequalities existed, but . . . they could never become gross and offensive to the social equality which was at the basis of communal life. And, third, "everyone had an obligation to work."[12] The return to tradition is selective, as seen by Nyerere's citing two inadequacies of the precolonial situation: (1) the unequal status of women and men; and (2) the generally low standard of living. Inequality must be eliminated, and the standard of living raised by overcoming technological ignorance and increasing the scale of economic activity. Using the three principles of traditional life — mutual respect, communal ownership, and work — and avoiding the two weaknesses — sexual inequality and poverty — the society being built will be one:

> in which all members have equal rights and equal opportunities; in which all can live at peace with their neighbours

[9] See Liebenow, *Colonial Rule and Political Development*, ch. 15.

[10] Reinforcing this notion of familyhood is the use of the word *Nduqu* as a term of address. Although Nduqu is frequently translated as "comrade," it is in fact the Swahili word for sibling (male or female).

[11] The following discussion is based on Nyerere's policy paper, "Socialism and Rural Development," reprinted in Julius K. Nyerere, *Uhuru na Ujamaa: Freedom and Socialism* (London: Oxford University Press, 1968), pp. 337–366.

[12] Nyerere, "Socialism and Rural Development," pp. 338–339.

without suffering or imposing injustice, being exploited, or exploiting; and in which all have a gradually increasing basic level of material welfare before any individual lives in luxury.[13]

Extreme differences in individual wealth are frequently found in developing countries. Limited access to capital and education in the colonial period enabled the few African property owners and secondary school graduates to augment their initial advantages after independence as the demand for their resources and skills increases dramatically when the colonial power pulls out. In fact, the gap between the rich and the poor in these new states frequently widens. In particular, the salaries paid to public servants, following the scales set by the colonial powers, are often exorbitant when compared to a country's average standard of living. To reduce such inequalities in Tanzania, not only have the salaries of government officials occasionally been cut or frozen, but a leadership code designed to prevent further inequality from developing has emerged. Since the government, government corporations, and the political party are the main employers of well-educated citizens, the establishment of behavioral norms for the political, bureaucratic, and state entrepreneurial elite can be an effective way to begin transforming the political culture. Two documents are especially important in setting out this leadership code — the Arusha Declaration of 1967 and the Mwongozo wa TANU (TANU Guidelines) of 1971.

The Arusha Declaration is very explicit as to what economic activities a leader may not engage in. Leaders are defined as officials, and their spouses, in the party, government, parliament, unions, affiliated party organizations (women's and youth groups), local government, and civil service. A leader may not: (1) hold shares in any company; (2) hold directorships in any privately owned enterprise; (3) receive two or more salaries; and (4) own houses that are rented. TANU Guidelines provide the ideological criteria which leaders must adopt, such as anti-imperialism, equalitarianism, and Pan-Africanism, and require them to participate in the economic development of the country. Thus, common practices of leaders in other developing countries are strictly prohibited. Suspension from the party and office has been used to enforce this behavior code. In the mid-1970s these restrictions became applicable to all party members, regardless of rank.

[13] Nyerere, "Socialism and Rural Development," p. 340.

Education

Prior to the advent of mission schools, each tribe or community developed formal and informal means of socializing young people to the roles they were expected to play in society. Frequently, the formal instruction was conducted during initiation ceremonies when boys and girls reached puberty. The length of such programs varied from several days to several months, and special bonds were created among those initiated at the same time. Informal socialization occurred when parents taught their children particular skills and values, when elders related tribal histories, and when disputes were reconciled in public by the community leaders. In the Muslim urban and coastal areas, Koranic schools assisted in the socialization of boys into the dominant Swahili culture. Neither tribal nor Muslim socializing agents have disappeared, but their influence has been reduced and modified. Some of the values espoused by the traditional socializers, after having been deemphasized during the colonial era, are now finding their way back into the school curriculum. Other old values, such as the position of women in society, are in conflict with ujamaa principles, and schools compete with families and religious institutions for dominance in areas like this.

Formal education usually provides the state its first opportunity to affect socialization, so education becomes important to a state seeking to transform the political culture. Influencing the values of children has always been the goal of those sponsoring schools, whether they be religious groups, the British colonial government, or the Tanzanian government. Creating good Christians, Muslims, or civil servants was the aim of the first two types of sponsors; creating good Tanzanians is the goal of the last. How Tanzanian educators hope to socialize students to ujamaa values is important for assessing the likelihood of their transforming political culture.

Having inherited a racially and religiously segregated school system, one of the first moves the government made was to deny the use of race and religion as admission criteria. Since the language of instruction in a school frequently depended on its racial composition, a policy of using Swahili as the teaching medium in primary schools and English and Swahili in secondary schools facilitated the absorption of African students into former European and Asian schools.

Fees were charged in the past, to limit the number of children in school to that which could be handled by the country's limited resources. In contrast, the Nyerere government has instituted a system of compulsory primary education, which was in place by the end of 1978. However, only a small proportion of those finishing primary school can go on to receive secondary education or find wage-earning employment. And there are other problems. Conflict between the desire to eliminate illiteracy, thereby increasing agricultural productivity and improving health, and the extremely academic education provided by schools, which encourages students to seek nonagricultural employment, has led those educators and politicians concerned with Tanzanian development to reconsider the goals and methods of education.

Indicative of the importance of education reform to President Nyerere is the fact that the first post-Arusha policy he presented concerned the nation's school system. In "Education for Self-Reliance" he pointed out that the form and content of colonial education were designed to socialize Africans to their place in colonial society.[14] He then argued that as the role of Africans in a colonized Tanganyika and that in an independent Tanzania were not the same, failure to revamp the educational system after 1961 meant that the schools were turning out young citizens prepared for a society that no longer existed. Four faults, in particular, were noted. First, education was aimed at meeting the needs of those who would eventually go on to secondary and higher education. Given the small number of students who would do so, one must conclude that most children received training unrelated to their future needs. Second, "education [was] such as to divorce its participants from the society it [was] supposed to be preparing them for."[15] Particularly at the secondary and higher levels, boarding schools provided most of the education. Besides physical isolation from the local community, an attitudinal separation occurred, in that cooking and cleaning were not done by students, but by the school staff.

Overreliance on books and certified teachers for information constituted a third difficulty. Education failed to give adequate recognition to sources of wisdom not found in books or gathered from teachers with degrees. Finally, the organization of the education system deprived the nation of the productive capabilities of some of its most physically and mentally able citizens. Schools were not designed so that students could work their way through, and as a result work and study were not seen as activities to be performed by the same person.

Correcting this situation has been no easy task. Proposals made in "Education for Self-Reliance" have only begun to be implemented. Nyerere insisted that "every school should also be a farm; that the school community should consist of people who are both teachers and farmers, and pupils and farmers."[16] While the role of agriculture in the schools has increased, the complete integration of farming and studying has yet to be achieved. Nor is it clear that the attempt to make primary education complete in itself has succeeded. Selection for secondary and higher education still relies heavily on examination scores — although examinations are now developed in Tanzania, rather than Nairobi or London — because a satisfactory method of evaluating students' nonacademic contributions has not been found. One area of success has been raising the age of school entry to seven years, meaning that pupils will be fourteen or older when they finish their primary education and, thus, physically able to assume productive roles in their villages.

A few private schools still exist in Tanzania. Although they are primarily intended to serve those who are not citizens, some wealthy Tanzanians send their children to these institutions, or to boarding schools abroad, assuming that they provide better education than government schools or at least that

[14] Reprinted in Nyerere, *Uhuru na Ujamaa*, pp. 267–390. Much of the material in this section is drawn from David R. Morrison, *Education and Politics in Africa* (London: C. Hurst Co., 1976).

[15] Nyerere, "Education for Self-Reliance," p. 276.

[16] Nyerere, "Education for Self-Reliance," p. 282.

their graduates find it easier to enter foreign universities. Some restriction on Tanzanian attendance at private schools will probably be imposed if one school begins to correlate strongly with future social status, as has occurred in England.

Perhaps the most significant hindrance to using schools as instruments of social change is the fact that the teachers are required to transmit a value system that they themselves do not hold. Those teaching school now are the same people who successfully passed through an education system Nyerere identified as fostering a sense of capitalistic individualism and feelings of superiority toward one's unschooled neighbors, the antitheses of ujamaa ideals. Teachers must reexamine the values they learned and try to eliminate those values incompatible with ujamaa. If not, courses in political education, which have replaced civics classes, are not taught from a perspective of "we believe . . .", but rather as "*Mwalimu* says. . . ."[17] It is claimed that this kind of authoritarian presentation of political ideals is unlikely to produce in the student the inquiring mind and the "basic confidence in his own position as a free and equal member of society."[18]

The government has tried to promote ujamaa values beyond the secondary level also. In an attempt to prevent continuing elitism and secure socialist commitment on the part of university students, they are required, in addition to scholastic achievement, to be nominated for admission by fellow workers or peasants. This requires students to work for a few years before continuing their education. National service obligations are usually fulfilled after secondary school as well. Nevertheless, the insistence on academic qualifications as well means that many students come from jobs in various government bureaucracies, rather than coming from farms and factories, and it is to those jobs they will probably return. Two kinds of students are exempted from these new rules — women, because it is felt that past discrimination must be compensated for, and engineering students, whose skills are desperately needed to implement development projects.

Socialization is also needed for adults, and takes the form of campaigns against illiteracy. Since literacy is defined as the ability to read and write Swahili, and there are few texts in that language, it has been necessary for Tanzania to produce its own teaching materials. This allows for some control over the information transmitted, which might not occur if English were used, since economic considerations might lead to reliance on preexisting foreign materials and on foreign instructors. Literacy campaigns have succeeded in increasing the literate proportion of the adult population from under 20 percent at independence to over 50 percent today.

Media

Mass communication in Tanzania is conducted primarily through newspapers and radio, although television broadcast facilities have been set up in Zanzibar.[19] In 1970, the government took over control of the foreign-owned newspaper, *The Standard*. President Nyerere, explaining this move, said, "In the future there can be no suspicion that this English language newspaper is serving the interests of foreign private owners." *The Standard* then competed with the TANU-run English-language *Nationalist* until the two merged in 1972 to become the *Daily News*. *Uhuru* and *Nqurumo* are Swahili-language daily papers. The former is published by the party, while the latter is privately owned.

Over the years the news has moved from focusing on events in the developed countries to more coverage of African and local events. Government and party presses are used by various officials to present policy statements. While it is difficult to determine whether or not prior censorship occurs, there is some contrary evidence — vigorous criticism of government personnel and program implementation can frequently be found in all the papers. Circulation figures for the newspapers are somewhat mis-

[17] *Mwalimu* is the Swahili word for teacher and is commonly used when speaking about Nyerere, who once was a schoolteacher. Another title with which he is addressed is *Baba wa (or ya) Taifa* which translates as "Father of the Nation."

[18] W. M. S. Chamungawa, "Socialization Problems in Tanzania," *Taamuli*, 5 (June 1975), pp. 3–17.

[19] See William W. Neher and John C. Condon, "The Media and Nation Building in Kenya and Tanzania," in David R. Smock and Kwamena Bentsi-Enchill (eds.), *The Search for National Integration in Africa* (New York: Free Press, 1976), pp. 220–239.

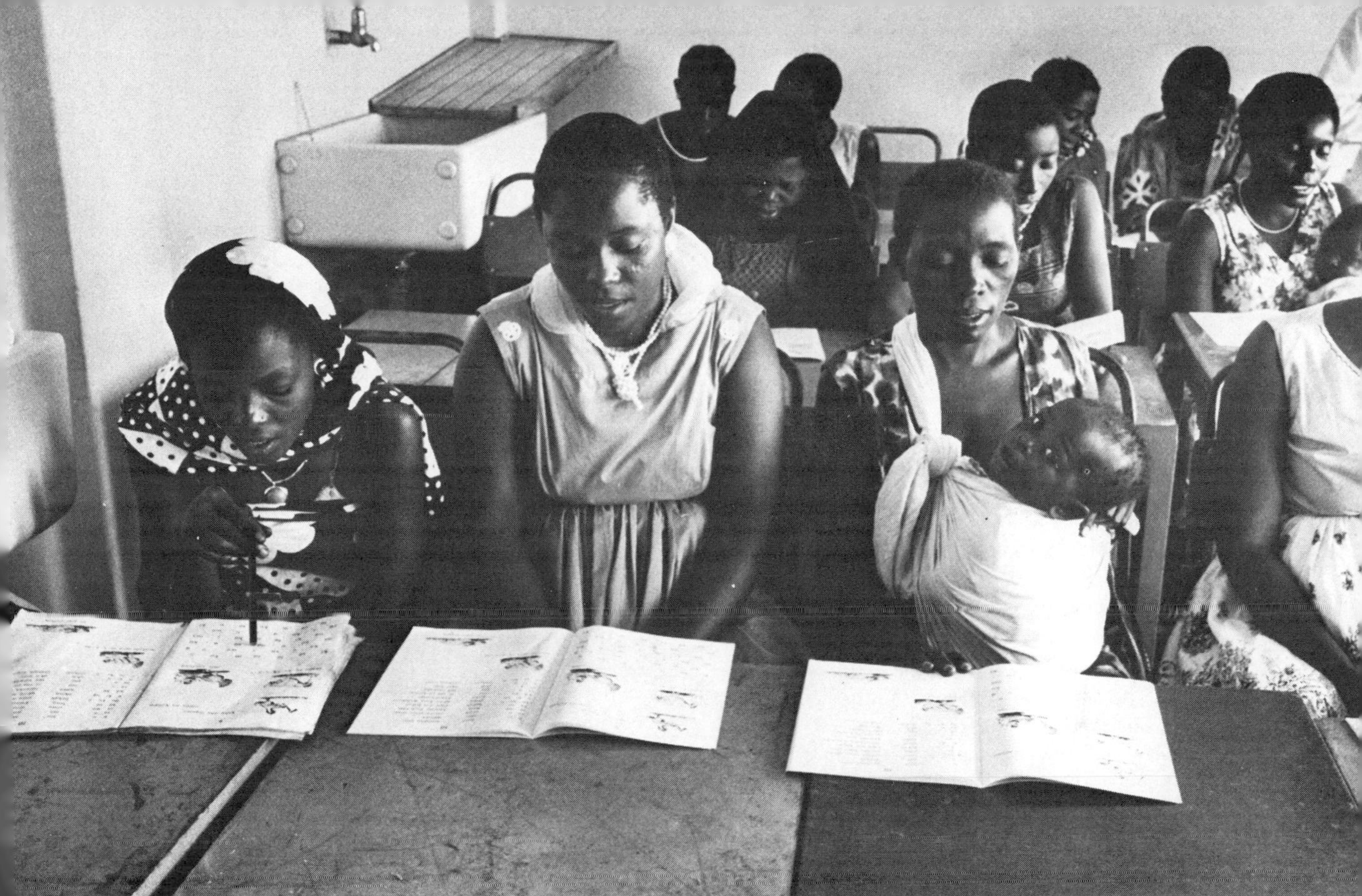

Tanzanian women learning to read Swahili in one of many literary classes throughout the country.

leading, as it is probable that several people read each copy. The fact that about half the circulation of the dailies is confined to the Dar es Salaam area suggests the limited range and impact of the newspapers.

Radios can be found in much of the country and the number of listeners is certainly much greater than the actual number of radios. Broadcasts in Swahili assist in the process of national integration by encouraging use of a common language. Radio and newspapers are used for educational purposes as well as providing information and entertainment. Programs about hygiene or the electoral procedures and editorials explaining a new government policy are common. Both sources of communication, however, are limited in their value as socializers because the individual is only exposed to what he or she chooses to read or hear.

It is difficult to judge how much influence these efforts at political socialization have had. A large majority of Tanzanians recognize themselves as members of one nation as well as members of tribes and churches. The problem of a brain drain — students from developing countries failing to return home after being educated abroad — does not seem as serious in Tanzania as in Nigeria or Uganda. This suggests, in part, that Tanzanian schools have engendered in students a commitment to serving the nation. Also, those of the present generation are being educated in ujamaa values; when they become parents, conflict between family values and school teaching may diminish accordingly. And, as the section on participation will discuss, many people seem to accept as legitimate the current institutional arrangements for participation, even though such institutions weaken the authority of more traditional figures. Whether this acceptance results from socialization or from the ability of the central government to provide rewards and sanctions is difficult to determine.

GOVERNMENT ORGANIZATION

Tanzania's government organization has elements of precolonial and colonial structures, but as the goals of the Tanzanian government have changed to focus on attaining internal economic development based on ujamaa values, so have the institutions, or at least the functions they perform. President Nyerere has summed up his attitude toward the structure of government by saying:

> We refuse to adopt the institutions of other countries even where they have served those countries well — because it is our conditions that have to be served by our institutions. We refuse to put ourselves in a strait-jacket of constitutional devices — even of our own making. The constitution of Tanzania must serve the people of Tanzania. We do not intend that the people of Tanzania should serve the constitution.[20]

In Tanzania the supreme political body is not the executive, legislative, or judicial branch but the party, the Chama cha Mapinduzi (CCM, or Party of the Revolution), formed in 1977 by the merger of TANU and the Afro-Shirazi party (ASP) on Zanzibar.[21] Thus, it must be remembered that any discussion of government institutions is describing the secondary organs of leadership and control.

In Tanzania, government reorganization and reform tends to result from a realization that the party's leadership role is being eclipsed by the government. The declaration of a republic in 1962, the decline of the cabinet as a policy-making body, the Arusha Declaration, and the 1977 Constitution are all examples of the reaction to the deliberate or accidental acquisition of power by the government at the expense of the party.

[20] From Nyerere's address to Parliament on June 8, 1965, cited in Robert Martin, *Personal Freedom and the Law in Tanzania* (Nairobi: Oxford University Press, 1974), p. 47.

[21] All material discussing conditions before 1977 will refer to TANU and ASP; all material referring to the present or future will use the CCM.

The Presidency

Before independence, executive and legislative power was concentrated in the hands of a governor. Independence in December 1961 led to a separation of the roles of head of state (a governor-general appointed by the Queen of England) and the head of government (a prime minister, elected by Parliament). By December 1962, the desire to reduce Tanganyikan dependence on Great Britain led to the creation of a republic and the establishment of a presidential-parliamentary system allowing for a strong president and a weak prime minister, similar to the French system. In form, the system has remained the same despite the union with Zanzibar in 1964, the formation of a one-party state in 1965, and the passage of a constitutional amendment declaring the party's supremacy in 1975.

Nyerere, as the sole incumbent of the Tanzanian presidency so far, has defined the powers of the position. Constitutionally, the president is endowed with broad authority. As prime minister, Nyerere relied heavily on counsel from his cabinet, but after the republican constitution came into force the president made more and more decisions independently, shifting the cabinet's role from policy making to policy implementing.

The president is elected in this one-party state by a method more closely resembling a plebiscite than a contest. A national conference of the CCM is convened to nominate a Tanzanian citizen, at least thirty years old, for the presidency.[22] Then it issues a ballot allowing registered voters (citizens over eighteen) to accept or reject the nominee. Should the candidate be rejected, the conference nominates a second person, likewise subject to acceptance or rejection, the process continuing until a majority of voters agree to the conference's choice. Elections must be held at least once every five years; although if the president dissolves parliament before its five-year term is up, he or she must also go through renomination and reelection. In the three elections held since the one-party state was created, the conference's first

[22] Before the mainland and island parties merged, a special electoral conference composed of the national conferences of TANU and the ASP was convened for this purpose.

Table 15.3

Presidential Vote in Tanzanian Elections

Year	*Yes*	*No*	*Spoiled ballots*	*Percentage yes*
1965	2,520,903	88,600	26,537	96.5
1970	3,465,573	109,828	74,888	95.0
1975	4,172,267	302,005	83,323	91.5

Sources: Lionel Cliffe (ed.), *One Party Democracy: The 1965 Tanzania General Elections* (Nairobi: East African Publishing House, 1967), p. 359; A. H. Rweyemamu, "The Presidential Election," in Election Study Committee, *Socialism and Participation: Tanzania's 1970 General Elections* (Dar es Salaam: Tanzania Publishing House, 1974), p. 197; and Colin Legum (ed.), *Africa Contemporary Record 1975–76* (London: Rex Collins, 1976), p. 323.

nominee (Nyerere) has never been rejected by the electorate (see Table 15.3).

Since Nyerere has been the only president, the problem of peaceful succession to the office has not yet been faced. (Nyerere did resign as prime minister early in 1962 and Deputy Prime Minister Rashidi Kawawa became the head of government for about ten months, after which Nyerere returned as the country's leader in becoming president, with Kawawa remaining in the now-weakened post of prime minister). The president has hinted that he will not seek reelection in 1980, in large part so that he can lend his legitimizing power to his successor.

Until 1977, the president was assisted by two vice-presidents. One of these people acted as the head of government for Zanzibar and the other served as prime minister in Parliament. The new Constitution provides for only one vice-president, who must come from the part of the country (mainland or islands) not represented by the president. Responsibilities for the vice-president have not been specified, and the role played is likely to depend on the personalities of the office-holder and the president.

Certain powers granted to the president could be abused by authoritarian leaders. Some of these powers, like the ability to deport any citizen from one area of the country to another or to declare a state of emergency allowing executive suspension or alteration of any law, have been modeled after powers possessed by the former colonial governors. Others, such as the preventive detention act, which allows the president to order the imprisonment of any person he deems a threat to the country's peace or security, have been created since independence. Actions taken under these acts are defended on the basis that individual rights can be abrogated when the security of the state is at stake.

The president also has broad appointment powers. The new Constitution no longer requires the selection of a popularly elected member of Parliament (MP) as prime minister, meaning that the president can choose the entire Cabinet from among all the MPs, whether elected or appointed. Of the approximately twenty-four ministers in office at any one time, one can find representatives of the various social groups in the country. Currently the Cabinet includes three nonblacks, two women, Muslims, Christians, and people from several different tribes, although in the early years Africans from the northern coastal and Lake Victoria regions were overrepresented. Significantly, the new prime minister, E. Sokoine, is from the Masai, a tribe on the border of Tanzania and Kenya, which has been among the most resistant to government penetration.

Tanzania has adopted the British practice of ministerial responsibility, holding ministers accountable for the actions taken by civil servants under their authority. In 1977, four Cabinet-rank officials resigned because of improper actions taken by their subordinates. Other presidential appointments include judges, regional and area secretaries, the highest-ranking civil servants, and thirty members of the Parliament.

Delegation of presidential powers to other members of the government is also allowed. When the president has felt it necessary he has brought certain ministries directly under his control and at other times he has allowed them to exist relatively independently; the ministries of foreign affairs, defense, regional administration, and development and planning have at various times received the direct attention of the president. The role of the Cabinet as a policy-making body has declined significantly in the last ten years. With the 1975 constitutional amendment declaring the party to be the nation's supreme political institution, the role of a Cabinet minister became that of a director of policy implementation.

Legislature

Tanzania has a unicameral legislature called the *Bunge* (National Assembly or Parliament). The Parliament seated in 1975 provided places for 218 members, who were chosen in a variety of ways. Ninety-six members were elected from mainland single-member constituencies; fifteen members were nominated by various national institutions and organizations (labor unions, the university), one member from each of the twenty mainland regions was selected by the ruling party; twenty members from Zanzibar were selected by the ruling party; twenty-five members were the regional secretaries of TANU; thirty-two members were nominated by the president.[23] The Zanzibar Revolutionary Council is the group of approximately thirty persons who have acted as the supreme executive and legislative bodies on the islands since January 1964. Members are not elected but rather selected or dismissed by the council itself. The current leader of the council is the vice-president of the republic. It was not until 1978 that parliamentary elections were held in Zanzibar. The fact that they still appoint twenty members to Parliament indicates that unification is not yet completed.[24]

The legislative meeting room bequeathed to Tanzania was modeled after the British House of Commons; it was arranged so that the government party sits facing the opposition. Moving the capital from Dar es Salaam to Dodoma provides an opportunity for Tanzanians to design a parliament building more suited to a one-party state.

The electoral process begins at the district level when the party's district conference examines all those party members who have submitted nomination petitions signed by at least twenty-five supporters. Members of the conference then vote for their preferred nominee and the candidates are ranked according to the number of votes received. Each district then forwards its rank-ordered list of names to the National Executive Committee (NEC) of the CCM, which selects the two candidates who will stand in the popular election. Only in a few cases has the NEC not ratified the top two candidates in the district conference's ranking. When a top-ranked nominee is not certified it is usually because the person is not considered a sufficiently active party member, rather than because a lower-listed candidate is more favored by the NEC. The NEC tries not to impose its preferences. Incumbent MPs and junior ministers have, in the past, failed to receive district endorsement and the people at party headquarters have not used their power to reinstate the unpopular politician.

Once two candidates have been selected for each constituency (in only a few districts is a candidate unopposed), the appeal for votes begins. There are strict limitations on campaigning. All expenses are paid by the party; personal expenditures on behalf of a candidate are forbidden. Candidates must always

[23] Under the 1977 Constitution, the future National Assembly will include 206 members. One hundred and six will be popularly elected from single-member constituencies (including ten from Zanzibar). Of the remaining one hundred, thirty will be appointed by the president (twenty from Zanzibar and ten from the mainland), twenty will be specially elected by the Revolutionary Council of Zanzibar, twenty will be appointed from the regions on the mainland and five from the regions of Zanzibar, and twenty-five will be the regional secretaries, by virtue of their government and party positions. Unlike the current Parliament, the 1980 legislature will have a majority of elected members.

[24] See Martin Bailey, *The Union of Tanganyika and Zanzibar: A Study in Political Integration* (Syracuse, N.Y.: Maxwell School of Citizenship and Public Affairs, Syracuse University, 1973), pp. 45–47.

appear together when campaigning and alternate the speaking order at each appearance. Speeches must be in Swahili. Debate on several topics is prohibited; candidates cannot challenge the principles of the party as presented in various published policy statements or election manifestos, nor can they appeal for support on the basis of race, tribe, religion, or sex. This means that candidates must run on the basis of past performance and their ability to convince voters that they will represent their constituents' views in the National Assembly. Elections are carried out by secret ballot, each containing the candidates' names and symbols — either a house or a hoe, with each symbol assigned by lot.

Given the restrictions on candidacy imposed by this nomination system, it is difficult to say just how much choice voters have. Because party membership is open to all citizens for only a small membership fee, participation in candidate nomination is not as limited as in countries that operate with a vanguard party of limited membership, like the Soviet Union and the Peoples' Republic of China. There is strong evidence that citizens have the opportunity to express their displeasure with incumbents. After the 1965 election, less than 20 percent of the new MPs had sat in the previous assembly; in 1970, over a third of the incumbent candidates were defeated; and in 1975, only half of the MPs seeking reelection succeeded. Even ministers have lost electoral contests, although Nyerere has appointed some defeated ministers to the special seats, so that he can keep them in his Cabinet. That this seems to ignore the wishes of the voters is recognized as a problem by Tanzanian leaders and it may be that incumbents fearing defeat at the polls will choose not to enter an election at all, hoping that they will be appointed to a special seat in the next session.

Before the creation of a de jure one-party state, parliamentary debate was lackluster. Following the British example, most intraparty disputes were settled behind closed doors and whips were used to enforce adherence to the party line when votes were taken. While this might be a good parliamentary strategy in a multiparty system, in Tanzania it meant that policies were not publicly debated in the legislature. After 1965, the party whip became less important and debates took place in the public eye. MPs have begun to play an increasingly critical role; several government bills have been defeated when they first came to a vote. And members have used their right to question ministers about government policy as a way to expose bureaucratic high-handedness.

Despite these exercises of power, several factors raise questions about the effectiveness of Parliament. For example, many of the bills defeated in the first round were later passed with few or no changes. In 1968, seven MPs were expelled from the party (and hence from Parliament) for having crossed the rather fine line between criticism and opposition. Many bills are introduced under "certificates of emergency," which limit the amount of time for debate. Also, Parliament is only in session for ten to twelve weeks a year, and the members have few facilities for office work or legislative research. As the CCM takes over more policy-making responsibility, Parliament's importance will probably continue to decline. However, recent decentralization measures have created a new role for nonminister MPs. The laws require them to live in their constituencies and serve on various local government bodies. It is too early to tell what effect these changes will have either on the role played by Parliament or on the MPs' chances for reelection.

So far, elections have not produced a Parliament demographically representative of the country's various social groups.[25] Women, for example, have never held more than a few of the constituency member seats. To partially rectify this, a fairly large proportion of the appointed members have been women. Tanzanians of European and Asian descent have sometimes defeated those of African descent in elections; there are currently two nonblack elected members and several who have been appointed. Most MPs have more education than the general population and a disproportionate number of MPs were employed by the government or the party prior to election. Only a few derive incomes solely from farming. Peasants and workers have not been particularly prominent in Parliament, despite a stated ideological preference for persons having such backgrounds. Most MPs are under forty.

[25] See Helge Kjekshus, *The Elected Elite: A Socio-Economic Profile of Candidates in Tanzania's Parliamentary Election, 1970* (Uppsala: Scandinavian Institute of African Studies, 1975).

Civil and Military Services

Assisting the president and Cabinet in the implementation of policy are the civil and military services. The political neutrality of these two organizations was abandoned when the one-party state was instituted. While nonpolitical public services might be desirable in multiparty states where government leadership may periodically change hands, excluding government employees from party politics in Tanzania would mean that much of the educated population would be denied a chance to contribute to public policy. Therefore, both civil and military personnel are allowed to run for all local and national offices and leaves of absence are arranged for those who win offices that may conflict with their jobs.

Prior to 1972, the organization of the civil service followed the British pattern fairly closely. Each minister was assisted by a principal secretary (equivalent to a British permanent secretary). Beneath this officer were department heads, their deputies, and other managerial and operational personnel who were organized into cadres or classes — administrative, executive, professional, technical, clerical. Decentralization (see the section on local government, page 503) has modified what used to be a fairly direct hierarchical chain of command by making field personnel responsible not only to central headquarters, but also to regional secretaries, who resemble French prefects. Like most African civil services, the number of public employees in Tanzania has grown rapidly. Budget provisions for 37,273 positions in the 1961–1962 estimates rose to over 75,500 by 1970–1971. The senior and middle levels grew at a particularly fast rate. In 1977, about 10,000 low-level civil servants were laid off, as their services were no longer needed.

At the time of independence, only 16.5 percent of middle- and senior-level posts were held by Tanzanians (African and non-African); the remainder were filled by foreigners or were vacant. In an attempt to change the anomalous situation of a national government carrying out its programs through a public service dominated by foreigners, Tanzanian leaders implemented a policy of rapid Africanization, which meant the replacement of expatriate employees with African citizens (and later any citizen, regardless of race). By 1972, just over 94 percent of the filled posts at these levels were held by citizens and that figure has not changed much in the last few years.[26] Despite the high proportion of local officers, expatriates who act as advisers still have a great deal of influence. Information provided by such foreign experts frequently provides an unchallenged basis for subsequent policies.

There are still problems with the civil service. As the new incumbents did not have the experience of their predecessors, some decline in efficiency and effectiveness has taken place. But this decline is less noticeable in the top management positions than in the junior executive jobs, where corruption and malfeasance are periodically encountered. Also, changing the colonial tradition of tight bureaucratic control over information needed for decision making is proving to be difficult. If citizen participation in political life is to become meaningful, the expertise and knowledge held by government officials must be shared.

A similar situation existed in the armed forces where, although the soldiers were predominantly Africans, the majority of officers were British. An army mutiny in 1964 led to the quick replacement of alien officers and the politicization of the military. A regional commissioner, S. J. Kitundu, was appointed the political commissar of the newly named Tanzanian Peoples' Defense Force (TPDF). Soldiers were encouraged to join the ruling party and heavy recruitment of soldiers from the TANU Youth League helped ensure the political loyalty of the troops. Leaders feel that a developing country cannot afford to allow military personnel to be idle in times of peace, so Tanzania uses soldiers on various public projects like building roads and digging irrigation ditches. During the recent drought, soldiers were required to grow their own food, since national supplies were so low. Participation in the daily tasks of economic development is meant to prevent the physical, social, and psychological isolation of soldiers from civilians. In the first significant test of Tanzania's military capabilities, the TPDF provided

[26] See Adebayo Adedeji, *The Tanzanian Civil Service a Decade After Independence* (Ile-Ife, Nigeria: University of Ife Press, 1974), pp. 11–13; and G. Mutahaba, "The Effect of Changes in the Tanzanian Public Service System upon Administrative Productivity, 1961–1972," *The African Review*, 5:2 (1975), pp. 201–208; and Manpower Planning Division, *Annual Manpower Report to the President*, 1975 (Dar es Salaam: Government Printer, 1977), p. 119.

assistance to Ugandan exiles in their overthrow of Ugandan leader Idi Amin in 1978 and 1979. The success of that operation suggests that their military training and leadership are of a high standard.

Local and Regional Government

Tanzania is divided into twenty-five regions (twenty on the mainland and five on the islands), which are further subdivided into 106 districts. Until 1972, elected district councils (on the mainland) were responsible for designing and implementing various projects and levying taxes to do so. As in most countries, though, some wealthier districts were better able to provide social services than poorer ones. To prevent geographic inequalities from widening, the government reorganized the system of local government, calling the process decentralization. This new system is only a few years old, and evaluating its performance so far is difficult. The new structures can, however, be described.[27]

One step in reorganization was the elimination of most local taxes, meaning that financial control could no longer be exercised by district councils. Now, all tax revenues are collected by the central government and distributed among the regions and districts. Each region is headed by a political appointee, the secretary of the regional party organization. These regional secretaries are equivalent in rank to Cabinet officers. Assisting each is a career civil servant, also appointed by the president, called the regional development director. Much as prefects in France, these two officers supervise and coordinate most of the activities in their regions, regardless of which ministry sponsors a project. Medical personnel, primary schoolteachers, and agricultural extension officers, therefore, have primary operational responsibility to their regional secretary and director, but depend on their respective ministries for career advancement.[28] Each region also has a Regional Development Committee, composed of the senior civil servants from each ministry represented in the region, the local MPs, senior party officials, and such other persons as may be invited. Discussion of various regionwide projects takes place at their meetings, which are directed by the regional director.

At the district level the regional structure is repeated. A political area secretary is also the district party secretary; that official works with a district development director. Both are appointed by the president and exercise functions similar to their regional counterparts. The district councils have been replaced by district development councils, which include elected representatives — one from each ward — as full members and several government and party officials as ex officio members. The power of these councils to make decisions about local development is much less than that held by the old district councils. Primarily they advise government officials as to what they would like to see done.

Two additional levels of government, divisions and wards, are administrative units for project implementation, although wards also are important in the party hierarchy.

As a result of the recent government program to move people from scattered rural homesteads into villages (see pages 516–518) and of the policy of decentralization, local government activities have become more important than they were in the first few years of independence. Until 1976, Tanzanians could join one of the many production or marketing cooperatives that had existed since the late colonial period. After voluntary cooperatives were abolished in 1976, villages took over most of their functions. Village assemblies, open to all residents, have replaced the annual general meetings of the cooperatives, and the role of the Village Development Committee is like that of the old cooperative boards of directors. Thus, villages now have their own sources of revenue in the form of surpluses produced by cooperative projects. Disposal of part of the surplus into a village development fund creates a local treasury to finance community projects.

Courts

Like most colonial countries, Tanzania had two court systems, one for Africans and the other for immigrant races. In the African court system, district administrators operated as both the executive who

[27] See A. H. Rweyemamu, "Some Reflections on Decentralization in Tanzania," in A. H. Rweyemamu and B. U. Mwansasu (eds.), *Planning in Tanzania* (Nairobi: East African Literature Bureau, 1974), pp. 121–131.

[28] Central ministries are now left chiefly with responsibility for nationwide development projects in secondary and higher education, state farms, parastatals (government-run corporations), and major transportation routes.

implemented the laws and the judge who enforced them. Even at the highest level, the courts viewed themselves as having a role in policy implementation as well as adjudication. As such, the people viewed courts primarily as instruments for the colonial government to enforce its decrees, rather than as protectors of individual rights.[29]

Citing Britain as its model, Tanzania has not included a formal bill of rights in any of its constitutions. The Presidental Commission on the Establishment of a One-Party State gave several reasons for its decision not to incorporate a specific list of rights in the 1965 (interim) Constitution, including: (1) that such a bill of rights "limits in advance of events the measures which Government may take to protect the nation from the threat of subversion and disorder"; (2) "the danger that a Bill of Rights would invite conflict between the Judiciary and the Executive and Legislature"; and (3) "decisions concerning the extent to which individual rights must give way to wider considerations of social progress are not judicial decisions."[30]

Imposing universal principles of rights on a society previously ruled without regard for those principles precludes any possibility of making politically desirable changes. For example, at independence, any attempt to ignore race as a criterion for promotion in the civil service would have meant that European and Asian personnel, by becoming citizens, could remain in office and rise to the highest positions in the bureaucracy. To redress a racial imbalance inherited from the colonial period, race was an important factor for advancement at first. Once a more representative racial balance was achieved, nondiscrimination on the basis of race became effective. A constitutional ban on discrimination would have removed the needed flexibility.

Today Tanzania has a unified court system. At the lowest level are the primary courts, rural or urban. These courts compete with traditional authorities (ex-chiefs, elders) for the right to decide minor cases not involving long prison terms or high fines. The inability of the lower courts to handle a large number of cases quickly has prevented strong government action against the traditional, unofficial adjudicators. Magistrates in the primary courts are generally lay persons who have received at least six months of specialized judicial training. Assisting primary court judges are two assessors who come from the area served by the court. Decisions are rendered by a majority of the three people hearing the case. Professionally trained magistrates preside over district courts, which hear appeals from primary courts and hear cases involving serious criminal offenses or involving large fines. The High Court of Tanzania takes appeals from lower courts and has original jurisdiction over crimes like treason.

One factor that delayed the development of public confidence in the courts was the fact that judicial personnel at the higher levels have been largely expatriates. No Tanzanian citizens served on the High Court until 1964, and it was not until 1971 that the chief justice was a Tanzanian. Independence of the judiciary has not been abridged, however, although dissatisfaction with particular decisions has been expressed by the president and other government officials.

Permanent Commission of Enquiry

As a means of protecting an individual from administrative abuses of power, the 1965 Constitution, an interim document, established an ombudsman-like agency called the Permanent Commission of Enquiry. The commission is composed of five persons appointed by and responsible to the president. They are empowered to hear complaints against any government ministry or department and a variety of cooperative, voluntary, and parastatal organizations, but they cannot review judicial decisions.

Investigations are usually begun after an oral or written complaint is received, but the commission can initiate its own studies as well. Although they have many powers similar to those of courts, such as summoning witnesses and evidence, commissioners are not constrained to merely finding innocence or guilt. Where administrative powers are found to have been abused and no other means of complaint are available (that is, it is not under the jurisdiction of

[29] This section relies heavily on information presented by David R. Martin, *Personal Freedom and the Law in Tanzania* (Nairobi: Oxford University Press, 1974).

[30] Tanzania. Presidential Commission on the Establishment of a Democratic One Party State, *Report* (Dar es Salaam: Government Printer, 1965), pp. 30–33.

the courts or an administrative grievance board) the commissioners try to negotiate a settlement. Finally, the commission makes recommendations to the president about what action, if any, should be taken to rectify particular instances of maladministration. Since the proceedings of the commission and its recommendations to the president are not public, it is difficult to evaluate the success of this institution in protecting individual rights.

POLITICAL STRUCTURE AND PROCESS

The Party of the Revolution (CCM)

Nyerere views democracy and socialism as mutually reinforcing. But participation poses two difficult problems in a developing country pursuing socialism. First, given the extremely unequal distribution of political resources (education, money, time, experience), uncontrolled participation means domination by those persons whose immediate interests would be least served by redistributive policies. Second, many aspects of running a modern state are highly technical and unlikely to be easily understood by a largely uneducated citizenry. Participation by the masses in this situation is either meaningless or viewed as a hindrance by technocratic officials. Developing a means of effective participation for the entire population has been one of the most important goals of the Tanzanian leadership.

In Tanzania, the party is attempting to provide the major means of contact between the government and the people. Although party transmission of information from the government to the people has been somewhat successful, involvement of the public in decision making (as opposed to merely approving or disapproving decisions already made) has not been well established.

Until February 1977, Tanzania was unique in being the only one-party state with two parties — the Tanganyika African National Union (TANU) on the mainland and the Afro-Shirazi Party (ASP) on Zanzibar. Leadership and geographical jurisdiction were separate, but it was claimed that the two parties were aiming at the same goal, a socialist Tanzania. However, on the issue of democratic participation, the differences between TANU and ASP have been immense. No popular elections were permitted on the islands between 1964 and 1977, and it was only with difficulty that Zanzibaris were allowed to vote in the presidential plebiscites. After nearly fifteen months of negotiations, a draft constitution merging TANU and ASP into the Chama cha Mapinduzi (CCM), the Party of the Revolution, was accepted by the leaders of the two parties. Much of the organization of CCM follows the forms established by TANU.

CCM's highest body is the National Conference, which meets every two years, although special sessions can be convened. Its voting membership includes the party's chairperson and deputy chairperson,[31] all the party regional secretaries and district chairpersons, all MPs and Tanzanian members of the East African Legislative Assembly, members of the party's National Executive Committee (NEC) and Central Committee (CC), ten delegates from each district (elected by the district conferences), and four members from each district representing each of the party's four affiliated organizations — youth, women, cooperatives, and workers. Given the large size of this conference (nearly 2,000 people), its activities are limited to laying down general policies and electing committees to deal with more specific issues. The chairperson and deputy chairperson are elected by the conference for five-year terms and are subject to removal by a two-thirds vote. Rules require that these two officials come from different parts of the republic.

The NEC is composed of the two chief officers, forty members selected by the National Conference, all Central Committee members, and the heads and secretaries of all the regions and affiliated organizations. Here is where policy is made. The NEC is also responsible for selecting parliamentary candidates, as discussed earlier, and providing general supervision over internal and external security. Although NEC meetings are closed to the public, examination of minutes suggest that they are the scene of vigorous debate and have not been completely dominated

[31] In Swahili, titles are neither masculine nor feminine. Thus chairperson is the most accurate translation.

by any individual, including Nyerere.[32] While it is not an official doctrine, a kind of democratic centralism seems to exist, in that the principles on which policy is based are not to be questioned outside of the NEC or the National Conference.

Supervision of the day-to-day activities of the party is performed by the Central Committee (CC), which includes the chairperson and deputy chairperson, thirty members elected by the NEC, and anyone else the chairperson selects. Unlike the NEC, which meets only twice a year, the CC meets at least every other month. Most of its activities, like the recruitment and management of paid party staff, are carried out by specialized departments under the general direction of an executive secretary and two deputy secretaries, one for the mainland and one for the islands.

Much of the central party structure is replicated at the regional and district levels, where general meetings are held once every two and one-half years, with executive and steering committees guiding the local party in the interval. The chief officers at each level are a chairperson, elected by the regional and district conferences respectively, and a secretary appointed by the national chairperson.

At the next level are the party branches. Branches are usually organized at the village or, in urban areas, ward level. They have an annual Branch Conference and an executive committee. The branch chairperson is elected by the branch conference and the secretary is appointed by the national Central Committee.

Finally, the grass roots of the party are organized cells consisting of CCM members living near each other, ideally in ten-house groups. (The new party Constitution provides for the possibility of cells organized at the workplace too.) First instituted in 1965, the cells and their leaders are supposed to perform several functions. Dues are collected and memberships recorded. Cell leaders are expected to serve as liaison between the cell members and various local party and government officials, act like police officers by reporting on local troublemakers to higher authorities, and arbitrate minor disputes. Conceiving and implementing small-scale development projects is also presumed to be a function of cells.

Obviously the success of a cell depends on the quality of its leader. In electing cell leaders, the problem is choosing between older, more experienced persons who may have some traditional status in the community and younger, better educated, and probably more progressive members. The openness of party membership has resulted in the election of some cell leaders who resist ujamaa policies, which threaten either their traditional status or their wealth, if it is derived from large private landholdings. Recognizing this problem, some officials have called for stricter requirements on party membership and strong disciplinary measures against those who violate party guidelines. It is at this level that leaders who believe in and practice socialism are most important and most difficult to secure.[33] Another problem is that some cells elect leaders who command no respect. Attempting to resist government penetration of their daily lives, these cells choose incompetent leaders who will be of little use to the central government when it requests information about cell members.[34] If this last situation becomes too widespread, government will encounter serious difficulties in implementing programs.

A lack of central control characterized the party in the first few years after independence. TANU aspired to be both a nation-building and a mobilizing party, but only since the Arusha Declaration has the party begun to challenge the government for leadership in society. Several reasons explain this change. In the early sixties, educated Africans were needed to fill the government posts vacated by departing colonial civil servants. Given the few administrators and professionals available and the prestige and financial rewards of government employment, few people chose to enter or could be afforded by the party organization. Thus, a central headquarters staff of less than two dozen was responsible for controlling the

[32] See Henry Bienen, *Tanzania: Party Transformation and Economic Development*. Expanded edition (Princeton: Princeton University Press, 1970), ch. 5.

[33] A. H. Mshangama, "TANU Cells: Organs of One Party Democratic Socialism," in J. H. Proctor (ed.), *The Cell System of the Tanganyika African National Union* (Dar es Salaam: Tanzania Publishing House, 1971), pp. 20–31.

[34] Descriptions of this situation can be found in James R. Finucane, *Rural Development and Bureaucracy in Tanzania: The Case of Mwanza Region* (Uppsala: Scandinavian Institute of African Studies, 1974), pp. 65–66.

numerous regional, district, and branch offices throughout the country. Also, many simultaneously held party and government posts seriously restricted the time available for party work. And, after 1961, the enthusiasm generated by the drive for independence tapered off. Nyerere resigned as prime minister in 1962, ostensibly to rejuvenate an increasingly moribund party organization. Although few changes in the party appear to have occurred as a result, the symbolic value of a nation's leader returning to the people for ten months was important in retaining popular support for TANU.

Today, however, the ability of the party to oversee its subdivisions has improved and the party's position as the supreme political body has increased its attractiveness as a place to build a career. Improvements in and expansion of education have resulted in more middle- and high-level personnel being eligible for employment than the government has jobs (at least in jobs requiring nontechnical skills). And, as time passes, the availability of retired government officials for party positions will also rise. Now the most important organizational problem faced by the CCM is to ensure that cell leaders are committed to party principles. Recent efforts to group citizens into villages (see pages 516–518) will allow closer party supervision of cell activities than was possible in the past. If, as is planned, young people socialized with ujamaa values remain in the villages, grass-roots socialist leadership positions will be more easily filled.

Political Participation

In addition to the structures for participation, actual participation should be examined. Prior to independence, opportunities for conventional participation by Africans were severely restricted. With no opportunity to call their rulers to account for their actions, Africans turned to riots, demonstrations, and passive resistance to protest various policies. Independence has not eliminated unconventional forms of participation, but in Tanzania, unlike a majority of other African countries that have experienced military coups, the predominance of conventional forms is striking.

VOTING Only a few African countries have held all their scheduled elections on time. Tanzania is one of them. Even more significant is the extent to which Tanzanian election results have been analyzed. Two major election studies have been conducted, making it possible to examine voter turnout as a measure of popular participation.[35] Figures in Table 15.4 show that about half of the voting-age population participated in the first two post-independence elections, despite the fact that more voters were registered in 1970 than in 1965.

One hundred percent turnouts do not occur in Tanzania as they do in other socialist or one-party regimes. While it might be argued that this means that Tanzanian leadership has been unable to generate popular involvement, the lower turnout probably reflects the absence of official penalties for nonvoting.

INDIVIDUAL CONTACTING Looking at how individuals deal with government and party officials is another means of understanding participation. Two surveys have clearly shown the methods Tanzanians prefer for making complaints about government.[36] Most contact a local party official. Elected town councillors and MPs are more likely to hear complaints than are government officials or other family members. The survey also revealed that most people expected fair treatment by civil servants and believed that appeals concerning perceived administrative injustice will at least be heard. While actual behavior is not seen in attitude surveys, the data suggest that Tanzanians have a great deal of confidence that party and government officials usually respect the individual citizen and are not oppressive. Confirmation of this feeling is seen in the findings of a study in the West Lake Region, which reported feelings of political efficacy among 80 percent of that population.[37]

[35] Lionel Cliffe (ed.), *One Party Democracy: The 1965 Tanzania General Elections* (Nairobi: East African Publishing House, 1967); A. H. Rweyemamu, "The Presidential Election," in Election Study Committee, *Socialism and Participation: Tanzania's 1970 General Elections* (Dar es Salaam: Tanzania Publishing House, 1974).

[36] K. Prewitt and G. Hyden, "Voters Look at the Elections" in Cliffe, *One Party Democracy*, pp. 273–298; J. R. Morris, "The Voter Level Surveys" in Election Study Committee, *Socialism and Participation*.

[37] G. Hyden, *Political Development in Rural Tanzania: TANU Yajenga Nchi* (Nairobi: East African Publishing House, 1969), ch. 12.

Table 15.4

Participation in the 1965 and 1970 Tanzanian General Elections

	1965	1970
Eligible Population (est.)	5,000,000	6,582,299
Registered voters	3,187,215	4,860,456
Percent registered	63.7	73.7
Parliamentary vote	2,289,602	3,327,255
Percent eligible voting	45.8	49.2
Percent registered voting	71.8	66.6
Presidential vote	2,451,938	3,407,083
Percent eligible voting	49.0	51.8
Percent registered voting	76.9	70.1

Sources: Lionel Cliffe (ed.), *One Party Democracy: The 1965 Tanzania General Elections* (Nairobi: East African Publishing House, 1967), pp. 358–409; Election Study Committee, *Socialism and Participation: Tanzania's 1970 General Elections* (Dar es Salaam: Tanzania Publishing House, 1974), pp. 447, 456.

UNCONVENTIONAL FORMS OF PARTICIPATION Mainland Tanzania has not been characterized by a high degree of political violence.[38] Nevertheless, participation has not been limited to conventional forms, as three examples will illustrate.

In January 1964, primarily as a protest to the rather slow rate at which British officers in the Tanganyikan army were being replaced by Africans, an army mutiny took place. This was not an attempt to overthrow the government, but only a move to speed up the implementation of an accepted policy. In the ensuing confusion, labor leaders also took to the streets, pressing similar demands for civilians. The president was forced into hiding and it was only with the assistance of British troops that order was restored. Although judicial proceedings against the mutineers were instituted and those involved found guilty and punished, many of their demands were in fact met. When order was restored, politicization of military and civilian officials was begun to ensure loyalty to the ruling party and the government, and to reduce the likelihood of such an incident recurring.

Events in late 1966 illustrate two ways that demonstrations provide avenues for political participation. A new law was passed requiring all university graduates to perform two years of national service — three months in National Service camps and twenty-one months in their professional capacities, but receiving only two-fifths of the normal salary. In response, students marched on government offices. After presenting their demands to the president and most of the Cabinet, they were told that they would not be forced unwillingly into the National Service — nor would they be allowed to continue their education, almost completely paid for by the government. Nearly two-thirds of the Tanzanians at the University of Dar es Salaam were expelled and sent back to their homes. However, acknowledging the validity of student criticism of the luxurious lifestyles of politicians and senior civil servants, the president also substantially cut the salaries these groups were

[38] Zanzibar, on the other hand, has been the scene of some very violent activities, beginning with the overthrow of the first independent government in January 1964. In 1972, Sheikh Abeid Karume, the first vice-president of Tanzania, was assassinated in Zanzibar.

receiving. The government originally planned to readmit the students after two years, but political pressures resulted in their returning a bit earlier. In response to the original protest, demonstrations occurred across the country condemning the elitist presumptions of the students. While feelings against the students did run high, most of these counter-demonstrations were organized by government or party officials. Occasionally schools were closed and pupils required to join in marches and rallies. This incident indicates that demonstrations can be of two kinds — self-organized protest or government-organized support.

Assassinations of public officials also are forms of unconventional participation. Tanzania has not been immune from such acts of violence, although they are rare. Dr. Wilbert Klerru, commissioner for Iringa, was assassinated in December 1971. Because he was responsible for implementing policies designed to communalize farming in an area inhabited by a relatively large number of successful private farmers, Klerru was not very popular. He was killed by a prosperous farmer who confessed to the crime. Local support for the assassin's action can be seen by the fairly sizeable defense fund raised for his trial.

WORKER PARTICIPATION IN MANAGEMENT Ujamaa ideology insists on economic as well as political democracy. To secure democratic participation in the economy, Tanzania has experimented with several forms of worker input into the running of industries, plantations, large commercial firms, and the lower levels of public service. First, to be established were conciliation boards and workers' committees. The boards are designed to arbitrate employee grievances by a three-person panel, a workers' representative, a management representative, and an independent member. Workers' committees have two purposes: (1) "to consult with the employer on matters relating to the maintenance of discipline"; and (2) to help increase productivity and efficiency.[39]

[39] In William Tordoff, *Government and Politics in Tanzania* (Nairobi: East African Publishing House, 1967), p. 150. Additional information about labor relations can be found in Issa G. Shivji, *Class Struggles in Tanzania* (Dar es Salaam: Tanzania Publishing House, 1975), ch. 12.

After the Arusha Declaration, an attempt was made to involve workers in planning by setting up workers' councils to advise management. More recently this advisory role has been strengthened by appointing workers to the boards of directors of the parastatal organizations. A goal of having 40 percent of the directors being workers was set for the end of 1977. Professional managers and civil servants, however, still have the final say. When workers object to management behavior, they tend to lock out managers rather than strike. In a few instances they have attempted to continue operating the factories under complete workers' control. Usually, however, the government has sided with management and instructed workers to resume work and readmit the managers while their grievances are being investigated.

INTEREST GROUPS Prior to independence, trade unions, cooperative societies, and TANU's affiliated organizations — the Youth League, the Union of Tanganyikan Women (UWT), and the Union of Tanganyikan Parents (TAPA) — were the major interest groups. Muslim and Christian leaders also attempted to influence colonial policy, particularly in the area of financial aid to parochial schools. Traditional tribal rulers can also be considered as representatives of interest groups in two ways. First, they were guardians of their particular tribe's interests. Second, they were lobbyists for the preservation of their traditional powers, that is, for the interests of chiefs in general.

Under TANU, however, the independence of these traditional groups began to decline. Abolishing the chieftaincy in the early 1960s was the beginning of the attempt to substitute broader national loyalty for local ties. As noted in the section on local party leadership, these traditional loyalties have not completely disappeared. In fact, tribal leaders were frequently the only people in rural areas who had developed any leadership skills. Some traditional personalities, like chiefs A. S. Fundikira and S. N. Eliufoo, were brought into the Cabinet not just because of their personal abilities, but because their presence would help secure legitimacy for the new government.

In the first few years after independence, when the establishment of a one-party state idea was being considered, the articulation of interests outside the party was looked on with increasing disfavor. As a result, both trade unions and cooperative societies became affiliated with TANU. Leaders of these groups became coopted into the Cabinet at independence. Rashidi Kawawa of the trade unions served successively as deputy prime minister, prime minister, and second vice-president, and is now minister of defense. Paul Bomani had headed the country's most important cooperative society prior to becoming minister of finance, and is Tanzania's ambassador to the United States. Leaders of other interest groups, such as Bibi Titi Mohamed of the Union of Tanganyikan Women, were also given top government spots in the early years. This meant that few experienced leaders were available to these groups exclusively, and that the groups' incorporation into the party was not easily resisted. Today there are five organizations affiliated with the CCM — the Youth League, the UWT, TAPA, the National Union of Tanzanian Workers (NUTA), and the Cooperative Union of Tanzania. Their role now seems to be less to represent their members' interests to the policy makers than it is to explain and enforce their members' adherence to government policies.

Leaders of these organizations are appointed by the party chairperson, although there is generally some consultation with the membership before a selection is made. In the past this appointive power has resulted in conflicts of interest. For example, one minister of labor was the head of NUTA. Since the minister is the final arbiter in labor disputes, many of which are between workers and government corporations, he found himself simultaneously promoting the interests of both sides.

Lobbying by private interest groups, such as Christian churches, Muslim associations, and chambers of commerce, is carried out through individual group members who hold high political office or have close personal connections with decision makers. One other important group whose role has been significant in putting pressure on the government is the association of university students. Because they are so few in number and so essential to the future development of the country, Tanzanian students have an influence on government policies far beyond that of students in developed countries. Harnessing this group, which in some senses regards itself as the national protector of socialist ideology and a government critic, has proved to be one of the politicians' most difficult tasks. Recently students demonstrated against salary increases for top government and party officials, arguing that such raises could only come at the expense of workers and peasants and were therefore not in accord with ujamaa principles. The government response, as in 1966, was to expel and rusticate the demonstrators (on this occasion nearly 20 percent of the student body, including President Nyerere's daughter), abolish the student association, and strengthen the campus branch of the CCM Youth League. Within a few months, however, most of the students were pardoned and only the alleged ringleaders were barred from institutions of higher learning for five years.

PUBLIC POLICY AND PERFORMANCE

At independence, the structure of the Tanzanian economy was like that of most new states. The colonial government was less concerned with developing a balanced domestic economy than with maximizing the production of exportable raw materials. As a result, twenty years ago the country had an economy characterized by dramatic inequalities of individual income and wealth and by uneven economic development among the various regions. Socialism in Tanzania has meant attacking these inequalities in two ways. One is for the central government, through its control of prices, wages, and the distribution of public revenues to local government, to prevent the wealthiest individuals and regions from enlarging the gap between themselves and the poorest people and areas.

Second, by reorganizing agricultural production along more communal lines, the leaders believe that rural incomes will rise from increased productivity. The combined effect of these two strategies, if successful, will be a more egalitarian distribution of the society's wealth. Evaluation of the performance of the Tanzanian government, especially since the 1967 Arusha Declaration, must be made with this goal in mind.

Economic Development

Economies like Tanzania's are extraordinarily susceptible to two factors beyond the control of national leaders. First, the large agricultural sector makes good weather essential for productivity. Second, as a relatively small producer and consumer in the world market, Tanzania has very little control over the prices of exports and imports. This last problem is compounded by the fact that the price of raw material exports (agricultural and mineral) fluctuates greatly, while the prices of capital equipment imports steadily rise. At independence, Tanzania entered the international economic system, producing goods that were weather-dependent and for which increased production did not necessarily mean increased income, while it was buying products that were continually more expensive. Bad weather and tremendous inflation in the price of oil and manufactured goods combined in the mid-1970s to push the Tanzanian economy to the edge of a disaster. The timely return of rain allowed production to increase again.

An additional economic problem at independence was that all the major industrial, commercial, and financial enterprises, along with most of the large plantations, were owned by foreigners. Profits were frequently sent overseas, to company headquarters in the developed countries. An economy they could not control was not satisfactory to Tanzanian political leaders. Beginning with the 1967 Arusha Declaration, Tanzania began to try to restructure its internal economic system by nationalizing what leaders called the "commanding heights" of the economy — large factories, banks, insurance firms, export-import businesses, and plantations. The subtitle of this speech, "Socialism and Self-Reliance," reflected the leaders' economic goals.

AGRICULTURE Tanzania was one of the first African countries to announce that it would base development on agriculture. Leaders rejected the conventional wisdom of the mid-sixties, which emphasized industrialization as the quickest route to development. In addition to the general desire to increase agricultural production, two short-term aims were: (1) to increase the production of locally consumed foodstuffs, so imports could be reduced; and (2) to diversify exports (both between agricultural and nonagricultural sectors and within the agricultural sector), so that price fluctuations in the world market would be less disruptive to the national economy.

Overall agricultural growth rates have been declining since 1967. Prior to that time production grew at about 6 percent annually. During the first six years after the state took over the large estates, the overall annual growth rate fell to around 4.6 percent, and during the drought (1973–1974), total production actually declined (see Table 15.5). Although the post-drought growth rates hover around 5 percent, much of this figure represents a return to 1973 levels. Good weather accounts for much of the improvement, although floods in 1979 threaten to set back agricultural production once again. Sustaining this growth rate by improvements in technology and organization is essential to create the wealth needed to provide services and expand nonagricultural production.

Low levels of technology, for example, the use of hoes rather than ox plows, account for low production, but do not necessarily explain the decline in growth rates. A more probable explanation is that the prices offered to peasant producers by government marketing boards were, until recently, extremely low. Also, removal of the direct tax on peasant income may have resulted in smaller surpluses, since cash for taxes was no longer needed, although the government had hoped the increased savings would be used for capital improvements resulting in increased production. To the extent that prices were too low, higher prices should stimulate production. Assuming that reinstituting the peasant taxes is politically unacceptable, only strong leadership at the village level will compensate for productivity lost due to tax removal. Another possible reason for the decline in output is resistance to villagization (see pages 516–518).

With respect to the two short-term goals, results have been more encouraging. In the first five years after the Arusha Declaration, food production averaged an annual growth rate of about 2 percent.[40] During the drought, however, production of locally

[40] Based on figures in FAO, *1976 FAO Production Yearbook*, Vol. 30 (Rome: Food and Agricultural Office of the United Nations, 1977).

Table 15.5

Gross Domestic Product of Tanzania (in millions of U.S. dollars)

Sector	*1960*	*1965*	*1970*	*1973*	*1975*
Agriculture, forestry, hunting, and fishing	$316.3	$363.4	$473.3	$647.1	$944.9
Mining and quarrying	14.0	19.4	14.7	17.3	13.2
Manufacturing and electricity	19.6	66.5	127.6	205.6	257.5
Construction	12.6	25.7	56.5	84.2	97.8
Commerce	81.2	174.1	249.1	357.7	505.9
Transportation and communication	23.8	54.0	99.8	142.8	179.6
Public administration and defense	30.8	54.1	70.5	105.9[a]	145.2[a]
Other services	19.6	36.4	58.2	82.8[a]	109.0[a]
Total	517.9	793.6	1149.7	1643.4	2253.1

[a] An estimate or an adjustment by the Economic Commission for Africa.

Source: United Nations Economic Commission for Africa, "National Accounts Estimates, 1970–1975," *Statistical and Economic Information Bulletin for Africa*, No. 10 (May 1977), p. 126.

consumed maize was especially hard hit, although by 1977, more maize was produced than could be sold domestically. In the years just after the drought, there was a dramatic shift away from export crops to food for domestic consumption which resulted in food production increases averaging near 8 percent, although total agricultural production increased less significantly.

Diversification of export crops has also taken place in Tanzania. Sisal, cotton, and coffee are still important crops, but tobacco, tea, and sugar are increasing their share of export earnings (see Table 15.6). Zanzibar, 95 percent of whose export earnings comes from cloves, is also trying to diversify its agricultural production, but has not yet been notably successful.

INDUSTRY Industrial development is also conditioned by the desire for self-reliance announced in 1967.[41] Many countries, in order to secure economic development, have tried to produce those consumer goods that make up a large part of their import bills. While in some cases, these efforts may have benefited the general population — for example, in the production of textiles — other times import substitution has meant manufacturing products whose consumption is limited to the more privileged sectors, as with bottled beer and machine-made cigarettes. A second approach to industrial development has been to attempt to add value to raw products by processing them before export. Sugar refining, grain milling, meat canning, gem cutting, and nut shelling fall into this category.

Both of these kinds of industries can currently be found in Tanzania. Manufacturing now accounts for about 12 percent of the gross domestic product (GDP), a moderate proportion by African standards, but a share leaders want to increase. With the probable exploitation of coal and iron-ore deposits in the southern part of the country, a basic industries strategy will be adopted. Steel production, for example, will enable Tanzania to produce those basic capital goods necessary for increasing production in other sectors of the economy, including agricul-

[41] Justinian Rweyemamu, *Underdevelopment and Industrialization in Tanzania* (London: Oxford University Press, 1973).

Table 15.6

Diversification of Tanzanian Exports[a]

Product	*1964 Percentage*	*1973 Percentage*
Sisal	30.1	9.6
Cotton	13.6	14.9
Coffee	15.2	22.3
Cashew nuts	4.5	7.9
Tea	2.1	2.4
Tobacco	—	2.5
Cloves	3.0	10.5
Other	31.5	29.9
Total	100.0	100.0

[a] Excludes exports to Kenya and Uganda.

Source: Reprinted by permission from *Africa South of the Sahara, 1978–79* (London: Europa Publications Ltd., 1978), p. 984.

tural and food-processing equipment. These plans will not be realized until some future date. In the meantime, there has been an emphasis on creating small-scale rural industries to provide jobs in the villages. By providing employment in the villages, leaders hope to stem the migration from rural to urban areas.

Recently the Tanzanian government has begun to allow foreign private investors to participate in the economy on more than a minority shareholder basis. This new attitude toward foreign investment is the result of the need for more managerial and entrepreneurial skills in order for the economy to expand satisfactorily. It also reflects the leaders' greater confidence that the major sectors of the economy are firmly under local control.

In both agriculture and industry, but especially the latter, large amounts of capital are needed to get started. Most revenues raised in Tanzania go to meet the nation's recurrent expenditures, leaving few resources for new development. Therefore, to finance these projects, assistance is sought elsewhere. Socialist policies preclude large amounts of private foreign capital being invested in Tanzania by multinational corporations, so a large part of Tanzania's foreign policy is concerned with finding new sources of grants and loans. Grants are essentially outright gifts to the government, although the politics of gratefulness implies some kind of reciprocity, not necessarily financial. Grants do not encourage self-reliance. Loans, on the other hand, must be repaid and, though the repayment period may be long and the interest rate low, money borrowed must be put to productive use.

In fiscal 1975–1976, the country secured approximately \$79 million in loans and nearly \$55.7 million in grants from international organizations and foreign countries. Grants came primarily from Sweden, Norway, Denmark, and Finland. The largest loans were contracted with the World Bank, Canada, Denmark, and the United States.[42] In the early 1970s, the People's Republic of China was the largest single donor of aid to Tanzania. The policy of self-reliance has not kept Tanzanian officials from seeking foreign assistance, although they ensure that the terms for such aid do not compromise the country's independence. Ironically, it seems that a number of developed countries are more willing to assist Tanzania's development because of its effort to become self-reliant.

COMMERCE Government involvement in trade and commerce has not been successful. Trade in East Africa, as in many parts of the world, was the province of immigrants, in this case, Asians. Partly to prevent profits from leaving the country and partly to satisfy the nationalist demand for Africanization of retail trade, all East African governments have intervened in this sector of the economy. At first, Tanzania set up a State Trading Corporation (STC) to handle export-import business and wholesale trade. Mismanagement in this parastatal assumed scandalous proportions. Recently the organization was broken up into regional trading corporations (RTC) in the hope that decentralization will provide better marketing arrangements for local products.

Government intervention at the retail level has

[42] Tanzania, Controller and Auditor General, *Appropriation Accounts, Revenue Statements, Accounts of the Funds, and Other Public Accounts for the Year 1975/76, Part I* (Dar es Salaam: Government Printer, 1977), pp. 59–60.

been no more successful. Operation *Maduka* (Swahili for shops) was intended to complement the villagization program. As villages were formed, private shopkeepers were to have their licenses revoked, with cooperative stores established in their place. The result was that many areas ended up having no stores, since the necessary entrepreneurial skills and capital were not available to establish cooperatives. Reversal of the policy now means that licenses will be available to private persons until such time as sound cooperative shops can be set up.

INFRASTRUCTURE Prior to independence, the transportation network was designed to move coffee and sisal crops from the fertile north to the coast for export. After 1961, the government emphasized improved communication links with Kenya in an attempt at regional integration. The next major transportation policy resulted from Southern Rhodesia's declaration of independence. Zambia feared its normal route to the sea might be closed and Tanzania helped it in an effort to provide rail, road, and pipeline connections between the copperbelt of Zambia and the port of Dar es Salaam. With the completion of the Chinese-aided Tanzania-Zambia Railway (Tazara) in 1975 (two years ahead of schedule), Tanzania now plans to develop stronger internal communications by building feeder lines to the main routes and expanding the network of secondary roads.

Potential for hydroelectric power in Tanzania is quite good. Current electricity supplies are suitable for current needs, but expansion of the manufacturing sector will require new dams to be built. Several foreign donors, notably Sweden and Norway, are interested in sponsoring such projects. Significant deposits of coal will also help the country reduce its dependence on expensive imported oil. Negotiations with the People's Republic of China for the initial financing of a coal mining industry are in progress.

SKILLED PERSONNEL A final factor of economic development that must be considered is the availability of skilled personnel. Although dependence on expatriates in the civil service has lessened significantly, reliance on foreign skills in the parastatal sector is still substantial. Industry and commerce have suffered more from the appointment of inexperienced directors than has the civil service. Ability to balance accounts is tested annually and returns on investments and sales receipts are easier to measure than the productivity of government administrators, who are not concerned with profit making. One report claims that nearly 40 percent of the 175 parastatals engaged in manufacturing showed losses in the 1975–1976 fiscal year.[43] The same report cited the major problems faced by these state corporations as overstaffing, lack of capital, poor and unaccountable management, poor record keeping, and corruption. Time lost from such activities as parades, public meetings, worker education, and cultural events partially accounts for below-capacity operations.

Laying off workers, as was recently done, will help some. So will holding managers responsible for organizational finances. But until such time as enough Tanzanian managers have the training and experience to run large firms, the government must choose between employing foreigners already possessing the requisite skills or using local people who may not be as efficient. Compromise solutions, whereby a Tanzanian is formally in charge but is assisted by a team of expatriate advisers, are being tried, but these arrangements are only temporarily acceptable.

Extractive Performance

NATIONAL SERVICE Recruits for national service were not always easily procured, as the university demonstrations of 1966 indicated. But this situation now seems to have changed. All students who complete eleven or more years of schooling are required to perform national service, which they now accept as a return payment for education provided at state expense. Others with less education may volunteer. Their training is partly military and partly vocational, and they generally provide the foot soldiers for development projects such as public works construction and literacy training.

TAXATION Colonial governments originally instituted taxes for two purposes: (1) so that the costs

[43] U.S. Department of Commerce, Bureau of International Commerce, *Foreign Economic Trends and Their Implications for the United States: Tanzania* (August 1977), p. 5.

of territorial administration could be raised locally and not require expenditures by the colonial power; and (2) to force Africans to seek wage employment in various agricultural, mining, and industrial enterprises by requiring taxes to be paid in cash. In the first few years of independence, colonial tax structures were modified little. Since Arusha, however, significant changes in the tax structure have been made. Income taxes on peasant farmers were abolished, income taxes on wage earners have become increasingly progressive, and heavy taxes and duties on luxury goods were imposed. Not having to collect taxes from scattered peasants has reduced the administrative costs of raising revenue. Almost three-quarters of domestically generated revenues came from three tax sources — excise duties (6.3 percent), sales taxes (38.5 percent), and income taxes (29.4 percent).[44] The result is that the gap between the highest and lowest paid workers has been drastically reduced (the after-tax ratio is about 9.1) and the trend toward an increasing rural-urban gap in income has been reversed.[45]

Tanzania's ability to procure international aid for its development projects (as described earlier) should also be considered when evaluating the country's extractive performance.

Distributive Performance

Providing services was not, until the decade before independence, a major concern of the colonial government. TANU's criticism of the lack of services was an important part of the nationalist campaign. At independence, the new government found that its supporters were expecting a great deal of social welfare from the government. Three services were of particular importance — education, health, and clean water.

EDUCATION Education policy was described in the section on socialization. Here it can be noted that in 1973 expenditure on education was about 3.5 percent of the gross national product; military costs were about 2.3 percent of the GNP. Table 8.3 shows that Tanzania, along with Japan and Mexico, is one of the countries with a proportionally greater outlay on public education than on defense. The $62 million spent on education that year represented about 15 percent of total government expenditures.

Even prior to the implementation of universal primary education in 1977–1978, the number of pupils had been increasing.[46] Enrollment in primary and secondary schools in 1975 was up over 100 percent from the 1965 figure. This represents a significant change in the proportion of the appropriate age group receiving schooling: from 17 percent in 1965 to 43 percent in 1975. Primary schools enrolled 70 percent of children ages seven to thirteen, although only 3 percent of those aged fourteen to nineteen were in secondary school in 1975. As noted earlier, a vigorous program of adult education has produced dramatic changes in the literacy rate as it did in Cuba, so that today at least 50 percent of the population over fifteen can read and write Swahili with some proficiency.

HEALTH Another area of social welfare particularly important in Tanzania is health care. Although reliable statistics are hard to come by, it seems there has been some improvement in important health indicators, such as life expectancy, now estimated between forty-one and forty-seven years, compared with about thirty-eight years at independence, and infant mortality, which has declined from near 160 per thousand births to 152 per thousand. Discernible changes in health policy since the Arusha Declaration can be noted with more certainty.[47] New policies deemphasize the role of large central hospitals in the provision of health care. Instead, the government has increased the number of health centers, dispensaries, and medical auxiliaries in the rural areas. It has increased the number of mobile health teams, enabling specialists and

[44] Tanzania, Controller and Auditor General. *Appropriations Accounts*, pp. 38–41.

[45] Richard N. Blue and James H. Weaver, *A Critical Assessment of the Tanzanian Model of Development* (New York: Agricultural Development Council, 1977), pp. 5–8.

[46] Statistics cited in this section are taken from UNESCO, *Statistical Yearbook*, 1977 (New York: UNESCO, 1978), Tables 3.2, 4.2, and 4.5.

[47] G. M. van Ettien and A. M. Raikes, "Training for Rural Health in Tanzania," *Social Science and Medicine*, 9 (February 1975), pp. 89–92. See also Oscar Gish, *Planning the Health Sector* (London: Croom Helm, 1975).

equipment to visit areas outside the major towns. Along with this, the government has attempted to provide health services to each newly formed ujamaa village. Village medical helpers, in some ways modeled after the "barefoot doctors" of the People's Republic of China, have been trained to provide first aid and treat minor illnesses. In both instances, the necessary reduction in the qualifications of medical personnel has resulted in inappropriate treatment for some patients. As can be seen, most efforts provide curative services. Preventive medicine, while acknowledged as important, is less widespread. However, the literacy campaign was used to provide information on basic health care and nutrition, an ingenious use of limited resources to accomplish these goals.

WATER Part of preventive health care is to ensure that clean water and adequate waste removal facilities are available. Improving rural water supplies is important for a number of reasons. Obviously, clean water reduces the incidence of waterborne diseases. If improving the water supply also means that less time is spent fetching water, there will be more time for development projects or self-improvement, such as literacy training. Providing good water to rural Tanzanians has been difficult. By 1974, it was estimated that only about 15 percent of the rural population had access to clean water.[48] In urban areas the figure is well over 50 percent. The number of people being served increased rapidly in the past few years. A serious outbreak of cholera in 1977, which caused at least three hundred deaths, adds urgency to the need for government to provide access to clean water for everyone, a goal not expected to be reached until 1991.

Regulative Performance

The effort to establish communal villages is probably the most significant single policy adopted by the government. Known as "villagization," this policy is meant to move all people living on isolated farms into villages of at least a few hundred families. The implementation of this program provides a case study of government regulative behavior.[49]

Several villages were set up in the first few years after the Arusha Declaration, but a major effort began in 1972. By 1977, the government claimed that nearly 11 million people (more than two-thirds of the population) had moved to new or existing villages, although most moves were of only a few miles. To effect these moves, the government used intensive publicity, promised social services and goods, and occasionally applied coercion. Two kinds of situations provoked coercion from local officials. First, protocapitalist farmers ignored instructions to move into villages, as happened in Iringa. To compensate these farmers forced off their land the government offered limited payments. The second situation was more complicated. Some overeager local officials, trying to please their superiors, attempted to move people before preparation of the new village site had been completed; this occurred in Morogoro. Peasants resisted and force was used. Investigations of complaints about this episode led to a halt on all moves before site preparation was complete.

Grouping people into villages is expected to provide several advantages. First, it will make it easier to provide social services (education, health care, clean water), and increase the number of people able to take advantage of them. Second, increased interaction among villagers is hoped to lead to cooperative, and thereby increased, production. Reduction of inequalities in land holdings is also achieved.

Villages are not automatically communal (or ujamaa) villages when they are established. Forced collectivization of agricultural production on the Soviet model has not been attempted. Rather, there are three stages of productive organization. At first, most villages consist of privately held plots of land farmed by individual families. These are called development villages. Once members of the village have decided to produce or market their products cooperatively they are registered as a cooperative village. It is hoped that the villages will ultimately qualify as ujamaa villages, multipurpose cooperative societies with most productive, marketing, and retail activities carried out communally.

[48] G. Tschannerl, "The Political Economy of Rural Water Supply," *African Environment*, 1 (October 1975): 62.

[49] P. L. Raikes, "Ujamaa and Rural Socialism," *Review of African Political Economy*, No. 3 (1975), pp. 33–52.

To achieve this goal of ujamaa villages, the government has modified the previous practice of rewarding progressive farmers, those who adopt modern agricultural methods. Instead the government rewards progressive villages with credit, advice, and improved seed and fertilizer. Although the number of villages in Tanzania has increased dramatically in the last few years, the number of ujamaa villages is still relatively small, despite the rather loose employment of the term by officials. Abandoning the known results of traditional and protocapitalist modes of production, however unsatisfactory those results may have been, for the uncertain benefits of ujamaa production is neither psychologically nor economically easy to achieve.

Evaluation of villagization is difficult after such a short period of operation, but we can outline what should happen if the program were successful. Two criteria are important: (1) popular participation in decisions affecting everyday life should increase; and (2) the productive capacity of the country should increase. Early trends indicate mixed results. First, the decision to move into villages was not made by a majority of the people until they were either coerced or enticed into them during the 1973 to 1976 campaign. Whether or not most villages will be willing or able to take over the operation of local services from the central authorities remains to be seen.

On the second question, the coincidence of the villagization campaign with a severe drought makes analysis of agricultural production somewhat uncertain. However, figures for the more recent period of good weather show two opposing trends in productivity. Those regions where large, heavily capitalized private farms were reorganized into villages with smaller holdings show a decline in production. Re-

Communal farming in Ujamaa villages allows greater access to equipment like the combine pictured here in the southern village Kilolo.

gions where subsistence agriculture dominated before 1975 have recently increased output. In some areas where production has dropped due to resistance to villagization, the government has eased up on its pressure for complete communalization. Villagers are also permitted to return to their former lands to harvest existing crops or to gather fruit from trees, which represent long-term capital investments by the peasants. Such modifications are only temporary, however, and the creation of ujamaa villages is still the goal.

Regulative performance in other areas should also be mentioned. The leadership code, discussed earlier, regulates the economic behavior of government officials. The control of some crimes is handled outside the judicial system. For example, in areas where cattle theft has been pronounced and is part of the traditional culture, the government has simply rounded up large numbers of suspected rustlers and their supporters and resettled them away from their traditional victims. In a like manner, prostitutes in large cities are periodically picked up and sent back to their rural homes.[50] Officials occasionally search Dar es Salaam looking for the unemployed, who are usually sent to jobs in rural areas, but this practice has met with some political resistance, as it obviously infringes freedom of movement. The government contends that the alternative to this policy is the development of extensive urban slums and an increase in crime.

In a sense, the removal of the urban unemployed has a legal counterpart in the preventive detention law. It is not certain just how many people are held under this law, but Amnesty International claims that there are about 1,500 political prisoners in Tanzanian jails; many are in Zanzibar, having been arrested during the 1964 coup.[51] A number of exiles from various competing southern African liberation movements, residing in Tanzania, have also been detained, as their activities were deemed dangerous to state security.

[50] Marshall B. Clinard and Daniel J. Abbott, *Crime in Developing Countries* (New York: Wiley, 1973), pp. 269–270.

[51] "Tanzania," *Africa Report* (May–June 1978), p. 32. Twenty-six political detainees were released as part of a general amnesty celebrating the first anniversary of the founding of CCM.

Symbolic Performance

There is little doubt that in the area of symbolic performance, Tanzania has had enviable success. Compared to other African leaders, Nyerere has been able to forge a stronger sense of nationhood among citizens. While not entirely successful in increasing productivity through exhortation, party leaders have used egalitarian rhetoric in their efforts to hold down high civil service salaries for several crucial years.

Popular loyalty toward political leaders is often lacking because the leaders separate themselves from other citizens by their clothing styles, big houses and cars, or by speaking a foreign language. While these distinctions can be found in Tanzania, the personal lifestyles of the top leadership are austere by Third World standards. For instance, Nyerere lives in his private home rather than in the luxurious State House, and the dress of officials of all ranks is a simple collarless cotton shirt and loose-fitting pants. The leadership code set forth in the Arusha Declaration and the TANU Guidelines is also of symbolic importance as it makes wide differences in wealth between officials and citizens politically unjustifiable.

The insistence on Swahili instead of English as the national language has been extremely important as a means of nation building. And the form of address for all citizens, ndugu, fosters a spirit of equality. Ujamaa and the sense of familyhood it imparts is equally important in minimizing perceived differences among people.

International Performance

In terms of population size, land area, or wealth, Tanzania is not a particularly important member of the international system. Indeed, much of the developing world it is a part of has been the arena in which superpower disputes are acted out. Remembering this fact is essential to understanding Tanzania's behavior in foreign affairs.

Today Tanzania is a nonaligned nation. Tanganyika was essentially pro-Western, although in colonial days, national leaders insisted on the withdrawal of South Africa from the British Commonwealth and refused to accept unconditionally treaties signed by Britain on the country's behalf, indicating some independence in foreign policy from the beginning. The merger with pro-Eastern Zanzibar forced these leaders to reassess their position. The first major foreign policy issue in 1964 and 1965 was the problem of Germany. East Germany was the major donor of aid to Zanzibar, and West Germany was an important source of assistance for Tanganyika. At the time, however, West Germany refused to recognize any country that recognized East Germany. As a compromise, Nyerere proposed to downgrade the East German embassy to an unofficial consulate. This was unacceptable to the Bonn government, which withdrew all military aid. Angered, Tanzania refused to allow other German personnel to remain. It was several years before relations between Tanzania and West Germany normalized.

These two years also saw relations with the United States and Great Britain deteriorate. American operations in the Congo in 1964 offended most independent African nations, who were trying to use the newly formed Organization for African Unity (OAU) to find an African solution to an African problem. A forged letter suggesting an American attempt to overthrow Nyerere and a misinterpreted diplomatic phone call hinting at an American-supported coup in Zanzibar worsened United States — Tanzanian relations. And formal relations were broken off with Great Britain when Southern Rhodesia declared independence unilaterally in 1965 and Britain failed to do more than denounce the move. Relations with the Carter administration and the Labour government under Prime Minister Callaghan were good in 1978, based primarily on their similar policies toward Southern Rhodesia. Should Margaret Thatcher, the Conservative Prime Minister elected in 1979, decide to recognize as legitimate the government of Bishop Abel Muzorewa in Southern Rhodesia, Tanzania will probably lead African nations in breaking off diplomatic relations with Great Britain.

As stated earlier, a large proportion of the budgets of developing countries depends on foreign loans and grants. Reductions in aid from West Germany and Britain after the crises just described forced Tanzania to look elsewhere for help. The Soviet Union imposed stringent conditions on their assistance, making it unattractive to Tanzanian leaders. Two other sources of aid, however, were willing to fill the gap left by the major Western powers. One was China, which has made Tanzania the showpiece of its development aid to Africa. The second source was smaller Western nations, particularly the Scandinavian countries, the Netherlands, and Canada. Aid has not prevented criticism of these new donors either, as evidenced by the split between Tanzania and China over which side to support in the Angolan civil war in 1975.

While Tanzania's position in the world may be relatively minor, its position in Africa is important. From the early days of independence, Dar es Salaam has served as headquarters for numerous southern African liberation groups and its border areas shelter refugees from many less stable neighbors. In the early phases of the revolution in Mozambique and during the present struggle to free Zimbabwe (the African nationalist name for Southern Rhodesia), Tanzania has been the site of guerrilla training camps. Also, two Tanzanian infantry battalions are stationed in Mozambique, to protect the border from Southern Rhodesian incursions. As a leader of the front-line states who are working for a solution to the fighting in Southern Rhodesia, Nyerere has become an important figure in international politics.

Relations with neighbors, Kenya and Uganda, have been quite unsatisfactory. The dream of a Federation of East Africa, which seemed possible twenty years ago, is almost unimaginable today. Most of the public services once shared — currency, harbor operations, airline, railways — are now run nationally. A dispute over the sharing of community assets after the jointly-run East Africa Airways collapsed in 1977 led Tanzania to close its entire border with Kenya, ending all travel and commerce between the two countries.

Relations with Uganda have deterioriated steadily since 1971 when Idi Amin overthrew Ugandan president Milton Obote, a personal friend of Nyerere. Border skirmishes and name-calling characterized the next seven years. After Ugandan troops invaded the West Lake Region in late 1978, Tanzanian troops not only repelled Amin's army, but, allied with Ugandan exile forces, invaded Uganda, determined to topple Amin. Success in that effort came in the spring of 1979. Tanzanian soldiers will probably remain in Uganda during the transition to civilian government and until the Ugandan police and defense forces can be rebuilt.

While the reasons behind the collapse of particular services are complex, much of the failure of the East African Community can be traced to three related problems: (1) the economic imbalance between Tanzania and the two other countries, especially wealthier Kenya, which began in the colonial era, but has not changed since independence; (2) the different approaches to economic development pursued by Kenya (predominantly capitalist, relying on private foreign investment) and Tanzania (primarily socialist, relying on state ownership); and (3) the economic chaos reigning in Uganda. Investigations of the feasibility of a new common market with Zambia and Mozambique, more ideologically compatible neighbors, are now underway. And talks concerning some sort of coordination (as yet unspecified) between the CCM and Zambia's single party are also being held.

Thus, it seems that what one author has called "principled non-alignment" is an accurate description of Tanzania's foreign policy.[52] Because Tanzania diversifies its sources of aid, neither the East nor the West can expect to force Tanzania to follow a particular line. Nor has a false notion of racial solidarity prevented Nyerere from criticizing the despotism of Uganda's Amin. But, as in most countries, foreign policy is the prerogative of the chief executive and it remains to be seen whether Nyerere's policies will be continued by his successors.

Future Prospects

That Tanzania has faced the problems of economic, social, and political development head-on cannot be disputed. Nor can it be denied that the country's leadership has attempted to define national goals and to devise original and innovative policies to achieve those goals.[53] For these reasons, Tanzania has become a model for many other Third World countries who admire not so much the specific policies as the relative independence with which they were made. Not all the projects undertaken have been successful, but the ability to recognize shortcomings and modify plans has so far prevented the system from breaking down. Nor have all conflicts between various social and economic groups been eliminated. In fact, such conflicts may actually be more intense in Tanzania than in other African states. Since the government has been unusually clear about its goals, failure to reach them has been all the more obvious. As a result of changes in Tanzania's political system over the past two decades, a number of new problems have emerged. How these problems are dealt with will determine, to a large extent, the direction of future Tanzanian development.

Decentralization, and its supposed transfer of power from central authorities to the people, poses some potential problems when combined with a doctrine of self-reliance. First, decentralization seems only to mean a rearrangement of the centers of decision making within the government, not a transfer of power to citizens. Insofar as the gap between rhetoric and reality becomes apparent to the public, mounting discontent or cynicism can be anticipated. Second, in order to avoid the danger of uneven development leading to separatism in wealthier regions, all people must agree that self-reliance refers to the nation as a whole as well as to the villages, districts, and regions. The self-reliance of the subsistence farmer must be extended to the national community.

Class divisions arising out of differential access to the means of production are well known to Tanzanian leaders. Many policies are aimed at preventing these divisions. But the emergence of a different class, called by some the "bureaucratic bourgeoisie," is a very real danger to the goal of equality.[54] Those who manage state-owned enterprises frequently operate with the same goals as privately owned firms — reducing costs and increasing profits. Inequality is then reinforced as long as these concerns supercede consideration of the needs of the workers and consumers and as long as the salaries of these managers allow for a substantially higher standard of living than that of most people. Similarly, if the surpluses produced by ujamaa villagers go to pay the salaries of nonproductive bureaucrats, the peasants' economic

[52] Cranford Pratt, *The Crucial Phase in Tanzania, 1945–1968* (Cambridge, Eng.: Cambridge University Press, 1976), ch. 6.

[53] See J. K. Nyerere, *The Arusha Declaration: Ten Years After* (Dar es Salaam: Government Printer, 1977).

[54] Issa G. Shivji, *Class Struggles in Tanzania*.

conditions and social position will change little. The problem is balancing increased productivity with reduced inequality.

Another problem is related to maintaining mobilization over an extended period of time. In 1967, Nyerere claimed that Tanzania's economic situation demanded the same levels of commitment and sacrifice exhibited by the Allied nations in World War II. But developing an economy and fighting a war are not the same. People need little encouragement to defend themselves from attack. But to increase production with only limited prospects for material rewards is not as easily induced. In this case, great leadership is required to convince people of the need for action. Perhaps the majority of the people have so far viewed government policies as improving their lives — clean water, health care, and education are more widespread than they were twenty years ago. But, especially in the last few years, these services have been provided as inducements to move into villages. People were given the impression that the government has a large supply of goods and services to distribute. Obtaining these prizes has required little or no productive activity on the part of the villagers. Whether self-help will be adopted in order to maintain and expand these services remains to be seen. There is some question as to how long austerity can be enforced on middle- and upper-income groups. Restriction on the import of luxury consumer goods (automobiles, refrigerators) could be accepted during the drought, but as the crisis subsides, demand for such goods can be expected to increase.

Perhaps the most important question is "What happens after Nyerere is no longer in charge?" He is responsible for much of the success of the Tanzanian experiment, which has moved the country toward an egalitarian society with a minimum of violence. He has laid out the major philosophical guidelines within which policies have been formulated. He has personally selected important decision makers and policy implementers. The union with Zanzibar, although beginning to become institutionalized, still depends heavily on the personal commitments of Nyerere and Vice-President Sheikh Mwinyi Aboud Jumbe for its success. And Tanzania's leadership in African affairs stems from Nyerere's position as an elder statesman and the respect he receives from all parts of the international community.

The president clearly recognizes that the problem of succession has plagued most African countries. If he acts on his intention of not seeking reelection he will be one of the few Third World leaders to step down of their own volition. Jumbe appears to be Nyerere's choice as successor, and the vice-president has begun expanding his participation in national politics by regularly touring the mainland. A peaceful transfer of state power will demonstrate the degree to which the president's democratic ideals have taken root in Tanzanian society. Tanzania's ability to peacefully change leaders at the parliamentary and local government levels provides some reason to expect the presidential transition to go smoothly also. But the failure of most other African countries to establish legitimate succession procedures leads most observers to wait and see.

KEY TERMS

Julius Nyerere
indirect rule
Tanganyika African National Union (TANU)
multi-racism
United Tanganyika Party (UTP)
ujamaa
Arusha Declaration
Bunge
The Party of the Revolution (CCM)
Afro-Shirazi Party (ASP)
Organization for African Unity (OAU)

Analytic Appendix

A Guide to Comparative Analysis in Comparative Politics Today

Comparative analysis is a powerful and versatile tool. It enhances our ability to describe and understand politics in any country, by offering the concepts and reference points of a broader perspective. It stimulates the formation of general theories of political relationships through the comparative consideration of different types of political systems. It encourages us to test the theories we have about politics by confronting them with the experience of many different institutions and settings. It helps expand our awareness of human possibilities in politics, taking us out of the network of assumptions and familiar arrangements within which we all operate.

The text of *Comparative Politics Today* attempts to make use of comparative analysis in all these ways. The initial chapters introduce a set of concepts for discussing and comparing the system, process, and policy aspects of different political systems. The theoretical discussions in Chapters 3 to 8 expand on these concepts and present some general theories for describing and analyzing various aspects of political life. The seven country studies build on these concepts and theories in their description and analysis of politics in a wide range of situations.

This appendix is designed to facilitate further the use of comparative analysis by the readers of *Comparative Politics Today*. We hope to make it easier to go back and forth between the general discussion of concepts and theories and their application to specific countries. Perhaps more importantly, we want to encourage the readers to ask and try to answer their own comparative questions, engaging in comparative analysis of their own by confronting the abstract concepts and theories with the evidence of the countries, or the explanations of events in one nation with the political experiences of other nations.

Although the authors of the analytic and country chapters of this book have adopted a common analytic framework, the country discussions presented are far from identical, and not all of the topics treated in the general introductory chapters are discussed in the country chapters. General headings differ somewhat; sub-headings differ substantially; the extensiveness of treatment of topics varies greatly at some points. There are good reasons for such difference: the processes and problems of politics in these seven countries are quite different. Political parties are, as it happens, important in the politics of each of these countries. But the dominance of the whole society by the Communist Party in the Soviet Union contrasts sharply with the more limited and specialized role of political parties in England, West Germany, and France. In discussing the different functions, then, the role of the party must be stressed again and again in the U.S.S.R. and China, less frequently in some of the other countries.

Moreover, the authors wish to bring out some of the unique features of their countries, as well as characteristics they have in common. One way to give the reader a feel for the special configuration of structures, policy problems, and political resource balances in each country is to stress different key elements in the larger picture. Hence, we see the emphasis on the accumulated layers of political tradition in France, the revealing nature of succession crises in the U.S.S.R., the search for nation-building and economic development in Tanzania.

While these divergences from chapter to chapter are both desirable and necessary, the reader will also find it helpful to have a comparative guide to the presentation of concepts in the analytic chapters and descriptions in the country chapters. The three tables in this appendix can serve as such a guide. By listing headings and subheadings in the text (often in abbreviated form) and page numbers, the tables indicate where discussions of the major concepts associated with the three general levels of the political system — system, process, and policy — can be found. They also show where these concepts are applied in the discussions of politics in each of our seven countries: England, France, West Germany, the U.S.S.R., China, Mexico, and Tanzania. All the tables are organized in the same way. In the column on the far left of the table we find the major analytic topics, including the most significant functions and structures of the political system. Reading across the table we can find the location of the theoretical and country-specific discussions of each concept.

For example, political socialization is one of the major concepts associated with the system level — it is a critical system function in all political systems. In Table A.1 we see political socialization listed as the third topic. Reading across the table, we see first where the theoretical discussion of this function is to be found (Chapter 3), and under what sub-headings. Then, reading further to the right across the table, we see the sub-headings and page numbers where political socialization in each of the seven countries is discussed. The similarities and differences in the sub-headings themselves are interesting, for they reveal aspects of socialization that the author of each country study emphasizes. We see, for example, the emphasis on communication networks in the U.S.S.R. and China, where the government makes specific efforts to shape citizen attitudes through controlling information. Further, each author discusses education or schools as a distinct topic, and almost all devote special attention to the family in political socialization.

Table A.1 lists six separate analytic topics, covering both comparative analysis in general and the system level in particular. The reader can check the ideas put forth in the analytic chapter against the facts and interpretations presented later in the specific country chapters.

Table A.1 can be used to seek the answers, or promote discussion about, questions like these:

1. *Comparative Analysis*
   What are the major obstacles to comparing political systems that are very different in language, size, customs, organization, and policy? How and to what extent can these be overcome?
   What are the major uses of comparative analysis?
   Why have the authors of the country studies chosen the particular sub-headings and emphases that appear in their chapters? What do these tell us about their country?
2. *Environment of the Political System*
   What are the effects of the level of social and economic development on the processes of the political system? On the problems faced by citizens and leaders?
   How does the international environment shape national political life?
   How may ethnic, religious, or linguistic divisions in a political system affect its processes and problems?
3. *Political Socialization*
   What are the agents in a society that contribute to political socialization?
   Can these agents be united and controlled so as to present a unified picture of political life? How and with what consequences?
   Under what conditions and to what extent can the images and ideas acquired in childhood be modified in later life?

4. *Political Culture*
   How is the legacy of the past transmitted to the present? Under what conditions can such a legacy be a burden to contemporary politics? Under what conditions can it help achieve political goals?
   What are political sub-cultures? When are they stabilizing or destabilizing influences?
   How does the political culture work to constrain the processes and policies of a society?
5. *Political Recruitment: Citizen Participation*
   What are the major types of citizen participation? When does citizen participation "make a difference" in politics?
   What types of citizens are likely to participate?
   How can citizen participation levels be modified or their composition altered?
6. *Elite Recruitment*
   What types of citizens are likely to become "elites"? How do they choose themselves and how are they chosen in different types of political systems?
   Why is the recruitment of leaders a major means for controlling public policies?
   How is this control attempted and by whom in democracies? In one-party systems? What are the limitations on such control?

In Table A.2 we find the major analytic concepts associated with the process level of the political system — the major structures and functions involved in the expression of political interests, the mobilizing of political resources around those interests, and the making and implementation of public policies.

Table A.2 can be used to seek the answers, or promote discussion about, questions like these:

1. *Interest Articulation and Groups*
   What different types of interest groups predominate in different political systems?
   Why is the autonomy of interest groups so important for the distinction between democratic and authoritarian political systems?
   Where are institutional groups dominant? How might they be checked?
2. *Interest Articulation and Access Channels*
   What types of access channels do different groups find effective? Under what conditions?
   How is access to the influential policy makers different in democratic and authoritarian systems?
   What is the role of political protest in interest articulation? Of political violence?
3. *Political Parties*
   Why are political parties so important in political systems and societies as different as those in England, France, Germany, the U.S.S.R., China, Mexico, and Tanzania?
   How do these parties differ from each other in their role in leadership selection?
   How do these parties differ in their goals and organizational bases?
4. *Interest Aggregation*
   What types of interest aggregation structures predominate in different political systems?
   How do the interest aggregation structures affect the types of interests taken seriously in the policy-making process?
   In what different ways do competitive party systems shape interest aggregation?
   Why do some interest aggregation structures seem to be more effective than others in developing stable bases for policy?
5. *Policy Making: Decision Rules*
   Why do some decision rules make it easy to adopt new policies, while others make new policy making the exception?
   What structures act to create change-oriented or *status quo*–oriented decision rules?
   Under what conditions are citizens likely to favor various decision rules?
6. *Policy Making: Structures and Functions*
   Why have executives become more important and legislatures less so, even in the democratic countries?
   Why are bureaucracies so important everywhere? How can they be controlled and by whom?
   How can leadership play a role in overcoming the constraints of decision rules?
   How can implementation result in fundamental modifications of chosen public policies?

In Table A.3 we find the major analytic concepts associated with the policy level of the political system: the different ways that political systems attempt to achieve chosen goals through extracting resources, regulating behavior, and so forth; the successful and unsuccessful outcomes of these performance efforts; and the different strategies of organization and performance used to seek achievement of various political "goods."

Table A.3 can be used to seek answers for, or promote discussions about, questions like these:

1. *Policy Performance*
   How do political systems extract resources with which to implement policies?
   What differences in the size and role of the political system do we find in resource extraction and distribution in different societies?
   What different areas of life are regulated in different kinds of political systems?
2. *Policy Outcomes*
   Why are some political systems oriented to equality, others to seeking citizen welfare? How does the role of government vary in this regard?
   Why must some political systems make much greater demands on their citizens than do other systems to achieve the same policy outcomes?
   Why do policy efforts — policies and outputs — often fail to achieve desired policy outcomes?
3. *Policy Evaluation and Strategy*
   What different types of "political goods" are desired by people in different societies?
   How may the search for one kind of political good affect other political goods in positive and negative ways?
   What seem to be advantages and disadvantages of "democratic" and "authoritarian" strategies of seeking political goods in the industrial nations?
   What kinds of strategies have pre-industrial nations attempted in efforts to achieve their goals? How have these worked in practice?

By asking these and other questions in the context of the analytic chapters and the appropriate sections of country chapters, the reader can enhance his or her understanding of the issues of comparative politics today.

Table A.1

A Guide to Analysis in Comparative Politics Today: Theory and System Level

Analytic topics	*Theoretical discussion:*	*England*	*France*	*West Germany*
1. Comparative analysis	Chapter 1 Comparative analysis 2–3 System and environment 4–6 Structure and function 6–12 The policy level 12–13	All of Chapter 9 (147–209)	All of Chapter 10 (211–258)	All of Chapter 11 (261–315)
2. Environment of the political system	Chapter 2 Historical setting 16–18 Size 18 Economic development 18–22 International setting 22–23 Inequality 23–25 Cultural heterogeneity 25 Policy problems 26–30 Goals and challenges 30–32	Constraints of history and place 150–159 Making of modern England 151–154 Mixed inheritance 154 Insularity and involvement 154–156 One Crown and many nations 156–158 Multi-racial England 158–159	Historical retrospective 211–212 Economy and society 212–213	Meaning of the past 261–263 Policy environment 269–277 Domestic setting 269–275 External setting 275–277
3. Political socialization	Chapter 3 Political socialization 34–36 Resocialization 36–38 Agents of socialization 38–42 School 38–39 Peer groups 39 Occupation 39 Mass media 39–40 Parties 40–41 Contacts 41 Environment 41 Political self 41–42	Political socialization 177–181 Influence of family 177–178 Sex 178 Schooling 178–179 Class 179–181 Cumulative effect 181	Political socialization 221–227 Church and religion 222–223 Family 223 Class and status 223–224 Associations 224 Education 225–226	Political socialization 280–282 Family and school 280–281 Political learning in adulthood 282
4. Political culture	Chapter 3 Political culture 42 System propensities 42–44 Process propensities 44–45 Policy propensities 45–48 Subculture and comparison 48	Political culture and political authority 171–177 Allegiance to authority: legitimacy of the system 171–174 The role of law 174–175 Whose authority? 175–176	Themes of political culture 219–221, 226–227 Burden of history 219 Abstractions and symbolism 219 Representative versus plebiscitarian traditions 219–220	Legacy of the past 277 Sense of political community 277–278 Concepts of the state 278 Perceptions of authority 278–279 Perceptions of the citizen's role 279–280

U.S.S.R.	*China*	*Mexico*	*Tanzania*	*Analytic topics*
All of Chapter 12 (317–375)	All of Chapter 13 (381–432)	All of Chapter 14 (435–478)	All of Chapter 15 (481–521)	1. Comparative analysis
Significance of Russian Revolution 317–327 Historical background 320–321 Society and economy 321–322 Social structure and political subcultures 329–338 Party 330 Intelligensia 333 Workers 336 Farms 336 Ethnic pluralism 337	Introduction 381–382 Revolutionary setting 384–385 Soviet communism 385–387 CCP history 387–390 History of P.R.C. 390–396 Socioeconomic change 396–399	General setting 437–454 Historical perspective 437–448 Economic and social change 448–454	Sub-Saharan Africa and Tanzania 481–482 Land and resources 482–483 People 483–487 Early history 487–488 German rule 488–489 British rule 489–492	2. Environment of the political system
Political socialization 338–345 Schools 338–340 Komsomol 340–342 Family 342 Adults 342–345 Political communication 345–350 Oral agitation 346 The press 346–348 Unauthorized communication 348–349	Agents of socialization 407–411 Family 407 Education 407–408 Communication net 408–411 Political and social experience 411 Socialization and the Cultural Revolution 411–413	Political socialization 456–459 Family 457–458 Education 458–459 Daily life 459	Political culture and socialization 492–498 Education 494–496 Media 496–498	3. Political socialization
The dominant political culture 327 Ideological themes 327–328 Leadership and changing political culture 328–329	The Chinese political tradition 383–384 Political culture and socialization 406–407	Culture and socialization 454–459 Three political subcultures 454–456 Clash of political cultures 472–473	Political culture and socialization 492–498 The traditional colonial mix 492–493 Ideology 493–494 (Also see 407.)	4. Political culture

(*table continued on next page*)

Table A.1 (*continued*)

Analytic topics	*Theoretical discussion:*	*England*	*France*	*West Germany*
4. Political culture (*continued*)	Change in political culture 48–51	Cultural limits on policy 176–177	Distrust of politics 220 Crisis and apathy 220–221 Class and status 223–224	The incoming generation 282–283 Political institutionalization and change 283–287 Elite homogeneity and heterogeneity 286–287 The coming changing of the guard 287–288
5. Political recruitment: citizen participation	Chapter 4 Democratic and authoritarian structures 53–54 Types of citizen involvement 54–56 Who participates 56–59 Citizens as subjects 59–60 How much participation 67–69	Popular participation 181–182 (Also see 173, 184.)	Political participation 227–233 Participation in local politics 227–228 Voting in parliamentary elections 228–229 Voting in plebiscitarian contests 229–233	Participation and recruitment 284–288 The electorate 284–285 Middle range participants 285 Participation and political stability 288
6. Political recruitment of elites	Chapter 4 Eligibility biases 60–62 Selection of elites 62–64 Control of elites 64 Coercive and violent participation 64–66	Recruiting for central political roles 182–185 Politicians and society 185–186 (Also see Class, especially 179–181.)	Recruitment and style of elites 233–236 The political class 233–234 The bureaucracy 234–236 (Also see 253–254.)	Leading participants 285–286 Elite recruitment 286 Elite homogeneity and heterogeneity 286–287 The coming changing of the guard 287–288

U.S.S.R.	China	Mexico	Tanzania	Analytic topics
				4. Political culture (*continued*)
Recruitment and participation 350–353 Directed political participation 352	Political and social experience 411 Participation 413–414	Political recruitment 459–463 Political mobilization 466–468 Political abstention 473–475 (Also see 440–441.)	Political Participation 507 Voting 507 Individual contacting 507 Unconventional participation 508–509 Worker participation in management 509	5. Political recruitment: citizen participation
The Komsomol 340–342 Recruitment of elites 350–352 Within the apparatus 350–351 Role of Apparatchik 351 Access to elite membership 351–352 Power struggles 353–362 Succession crises 354–358 The late Brezhnev era 358–359 Policy issues 359–362 Party control of the bureaucracy 365–368	Recruitment 414–417	Political recruitment 459–463 Political leaders 460–463	The presidency 498–500 The legislature 500–502 Unconventional participation 508–509	6. Political recruitment of elites

Table A.2

A *Guide to Analysis in* Comparative Politics Today: *Political Process Level*

Analytic topics	*Theoretical discussion*	*England*	*France*	*West Germany*
1. Interest articulation: groups	Chapter 5 Types of groups 70–75 Individual contactors 71–72 Anomic groups 72–73 Nonassociational groups 73–74 Institutional groups 74–75 Associational groups 75 Interest groups in different political systems 84–86	Interest groups 188–190	Interest groups 236 Interest articulation 236–238	Interest group politics 288–289 Key peak associations 290–293 Organized business 290–291 Organized labor 291–293 Organized agriculture 293 Religious organization 293
2. Interest articulation: access channels	Chapter 5 Access to the influential 75–80 Personal connection 76 Direct representation 76 Mass media 76–77 Parties 77 Legislatures and bureaucracies 77 Protest 77 Coercive tactics 78 Effectiveness of groups 80–81 Policy perspectives 81–84	Articulation interests 186 Political communication 186–188 (Also see 190, 156.)	Means of access and styles of action 238–240	Interest group politics 288–290 Functional representation 289 Political representation 289–290 Interest groups and public policy 293–294
3. Political parties	Chapter 6 Social bases and goals of parties 87–91 Functions of political parties 91–95 Socialization 91–92 Recruitment 92 Communication 92–93 Interest articulation 93 Interest aggregation 93–94 Policy Making 94 Implementation and adjudication 94–95	The party system: aggregation and choice 190–196 Electoral choice 190–193 Control of organization 193–194 Party preferences 194–196 (Also see Recruiting for central roles, esp. 182–184 and Class, 179–181.)	Political parties 240–249 The traditional party system 240–242 The RPR 242–245 Republicans and center 245–246 The socialists 246–247 The communists 247–249	Party politics 294–299 To them that have shall be given 294–296 Parties and voters 296–297 Party organization 298–299
4. Interest aggregation	Chapter 6 Structures performing aggregation 95–105	The party system: aggregation and choice 190–196	Voting in parliamentary election 230–231	Party politics 294–299 Parties and voters 296–297

U.S.S.R.	China	Mexico	Tanzania	Analytic topics
Unauthorized communication: dissent and repression 348 Groups and strata in the communist party 330–333 The intelligentsia 333–335 The workers 336 The collective farmers 336–337	Mass organizations 405–406 Interest articulation 417–420	Political mobilization 466–469	Interest groups 509–510	1. Interest articulation: groups
Unauthorized communication: dissent and repression 348 Group interests and policy making 354	Interest articulation 417–420	Political mobilization 466–469 Political aggregation 469–472 Clash of political cultures 472–473	Interest groups 509–510 Unconventional participation 508–509 Permanent commission of enquiry 503–505	2. Interest articulation: access channels
Groups and strata in the communist party 330–333 Role of apparatchik 351 Succession crises 354–358 Governmental characteristics 322–326 Political communication 345–346 Recruitment of elites 350–352 Party control of the bureaucracy 365–368	CCP history 387–390 The party 403–415 Recruitment 414–417 Interest articulation 417–420 Interest aggregation and conflict 420–423 Policy making and implementation 423–428	The PRI 466–472 Political mobilization 466–469 Political aggregation 469–470 Political recruitment 459–463 Political leaders 460–463 Constitutional and legal norms 463–466 (Also see 439–445.)	British rule 489–492 The presidency 498–500 The party of the revolution (CCM) 505–507	3. Political parties
Power struggles and policy making 353–354	Interest aggregation and conflict 420–423	Political aggregation 469–472 (Also see 441–447.)	The party of the revolution (CCM) 505–509	4. Interest aggregation

(table continued on next page)

Table A.2 (*continued*)

Analytic topics	*Theoretical discussion*	*England*	*France*	*West Germany*
4. Interest aggregation (*continued*)	Individual elites 95–96 Interest groups 96–98 Competitive party systems 98–100 Noncompetitive parties 100–102 Military governments 102–105 Significance of interest aggregation 105–106	Electoral choice 190–193 Control of organization 193–194 Policy preferences 194–196 A community of interests 169–170 Cabinet and prime minister 159–164 House of Commons 166–168 Policy preferences 194–196 A ruling clique 202–203	Voting in plebiscitarian contests 231–25 Political parties 242–251 The traditional party 242–244 (Also see 241–242 on coercive action.)	Rule by party elites 297–298 Parties and representative democracy 299 The executive arena 300–302
5. Policy making: decision rules	Chapter 7 Policy making 107–108 Rules for policy making 108–111 Geographic power distribution 108–109 Separation of powers 109–110 Limitations on power 110–111	The constitution of the Crown 159–170 Cabinet and prime minister 159–164 A community of interests 169–170 One Crown and many nations 156–158 Limits of centralization 196–199 Limits of decentralization 199–202 A ruling clique? 202–203 The role of law 174–175	Constitution and governmental structure 213–219 Policy processes 249 The executive 249–251 The civil service 251–252 Regional reform 252 Parliament 252–254 Checks and balances 254–255 (Also see participation in local politics, 227–228.)	Constitutional organization 263–269 Rulers and ruled 264 Federalism 264–265 Federal president 265–266 Federal government 266–267 Federal diet 267 Judiciary 267–269 Public policy administration 269 The context for policy-making 300 Arena of federalism 304 (Also see 284–285.)
6. Policy making: structures and functions	Chapter 7 Policy making structures 111–112 Assemblies 112–115 Functions of assemblies 112–114 Structures of assemblies 114–115 Executives 115–118 Types of executives 116–118 Functions of executives 118–119 Bureaucracies 119–124 Structures of bureaucracies 120–121 Functions of bureaucracies 121–124	Policy making and implementation 196–203 Limits of centralization 196–199 Limits of decentralization 199–202 The constitution of the Crown 159–170 Cabinet and prime minister 159–164 The civil service 164–165 The role of parliament 165–169 A community of interests 169–70	Policy processes 249 The executive 249–251 Civil service 251–252 Parliament 252–254 Checks and balances 254–255	Policy making 299–306 Executive arena 300–302 Legislative arena 302–304 Arena of federalism 304–306 (Also see 263–269.)

U.S.S.R.	China	Mexico	Tanzania	Analytic topics
Succession crises 354–358 The late Brezhnev era 358–359 Policy issues 359–362 Governmental characteristics 322–326				4. Interest aggregation (*continued*)
Governmental characteristics 322–326 Power struggles and policy making 353–354 Policy issues 359–362 Party control of the bureaucracy 365–372	Constitution and political structure 399 The state 400–403 The party 403–405 The army 405	Constitutional and legal norms 463–466 (Also see 462–463.)	Government organization 498–506 The presidency 498–500	5. Policy making: decision rules
The schools (policy making) 338–340 Policy implementation 362 Structure of the soviets 363–365 Party control of bureaucracy 365–368 Law enforcement and judicial process 368–369 The legal professions 369–370 The court system 370–371 Police agencies 371–372	The state 400–403 The party 403–405 The army 405 Mass organizations 405–406 Policy making and implementation 423–428 Decision making 424–425 Administration 425–426 Rule enforcement and adjudication 426–428	Constitutional and legal norms 463–466	The presidency 498–500 The legislature 500–501 Civil and military services 502–503 Local and regional government 503 The courts 503–504 Permanent commission of enquiry 504 Political structure and process 505 The party of the revolution (CCM) 505–507	6. Policy making: structures and functions

Table A.3

A *Guide to Analysis in* Comparative Politics Today: *Policy Level*

Analytic topics	*Theoretical discussion*	*England*	*France*	*West Germany*
1. Policy performance	Chapter 8 Policies as goals 125–133 Performance 125–126 Extraction 126–129 Distribution 129–131 Regulation 131–133 Symbolic performance 133	The proof of policy 203–209 Policy performance 203–206	Performance and prospects 255–258	Policy performance and consequences 306–313 Public finance 306–309 Social Welfare 309–310 Economic concentration 310–311 Economic democracy 311 European integration 311–312 Armament 312–313
2. Policy outcomes	Chapter 8 Outcomes of performance 133–140 Domestic welfare 134–36 Domestic security 136–139 Feedback 140	Policy outcomes 206–208 (Also see 154–156.)	Performance and prospects 255–258	Policy performance and consequences 306–313 Public finance 306–309 Social welfare 309–310 Economic concentration 310–311 Economic democracy 311 European integration 311–312 Armament 312–313 Unanticipated consequences 313
3. Policy evaluation and strategy	Chapter 8 Political goods and productivity 140–142 Types of political goods 140–142 Trade-offs and opportunity costs 142 Strategies for producing goods 142–143 Types of systems 142–143 Industrial democracies 143 Industrialized authoritarianism 144–145 Pre-industrial nations and strategies 145–146	Adaptability and stability 208–209	Performance and prospects 255–258 Conclusion 226–227 (Also see The coming changing of the guard, 285–286.)	Problems and prospects 313–315 Military security and peace 314 Economic security and growth 314 Internal security and civil liberties 314–315 (Also see The coming changing of the guard 287–388.)

U.S.S.R.	China	Mexico	Tanzania	Analytic topics
Policy issues 359–362 The schools 338–340 Unauthorized communication: dissent and repression 348–350 Law enforcement 368–369 Performance 372–376 Extraction 373–374 Regulation 374–375 Distribution 375–376	Political history of the PRC 390–396 Soviet model 390–392 Maoist model 392–396 Post-Mao period 396 Socialization and the Cultural Revolution 411–413 Performance capabilities 428–429	Governmental performance and political system performance 475–478	Public policy and performance 510–520 Extractive performance 514–515 Distributive performance 515–516 Regulative performance 516–518 Symbolic performance 518 International performance 518–520 (Also see 493–494.)	1. Policy performance
Policy issues 359–362 Performance 372–376 Extraction 373–374 Regulation 374–375 Distribution 375–376 Alternative paths of development 376–378	Socioeconomic change 396–398 Performance outcomes 429–432	Governmental performance and political system performance 475–478 (Also see 448–454.)	Economic development 511–514 Agriculture 511–512 Industry 512–513 Commerce 513–514 Infrastructure 514 Skilled personnel 514 Public policy and performance 510–520	2. Policy outcomes
Alternative paths of development 376–378	Introduction 381–382 Performance outcomes 429–432	The Mexican miracle 435–437	Future prospects 520–521	3. Policy evaluation and strategy

Selected Bibliography

CHAPTER 1

Almond, Gabriel A., and Powell, G. Bingham, Jr. *Comparative Politics: System, Process, Policy*. Boston: Little, Brown, 1978.

Blondel, Jean. *An Introduction to Comparative Government*. New York: Praeger, 1969.

Deutsch, Karl W. *The Nerves of Government*. New York: Free Press, 1963.

Easton, David. *A Systems Analysis of Political Life*. New York: Wiley, 1965.

Holt, Robert, and Turner, John, eds. *The Methodology of Comparative Research*. New York: Wiley, 1970.

Lijpart, Arend. "Comparative Politics and Comparative Method," *American Political Science Review*, September 1971.

Przeworski, Adam, and Teune, Henry. *The Logic of Comparative Social Inquiry*. New York: Wiley, 1970.

CHAPTER 2

Bell, Daniel. *The Coming of Post-Industrial Society*. New York: Free Press, 1973.

———. *The Cultural Contradictions of Capitalism*. New York: Basic Books, 1976.

Black, Cyril E. *The Dynamics of Modernization*. New York: Harper and Row, 1966.

Chenery, Hollis, et al. *Redistribution With Growth*. London: Oxford University Press, 1974.

Enloe, Cynthia. *Ethnic Conflict and Political Development*. Boston: Little, Brown, 1973.

Huntington, Samuel P. *Political Order in Changing Societies*. New Haven, Ct.: Yale University Press, 1968.

——— and Dominguez, Jorge. "Political Development." In F. I. Greenstein and N. W. Polsby. *Handbook of Political Science*, Vol. 3, Ch. 1. Reading, Ma.: Addison-Wesley, 1975.

Keohane, Robert O., and Nye, Joseph S. *Transnational Relations and World Politics*. Cambridge, Ma.: Harvard University Press, 1972.

———. *Power and Independence: World Politics in Transition*. Boston: Little, Brown, 1977.

Lindberg, Leon N., and Scheingold, Stuart A. *Europe's Would-be Polity*. Englewood Cliffs, N.J.: Prentice-Hall, 1970.

Lindberg, Leon, ed. *Politics and the Future of Industrial Society*. New York: David McKay, 1976.

Moore, Barrington, Jr. *Social Origins of Dictatorship and Democracy*. Boston: Beacon, 1966.

Nordlinger, Eric A., ed. *Politics and Society*. Englewood Cliffs, N.J.: Prentice-Hall, 1970.

Pye, Lucian W. *Aspects of Political Development*. Boston: Little, Brown, 1966.

Rustow, Dankwart A. *A World of Nations*. Washington, D.C.: Brookings Institution, 1967.
Young, Crawford. *The Politics of Cultural Pluralism*. Madison, Wis.: University of Wisconsin Press, 1976.
Sigel, Roberta S., ed. *Learning About Politics*. New York: Random House, 1970.
Wylie, Laurence. *Village in the Vaucluse*. Cambridge, Ma.: Harvard University Press, 1957.

CHAPTER 3

Almond, Gabriel A., and Verba, Sidney. *The Civic Culture*. Princeton, N.J.: Princeton University Press, 1963.
———, eds. *The Civic Culture Revisited*. Boston: Little, Brown, 1980.
Brown, Archie, and Gray, Jack. *Political Culture and Political Change in Communist States*. New York: Holmes and Meier, 1977.
Dawson, Richard E., Prewitt, Kenneth, and Dawson, Karen S. *Political Socialization*. Boston: Little, Brown, 1977.
Dennis, Jack, ed. *Socialization to Politics: A Reader*. New York: Wiley, 1973.
Easton, David, and Dennis, Jack. *Children in the Political System: Origins of Political Legitimacy*. New York: McGraw-Hill, 1969.
Greenstein, Fred. *Children and Politics*. New Haven, Ct.: Yale University Press, 1965.
Hess, Robert, and Torney, Judith. *The Development of Political Attitudes in Children*. Garden City, N.J.: Doubleday, 1968.
Hyman, Herbert H. *Political Socialization: A Study in the Psychology of Political Behavior*. New York: Free Press, 1959.
Inglehart, Ronald. *The Silent Revolution: Changing Values and Political Styles Among Western Publics*. Princeton, N.J.: Princeton University Press, 1977.
Jennings, M. Kent, and Niemi, Richard. *The Political Character of Adolescence*. Princeton, N.J.: Princeton University Press, 1974.
Kavanagh, Dennis A. *Political Culture*. London: Macmillan, 1972.
Langton, Kenneth P. *Political Socialization*. New York: Oxford University Press, 1969.
Putnam, Robert. *The Beliefs of Politicians*. New Haven, Ct.: Yale University Press, 1973.
Pye, Lucian W., and Verba, Sidney, eds. *Political Culture and Political Development*. Princeton: Princeton University Press, 1965.
Sears, David O. "Political Socialization." In F. I. Greenstein and N. W. Polsby. *Handbook of Political Science*, Vol. 2, Ch. 2. Reading, Ma.: Addison-Wesley, 1975.

CHAPTER 4

Barnes, Samuel H., and Kaase, Max. *Political Action: Mass Participation in Five Western Democracies*. Beverly Hills, Ca., Sage Publications, 1979.
Bendix, Richard. *Nation-Building and Citizenship*. New York: Anchor, 1969.
Blau, Peter. *On the Nature of Organizations*. New York: Wiley, 1974.
Burling, Robbins. *The Passage of Power: Studies in Political Succession*. New York: Harcourt Brace Jovanovich, 1974.
Campbell, Angus, et al. *The American Voter*. New York: Wiley, 1960.
Dahl, Robert A. *Polyarchy: Participation and Opposition*. New Haven, Ct.: Yale University Press, 1971.
———. *After the Revolution*. New Haven, Ct.: Yale University Press, 1971.
Eisenstadt, S. N. *The Political Systems of Empires*. New York: Free Press of Glencoe, 1963.
Gurr, Ted Robert. *Why Men Rebel*. Princeton, N.J.: Princeton University Press, 1970.
Hibbs, Douglas A. *Mass Political Violence*. New York: Wiley, 1973.
Hirschman, Albert. *Exit, Voice, and Loyalty*. Cambridge, Ma.: Harvard University Press, 1970.
Lane, Robert E. *Political Life*. Glencoe, Ill.: The Free Press, 1959.
Lijpart, Arend. "Typologies of Democratic Systems." *Comparative Political Studies*, April, 1968.
Linz, Juan. "Totalitarian and Authoritarian Regimes." In F. I. Greenstein and N. W. Polsby. *Handbook of Political Science*. Reading, Ma.: Addison-Wesley, 1975.
Lipset, Seymour M. *Political Man*. London: Mercury, 1963.
Marshall, T. H. *Class, Citizenship and Social Development*. New York: Doubleday, 1964.
Matthews, Donald R., and Prothro, James W. *Negroes and the New Southern Politics*. New York: Harcourt Brace Jovanovich, 1962.
Nie, Norman, Verba, Sidney, and Petrocik, John R. *The Changing American Voter*. Cambridge, Ma.: Harvard University Press, 1976.
Pateman, Carole. *Participation and Democratic*

Theory. New York: Cambridge University Press, 1970.

Putnam, Robert D. *The Comparative Study of Political Elites*. Englewood Cliffs, N.J.: Prentice-Hall, 1976.

Skolnick, Jerome H. *The Politics of Protest*. New York: Simon and Schuster, 1969.

Thompson, Dennis F. *The Democratic Citizen*. New York: Cambridge University Press, 1970.

Verba, Sidney, and Nie, Norman. *Participation in America: Political Democracy and Social Equality*. New York: Harper and Row, 1972.

Verba, Sidney, Basheruddin, Ahmed, and Shatt, Anil. *Caste, Race, and Politics*. Beverly Hills, Ca., Sage Publications, 1971.

Verba, Sidney, Nie, Norman, and Kim, Jae-on. *Participation and Political Equality*. Cambridge, Eng.: Cambridge University Press, 1978.

CHAPTER 5

Beer, Samuel H. *British Politics in the Collectivist Age*. New York: Knopf, 1965.

Bentley, Arthur F. *The Process of Government*. Cambridge, Ma.: Harvard University Press, 1967.

Castles, Francis G. *Pressure Groups and Political Culture*. London: Routledge and Kegan Paul, 1967.

Ehrmann, Henry W. *Interest Groups on Four Continents*. Pittsburgh, Pa.: University of Pittsburgh Press, 1958.

———. *Organized Business in France*. Princeton, N.J.: Princeton University Press, 1957.

La Palombara, Joseph. *Interest Groups in Italian Politics*. Princeton, N.J.: Princeton University Press, 1964.

Oberschall, Anthony. *Social Conflict and Social Movements*. Englewood Cliffs, N.J.: Prentice-Hall, 1973.

Olson, Mancur. *The Logic of Collective Action*. Cambridge, Ma.: Harvard University Press, 1965.

Schmitter, Philippe, ed. "Corporatism and Policy-Making in Contemporary Western Europe." *Comparative Political Studies*, April, 1977.

———. *Interest Conflict and Political Change in Brazil*. Stanford, Ca.: Stanford University Press, 1971.

Scott, James C. *The Moral Economy of the Peasant: Rebellion and Subsistence in Southeast Asia*. New Haven, Ct.: Yale University Press, 1976.

Skilling, H. Gordon, and Griffiths, Franklyn. *Interest Groups in Soviet Politics*. Princeton, N.J.: Princeton University Press, 1971.

Truman, David. *The Governmental Process*. New York: Knopf, 1951.

Weiner, Myron. *The Politics of Scarcity: Public Pressure and Political Response in India*. Chicago, Ill.: University of Chicago Press, 1962.

Wilkinson, Paul. *Political Terrorism*. London: The MacMillan Press, 1974.

Wilson, James Q. *Political Organizations*. New York: Basic Books, 1973.

Wootton, Graham. *Interest Groups*. Englewood Cliffs, N.J.: Prentice-Hall, 1970.

CHAPTER 6

Alford, Robert. *Party and Society*. Chicago: Rand McNally, 1963.

Converse, Philip E. "Public Opinion and Voting Behavior." In F. I. Greenstein and N. W. Polsby. *Handbook of Political Science*, Vol. 4, Ch. 2. Reading, Ma.: Addison-Wesley, 1975.

Dahl, Robert A., ed. *Political Oppositions in Western Democracies*. New Haven, Ct.: Yale, 1966.

———. *Regimes and Oppositions*. New Haven, Ct.: Yale University Press, 1973.

Dodd, Lawrence C. *Coalitions in Parliamentary Government*. Princeton, N.J.: Princeton University Press, 1976.

Downs, Anthony. *An Economic Theory of Democracy*. New York: Harper and Row, 1957.

Duverger, Maurice. *Political Parties*. New York: Wiley, 1955.

Epstein, Leon D. *Political Parties in Western Democracies*. New York: Praeger, 1967.

Huntington, Samuel, and Moore, Clement. *Authoritarian Politics in Modern Society*. New York: Basic Books, 1970.

Key, V. O. *Politics, Parties, and Pressure Groups*. New York: Crowell, 1964.

La Palombara, Joseph, and Weiner, Myron. *Political Parties and Political Development*. Princeton, N.J.: Princeton University Press, 1966.

Lijpart, Arend. *The Politics of Accommodation*. Berkeley and Los Angeles, Ca.: University of California Press, 1976.

Lipset, Seymour M., and Rokkan, Stein. *Party Systems and Voter Alignments*. New York: Free Press, 1967.

Mackie, Thomas T., and Rose, Richard. *The International Almanac of Electoral History*. New York: Free Press, 1974.

Michels, Robert. *Political Parties*. New York: Collier, 1962.

Nordlinger, Eric A. *Soldiers in Politics: Military Coups and Governments*. Englewood Cliffs, N.J.: Prentice-Hall, 1976.

Ostrogorski, M. J. *Democracy and the Organization of Political Parties*. New York: Anchor, 1964.

Rae, Douglas. *The Political Consequences of Electoral Laws*. New Haven, Ct.: Yale University Press, 1971.

Riker, William H. *The Theory of Political Coalitions*. New Haven, Ct.: Yale University Press, 1962.

Rokkan, Stein. *Citizens, Elections, Parties*. New York: McKay, 1970.

Rose, Richard, ed. *Elective Behavior: A Comparative Handbook*. New York: Free Press, 1974.

Sartori, Giovanni. *Parties and Party Systems*. Cambridge, Eng.: Cambridge University Press, 1976.

Schattschneider, E. E. *Party Government*. New York: Rinehart, 1942.

La Palombara, Joseph, ed. *Bureaucracy and Political Development*. Princeton, N.J.: Princeton University Press, 1964.

Loewenberg, Gerhard, and Patterson, Samuel. *Comparing Legislatures*. Boston, Ma.: Little, Brown, 1979.

Neustadt, Richard E. *Presidential Power: The Politics of Leadership*. New York: Wiley, 1960.

Vile, M. J. *Constitutionalism and the Separation of Powers*. New York: Oxford University Press, 1967.

Wheare, K. C. *Federal Government*. New York: Oxford University Press, 1964.

Wheeler, Harvey. "Constitutionalism." In F. I. Greenstein and N. W. Polsby. *Handbook of Political Science*. Reading, Ma.: Addison-Wesley Press, 1975.

Wildavsky, Aaron, ed. *American Federalism in Perspective*. Boston: Little, Brown, 1967.

———. *Budgeting: A Comparative Theory of Budgetary Processes*. Boston: Little, Brown, 1975.

CHAPTER 7

Armstrong, John A. *The European Administrative Elite*. Princeton, N.J.: Princeton University Press, 1973.

Blondel, Jean. *Comparative Legislatures*. Englewood Cliffs, N.J.: Prentice-Hall, 1973.

Crozier, Michael. *The Bureaucratic Phenomenon*. Chicago: University of Chicago Press, 1963.

Duchacek, Ivo. *Power Maps*. Santa Barbara, Ca.: California ABC Clio Press, 1973.

———. *Rights and Liberties in the World Today*. Santa Barbara, Ca.: California ABC Clio Press, 1973.

Frederich, Carl J. *Limited Government: A Comparison*. Englewood Cliffs, N.J.: Prentice-Hall, 1974.

Goodnow, Frank. *Politics and Administration*. New York: The MacMillan Company, 1900.

Hoebel, Adamson. *The Law of Primitive Man*. Cambridge, Ma.: Harvard University Press, 1954.

Interparliamentary Union. *Parliaments: A Comparative Study of the Structure and Functioning of Representative Institutions in 41 Countries*. London: Cassell, 1962.

Katz, Elihu, and Danet, Brenda. *Bureaucracy and the Public*. New York: Basic Books, 1973.

King, Anthony. "Executives." In F. I. Greenstein and N. W. Polsby. *Handbook of Political Science*. Reading, Ma.: Addison-Wesley, 1975.

Kornberg, Allan, ed. *Legislatures in Comparative Perspective*. New York: McKay, 1973.

CHAPTER 8

Adelman, Irma, and Morris, Cynthia. *Economic Growth and Social Equity in Developing Countries*. Stanford, Ca.: Stanford University Press, 1973.

Almond, Gabriel A., Flanagan, Scott, and Mundt, Robert. *Crisis, Choice and Change*. Boston: Little, Brown, 1973.

Almond, Gabriel A., and Powell, G. Bingham, Jr. *Comparative Politics: System, Process, Policy*. Boston: Little, Brown, 1978.

Anderson, Charles W. *Politics and Economic Change in Latin America*. Princeton, N.J.: D. Van Nostrand, 1967.

Bill, James A., and Leiden, Carl. *Politics in the Middle East*. Boston: Little, Brown, 1979.

Binder, Leonard, et al. *Crises and Sequences in Political Development*. Princeton, N.J.: Princeton University Press, 1971.

Chenery, Hollis, et al. *Redistribution with Growth*. London: Oxford University Press, 1974.

Eckstein, Harry. *The Evaluation of Political Performance: Problems and Dimensions*. Beverly Hills, Ca.: Sage Publications, 1971.

Eisenstadt, S. N. *Traditional Patrimonialism and Modern Neo-Patrimonalism*. Beverly Hills, Ca.: Sage Publications, 1973.

Enloe, Cynthia. *The Politics of Pollution in a Comparative Perspective*. New York: David McKay, 1975.

Field, Mark G., ed. *Social Consequences of Modernisation in Communist Societies*. Baltimore, Md.: Johns Hopkins University Press, 1976.

Grew, Raymond, ed. *Crises of Political Development in Europe and the United States*. Princeton, N.J.: Princeton University Press, 1978.

Heclo, Hugh. *Modern Social Politics in Britain and Sweden*. New Haven, Ct.: Yale University Press, 1974.

Heidenheimer, Arnold, Helco, Hugh, and Adams, Carolyn T. *Comparative Public Policy*. New York: St. Martin's Press, 1975.

Herber, Bernard P. *Modern Public Finance*. Homewood, Ill.: Richard Irwin, 1971.

Hirschman, Albert. *A Bias for Hope*. New Haven, Ct.: Yale University Press, 1971.

———. *Journeys Toward Progress*. New York: Doubleday and Company, 1965.

Huntington, Samuel P., and Moore, Clement H., eds. *Authoritarian Politics in Modern Society*. New York: Basic Books, 1970.

Huntington, Samuel P., and Nelson, Joan M. *No Easy Choice: Political Participation in Developing Countries*. Cambridge, Ma.: Harvard University Press, 1976.

Jackman, Robert W. *Politics and Social Equality*. New York: Wiley, 1975.

Lindblom, Charles E. *Politics and Markets*. New Haven, Ct.: Yale University Press, 1978.

Linz, Juan J., and Stepan, Alfred. *The Breakdown of Democratic Regimes*. Baltimore, Md.: Johns Hopkins University Press, 1978.

McNamara, Robert S. *One Hundred Countries, Two Billion People*. New York: Praeger, 1973.

Packenham, Robert. *Liberal America and The Third World*. Princeton, N.J.: Princeton University Press, 1973.

Pryor, Frederic L. *Public Expenditures in Communist and Capitalist Nations*. Homewood, Ill.: Richard Irwin, 1968.

Rawls, John. *A Theory of Justice*. Cambridge, Ma.: Harvard University Press, 1971.

Siegel, Richard L., and Weinberg, Leonard. *Comparing Public Policies*. Homewood, Ill.: Dorsey Press, 1977.

Singer, J. David, and Small, Melvin. *The Wages of War 1816–1965*. New York: Wiley, 1972.

Tilly, Charles, ed. *The Formation of National States in Western Europe*. Princeton, N.J.: Princeton University Press, 1975.

Wilensky, Harold. *The Welfare State and Equality*. Berkeley, Ca.: University of California Press, 1975.

CHAPTER 9: *England*

Beer, Samuel H. *British Politics in the Collectivist Age*. New York: Random House, 1969.

Butler, David E., and Sloman, Anne, eds. *British Political Facts, 1900–1974*. New York: St. Martin's, 1975.

Butler, David E., and Kavanagh, Dennis. *The British General Election of 1979*. London: Macmillan, 1980.

Butler, David E., and Stokes, Donald. *Political Change in Britain*. New York: St. Martin's, 1969.

Dictionary of National Biography. Part I: From the Beginning to 1900. Part II: 1900–1950. New York: Oxford University Press, 1953 and 1961.

Headly, Bruce. *British Cabinet Ministers*. London: Allen and Unwin, 1974.

Heclo, Hugh, and Wildavsky, Aaron. *The Private Government of Public Money*. Berkeley, Ca.: University of California Press, 1974.

Gwyn, William B., and Rose, Richard, eds. *Britain—Progress and Decline*. New Orleans: Tulane University Press, 1980.

Macintosh, John P. *The British Cabinet*. London: Methuen, 1969.

McKenzie, R. T. *British Political Parties*. New York: Praeger, 1964.

Putnam, Robert D. *The Beliefs of Politicians*. New Haven, Ct.: Yale University Press, 1973.

Rose, Richard. *Studies in British Politics*. New York: St. Martin's, 1976.

———. *Policy-Making in Britain*. New York: Free Press, 1969.

———. *The Problem of Party Government*. New York: Free Press, 1974.

Sampson, Anthony. *The New Anatomy of Britain*. New York: Stein and Day, 1972.

Social Trends. London: Her Majesty's Stationery Office, annually.

Walkland, S. A., and Ryle, M. *The Commons In The Seventies*. London: Fontana, 1977.

CHAPTER 10: *France*

Ardagh, J. *The New France; A Society in Transition*. Baltimore, Md.: Penguin Books, 1973.

Charlot, Jean. *The Gaullist Phenomenon: The Gaullist Movement in the Fifth Republic*. London: Allen and Unwin, 1971.

Harrison, Martin, ed. *French Politics*. Lexington, Ma.: D. C. Heath, 1969.

Hayward, Jack. *The One and Indivisible French Republic*. New York: Norton, 1973.
Hoffmann, Stanley, et al. *In Search of France*. Cambridge, Ma.: Harvard University Press, 1965.
Hoffmann, Stanley. *Decline or Renewal? France since the 1930s*. New York: The Viking Press, 1974.
Kesselman, Mark. *The Ambiguous Consensus: A Study of Local Government in France*. New York: Knopf, 1967.
Rémond, René. *The Right Wing in France from 1815 to de Gaulle*. Philadelphia: University of Pennsylvania Press, 1969.
Ridley, F., and J. Blondel. *Public Administration in France*. New York: Barnes and Noble, 1964; 2nd edition, 1969.
Suleiman, Ezra N. *Politics, Power and Bureaucracy in France: The Administrative Elite*. Princeton, N.J.: Princeton University Press, 1974.
Thomson, David. *Democracy in France Since 1870*. New York: Oxford University Press, 1964.
Tiersky, Ronald. *French Communism, 1920–1972*. New York: Columbia University Press, 1974.
Williams, Philip M. *The French Parliament: Politics in the Fifth Republic*. New York: Praeger, 1968.
Wright, Gordon. *France in Modern Times, 1760 to the Present*. Chicago: Rand McNally, 1962.
Wylie, Laurence. *Village in the Vaucluse*. Cambridge, Ma.: Harvard University Press, 1957.

CHAPTER 11: *China*

Barnett, A. Doak. *China and the Major Powers in East Asia*. Washington, D.C.: Brookings Institution, 1977.
Bennett, Gordon. *Huadong: The Story of a Chinese People's Commune*. Boulder, Co.: Westview Press, 1978.
Bianco, Lucien. *Origins of the Chinese Revolution, 1915–1949*. Stanford, Ca.: Stanford University Press, 1971.
Chang, Parris H. *Power and Policy in China*, 2nd enlarged ed. University Park, Pa.: Pennsylvania State University Press, 1978.
Dittmer, Lowell. *Liu Shao-ch'i and the Chinese Cultural Revolution*. Berkeley, Ca.: University of California Press, 1974.
Dreyer, June Teufel. *China's Forty Millions*. Cambridge, Ma.: Harvard University Press, 1976.
Fairbank, John King. *The United States and China*, 4th ed. Cambridge, Ma.: Harvard University Press, 1979.
Hinton, Harold C., ed. *The People's Republic of China: A Handbook*. Boulder, Co.: Westview Press, 1978.
Li, Victor H. *Law Without Lawyers: A Comparative View of Law in the United States and China*. Boulder, Co.: Westview Press, 1978.
Meisner, Maurice. *Mao's China: A History of the People's Republic*. New York: Free Press, 1977.
Parish, William L., and Whyte, Martin King. *Village and Family in Contemporary China*. Chicago: University of Chicago Press, 1978.
Pye, Lucian W. *China: An Introduction*, 2nd ed. Boston: Little, Brown, 1978.
Schram, Stuart R. *The Political Thought of Mao Tse-tung*. Revised and enlarged ed. New York: Praeger, 1969.
Selden, Mark, ed. *The People's Republic of China: A Documentary History of Revolutionary Change*. New York: Monthly Review Press, 1979.
Townsend, James R. *Politics in China*, 2nd ed. Boston: Little, Brown, 1980.
United States Congress, Joint Economic Committee. *Chinese Economy Post-Mao: Volume 1, Policy and Performance*. Washington, D.C.: Government Printing Office, 1978.
Whiting, Allen S., and Dernberger, Robert F. *China's Future: Foreign Policy and Economic Development in the Post-Mao Era*. New York: McGraw-Hill, 1977.
Whyte, Martin King. *Small Groups and Political Rituals in China*. Berkeley, Ca.: University of California Press, 1974.
Wilson, Dick, ed. *Mao Tse-tung in the Scales of History*. Cambridge, Eng.: Cambridge University Press, 1977.

CHAPTER 12: *Russia*

Barghoorn, Frederick C. *Detente and the Democratic Movement in the USSR*. New York: Free Press, 1976.
Brown, Archie, and Gray, Jack, eds. *Political Culture and Political Change in Communist States*. New York: Holmes and Meir, 1978.
Brzezinski, Zbigniew, and Huntington, Samuel I. *Political Power: USA/USSR*. New York: Viking, 1964.
Bukovsky, Vladimir. *To Build a Castle—My Life as a Dissenter*. New York: Viking, 1979.
Churchward, L. G. *The Soviet Intelligentsia*. London: Routledge and Kegan Paul, 1973.
Cohen, Stephen F. *Bukharin and the Bolshevik Revolution*. New York: Knopf, 1973.

Conquest, Robert. *Power and Policy in the U.S.S.R.* New York: St. Martin's, 1961.

Hollander, Gayle Durham. *Soviet Political Indoctrination*. New York: Praeger, 1972.

Hollander, Paul. *Soviet and American Society: A Comparison*. New York: Oxford University Press, 1973.

Hough, Jerry F., and Fainsod, Merle. *How the Soviet Union is Governed*. Cambridge, Ma.: Harvard University Press, 1979.

Juviler, Peter. *Revolutionary Law and Order*. New York: Free Press, 1976.

McCauley, Mary. *Politics and the Soviet Union*. New York: Penguin Books, 1978.

Medvedev, Roy A. *On Socialist Democracy*. New York: Knopf, 1975.

Meyer, Alfred G. *Leninism*. Cambridge, Ma.: Harvard University Press, 1957.

Mickiewicz, Ellen P., ed. *Handbook of Soviet Social Science Data*. New York: Free Press, 1972.

Moore, Barrington, Jr. *Terror and Progress USSR*. Cambridge, Ma.: Harvard University Press, 1954.

Reddaway, Peter. *Uncensored Russia*. New York: American Heritage, 1972.

Rigby, T. H. *Communist Party Membership in the U.S.S.R. 1917–1967*. Princeton, N.J.: Princeton University Press, 1968.

Ryavec, Karl W., ed. *Soviet Society and the Communist Party*. Amherst, Ma.: University of Massachusetts Press, 1978.

Sharlet, Robert. *The New Soviet Constitution of 1977: Analysis and Text*. Brunswick, Oh.: King's Court Communications, 1978.

Skilling, H. Gordon, and Griffiths, Franklyn, eds. *Interest Groups in Soviet Politics*. Princeton, N.J.: Princeton University Press, 1971.

Tokes, Rudolf L., ed. *Dissent in the USSR*. Baltimore, Md.: Johns Hopkins University Press, 1976 (paperback).

Tucker, Robert. *Stalin As Revolutionary*. New York: W. W. Norton, 1973.

CHAPTER 13: *West Germany*

Bracher, Karl D. *The German Dictatorship: The Origins, Structure, and Effects of National Socialism*. New York: Praeger, 1970.

Braunthal, Gerard. *The West German Legislative Process*. Ithaca, N.J.: Cornell University Press, 1972.

Cerny, Karl, ed. *Germany at the Polls: The Bundestag Election of 1976*. Washington, D.C.: American Enterprise Institute, 1979.

Conradt, David P. *The German Polity*. New York: Longman, 1978.

Craig, Gordon A. *Germany, 1866–1945*. Oxford, Eng.: Clarendon Press, 1978.

Dahrendorf, Ralf. *Society and Democracy in Germany*. New York: Doubleday, 1967.

Grosser, Alfred. *Germany in Our Time*. New York: Praeger, 1971.

Johnson, Neville. *Government in the Federal Republic: The Executive at Work*. Oxford, Eng.: Pergamon, 1973.

Kommers, Donald P. *Judicial Politics in West Germany*. Beverly Hills, Ca.: Sage Publications, 1975.

Loewenberg, Gerhard. *Parliament in the German Political System*. Ithaca, N.Y.: Cornell University Press, 1966.

Mayntz, Renate, and Scharff, Fritz W. *Policy-Making in the German Federal Bureaucracy*. Amsterdam, Hol.: Elsevier, 1975.

Schoenbaum, David. *Hitler's Social Revolution*. New York: Anchor, 1967.

CHAPTER 14: *Mexico*

Almond, Gabriel A., and Verba, Sidney. *The Civic Culture*. Princeton, N.J.: Princeton University Press, 1963.

Bock, Peter G., and Rothenberg, Irene Fraser. *Internal Migration Policy and New Towns: The Mexican Experience*. Urbana, Ill.: University of Illinois Press, 1979.

Carlos, Manuel L. *Politics and Development in Rural Mexico: A Study in Socio-Economic Modernization*. New York: Praeger, 1974.

Casanova, Pablo G. *Democracy in Mexico*. New York: Oxford University Press, 1970.

Cline, Howard F. *Mexico, Revolution to Evolution*. New York: Oxford University Press, 1962.

Fagen, Richard, and Tuohy, William. *Politics and Privilege in a Mexican City*. Stanford, Ca.: Stanford University Press, 1972.

Fromm, Erich, and Maccoby, Michael. *Social Character in a Mexican Village*. Englewood Cliffs, N.J.: Prentice-Hall, 1970.

Glade, William, and Anderson, Charles. *The Political Economy of Mexico: Two Studies*. Madison, Wis.: University of Wisconsin Press, 1963.

Hansen, Roger D. *The Politics of Mexican Development*. Baltimore, Md.: Johns Hopkins University Press, 1971.

Lewis, Oscar. *The Family of Sánchez*. New York: Random House, 1961.
———. *Five Families: Mexican Case Studies in the Culture of Poverty*. New York: Basic Books, 1959.
———. *Life in a Mexican Village*. Urbana, Ill.: University of Illinois Press, 1951.
———. *Pedro Martinez: A Mexican Peasant and His Family*. New York: Random House, 1963.
Paz, Octavio. *The Labyrinth of Solitude*. New York: Grove Press, 1962.
Purcell, Susan Kaufman. *The Mexican Profit Sharing Decision: Politics in an Authoritarian Regime*. Berkeley, Ca.: University of California Press, 1975.
Quirk, Robert E. *Mexico*. Englewood Cliffs, N.J.: Prentice-Hall, 1971.
Ramos, Samuel. *Profile of Man and Culture in Mexico*. Austin, Tx.: University of Texas Press, 1963.
Ross, Stanley R. *Is the Mexican Revolution Dead?* New York: Knopf, 1966.
Scott, Robert E. *Mexican Government in Transition*. Urbana, Ill.: University of Illinois Press, 1964.
Smith, Peter H. *Labyrinths of Power: Political Recruitment in Twentieth Century Mexico*. Princeton, N.J.: Princeton University Press, 1979.
Stevens, Evelyn P. *Protest and Response in Mexico*. Cambridge, Ma.: Massachusetts Institute of Technology Press, 1974.
Tax, Sol, ed. *Heritage of Conquest*. Glencoe, Ill.: Free Press, 1952.
Wolf, Eric. *Sons of the Shaking Earth*. Chicago: University of Chicago Press, 1959.

CHAPTER 15: *Tanzania*

Bienen, Henry. *Tanzania: Party Transformation and Economic Development*, expanded ed. Princeton, N.J.: Princeton University Press, 1970.
Cliffe, Lionel, ed. *One Party Democracy: The 1965 General Elections*. Dar es Salaam, Tanzania: Tanzania Publishing House, 1967.
——— and Saul, John, eds. *Socialism in Tanzania*, 2 vols. Nairobi, Kenya: East African Publishing House, 1972–73.
Dryden, Stanley. *Local Administration in Tanzania*. Nairobi, Kenya: East African Publishing House, 1968.
Duggan, William R., and Civille, John R. *Tanzania and Nyerere*. Maryknoll, N.Y.: Orbis Books, 1976.
Election Study Committee. *Socialism and Participation: Tanzania's 1970 National Elections*. Dar es Salaam, Tanzania: Tanzania Publishing House, 1974.
Finucane, James R. *Rural Development and Bureaucracy in Tanzania*. Uppsala, Sweden: Scandinavian Institute of African Studies, 1974.
Gish, Oscar. *Planning the Health Sector: The Tanzanian Experience*. London: Crrom Helm, 1975.
Hyden, Goran. *Political Development in Rural Tanzania: TANU Yajenga Nchi*. Nairobi, Kenya: East African Publishing House, 1969.
Ingle, Clyde R. *From Village to State in Tanzania*. Ithaca, N.Y.: Cornell University Press, 1972.
Kjekshus, Helge. *The Elected Elite: A Socio-Economic Profile of Candidates in Tanzania's Parliamentary Election, 1970*. Uppsala, Sweden: Scandinavian Institute of African Studies, 1975.
Martin, Robert. *Personal Freedom and the Law in Tanzania*. Nairobi, Kenya: Oxford University Press, 1974.
Nyerere, Julius K. *Freedom and Development*. London: Oxford University Press, 1973.
———. *Freedom and Socialism*. London: Oxford University Press, 1968.
Pratt, Cranford. *The Critical Phase in Tanzania, 1945–1968*. Cambridge, Eng.: Cambridge University Press, 1976.
Rweyemamu, A. H., and Mwansasu, B. U., eds. *Planning in Tanzania*. Nairobi, Kenya: East African Literature Bureau, 1974.
Rweyemamu, Justinian. *Underdevelopment and Industrialization in Tanzania*. London: Oxford University Press, 1973.
Shivji, Issa G. *Class Struggles in Tanzania*. London: Heinemann Books Ltd., 1975.
Taylor, J. Clagget. *The Political Development of Tanganyika*. Stanford, Ca.: Stanford University Press, 1963.
Tordoff, William. *Government and Politics in Tanzania*. Nairobi, Kenya: East African Publishing House, 1967.

Index